"I have always loved the Holy Tongue"

BASED ON THE

CARL NEWELL JACKSON LECTURES

"I have always loved the Holy Tongue"

Isaac Casaubon, the Jews, and a

Forgotten Chapter in Renaissance Scholarship

Anthony Grafton ✳ Joanna Weinberg

WITH ALASTAIR HAMILTON

The Belknap Press of Harvard University Press

CAMBRIDGE, MASSACHUSETTS   LONDON, ENGLAND   2011

Library of Congress Cataloging-in-Publication Data

Grafton, Anthony.
"I have always loved the holy tongue" : Isaac Casaubon, the Jews, and a forgotten chapter
in Renaissance scholarship / Anthony Grafton, Joanna Weinberg.
p. cm.
Includes bibliographical references and index.
ISBN 978-0-674-04840-9 (cloth : alk. paper)
1. Casaubon, Isaac, 1559–1614.   2. Old Testament scholars—Biography.
3. Christian Hebraists—Biography.   4. Bible—Criticism, interpretation, etc.—
History—16th century.   5. Bible—Criticism, interpretation, etc.—
History—17th century.   I. Weinberg, Joanna, 1949–   II. Title.
PA85.C3G73 2011
296.092—dc22
[B]   2010012951

To the memory of A. M. Meyer

Contents

Illustrations

A Note to Readers

Latin and Greek texts are presented as they appear in the manuscripts and printed sources, although we have suggested corrections where they seemed unavoidable. Thus we have retained most of Casaubon's preferred abbreviations, such as σηαι for σημείωσαι (note, N.B.). Passages in Casaubon's *Ephemerides* have been corrected against the holograph (Canterbury Cathedral Archive, Lit MS D/1). Because Hebrew vocalization was often inaccurate and sometimes wild in the sixteenth and seventeenth centuries, we have reproduced only the consonantal texts of passages cited. When transliterating Greek or Hebrew, we have striven for simplicity. In particular, we have cited Hebrew works by the most familiar forms of their titles, even when inconsistencies result: hence the reader will encounter *Josippon* and *Yuchasin*. We hope that ease of recognition will compensate for the oddities occasioned by our method. For the same reason, we have given the names of individuals in the forms most likely to be familiar to readers, whether Latin or vernacular.

Although our predominant mode of citation in the notes is by author and date, for readers' convenience we have adopted an alternative system for the large number of annotated editions quoted, citing these by the shelfmarks by which they are cataloged in some depositories. Frequently cited depositories are abbreviated in the notes as follows:

BL   British Library, London
Bod   Bodleian Library, Oxford

ONE

Rabbi Isaac Casaubon

A Hellenist Meets the Jews

The Houghton Library at Harvard possesses two books previously owned by Isaac Casaubon (1559–1614): a 1578 edition of Plautus with a massive commentary, which he gave to his son Meric; and a Hebrew translation of Calvin's catechism, in which he left a few annotations—enough to show that he understood the text very well.[1] Whereas the former title is predictable, the latter seems a surprising choice of reading for someone who has always been best known as a Hellenist. And yet it was by no means the only Hebrew book that Casaubon filled with the characteristic chicken scratches of his marginalia. More than a century ago, the Jewish scholar Solomon Schechter happened on a curious note in the *Otsar haSefarim* (Thesaurus librorum, 1880) of the Hebrew bibliographer Isaac ben Jacob. Ben Jacob mentioned a profusely annotated copy of the medieval scholar David Kimhi's grammar *Mikhlol* (Completeness), which belonged to what was then the British Museum.[2] He attributed the notes to one "Rabbi Yitzchak Kasuban," with whom even the legendarily erudite Schechter was not acquainted. By consulting Joseph Zedner's catalogue of the Hebrew books in the British Museum, Schechter cleared up the little mystery: "it was no other than the famous Christian scholar, Isaac Casaubon." With characteristic good humor he reflected, "when Philo was regarded as a Father of the Church, Ben Gabirol quoted for many centuries as a Mohammedan philosopher, why should not Casaubon obtain for once the dignity of a Rabbi?"[3]

---

1. Birrell 1980, 66, 68 n. 39. The Calvin text is Houghton Library, Harvard University, Heb. 7103.978.5/*FC5.C2646.Zz554c; the Plautus is Houghton Library *FC5.C2646.Zz578p.
    2. BL 1984.a.10.(1).
    3. Schechter 1896, 315.

סֵפֶר חִנּוּךְ בְּחִירֵי יָהּ

חברו הֹרֹ' עמנואל טרמליאוס מעיר
פרארא בארץ איטליאה :

אב לבנים יודיע אל־אמתך ; ישעיה ל"ה׃

עֶטֶס בְּבֵית רוברטוס סטעטוס איש צרפתי בשנת
שֵׁיֹל לְפָ"ק בְּקוֹדֶשׁ חִילוֹל בְּיוֹסְכֹל לְקוֹדֶשׁ׃

Isaac Casaubonus.

FIGURE 1.1. Casaubon's copy of Calvin's catechism, in Hebrew. Houghton Library, Harvard University, Heb. 7103.978.5/*FC5.C2646.Zz554c.

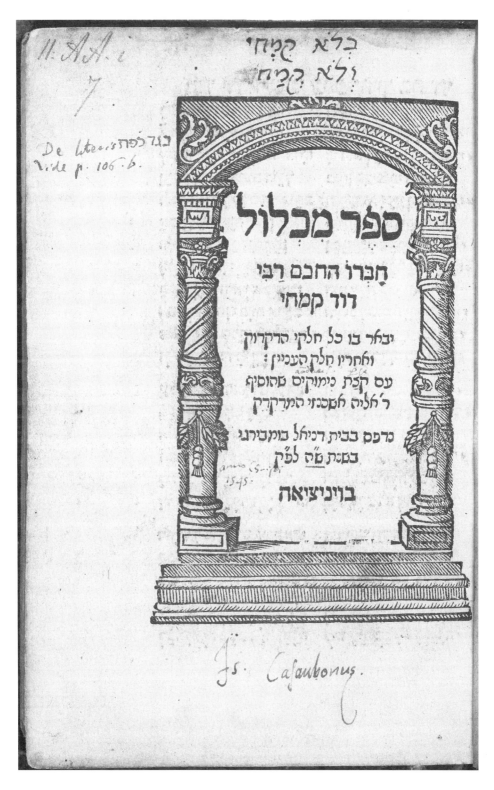

בלא קמחי
ולא קמח

De literis
vide p. 106. b.

כגד כפה

ספר מכלול

חברו החכם רבי
דוד קמחי

יבאר בו כל חלקי הדקדוק
ואחריו חלק הענין :
עם קצת נימוקים שהוסיף
ר׳ אליה אשכנזי המדקדק

נדפס בבית דניאל בומבירגי
בשנת שֿה לפֿק

anno Chr.
1545.

בויניציאה

Is. Casaubonus.

FIGURE 1.2.   Casaubon's copy of David Kimhi's *Sefer Mikhlol*. British Library 1984.a.10.(1).

In fact, as this book will show, Casaubon was certainly no rabbi, but he was a serious student of Jews and Judaism. His reading embraced works by Jews in Hebrew, Aramaic, and Greek, as well as books about Jews by Christian Hebraists. His personal library included works of all these types, and even one or two texts in Yiddish. And his interest in Jewish texts, customs, and institutions ranged the centuries from biblical times to his own. Casaubon self-consciously applied the same methods to Jewish texts and problems that he used in his much better-known studies of ancient Greek and Latin literature—the fields in which he won the admiration of the legendarily unrespectful Joseph Scaliger, who told his students that "Casaubon is the greatest Greek scholar that we have: he is my superior."[4] More important still, he saw these studies as intimately, even organically, connected. To know Casaubon the Judaist is, we will argue, to know Casaubon the classicist in a new way.

Casaubon the Hellenist

Casaubon lives on in scholarly memory as a classical philologist of supreme skill and learning, whose name still adorns the critical apparatuses of a dozen classical authors. In the last days of 1591, he finished his commentary on the *Characters* of Theophrastus. The author, who was Aristotle's star pupil and became his successor as head of the Lyceum, composed this lively set of character sketches for unknown reasons, at an uncertain date.[5] The figures Theophrastus describes, all of whom exemplify bad qualities, seem to have stepped out of the cartoons of an Athenian James Thurber. They include the Toady, who laughs so hard at a great man's jokes that he has to stuff his cloak into his mouth to control himself; the Superstitious Man, who will not step on a tombstone, approach a pregnant woman or a corpse, or pass a crossroads without making a libation; the Chatterbox, who is as likely to tell you "I threw up yesterday" as to give you the price of wheat, and does not care if either fact interests you; and the Talker, whose logorrhea menaces the entire city: "on a jury he prevents others from reaching a verdict, at the theatre from watching the play, at dinner from getting on with their meal."[6] As so often, an ancient text turns out, like the Mad Gardener's rattlesnake, to be

---

4. Scaliger 1695, 83; 1740, II, 259: "C'est le plus grand homme que nous ayons en Grec: Je luy cede; est doctissimus omnium qui hodie vivunt." The fullest study of Casaubon as a philologist is now Parenty 2009.

5. See in general Millett 2007 and the splendid introduction to Diggle 2004.

6. Theophrastus, *Characters* 7.1; 2.4; 16.5, 9; 3.3; 7.8, trans. Diggle 2004.

the Middle of Next Week—or at least next week's faculty meetings and dinner parties.

Though short and entertaining, the text bristles with difficulties of every kind, from interpolations to simple corruptions. More important, as a whole it is unlike anything else in classical Greek prose generally, or the works of Theophrastus in particular.[7] The Florentine Hellenist Pier Vettori, who produced a pioneering critical edition of the tragedies of Aeschylus for Casaubon's father-in-law, the classical scholar and publisher Henri Estienne, rejected the *Characters* out of hand as spurious, as Casaubon knew.[8] Casaubon, moreover, had to work through the text while traveling, deprived of the books and notes that remained in his study in Geneva.[9] Nonetheless, he composed a little masterpiece of divination and interpretation. He proved the work authentic and did more than any of his predecessors and most of his successors to clarify its meaning.[10]

In the Greek text and Latin translation published by the scholar-printer Fédéric Morel in 1583, Theophrastus describes the Boastful Man as follows: "He stands right in the *diazeugma* and tells foreigners how much money he has invested at sea."[11] Reading this, Casaubon asked one simple but vital question: "What is he calling a *diazeugma?*"[12] He had every reason to wonder. Although Morel printed the Greek word in his text, he had not a clue what it meant in this context. He transliterated it, rather than translated it, in his Latin version, and when he tried to explain the term in a marginal

---

7. Diggle 2004, 4–37.

8. Casaubon 1592, 4: "Quare non assentior doctis quibusdam viris, qui ab Aristotelis discipulo hunc librum abiudicarunt: qui praeter illud unicum argumentum de quo mox dicemus, nihil penitus habent quo suam sententiam tueri possint. An enim illud dicent? parum tanto scriptore dignum hoc esse scriptum. Ita video doctissimum Victorium existimasse. Mihi vero contrarium prorsus videtur: nam et opus hoc, esset modo integrum, et quale auctor ediderat, dignissimum iudico quod tanto viro tribuatur: et vicissim, eo fuisse comperior Theophrastum ingenio, ut nemo aptior huic argumento isto modo tractando inveniri potuerit." See, e.g., Vettori 1582, 196 (17.7): "nec tamen me fallit ita quoque bestiolam appellatam, cuius meminit auctor libelli, quo describuntur naturae hominum ac mores: Theophrasto autem nunc ille falso attribuitur"; and 1582, 434 (37.5), on the "Vetus proverbium . . . de ficorum inter se similitudine" (Theophrastus, *Characters* 5.5): "proverbium autem, quod significavi, legitur in libello, quo describuntur mores diversorum ingeniorum, qui inscribitur ea de causa, χαρακτῆρες, et Theophrasto vulgo attribuitur." There is also what looks like a draft for a polite dissent in Bod MS Casaubon 11, 14: "Δ sed cum ille nullam huius suae sententiae rationem attulerit, liceat nobis ab optimo viro et doctissimo [added below line: cum bona manum eius gratia] dissentire."

9. Diggle 2004, 53 n. 169.

10. See in general Parenty 2009, 154–163.

11. Theophrastus, *Characters* 23.2, as translated in Morel 1583, 11 recto: "Arrogantis autem hominis proprium est, dum rectus stat in diazeugmate commemorare hospitibus quam multas in mari divitias habeat." Cf. Diggle 2004, 53: "F. Morel (1583) contributes little or nothing."

12. Casaubon 1592, 260 (misnumbered 262): "Quid appellat διάζευγμα?"

note, he lunged in every direction, less like a purposeful commentator than the proverbial cow caught in barbed wire: "it seems to be some kind of gap or transverse beam on a bridge, or a port, or the vestibule of a building."[13] Casaubon replaced wild guesses with systematic reasoning and precise information. He thought it clear that Theophrastus must have brought his imaginary braggart onstage in "some public place at Athens where meetings used to take place."[14] A chorus in Aristophanes' *Knights* (979) mentioned the "*Deigma*." And a note in the Greek scholia on Aristophanes explained that the term referred to exactly the sort of public spot Casaubon had in mind: "the *Deigma* is a place in the Piraeus where many foreigners and citizens met and told stories."[15] "I think," Casaubon concluded, "that the passage must be corrupt, and I read *Deigmati* [(in the) *Deigma*]. For the *Deigma* was a place in the Piraeus that took its name from its function. For it was where foreign merchants laid out a sample [*deigma*] of their wares."[16] The fact that the scholium mentioned foreigners clinched his case. Theophrastus' braggart, after all, spent his time "explaining" his business "to foreigners."[17] As emended, the whole passage became a vivid, concrete description of a boastful man, "standing in the market in the Piraeus" rather as Antonio stands on the Rialto in Shakespeare's *Merchant of Venice*, telling strangers about what should have been his private business.[18]

This emendation is only one of the many cases in which Casaubon focused his vast learning, like a great philological laser, on individual passages in the text, and transformed them from gobbledygook to coherent Greek. Again and again he used his knowledge of parallels from Athenian literature to set the *Characters* into context. Theophrastus' Obsequious Man, for example, not only has his hair cut and his teeth whitened and changes his clothes too often, and frequents bankers, but also "dallies in the gymnasia

13. Morel 1583, 11 recto, printed marginal note on "in diazeugmate" (in the Latin translation of 23.2): "Id genus quoddam esse videtur interstitij vel transversi tigni in ponte, portuve aut aedium vestibulo."

14. Casaubon 1592, 260 (misnumbered 262): "non est dubium, publicum aliquem Athenarum locum intelligi ubi conventus fieri solebant."

15. Casaubon, as we will see, read this in Aristophanes 1547, 243: "σύμμαχος. σκέψασθε τί δή ποτέ ἐστι τὸ δεῖγμα τῶν δικῶν. παρεῖται γάρ φησιν, εἰ μὴ τὸ δεῖγμα τόπος ἐστὶν ἐν πειραιεῖ, ἔνθα πολλοὶ συνήγοντο ξένοι καὶ πολῖται καὶ ἐλογοποίουν."

16. Casaubon 1592, 260 (misnumbered 262): "Quare arbitror locum esse corruptum, et lego Δείγματι. Digma appellabatur locus in Piraeeo e re nomen habens. Ibi enim peregrini mercatores suarum mercium δεῖγμα et specimen producebant, ἐν τρυβλίῳ credo περιφέροντες, ut alicubi Plutarchus ait [Plutarch, *Demosthenes* 23.6]. Itaque peregrinis hominibus fere erat ille locus refertus."

17. Ibid., 260 (misnumbered 262): "Auctor scholiorum Aristophanis: Δεῖγμα τόπος ἐστὶν ἐν Πειραιεῖ ἔνθα πολλοὶ συνήγοντο ξένοι καὶ πολῖται καὶ ἐλογοποίουν. quae postrema verba ita hanc emendationem confirmant, ut nihil supra."

18. Diggle 2004, 53–54, offers this emendation as an example "of the wonders worked by his [Casaubon's] first-hand learning" (53).

where the ephebes exercise."[19] This phrase, Casaubon admitted, might simply mean that the Obsequious Man liked to work out with the young. But he thought it also had a "more hidden sense, which must be recovered from the ancient customs of the men who lived in Theophrastus' time."[20] In Athens, Casaubon explained, men who nourished a particularly sharp thirst for glory liked to spend their time "in the places where youths exercised, so that they could be seen by them, and enjoy, as one way to profit from their high position, the attention of the young."[21] The Obsequious Man, accordingly, might haunt the gymnasium in order to praise the great men who regularly appeared there. Casaubon's evidence came from the Athenian comic poets. Eupolis, in a lost work, mocked Aristophanes for hanging around the ephebes' gymnasia after winning the year's competition for comedy; and Aristophanes denied in the *Wasps* that he had done so.[22] For Casaubon, the simple fact that the *Characters* also mentioned this practice "was enough in itself to supply a basis for judging the age of this text and its author."[23] Casaubon knew that the text was genuine, as Vettori had not, because his reading had steeped him in the Athenian mores of the fourth century B.C.E., which he recognized everywhere in the text.

Casaubon's edition displays his mastery of Greek and his skill at conjectural emendation. More important, it shows him thinking in a richly historical way about an ancient book.[24] Again and again, Casaubon explained

19. Theophrastus, *Characters* 5.7, trans. Diggle 2004.

20. Casaubon 1592, 83, a gloss on οὗ ἂν ἔφηβοι γυμνάζονται: "An ut se ipse exerceat cum illis, quod erat hominis elegantis et liberalis, quam famam captat iste? Potest quidem ita accipi: caeterum alius omnino est, isque reconditior huius loci sensus: ex veteri more eorum hominum qui Theophrasti aetate vixerunt petendus."

21. Ibid., 83: "Sciendum igitur, moris fuisse Athenis hominibus iis quos inanis gloriolae γαργαλισμὸς titillaret, in illis locis ut plurimum versari ubi se adolescentes exercebant: quo nimirum possent ab illis conspici, atque hunc ipsi sui honoris fructum perciperent, dum in se iuniorum ora obverterent [changed to converterent in Casaubon's copy]."

22. Aristophanes, *Wasps* 1025; Casaubon's source for Eupolis is the scholium on that line (Aristophanes 1547, 348). On these accusations and their larger context in the public, performative world of Athens, see esp. Scanlon 2002, 211–219; and Storey 2003, 288–290.

23. Casaubon 1592, 83–84: "Atque hoc nomine multi olim irrisi a veteribus poetis comicis: in his Eupolis poeta: cui obiicit Aristophanes quod parta victoria palaestras obambularet, ut ab adolescentibus spectaretur, ob recens partam victoriam insignis et δακτυλόδεικτος. Περιῄει, ait Aristophanes, τὰς παλαίστρας σεμνυνόμενος Καὶ τοῖς παισὶν ἑαυτὸν δῆλον ποιῶν τῆς νίκης ἕνεκα. Quare idem Aristophanes in Vespis laudi sibi tribuit, quod tale nihil unquam fecerit: se enim nunquam solitum παλαίστρας περικωμάζειν περιίοντα. ⋀ Profecto vel ex uno hoc loco de antiquitate huius scripti et scriptoris ipsius licet existimare." Casaubon's ink caret in his copy of the text (BL 525.a.10) indicated a marginal note in which he added a further testimonium: "Aeschines quoque Demosthenem facit σεμνυννόμενον ἐν τῇ τῶν μειρακίων διατριβῇ [In Timarchum 175]." He incorporated this in the second edition in Casaubon 1599, 161.

24. Naturally, Casaubon's mastery of Athenian institutions seems very limited when judged in modern, or even in eighteenth-century, terms: see Parenty 2009, 97–109.

to his readers that "the contents of this book were not examples made up by the author but drawn from everyday life."[25] With his usual precision, he noted that the closest parallels to the *Characters* occurred not in other works by Theophrastus, or those of his teacher Aristotle, but in Athenian comedy—the source, as we have already seen, for much of his information about the historical world through which Theophrastus' superstitious and obsequious men bumbled their way.[26] True, Casaubon's instincts and erudition did not always lead him down the right paths. Following the preface, now seen as spurious, Casaubon described the work as moral in its purpose, even though it contained only examples of bad conduct (the positive examples that had once formed part of the text, he insisted, had been lost, along with some of the bad ones).[27] This misinterpretation would shape readings and adaptations of the *Characters* for a long time to come.[28] Casaubon also seems not to have guessed that in Athens, "loiterers in gymnasia are usually suspected of looking for boys to pick up"[29]—although his own statement that celebrity loiterers sought the applause of the young was not wholly off the mark.[30] Still, in these and many other cases, Casaubon's little book reveals the vast learning, lucid interpretations, and precise, unexpected connections drawn between disparate texts that one might expect of a great classical scholar.[31]

25. Casaubon 1592, 131: "Etiam hic meminisse lectorem velim eius quod alibi diximus: quaecunque hoc libro continentur, ea non ficta esse ab auctore exempla: sed e vita quotidiana desumpta: et ex iis quae vere facta dictave essent, hunc librum esse concinnatum."

26. Ibid., 9: "Fit autem hoc a Theophrasto magna ex parte $\mu\iota\mu\eta\tau\iota\kappa\hat{\omega}\varsigma$: quod poetarum esse, supra posuimus. Itaque plurima in his brevibus reliquiis, quae veluti tabulae e naufragio superstites utcunque remanserunt, legas, ex quibus huius operis cum poetis, scenicis maxime et comicis, quos esse optimos exprimendorum morum artifices scimus, affinitas percipi queat: ut suis locis cum cura est a nobis indicatum." Note Casaubon's use of the phrase "veluti tabulae e naufragio," normally used by antiquaries to refer to their method of reconstructing objects or institutions from fragmentary evidence (see Fubini 2003). It gives a sense of his own view of his historical method as an editor.

27. Casaubon 1592, 9: "Nunc, melior eius pars, proh dolor! intercidit: nam et ea pars quae erat de virtutibus tota hodie desideratur: et illius quae de vitiis, haut scio an portio saltem $\dot{a}\xi\iota\acute{o}\lambda o\gamma o\varsigma$ fuerit, quantumcunque est quod ad nos pervenit. Quota enim est obsecro vitiorum pars quae hic continetur?"

28. Ibid., 8–9: "Quorsum haec? ut appareret libellum hunc medii cuiusdam esse inter philosophorum et poetarum scripta generis. Subiectum quidem est de moribus: quos emendare, unicus est auctori in hoc opere finis propositus: atque hoc saltem illi cum ethico philosopho commune est, et ambobus proprium. Caeterum tractatur hoc subiectum, non more philosophorum: sed novo quodam docendi genere, quod descriptione constat eorum quae homines aut hac aut illa virtute vitiove praediti, facere $\hat{\hat{\eta}}$ $\tau o\iota o\hat{v}\tau o\acute{\iota}$ $\epsilon\dot{\iota}\sigma\iota$ consueverunt." On Casaubon's moral interpretation of the text and its impact see Boyce 1947, 44, 122, 160.

29. Diggle 2004, 236.

30. Cf. Fisher 2000, 377.

31. For an excellent recent account of Casaubon's life and work see John Considine, "Casaubon, Isaac," in *ODNB* 2004.

But what does it mean to study a classical scholar historically? Much of the work Casaubon did on classical Greek and Latin texts was, like his work on Theophrastus, highly technical in character, and by its nature not easy to link with the larger contexts, social, cultural, religious, in which he lived and worked. Putting into context the Casaubon who emended and explicated Greek texts is a little bit like doing the same for a great mathematician—very hard to do without imprisoning the subject in an iron cage of forced analogies. The difficulty of connecting the work to the man and his world has long been clear, for it forms a central theme of the one great book on Casaubon, Mark Pattison's eloquent biography. This magnificent book, first published in 1875, traced Casaubon's career in precise detail.[32] Pattison followed Casaubon on the crooked, difficult path that led from modest professorships at Geneva and Montpellier, where he taught from 1596 to 1600, to the royal library in Paris, where he spent the decade 1600–1610, and finally to London, where he served James I for the last four years of his life. He summarized Casaubon's work as teacher and scholar, described his personal circumstances, and made clear how prominent a star this philologist had been in the intellectual galaxies of his time. Though long, Pattison's book had a Theophrastan side: it bristled with sharply observed pen portraits of Casaubon's friends and enemies, patrons, and correspondents. These, like Pattison's sharp observations on the world of learning, made his book a classic of Victorian literature.

In some ways, Pattison turned Casaubon himself into a mammoth Theophrastan character. Mesmerized, as a young writer, by Casaubon's thousand-page Latin diary,[33] Pattison saw his subject—as the diary suggested—as a tragic figure, who had driven himself to despair, vainly trying to master an infinite universe of knowledge in a finite lifetime. He used the rich evidence of Casaubon's letters—as full of complaints as the e-mails of our contemporaries—to fill in a scarifying portrait of the unworldly scholar, endlessly tormented by his inability to work as hard or produce as much as he wished, patronized and exploited by lesser men, and distinguished, in the end, not for his intellect but for his industry.[34] No one who has read Pattison's book will forget his account of Casaubon's autopsy. The distinguished physician

---

32. Pattison 1892. On Pattison and his career see H. S. Jones 2007.

33. Casaubon's diary showed Pattison the possibility for writing a new and vivid style of history. See H. S. Jones 2007.

34. Pattison 1892, 449, defending Casaubon and other scholars against the critique of Thomas De Quincey that they "were poor as thinkers": "The scholars were not 'poor as thinkers,' because thinking was not their profession. They were busy interpreting the past. The fifteenth century had rediscovered antiquity, the sixteenth was slowly deciphering it. For this task, memory, not invention, was the faculty in demand." This assessment is cited approvingly in Momigliano 1950, 307.

Theodore Turquet de Mayerne found that Casaubon's bladder had become malformed and full of "mucous calculous matter": "The malformation was congenital, but had been aggravated by sedentary habits, and inattention to the calls of nature, while the mind of the student was absorbed in study and meditation."[35] Casaubon emerged as a Protestant counterpart to the Baroque saints of the same period, who suffered the pains of martyrdom as they made the mystical ascent—one who suffered his pains, however, in pursuit of human, historical knowledge, some of which inevitably eluded him.[36] And the lesson has not been lost on Pattison's many readers. Harold Laski repeatedly took *Casaubon* with him on holiday.[37] "It sets me all on fire every time I read it," he wrote to Oliver Wendell Holmes in 1918, "to think of that lonely fellow ploughing through his manuscripts unwelcomed because one day the path might be clear for the inspired genius to travel by."[38]

Pattison made clear that Casaubon not only read but also wrote enormous commentaries, many of them on even more enormous texts. But he dismissed these enterprises, which represented a form of learning totally cut off from life, devoid of literary taste or passion:

> Admitted thus behind the scenes to a sixteenth-century workshop, we feel that we are now in the age of erudition. The renaissance, the spring-tide of modern life, with its genial freshness, is far behind us. The creative period is past, the accumulative is set in. Genius can now do nothing, the day is to dull industry. The prophet is departed, and in his place we have the priest of the book . . . The scholar of 1500 gambols in the free air of classical poetry, as in an atmosphere of joy. The scholar of 1600 has a century of compilation behind him, and "drags at each remove a lengthening chain."[39]

35. Pattison 1892, 417: "After death was discovered, what no diagnosis could have detected, a monstrous malformation of the vesica. The bladder itself was of natural size and healthy. But an opening in its left side admitted into a second, or supplementary bladder. This sack was at least six times as large as the natural bladder, and was full of mucous calculous matter."

36. See Siraisi 2007, 71–72. She shows that for all its vividness, Mayerne's autopsy in fact drew on a well-established tradition of connecting scholars' illnesses to their absorption in their work.

37. Holmes and Laski 1953, I, 441: "the book I [Laski] never fail to take away on vacation, the *Life of Casaubon* by Mark Pattison which I read again with great joy [1922]"; I, 633: "I [Laski] read also Pattison's *Life of Casaubon* which I found wholly delightful [1924]"; II, 1195: "I [Laski] have enjoyed greatly re-reading Mark Pattison's *Life of Casaubon* and Diderot's *Life* by Scherer—both of them, I think, tip-top in their way [1929]."

38. Ibid., 155. Here and elswhere, especially at II, 1195, Laski's remarks about the book are accurate enough that they seem to reflect a real reading. We are less certain about a 1923 remark to Holmes, I, 571—"Also I have read an old German, Bernays on *Scaliger* with something of the same delight that I had in 1918 reading Pattison's *Life of Casaubon*"—since the two books are very different in character.

39. Pattison 1892, 109–110. The internal quotation comes from Oliver Goldsmith.

Casaubon embodied the scholar's search not for insight but for knowledge—a quest inevitably condemned to failure, as the scholar who undertook it was condemned to melancholy, by his own fallibility, forgetfulness, and mortality. No wonder that, in the century and a quarter since Pattison's book appeared, Casaubon's name has most often been remembered in connection with the fictional antihero often seen as a portrait of the melancholy Pattison: George Eliot's Mr. Casaubon.[40]

In fact, as the late Tony Nuttall pointed out in a wonderful book-length essay, Pattison—himself an extraordinarily productive writer and an extremely neurotic man—projected his own feelings of dissatisfaction onto his subject.[41] Like Pattison himself, the depressive, melancholy Casaubon worked frenetically: "I rose at five: alas, how late!" begins one characteristic journal entry.[42] More important, he was consistently creative, in a wide range of fields. Casaubon produced seventeen children as well as a vast stream of learned works, some of which he wrote while using one foot to rock the current infant's cradle. He edited and wrote commentaries on Diogenes Laertius, Theocritus, Athenaeus, Strabo, Suetonius, the younger Pliny, the *Scriptores historiae Augustae*, and Persius; translated Polybius freshly into Latin; assembled, though he did not publish, brilliant notes on Polybius and Aeschylus; and wrote both the first modern treatise on the nature of ancient satire and a vast critique of Cardinal Cesare Baronio's history of the early church, the *Exercitationes*, published with no small splendor in 1614. He also annotated hundreds of books and filled almost sixty notebooks, now in the Bodleian Library, with his reflections on texts of every sort. A number of the greatest classical scholars of the last half-century—Eduard Fraenkel, Arnaldo Momigliano, James Diggle—have occupied themselves with Casaubon's technical work. Every one of them has confirmed Casaubon's brilliance as an emender and interpreter of texts—as Nuttall, himself a formidable Greek scholar, did in his turn.[43]

It is not hard to explain why Pattison, for all his gifts, failed to do justice to Casaubon's scholarship. In the first place, he lacked sympathy with some of Casaubon's central interests. Pattison knew classical scholarship in many forms—from the Latin and Greek verse composition, ancient history, and classical philosophy that occupied Oxford tutors and their pupils to the cutting-edge philology of Jacob Bernays and his contemporaries in Germany. But his vision of the discipline was narrow: far narrower than that of

---

40. For recent reviews of the endless debates on this topic see Nuttall 2003 and H. S. Jones 2007.

41. Nuttall 2003.

42. Casaubon 1850, I, 4.

43. Fraenkel 1950, I, 61–77; Momigliano, 1974 and 1977; Diggle 2004, 8, 53–54; Nuttall 2003. See now Parenty 2009.

German classicists like Bernays or Hermann Usener. As a young follower of Newman in the Tractarian Movement, Pattison had studied the fathers of the church intensively. As the master of Lincoln College and Oxford's most eloquent advocate of German *Wissenschaft,* he insisted on the supreme importance of a limited canon of Greek texts.

By contrast, as Pattison regularly complained, Casaubon devoted as much time and energy to the fathers of the church and other late antique writers as he did to the so-called classics. A passionate Protestant, living in a world of religious war, one in which many of his friends suffered persecution or death for their beliefs, he believed that he had a duty to use his skills as a scholar to work out the true story of Christian origins—and, by doing so, to reveal what a true Christian church should be like in his own day. From the late 1590s, he plunged into the study of the Greek fathers with the precision he brought to all his reading and to the texts that mattered most to him.[44] To Pattison, however, Casaubon's engagement with late antique and Christian writers only proved his lack of true taste. Like many of his contemporaries, he cared less—as Pattison said of King James—for "the grand classical antiquity, for which none about him had eye or ear," than for "the bastard antiquity of the fourth century."[45]

Thanks to Marrou and Momigliano, Bowersock and Brown, Hopkins and Shaw, we have all learned to see the centuries that gripped Casaubon as central ones in the history of the Mediterranean world.[46] We read the many forms of literature they produced with sympathy and interest, and we see in the earlier scholars who knew this world so well creative philologists and historians whose work still demands and rewards attention. When Casaubon carefully notes in 1611 that Eunapius is worth reading because he offers such rich information on "the last efforts of a dying paganism" to rival Christianity, we hear a voice that will later sound in the pages of Tillemont and Gibbon.[47] The progress of scholarship in our own time has enabled us to appreciate the scholarship of the late sixteenth and the seventeenth centuries—an age when the *Corpus Iuris* and the church fathers, the poetry of Ausonius and the bilingual glossaries from which young Romans learned

44. Parenty 2009, 93–96.

45. Pattison 1892, 263.

46. See in general Bowersock, Brown, and Grabar 1999.

47. Bod MS Casaubon 25, 113 recto: "Lectio Eunapii ad quid praecipue utilis. Ad cognoscendum extremos deficientis paganismi conatus. Notandum autem istos noviss. philosophos deditos fuisse ϑειασμοῖς, aemulatione Christianorum. sed quam frivolus ille ϑειασμὸς. sic Porphyrius scripsit de philosophia ἐκ τῶν λογίων, de quo libro Junius in Animadversis." For the date of this note see Casaubon 1850, II, 865, 867; and for the larger context of such thoughts see Pocock 1999–. Also relevant are the notes in Casaubon's copy of the works of Julian (Wren Library, Trinity College Cambridge, Adv.d.1.30).

Greek were the common currency, not only of Casaubon, but of all the contemporaries he admired most—in a way that Pattison could not.[48]

The conditions of scholarly life in Victorian Britain, as Pattison understood them, also limited the scope of his project. Pattison knew that Casaubon had much to say about authors whom he would have seen as classical: Aeschylus, Sophocles, Theophrastus. But Pattison did not believe that he could expect English readers to follow an exposition of obsolete commentaries.[49] Although he read Casaubon's classical publications, he said little about them. Early in his twenties Casaubon published a commentary on Diogenes Laertius' *Lives of the Philosophers.* At one point in this anecdotal book, Diogenes represents the poet and Homeric critic Aratus as asking Timon of Phlius how he can get hold of a sound text of Homer. Timon tells him to find an old one—one that no one (that is, no one like Aratus) has tampered with (9.113). This lackluster anecdote inspired Casaubon to rethink everything he knew about the origin, transmission, and state of preservation of the Homeric epics. He connected Diogenes' story with a remark by the Jewish historian Josephus,[50] and he drew conclusions as revolutionary as they were concise from this evidence:

> Josephus says that Homer did not leave his poems in written form, but they were preserved by memorization and written down much later. If this is true, then I do not see how we can ever have them in a correct form, even if we have the oldest manuscripts. For it is likely that they were written down in a form quite different from that in which he first composed them.[51]

The German scholar Friedrich August Wolf, who mounted a far more systematic attack on the authenticity of the Homeric epics in his *Prolegom-*

48. For the prevalence of late antique and early medieval studies in the sixteenth and seventeenth centuries, see, e.g., Grafton 1983–1993, I, chap. 5; and see more broadly Quantin 2009.

49. In fact Pattison's *Casaubon,* though enthusiastically reviewed, sold poorly—to the surprise of the author's tax inspector, who thought, after reading the enthusiastic review in the *Times,* that Pattison would have substantial royalties to report (H. S. Jones 2007, 173).

50. Josephus, *Contra Apionem* 1.12: "Of the works generally accepted as genuine by the Greeks, none is older than the poems of Homer. And it is obvious that he came later than the siege of Troy. Now some say that even he did not leave his poems in writing, but that they were committed to memory as songs and put together afterward, and that this is the reason why they have so many variations." Casaubon wrote "No" beside this passage in his working copy of Josephus, BL C.76.g.7, 917.

51. Casaubon 1583, 270; 1593, 114: "Si verum est quod Iosephus ait, Homerum sua carmina [changed in 1593 to poemata] scripta non reliquisse, sed διαμνημονευόμενα multo post scripta fuisse, non video quomodo satis emendata possint ea haberi, vel si antiquissimos habeamus codices: siquidem verisimile est non paullo aliter ea fuisse scripta, ac essent ab ipso composita."

ena to Homer of 1795, still quoted Casaubon's astounding remark as an important precedent.[52] Yet Pattison—who wrote a famous essay on Wolf—found no room for this point in his massive book.

Much of Casaubon's writing, moreover, remained unpublished, in his manuscript copybooks and the margins of his books. Pattison examined these materials with interest and insight. They showed him that Casaubon had developed a distinctive personal style for reading and taking notes—a point that Pattison expounded at length in one of the most striking parts of his book.[53] Casaubon, he explained, "read pen in hand, with a sheet of paper by his side, on which he noted much, but wrote out nothing."[54] These pages gradually grew into notebooks: "When he had accumulated a number of sheets, he tied them up in a packet, or stitched them up in a book, and called it 'indigesta ὕλη'—materials."[55] Casaubon decorated the margins of his books in the same way.

In the end, though, Pattison found these materials largely indecipherable. Even Casaubon's younger contemporaries, he knew, had found it almost impossible to use these notes: "'Casaubon's way,' Grotius tells Camerarius, 'was not to write out what he designed to publish, but to trust to his memory, with at least a few jottings, partly on the margin of his books, partly on loose sheets—true sibylline leaves' . . . Casaubon's notes are bare references, and references not to places in books, but to the thing or word to which he intended to recur. To this vast mass of material his own memory was the only key."[56] Similarly, although Casaubon annotated his books heavily, they were

---

52. Wolf 1884, 137–138 n. 42. For the larger story see Ferreri 2007.

53. The novelty of Pattison's approach is well brought out by G. O. Trevelyan to Pattison, 25 May 1876, Bod MS Pattison 57, 260 recto–261 recto, quoted in part by H. S. Jones 2007, 174: "Dear Mr Pattison, Your kind letter gave me very real pleasure. It so happens that I had the rare advantage of reading your Casaubon exactly at the time when I had still before me the whole task of portraying Macaulay's methods and habits as a writer and reader. I read it, in fact, during the Whitsuntide holidays in last year, when I had just completed my tenth chapter. How much I owe to the Life of Casaubon I can not exactly define; but without it I do not think that I should ever have had the courage deliberately, and at length, to dwell for so long on Macaulay's ways as a scholar. I venture to hope that you detected traces of its influence."

54. Pattison 1892, 428–429.

55. Ibid., 428.

56. Ibid. The original source is Grotius to Ioachim Camerarius, 27 July 1628, in Grotius 1687, 809: "Casauboni gaudeo a te mentionem fieri, cujus ingenium vere apertum ac probum non minus ego semper veneratus sum quam raram eruditionem. Quam mihi amicus fuerit satis testari poterunt literae quas nuper in Batavos misi cum editio ejus epistolarum adornari diceretur. Dixit mihi ipse cum Londini quotidie simul essemus anno hujus saeculi XIII se post migrationem e Gallia omnes illas militares literas ex animo abjecisse, quarum incitamentum illi fuerat Regum idem ac militum maximus: translatum vero in Britanniam studia quoque se eo transtulisse, quo vergeret animus Regis cui non tam arma quam pax et Religio cordi. Deinde is erat Casaubonus qui nihil parati penes se haberet, nisi in memoria et si forte in oris librorum aut brevibus schedis, Sibyllae foliis. Itaque in Polybium notas nullas habemus nisi

"scored under, and marked anyhow, to catch the eye in turning over the leaves"—filled with notes that served as reminders of passages in the text but did not themselves preserve any original thoughts. As Pattison pointed out, moreover, Casaubon himself described note-taking, in his commonplace book, as an art of memory: "Remember to set down everything you read in books of excerpts. This is the only way to aid your failing memory. As the proverb has it, One knows as much as his memory holds."[57] In taking these statements literally—as Eduard Fraenkel first showed in detail—Pattison was simply wrong.[58] Casaubon's notes bulge with everything from conjectural emendations to historical theories. They allow us to reconstruct in extraordinary detail his ways of working with texts, and in scores of cases they reveal novel literary, historical, and cultural interpretations taking shape.

Take the case of Theophrastus. The British Library possesses Casaubon's annotated working copies of both his first, 1592 edition of the *Characters* and the expanded one of 1599.[59] He used his copy of the first edition to accumulate material for the second, ranging from citations about men who haunted the ephebes' gymnasiums to five previously unknown character sketches, provided by his friend the jurist Marquard Freher from a manuscript in the Palatine Library in Heidelberg. And he continued working in the second, in some cases devising elegant new conjectures and arguments.[60] He also took separate notes on Theophrastus, which survive in two of his manuscript copybooks in the Bodleian Library. The first of these, Casaubon 7, contains the working draft of his commentary.[61] Finally, the British Library possesses Casaubon's copy of Aristophanes and the Aristophanic scholia—a work that, as we have seen, provided essential aid as he navigated the rocky archipelago of Theophrastus' little book.[62]

To bring these materials together is to descend from the thin air of "history of classical scholarship" into a far more vivid and concrete realm, one in which we can actually watch Casaubon spin the webs of annotation that made his discoveries possible. We have seen that the scholia to Aristophanes

---

in primum librum, et has quoque non perfectas, quae post editum ab ipso in angusta forma Polybium, cum minoris figurae edito prodierunt. Nec in Aelianum quicquam ipsius est."

57. Bod MS Casaubon 16, 5 verso: "Quicquid legis in Excerptorum libros referre memineris: haec unica ratio labenti memoriae succurrendi. Scitum a. illud est, Tantum quisque scit, quantum memoria tenet."

58. Fraenkel 1950, I, 61–77.

59. BL 525.a.10 and 1089.h.7.(2). On these and what follows see Diggle 2004, 53–54.

60. Diggle 2004, 340–341 and 341 n. 72.

61. Bod MSS Casaubon 7 and Casaubon 11; see Diggle 2004, 340–341.

62. BL C.77.g.12.

supplied Casaubon with vital information. His copy reveals much more. Casaubon believed in principle that the scholar had a duty to master all the commentaries on his texts. Accordingly, he read these dry but often corrupt or cryptic notes from end to end.[63] Casaubon, moreover, was interested not only in ancient texts, but also in the full world of material remains and institutions that the antiquaries of the preceding century and beyond had reconstructed. He read the works of earlier antiquaries like Onofrio Panvinio and Pedro Chacon. In 1605 he discussed material remains with the brilliant young dean of antiquaries in his own time, Nicolas-Claude Fabri de Peiresc, who taught him to trust only the actual coins, not modern publications of them, and showed him unpublished inscriptions.[64] In 1607, when the Triopian inscription of Herodes Atticus was discovered on the Appian Way, Casaubon was the natural choice to edit the verse text by Marcellus of Side (unfortunately, he attributed the shrine of Regilla, for which the inscription was composed, to Herod the Great rather than to the second-century orator and sponsor of monumental projects, Herodes Atticus).[65]

Casaubon, in other words, knew how to set texts against a three-dimensional historical backdrop—and how to construct that backdrop, as the scholar must, from the texts themselves. Again and again, he noted down in his copy of Aristophanes, often with the comment "Mos" (custom), exactly the sorts of information about Athenian rituals and institutions that he used so effectively in his commentary.[66] He found a place on the title page for a reference to the rivalry between Eupolis and Aristophanes, which the

63. On the origins and transmission of the scholia on Aristophanes see Dunbar 1995, 31–51; Dickey 2007, 28–31. Casaubon was studying these scholia in 1590; see Parenty 2009, 385, 409. For Casaubon's own sense of the importance of commentaries see Bod MS Casaubon 16 (a real commonplace book), 4 verso (margin): "In primis conquirendi magnorum scriptorum interpretes, ut et recte citentur intellecti et locorum collatio fieri possit."

64. For Casaubon's readings of antiquarian works see Bod MS Casaubon 25, 84 recto; Bod MS Casaubon 60, 130 recto–131 recto; and Casaubon 1710, 10–11; for his conversation with Peiresc see Gassendi 1641, 82–84; and Bod MS Casaubon 60, 15 verso: "COL. JULIA PATERNA. COL. Julia Augusta. In antiquis monumentis reperiuntur multae his nominibus appellatae coloniae. et didicimus ab eruditiss. Aquensi senatore Chalasso Peires, in veteri insc. quae non est edita Arelate dici COL. Jul. Pater. Ac Juliae q. omnes et leges et colonia a Julio Caes. et Augusto dictae sunt. sed videntur col. Julii Caes. a coloniis Augusti separatae cognomine PATERNA." On the traditions of antiquarianism see the classic study by Momigliano 1950, and for more recent perspectives Miller 2000; Stenhouse 2005; and Miller 2007.

65. Casaubon 1606?, reprinted as Baremius 1608 (the inscription is Kaibel, *Inscr. Graec. Ital. et Sicil.* 1390). His mistake was corrected by the Augsburg humanist Marx Welser, himself a very eminent antiquary. See Welser to Hoeschel, n.d., in Welser 1682, 838; Welser to Casaubon, 4 June 1608, BL MS Burney 366, 312 recto; Welser to Hoeschel, n.d., ibid., 297 verso = Welser 1682, 838–839. Pattison 1892, 463, offers a strange and unfounded interpretation of the episode.

66. Casaubon, marginal notes in BL C.77.g.12, 13, on *Plutus* 227: "Mos. Qui ex sacrificio Delphic[o] redibant suis partem aliquam victimae caesae asportabant"; ibid., 42, on *Plutus* 845: "Mos. Vestes quibus

scholia documented, and on the margin of the relevant page for the term "Digma."[67] This close reading of a difficult and demanding anthology of ancient and medieval commentaries, often abridged or corrupt, must have taken place before Casaubon set to work on Theophrastus. Slow, systematic exploration of this unpromising, rubble-strewn landscape underpinned his ability to master the fragmentary *Characters*. Casaubon read the scholia themselves, moreover, as critically as the ancient text they illuminated. He realized that the version printed by Sigismund Gelenius in 1547, which he used, was itself both late and composite: "Note: this passage on its own shows that these scholia were clearly compiled not so long ago by some scholar from a variety of manuscripts. It is clear that he often found himself at a loss, since he was using corrupt and lacunose manuscripts."[68] Here, as in his remark about the text of Homer, Casaubon opened trails that the Dutch and German scholars of the eighteenth and nineteenth centuries would travel.[69]

Casaubon's draft commentary on Theophrastus does not add materially to our understanding of how he realized where the Boastful Man took his stand. But it does show Casaubon presenting his emendation in an articulately aggressive way, which he later softened for print: "Perhaps someone can explain to me exactly what the word διάζευγμα means in this passage. If not, let him admit that the passage should read as I think it should be emended, 'In the *Deigma*.'"[70] His other manuscript notes, for their part, reveal him drawing a general lesson from this particular case. For Casaubon, his success in dating the *Characters* revealed, with stark precision, that the scholarly interpreter of texts should always take, or at least begin from, a historical approach: "Note that if you compare this book with the early Attic Greek writers, it is as easy to judge the period when it was written as it is to judge that of Juvenal or Martial. For the authors of any particular period have a special quality that does not fit the writers of another period. That is

erant induti qui initiabantur, alicui deo consecrabantur. sed perlege annotationem totam"; ibid., 48, on *Plutus* 1014: "Mos. Atticae mulieres lectica deferebantur Eleusinem."

67. Casaubon, note on the title page of BL C.77.g.12: "Conqueritur suas fabulas paucis immutatis ab Eupolide surripi et Hermippo. pag. 91." For "Digma" see ibid., 243.

68. Casaubon, marginal note in ibid., 96: "† No. vel ex hoc loco apparet haec scholia fuisse ab aliquo docto viro ante annos non ita multos ex variis codd. collecta: saepe autem haesisse illi aquam apparet: quippe codd. utenti depravatis et mutilis." Cf. his note on *Plutus* 1110, ibid., 52: "Nota. Interpres hic non est antiquus quando Eustath. laudat."

69. Grafton 1981, 115–120.

70. Bod MS Casaubon 7, 53 recto: "Aut doceat me aliquis quid sibi vox διάζευγμα velit hoc loco: aut fateatur legendum esse ut nos emendandum censemus, ἐν τῷ Δείγματι." Signs of Casaubon's revision of the passage are visible in the MS.

why it is also best to explain writers by others of the same period."[71] The Casaubon made visible by the remains of his work on Theophrastus, printed and manuscript, is a figure more energetic, insightful, and directed than the one portrayed so memorably by Pattison. Yet the book in question is of modest size and scope, and offers little enlightenment on Casaubon's religious life and his application of scholarship to the Christian tradition.

"The twentieth century," writes John Considine, author of the excellent life of Casaubon in the *Oxford Dictionary of National Biography*, "has tended to see interest in Casaubon divided between specialists, and therefore impoverished: historians of classical scholarship, for instance, have sometimes seen the *Exercitationes* as a regrettable diversion of his talents rather than as the culmination of a lifetime's concern with philology and religious reformation."[72] We would argue that this tendency goes back all the way to Pattison himself: and we agree that it has made Casaubon very hard to appreciate in his own terms. And we propose to approach Casaubon with these cautions in mind: by treating all of Casaubon's writings, from marginalia to published commentaries and from informal notes to formal texts, as part of the same, as yet undefined project. For webs of thought, given a partially material form in Casaubon's scratchy script, connect the published and unpublished, formal and informal parts of his work. Casaubon often found his way into a text or a topic by taking notes, in the margins of a printed book, in a notebook, or on loose sheets of paper. The ideas that his reading sparked in him he then explored further in the entries in his journal and in letters to friends, as well as in his drafts and published works. Even the most personal documents reflect the life of Casaubon's mind, a life consumed in reading and interpretation. Pattison rightly saw that writing letters, for Casaubon, was a profound moral and spiritual enterprise. In agony on his deathbed, he still found the strength to keep up his correspondence, if more slowly than he liked, in lucid, correct Latin, and he still insisted that formal letter-writing held the larger Republic of Letters together. Correspondents of similar tastes and minds, he believed, could forge links stronger than those that connected

71. Bod MS Casaubon 11, 14: "Σηαι de aetate qua scriptus hic liber tam facile existimare si conferas cum priscis Gr. Att. quam de Juvenale aut Martiale est. Nam singularum aetatum auctores peculiare aliquid habent, quod alius aetatis script. non conveniat. Quare etiam optime scriptores per alios eiusdem aetatis explicantur." In fact, as one might expect, Casaubon's tastes in interpretation were more catholic, and more traditional, than this note suggests. Cf. Bod MS Casaubon 60, 5 recto: "Σηαι de initiis veteris philosophiae et tota philosophandi ratione antiqua Plato in Protagora doctissime disputat. Ibidem habes exemplar verae κριτικῆς et quo judicio, quo modo versandum sit in interpretatione auctorum praesertim poetarum"; and the remarkable historical analysis of patristic exegesis in Casaubon 1850, II, 882–884.

72. Considine, "Casaubon, Isaac," in *ODNB* 2004.

members of the same church.[73] But Casaubon's letters were also scholarly enterprises, in which he pursued the same philological problems that caught his eye as a reader. As we will see, they often provide detailed accounts of his analyses of texts, as well as revelatory statements of his attitudes toward them and toward his colleagues.

The same holds for his diary and his copybooks. Like many of his contemporaries, Casaubon seems to have taken rough notes in an erasable pocket notebook of donkey-skin,[74] and then transferred these materials to the diary and his copybooks, where he elaborated and refined them. It is not always easy to find the key to these sprawling, scattered notes. Casaubon's learned son Meric, who knew these materials and how they came into existence better than anyone else, wrote to John Evelyn in 1669: "Presently after the reading of yours I set my self to search my Fathers Adversaria and papers, and after a little search I found a proper head or title *de Baculis,* as an addition to what he had written upon Theophrastus; and under that title, many particular references to all kind of ancient Authors: but soe confusedly, that I think noe man, but I, that had been used to his hand and way, can make any thing of it."[75] Many of the plates in this book will give the reader a sense of what Meric had in mind. Yet the determined explorer can often find a way to the jewel at the heart of the lotus.

The material is dauntingly rich. Casaubon's correspondence includes some 2,500 letters, mostly in Latin (though some are in Greek and a few are in Hebrew).[76] Hundreds of his books survive, many of them profusely annotated. And then there are his notebooks, his publications, his diary. It will

73. Casaubon to Johannes Polyander, 23 April 1614, Bod Rawlinson Letters 76ᵃ, 213–214: "Diu est, Vir Clarissime Nobilissimeque, cum ad te scribere gestiebat animus. Nam qui saepe multos multa praeclara de [MS te] tua singulari pietate pari eruditione juncta audissem praedicare: Optabam, non ea duntaxat conjunctione animorum, quae pios omnes ubivis locorum positos, invicem conciliat, sed illa etiam arctiore amicitia, quae literarum commercio fovetur, tibi conjungi. Haec cogitanti mihi allata est tua Epistola, quae per hanc Urbem diu jactata aegre tandem pervenit quo mittebatur. Gaudeo, Vir Doctissime, esse tibi datam occasionem antevertendi cunctationem meam; posthac si ita tibi videbitur, mutua scriptione hoc officium diligenter colemus. Ego, si per curas, quibus obruor, et morbum gravissimum licuisset, post tuas acceptas horam unam responsionem non distulissem. Scripsi nuper decumbens e morbo ad singularem amicum meum Dom. Erpenium, ut meum silentium apud te excusaret. Si vitam Deus Opt. Max. concesserit dabo deinceps operam ut intelligas, eas amicitias facere me plurimi quas cum pijs viris contraxi." Note also the remarkable analysis of the fathers' republic of letters in Casaubon 1606, 53–54, and the splendid analysis of Casaubon's commitment to collegiality and intellectual exchange in Considine 2003.

74. One of these survives: Bod MS Casaubon 61. We thank Peter Stallybrass for his advice on this document.

75. Casaubon 1709, 25.

76. We thank Paul Botley, who is currently preparing an inventory of Casaubon's correspondence, for this estimate.

clearly take many historians, and many years, to collate all of this material and use it to map the full, complex contours of Casaubon's life and work. For the moment, we plan to move forward through offering a series of case studies, in each of which we will explore as wide as possible a range of the paths Casaubon broke. By sticking to this method and seeking to use all of the materials Casaubon has left us, we will necessarily set limits to the territory we can explore. But this comprehensive approach, though taxing, has many advantages. In the first place, it brings the history of classical scholarship into direct contact with one of the liveliest branches of early modern intellectual and literary history—the study of material texts, of books and those who read and used them. Ann Blair, Daniel Rosenberg, Richard Yeo, and many others have taught us to see the early modern period as an age of "information overload," when scholars of encyclopedic and passionate curiosity fought to master the sludgy mass of old and new texts that the presses flung into studies and libraries across Europe.[77] Marginal notes and notebooks were most scholars' primary devices for the storage, processing, and retrieval of information. As these dedicated readers tried to keep abreast of new publications and new data, they rang many ingenious changes on what might seem, at first, the simple task of taking notes.[78] Through the seventeenth and eighteenth centuries, Bacon, Newton and Leibniz, Voltaire and Winckelmann—long seen as the heroes who liberated Europeans from the paper-chase culture of the humanists—continued to use and adapt these text-based ways of processing information.[79]

Classical scholars spent even more time and energy than the scientists on constructing memory theaters out of paper. Pattison regarded Casaubon's ways of taking notes as basically random: "The blank pages, the title page, or any page, serve to hold a reference. Hence, while the scholar reckons among his choicest treasures a greek volume with marginal corrections in Scaliger's hand, a volume which has belonged to Casaubon is merely defaced by the owner's marks and memoranda."[80] In fact, as we will see, the procedures Casaubon followed as he collected information were varied, but not random. Some of his methods were standard. Jean Bodin, whose influential manual on how to read historical texts appeared in 1566, urged readers to form and record general judgments of historians' value. Montaigne, among many other skilled readers, did just that, as he explained in one of his essays, en-

77. See, e.g., Blair 2000a, 2003, 2004a, 2004b, 2005.
78. For an excellent survey see Sherman 2008.
79. For futher case studies see Frasca-Spada and Jardine 2000; Décultot 2000, 2003; and Malcolm 2004. Blair 2010 offers the richest survey of this story.
80. Pattison 1892, 429.

tering summary judgments in the endpapers of his copies.[81] Casaubon did the same, often using title pages to set down prominent general notes on what he considered central to a particular writer or book. Thus, the title page of his copy of Josephus, now in the British Library, has at its top a cogent general estimate of Josephus' unique value as a historian, as well as a sharp critique of his habit of diverging from the Old Testament and reducing its marvels to myths in his account of Jewish history.[82]

Casaubon resembled many scholars and writers of his period when he treated reading as a formal activity, to be conducted according to set rules and accompanied by elaborate rituals, in conditions of strenuous attentiveness.[83] Machiavelli imagined his reading of the ancient historians in his study as a formal dialogue with them, for which he put on regal clothing. Casaubon combed his hair—and prayed for divine help—before he sat down to work through his books.[84] Yet some of his ways of reading were distinctive. His heavily annotated copy of Polybius, now incorporated in a manuscript in the Bodleian Library, offers on its title page instructions on how to collect the fragments of the lost books from the lexicon then known as Suidas—a philologist's approach that Montaigne or Bodin would probably not have adopted.[85] More generally, as we will see, Casaubon often began his reading of texts—biblical and classical, ancient and modern—by reflecting on the proper approach to adopt and the utility of the work he applied it to. These comments, as will become clear, reveal the unity of his approach to

81. Grafton 2007, esp. chap. 3.

82. Casaubon, note on the title page of BL C.76.g.7: "Auctor est in historia φιλαλήθης φιλόπονος, et multis eximiis virtutibus historico necessariis excellens: vt per me quidem provocare possit quemvis e Graecis historicis. Illud excusare non possum, quod libros sacros non semper sequatur accurate: addit enim aliquando τοῖς ἐν αὐτοῖς: detrahit saepe, et omittit non omittenda. causas etiam rerum alias longe assignat multis locis quam Moses: et in summa non fuit in rebus iis referendis quae sacris literis continentur tam religiosus quam par erat. πολλοῦ γε καὶ δεῖ. In primis offendit me quod saepe res narrans sacra historia comprehensas vocat illa μυθευόμενα: ut p. 819 de Sodomorum eversione loquens. et p. 821. μυθεύουσιν, ait, Abraham habitasse in Chebron. Atqui diserte id notat Moses Genes. 35.27. Scio posse hoc flagitium molliri si μυθεύειν expones non fabulantur sed aiunt. Verum nescio q. caret culpa graviss. Josephus. Sed omnia superat quod p. 882. notamus." Casaubon refers to Josephus, Bellum 4.485, 4.531, and 6.313.

83. Parenty 2009, 247–253.

84. See the brilliant account in Nuttall 2003, 143.

85. Casaubon, note on the title page of his 1549 working copy of Polybius, incorporated in Bod MS Casaubon 19: "Σηαι Ad editionem Polybii possunt colligi multa egregia fragmenta ex Suida quae quod non haberent nomen Polybii adiectum, praetermissa sunt a Fulvio Vrsino. Versato in historia Polybii facile erit dignoscere. Nos in nostro libro pleraque omnia notata habemus." Casaubon actually worked through his copy of the Basel 1544 Suidas, identifying fragments of Polybius: Leiden University Library 759 B 16. Note also his appreciative note in his copy of Chemnitz 1606, Wren Library, Trinity College Cambridge, Adv.d.1.32, III, flyleaf: "Eruditio Chemnitii. Prorsus est eximia: et in eo illud singulare quod textus locorum de quibus agit, ex ipsis fontibus petit: vnde saepe illi nascuntur observationes eruditae."

books of very different origins and genres, and offer a vital new source for understanding his interpretative strategies and tactics.

Many of Casaubon's notes seem unenlightening because, as Pattison remarked, they take the form of individual words or larger quotations from the text in question. But Renaissance humanists argued as often by allusion and quotation as by syllogism. Arnaldo Momigliano showed long ago, in an article as rich with content as it is short, that Casaubon reflected about problems of religious coexistence and toleration as he read one of the late antique texts that he loved so much, the *Variae* or state papers of the sixth-century politician and scholar Cassiodorus. As one who in boyhood had been hunted for his own beliefs and in manhood suffered endless harassment from both Catholics and coreligionists, Casaubon had thought hard about these issues. Instead of offering a formal conclusion of his own, however, he scrawled salient passages from the emperor Theodoric on the title page: "We cannot command religion"; "Because no one is forced to believe against his will . . ."; "Since divinity allows many religions to exist, we do not dare to impose a single one of them."[86] In an age of religious war and persecution, as Momigliano saw, these extracts amounted to powerful, even daring statements about the importance of toleration. By retracing Casaubon's steps and reweaving his webs of annotation, we can learn how this most erudite of men stocked his memory in the first place, and then how he drew on those stocks when working on concrete texts and problems. More exciting, we can master the code of his quotations, and rediscover the arguments, about antiquity and modernity, that they put.

Casaubon's notes admit us to what he called his "museum" and show us the scholar at work. But they do much more. They help us to see Casaubon as a richly human figure. In 1995 the historian of medicine Gerald Geison devoted a book to what he called *The Private Science of Louis Pasteur*—Pasteur's science not as he presented it in his formal publications, but as he developed it in his notebooks, where he went off on tangents, stumbled, and made mistakes, which he excised or smoothed away when he wrote up his definitive results.[87] Like Pasteur's notebooks, Casaubon's annotated books and copybooks contain the record of a private science, an imperfect, unfinished, deeply human pursuit. At times, their tone and style sharply contrast

86. Arnaldo Momigliano called attention long ago (1977) to Casaubon's copy of the *Variae* of Cassiodorus. In the central position on the title page in which Casaubon liked to place his judgments on what he saw as most important in the books he annotated, as well as quotations of central importance, he wrote: "Religionem imperare non possumus" and "66. Theodoricus ad Judaeos: quia nemo cogitur ut credat invitus. sic p. 348 cum divinitas patiatur multas esse religiones, nos non audemus unam imponere" (BL C.80.a.1). The first two of these three apparently separate remarks originally made up a single line in Theodoric's letter to the Jews (Cassiodorus, *Variae* 2.27; the other letter quoted is 10.26).

87. Geison 1995.

with those of the work he allowed to reach the public. As a student of Polybius and other historians, Casaubon insisted on the venerable Ciceronian
doctrine that history was *magistra vitae,* the best source of moral and practical instruction for those who planned to lead active lives in the political world. He stated these views in marmoreally formal Latin in the 1609
introduction to his translation of Polybius, and to a considerable extent he
believed in them.[88] During his first meeting with King James, he was delighted to find that the erudite monarch shared his belief that modern readers should not take political guidance, as fashionable humanists advised,
from Tacitus, whom fate had compelled to write the histories of tyrants.[89]

Yet when Casaubon praised Polybius, to his readers, for writing a history
that aspired to cover the entire Mediterranean world and devoted long digressions to explaining the causes of events, he deliberately assumed a conventional, respectable stance.[90] A note on the title page of his copy of Poly-

88. Casaubon 1609, i iij recto: "Quamobrem, sicut verum est dicere, Polybium historiam sui temporis scripsisse; ita non minus verum est dicere, Polybium in historia quam scribebat, praxin politicae
doctrinae et disciplinae militaris exercuisse."

89. See ibid., o ij verso–iij recto: "Sed Tacitum nascendi sors huic durae conditioni alligaverat (qua
de re saepius ipse gravissime queritur), ut vel silendum ei esset, vel ista scribenda. Tacitum igitur facile
nos quidem excusamus: illos excusari non posse iudicamus, qui unicum hunc historicum omnibus alijs
anteponunt: unum Tacitum politicis hominibus assidue terendum pronuntiant: unum esse unde Principes et principum consiliarij documenta regendae Reip. petere debeant. cuius absurditatem sententiae si
vellemus exagitare: facile probaremus, qui ita sentiunt, eos tyrannidis principes hodiernos tacite ac-
cusare; vel palam tyrannidis instituta videri velle eos docere"; and Casaubon 1850, II, 786 (9 November
1610): "Incidit sermo de Tacito, Plutarcho, Commineo, aliis. Quum dixisset Rex errare eos qui Tacitum
magistrum civilis prudentiae unicum facerent, atque ego dixissem, ante annum idem judicasse me in
praefatione ad Polybium, non mediocriter se gaudere Rex doctissimus dixit, quod ego idem secum sentirem. In Plutarcho reprehendebat iniquitatem erga Julium Caesarem, in Commineo levitatem judiciorum et malignum elogium Anglorum. Quid multa? Non sine stupore tantum Regem de literis audivi
pronuntiare." Casaubon here was chiefly criticizing Lipsius, the grand master of late Renaissance Tacit-
ism. See Parenty 2009, 194–203. Note also Casaubon's comment on the beginning of Polybius 6, Bod MS
Casaubon 19, printed text of Polybius (incorporated in MS), 176: "Indagatio subtilis unde orta sit primum in animis hominum ἡ τοῦ καλοῦ καὶ κακοῦ ἔννοια." For the enthusiastic responses of early readers of Casaubon's translation and preface see, e.g., Thompson to Casaubon, 24 October 1609, BL MS
Burney 366, 260 recto; and Molino to Casaubon, 18 January 1609, BL MS Burney 367, 28 verso. On the
late humanists' tastes in historiography see in general, e.g., Tuck 1993; Pocock 1999—; Soll 2005; and
Grafton 2007.

90. Casaubon 1609, i iij recto: "Nihil ille, paullo praesertim majoris momenti narrat factum, cuius
non afferat et antecedentes et cohaerentes caussas cur ita sit factum, aut cur eum habuerit res exitum.
simul autem et modum accurate explicat, quo singula fuerint administrata. Hinc illae non infrequentes
digressiones, quibus aut naturam locorum declarat . . . aut aliquod theorema politicum ex professo
persequitur"; ibid., v verso: "Est hoc quoque historiae Polybianae grande atque insigne decus; quod non
de una tantum aut altera natione fuerit instituta; verum de omnibus quae toto Orbe illis temporibus
noscebantur. Cuius generis historia, quum reliquas eius formas tantum dignitate superet, quantum
parte aliqua sui totum est praestantius; ijs cum difficultatibus est coniuncta, ut post hominum memoriam perquam pauci fuerint reperti, qui oneri tanto subire auderent; quorum autem humeris onus illud
bene sederet, paucissimi." For Casaubon's Polybian studies see esp. Momigliano 1974; Tournoy 1998; and
Parenty 2009, 168–206.

bius takes a much more critical view of the historian's efforts at global coverage: "Note that Polybius' history is quite hard to follow, both for other reasons and because it is universal. It is hard for those who write this sort of history to avoid obscurity and confusion. For often, as they try to give an account of everything at once, they give a satisfactory account of nothing."[91] Another note treats the Greek historian's frequent digressions on historical method as a bug, rather than a feature, of his style: "Note: one thing we do not like in this author is that he repeats, and sets out, his plans, his goals, and his ends, so many times. Why did he bother to do this? Did he think he was going to be read only by Greek soldiers or centurions who smelled like goats?"[92] Here, as in his notes on Cassiodorus, Casaubon made artful use of quotation. The goatish centurion came from Persius, whose *Satires* Casaubon edited with a vast commentary in 1605.[93] But the Casaubon who artfully juggled textual allusions in margins and manuscripts was considerably less decorous than the one who composed set pieces in Latin about the moral uses of history. It comes as no surprise that he had a taste for satire. Our chosen path enables us to meet both the respectable Casaubon, on his way to meet the world with bowler hat and umbrella, and his subversive twin, with his bladder and false nose—and to work out, so far as we can, their relation to each other.

Setting Casaubon into the context of the history of reading sheds light not only on his practices, but also on the positions he occupied. Pattison deplored the fact that Casaubon, from 1600 until his death in 1614, lived not as a scholar in retirement but as, in effect, an expert reader, serving first Henri IV of France and then James I of England. Pattison's biography portrayed his relations with both Henri and James as catastrophically disappointing, a view in which most later historians have followed him.[94] He rebuked his hero even more bitterly for his folly in agreeing to serve, at Fontainebleau in 1600, as a judge in the controversy about whether the Protes-

91. Bod MS Casaubon 19, note on the title page of printed Polybius: "Σηαι Polybii historia cum alias ob caussas subobscura est, cum quia est καθολικὴ. Aegre enim fieri potest ut qui talem hist. scribunt vitent obscuritatem et confusionem: saepe enim dum omnia volunt docere simul, nihil satis docent. Exemplo sit Chalcondylae historia mirifice perturbata confusa et caliginosa."

92. Ibid.: "Σηαι In hoc auctore non placet nobis quod toties suum institutum, scopum et finem repetit et ob oculos ponit. Nam quorsum idem toties? nisi putaret solum se a militibus Graecanicis lectum iri, aut hircosis centurionibus. Tale omnino vitium licet notare in Varronis lib. De L. L. Perlege principia et fines singulorum librorum, eadem ubique reperies non sine aliquo taedio, meo certe, repetita."

93. Casaubon refers to Persius' unflattering portrait of "aliquis de gente hircosa centurionum" (3.77). In his commentary ad loc., he remarked (Persius 1812, 86): "*De gente hircosa Centurionum.* Centurionum *hircosam gentem* (quae hircum olet) nominat, illuviem eorum et δυσχέρειαν notans, qua viri fortes videri vellent."

94. See most recently Trevor-Roper 2006.

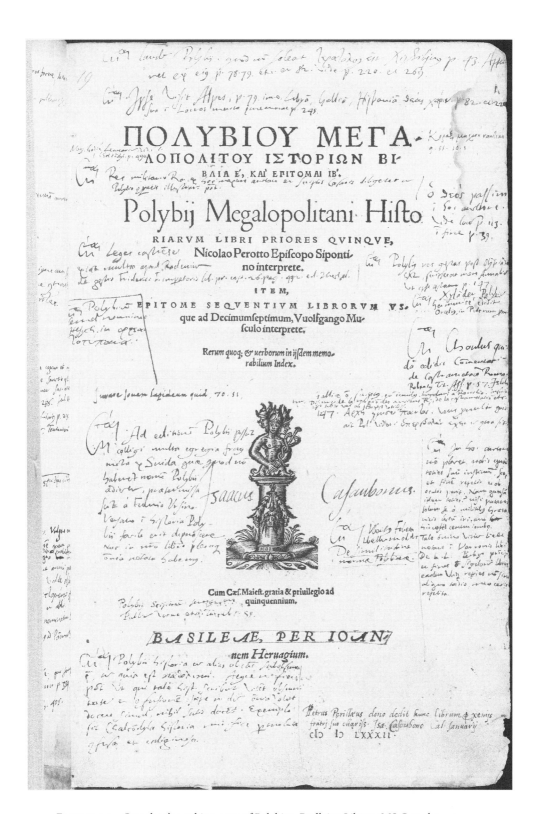

FIGURE 1.3. Casaubon's working copy of Polybius. Bodleian Library MS Casaubon 19.

tant Philippe Duplessis-Mornay had distorted the quotations in a work of theological polemic.[95] Casaubon certainly had his disappointments at court, in England as well as France. But in choosing to serve as what Sir Philip Sidney called "a discourser," a scholar who interpreted ancient texts for modern grandees, Casaubon followed a course that many of his most intelligent and cultivated contemporaries chose—one that had advantages that a career at the university lacked.

The British humanist Gabriel Harvey moved between Cambridge and the circle of Leicester in the 1570s. At court and in country houses, he read Livy's account of the origins of Rome with Philip Sidney, in order to help him prepare for his first major political mission as ambassador to the Holy Roman Emperor. He also went through Livy's narrative of Hannibal's wars with Rome with the young Thomas Smith, before the latter went off to apply the policies of Hannibal to the refractory Irish in the Ards. Casaubon himself recorded the case of Henry Cuffe, who read Lucan and Aristotle with Essex and was blamed by many—including Essex himself—for leading him to rebel against Queen Elizabeth.[96] Friction was inevitable, and collisions likely, when scholars tried to impose their knowledge, their values, and their beliefs on great men and women. Yet these choices, as we will see, gave Casaubon—as they gave others—the opportunity to pursue studies he loved and even, on occasion, to influence a royal decision.

To see Casaubon as a reader, moreover, is to see him in his own terms—as one who tried to reduce the practices of reading to formal rules, which he then applied with scrupulous care. He took the time to warn himself, as he compiled a commonplace book, not to pull quotations out of context in taking notes, lest he misuse them when he set out to write:

> we must see to it, in the first place, when passages from authors are cited, that they are relevant, and that we are not being deceived by something that looks appealing at first sight. Therefore when you copy passages down, examine the author himself closely, and do a serious job of working through everything. For it often happens that as we read some author, we note down passages in the margin, and then go gravely wrong when we use these in our writing.[97]

95. Pattison 1892, 135–147.

96. See Jardine and Grafton 1990; and cf. the more recent work of Soll 2005 and N. Popper 2005. For all the differences between Harvey and Casaubon, the two men shared a propensity for framing and setting down as explicitly as possible the standpoint from which they read a given book.

97. Bod MS Casaubon 16, 4 verso: "In primis videndum, cum loci ex auctoribus citantur, ut ad rem faciant: nec decipiat species quaedam primo blandiens. Itaque cum locos describis, attente vise autorem

No wonder that the scholar who set himself such high standards in citation felt that he could not refuse the demand that he judge Mornay's practices. The richer and more detailed the background against which we chart the particular arc of Casaubon's career, the better we can understand both.

Working from the material texts is most important, however, for the light it can shed on Casaubon's passions and priorities as a scholar—especially the unexpected ones. Consider, one more time, Casaubon's first working copy of Theophrastus. Between the end of his text and his commentary is a set of twenty small leaves, containing what Casaubon identifies as "Capita aliquot Theophrasti"—*Characters* 24–28, then unpublished. Casaubon often began his sets of notes on a text, as we will see, with a fervent little reference to his divine vocation for scholarship: σὺν θεῷ (with God). In this case, however, he wrote something different. On the first page appears, along with his name and a reference to Plato, the Hebrew phrase שבח לאל בורה עולם (Praise to God, Creator of the Universe [the word for Creator should be spelled בורא]). On the last page of the text he wrote, in cursive, a second Hebrew phrase under the Greek word τέλος (end): תם ונשלם, "Finished and completed," a phrase often used, with שבח לאל בורא עולם, in the colophons of Hebrew books.[98]

At this point, attending to the material text reveals something that few previous writers on Casaubon have discussed: he found it easy and natural to move from Latin and Greek to Hebrew—even when expressing a pious sentiment. Pattison remarked that "of the canonical books, the Hebrew Psalter is a constant companion, and never fails to move him."[99] A quarter of a century later, as we have seen, Schechter noted that Casaubon had annotated Kimhi's grammar.[100] But even Schechter found the existence of these notes surprising: "It is not known that Casaubon's ambition lay in this direction." Otherwise, Casaubon's Hebrew interests and studies have received, in essence, no attention.[101] And yet, when we take this hint and begin to look for more Hebrew, we find a number of points, even in the seemingly un-

---

ipsum, et diligenter omnia expende. saepe enim accidit ut inter legendum aliquem auctorem locos in margine annotemus: quos postea literis mandantes, graviter peccamus."

98. BL 525.a.10.

99. Pattison 1892, 441. Pattison also (1892, 368–371) gives a brief but excellent account of Casaubon's interaction with a young Jew, Jacob Barnet, in 1613; see Chapter 5 below for a detailed discussion. But Pattison does not connect these dots.

100. Schechter 1896, 315.

101. For an honorable exception, see Secret 1998, 102 ("Mais la vocation de Scaliger pour les langues orientales ne peut faire oublier celle d'Isaac Casaubon"), 217–220. Colomiès 1665 does not include a life of Casaubon, and Colomiès 1730, which does, touches only briefly on Casaubon's Oriental studies, 129 n.q.

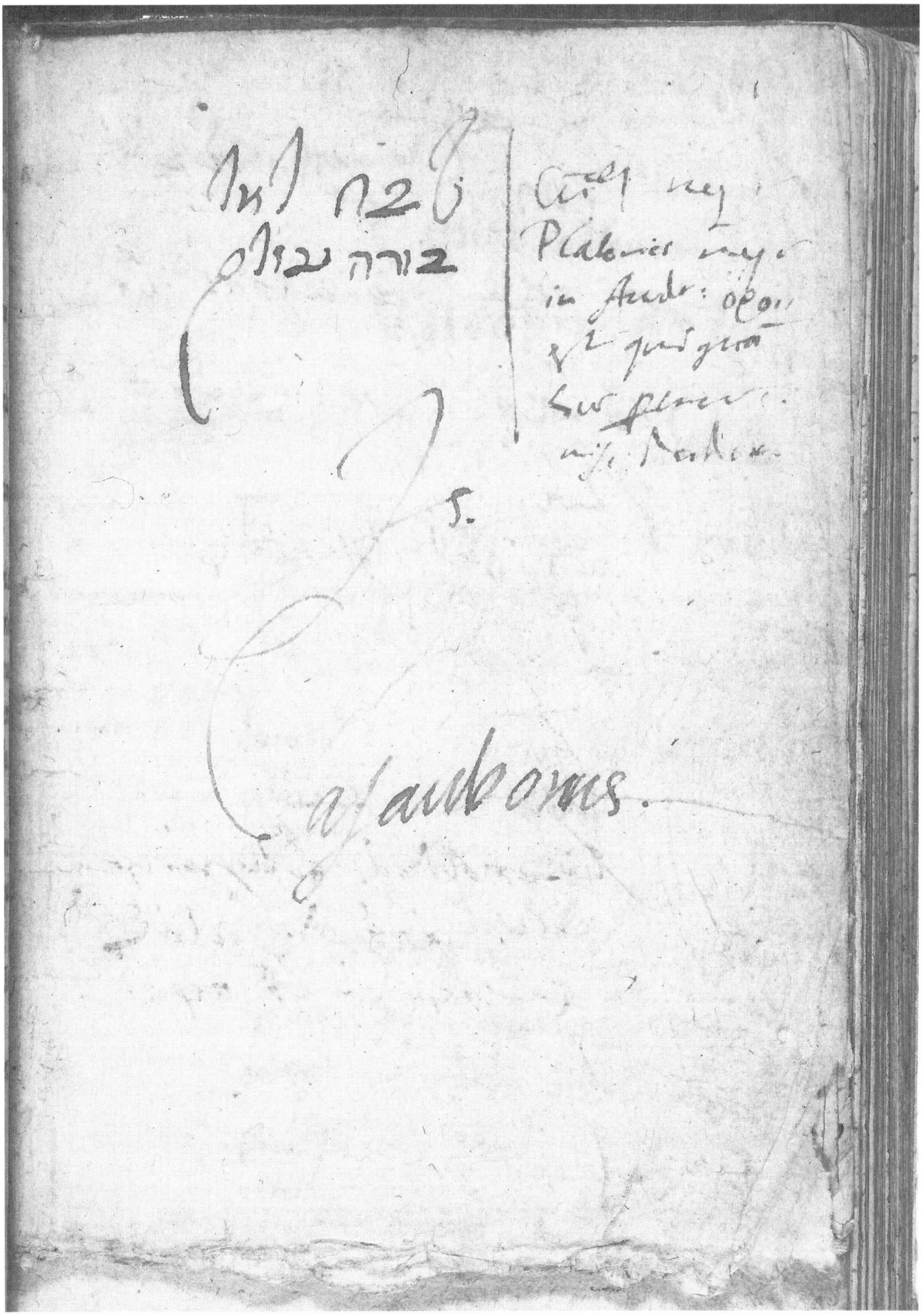

FIGURE 1.4. A Hebrew note by Casaubon in a working copy of his edition of
Theophrastus' *Characters*. British Library 525.a.10.

likely case of Theophrastus, in which Casaubon cites Hebrew parallels.[102] In this instance, the presence of Greek far outweighs, even overwhelms, that of Hebrew. But when we prospect for Hebrew in the whole vast field of evidence, we learn that Casaubon devoted a great deal of time, effort, and attention to the Hebrew language and its relative, Aramaic; to the literature of the Jews, in Greek as well as in Semitic languages; and to the relations between Jewish history and religion and Christianity.

In one sense, it is not surprising that Casaubon took a serious interest in Jewish studies. The fifteenth and sixteenth centuries, as many scholars have shown, saw the rise, alongside Greek and Latin humanism, of a new form of scholarship, usually called Christian Hebraism. Its practitioners included Christian grammarians, lexicographers, and editors like Paul Fagius, Sebastian Münster, Benito Arias Montano, and Johann Buxtorf; Jewish and convert scholars like Elijah Levita and Johannes Isaac; students of the Jewish mystical tradition like Johannes Reuchlin, Guillaume Postel, and Pietro Galatino; and students of Jewish practices and institutions like Joseph Scaliger and Petrus Cunaeus. Its products ranged from dry and precise editions of the Hebrew Bible, often with rabbinical commentaries, to speculative discussions of the Kabbalah, and included detailed investigations of Jewish history in the ancient world and vivid accounts of contemporary Jewish life and ritual.[103] To someone with Casaubon's passion for the history of Christianity and its background, this body of scholarship naturally seemed extremely attractive. The study of Christian Hebraism, however, has for the most part occupied Judaists rather than students of Western humanism. Too few sophisticated efforts have been made, as yet, to compare the forms of scholarship applied to Jewish materials with those applied to Greek and Latin texts and topics, or to examine what the new Hebrew scholarship meant to scholars who did not specialize in the field. Casaubon taught Hebrew only briefly and did not publish in the standard Christian Hebraist genres. He, and others like him, have never played even a modest part in modern accounts of Christian Hebraism. But once we take all the evidence into account—once we retrace Casaubon's full webs of annotations and diary entries, letters, and publications, strand by strand—it will become clear

102. See BL 525.a.10, 10 (a manuscript note that Casaubon worked into the text of Casaubon 1599, 89); BL 525.a.10, 48, on 3 (Casaubon 1599, 126); BL 525.a.10, 62, on 4.4 (Casaubon 1599, 141); BL 525.a.10, 173, on 30.11 (not in Casaubon 1599, 246); BL 525.a.10, 174, on 30.1 (not in Casaubon 1599, 247–249); BL 525.a.10, 225, on 17.2 (Casaubon 1599, 296); and cf. Casaubon 1592, 105, on 6.5, reprinted in Casaubon 1599, 181.

103. See in general Manuel 1992; Zinguer 1992; Burnett 1996; Hess 2002; Sutcliffe 2003; Shoulson and Coudert 2004; Veltri and Necker 2004; Rosenblatt 2006; Toomer 2009.

that Hebrew studies played a vital role in his life and thought, and that they shed a necessary light on his methods as a scholar.

Hermes Trismegistus and His Jewish Cousin

Consider, to begin with, what is now the most famous scholarly argument Casaubon ever made: his demonstration that the Greek dialogues ascribed to Hermes Trismegistus had been written not in hieroglyphs during the early centuries of Egyptian history, but in Greek, under the Roman Empire. In the middle of the fifteenth century, Marsilio Ficino put off finishing his translation of Plato in order to translate the dialogues of the *Hermetic Corpus* into Latin. From then on, most Western readers believed that Thrice-Wise Hermes, an Egyptian sage, really composed these dialogues, with their detailed description of the creation of the world and the life of the soul.[104] The writings of Hermes showed that a virtuous pagan could have vivid inklings of the truths that God revealed directly to the Jews. They were also, Ficino held, the source from which Plato drew the core of his philosophy— itself strikingly compatible with Christianity. Throughout the later fifteenth and the sixteenth centuries, accordingly, Hermes enjoyed the status of a pagan prophet. Like David and the Sibyls, he appeared, handsomely turned out in oriental garb, on the floor of the Siena cathedral. Like them, too, he received the honor of a citation in Cesare Baronio's church history. The hardworking Catholic church historian naturally cited the prophetic testimony of David and the Sibyls, as the Mass did. But then he unwisely followed fashion, adding a last-minute reference to Hermes in the margin of his manuscript. The note was included in the published text.[105]

Casaubon devoted several pages of his vast attack on Baronio to a set-piece demonstration that the Hermetic texts must be centuries older than they claimed, or than Baronio believed.[106] A jewel of precise philological argument that gleams all the more brightly in the vast, dark setting of Casaubon's polemic, his demonstration reveals, in miniature, the qualities that made him so penetrating a philologist—and that show just how powerful an intellectual weapon the philology of the humanists could be.[107] As in the case

104. See in general Kristeller 1937; Yates 1964; Garin 1988; Copenhaver 1992. For the larger context of the rediscovery of Hermes in Florence see esp. Gentile and Gilly 1999.

105. Biblioteca Apostolica Vaticana, MS Vat. lat. 5684, 11 recto.

106. The most detailed study is Grafton 1983; and Mulsow 2002, a valuable collection that sets the whole story in context; for the larger implications see also Mulsow 2006. As will be clear, Grafton 1983 failed to take into account the relevance of Jewish and Hebrew materials.

107. Cf. Levine 1977 and 1999.

of Theophrastus, he began by writing in a book—a copy of the 1554 Paris edition of the *Hermetic Corpus,* now in the British Library.[108] Sometimes he merely noted points of fact: for example, the references to the Greek sculptor Phidias and the cithara-player Eunomus that appear in a separate part of the *Corpus,* the so-called Horoi, showed, as he argued in his attack on Baronio, that the text could not be preclassical.[109] He also remarked on what he took to be clear borrowings from Plato and from the Old and New Testaments.[110] And he drew on his vast stores of knowledge about Greek literature, from all periods, to show that late texts, rather than early ones, offered the most striking linguistic parallels to the *Corpus.*[111] Once Casaubon had lined the margins of the entire book with notes like these, he felt confident that the Hermetic texts could not be genuine. Written in a philosophical Greek he knew from many other, late sources, they clearly reflected their origin in a world very distant from that of the Egyptian Hermes: "The style of this book could not be farther from the language that the Greek contemporaries of Hermes used. For the old language had many words, phrases, and a general style very different from that of the later Greeks. Here is no trace of antiquity, no crust, none of that patina of age that the best ancient critics found even in Plato, and even more in Hippocrates, Herodotus, and other older writers. On the contrary, there are many words here that do not belong to any Greek earlier than that of the time of Christ's birth."[112]

In building this case, Casaubon wielded tools—above all the historical approach to language—that earlier humanists had forged. In the mid-fifteenth century, Lorenzo Valla had produced the mother of all demolitions of forgeries. Using parallels carefully drawn from sources dating to the third and fourth centuries, the age of Constantine, he showed that the *Donation of Constantine* could not be genuine because it was written in the wrong sort of Latin and mentioned the wrong terms and customs.[113] During the six-

108. BL 491.d.14.

109. Casaubon, notes in ibid., 97, on *Corpus Hermeticum* 18.4: "Phidias"; and 98, on 18.7: "historia extat apud Strabonem, Clem. etc."

110. Casaubon, notes in BL 491.d.14, 19, on *Corpus Hermeticum* 4.3: "Plato in Tim. p. 477"; and 15, 17, 56 (see Grafton 1983, 82).

111. Casaubon, notes in BL 491.d.14, e.g., 12, on *Corpus Hermeticum* 2, where he piles up parallels from Pseudo-Dionysius the Areopagite (Grafton 1983, 82–83).

112. Casaubon 1614, 86; 1654, 79; 1663, 79: "Stylus huius libri alienissimus est a sermone illo quo Graeci Hermetis aequales sunt usi. nam illa vetus lingua multa habuit vocabula, multas phrases, imo totius elocutionis ideam ab illa diversissimam qua posteriores Graeci sunt usi. Hic nullum penitus vestigium antiquitatis, nullus χνοῦς, nullus πῖνος τῆς ἀρχαιότητος qualem praestantissimi veterum Criticorum etiam in Platone observant, nedum in Hippocrate, Herodoto et alijs antiquioribus. contra, multa hic vocabula, quae ne vetustior quidem Hellenismus agnoscat eo qui vigebat circa nativitatem Domini."

113. See Valla 2007.

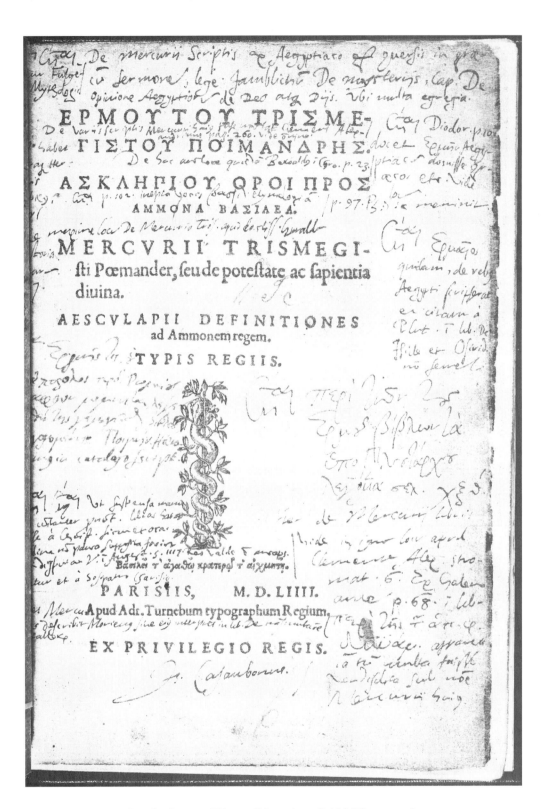

FIGURE 1.5. Casaubon's copy of Hermes Trismegistus. British Library 491.d.14.

teenth century, many scholars—including Casaubon's much-admired friend Joseph Scaliger—wielded similar arguments against the historians of the ancient world forged by the Dominican Giovanni Nanni, or Annius, of Viterbo.[114] Even in little Geneva, Casaubon had encountered a master of the historical approach to ancient texts. Henri Estienne published an anthology of Greek hexameter poets in 1566. He had already edited many Greek texts and begun collecting material for the great dictionary of Greek that he would publish in 1572–73. And he drew on this experience when he put the *Hero and Leander* of Musaeus—traditionally, but wrongly, ascribed to the legendary companion of Orpheus—at the end, not the beginning, of his corpus of poets. Casaubon noted in his own copy of this collection that one of the words Musaeus used, ἐξολόλυξε, was enough to show that his poem could not be "by Homer or any other poet of the first rank." In doing so, as he knew, he was simply corroborating his father-in-law's observation.[115]

Although others had devised the method Casaubon applied, he assembled the evidence for his critique of Hermes alone and without a leader. In the "Horoi," one of the originally unconnected texts that came to be seen as parts of the *Hermetic Corpus,* the author remarks that when his texts are translated "later" into Greek, their words will lose much of the power that they had in their original Egyptian form (16.1–2). "Note that 'later,'" Casaubon wrote in the margin, calling attention to the writer's effort to give his work an Egyptian coloring: "What a tricky fellow it was who wrote this."[116] One reason this passage struck Casaubon so forcibly was that he had noticed, earlier on, a related one in dialogue 8 of the *Corpus.* Here Hermes remarks that the universe is rightly named κόσμος: κοσμεῖ γὰρ τὰ πάντα (it sets everything into order) (9.8). At this point Casaubon wrote only κόσμος in the margin.[117] But in the final attack on Baronio, he drew the threads together in a neat philologist's knot. "Are κόσμος and κοσμεῖν," he mercilessly inquired, "words from the ancient Egyptian language?"[118] The text claimed to be translated from Egyptian, and the author had done his best to make it seem like a translation: yet it contained Greek plays on words.

More than a millennium before, Julius Africanus had condemned the

114. Grafton 1991; 1983–1993, II.

115. Casaubon, note in Cambridge University Library Adv.a.3.3, I, 729: "Hom. hac voce nunquam sic est usus: nec Hom. est hoc carmen, nec ullius optimi poetae, nedum Hom." For Henri Estienne's observation that Musaeus' style was that of late Greek see ibid., II, 488, underlined by Casaubon.

116. Casaubon, note in BL 491.d.14, 90: "No. ὕστερον. Nae hic homo suaviludius est, qui haec scribat."

117. Casaubon, note in ibid., 39.

118. Casaubon 1614, 86; 1654, 79; 1663, 79: "an . . . κόσμος et κοσμεῖν voces sunt antiqui sermonis Aegyptiaci?"

story of Susanna, which appears in the Greek text of the book of Daniel. Its Greek plays on words, he argued, showed that it could not have come from a Hebrew original. So Casaubon demolished Hermes—but with the further twist that he revealed not only the text's flaws, but also the author's conscious effort at deception.[119] A number of Catholic scholars tried to rebut Casaubon's critique in the course of defending Baronio against him, and Protestants as well as Catholics did their best to prove that the treatises contained Egyptian elements even if their language, in this version, was Greek.[120] From the 1990s on, the view that these texts contain fragmentary but real elements of Egyptian belief and ritual has gained favor. But the core of Casaubon's arguments about the transmitted text itself remains unshaken.[121] The demolition of Hermes was a masterpiece of iconoclastic classical scholarship, and it helped to unleash a wave of destructive criticism that would eventually reach the Bible itself: "the advent of the critical philology of Joseph Scaliger's and Isaac Casaubon's generation, which engaged in a search for classical forgeries, initiated a massive process of realignment of authority. The writings of figures such as Orpheus, Zoroaster, Hermes Trismegistus, and the Sibyls, who had been prominent figures of the *prisca theologia* during the Renaissance, were identified as late antique forgeries or pseudepigraphic. This had unexpected consequences for the reconstitution of the philosophical and theological canons."[122]

Yet the web of annotation and discussion that Casaubon wove as he fought and thought his way through the *Corpus* extended beyond the bounds of Greek philology or, for that matter, Greek philosophy, and the rich evidence he left enables us to date and understand his work on Hermes with new precision. We can start with the crowded title page of his copy of the text. Most of the notes that make up this tightly packed textual mosaic refer to Greek texts that mentioned Hermes or the Hermetic writings, and which Casaubon thought might play a part in his argument. But one of them shows that Casaubon felt nowhere near so confident about his revisionist thesis while he was developing it as he sounded when he published it: "Note!

119. On Africanus see Grafton 1990. For another instance in which Casaubon applied a similar method, see his copy of Pseudo-Hegesippus, BL 1112.b.1, note on the title page verso: "Non esse illum antiquum Egesippum suadet haec maxime ratio, praeter allatas a Gualthero. Videtur enim, imo ferme constat hunc librum Latine scriptum esse, non de Graeco versum. Itaque τοῦ παλαιοῦ Heg. esse non potest: quem scripsisse Graece nemo nescit. [new ink] Neque nego pleraque descripta esse e Graec[o] auctore. Inde est ordo pro leg. i. τάγμα. chiliarchus pro tribunis mil. 394. Judaeum fuisse auctorem palam est. Vide 429 et 628."

120. Grafton 1983.

121. See Fowden 1986; Copenhaver 1992.

122. Mulsow 2006, 221–222.

Note! The arguments that Vives makes in his commentary on Augustine require that one state in a gentle way, and hesitantly, that these books were forged by Christians, like a good many Sibylline oracles. This is a very delicate matter."[123] Juan Luis Vives, friend of Erasmus and great authority on the church fathers, drew up in the 1520s the grandest of all Renaissance commentaries on the grandest of all patristic texts, the *City of God*. Even though Vives had to cut his immense text when Erasmus, his editor, found it too long, it became legendary for its erudition, its philological acuteness, and its splendid digression on Renaissance performers who, like Adam before the Fall, could control all their bodily organs, as they showed by farting tunes.[124]

In XVIII.46, Augustine mentioned the possibility that Christians could be suspected of having forged "those prophecies of Christ which circulate under the name of the Sibyl, or of others, if they exist, that do not belong to the Jewish people."[125] Vives denounced such suspicions retrospectively:

> It is clear that these prophecies were not forged. For Lactantius and Eusebius, in whose times the Sibylline prophecies were in the hands of all, cite them, and they would never have been so impudent as to claim that the Sibylline books contained things that are not in them. Moreover, they would have hurt the Christian cause more by doing so than they could ever have helped it by arguments, once men clearly saw that they were relying on fake authorities.[126]

The clear prophecies of Christ that appeared in the poetry of Virgil and Ovid, which derived from the verses of the Sibyls, confirmed that pagans had foreseen the coming of the Messiah—an idea dear to Vives.[127] In de-

123. Casaubon, note on the title page of BL 491.d.14: "Σηαι Σηαι vt suspensa manu et cunctanter pronunt. libros hos fuisse a Christ. sicut et orac. Sibyllina non pauca supposita faciunt quae disputat V. in August. s. 1117. Res valde est anceps."

124. Vives' remark on *City of God* XIV.24 is discussed by Montaigne in a famous passage, *Essais* 1.21.

125. Augustine, *City of God* XVIII.46: "nisi forte quis dixerit illas prophetias Christianos finxisse de Christo, quae Sibyllae nomine vel aliorum proferuntur, si quae sunt, quae non pertinent ad populum Iudaeorum."

126. Vives 1555, 1117, on "Illas prophetias Christianos finxisse": "Non esse confictas hinc apparet quod Lactan. et Euseb. eas citant, quorum tempore Sibyllini libri in manibus omnium erant. nec ipsi fuissent tam impudentes, qui ea dixissent esse in Sibyllinis libris, quae nusquam erant: adde quod plus sic obfuissent Christianae causae, quam alijs omnibus argumentis potuissent prodesse, quum homines aperte cernerent eos fictis in rem suam autoritatibus inniti, quumque hoc falsum et impudens deprehendissent caetera omnia suspecta haberent, et tanquam similia repudiassent reiecissentque."

127. Ibid.: "Quid quod Verg. et Ovidius manifesto in poemata sua de Sibyllinis carminibus versus mutuantur, quos nemo ita caecus est, quin esse de Christo dicta perspiciat, qualis est tota quarta aegloga Vergilii, et digressus de morte Caesaris in fine primi Georg. apud Ovidium vero illa sunt, Et deus humana lustro sub imagine terras: tum: Esse quoque in fatis reminiscitur affore tempus Quo mare, quo

throning Hermes, Casaubon defied, as he knew, a more than respectable body of Christian humanist opinion. Many humanists from Ficino onward had drawn on Eusebius and other early Christian writers as they emphasized the clarity with which the best of the pagans had written of God and foreseen the Messiah. At first, accordingly, he felt himself obliged to tread cautiously—and, as we have seen, to marshal the philological evidence with enormous energy and precision.

Another of the notes on the title page of Casaubon's Hermes shows that he was not isolated in his interests—and that the case of the *Hermetic Corpus* was not unique either. "Beroaldus," Casaubon wrote, "has something on this author on p. 23 of his *Chronicum*."[128] Here he admitted to himself—as he did not admit to readers in his attack on Baronio—that he was not the first to attack Hermes. Two Hebraists and chronologers—the Paris Hebraist Gilbert Génébrard, a fanatical Catholic, and the Geneva professor Matthieu Béroalde, a ferocious Calvinist—denounced the *Corpus* as a fake, in public, before Casaubon did.[129] In general terms, Casaubon did not admire Béroalde, who insisted that one must base chronology not on the lying Herodotus, who was now in hell, repenting his sins at leisure, but on scripture. But he completely agreed with the chronologer that any text that mentioned Phidias must come from the age of Pericles or after, not that of Pharaoh.[130]

Casaubon's copy of Béroalde makes clear, moreover, that Hermes was far from the only problematic prophet that interested him. Béroalde discussed rabbinic, as well as pseudo-Egyptian, prophecies about the coming of the

---

tellus, correptaque regia coeli Ardeat, et mundi moles oporosa laboret. primo Transfor. item apud Lucanum de ijs, quae praecedent iudicium domini primo Pharsa. Sic quum compage soluta, Secula tot mundi suprema coegerit hora, Antiquum repetens chaos etc. quod si nostra quae magni autores tradiderunt dicunt commentitia, ostendant ipsi quae possint dici sine ulla controversia vera, et afferemus Academicum aliquem, qui se dubitare respondeat."

128. Casaubon, note on the title page of BL 491.d.14: "De hoc auctore quaedam Beroaldus in Chro. p. 23."

129. Purnell 1976, reprinted in Mulsow 2002.

130. Béroalde 1575, 23: "Quod vero aiunt Mercurium istum fuisse antiquiorem Pharaone, sicuti prodidit Suidas, falsum esse arguit ipsum Paemandri, quod ad illum refertur, scriptum. Nam Sibyllarum meminit quae multis post Pharaonem seculis extiterunt. Item Aesculapius is, ad quem scribit iste Mercurius, Phidiae meminit, qui Periclis aetate vixit. Ita librum illum Mercurii Trismegisti subdititium esse apparet, in quo multa dicuntur, quae nec ratione, nec autoritate fulciantur idonea, qui Ilerdam mittendus sit cum suo autore. Quod monendum putavi propter eos, qui titulis et librorum nominibus decepti, sine delectu quaevis non modo legunt, sed quod longe periculosius est, credunt quoque, antiquitatis quadam veneratione et admiratione permoti: eorum more, qui signa quamvis rudia, si modo sunt antiqua, putant omnium esse optima et praestantissima. Aetate autem Augustini alia fuisse nota Hermetis huius Trismegisti scripta apparet, ex capite 23. libri 8. de Civitate Dei, et aliis aliquot eiusdem libri locis, e quibus impietas huius Trismegisti facile deprehendi potest." In his copy, BL C.79.e.12.(1), Casaubon writes: "Contra Mercuri[um] Trismegist[um]."

Messiah. One of his chief sources for these was an early Christian Hebraist work: the *De arcanis Catholicae veritatis* of the Franciscan Pietro Galatino, first published in 1518. Galatino's vast compendium included both material from the long-standing tradition of Christian controversial writing against the Jews and alluring scraps of Christian Kabbalah. He praised the ancient rabbis who, he claimed, had foreseen the coming of Jesus and proclaimed, long in advance, the truths of Christianity. But he damned their more recent successors, who had corrupted the true doctrines of Judaism in order to support their own stiff-necked refusal to convert. Like many others, Béroalde cited and drew on this immense and informative, if ill-organized, work. But he accorded it little intrinsic worth, since, as he pointed out, Galatino had not written his own book but merely "published as his own the works of Ramon Martí," a thirteenth-century Spanish Dominican, "changing the order and making small alterations in the arguments; so it would be fair to accuse Galatino of plagiarism." Béroalde planned to make this clear to all by publishing a manuscript of Martí's work, the *Pugio fidei,* which he possessed.[131] Excited, Casaubon noted on the title page of his copy of Béroalde—preserved, like his Hermes, in the British Library—that Galatino had stolen a great deal from Martí, whose work in turn was important for Hebrew scholarship.[132] In Casaubon's web of annotations, in other words, the same strands lead to questions of Hermetic and Hebrew scholarship—on different pages of the same book.

But the strands of the web stretch further, and reveal more. Reasonably enough, historians have associated Casaubon's attack on Hermes with his much larger attack on Baronio: both stemmed from religious motives, and both reflected Casaubon's scorn for what he saw as shoddy scholarship. Casaubon's diary reveals that he began to write up his final attack on Hermes—

131. Béroalde 1575, 64: "His autem fere verbis ista dicuntur a Talmudistis. Traditio a schola Eliae: Sex millibus annorum erit mundus, et postea destruetur. Bis mille anni, inanitati: Bis mille, legi: Bis mille, diebus Messiae erunt. hactenus traditio. de qua qui plura scire expetit, adeat Galatinum libro de Arcanis catholicae fidei quarto, capite 20. Item legat Pugionem Martini Raymundi, capite decimo secundae partis. Galatinus autem (ut hoc obiter moneam) Martini Raymundi scripta pro suis edidit, commutato rerum ordine, et argumento nonnihil variato, ut plagii possit accusari Galatinus. quod planum me facturum spero, si dederit Dominus, ut Pugionem ipsius Raymundi scriptum ad impiorum perfidiam iugulandam, maxime autem Iudaeorum, in lucem proferam. Is autem liber, studiis Hebraicis maxime utilis pervenit ad me ex bibliotheca Francisci Vatabli Mecoenatis mei, primi Hebraicarum literarum professoris, sub Francisco rege huius nominis primo, per quem Deus bonarum literarum studia revocavit in Galliam." Béroalde and Casaubon do not refer to the fourteenth-century work of Porcheti de Salvaticis, *Victoria adversos impios Hebraeos* (first printed by Giustiniani in Paris in 1520), which belongs to the tradition of Martí.

132. Casaubon, note on the title page of BL C.79.e.12.(1): "p. 64 Pugio Martini R . . . mundi: liber utilis a[d] literas Hebr. intell[igendas]. ex quo pleraque furat[us est] Galatinus."

which, when he read it over, disappointed him — in August 1612.[133] But it also shows that he read Galatino with care much earlier, in June 1601.[134] And Casaubon's notes, preserved in the Bodleian Library, make clear that he read Galatino much as he read Hermes. In fact he was infuriated, as he read Galatino, by exactly what irritated him most in Hermes. Casaubon's objection to the *Hermetic Corpus* rested on more than philological grounds—rested, in fact, on deep theological convictions. As a committed Calvinist, Casaubon knew, in his soul, that scripture took precedence over all other books.[135] As a reader of the true, Jewish prophets, he also knew that they had genuinely expressed themselves in difficult, obscure terms. Mere mortals could not even devise a full explanation for the character of prophetic language, much less understand that language.[136] They could only revere these writings, and use every resource at their disposal to appreciate their power:

> We can note some intermediate causes of their obscurity. Some have
> to do with the subject matter, which is lofty, sublime, and sometimes
> also in the future, so that the prophets could only speak obscurely
> about them. Others belong to their style, which fits their subject: a
> sublime medium for sublime things. Every quality that, according
> to Longinus and other rhetoricians, can produce the effect of sub-
> lime language will be found, in a most exquisite form, in the writ-
> ings of the prophets.[137]

133. Casaubon 1850, II, 942 (25 August 1612): "Quaedam hodie de Mercurio Trismegisto, sed quae mox displicuerunt."

134. Ibid., I, 354 (11 June 1601): "In Galatino et Reuchlino fuimus per hosce dies, nec poenitet insumti in illorum lectione temporis, etsi non carent eruditi homines suis magnis naevis, de quibus si voles tu, O Deus, utiliter fortasse aliquando disputabimus."

135. For a general reflection see Bod MS Casaubon 60, 61 verso: "Auctoritas sacrae paginae. Qui negant hodie sacram paginam ἁπλῶς esse ad salutem necessariam, quantum scelus admittunt? Nullum scelestius dictum ne fingi quidem potest. Ego non censeam temere damnandas consuetudines et παρ-αδόσεις veteris ecclesiae. Sed dogmata non aliunde confirmant patres, nisi ex sacra script. lege Epiph. et alios."

136. Bod MS Casaubon 51, 19 recto: "Obscuritas prophetarum. Nemo leviter prophetarum scripta attigit quin eorum obscuritatem animadverterit. huius rei multiplex est causa. Ac caussam quidem caussarum investigare cur Deus OPT. MAX. voluerit sic eos loqui non est tenuitatis nostrae: quibus per-suasissimum est, ita Deo visum quia ita optimum: ita esse optimum quia sic Deo visum."

137. Ibid.: "Sed propiores huius obscuritatis causae multae possunt adnotari. aliae e rebus ipsis profi-ciscuntur: quae altae, sublimes, interdum etiam futurae: ut de iis non potuerint prophetae nisi obscure loqui. aliae sunt in ipso dicendi genere: quod sane rebus est accommodum, ὑψηλὸν ὑψηλαῖς. Itaque quicquid est apud Longinum et alios rhetoras quod τὸ ὕψος τῷ λόγῳ conciliet, id omne reperietur in prophetarum scriptis luculentissime expressum."

In keeping with these views, Casaubon found it intolerable when the narrator of the *Corpus,* Pimander, proclaimed that "this is the mystery that has been hidden until this day." Pimander, after all, told the story of the Creation, and much more, in terms parallel to those used in the Old Testament itself. "Note," Casaubon wrote in the margin, "if this is true, then God revealed his mysteries not through Moses but through this man."[138]

Similarly, as Casaubon read and took notes on Galatino, he found himself particularly irked by the Franciscan's repeated claims that the rabbis whose words he quoted had offered exact prophecies about the Virgin, the Messiah, and the Catholic doctrine of the Eucharist.[139] Of one of these figures, whom Galatino called Rabbenu Haccados (Our Holy Rabbi), Galatino wrote: "He was rightly called the holy teacher, since with the inspiration of the Holy Spirit he opened up all the mysteries of our lord Jesus Christ so clearly in that book, that he seems not to have predicted the future, but to have recounted the actual events, like an Evangelist."[140] As Casaubon turned the massive pages of Galatino's book, his irritation grew—though it was not always sparked by the points most likely to provoke a modern scholar, such as the apparent suggestion that the great teacher known as "our holy rabbi," Judah haNasi, had lived before the Incarnation rather than in the years around 200 C.E.[141] Galatino's Rabbenu Haccados, writing supposedly before the Incarnation, managed to predict not only the Crucifixion, but the much later rediscovery of the True Cross: "This tree will be hidden away, unknown to all men, in the ground. But when Queen Elena rules the land,

138. Casaubon, note in BL 491.d.14, 5: "No. si hoc verum est et hic scripsit ante Mosem, per hunc non per Mosem Deus mysteria revelavit."

139. Bad forgery always irked Casaubon. Cf. his comment in his copy of the spurious history of Abdias, BL 1020.f.2, 94 verso: "—missa. O asinos qui putant haec esse genuina." Casaubon was by no means the first to detect this forgery: see Lyon 2003, 265.

140. Galatino 1603, 8 (I.3): "qui certe non ab re doctor sanctus dictus est, cum Spiritu sancto afflatus, ita plane eo in libro cuncta Domini nostri Iesu Christi mysteria aperuerit, ut non futura praedixisse, sed res gestas tanquam Evangelista narrasse videatur."

141. Casaubon would have known the traditional title and dating of Judah haNasi from Abraham ibn Daud's *Sefer haKabbalah.* In his copy, BL 1939.b.63, he underlined the name of Judah haNasi (60 recto) and wrote "Misna" and "R. Hakkados." (60 verso). In fact, however, Galatino knew that chronology made it impossible for the Rabbenu Hakkados who appeared in Heredia as a prophet before the Incarnation to be Judah haNasi, and he solved the problem with a method widely used by both Jewish and Christian scholars: multiplication of entities with the same name. He took care to claim that two distinct rabbis had been known by this title, and that later Jews had conflated them. Galatino 1603, 6: "Quem [Judah haNasi] Iudaei pro eius doctrinae probitatisque excellentia, Rabbenu Haccados, id est, magistrum nostrum sanctum cognominant. Fuit tamen et alius Rabbenu Haccados, qui tempore Romanorum consulum et doctrina et spiritu prophetiae claruit, ac multa et quidem miranda de Christo scripsit. Quamobrem Iudaei recentiores nominis similitudine decepti, illum hunc fuisse existimant."

all Israel will suffer. For she will seek this tree, and they will have no knowledge of it, nor will it be found until the mercy of God is fulfilled, and he makes it come forth from the ground."[142] "Rubbish, rubbish, rubbish," Casaubon wrote at this point in his notes; "and yet it is astonishing, and more than astonishing, to see the confidence which Galatino displays whenever he cites this pseudo-rabbi, who, he says, spoke so many years before the birth of the Lord, so clearly, about the mysteries of the faith, and all that pertains to the Blessed Mary."[143] In the case of the "ancient rabbis," as in that of the ancient Near Eastern prophets, Casaubon simply could not accept the idea that an otherwise unknown sage had spoken "a good bit more clearly about the mysteries of our faith than the prophets, or the rabbis contemporary with him, but also more openly, in many cases, than the Evangelists or the Apostles."[144] The very precision with which both Hermes and Rabbenu Haccados described the Creation and predicted the future proved that they must be the inventions of later writers, out to win authority for their peculiar revelations.

In this case, as in that of Hermes, Casaubon was right on the points at issue. The Rabbenu Haccados who appeared in Galatino's work, and his words, came from a text titled *Galerazaya* (Revealer of Secrets). This was a set of queries from "Antoninus, consul of the city of Rome," and answers from "Rabbenus hacchados," which in turn figured in a Latin letter ascribed to Neunia son of Haccana. Rabbi Nehuniah ben haKanah was a historical figure of the first century.[145] But from Gershom Scholem on, modern schol-

---

142. Galatino 1603, 375–376 (VI.15): "Et quoniam ex arbore vitae haec arbor excisa fuerat, fructus eius vitam afferrent mundo. Haec tamen arbor abscondetur in terra cunctis mortalibus ignota. Cum autem dominabitur in terra sancta Regina Elena, omnis Israel in angustiis erit ac detrimento. Quippe quod ab ea perquiretur haec arbor, et nulla ipsius apud eos extabit notitia, neque ipsa invenietur, quousque Deus impleatur misericordia, et ex terra eam prodire faciat. Et reperietur una de iis arboribus, de quibus dixit Isaias, Et dedit cum impiis sepulturam suam. Hoc autem erit, ut notum faciat Deus, quam magna sint sua miracula, ac mirabilia sua quam fortia. Haec omnia ad verbum ille, quem vel ipsi Magistrum nostrum sanctum appellant."

143. Bod MS Casaubon 27, 209 recto: "Imo vero totum argumentum fictitium esse et supine confictum docent plurima. Maxime vero illa disputatio longa de arbore Crucis et praedictio de futura illius revelatione cum regnaret regina Helena. quis tam stultus tam fatuus tam ridicule simplex, qui illa putet scripta ante Domini nativitatem, aut omnino ante quam res gesta esset, quae omnino notissima. Nugae, nugae, nugae. et tamen mirum bis mirum quam πληροφορίαν adhibeat Gal. quoties hunc ψευδοραβ-βίνον laudat: qui, inquit, tot annis ante nativitatem DNI tam clare de fidei mysteriis disseruit: utique de iis quae pertinent ad B. Mariam."

144. Ibid., 209 verso: "Fragmenta ex libris Rabbenu Haccados [left margin: σηαι etiam Baronius fidem abrogat huic Rab. t. 1. p. 19]. Hic est ille Rabbinus quem volunt de nostrae fidei mysteriis locutum esse non paullo apertius quam Prophetas aut aequales etiam suos Rabb. sed saepe etiam apertius quam Evangelistas vel Apostolos."

145. The form here was probably modeled on the dialogue between Rabbi and Antoninus in Babylonian Talmud, Sanhedrin 91a–b.

ars have held that his letter was confected by its purported translator, a converted Jew from Aragon named Paulus de Heredia, whose work reached print around 1487.[146] "Rabbenus Haccados" served as a ventriloquist's puppet for his creator. The name that Paulus gave him was in fact a Latinized version of a standard Jewish title for Judah haNasi, the compiler of the Mishnah (second century), whom Paul described as the "trinepos" (great-great-great-great-grandson) of Rabbenus Haccados.[147] And his prophecies about Helena and the discovery of the True Cross, which Galatino recycled with modest variations, were Christian back-formations, exactly as Casaubon held.[148] The method that Casaubon used to demolish the quotations in Galatino was the same one he used in the case of Hermes, in the same period. Yet without the diary entry, letters, and notes that fix Casaubon's critical reading to a particular date and identify the whole range of books on his desk, the connection between the two enterprises would remain invisible.

Casaubon's correspondence, finally, also contains a small but vital section of his Hermetic web. Through the first decade of the seventeenth century, Casaubon and his close friend Scaliger exchanged detailed letters on a wide range of issues, from manuscripts that Scaliger needed for his edition of Eusebius to the identification and exposure of forgeries. Both men believed that many Jews and early Christians had forged texts in the hope of promoting the kingdom of God. Both strongly disapproved of this supposed *dolus bonus*. In one pointed letter, written on 28 August 1603, Casaubon asked Scaliger for his opinion of that "Rabbi Haccados, whom Galatino uses to prove that all the mysteries of the Christian religion, and especially that of transsubstantiation, and all those sorts of bells and whistles, were known to the ancient Jews."[149] This loaded question supplies a terminal date for Casaubon's critical reading of the problematic rabbinical texts in Galatino. It took place between 1601, when he began looking seriously at the text, and mid-1603. But the letter reveals even more. It confirms that he attacked these texts for exactly the same reasons that he attacked Hermes. And it shows that he went through both corpora, Greek and Hebrew, at exactly the same time. For in the next sentence, Casaubon not only declared the rabbinical texts in

146. Heredia 1487?, translated in Heredia 1998. See in general Dan 1997, 30–35, for a translation of Scholem's arguments; and Secret 1966.

147. Heredia 1487?, unpaginated; Heredia 1998, 39.

148. See Heredia 1487?: "cum autem dominabitur in terra sancta regina Helena omnis israhel in angustiis erit et detrimento. quippe quod ab ea perquiretur haec arbor et nulla apud eos extabit noticia: neque invenient quoad deus implebitur misericordia et ex terra prodire faciet": 1998, 17.

149. Casaubon 1709, 186: "dic mihi quid judicii tui sit super Rabbino illo Haccados, unde probat Galatinus, omnia τῆς Χριστιανῆς θρησκείας μυστήρια, maxime autem τὰ περὶ τῆς μεταστοιχειώσεως, atque id genus τερετίσματα fuisse antiquissimis Judaeis cognita."

Galatino to be pseudepigrapha, but also assigned the "works of Trismegistus" to the same category. "I will believe they come from that very ancient Egyptian," he confided to Scaliger, "on the day when I begin divorce proceedings from the art of criticism."[150] Casaubon confronted Galatino and Hermes, in other words, in the same years, between 1601 and 1603; and he condemned them in the same terms, and in the same sentence. For Casaubon's attack on Hermes and his attack on Galatino, the critical reading of a Greek and of a Hebrew text formed parts of the same enterprise. He saw himself as using the same method on both, and arriving at the same results. But because Baronio also denounced Rabbi Haccados as a fake, Casaubon only registered his agreement, and did not publish the details of that part of his investigation.[151] Only by tracing all the strands of Casaubon's web can we see that, even as he carried out his most famous philological analysis of a Greek text, he wove Hebrew and Greek threads together at every point. The philologist's powers, and his discovery of them, did not belong to Hellenistic philology alone. As we will see, the threads continued to be tightly bound to one another as Casaubon moved, much deeper than anyone has realized, into the enchanted forests of Jewish learning, ancient and modern.

Prayer, Psalms, and Pious Devotions

"To live, using prayers to which all may listen" (*et aperto vivere voto*).[152] Glossing this dictum of Persius in his annotations on the Roman writer,[153] Casaubon invoked a Senecan precept that seems to clinch the sense of the poet's line: "A person should live among his fellow human beings as though God were watching him, and speak to God as though his fellow humans were listening in."[154] Casaubon's clarification of the meaning of Persius' terse phrase is philologically helpful. For the reader, however, the Stoic precept enunciated here would seem to represent Casaubon's own aspirations, as expressed on virtually every page of his diary.[155] His outpouring of prayers, pious devotions, and confessions and his daily accounting of time belong to the human as much as to the divine realm. It may be for this reason that Arnaldo Momigliano asserted that Casaubon composed his diary self-

---

150. Ibid.: "Ego rationibus ut existimo non levibus adducor, ut et quae ex hoc adducuntur, et quae ex aliquot aliis τοιουτότροπα, credam esse ψευδεπίγραφα, non minus quam τὰ τοῦ Τρισμεγίστου, quae ab antiquissimo illo Aegyptio esse profecta tum credam, cum τῇ κριτικῇ nuntium remisero."

151. Casaubon 1614, 102; 1654, 93; 1663, 93. Cf. Baronio 1593–1607, I, 14.

152. Persius, *Saturae* 2.7, cited by Millet 2006, 152.

153. Casaubon 1605a, 180, one of several references to Seneca.

154. Seneca, *Epistulae* 10.5: "Sic vive cum hominibus tamquam Deus videat, sic loquere cum Deo tanquam homines audiant."

155. On Casaubon's Stoicism see Millet 2006.

consciously, knowing that it was to reach the public domain.[156] Whether or not we accept his view, it is nevertheless true that all the elements that make up the divine office are contained in Casaubon's diary: doxology, petitionary prayer, confessions of the most intimate kind, recitation, or rather meditation, on the Psalms and readings from early Christian writings, in particular the Greek fathers. As Pattison wrote: "what stirs his soul is Christian Greek."[157] But like his friend Lancelot Andrewes, the bishop of Winchester, who was also attracted to the patristic writings of the Eastern Orthodox tradition, Casaubon could pray in any language, and he was undoubtedly fascinated by the forms of prayer adopted by different religious communities.[158]

In his remarkable manual of private prayer Andrewes had interspersed his devotions with a dazzling zigzag mosaic of Hebrew prayers taken not only from the Hebrew Bible but also from the Jewish prayerbook.[159] He even introduced one section of petitionary prayer with the phrase taken from tractate Avot, "the fence of the law" *(seyyag haTorah).*[160] Casaubon, for his part, filled his diary with the same amalgam of the three sacred languages. But in his case we have material proof of his interest in Jewish liturgy, in the form of his own copies of three different Hebrew liturgies which are now kept in the British Library. These prayerbooks, printed at the end of the sixteenth century, represent the Ashkenazi (German/central European) rite in one case[161] and the Sephardi (Spanish and Portuguese) rites in the other two.[162] They testify to Casaubon's spiritual quest, which knew no denominational boundaries. This is by no means a conventional expression of what is

156. Momigliano 1977, 189. He also referred to Casaubon's use of Jewish liturgical formulas and to his avoidance of theologically charged vocabulary.

157. Pattison 1892, 441.

158. Not only Protestants but also Catholics considered Hebrew an appropriate medium for prayer. See Stow 1976, who discusses use of Hebrew and translation of Christian prayers into Hebrew by the abbot of Vallombrosa at the beginning of the seventeenth century. The Hebrew prayers were used for 150 years.

159. There were many editions of Andrewes's *Preces privatae.* The English translation published in 1648 became a model for Anglican private devotions. A prized autograph manuscript of the manual was given to Archbishop Laud, and this was published as Andrewes 1892.

160. See, e.g, Andrewes 1892, 46, where the Hebrew texts are identical with a passage in the afternoon prayer for the sabbath, and another from the *Amidah* prayer for the New Year. The expression "fence around the Law" is the heading for a petitional prayer (Andrewes 1892, 27). (In the English version of Andrewes' work no trace of the Hebrew remains. It simply reads: "The Fence of the Law . . . Give me grace, o Lord. Bruise the serpent's head.") On Andrewes and Jewish traditions see Lossky 1991, 70, who refers to a statement in which Andrewes condemns those who refuse to mention the Talmud, asserting that Saint Paul had already referred to it. See also Lloyd Jones 1983, 148–149.

161. *Seder Tefillot* (BL 1970.c.2 [formerly 481.a.11]). This may be the book described as *Liber Tephilloth Hebr.* in the list of Casaubon's books in Bod MS Casaubon 22, 104 recto.

162. *Temunot Tehinot Tefillot Sefarad* [Sephardi prayerbook] (Venice: Zanetti, 1558) (BL 1972.c.1); *Mahzor sefardim miyamim nora'im* (Venice: Zanetti, 1598) (a Sephardi prayerbook for high holy days [BL 1972.c.14]).

generally known as Christian Hebraism. True, both Protestants and Catholics had made Jewish prayer a Christian affair when they published Latin translations of parts of the Jewish liturgy. In 1566, for example, Antoine Chevalier published an *Alphabetum Hebraicum* in which he included a kind of catechism containing translations of certain Jewish prayers; in 1542 Paulus Fagius printed translations of the grace after meals and other such prayers. But although, as we will see, these attempts at epitomizing the life of Jesus in its Jewish context were not unimportant to Casaubon, they were not the sole reasons that propelled him to familiarize himself with and to reflect upon the Jewish mode of praying.[163]

All three prayerbooks are inscribed with typical Casaubon marginalia, revealing the determined student of Hebrew as much as the inquisitive scholar and pious individual. Thus, prayers and the names of the services are, as is his wont, translated into Greek. Particularly striking is the way Casaubon read the 1598 Sephardi prayerbook for the high holy days.[164] One of the focal elements in the service of penitential prayers recited during the ten days of penitence that connect the New Year's Day with the Day of Atonement is the *viddui,* the confession of sins. This collection of prayers combined with supplications for forgiveness clearly resonated with Casaubon. As he makes his way through the prayerbook, he stops to reflect as he reads the prayer based on a talmudic text (Babylonian Talmud, Yoma 87b): "My God, before I was formed, I was of no worth, and now that I have been formed it is as though I had not been formed. I am dust in my life, how much more so in my death. Behold, I am before You like a vessel full of shame and reproach." Casaubon renders the phrase "full of shame and reproach" into Latin.[165] Similarly, he dubs the central prayer, *ashamnu* (we have incurred guilt)—a confession of sins listed in alphabetical order—"a remarkable confession" ("egregia confessio").[166] These artfully composed penitential

---

163. He also treats liturgy in a comparative mode, examining the order of Jewish and Christian daily prayers, in Casaubon 1614, 536; 1654, 472; 1663, 472. See also Casaubon 1614, 590–591; 1654, 520–521; 1663, 520–521, where he attacks Baronio for suggesting that the saying of grace originated with Jesus. Instead Casaubon cites Zacuto's *Yuhasin* (Zacuto 1580/81, 9 verso), which mentions the grace after meals among the three *takkanot* (enactments) traditionally ascribed to Moses.

164. BL 1972.c.14. On the flyleaf Casaubon wrote out the names of the different parts of the service and noted that the Hebrew letters used to indicate the date of publication make up the word *mashiah* (Messiah): [5]358 = 1598. In his copy of Génébrard's *Eisagoge* (BL 622.h.32), 140 (wrongly numbered 132), Casaubon annotated the list of Hebrew books provided by the author. He glossed the entry for *Mahzor* with the words "Est editus, et vidimus apud ampliss. Thuanum eo nomine librum magnum." At some point in his Paris years, in other words, he did not yet have his own copy of the *Mahzor* and had little knowledge of it.

165. Casaubon, marginal note in BL 1972.c.14, 116 recto: "vas plenum pudoris et ignaviae."

166. Casaubon, marginal note in ibid., 128 recto: "egregia confessio."

prayers recited by Jews in their synagogues every year appealed to Casaubon's Huguenot soul.[167]

But it was not simply the call to repentance that attracted Casaubon's attention, but also the legal prescriptions regarding the blowing of the ram's horn, the *shofar*, which is the essential ingredient of the New Year's Day service. All prayerbooks include instructions as to when and how the *shofar* is to be blown at different stages of the service. Casaubon notes that on the sabbath the *shofar* is to be mentioned in the prayer, but not sounded.[168] He passes no judgment on this practice, simply records it. Perhaps he connected this prohibition with the veto on playing musical instruments in the Calvinist church.

The annotations described so far indicate that Casaubon had some proficiency in reading prayerbook Hebrew. Indeed, he demonstrates his knowledge of Jewish prayers that had become infamous among Christians and, consequently, censored. In its original formulation the *Aleinu* prayer, which begins "It is our duty to praise the Lord of all," included a sentence describing other peoples as "kneeling and prostrating themselves to pointless folly and praying to a god that does not procure salvation." In some manuscript prayerbooks and in printed editions these words were censored; only the blank space in the printed text would have indicated to those in the know that words had been omitted.[169] On coming across the *Aleinu* prayer in its original setting, in the section dealing with God's kingship in the additional service (*Musaf*) for the high holy days, Casaubon simply glossed, "Here the anti-Christian words have been omitted."[170] Casaubon was less thorough in his examination of the 1579 Ashkenazi prayerbook.[171] But he did make a Latin rendition of two texts that were totally alien to the religious world in which he had been raised. One is the long blessing recited after every visit to the lavatory, which expresses the duty to thank God for maintaining the movements of the requisite physical organs. For this text Casaubon translates some of the more unusual words. Interestingly, he misinterprets the

---

167. He is also impressed by Solomon ibn Gabirol's poem "Keter malkhut" ("*Corona regis,*" The King's Crown), which is recited on the morning of the Day of Atonement (see his notes in ibid., 132 verso ff.) and makes some attempt at translating the typical religious vocabulary used in the poem.

168. Casaubon, marginal note in BL 1972.c.14, 87 recto: "sabbato fit mentio clangoris at non clangitur."

169. The classic treatment of this phenomenon is W. Popper 1899; for recent discussion of this form of censorship and its impact see Raz-Krakotzkin 2007, 164.

170. Casaubon, marginal note in BL 1972.c.14, 132 recto: "hic desunt verba contra Christianos." On Casaubon's reaction to Buxtorf's discussion of anti-Christian prayers see Chapter 3 below. Buxtorf 1604, 175–176, discusses the *Aleinu* prayer and its censorship.

171. BL 1970.c.2.

Figure 1.6. Casaubon's copy of a Hebrew prayerbook. British Library 1970.c.2.

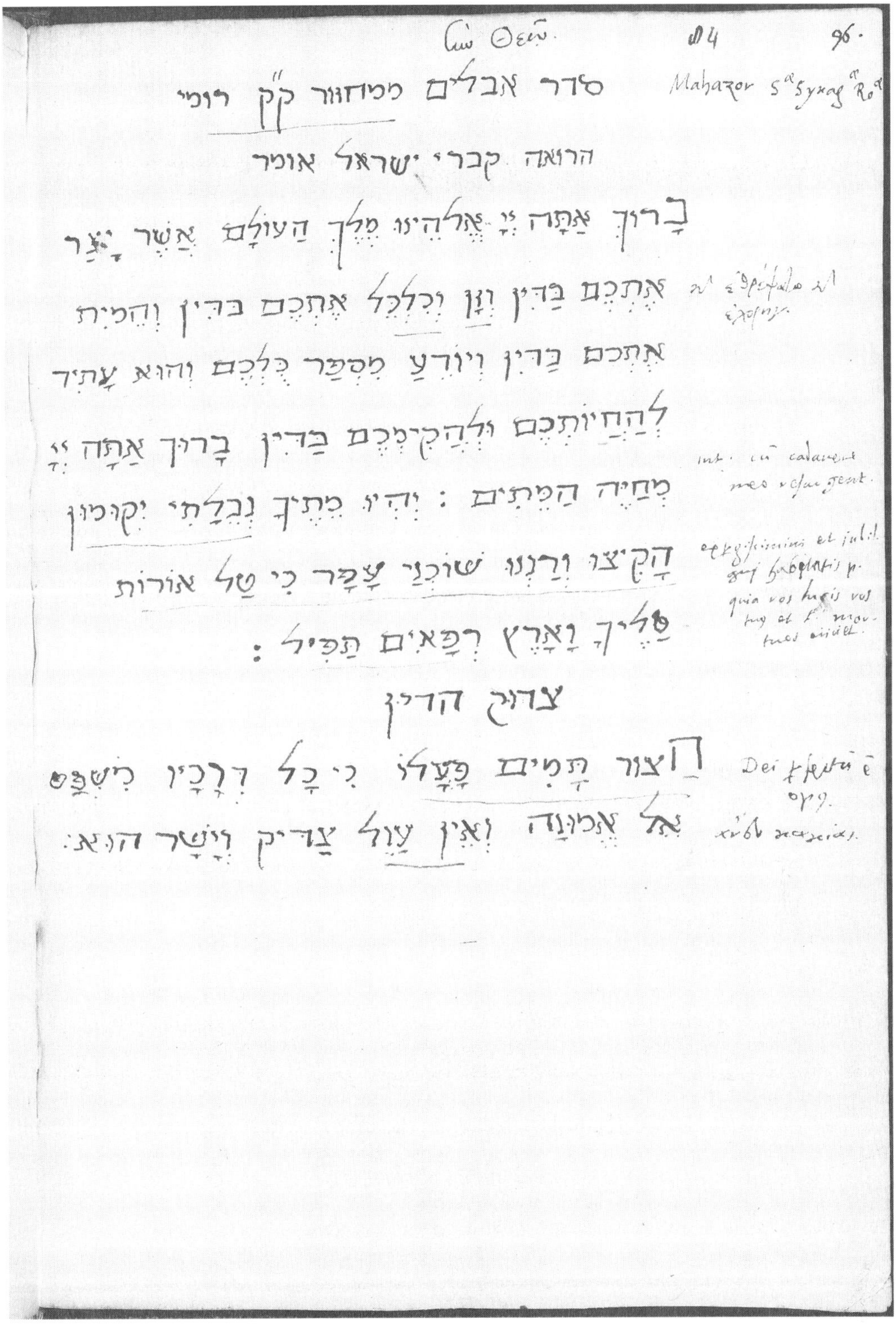

סדר אבלים ממחזור קק רומי   *Mahazor Sᵃ Synagᵃ Roᵐ*

הרואה קברי ישראל אומר

בָּרוּךְ אַתָּה יְיָ אֱלֹהֵינוּ מֶלֶךְ הָעוֹלָם אֲשֶׁר יָצַר

* in epistola ʼiⁱ*
אֶתְכֶם בַּדִּין וְזָן וִיכַלְכֵּל אֶתְכֶם בַּדִּין וְהֵמִית

אֶתְכֶם בַּדִּין וְיוֹדֵעַ מִסְפַּר כֻּלְּכֶם וְהוּא עָתִיד

לְהַחֲיוֹתְכֶם וּלְהַקִימְכֶם בַּדִּין בָּרוּךְ אַתָּה יְיָ

int. cū calavere
res resurgent.
מְחַיֶּה הַמֵּתִים : יִֽהְיוּ מֵתֶיךָ נְבֵלָתִי יְקוּמוּן

et gigniminis et jubil
quia vos tegis vos
tug et f. mor-
tues viuet.
הָקִיצוּ וְרַנְּנוּ שׁוֹכְנֵי עָפָר כִּי טַל אוֹרֹת

טַלֶּיךָ וָאָרֶץ רְפָאִים תַּפִּיל :

צדוק הדין

Dei perfectū ē
opꝰ
הַצּוּר תָּמִים פָּעֳלוֹ כִּי כָל דְּרָכָיו מִשְׁפָּט

viæ rectæ.
אֵל אֱמוּנָה וְאֵין עָוֶל צַדִּיק וְיָשָׁר הוּא :

Figure 1.7. Casaubon's copy of a blessing from the Roman *Mahzor.* Bodleian Library MS Casaubon 30, 96 recto.

phrase "if one of them [the orifices] is opened or closed it is impossible to stand and set oneself before You" as a reference to the resurrection of the dead.[172] But even more intriguing is Casaubon's Latin translation of the morning blessing recited by men, "Blessed art thou, O Lord, who did not make me a woman."[173] It is impossible to know what such a blessing signified for Casaubon. His society was no less patriarchal than that of the Jews, which the blessing, on a superficial reading, would seem to emphasize. But he was nevertheless accustomed to participating in public religious devotions together and on equal terms with his wife and children—or so his diary entries would have us understand.[174]

The notes in these prayerbooks present a picture of a dispassionate reader of the Jewish prayerbook, who simply wishes to know how others pray. But sometimes it appears that the rifling through the pages was fired by some hidden or less hidden agendas. One page of Casaubon's notebooks, inscribed as usual to God, contains his transcription with some marginal notes of the prayer recited on visiting burial grounds.[175] He had copied it out from yet another prayerbook, the *Mahzor of the Holy Community of Rome*. The blessing ends with the words: "He will resurrect you and set you up with justice for life in the world to come. Blessed art Thou, O Lord, who revives the dead." The choice of this particular benediction and this particular prayerbook requires explanation.[176]

In 1569 Gilbert Génébrard, the erudite professor of Hebrew at the Collège Royal in Paris, renowned equally for his devotion to the Catholic cause and

172. Ibid., 2 verso: "mortuorum resurrectio."

173. Ibid.: "Benedictus D. quod non creavit me foeminam."

174. See, e.g., Casaubon 1850, II, 1050: "Ego, uxor et liberi concioni sacrae Dei beneficio interfuimus"; ibid., 1051: "Concioni Gallicae ego et uxor hodie interfuimus"; ibid., 1061: "Ego, uxor et liberi sacram Eucharistiam participavimus in Ecclesia Gallica." See also ibid., 1021–1022, for Casaubon's delight in the company of pious women. Casaubon's reaction to Fagius' compilation of Hebrew adages in praise of women in his commentary on Genesis 2:18 (BL 481.c.4.[2], 59) confirms this. This is one of the passages indexed on the title page ("uxoris encomia"), and in this context he writes in the margin "mulierum laudatio."

175. Bod MS Casaubon 30, 96 recto. The justified right margin and other features of this copy suggest that Casaubon was transcribing a manuscript original. Our thanks to Malachi Beit-Arié for discussing the manuscript with us and for making this suggestion.

176. The importance of the Italian rite was stressed by S. D. Luzzatto 1966 in his notable introduction to the *Mahzor Bene Roma*, and by Goldschmidt 1978 in his addenda to Luzzatto's introduction. Both stressed the importance of this rite for the history of the liturgy, even though it was used only in Italy, in a few synagogues in Salonika and Constantinople, and in the Italian synagogue in Jerusalem. The *minhag Roma, minhag haItaliani,* or *minhag haLo'azim* is found in many manuscripts from the thirteenth through fifteenth centuries and bears much affinity to the *minhag Romania*. It is not surprising that the Roman *Mahzor* was the first Jewish liturgical work to be printed. Christians seem to have been especially interested in this prayerbook because Roman Jewish traditions could be regarded as harking back to the time of Jesus.

for his hostility to Huguenots, produced a compilation of Hebrew writings and prayers with Latin translations.[177] The collection included a section on the duties of mourners, extracted from the Roman *Mahzor*.[178] Génébrard's preface reveals the purpose of his rendition of these particular prayers from the Roman rite. In it he launches an offensive against the Protestant Sebastian Münster and "those of his ilk," who had denied that Jews prayed for the dead. They had gone so far as to assert that the unequivocal statement about resurrection of the dead in 2 Maccabees (12:39–45) was an interpolation, the work of an insolent Jew. Their vicious purpose in insisting that the Jews had never up to these days used such a prayer was to undermine the Catholic church's established custom of praying for the dead.[179]

During his own years in Paris, Casaubon managed to lay hands on Génébrard's copy of Sebastian Münster's Latin translation of the Hebrew Josephus—a medieval work known as the *Josippon*.[180] In his annotations on the book he copies down Münster's provocative denial that Jews pray for the dead, but he registers his own serious reservations about the truth of Münster's assertion.[181] In particular, he was struck by Génébrard's marginal note, in which he dismissed as an aberration the idea that Jews did not pray for the dead. Génébrard invoked an unimpeachable authority, his Hebrew teacher, the convert Cesar Brancassius, who corroborated his view on the basis of contemporary Jewish practice. Moreover, the Protestant Paulus Fagius had referred to "a certain great prayer in which they praise God, in

177. Génébrard 1569.

178. Génébrard 1608, 68: "Supremum lugentium officium ex libro precationum Hebraicarum, qui inscribitur Mahzor Sanctae Synagogae Romanae. Quis conspicit sepulchra Israelitarum, dicit."

179. Ibid., 64: "Perspicient in solennibus ipsorum sacris usurpari, quae a Munstero et consimilis metalli hominibus, ut enervent librorum de Machabaeorum gestis veritatem, ut receptam Ecclesiae de orando pro mortuis consuetudinem infirment, maligne asseverantur nunquam in hunc usque diem fuisse apud ipsos usitata." In the margin is a printed note referring to *Josippon* 3.19 and Münster's discussion of it. For further evidence of Catholic views see Serarius 1611, 715: "Ipsi vero etiam Hebraei preces pro mortuis olim fuderunt, et hodie fundunt, uti testatur libellus, quem e *Machzor* vertit Genebrardus." He also speaks about the great synagogue in Frankfurt and the use of the the mourner's Kaddish and the "eternal light" *(ner tamid):* "In maiore Francofordensium Iudaeorum Synagoga, in ipso ingressu ad laevam, fere semper ardens lumen, aut etiam lumina plura videas. quia, si cuiusquam parens moriatur, praeter preces, hos etiam cereos, anno integro, accendit." See also Garetius 1565.

180. For a full discussion of this text see Chapter 3 below.

181. Münster 1541, 61, on 3.19: "Adduntur tamen ibi nonnulla quae hic in hebraeo non sunt, potissimum in fine subjicitur, quod oratio vivorum pro defunctis facta prosit mortuis ipsis in alia vita. Id cum in alio scripturae loco non inveniatur, neque Iudaeis in hunc usque diem in usu sit, orare pro his qui iam sunt sub iudicio dei, videtur coronis ista per audaculum aliquem adiecta. Et ne quisquam hic garriat, me fidelem hebraismi interpretem non extitisse, hunc ego ad exemplar Constantinopoli a Iudaeis impressum mitto, quod passim hodie apud Iudaeos nostrates invenitur, quodque ego sequutus sum, et ibi inveniet, me alia non reddidisse quam quae in codice illo inveni." The learned owner of the copy of the work in Lambeth Palace Library (E2574H.3) also indicated that this is an important passage.

whose power our worldly and heavenly existence lies."[182] Casaubon's final verdict on the whole matter is—probably deliberately—ambiguously cynical: "This was the view of that man, who was, I believe, more learned than honorable, and certainly possessed the most vicious tongue of any man alive. As his death showed, he was born to harm the public, and died to serve it."[183]

It seems, therefore, that Génébrard's Latin translation and discussion of the prayer for the dead inspired Casaubon to acquire a copy of the Roman *Mahzor*. But Casaubon's careful transcription of the Hebrew text, accompanied by a few translations of the expressions, shows us that his interest in the prayerbook and its prayer went beyond religious polemic; rather, his efforts demonstrate a genuine desire to deepen his understanding of Hebrew prayer. The same kind of motivation led him to examine the *Officium Beatae Mariae* (Office of the Blessed Maria), which he happened to read in its official version sanctioned by Pope Pius V in 1571. In 1610 Casaubon entered a description of the breviary in his diary, combining praise and censure: "The book is beautifully bound and contains some pious prayers."[184] But

182. This is a reference to the Aramaic *Kaddish* prayer, which is recited by mourners.

183. Bod MS Casaubon 27, 174 recto: "Caeterum historia hujus cap. extat 2 Macc. 12. sed notat M. ibi dici orationem vivorum pro defunctis factam prodesse mortuis [i.e., 2 Maccabees 12:45]: quod cum non legatur in hoc libro Hebr. neque ea sententia aut in ullo sacrae scripturae loco inveniatur, aut etiam in ritualibus Hebr. τῶν νῦν ὄντων: putat M. ab aliquo audaculo eam sententiam libris Mac. fuisse appictam. De quo sane cogitandum: nam etsi fortasse minus vera est M. sententia: tum ille gravissimas caussas habuit, cur id suspicaretur. At reperi scriptum in ora libri qui olim fuit Genebrardi, manu ipsius Genebrardi e regione superiorum M. verborum, sic, Falsum. Nam Judaei hodierni orant pro mortuis, ut a Brancacio accepi. Quinetiam Fagius alioquin infestus orationi pro defunctis in 14. cap. sui deuteronomii quod e Chaldaeo Latinum fecit, dicunt, inquit, orationem quandam magnam, in qua laudant Deum quod in eius potestate sit vita nostra, atque inter coetera sic dicunt: תנוח נפשו ומשכבו בשלום ישכב בשלום ויישן בשלום עד יבא מנחם משמיע שלום אבות עולם ישיני חברון etc. Vide ipsum fagium. Sed addit G. Vide et quae Judaeus baptizatus Antonius Margarita in libro suo Germanico habet, quem de superstitionibus Judaicis conscripsit. Haec ille, vir, meo judicio, doctior quam probior: certe quidem omnium mortalium maledicentissimus. Et quod exitus docuit malo publico natus, bono denatus." See also Casaubon's note on the discussion of prayer for the dead in Maccabees on the flyleaf of Wren Library, Trinity College Cambridge, Adv.d.1.32: "Eruditio Chemnitii. Prorsus est eximia: et in eo illud singulare quod textus locorum de quibus agit, ex ipsis fontibus petit: vnde saepe illi nascuntur observationes eruditae. exemplo sit locus Maccab. de purgatorio. nam in voce ἐπίνοια latet magna vis argumenti vt recte hic observat, pag. 147." Cf. also Casaubon's notes at ibid., III, 146–147.

184. Casaubon 1850, II, 710–712; 711 (25 January 1610): "Liber est excellenter compactus, et plures preces pias continens, in his unam Thomae non vulgarem ut erat illius viri admirandum ingenium. In hoc igitur libro quum casu in illum incidissem, et forte aperuissem, duo statim deprehendi quae visa mihi nefanda cum impietate conjuncta. Prius est quod Papa in praefatione diserte vetat omnem precum id genus usum in vernacula lingua. At, Deus bone, quoties mihi contrarium affirmatum est? Quoties dictum moneri viros foeminasque ut preces vernacula lingua scriptas usurpent? Sane negari non potest in Gallia hodie multum earum esse usum. Sed hoc profecto nos ab invitis pudore quodam expressimus. Qui si hodie non essemus, periret miseris libertas aliquid cognoscendi eorum quae ad pietatem pertinent. Et diserte Papa superstitionem id vocat. O monstrum iniquitatis! O vere hac quidem in parte

then admiration turns to attack. Denounced in no uncertain terms is the "iniquitous" pronouncement of the pope in the preface in which he banned all use of vernacular prayer, even going so far as to call it a "superstition." Casaubon pours out his wrath, describing the situation of his wretched French coreligionists, men and women, who, if the pope had his way, "would be deprived of the freedom to know something of that which pertains to the pious life." In this furious stream of invective, Casaubon supports the individual's inalienable right to pray in any language. It is not surprising, therefore, that when he came to examine other prescriptions related to the liturgy, Maimonides' Laws of Prayer, he noticed and copied out the law that permitted a person to recite some prayers in the vernacular "provided the traditional formulas [of the Hebrew text] are used."[185]

Prayer is indeed a contentious issue, and when it comes to clarification of Jesus' words in the Gospel, and Baronio's misinterpretation of them, Casaubon again shows his colors. He castigates Baronio while at the same time demonstrating the importance of prayer for him as individual and member of a religious community. According to Casaubon, Baronio had offered an interpretation of Matthew 6:7—"But when ye pray, use not vain repetitions [$\beta\alpha\tau\tauo\lambda o\gamma\acute\eta\sigma\eta\tau\epsilon$], as the heathens do: for they think that they shall be heard for their much speaking [$\pio\lambda\upsilon\lambda o\gamma\acute\iota\alpha$]"—that was both incorrect and confused.[186] Baronio had not made the requisite distinction between public and private prayer, for he interpreted the verse in relation to the recitation of the Psalms. In fact, as Augustine had explained, Jesus was decrying a certain mode of composing private, petitionary and penitential, prayers. Aside from Casaubon's usual denunciation of Baronio, the passage is notable for highlighting his spiritual cast of mind: "Although the Psalms, with their prophetic doctrine and doxology, are not infrequently intermingled with

---

$\dot\alpha\nu\tau\acute\iota\chi\rho\iota\sigma\tauo\nu$. Alterum fuit, quod sum abominatus, in Decalogo, unde totum de imaginibus praeceptum est sublatum. Euge fidelis Pastor. Hoc est Dei mandata servare."

185. Bod MS Casaubon 30, 106 verso: "Addit posse orari in quavis lingua, modo serventur traditae formulae." See Maimonides, *Mishneh Torah,* Hilkhot Berakhot, 1, 6.

186. Baronio 1593–1607, I, 115: "Multa cum inculcasset Dominus de absolutissima Christianae legis perfectione, quod suos quam maxime a fastu Pharisaeorum cuperet esse alienos, ne quid facerent quo videantur ab hominibus, admonuit: neve Ethnicis assimilarentur, qui in multiloquio se exaudiri putarent, compendiosam eosdem precum formulam docuit. Non tamen ex eo inferendum vel existimandum quod reprehenderit Dominus prolixum psalmorum cantum: nam et in templo frequens multiplexque erat usus psalmorum. Sed dum ait: Quod Ethnici faciunt] ad superstitiosam illorum observationem alludit. unde textus Evangelistae non habet $\pio\lambda\upsilon\lambda o\gamma\acute\iota\alpha\nu$, sed $\beta\alpha\tau\tauo\lambda o\gamma\acute\iota\alpha\nu$, quod non simpliciter multiloquium sed inanem sermonem demonstrat . . . Putamus insuper Dominum alludere voluisse ad eam, quae in Syria erat, idololatriam, cum videlicet deam Syriam circumferentes, quasi divino quodam perciti spiritu essent, phanatice multa iactabant; cuius ritus meminit Apuleius. Ceterum quam pie, quamque salubriter traditione Apostolorum instituta sit in Ecclesia psalmodia, opportunius suo loco dicemus inferius."

prayers, their recitation really entails the enunciation of praises of God. But nobody can spend too much time, be it day or night, in the pious duty of lauding God with the texts taken from the holy page."[187]

The Psalms played a central and distinctive role in the Reformed church. The metrical French Psalms composed by Calvin, and in particular those written by the accomplished poet Clément Marot, were widely disseminated, and the singing of the Psalms became the "core congregational activity of a reformed service":[188] "When we sing them we can be certain that God puts the words into our mouths; it is as if He sings them with us for his aggrandizement." Thus Calvin, who oversaw the composition of the 128 melodies used in the psalter, which was rarely published without the musical notation.[189] This was Casaubon's tradition. Although he did not, unlike some Huguenots, use the Psalms as a vehicle for political activity, they were often on his lips, as a story from his diary most eloquently expresses.

In 1608 Casaubon realized, while in church, that he had lost in the accidental sinking of a boat the copy of the psalter that his wife had given him as a wedding present and that he had used for twenty-two years. "There was a young man sitting in front of me," he recalled, "and I peeked at his book so that I could join those singing the psalm. By chance they were singing the later part of Psalm 86." He quotes the text in Hebrew and Greek, and in the "metrical version": "Tirant ma vie du bord, Du bas tombeau de la mort"— the text that he presumably saw in his neighbor's book.[190] Clearly, Casaubon knew the Psalms so well that he could meditate on the original Hebrew text, line by line, and on its Greek counterpart, even as he joined his fellow congregants in singing the rhymed and less literal French. But Casaubon owned other psalters. One was the only book that traveled with him in that most difficult transition of his life, when he left France for England. Alone in England—his wife and children did not join until more than a year later—he turned to the psalter for consolation.

Like Ambrose, a church father close to his heart, Casaubon drew inspira-

187. Casaubon 1614, 325; 1654, 287–288; 1663, 287–288: "Cantus enim Psalmorum, etsi vaticinijs, doctrinae, et δοξολογία habet preces permixtas non raras, proprie tamen ad praedicationem laudum Dei spectat. Deum autem laudare, et quidem formulis e sacra pagina depromptis, nemo queat nimis, vel si dies totos, noctes totas, illi officio pietatis impenderit. Christus vero non de praedicatione Dei laudum agit; sed ut recte monet Augustinus, de modo concipiendi preces privatas, quoties piorum aliquis opem atque auxilium Dei, aut delictorum veniam vult impetrare. Male igitur haec confundit Baronius, male etiam multiloquium negat a Domino prohiberi, quia textus Matthaei non habeat πολυλογίαν, sed βαττολογίαν. Atqui hoc falsum est, et mire hic hallucinatus est scriptor Annalium."

188. Pettegree 2005, 55.

189. See ibid., 56–59.

190. Casaubon 1850, II, 621: "Erat juvenis ante me sedens, in cujus librum oculos conjicio, ut psallentibus me adjungam. Forte canebatur pars posterior psalmi octogesimi sexti."

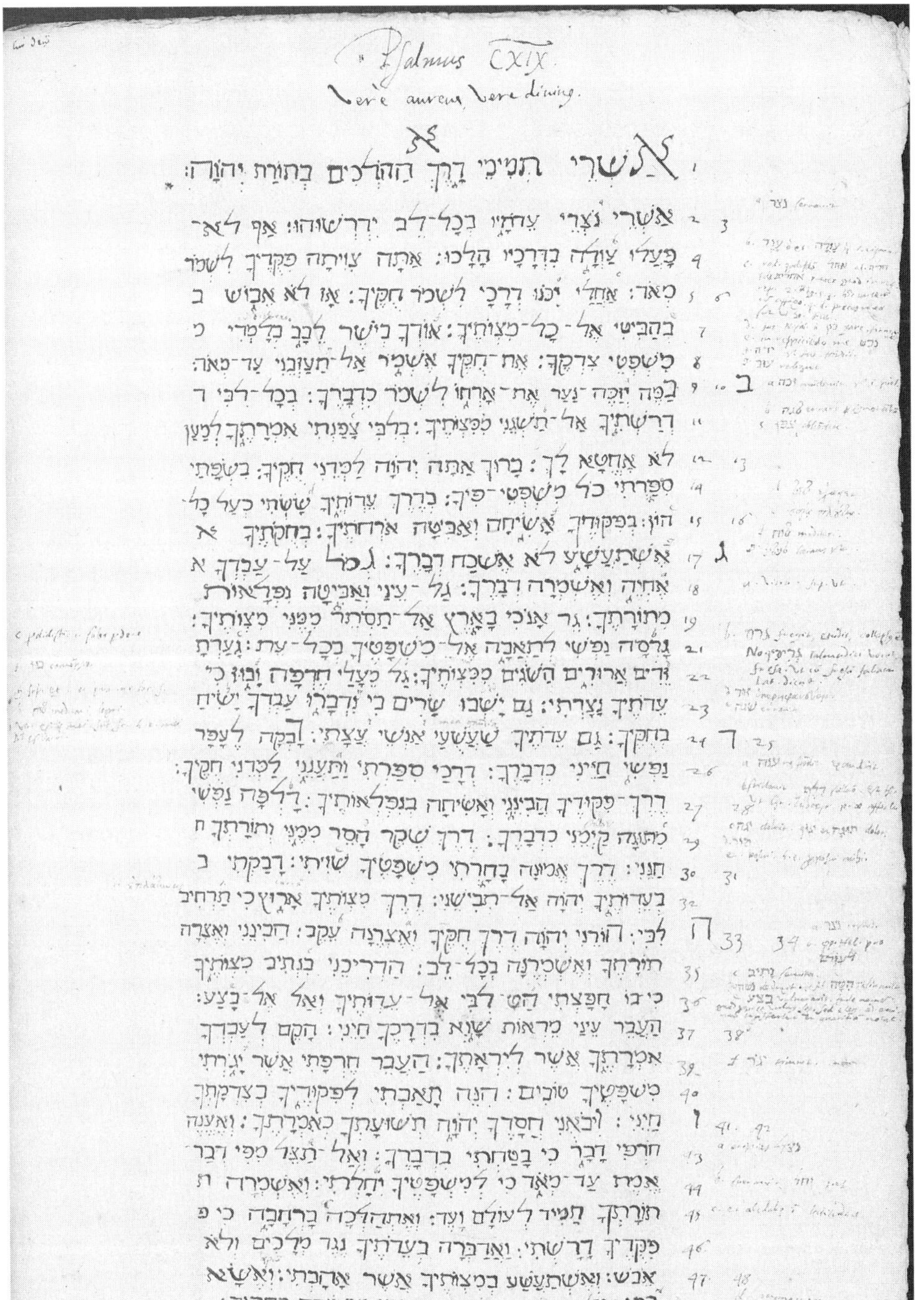

Psalmus CXIX.

vere aureus, vere divinus.

א

אַשְׁרֵי תְמִימֵי דָרֶךְ הַהֹלְכִים בְּתוֹרַת יְהוָה׃

אַשְׁרֵי נֹצְרֵי עֵדֹתָיו בְּכָל־לֵב יִדְרְשׁוּהוּ׃ אַף לֹא־
פָעֲלוּ עַוְלָה בִּדְרָכָיו הָלָכוּ׃ אַתָּה צִוִּיתָה פִקֻּדֶיךָ לִשְׁמֹר
מְאֹד׃ אַחֲלַי יִכֹּנוּ דְרָכָי לִשְׁמֹר חֻקֶּיךָ׃ אָז לֹא־אֵבוֹשׁ בְּ
הַבִּיטִי אֶל־כָּל־מִצְוֹתֶיךָ׃ אוֹדְךָ בְּיֹשֶׁר לֵבָב בְּלָמְדִי
מִשְׁפְּטֵי צִדְקֶךָ׃ אֶת־חֻקֶּיךָ אֶשְׁמֹר אַל־תַּעַזְבֵנִי עַד־מְאֹד׃

ב

בַּמֶּה יְזַכֶּה־נַּעַר אֶת־אָרְחוֹ לִשְׁמֹר כִּדְבָרֶךָ׃ בְּכָל־לִבִּי ד
דְרַשְׁתִּיךָ אַל־תַּשְׁגֵּנִי מִמִּצְוֹתֶיךָ׃ בְּלִבִּי צָפַנְתִּי אִמְרָתֶךָ לְמַעַן
לֹא אֶחֱטָא־לָךְ׃ בָּרוּךְ אַתָּה יְהוָה לַמְּדֵנִי חֻקֶּיךָ׃ בִּשְׂפָתַי
סִפַּרְתִּי כֹּל מִשְׁפְּטֵי־פִיךָ׃ בְּדֶרֶךְ עֵדְוֹתֶיךָ שַׂשְׂתִּי כְּעַל כָּל־
הוֹן׃ בְּפִקּוּדֶיךָ אָשִׂיחָה וְאַבִּיטָה אֹרְחֹתֶיךָ׃ בְּחֻקֹּתֶיךָ א

ג

אֶשְׁתַּעֲשָׁע לֹא אֶשְׁכַּח דְּבָרֶךָ׃ גְּמֹל עַל־עַבְדְּךָ א
אֶחְיֶה וְאֶשְׁמְרָה דְבָרֶךָ׃ גַּל־עֵינַי וְאַבִּיטָה נִפְלָאוֹת
מִתּוֹרָתֶךָ׃ גֵּר אָנֹכִי בָאָרֶץ אַל־תַּסְתֵּר מִמֶּנִּי מִצְוֹתֶיךָ׃
גָּרְסָה נַפְשִׁי לְתַאֲבָה אֶל־מִשְׁפָּטֶיךָ בְכָל־עֵת׃ גָּעַרְתָּ
זֵדִים אֲרוּרִים הַשֹּׁגִים מִמִּצְוֹתֶיךָ׃ גַּל מֵעָלַי חֶרְפָּה וָבוּז כִּי
עֵדֹתֶיךָ נָצָרְתִּי׃ גַּם יָשְׁבוּ שָׂרִים בִּי נִדְבָּרוּ עַבְדְּךָ יָשִׂיחַ

ד

בְּחֻקֶּיךָ׃ גַּם־עֵדֹתֶיךָ שַׁעֲשֻׁעָי אַנְשֵׁי עֲצָתִי׃ דָּבְקָה לֶעָפָר
נַפְשִׁי חַיֵּנִי כִּדְבָרֶךָ׃ דְּרָכַי סִפַּרְתִּי וַתַּעֲנֵנִי לַמְּדֵנִי חֻקֶּיךָ׃
דֶּרֶךְ־פִּקּוּדֶיךָ הֲבִינֵנִי וְאָשִׂיחָה בְּנִפְלְאוֹתֶיךָ׃ דָּלְפָה נַפְשִׁי
מִתּוּגָה קַיְּמֵנִי כִּדְבָרֶךָ׃ דֶּרֶךְ שֶׁקֶר הָסֵר מִמֶּנִּי וְתוֹרָתְךָ ח

ה

חָנֵּנִי׃ דֶּרֶךְ־אֱמוּנָה בָחָרְתִּי מִשְׁפָּטֶיךָ שִׁוִּיתִי׃ דָּבַקְתִּי ב
בְעֵדְוֹתֶיךָ יְהוָה אַל־תְּבִישֵׁנִי׃ דֶּרֶךְ מִצְוֹתֶיךָ אָרוּץ כִּי תַרְחִיב
לִבִּי׃ הוֹרֵנִי יְהוָה דֶּרֶךְ חֻקֶּיךָ וְאֶצְּרֶנָּה עֵקֶב׃ הֲבִינֵנִי וְאֶצְּרָה
תוֹרָתֶךָ וְאֶשְׁמְרֶנָּה בְכָל־לֵב׃ הַדְרִיכֵנִי בִּנְתִיב מִצְוֹתֶיךָ
כִּי־בוֹ חָפָצְתִּי׃ הַט־לִבִּי אֶל־עֵדְוֹתֶיךָ וְאַל אֶל־בָּצַע׃
הַעֲבֵר עֵינַי מֵרְאוֹת שָׁוְא בִּדְרָכֶךָ חַיֵּנִי׃ הָקֵם לְעַבְדְּךָ
אִמְרָתֶךָ אֲשֶׁר לְיִרְאָתֶךָ׃ הַעֲבֵר חֶרְפָּתִי אֲשֶׁר יָגֹרְתִּי

ו

כִּי מִשְׁפָּטֶיךָ טוֹבִים׃ הִנֵּה תָּאַבְתִּי לְפִקֻּדֶיךָ בְּצִדְקָתְךָ
חַיֵּנִי׃ וִיבֹאֻנִי חֲסָדֶךָ יְהוָה תְּשׁוּעָתְךָ כְּאִמְרָתֶךָ׃ וְאֶעֱנֶה
חֹרְפִי דָבָר כִּי־בָטַחְתִּי בִּדְבָרֶךָ׃ וְאַל־תַּצֵּל מִפִּי דְבַר
אֱמֶת עַד־מְאֹד כִּי לְמִשְׁפָּטֶךָ יִחָלְתִּי׃ וְאֶשְׁמְרָה ת
תוֹרָתְךָ תָמִיד לְעוֹלָם וָעֶד׃ וְאֶתְהַלְּכָה בָרְחָבָה כִּי פ
פִקֻּדֶיךָ דָרָשְׁתִּי׃ וַאֲדַבְּרָה בְעֵדֹתֶיךָ נֶגֶד מְלָכִים וְלֹא

ז

אֵבוֹשׁ׃ וְאֶשְׁתַּעֲשַׁע בְּמִצְוֹתֶיךָ אֲשֶׁר אָהָבְתִּי׃ וְאֶשָּׂא
כַפַּי אֶל־מִצְוֹתֶיךָ אֲשֶׁר אָהָבְתִּי וְאָשִׂיחָה בְחֻקֶּיךָ׃
זְכֹר־דָּבָר לְעַבְדֶּךָ עַל אֲשֶׁר יִחַלְתָּנִי׃ זֹאת נֶחָמָתִי
בְעָנְיִי כִּי אִמְרָתְךָ חִיָּתְנִי׃ זֵדִים הֱלִיצֻנִי עַד־מְאֹד מִ

FIGURE 1.8. Casaubon's transcription of Psalm 119. Bodleian Library MS Casaubon 6, 25 recto.

tion, scholarly as well as spiritual, from one particular psalm (119/118), the longest in the book (176 verses).[191] This great acrostic of twenty-two stanzas of eight lines, each following alphabetic order, is characterized by its use of multiple designations for the words for Torah: law, ordinances, and precepts. As Casaubon's copybooks and diary indicate, this psalm claimed his attention over and over again.[192] In September 1611 he wrote out a "pious meditation" on the psalm in one of his copybooks: "Long is best, as was said once upon a time about the poems of some poet. All Davidic Psalms are divine, but this one excels them all; it is, as it were, the embodiment of all Holy Scripture."[193] In another corner of his copybooks, dated 23 September 1611, he presents "observatiunculae" on the same psalm. His observations range from textual questions to conceptual reflections on its meaning. The designations for the heavenly doctrine (that is, Torah) and the structure of the psalm as well as the differences between the Hebrew and Septuagint are noted down with particular attention to the specific Greek terms.[194] A short while before he jotted down these notes, he had made a long entry in his diary.[195] Again he bewails his miserable lonesome life, bereft as he is of the companionship of his wife and children. But the suffering is transformed into "a singular desire and joy" as he reads the holy scriptures. He is imbued with a "pious joy"—the true joy of the spirit. The Hebrew word ששׂון, which occurs several times in his favorite Psalm 119, is the focus of his homily. What is striking is how Casaubon reads the psalm, with an almost modern understanding of the Psalms' intertextuality; indeed the way he construes the verses has something of a midrashic ring about it. In attempting to explain the omnipresence of a term that can so easily be associated with "false pleasures," he writes:

191. For the importance and centrality of Psalm 119 in the church see Deissler 1955 and Harl 1972.

192. For example, in Bod MS Casaubon 6 he transcribes Psalm 119, which he calls "vere aureus, vere divinus," in full (22 verso–24 recto).

193. Bod MS Casaubon 25, 125 recto: "Vere enim dici potest de psalmis Davidis quod olim de poetae nescio cuius poematis, optimum esse quod esset longissimum. Sunt sane omnes cantiones Davidis admirandae et uno verbo divinae: sed illa certa quadam ratione mihi videtur excellere quod doceat nos quasi $\pi\rho\hat{a}\xi\iota\nu$ totius Sacrae Scripturae."

194. Bod MS Casaubon 28, 14 recto–verso.

195. Casaubon 1850, II, 881–882 (19 September 1611): "Mane totum posui in lectione et meditatione $\Psi\alpha\lambda\mu\hat{\omega}\nu$ $\tau\acute{\iota}\nu\omega\nu$. Hanc ego in misera hac vita et praesenti mea solitudine miserrima solam voluptatem, solum gaudium percipio, quod ex librorum sacrorum lectione animo meo oboritur. Gaudium dico, quia etsi non permittit mihi gaudere sollicitudo de uxore et liberis, itemque aliae molestissimae curae; quia tamen animum, uti possum, attollo ad Creatorem et Redemtorem meum, dum in his sum cogitationibus, pia quadam laetitia perfundor et gaudeo, te, Deus aeterne, supplex venerans, ut meum, meae et meorum animos a falsis gaudiis ad verum illud traducas quod tui timentibus est proprium." These reflections on the psalm continue on 20–21 September 1611.

> I notice that this "joy" is mentioned throughout the Holy Scripture either when the righteous request it from God, or when gratitude is expressed for having obtained it. The word ששון and words derived from it occur so often in Psalm 119, indicating a special kind of joy. After having committed his sin David beseeches God in Psalm 51 to restore joy and gladness [verse 8]; and only later does he explain what is meant by the joy, for [he says] "Restore to me the joy in Your salvation" [verse 12].[196]

Casaubon searches for the meaning of this word which, in its absolute state, can carry so many varied and contradictory connotations. He invokes another psalm in which the incidence of the word in a historical context aids a nuanced understanding of its precise connotation. In the phrase "the joy of thy salvation" (51:14), where the word appears in a construct state (connected to another noun), it takes on a specific meaning: the joy of the sinner whose sin has been forgiven and on whom God's salvation is bestowed.

Casaubon's reflections on and philological meanderings among the Psalms, as with other parts of the Old Testament, reveal a fine understanding of the biblical text. Like so many Reformed Christians, he had learned Hebrew in his youth, and he had become intensely absorbed in the study of a wide variety of commentaries on the Bible, which enriched his reading. But his attraction to Hebrew literature was not confined to the Old Testament or prayerbooks. Among the Hebrew books in Casaubon's possession was a work not usually found on the shelves of Christian Hebraists (or, for that matter, known to all Jews). The *Sefer Hasidim,* or Book of the Pious, of Judah the Pious is a remarkable text, composed in the Rhineland in the late twelfth century.[197] It describes the lives of a circle of Pietists whose constant quest was to discover and follow the "will of their creator." This quest, expressed by fear and love of God and self-abnegation, went together with a strict adherence to the principles of Torah. The reader of the book is brought into the world of this pietistic community in which the tension between learning and familial obligations is constantly articulated, and where, even

---

196. Casaubon 1850, II, 882: "Observo enim in S. Scriptura passim gaudii huius fieri mentionem, et pios a Deo vel petere illud, vel pro obtento gratias agere. In Ψαλμ. 119 tot locis occurrit vox ששון et inde deducta, quae laetitiam quandam singularem denotant. David post peccatum suum in Ψ. 51 petit a Deo ut sibi restituat ששון ושמחה, deinde explicat quale gaudium intelligat sic: השיבה לי ששון ישעך Paulus quoque Apostolus ad Rom. XIV.17. docet Regnum Dei esse non escam, aut potum, sed δικαιοσύνην καὶ εἰρήνην καὶ χαρὰν ἐν πνεύματι ἁγίῳ. O bone Deus, gaudium hoc gaudere doce me, doce uxorem meam et liberos. Amen."

197. See Scholem 1946 and 1954; Marcus 1981.

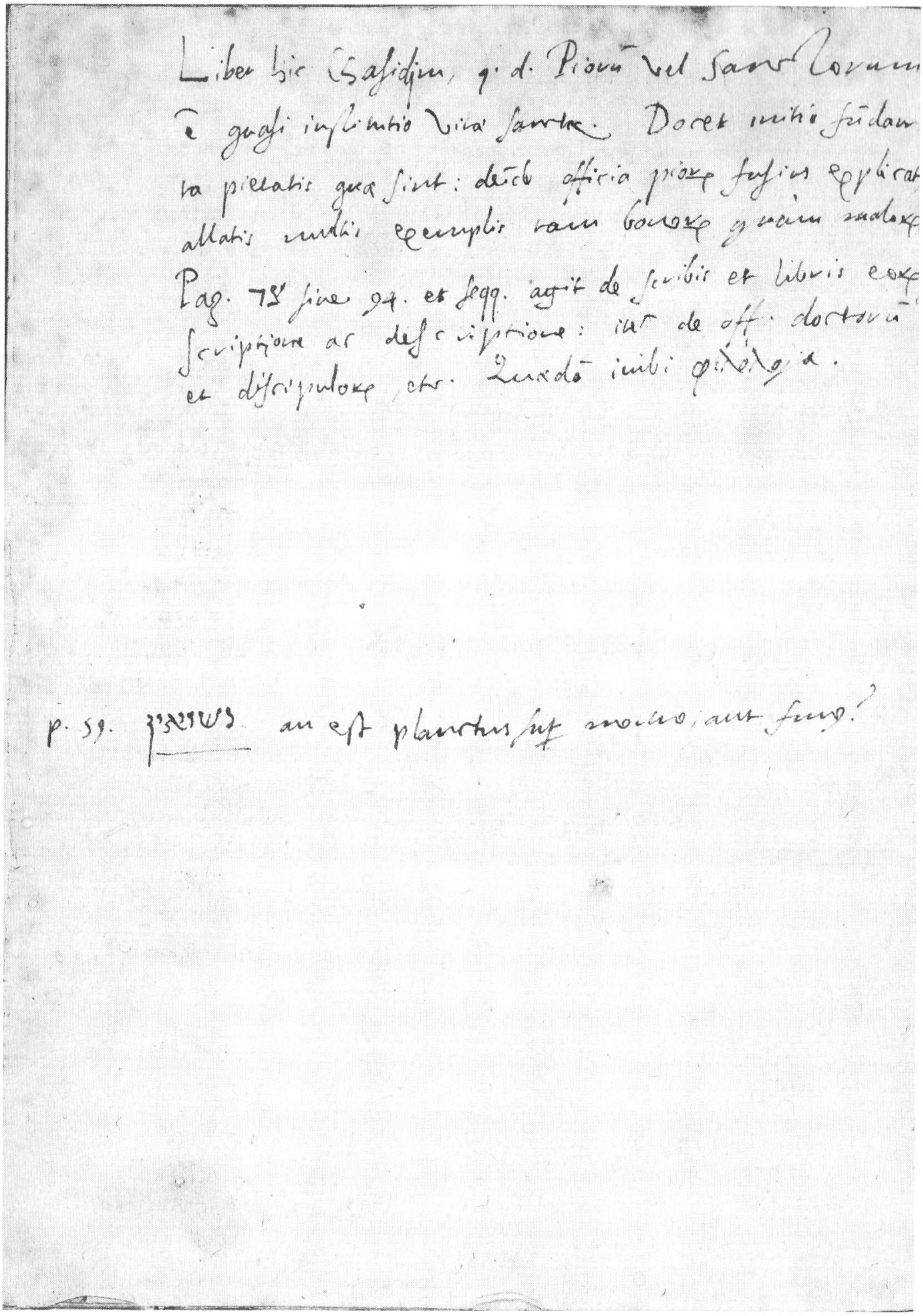

Liber his Casidim, q. d. Piorum vel Sanctorum
e quasi instrinsio vitae sanctae. Docet mihi judaeorum
ta pietatis quae sint: deïce officia piorum fusius explicat
allatis multis exemplis tam bonorum quam malorum

Pag. 78 sive 94. et seqq. agit de scribis et libris eorum
scriptione ac descriptione: itae de off: doctorum
et discipulorum, etc. Quaedam imbi φιλολογια.

p. 59. שעשועים   an est planctus sive mœror, aut finis?

FIGURE 1.9. Casaubon, note in his copy of Judah ben Samuel's *Sefer Hasidim*.
British Library 1934.f.13.

more distinctively, the pious Jews' devotion to the Torah and its traditions is enforced by their dedication to the material book and its production.[198]

In an exchange of letters with Scaliger, Casaubon had referred to his ownership of the book, which he offered to lend. But he appears to have been affected by Scaliger's unfavorable assessment of the work in his reply, for he did not reveal how carefully he had read it.[199] On the title page of his copy, as so often, Casaubon summarizes the book, "which teaches the basis of piety and then explains the duties of the pious, which are exemplified by many stories about the righteous as well as the wicked."[200] It is unlikely that Casaubon read the book with as much concentration and understanding as he did the works of the classical tradition, but there was clearly something about this book that made it worth reading. The pious Casaubon is struck by the prayers it contains,[201] and the bibliophile Casaubon is fascinated by its narratives about scribes and their books.[202] One story, in particular, earns his praise:

> There was a woman who was charitable but whose husband was stingy and did not wish to buy books or to give charity. So when the time came to perform her monthly immersion[203] she did not wish to do so. He asked her: "Why do you not immerse yourself?" She said: "I will not immerse myself unless you agree to buy books and give money to charity." And he was not willing to comply with her request, and she refused to immerse herself until he would agree to buy books and give charity. He complained about her to the sage, who told the man: "May your wife be blessed that she forced you to perform a religious duty." To his wife he said, "If you are able to ensure that he performs good actions, all well and good, but with re-

198. See Fishman 2006.

199. See Casaubon 1709, 246: "Habeo librum, qui inscribitur ספר חסידים, quem a te non invenio laudatum: puto tamen tibi visum: est enim Basileae editus. Uteris meo, cum voles: sed vereor ut sit tanti; pleraque enim alibi legi"; Scaliger 1627, 298: "Librum חסידים habeo; opus non vetustum, quaedam γνωμολογικὰ Iudaeorum Magistrorum continens." Casaubon's annotated copy of the book is BL 1934.f.13.

200. Casaubon, note on the flyleaf of BL 1934.f.13: "Liber hic Chasidim q.d. Piorum vel Sanctorum est quasi institutio vitae sanctae. Docet initio fundamenta pietatis quae sint: deinde officia piorum fusius explicat, allatis multis exemplis tam bonorum quam malorum."

201. On the phenomenon of prayer among the Rhineland Pietists and their use of number symbolism see Fishman 2004.

202. Casaubon, note on flyleaf of BL 1934.f.13: "Pag. צד sive 94 et seqq. agit de scribis et libris eorum scriptione ac descriptione: item de off. doctorum et discipulorum, etc. Quaedam inibi φιλόλογα."

203. This refers to ritual immersion, which a woman has to undergo a week after the end of her menstruation before she can resume sexual relations with her husband.

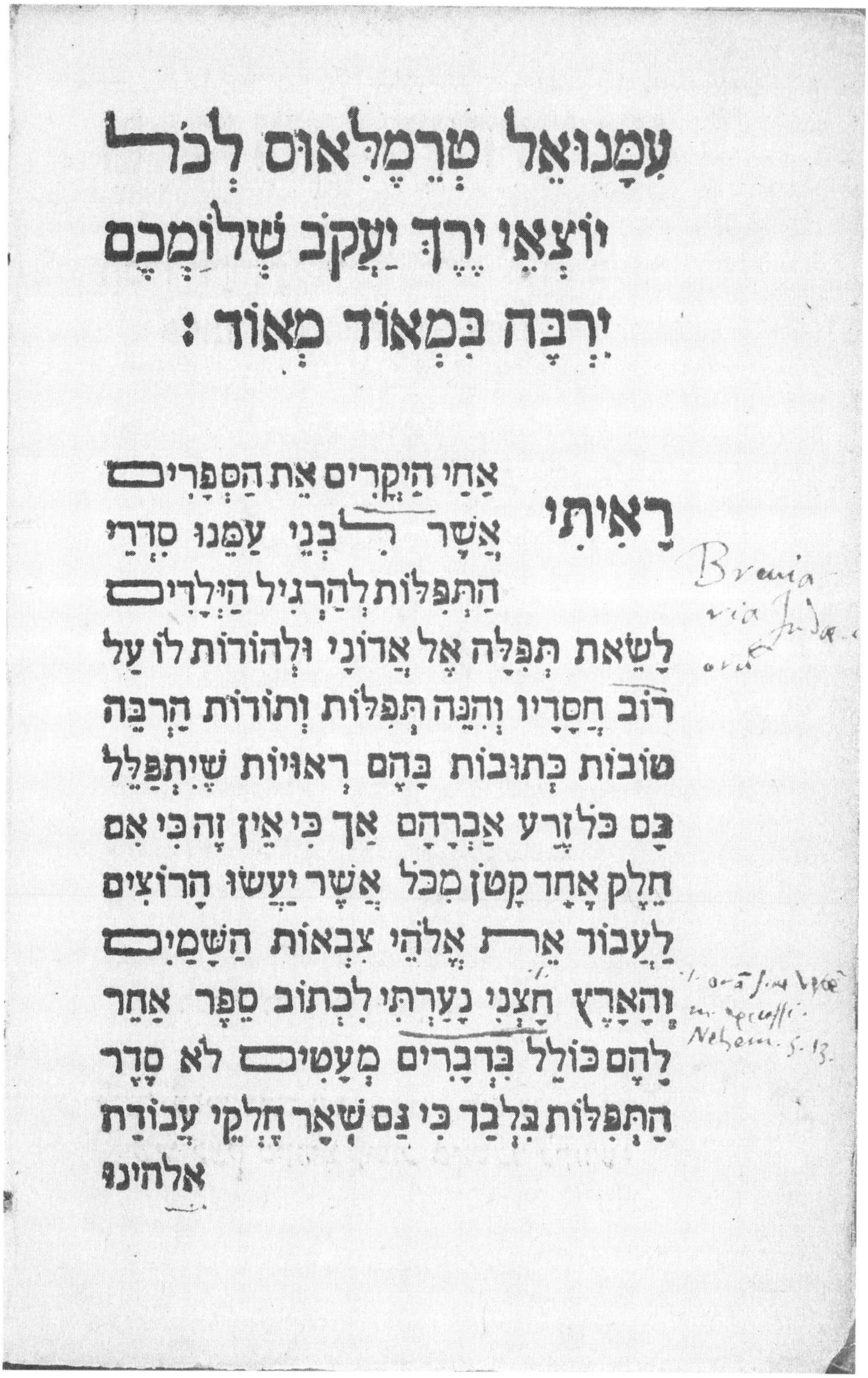

עֱמָנוּאֵל טְרֶמֶלְאוּס לְכָֽל
יוֹצְאֵי יֶרֶךְ יַעֲקֹב שְׁלוֹמְכֶם
יִרְבֶּה בִּמְאוֹד מְאֹד :

אַחַי הַיָּקָרִים אֶת הַסְּפָרִים
רָאִיתִי אֲשֶׁר ל־ לִבְנֵי עַמֵּנוּ סִדְרֵי
הַתְּפִלּוֹת לְהַרְגִּיל הַיְלָדִים
לָשֵׂאת תְּפִלָּה אֶל אֲדוֹנִי וּלְהוֹרוֹת לוֹ עַל
רוֹב חֲסָדָיו וְהִנֵּה תְּפִלּוֹת וְתוֹדוֹת הַרְבֵּה
טוֹבוֹת כְּתוּבוֹת בָּהֶם רְאוּיוֹת שֶׁיִּתְפַּלֵּל
בָּם כָּל זֶרַע אַבְרָהָם אַךְ כִּי אֵין זֶה כִּי אִם
חֵלֶק אֶחָד קָטָן מִכָּל אֲשֶׁר יַעֲשׂוּ הָרוֹצִים
לַעֲבוֹד אֶת אֱלֹהֵי צְבָאוֹת הַשָּׁמַיִם
וְהָאָרֶץ חָצְנִי נָעַרְתִּי לִכְתּוֹב סֵפֶר אַחֵר
לָהֶם כּוֹלֵל בִּדְבָרִים מְעַטִּים לֹא סֵדֶר
הַתְּפִלּוֹת בִּלְבַד כִּי גַּם שְׁאָר חֶלְקֵי עֲבוֹדַת
אֱלֹהֵינוּ

Brevia
via Juda
ot...

1. ora fuit oce
in quelli
Nehem. 5. 13.

FIGURE 1.10. Casaubon, note in his copy of Calvin's catechism, in Hebrew. Houghton Library, Harvard University, Heb. 7103.978.5/*FC5.C2646.Zz554c.

gard to sexual intercourse, do not put an obstacle before him, lest he contemplates sinning, and you therefore will be prevented from conceiving and he will become even more incensed."[204]

"Elegant" is the way Casaubon refers to this story, his marginal summary of which oddly omits any mention of male desire.[205] It exemplifies not so much women's love of books as their role as custodians of the book, for in the society of Rhineland Jewry women took it upon themselves to ensure that the books were copied out by scribes and then loaned out to students.[206] Casaubon was as passionate a book-buyer and as dependent for all practical purposes on his wife as any *yeshivah bocher*. On 19 May 1611 he recorded in his diary a typical book-buyer's vain resolution to improve: "Today I paid the booksellers what I owed, except for Norton, my debt to whom is the largest. I have emptied my purse. 'It is too late to save when all is spent' [Seneca, *Epistulae* 1.1.5]. I take no thought for my wife, I take no thought for my children. Today I decided that until my wife arrives I will not spend more than a gold sovereign on books—unless something truly rare turns up!"[207] No wonder, then, that this medieval short story, contained in a Jewish book, combining the acquisition of books, marital life, and charitable deeds, appeared to epitomize the things that mattered most in his life.

One point at least is now clearer than it was: why a Hebrew version of Calvin's catechism caught Casaubon's eye. He left very few notes in the book, but one of them appears right at the beginning. It refers not to Calvin's text but to the preface by the translator, Immanuel Tremellius, a converted Jew. Tremellius starts out by describing and praising the many Hebrew prayerbooks he has seen, before explaining the superiority of his Christian one. "The breviaries of the Jews," wrote Casaubon as he gathered one more tiny piece of source material for his wide-ranging and appreciative survey of Jewish prayer.[208] This Casaubon—Casaubon the Hebraist—is our subject.

---

204. Wistinetzki 1969, para. 670, 177; Margaliot 2004, para. 773, 490.

205. Casaubon, marginal note in BL 1934.f.13, 94 verso: "Historia eleg. de famula, quae ut librum posset emere suum defraudavit genium" (An elegant story of a girl who denied herself in order to buy a book).

206. See Grossman 2004, 192–193, who documents the same phenomenon in contemporary Christian society.

207. Casaubon 1850, II, 838: "Hodie librariis solvi, quae debebam, sed non Nortono, cui plurima debentur. Exhausi loculos. Sera in fundo parcimonia [Seneca, *Epistulae* 1.1.5]. Non cogito uxorem, non cogito liberos. Hodie constitui ante adventum uxoris in libros [non] amplius quam unum aureum impendere, excepto si quid forte occurrat rarius."

208. Houghton Library, Harvard University, Heb. 7103.978.5/*FC5.C2646.Zz554c, note on the dedicatory letter "Breviaria Judaeorum."

TWO

How Casaubon Read Hebrew Texts

Learning Hebrew

In September 1612, Casaubon wrote a letter to Franeker's distinguished professor of Hebrew, Johannes Drusius.[1] After a characteristic show of appreciation for his addressee's scholarship Casaubon admitted that the onset of old age, perhaps paradoxically, had brought on an even greater desire for learning ($\phi\iota\lambda o\mu\acute{a}\theta\epsilon\iota a$). He was now intent on spending all his spare time reading a Hebrew commentary on Pirke Avot that he had recently acquired. It was printed in Venice and contained the commentaries of "R. Samuel and Rasi." The work that had so engaged Casaubon's attention was the *Midrash Shemuel,* a commentary on Avot, the most popular tractate of the Mishnah. Traditionally designated *Pirke Avot* (Chapters of the Fathers), this collection of enigmatic adages and ethical pronouncements had attracted the exegetical creativity of Jews and Christians over the centuries. Of the many commentaries available by the beginning of the seventeenth century, the *Midrash Shemuel,* written by the Safed preacher and Kabbalist Samuel di Uceda,[2] would not seem the first port of call for a Christian scholar wishing to receive enlightenment about the meaning of Avot. But Casaubon did read the work—in its second edition, published by the Venetian press of di Gara in 1585—as his copy, now housed in the British Library, eloquently demonstrates. Nor was this his first copy of the text of Avot. Already in his possession was the Latin translation and commentary on Avot by the prolific Ger-

---

1. Casaubon 1709, 486: "Fit enim nescio quomodo, ut crescente aetate et iam ad senium vergente crescat in animo nostro $\acute{\eta}$ $\phi\iota\lambda o\mu\acute{a}\theta\epsilon\iota a$ . . . Nam quidquid superest vacui temporis, ejus magnam partem impendo a paucis diebus lectioni Commentarii Hebraici in Pirke Avot. Nactus nuper eum Codicem diu mihi desideratum. Continet autem liber, quo utor, Commentar. R. Samuel et Rasi, editus Venetiis."

2. On Samuel di Uceda (1540–?), see Pachter 1994, chap. 2; and Samuel di Uceda 1951.

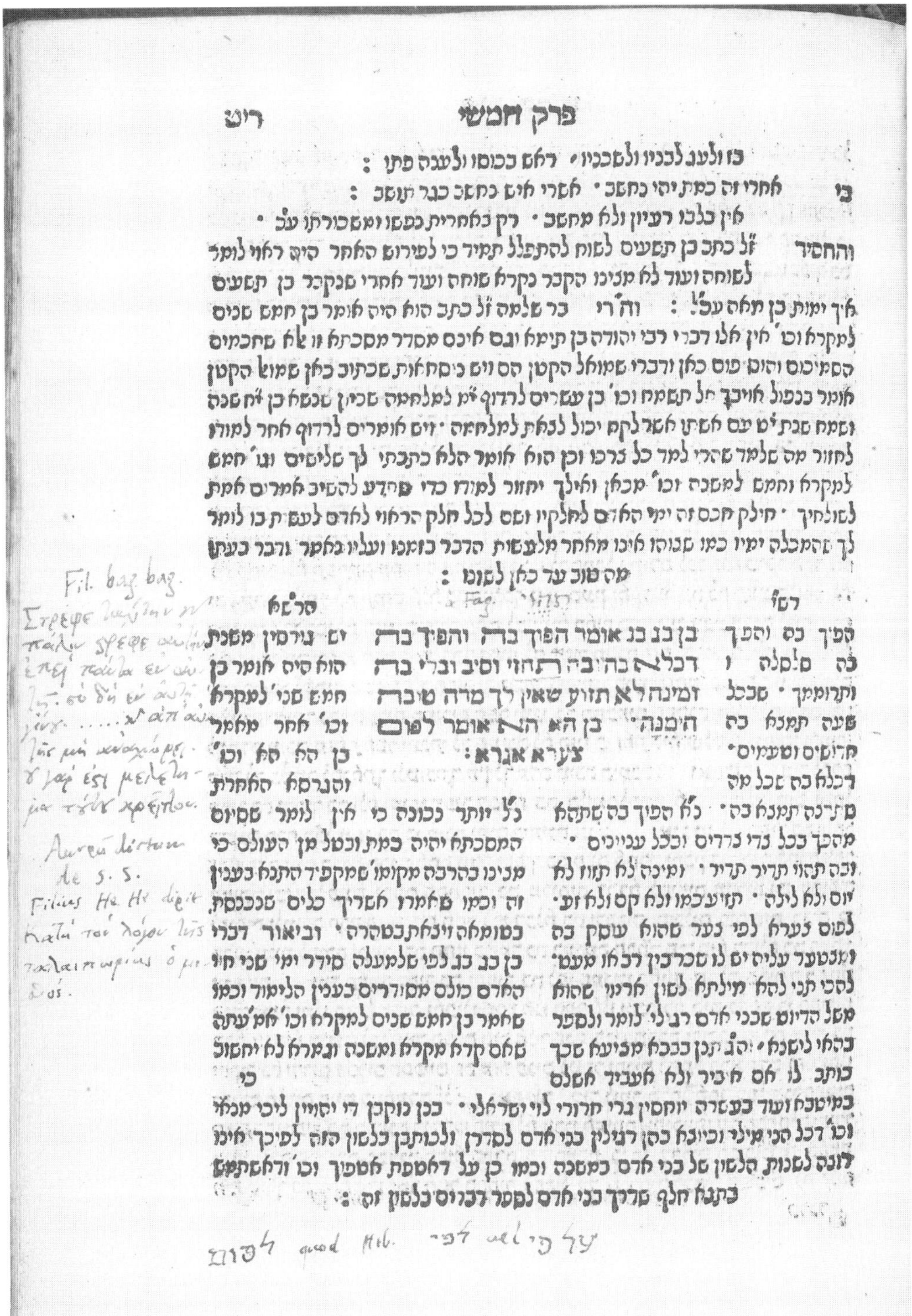

בז ולמב לבניו ולשכניו ♦ דאם ככוסו ולעגב פתו :

בן   אחרי זה כמת ,יהי כחשב ♦ אשרי חיע כחשב כגר תעשב :

אין כלבו רעיון ולא מחשב ♦ רק ב(אחרית כעשו ומסכרתו עב ♦

והחסיד   זל כתב כן תעשעס לשות להתפלל תמיד כי לפירוס האחר היה ראוי לומר
לשמחה וזעוד לא מנינו הקבר נקרא שמחה ועוד אחרי שנקבר כן תעשעס

איך ימות כן מאה עב! ♦ וה'ר'   כר שלמה זל כתב הוא היה אומר כן חמס שנים
למקרא וט' אין אלו דכרי רבי יהודה בן תימא ובס אינס מסדר מסכתא או צא שחכמים
הסמיכוס והוס פוס כאן ודכרי שמואל הקטן ודכרי שמואל הקטן הס יום כיסחאות שכתיב כאן שמואל הקטן
אומר בנפול אויבך אל תעמח וכו' כן עסרים לרדוף אים למלחמה שכין שנמא כן אח שנה
נשמח שבת'ים עם אעתן אשרלקם יכול לנבאת למלחמה ♦ זים אומרים לרדוף אחר למורד
לחזור מה שלומד שהרי למד כל ברכו וכן הוא אומר הלא כתבתי לך שליסיס וט' חמס
למקרא וחמס למשנה זכו' מכאן ואילך יחזור למזרח כדי שחדע להשיב אמרים אמת
לשולחיך ♦ חילק חכם זה ימי האדם לחלקין וגם לכל חלק הראוי לאדס לעשת וזכו לומר
לך שהמקבלה ימיו כמו שנוהו איבו מאחר מלנבשות הדבר כזעגו ועליו נאמר ורבר כעתו
מה טוב עד כאן לשונו :

Fil. bag.bag.   הר'שא   רסי

(marginalia in Latin and Greek on the left, Hebrew commentary in two columns)

הפוך כם והפך   בן בב בן אומר הפוך ברב והפוך ברב
כה כ!סלה ♦   דכלא בה יבה רתחזי וסיב ובל'י ברב
ותרומינך ♦ סבכל   זמינה לא תזוע שאין לך מדה טיברת
שעה תמצא כה   המנה ♦ בן הא הא אומר לפום
חדושים וטעמים ♦   צערא אגרא :
דכלא כה שכל מה
מ'ע'רנה תמצא בה ♦ נא הפוך בה שתהא
מהפך בכל ברי ברדיס וכבל עניויים ♦
ובה תהו תדיר תדיר ♦ נמיכה לא תזוז לא
יוס ולא נילה ♦ תזיעבכמו ולא קס ולא זע
לפום צערא לפי נער סהוא שוסק בה
ומנטער עליהים לו שכרדין דכלא סעט
להסי תני להא מילתא לשון ארמי שהוא
מעל הדיום שכני אדם רב לו' לומר ולמפר
בהאי לישנא ♦ יהב תנן בככא מביעא סכך
כותב לו אם חיבר לא חביד אעבד אשלם
ים   צירסין מסכת
הוא סיה אומר כן
חמם סני למקרא
וכו' אחר מאמר
בן הא הא וכו'
זהנרסא האחרת
צל יותר נכונה כי אין לומר סמיום
המסכתא יהיה כמת,וכטל מן העולם כי
מנינו כהרבה מקומו' שמקפי'ד התנא בעניני
זה וכמו שאמרו אשריך כלים שכנכנסת
בטומאה ויכאתבטהרה ♦ וביאור דברי
בן כב בן לפי שלמעלה סידר ימי שני חיו
האדם מולס מסודרים כעבין הלימוד וכמו
שאמר בן חמם שנים למקרא וכו' אם'עתה
שאס קדא מקרא ומשנה ונארא לא יחמוב כי

במיטבח וזעוד בעשרה יוחסין כבני חרורי לו ישראלי ♦ בכן נוקבן די יסוויין ליכי מגלאי
וכו' דכל הני מילי וכיובא כהן רגלין בני אדם לספרן ולכותבן כנלשון הזה לפיכך אימו
דובה לשנות הלשון של בני אדם כמסבה וכמו כן על דאתסת אטפך וכו' ודראתפצי
בתגא חלף עדיך בני אדם לספר רבניס כלשון זה :

עד הי וכו' דפ'   מ'ול quod Hil.

FIGURE 2.1. Casaubon's copy of Samuel di Uceda's *Midrash Shemuel*. British Library 1952.f.9.

man Hebraist Paulus Fagius;[3] but, as Casaubon noted on the flyleaf of his copy of the *Midrash Shemuel,* Samuel's text differed from that of Fagius in both length and layout.[4]

Like Gilbert Murray, who is said to have translated the leader of the *Times* into Greek every day during breakfast, Casaubon often translated sections of his current reading material into Greek. Hebrew texts, in particular, lent themselves to this sort of reading. Greek, apparently, was the language that could most effectively mirror the Hebrew original. As he perused Uceda's Avot, Casaubon's attention was attracted by the epithet given to Hananiah in chapter 3: "Rabbi Hananiah, the *segan hakohanim* [deputy of the priests], said, 'Pray for the welfare of the kingdom, since, but for fear of it, men would have swallowed up each other alive'" (3:2). In his Greek translation of this dictum Casaubon translated *segan hakohanim* as σύγκελλος ἀρχιερέων.[5] At the bottom of the page he wrote out the expression סגן הכהנים in Hebrew characters together with references to one of the period's standard Hebrew lexica, Elijah Levita's *Tishbi* (Isny, 1541),[6] and to the preface to the *Thesaurus temporum,* the reconstruction of the Greek and Latin texts of Eusebius' *Chronicle,* carried out by his soulmate Joseph Scaliger.[7] This careful

3. Possibly BL 481.c.4.(1).

4. Casaubon, note on the flyleaf of BL 1952.f.9: "Editio Fagii: Multa longe aliter disposita et ordo sententiarum multum diversus ab hac editione."

5. Ibid., 85 verso: "סגן הכהנים vide in Thisbi, et Scal. praef. in Euseb." Scaliger discussed this point in his *Elenchus* of Nicolaus Serarius, as Casaubon noted in the margin of his copy of the book, BL C.79.a.4.(2), 111, as well as in the text Casaubon cited here, Scaliger's *Thesaurus temporum,* Casaubon's annotated copy of which is Cambridge University Library Adv.a.3.4.

6. Levita 1541, s.v. *segen.* Levita comments that the word is always found in a construct form with the meaning of "vice–high priest." In his copy of the Basel 1601 *Tishbi* (BL 1936.c.5), Casaubon underlines the term under discussion.

7. Joseph Scaliger, "In chronica Eusebii Pamphili prolegomena" (1606), in Cambridge University Library Adv.a.3.4, *vi recto; Scaliger 1658, **verso–**2 recto: "Sed Eusebius rationem habuit quatuor Paschatum, id est trium annorum, quot designantur a Johanne Evangelista. Inscitia autem rerum Iudaicarum haec est, quod tam Annam quam Kaiapham apud Lucam, putavit esse summum pontificem: quum tamen Annas fuerit non ἀρχιερεὺς vere, sed ut Ecclesia Constantinopolitana loquitur, πρωτοσύγκελλος τοῦ ἀρχιερέως . . . Talmudice sive Iudaice כהן הגדול סגן *vicarius summi Sacerdotis.* Is ea de caussa summo sacerdoti socius dabatur, ut si per morbum, aut propter aliam caussam sonticam, ille non posset obire ea munia, quae neminem, praeter solum summum sacerdotem, obire fas est, vicarius eam necessitatem expleret, praesertim in decima Tisri, quando Sacerdos in Sancta adyta ingrediebatur, in quae nulli alii sacerdoti, praeterquam ipsi, ingredi liceret, aut vicario eius, si ille morbo impeditus, aut ὀνειρωγμῷ, quod ipsi vocant קרי, pollutus, id praestare non posset, cuius rei meminit Talmud, et exemplum extat apud Iosephum. Ideo tanta auctoritas illius vicarij erat ut minimo minus alter Pontifex esset. Nam qui in Evangelio ἀρχιερεῖς dicuntur . . . ij eo loco erant apud Pontificem Maximum, quo σύγκελλοι etiam hodie apud Patriarchas Constantinopolitanum, Antiochenum, Alexandrinum. Primicerius autem eorum, hoc est πρωτοσύγκελλος, secundum proxime a patriarcha locum obtinens, et olim ante Turcarum imperium patriarcha designatus, est instar vicarij Pontificis Ierosolymitani, de cuius auctoritate existimare licet ex illis Targum Ierosolymitani . . . Nam ambos [Annas and Kaiaphas] eodem

noting of the term סגן הכהנים with relevant bibliography alerts the reader that Casaubon had something in mind as he read the commentary on the Mishnah.

Casaubon's letter to Drusius is dated September 1612. It was around this time that he began a monumental project, his extended criticism of Cardinal Cesare Baronio's Roman Catholic version of church history, to which we will return.[8] Casaubon finished only one volume of his response to the cardinal, but the long text that came to print in 1614 under the title *De rebus sacris et ecclesiasticis exercitationes XVI ad Baronii annales* constituted a wide-ranging, often aggressive, sometimes venomous, refutation of the cardinal's reconstruction of the life and times of Jesus. In attacking Baronio Casaubon pulled out all the stops from his vast stock of erudition, using his expertise in Greek, Hebrew, Arabic, and relevant sources to demolish Baronio by exposing his scholarly deficiencies. In book 13, dealing with the year 31, Casaubon addressed Baronio's treatment of the knotty problem of the two high priests Annas and Kaiaphas, who, according to the Gospel of Luke (3:2) and Acts (4:6), held office simultaneously. The problem of the texts need not detain us here. What is significant is that as he berated Baronio for having tried to resolve the old problem by rejecting "the one and only true proof" culled from scripture itself and upheld by the rabbis, Casaubon revealed the order and manner of his own reading.

Baronio, Casaubon argued, got it wrong; he had been incapable of understanding how the institution of the priesthood functioned in antiquity. It was not true that the only function of the second high priest was to substitute briefly for the incumbent high priest in times of emergency. After all, scripture refers to high priests in twos: Nadav and Avihu, Eleazar and Ithamar. Furthermore—and here comes the jibe: "One has to be ignorant of Jewish antiquity in its entirety not to know that the title *'segan hakohanim'* occurs frequently in rabbinic texts.[9] Look at Elijah in his *Tishbi* and the scholia of R. Samuel and others on the second saying of chapter 3 of Pirke Avoth."[10] The term *segan hakohanim,* Casaubon explained, is similar to *av*

---

tempore summum sacerdotium gerere non potuisse, recte quidem iudicavit Eusebius . . . Itaque coniunctionem illam Annae et Kaiaphae apud Lucam ita interpretatur Eusebius, ut intelligendum sit, quantum ad sacerdotium, separatos esse, quod duo summi sacerdotes simul esse non possint: quantum ad tempus praedicationis, coniunctos, ita ut Annas in annum baptismi, Kaiaphas in annum Passionis conijciendus sit."

8. See Chapter 4.

9. Levita 1541, 121, s.v. "*Segen*": "The deputy of the high priest is called *segen.*"

10. Casaubon 1614, 242; 1654, 215; 1663, 215: "Et rudem esse oportet totius antiquitatis Iudaicae, cui non sit notus, qui toties nominatur in libris Rabbinorum סגן הכהנים. Vide Eliam in Thisbi, et Scholia R. Samuelis atque aliorum in Pirke Avoth cap. III. apophthegmate secundo."

64

HOW CASAUBON READ HEBREW TEXTS

bet din (he actually speaks of *abim beth din*),[11] who functioned as vice-president of the Sanhedrin. The relation between the *segen* and high priest, as indicated by Scaliger in his preface to Eusebius, is similar to that of the *syncellos* or *protosyncellos* and the patriarch of Constantinople. According to Casaubon, therefore, Baronio had failed to understand that the institution of the second high priest was attested both biblically and postbiblically, and not only from Jewish traditional texts but also from sources depicting the practices of the Eastern church of Constantinople.

It was no accident that this analogy occurred to Casaubon. The Greek word *syncellos,* which Casaubon used to render the word *segan* as it appears in Avot, was in the forefront of the minds of both Scaliger and Casaubon already in 1599. In fact, from the time that Scaliger started to work on his reconstruction of Eusebius' *Chronicle,* and with the help of Casaubon and other friends sought out the essential chronological materials for such an arduous endeavor, the eighth-century world chronicle of George the Syncellus was perhaps the source highest on his list of desiderata.[12] What we see here is the great Greek scholar studying a Hebrew text most assiduously, making connections as he reads and finally applying his recently acquired knowledge to a polemical disquisition on a delicate historical matter relating to New Testament times. One cannot help marveling at how nonchalantly Casaubon uses his newfound knowledge, just culled from Samuel di Uceda's commentary, as a standard by which to evaluate his opponent's expertise.[13]

But Casaubon did indeed invest much time reading Samuel di Uceda's commentary on Avot. He appears to have been undaunted by the closely printed Rashi type and by Uceda's constant allusions to contemporary authors. On the contrary, he singles out significant names, ideas, and words in the text. Having noted his appreciation of the "golden saying about Holy Scripture,"[14] "Turn it [Torah] around, turn it around; for it contains all (Avot 6:22)," he turns to Uceda's commentary to retrieve information—which he was to employ in print—about the supposed author of the adage, a certain Ben Bag Bag ("Fil. bag bag").[15] This unconvincing name, according to Uce-

---

11. A surprisingly elementary error: the plural of *av* is *avot.*

12. See Grafton 1983–1993, II, 536–548.

13. In a copybook (Bod MS Casaubon 30, 39 recto) that antedates this discussion, Casaubon inserts *segen* into a list of Hebrew roots, simply translating the word as "princeps."

14. BL 1952.f.9, 219 recto: "Aureum dictum de S.S."

15. Discussing Herod's parentage, he proceeds to discuss Jewish attitudes toward converts. He considers Ben Bag Bag's saying to be "worthy of Moses"; Casaubon 1614, 27; 1654, 25; 1663, 25: "Scimus etiam, doctorem quendam, cuius divina sententia et vel Mose ipso digna (non defuerunt qui Hilleli eam tribuerent, ut est in Iochasin pag. xix) extat in Pirke Aboth cap. v. sub finem, a Rabbinis caeteris

da's sources, was invented in order to protect proselytes from informers.[16] In the same vein, perhaps, is his underlining of a citation from Joseph ibn Nahmias, to the effect that it is the mental state of the sacrificiant that validates or disqualifies the sacrifice. In this case, Casaubon translates the words *poselet* (disqualifies) and *makhsheret* (validates) into Greek. Is he attracted by the idea expressed in this interpretation? After all, the notion of purity of intention was certainly in keeping with his own pietistic mentality. Or is the underlining and translation of these words simply one of hundreds of examples of Casaubon's mode of committing significant words and expressions to memory?

As he read Uceda, Casaubon made constant reference to Fagius' Latin translation and commentary of the text. A perusal of his annotations on Uceda's texts reveals that Casaubon was not tempted to adopt the Christian Hebraist's version of Avot in preference to that of the Kabbalist. The correct meaning of the text was what mattered; this was the rule according to which he read. If uncertain about the meaning of a word in Avot, Casaubon often supplied two possible translations.[17] Antigonus of Sokho, a sage of the Second Temple period, provided one of the text's most famous lessons: "Do not serve the master on condition of receiving a *peras*" (Avot 1:3).[18] At first, Casaubon translated *peras* by the Greek word *misthos,* reward. This was the dominant interpretation of the term, which gained currency through a gloss in *Avot d'Rabbi Nathan* identifying the Sadducees and Boethusians as the heretical disciples of Antigonus' disciples, who failed to understand the meaning of his saying. But he then added a note referring to Scaliger's rendering, *demensum,* or "portion," thus suggesting a meaning of the word that radically changed the interpretation of the dictum.[19] This second interpretation was proposed again more than four centuries later by the distinguished scholar of Hellenistic Judaism Elias Bickerman, in a famous article in the *Harvard Theological Review* (1951). Here Bickerman argued that Antigonus had told Jews who despaired under persecution that they must serve God

appellari Rabbi Bag Bag peregrinitatem illi objicientibus, quod ex utroque parente Gero sive Giora, id est proselyto, esset oriundus. neque ignoramus proverbium vetus, quo monebantur qui Iudaei erant ab origine prima, ut vel ad decimam usque generationem a proselytis sibi caverent. Verum haec et similia his alia, ex aemulatione et invidia profecta nequaquam evincunt, proselytos, et multo minus proselytorum filios aut nepotes, Iudaeos non esse, aut non vere dici. Nos apud Iosephum observamus, IVDAEI appellationem aliquando latius capi, aliquando angustius."

16. BL 1952.f.9, 220 verso: "Cur dicatur ben bag bag."

17. E.g., on the saying "love work" (Avot 1:10, 24 verso), he supplies both στέργε and φίλει.

18. BL 1952.f.9, 11 verso.

19. Ibid.: "פרס est demensum, σιτηρέσιον. de hac sententia vide Scal. Elench. p. 111." Casaubon refers to the discussion in his annotated copy of Scaliger's 1605 edition of *Elenchus Trihaeresii Nicolai Serarii,* BL C.79.a.4.(2).

even if they received absolutely nothing—not even enough to survive on—in return.[20]

Casaubon, as we have seen, was a great philologist, one of the greatest in an age when philologists enjoyed immense prestige. His unswerving defense of truth is emblazoned in one of his notebooks, where he decries the lies recounted by ancient ecclesiastical writers ostensibly "for the greater glory of God." He pursued this point in his correspondence with Scaliger and in a number of his publications, especially, as we have seen in the previous chapter, in relation to the Hermetic fantasies. Jews were by no means exempted from his critical scrutiny. He despised the Jesuit doctrine of the *dolus bonus,* the deceit that could be justified if practiced to attain a good end;[21] and he placed in the same evil category the "blasphemous pronouncement of the Jews: גדול השלום שדבר הכתוב בלשון בדוי Great is peace, for Scripture used deceitful speech [for the sake of maintaining peace between Joseph and his brethren]."[22] Writing out this saying taken from an extended oration on peace, and translating it, as is his wont, into Greek, Casaubon has only one comment to make, "ô scelus," what a crime![23]

Knowledge was to be pursued, but the perversion of truth, Christian or

20. Bickerman 1951.

21. See Bod MS Casaubon 25. On 64 recto Casaubon asks whether equivocation can be justified by the story of Jacob and Esau, and uses Chrysostom to show that it cannot. On 65 recto–66 verso he records: "Excerpta e Garneti epistolis, aut aliis eodem pertinentibus. Accepi a Praefecto Arcis Londini septem chartas, sive folia separata, eo spectantia, quarum haec est summa." What interested him about these papers of Henry Garnett, S.J., executed in 1606, in the wake of the Gunpowder Plot, for conspiring to overthrow the monarchy, was what they seemed to him to reveal about the Jesuits' practices. On 66 recto–verso he quotes Garnett's words, written in English in a script very different from his normal one, on how "in Cases of lawfull Equiuocation, the speech by equiuocation beinge saued from a lye. the same speeche may be without periury conteined by oath or by any other vsuall way though it were by receiuinge the sacrament yf iust necessity so require." On 66 verso Casaubon responds: "En doctrinam istorum hominum de aequiuocatione: en satanae discipulos." Casaubon used this material, which was clearly leaked to him, in Casaubon 1611, with copious attestations of the precision with which he reproduced it.

22. The passage is Leviticus Rabba 9:9, which presents several examples of scriptural personalities taking economies with the truth for the sake of effecting reconciliation. Casaubon is probably referring to the narration about a message sent to Joseph by his brothers in Gen. 50:16 ff.: "Your father commanded before he died, 'So shall you say to Joseph: Forgive, I pray you, the transgression of the servants of the God of your father.'" No such directive is actually found in scripture.

23. Bod MS Casaubon 27, 200 recto: "Veteres scriptores ecclesiasticae historiae et τοὺς μαρτυρογράφους multa secus quam acciderant atque adeo palam saepe falsa scripsisse, notum est eruditis. Hoc autem natum ex persuasione prava quod ad gloriam Dei etiam mentiri fas esset. Simillima persuasio scelestissimorum Judaeorum quorum est blasphema vox . . . ô scelus." Cf. Scaliger's remark to Casaubon in 1605, Scaliger 1627, 304: "Adeo verbum Dei inefficax esse censuerunt, ut regnum Christi sine mendaciis promoveri posse diffiderent." Quantin 2009, 147–148, points out that Casaubon's sharp criticisms of early Christian writers on grounds like these provoked the ire of Richard Mountagu and many others, who saw him, paradoxically, as an enemy of the church fathers.

Jewish, was not to be countenanced. Absorbed as he was in Hebrew and Judaic studies, and ever intent on acquiring knowledge to facilitate his reading of biblical, rabbinic, and medieval Hebrew literature, Casaubon does not appear to evince any real sympathy for Jews. Least of all does he show any for the rabbis. In his grand critique of Baronio's *Ecclesiastical Annals* he articulates his judgment on Jews and their texts: Christians should pay attention to the rabbis when they speak about the Hebrew language or talmudic institutions. But when it comes to actual content, to history or to explication of the antiquities of the ancient people, no confidence should be given to their testimony, "unless we want to be fooled."[24] Nevertheless, this stereotypical judgment, as we will ultimately demonstrate, is never taken to the letter.

Casaubon's career as a scholar included a lifelong engagement with the Hebrew language and with Jewish texts. As he wrote to the doyen of Hebrew studies, the elder Buxtorf, in 1610, "Although I am sorry about the [limited] progress I have made in your form of letters, I have always loved the Holy Tongue."[25] As early as 1592 he had elaborated an ambitious program, first to master rabbinic Hebrew and then to use the language actively as he explored the Levant and mastered Arabic. In pursuit of this aim he asked the distinguished Levantine traveler and state counselor Philippe Canaye de Fresnes to help him obtain a copy of one of the great rabbinic Bibles printed in Venice, as well as David Kimhi's Hebrew grammar and book of Hebrew roots.[26] As a student at Geneva he heard Theodore Beza lecture on the Old Testament and took Hebrew lessons with a noted scholar, Pierre Chevalier (Petrus Cevallerius).[27] In a letter to Scaliger written in 1604, he speaks of Chevalier with great respect, admitting that after the untimely death of his teacher he had not managed to make much progress in Hebrew.[28] Later he taught He-

24. Casaubon 1614, 455; 1654, 402; 1663, 402: "Rabbinis ubi de lingua Hebraica agitur, et vocis alicuius proprietate, vel aliquo Thalmudico instituto, merito a Christianis tribui non parum: ubi vero a verbis venitur ad res, aut ad historiam, vel rerum antiquarum veteris populi explicationem; nisi falli et decipi volumus, nihil admodum esse illis fidei habendum." This is a common attitude; see Hugo Grotius, *Annotationes ad Matt.* 24:24: "Nam ex quo patria expulsi sunt, omnis apud illos historia crassis erroribus et fabulis est inquinata; quibus proinde nihil credendum est, nisi alii testes accedant" (*Critici sacri* 1660, VI, 733–734).

25. Casaubon 1709, 606: "Nam etsi quantum in vestris literis profecerim, me sane poenitet, amavi tamen semper Linguam Sanctam."

26. Ibid., 569.

27. Campagnolo 2007, 195–217. For Casaubon's notes on Beza's lectures on Genesis and his sermons, preserved in Bod MS Casaubon 25, see the edition in Beza 1960—, XXV, 252–297.

28. Casaubon 1709, 206: "Equidem non dubito, multa in Sacris Literis ex Judaeorum scriptis posse, atque adeo debere illustrari. Sed quotusquisque nostrum est, qui de eo vel cogitet, vel qui eum usum τῆς Ῥαββινικῆς διαλέκτου habeat, ut par sit tanto incepto? Olim in eo studio aliquid operae atque olei consumpsimus, usi Magistro Petro Cevallerio Genevensi, quo nihil probius, nihil ἁπλοϊκώτερον. Verum amisso morte immatura amicissimo Praeceptore, non multum post illa profecimus." And see,

brew briefly in Calvin's Academy, and even set out to translate the *Josippon,* a medieval Hebrew adaptation of Josephus, into Latin.[29] His notes on the New Testament, written while he was only in his twenties, paid close attention to what he took as "Hebraisms": Greek words and phrases used in senses that derived from the Hebrew Old Testament.[30]

The pursuit of Jewish or Hebrew knowledge became a passionate commitment. Casaubon's famous diary, his notebooks, and his letters swarm with references to Hebrew texts.[31] The lists of the contents of his library (among his notebook collection in the Bodleian) and the books themselves, a good many of which, together with the *Midrash Shemuel,* are now in the British Library, testify to his constant preoccupation with Hebrew, Hebrew texts, and Jewish tradition in a multiplicity of forms.[32] When Casaubon made one of the momentous steps in his scholarly career and in 1599 left his impoverished but tranquil life in Montpellier for Paris, he also had to leave behind some of his books. In the list of books he subsequently ordered to be sent to him the Hebrew items are conspicuous.[33] Similarly, a fairly large concentration of books of Jewish content was shelved in his "small study."[34] According to a list compiled after his death, Casaubon even possessed various Hebrew manuscripts, including the *Zohar* and a fascicle of the Talmud. But

---

too, Meric Casaubon's polemical reply to the Jesuit Bulenger, who accused his father of relying for his knowledge of Hebrew on a Jewish informant, in his *Pietas,* in Casaubon 1709, 103: "Scito autem, Bulengere, illum mature ad illas literas animum applicuisse, et adhuc juvenem Rabbinorum sacris initiatum a Petro Cevallerio: a quo tamen non tantum didicit, quantum optabat, propter viri illius optimi et doctissimi immaturam mortem."

29. Pattison 1892, 43. For Casaubon's teaching see his letter to Prideaux, Casaubon 1709, 528: "Vixi annos quatuordecim Genevae Professor, primo Graecarum literarum, deinde etiam Latinarum, aliquando etiam Hebraicarum." For his early work on the *Josippon* see Bod MS Casaubon 27, 169 recto: "Vertere coeperam Genavae Hebraeum Josephum in Lat. sermonem: cum in secundo libro versarer, cognovi Munsterum totum opus pridem fecisse Latinum."

30. Casaubon 1587.

31. Casaubon is constantly adding to his bibliographical stock of Hebraica. See Bod MS Casaubon 52, 26 recto: "Auctorum apud Hebraeos nobiliorum elenchus." The alphabetical list on 26 recto–48 recto is a hodgepodge of authors and works: Casaubon even has an entry on Berosus. Since he refers to Scaliger's attack on Serarius, he must have been compiling it after 1605. The list begins with Abraham Zacuth, for whom his source of information is Augustinus Ricius, *De motu octavae spherae* (Paris, 1521). Astute as ever, Casaubon questions whether the author of the Astronomy is also the author of *Yuhasin*— a work that he later uses for authoritative information on Jewish history in his *Exercitationes* (see Chapter 4 below). Other fifteenth- and sixteenth-century authors include Moses Albelda, Gedalia ibn Yahya, Leon Modena, and Abraham Laniado. For some entries he simply refers to the titles of books, presumably because he did not know the names of the authors. For example, he refers to Abraham Saba's *Zeror hamor,* which had been cited by Fagius. He also translates the title page of the Cremona edition of the *Zohar* into Greek and has a long note on the *Sefer tikkunim (Tikkunei haZohar).*

32. See Appendix 3 below.

33. See Bod MS Casaubon 22, 60 recto.

34. Ibid., 57 recto: "Libri et manuscripti Is. Causaboni in parvo musaeo" (dated 2 August 1614).

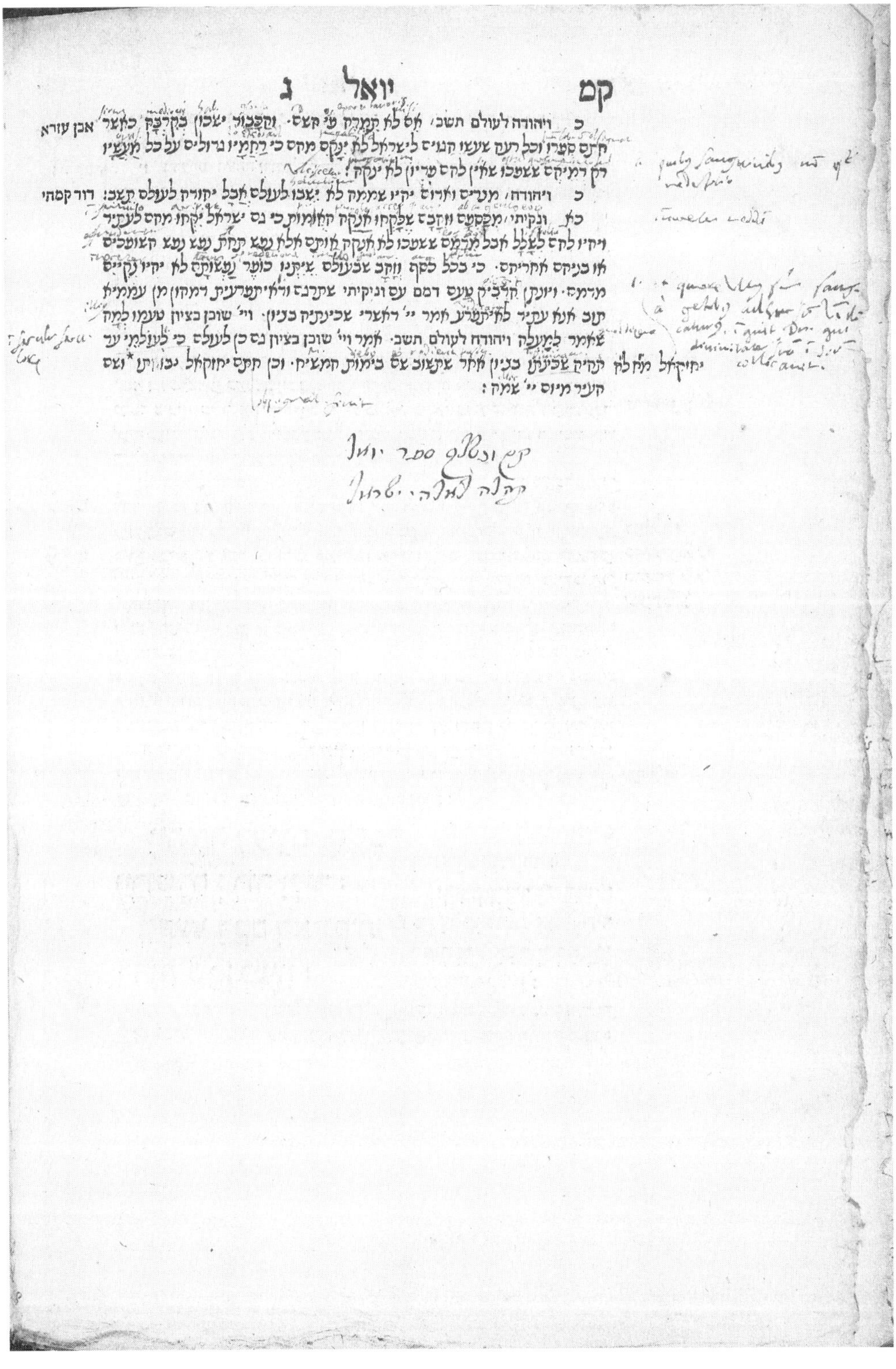

FIGURE 2.2. Casaubon's notes in Latin and in cursive Hebrew, in his copy of Jean Mercier's edition of the minor prophets. British Library 1942.g.3.

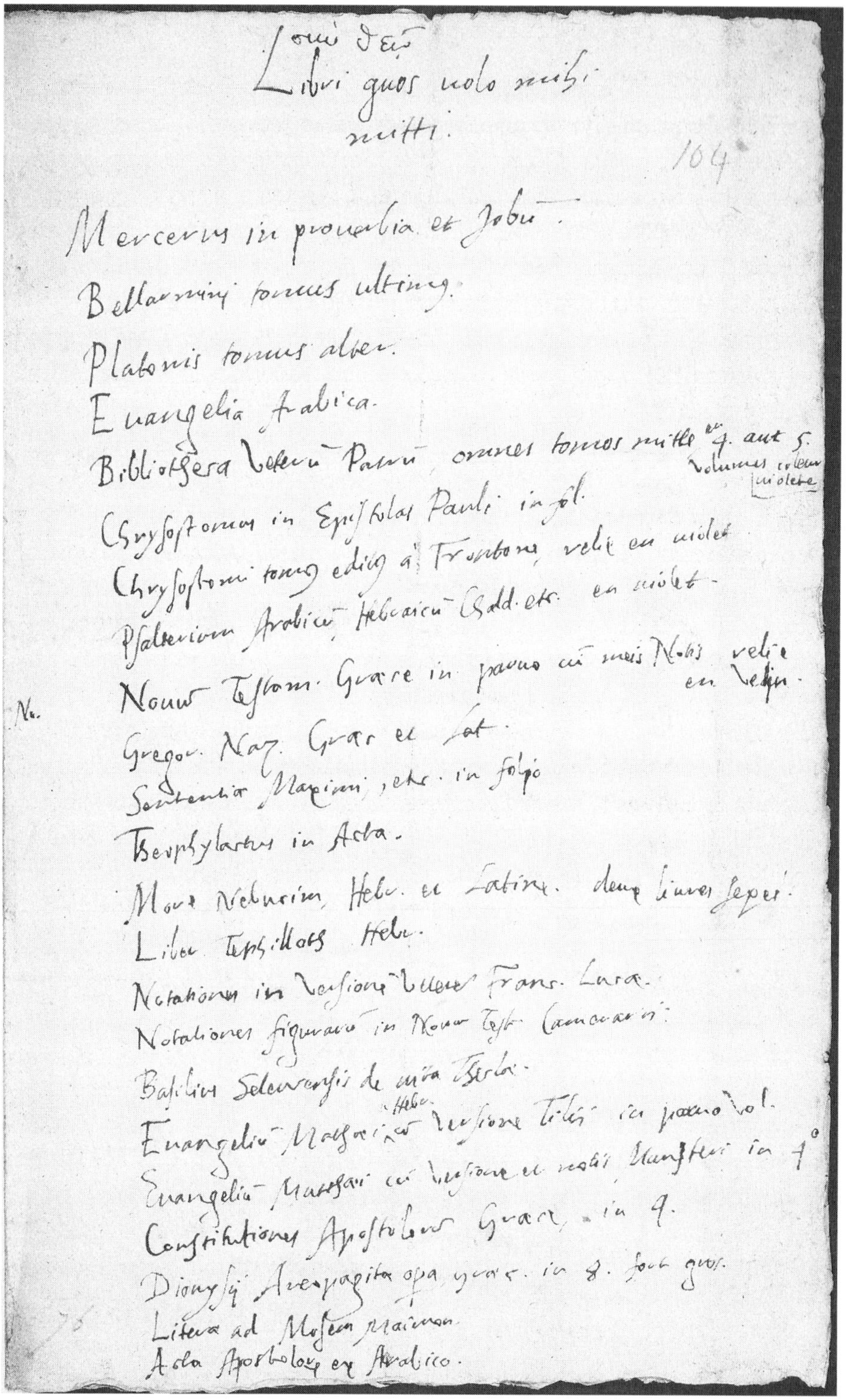

FIGURE 2.3.   Casaubon's list of books to be sent on from Paris to London. Bodleian Library MS Casaubon 22, 104 recto.

this coherent and sizable collection—perhaps the richest Hebrew collection in England when Casaubon arrived—dissolved, for the most part, in the vast ocean of the Royal Library in London, which acquired the lion's share of Casaubon's books after his death. The reconstruction that follows rests on many kinds of evidence, but above all on those of Casaubon's Hebrew books that we have been able to identify.[35]

Books were Casaubon's life breath, and the literature of antiquity his constant companion. He was fully cognizant, therefore, of what was required in order to decode the texts of the past. Greek and Latin were, according to one report, his mother tongues (whereas he spoke French "like a peasant").[36] As we have seen, from the period when he was still in France Hebrew was part of his daily curriculum, and he wrote out Hebrew words and texts in a beautiful, careful Hebrew hand, quite unlike the Greek and Latin scrawl that generations of scholars have tried—and occasionally failed—to decipher.[37] The different hands encapsulate the essential difference in Casaubon's command of these languages: a familiar, fluent, native Greek and Latin in contrast to a (mostly) correct but painstaking mode of reading Hebrew. His Hebrew script reflected the acquisition of Hebrew knowledge through books.

It will not come as a surprise that Casaubon possessed all the major grammars of Hebrew from Kimhi to Levita, from Chevalier to Buxtorf. Like most Christian Hebraists, he held the foremost Jewish grammarian and Massorete, Elijah Levita, in awe.[38] The desire to learn all the rules and peculiarities of the Hebrew language is manifested in all the Hebrew books that Casaubon possessed. In the copybook that contains his own running commen-

35. For a description of Casaubon's library and its fate see Birrell 1980. The Casaubon manuscripts include an itemized list of those of his books that remained in Paris at his death (Bod MS Casaubon 22, 94–103) and a numerical inventory—but not a list of titles—of the books that he had with him in London (Bod MS Casaubon 21, 19). Our conclusions about his later Hebrew reading rest chiefly on the evidence of his letters, his publications, his manuscripts in Oxford, and his annotated Hebrew books in the British Library, the presence of which was noted already by Schechter 1896, 315.

36. *Perroniana* 1669, 44: "Quand il parle François, disoit Monsieur du Perron, il semble que ce soit un paysan, et quand il parle Latin, il semble qu'il parle sa langue." Cf. Pattison 1892, 88.

37. Casaubon does also occasionally use a somewhat awkward cursive Hebrew script. See, e.g., his typical concluding "praise to God" at the end of his copy of the book of Joel: BL 1942.g.3, reproduced as Figure 2.2 here. According to Malachi Beit-Arié (personal communication), this script is basically Ashkenazic current semicursive, although the letter *tav* is more reminiscent of the Sephardic style.

38. Levita was certainly an indispensable authority for Casaubon, but not an infallible one. See, e.g., Casaubon 1614, 455; 1654, 402; 1663, 402. One of his copybooks (Bod MS Casaubon 10) is a partial translation of Levita's *Massoret haMassoret*, starting with the third preface. The hand is definitely not Casaubon's, and the catalogue suggests that the version is by his teacher, the Genevan Hebraist and censor Pierre Chevalier. Casaubon, in any event, read and annotated this text, and used it in an important letter on the Masorah to Jean Porthaise, Casaubon 1709, 173–174.

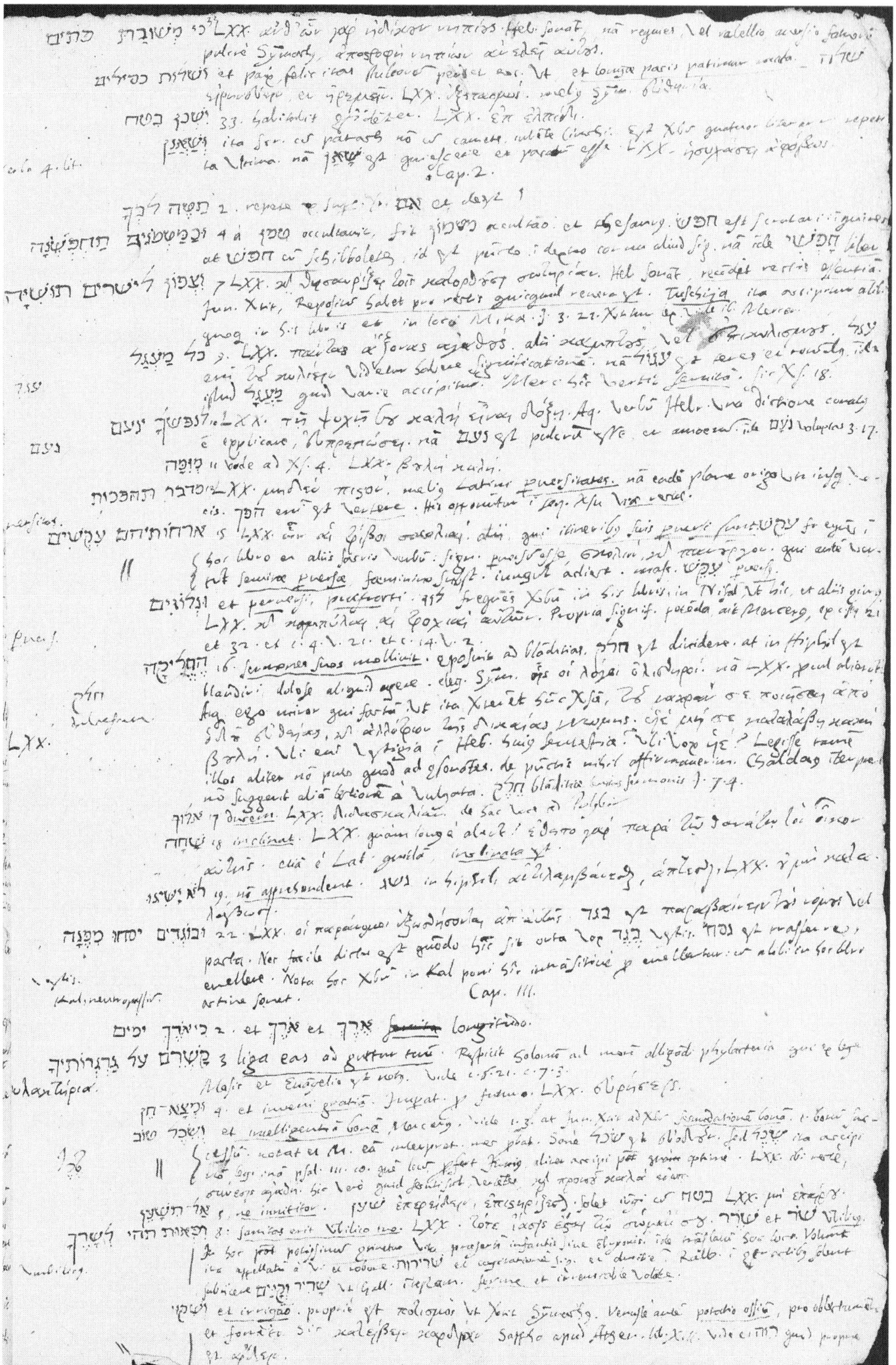

FIGURE 2.4. Casaubon's notes on Proverbs. Bodleian Library MS Casaubon 6.

tary on Proverbs, which he wrote in Montpellier,[39] Casaubon articulates the strain he is undergoing in trying to master the holy tongue. Glossing the word *yetsar* in "Your step should not be straitened [*yetsar*]" (4:12), he complains that there is nothing more irksome in Hebrew than the incidence of multiple verbs whose roots are similar, but not identical, and yet yield the same meaning.[40] But as he struggles to master the intricacies of Hebrew grammar—an effort that, as his various heavily annotated Hebrew textbooks demonstrate, he made over and over again—he absorbs and fine-tunes every word and every bit of information. Reading the introduction to the *Mikhlol,* in which Kimhi cites the rabbinic exhortation "one should always teach in a succinct manner," he adds the talmudic source, and recalls a similar sentiment expressed by Horace in the *Ars Poetica* (335): "Let whatever you teach be brief."[41] For Casaubon the wisdom of the ancients knew no religious or linguistic boundaries.

Aramaic and its relation Syriac were languages that no self-respecting student of early Christianity or rabbinic Judaism could ignore. By the late sixteenth century a variety of texts, translations, and grammars were available in print. Casaubon appears to have either possessed or read all the basic texts, which included the grammars of Münster and Canini, the Syriac New Testament text of Immanuel Tremellius,[42] and Latin translations of Targum Jonathan on the prophets. According to a letter written to the older Buxtorf, Casaubon possessed the copy of Münster's Chaldaic dictionary, which had passed through the hands of a worthy line of Christian Hebraists: Jean Mercier and Pierre Chevalier. The British Library's exemplum of the work, with its layers of marginal notes in hands other than Casaubon's, seems to be the copy in question.[43] Lexica in abundance filled his shelves, including Natan ben Yehiel's *Arukh* and Santes Pagninus' *Thesaurus.* Of particular note is

39. Bod MS Casaubon 6, 7 recto–21 verso. This is for the most part a philological commentary influenced by Mercier, with many references to the Septuagint and to Levita's *Tishbi.* On Proverbs 25:23 Casaubon makes a connection between the Aramaic word גרביתא, which the people of Narbonne still use, and "which we here in Montpellier call 'garbin.'": Bod MS Casaubon 6, 18 verso: "Ac notemus ventum צפון i.e. Aquilonem dici paraphrastae גרביתא quam vocem nostri Narbonenses hodie retinent. Vocamus enim hic Mompelii garbin ventum qui etesiarum loco aestus maximos refrigerat." That this was an important discovery for him is indicated by the fact that he records it again at the very beginning of his notes (7 recto).

40. Ibid., 10 recto: "Nihil in hac lingua molestius minus exercitatis, quam adfinitas radicum idem significantium, ut צרר צור יצר haec tria signif. idem."

41. BL 1984.a.10.(1), 3 recto in the margin: "i. cap pr. Tract. Pesacim in Tal. f. 3. Horat. Quicquid praecipies, esto brevis."

42. From a letter to Beza (Casaubon 1709, 71) in which Casaubon refers to the "Syrus interpres" it is clear that he was reading Tremellius' edition of the Syriac New Testament in Hebrew type as early as 1597.

43. BL 621.g.1.

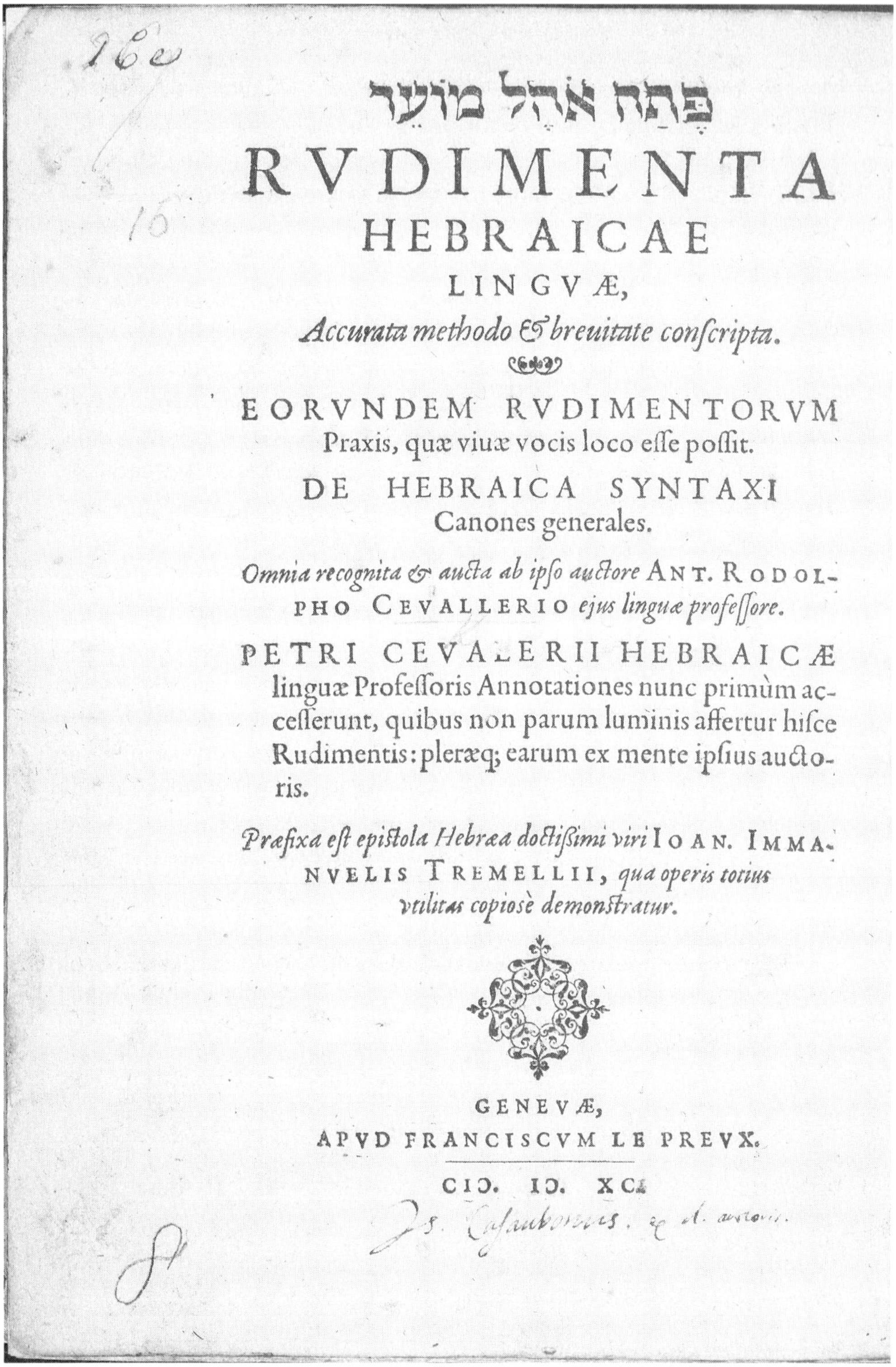

פֶּתַח אֹהֶל מוֹעֵר

RVDIMENTA
HEBRAICAE
LINGVÆ,

Accurata methodo & breuitate conscripta.

EORVNDEM RVDIMENTORVM
Praxis, quæ viuæ vocis loco esse possit.

DE HEBRAICA SYNTAXI
Canones generales.

Omnia recognita & aucta ab ipso auctore ANT. RODOL-
PHO CEVALLERIO *ejus linguæ professore.*

PETRI CEVALERII HEBRAICÆ
linguæ Professoris Annotationes nunc primùm accesserunt, quibus non parum luminis affertur hisce
Rudimentis: pleræq; earum ex mente ipsius auctoris.

Præfixa est epistola Hebræa doctissimi viri IOAN. IMMA-
NVELIS TREMELLII, *qua operis totius
vtilitas copiosè demonstratur.*

GENEVÆ,
APVD FRANCISCVM LE PREVX.

CIƆ. IƆ. XCI.

FIGURE 2.5. Casaubon's copy of Antoine Chevalier's Hebrew grammar. British Library
621.i.9.

David de' Pomi's trilingual lexicon *Tsemah David,* which Casaubon clearly used as a model for a lexicon of Arabic that he intended to compile, since only Arabic characters in his hand adorn the empty interlacing leaves of the lexicon.[44]

Casaubon owed much to the works of the great Christian Hebraists, such as Jean Mercier, Andreas Masius, Gilbert Génébrard, Sebastian Münster, Paulus Fagius, Johannes Buxtorf, and Johannes Drusius. The publications of lesser-known Hebraists also figured in his library. Sebastian Lepusculus, professor of Hebrew in Basel from 1556 to 1575, produced a potpourri of texts in a volume published in Basel in 1559.[45] He selected parts of Avot for partial commentary, and even added a Yiddish homily on R. Simeon's famous statement about the "three crowns": "There are three crowns: the crown of the Torah, the crown of priesthood, and the crown of kingship, but the crown of a good name surpasses them all" (4:13).[46] The work concludes with a brief text in Hebrew and Latin, titled "What prevents Jews from believing in Jesus?" Casaubon ignored the homily but did make inroads into the Yiddish text.[47]

Hebrew books printed by the press of Robert Estienne were tailor-made for students like Casaubon. He owned the text of Ruth, which contained a commentary wrongly attributed to Kimhi,[48] as well as a selection of the minor prophets with the commentaries of the three standard medieval exegetes, Rashi, Abraham ibn Ezra, and David Kimhi.[49] Both books were produced with very wide margins. The British Library copies of these books are virtually alive with Casaubon's annotations. He covered every page with writing that moves in all directions.

Casaubon's enthusiasm for the work of serious Christian humanists never left him. Very late in life, when he visited Oxford in 1613, he spent some of his precious time in the Bodleian Library taking notes on the work of the

44. BL C.79.d.6. It should be noted, as Alastair Hamilton has pointed out to us, that Casaubon's mode of compiling the Arabic lexicon on the basis of the Hebrew alphabet actually distorts the structure of the Arabic language. See Appendix 1 below. Occasionally, however, he does comment on the Hebrew terms, e.g., s.v. "*hazar*/go round" (60, col. b), where de' Pomi discusses the calendrical cycle. Casaubon glosses "cyclus solaris" as "cyclus lunaris" and refers to Münster's *Kalendarium.*

45. The contents of this work are described in detail by Prijs 1964, 151–153. According to Prijs, the homily was extracted either from a manuscript or from the Yiddish prayerbook printed in Venice in 1529.

46. Casaubon seems to have been intrigued by this saying, for he also refers to it on the flyleaf of his copy of *Midrash Shemuel,* BL 1952.f.9: "III coronae." The three crowns also served as the printer's emblem for Giustiniani.

47. BL 1982.c.34, 57.

48. BL 1942.g.4.

49. BL 1942.g.3.

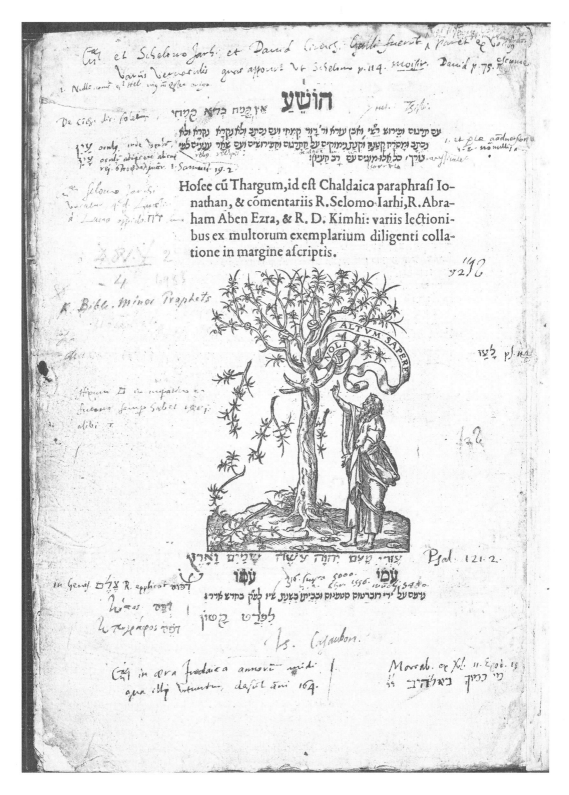

FIGURE 2.6. Casaubon's copy of Jean Mercier's edition of the minor prophets. British Library 1942.g.3.

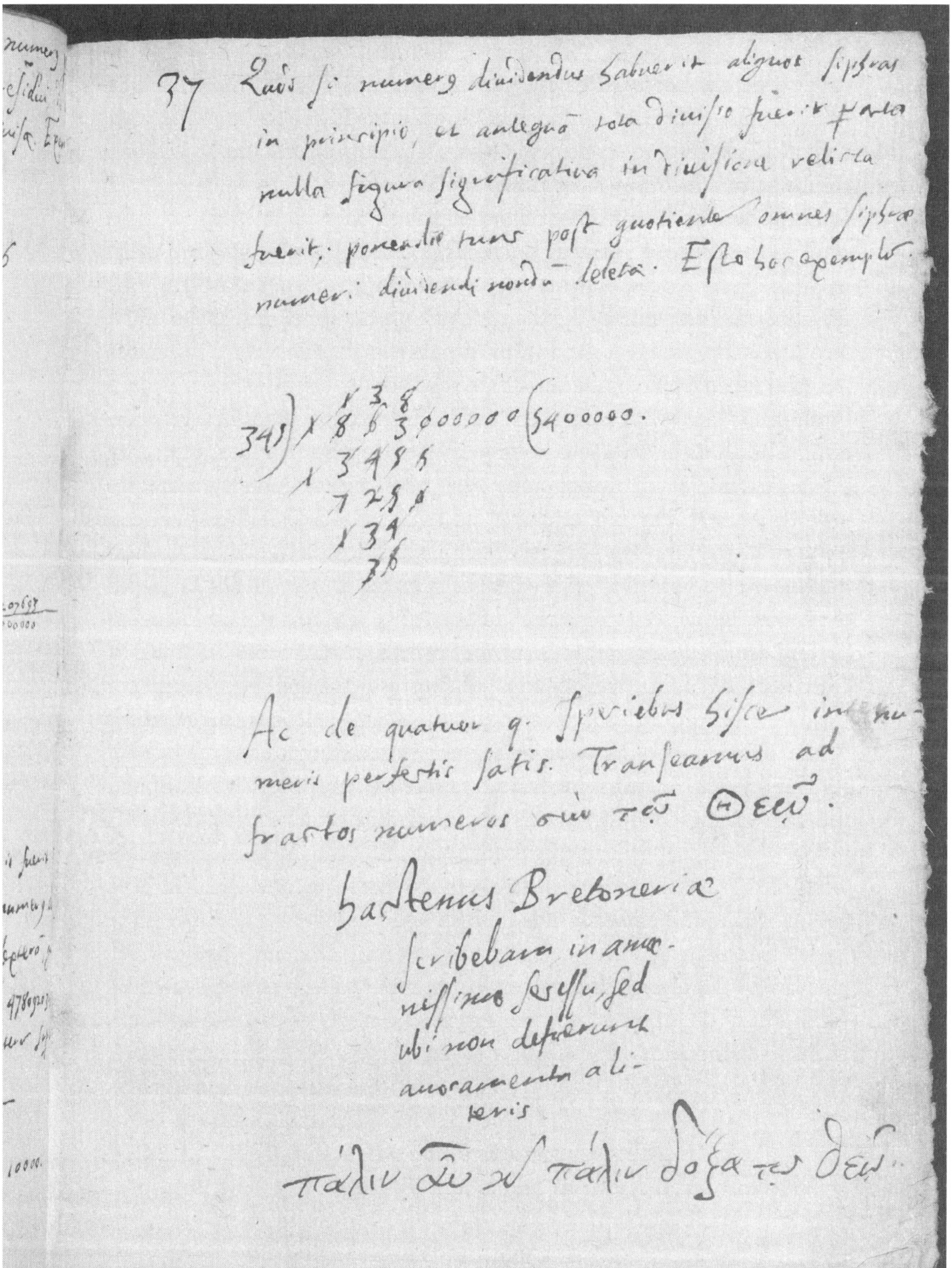

37 Quod si numerus dividendus habuerit aliquot siphras in principio, et antequam tota divisio fierit facta nulla figura significativa in divisore relicta fuerit, poneantur tuas post quotientem omnes siphras numeri dividendi nondum deleta. Esto hoc exemplum.

$$34)\ 18633000000\ (5400000$$

Ac de quatuor q. Speciebus siser in numeris perfectis satis. Transeamus ad fractos numeros σὺν τῷ Θεῷ.

hactenus Bretonoriae
scribebam in animo·
nissimo secessu sed
ubi non defuerunt
adiumenta ali-
teris

πάλιν ὧ ϗ πάλιν δόξα τῷ θεῷ.

FIGURE 2.7. Colophon to Casaubon's notes on Elijah Mizrahi. Bodleian Library MS Casaubon 27, 37 recto.

early sixteenth-century Hebraist Robert Wakefield, who had used his skills to support Henry VIII's position on his divorce. Casaubon was filled with enthusiasm to discover Wakefield's solid arguments against the belief—one that he ascribed to most Catholic theologians in his own day—that the Jews had deliberately corrupted the Hebrew text of the Old Testament.[50]

As a Hebraist Casaubon was, as always, an exemplary student. Unusually, he preferred to work with the Hebrew text, rather than using the Latin cribs that often accompanied Christian Hebraist editions of Jewish texts. At most, he employed the Latin text for supplementary annotation. For vacation reading in La Bretonnière—despite the nonliterary attractions around him[51]—he studied with painstaking care all the technicalities of a work on arithmetic, the *Sefer haMispar,* written by the Ottoman rabbinical authority Elijah Mizrahi.[52] It was an epitome of the work translated into Latin by Oswald Schreckenfuchs and annotated by Sebastian Münster. These holiday notes are extremely revealing; for Casaubon had also read one of the latest offerings in mathematics, namely Petrus Ramus' *Arithmetica,* and he brings the knowledge derived from the logician's textbook to bear on his reading of the Jewish writer's arithmetica, occasionally comparing Mizrahi's definitions with those of Ramus.[53] In addition, he clearly uses Mizrahi's text as a way of learning the relevant Hebrew terms. Discussing the Hebrew loanword for "geometry" *(handasah),* Casaubon laconically admits that he does not have Nathan ben Yehiel's lexicon to hand. Yet, in an astonishing feat of memory,

50. Bod MS Casaubon 28, 143 verso–144 recto: "ibidem sequitur libellus de incoru. codd. Heb. sane eruditus. Apparet illum valde fuisse versatum in libris Hebraicis et Rabbinicis et Arabicas etiam literas non plane ignorasse. Summa disputationis est: non esse verum, Hebraeos dolo corrupisse S.S. Non corrupisse ante Domini nativitatem apparet: quia nunquam D. hoc scelus illis obiicit. Non corrupisse postea probat ex Origene, Hieronymo, Augustino. Ostendit Hebraeos studio conservandi incorruptos libros sacros superasse longe omnes Graecos et Romanos." The book Casaubon found so appealing was Wakefield 1534.

51. Bod MS Casaubon 27, 37 recto: "Hactenus Bretoneriae scribebam in amoenissimo secessu, sed ubi non defuerunt avocamenta a literis." The notes begin with "Excerpta et notae in Arithmeticam R. Eliae מזרחי." The copy of the work from which he was transcribing is BL 532.f.1. There are underlinings and glosses throughout the book.

52. The Hebrew text was first published in Constantinople in 1534. On Mizrahi (1455–1526) as mathematician see Wertheim 1896.

53. Ramus promoted mathematics as the oldest of sciences and offered a new taxonomy of the subject, dividing mathematics of the *intelligibilia* (from which geometry is derived) from *sensibilia* (from which mechanics and astronomy and optics are derived). Casaubon refers to this division as "nova illa sententia P. Rami," and he pits Ramus against Mizrahi, although he does suggest that Mizrahi may have spoken more accurately in his fuller version of the book: "P. Ramus non sine ratione hanc partitionem reprehendit et divisit ipse in simplicem et comparativam. Elias noster cuius Epitome solum haec est, fortasse in opere integro accuratius de hoc egerat"; Bod MS Casaubon 27, 4 recto. On Ramus and mathematics see now Goulding 2006.

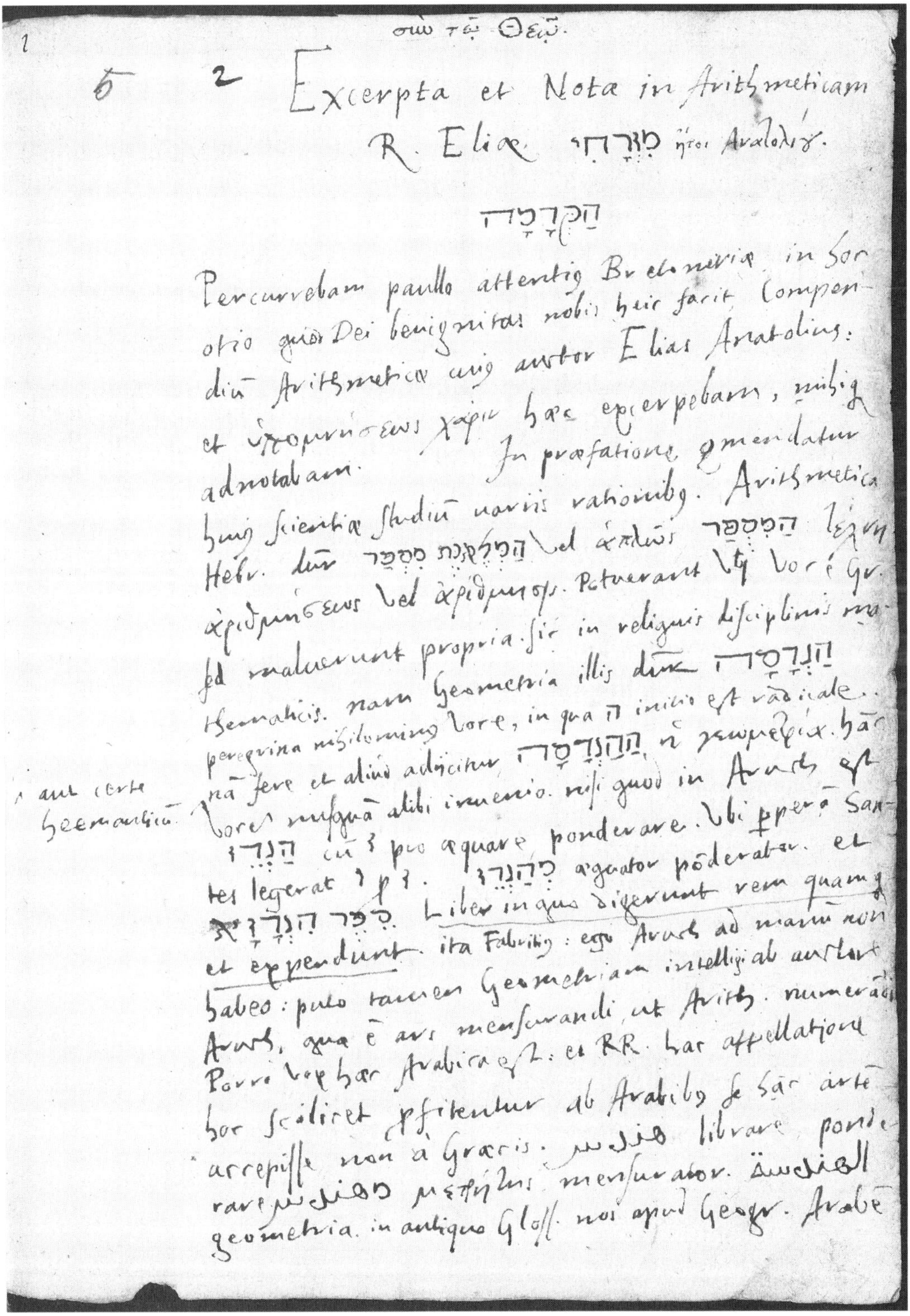

σὺν τῷ Θεῷ.

Excerpta et Nota in Arithmeticam
R. Eliæ מזרחי ἤτοι Ἀνατολίου.

הַמִּזְרָחִי

Percurrebam paullo attentiß Βρεχμένίω in Sor-
otio quod Dei benignitas nobis heic facit Compendium Arithmeticæ cuius autor Elias Anatolius:
et ὑπομνήσεως χάριν hæc excerpebam, nubiq
adnotabam.   In præfatione, commendatur
huius scientiæ studium variis rationibus. Arithmetica
Hebr. dicitur חָכְמַת מִסְפָּר vel הַמִּסְפָּר vel absolutè הַמִּסְפָּר
ἀριθμήσεως vel ἀριθμῶν. Potuerant vel vocé Gr.
sed maluerunt propria. Sic in reliquis disciplinis mathematicis. nam Geometria illis dicitur הַנְדָּזָה
peregrina nihilominus voce, in qua ה initio est radicale.
na fere et aliud adiicitur הַהַנְדָּזָה ἡ γεωμετρία. hā
voces nusquam alibi inuenio. nisi quod in Arabicis est
cui ? pro æquare ponderare. Ubi ἤπερ San-
tes legerat ל פ ?. מְהַנְדֵּז æquator poderator. et
סֵפֶר הַנְדָּז Liber in quo dicuntur rem quam
et eppendunt. ita Falritiy: ego Arabicè ad manum non
habeo: puto tamen Geometriam intelligi ab autori-
Arabicè, quæ è ars mensurandi, ut Arith. numerandi
Porro vox hæc Arabica est. et RR. hac appellatione
hoc scilicet profitentur ab Arabibus se hanc artem
arripuisse non a Græcis. librare, ponderare معيار metior. mensurator. هندسة
geometria. in antiquo Gloss. non apud Geogr. Arabes

FIGURE 2.8. Beginning of Casaubon's notes on Elijah Mizrahi. Bodleian Library MS Casaubon 27, 1 recto.

he seems able to recall the definition given by this eleventh-century Roman lexicographer.[54]

The Christian Hebraists of the fifteenth and sixteenth centuries paid more attention to Jewish exegetical and grammatical literature than to the complex and intricate workings of Judaism's legal tradition. A few works on the latter did, however, apparently merit attention and were translated into Latin. These included a listing of the positive and negative commandments by Moses of Coucy (Semag), an abbreviated version of which was provided by Sebastian Münster. Casaubon owned a copy of this work, and delved into the intricacies of what Jews may and may not do. But apparently, before he actually set this book on his desk he had already familiarized himself with this genre of Jewish literature; for on the flyleaf and title page of the book he advises comparison of this work with the divergent classification of the commandments in Menahem Recanati's *Ta´ame haMitsvot* (The Reasons for the Commandments) and in Moses Maimonides' writings.[55] Moreover, whereas Münster alludes only to the larger work from which he produced the epitome, Casaubon notes in Hebrew the proper title of the work, *Sefer Mitsvot gadol.*[56] By the time he came to write the response to Baronio, he was well equipped to use the fundamental rabbinic distinctions between *huqqim*, "statutes," for which no reason is traditionally given, and other laws or commandments, *mitsvot* (more correctly *mishpatim*). In an impressive disquisition on the meaning and origins of the word "mystery" and its connection with "sacrament," Casaubon introduces what surely must have been regarded as an alien concept, namely the rabbinic distinction between the two kinds of laws, proposing circumcision as an example of a statute for which no reason *(ta´am)* may be given, and the precept of honoring parents as an example of the nonepideictic law. It is in the former category of statute that he places the "sacrament of grace."[57] And just as he felt no qualms about

54. Bod MS Casaubon 27, 2 recto: "ego Aruch ad manum non habeo: puto tamen Geometriam intelligi ab auctore Aruch, quae est ars mensurandi, ut Arith. numerandi. Porro vox haec Arabica est, et RR. hac appellatione hoc scilicet profitentur ab Arabibus se hanc artem accepisse non a Graecis."

55. On the title page of his copy of Münster's 1533 work, BL ORB30/5652, Casaubon notes: "Confer cum libro Menahem Recanatensis qui omnia praecepta continet. Inscribitur טעמי המצות." On the flyleaf he also refers to *Guide for the Perplexed* III.36, in which Maimonides discusses the fourteen classes of commandments, and to the *Yad*, noting that this categorization as well as that of Recanati is different from the one given "in hoc libro."

56. Münster writes (BL ORB30/5652, 1 verso): "Visum autem fuit succincto illo commentario quam altero prolixo, unde haec pro maiori parte desumpsi, eum tibi commendare." Casaubon glosses "nempe huius R. libro *Sepher Mitzvoth gadol.*"

57. Casaubon 1614, 543; 1654, 479; 1663, 479: "Sacramenta enim et μυστήρια nuncuparunt rerum invisibilium signa visibilia, quae Deus ipse in Ecclesia sua instituit. Observant doctissimi e Rabbinis,

introducing non-Christian material into theological debate, so, too, did he introduce rabbinic material into a debate on Roman literature. In the first part of Casaubon's pioneering work on satire, to which we will return, he speaks of the festive days devoted to the honor of the Deity, a universal institution. In this context, he provides a learned discussion of festive days (*yamim tovim*) and days of expiation of sins, devoted to fasting and mourning. He supplies references to Maimonides ("in Iad Rambam") and Moses of Coucy ("R. Mosis Mikkotsi Praecepta"), and to the rabbinic classification of commandments.[58]

As an expert on ancient history Casaubon knew the importance of Josephus, and his interest in Josephus led him, as a similar interest had led Scaliger, to the medieval Hebrew *Josippon*. Such was his curiosity about this strange metamorphosis of the Greek Josephus that he began to translate the *Josippon* into Latin, stopping only when he realized that Münster had already put such an initiative into print (Basel, 1541).[59] The printed historical productions of the Jews, notoriously so meager, were all scanned and acquired by Casaubon. His heavily annotated copy of Génébrard's Latin and Hebrew volume of rabbinic and medieval Jewish historical writings is now in the British Library.[60] The impartiality with which he read is here particularly conspicuous. On the one hand, he was incensed by Abraham ibn Daud's notable unfamiliarity with Roman antiquity; but he was also impressed that the author was capable of praising the emperor Titus, the arch-

---

inter מצות et חוקים hanc esse differentiam: quod *mitsvoth* sive praeceptorum ratio aperta est; ut Deum cole: honora patrem et matrem. at *chukim* statuta sive decreta earum rerum esse dicunt, quarum טעם ratio soli Deo sit nota et comperta, ut circumcisionis et similium. Ad hoc genus pertinent Sacramenta Gratiae."

58. Casaubon 1605b, 6–7. He makes much more detailed reference to the Hebrew material in his notes in Bod MS Casaubon 23, 9 verso, including a ruling given in *Hilkhot Shevitat Yomtov* in Maimonides' *Mishneh Torah* about the prohibition against working on a *yom tov* (festival) apart from the preparation of food. In his *Discourse* on satire, which relies on Casaubon's tract, Dryden does not cite the Jewish material.

59. See Bod MS Casaubon 27, 169 recto: "Vertere coeperam Genavae Hebraeum Josephum in Lat. sermonem: cum in secundo libro versarer, cognovi Munsterum totum opus pridem fecisse Latinum. Destiti ig. avide cupiens Munsteri editionem nancisci. Ad Lutetiam tandem voti mei compos factus, ubi primum otii aliquantum sumus nacti in praetorio Geruiliano magni Praesidis Thuani, eum laborem ἐς πόδας ἐκ κεφαλῆς suscepimus percurrendum: quod tamen maiore cum fructu facturi eramus, si ad manum fuissent nostrae in hoc genere lucubrationes neglectae nobis ab aliquot annis." Detailed notes on the edition follow. Casaubon's copy of the Venice 1544 edition of the Hebrew text is BL 1938.f.21. His copy of Lepusculus' work, which contained a short version of the text with a Latin translation, is BL 1982.c.34.

60. BL 1939.b.63. The letter to Hubert in Casaubon 1709, 136, suggests that Casaubon was reading the second part of *Sefer haKabbalah* in 1602: "Legi adeo nuper Rabbini cujusdam de Romanis imperatoribus libellum, ubi exercuerunt me obscuri quidam loci."

enemy of the Jews.[61] As we will show, Casaubon did have a copy of Azariah de' Rossi's massive, innovative study of Jewish history and tradition, the *Me'or Einayim*. What apparently impressed, or rather irritated, him most in the book was what he refers to on more than one occasion as the "Jewish superstition" of employing the substitute letters *kuf* and *daled* for printing the divine name.[62] A rather easier book to read, despite its large number of citations from the Talmud in Aramaic, was Abraham Zacuto's chronology of rabbinic scholars and world history, *Sefer Yuhasin*.[63] Casaubon, like most Christian Hebraists, found the work immensely useful and informative, and often cited it as an unimpeachable authority in his attack on Baronio. In contrast to his obvious predilection for historical, scientific, and grammatical Jewish literature, and his rather conventional regard for medieval Jewish exegesis, Casaubon appears to have had little interest in Midrash. It may be that Casaubon associated this creative corpus of texts with the rabbinic "inanities" that he had come across in works such as Galatinus' anti-Jewish tract *On the Secrets of the Catholic Faith*. Whatever its gaps, Casaubon's Jewish library was not simply that of a typical Christian Hebraist. His ownership and reading of *Midrash Shemuel* is but one of several examples of his unfettered way of reading Hebrew and Jewish texts.

Casaubon, moreover, was not wholly dependent for Hebrew texts on his own and other private libraries. In Paris, he worked—or at least tried to work—in the Royal Library, to which he was nominally attached from the first, though largely frustrated by the elderly incumbent head librarian, Jean Gosselin.[64] After 1604, when Casaubon took Gosselin's place, his duties included sorting the rich contents of the library and identifying particularly recondite texts. These activities naturally brought him into contact with oriental texts and orientalists. Early in 1606, as he wrote to Scaliger, "a certain Scot, a very learned man," showed him an Arabic letter from the ruler of Morocco to Antonio, the pretender to the Portuguese throne. Casaubon could not make much of this text when he tried to decipher it.[65] He sent a

61. Casaubon, marginal note in BL 1939.b.63, 81 recto: "eius [Titus'] encomium. Mirum in ore Judaei."

62. Bod MS Casaubon 30, 112 verso. He calls this practice of substituting letters for Elohim a "superstitio Iudaica," "scribunt modo אלדים, ut in libro Azariae Mantuae edito passim, idque etiam in Isagoge Rabb. [i.e., Génébrard's work] est observatum p. modo scribunt אלקים ut in praefatione Abarbinel. in 12 proph. et in tract. de regibus Rom. pag. פא b [i.e., Ibn Daud's section on the kings of Rome in his *Sefer haKabbalah* [Mantua, 1513)]."

63. We have not yet located Casaubon's copy of *Yuhasin*. He had a copy of the 1580–81 Kraków edition, and refers to it several times in the *Exercitationes*.

64. See Delisle 1868, 197–198.

65. Casaubon to Scaliger, 19 January 1606, Casaubon 1709, 262: "Dederam viro nobili, qui isthuc iturus me convenit, quae est ejus humanitas, fasciculum tibi perferendum; cum postea Scotus quidam, vir

copy to Scaliger—who also found this example of chancery language and North African script largely impenetrable.[66]

The very learned Scot was James Hepburn, a mysterious graduate of St. Andrews who seems at this time to have been in the service of a friend of Casaubon's, the erudite royal councilor Georges Babou de la Bourdaisière.[67] At some point in 1606 or early in 1607, according to Hepburn, Casaubon asked him to decipher and transcribe a Hebrew manuscript: an illuminated kabbalistic scroll containing diagrams and materials on the names of God, the Sefirot, and other "mystical mysteries of the most occult theology," as Hepburn put it. His account of these events survives, written calligraphically on the cover of the transcript that he made for Casaubon:

> Isaac Casaubon—a man in other respects most expert—frankly confessed that he could not read or understand the text because of the old form of writing, and the teeny-tiny—so to speak—letters, and the fact that many of them, and some words, were missing, and the many holes, and his ignorance of many of the characters, and the wear that the parchment had undergone; and he could find no one in France who knew how to read or understand it.[68]

---

eruditissimus, ostendit mihi Epistolam, Arabice scriptam ad Antonium, Lusitaniae quondam Regem. Hanc percurrenti mihi non omnia quidem negotium facessebant, sed certa plurima; adeo ut de sententia Epistolae mihi non constaret; ac, nisi fallor, multa non vulgarem Arabismi dialectum praeferunt; quae longe discedunt ab Arabismo librorum editorum. Puto et multa scripta perperam, non in apographo tantum, quod videbis; sed in ipso autographo, cujus mihi facta est videndi potestas. Ejus Epistolae exemplum ad te misi, ut si per negotia tua liceret, doceres me, quid sibi illud velit; nam ego ne manum quidem satis assequor."

66. The letter in question was written in March 1588 from the ruler of Morocco, Aḥmad al-Mansur, to the Portuguese pretender Antonio. A copy made by Abudacnus, probably about 1608, survives in BL MS Burney 367, 199 recto–verso. Casaubon's efforts to decipher it appear in Bod MS Casaubon 11, 85 recto. Scaliger described the text as written in Chancery Arabic and copied in illegible African script. See Hamilton 2009, 122.

67. On Hepburn see Thompson Cooper, "Hepburn, James," in *DNB* 1885–1901; and Robert Cummings, "Hepburn, James," in *ODNB* 2004. Casaubon identifies Hepburn as the translator and interpreter of a gathering of Hebrew materials in Bod MS Casaubon 23, 1 recto–8 recto (Casaubon's note appears on 5 recto). It seems all but certain that Hepburn was the learned Scot who translated Hebrew letters from a Jewish convert, Julius Conradus Otto, into Latin for Casaubon's friend and patron Georges Babou de la Bourdaisière. Casaubon recorded the Scot's role in a note on one of these translations, which are in the same handwriting as the Latin segments of the materials in MS Casaubon 23 (BL MS Burney 365, 269 recto: "Vir illustris D. de la Bourdaisiere, cum Hebraei hominis epistolam videre optasset, mox a se versam Latine in hac charta transmisit: usus opera Scoti viri doctissimi quem secum habebat"). On this connection see Chapter 5 below.

68. Bod MS Add. C 279, 97 recto: "plurimaque id genus alia secretioris Theologiae mysteria mystica, quae omnia ex vetustissima M.S. pergamena (quae in Regis Galliarum bibliotheca Lutetiae Parisiorum instar nobilissimi et antiquissimi κειμηλίου a doctissimo Casaubono eiusdem bibliothecae custode conservatur) per quendam Juvenem Jacobum Hepburnum in orientalibus linguis apprime doctum et de

Hepburn, however, had the mastery of Hebrew and philology needed to copy the manuscript in full, which he promptly did.[69] A gift inscription in Latin shows that he had finished by 1607.[70]

In 1980 Gabrielle Sed-Rajna reconstructed these events.[71] As she noted, in 1599 a group of manuscripts from the library of Catherine de Médicis, derived from the collection of Cardinal Egidio da Viterbo, arrived in the royal library. One of the Egidian manuscripts, no longer in the Paris collection, was a diagram of the Sefirot in the form of a tree, along with material on the names and attributes of God, in many colors. It seems very likely that this was the manuscript that baffled Casaubon, and that Hepburn described in such detail.

In fact Hepburn did more than transcribe the manuscript into legible Hebrew. He copied out one segment of it—an illustration of a menorah and a related commentary on Psalm 67—in a more casual Hebrew script and translated it into Latin. He also added both a rough sketch and a careful new drawing of the menorah.[72] These materials, in turn, became part of a small notebook that ended up among Casaubon's papers.[73] They are preceded there by a series of Hebrew epitaphs translated into Latin.[74] After them appear a diagram of the houses of the zodiac with discussion, in Hebrew; a

<hr />

Rabbinorum scriptis optime meritum Scotobritannum fidelissime transcripta sunt, suoque studio et labore nunc primum studiosis communicata. Prius enim vir alioqui peritissimus Isaac Casaubonus ob scripturae vetustatem, et literarum, ut ita dicam, minusculeitatem earundemque plurium et nonnullarum dictionum defectum, foraminum multitudinem, characterum multorum inscitiam, ipsiusque pergamenae contritionem, se nec legere, nec intelligere posse, neminemque in Gallia invenire qui sciret, ingenue fassus est. Quare benevoli cuncti lectores studiosi qui fructum hinc divinum carpitis piis precibus pro ipso transcriptore apud Deum intercedite ut quemadmodum studium suum faelicibus inchoavit avibus faelicioribus procedat et faelicissimis finiat quo Dei gloriae propagandae et Reip. exornandae indies magis magisque inserviat. Amen."

69. Bod MS Huntington Add.E.(R.) (Neubauer 2429). The Hebrew colophon was added long after the manuscript was written. It reads: נצרי כתב כלם ושמו הוא יעקב חברון אסכוטי תנצבה תלח ("A Christian wrote all of them, and his name is Jacob Hebron [Hepburn], a Scot, may his soul be bound in the bundle of life, 1678"). Presumably whoever added the colophon drew the information in it from Hepburn's covering text in Latin.

70. Ibid.: "Ex dono Clementis Edmondes Remembratoris Civitatis London 1607." On Sir Clement Edmondes, a Fellow of All Souls who became remembrancer of the City of London in 1605, see Charles Welch, "Edmondes, Sir Clement," in DNB 1885–1901; and Stephen Porter, "Edmondes, Sir Clement," in ODNB 2004. According to Welch's article, "His name appears among the subscribers to Minsheu's polyglot dictionary in 1617." Marr 2004 gives a full account of Edmondes' scholarly and scientific interests. For his kabbalistic studies see 115–117 and 144 n. 46–145 n. 50. Marr was the first to connect the Huntington MS with the partial transcript in Bod MS Casaubon 23, discussed below.

71. Sed-Rajna 1980.

72. Bod MS Casaubon 23, 3 recto–5 recto. On 5 recto, under the handsome reproduction of the menorah diagram, Casaubon wrote: "Jacobus Hepburnus, nobilis Scotus." Hepburn calls the material on the menorah and Psalm 67 "res perpulchra, miranda et stupenda" (Bod MS Add. C 279, 97 recto).

73. Bod MS Casaubon 23, 2 verso–8 recto.

74. Ibid., 1 recto–2 recto.

similar diagram, in Arabic; and a large horoscope in Hebrew and Latin.[75] This is the natal chart of Nicolas Louis de France, Duc d'Orléans, born 16 April 1607. The second son of Henri IV, he died on 17 November 1611 at the Château de Saint-Germain-en-Laye. The dates suggest that Casaubon's dealings with Hepburn stretched on into 1607. More important, Hepburn added scattered materials to the translated segment of the kabbalistic scroll: a discussion, in Hebrew and translated into Latin, of the Hebrew mnemonic AGLA (*Atah gibbor le'olam Adonai;* Thou art mighty forever, O Lord), and drawings and explanations of the divinely revealed signs of the Maccabees, Antiochus, and Constantine the Great.[76] The last three were emblems of divine power that Johannes Reuchlin had long before brought together. These additions suggest that Hepburn was trying to set the manuscript into the larger context of Christian Kabbalah—a tradition in which he firmly believed in later life.[77]

The episode is revealing in many ways. Hepburn's testimony confirms that younger scholars interested in Eastern languages respected Casaubon's passion for their study and knowledge of them. His account also suggests that as Casaubon worked through the oriental materials in the royal library, he examined and discussed Hebrew texts in varied scripts, as well as manuscripts in different states of preservation. Hepburn also confirms that Casaubon's expertise had limits: unfamiliar characters and vocabulary could baffle him in Hebrew (or Arabic), as they could not in Latin or Greek, and he turned to younger scholars with more specialized knowledge for help. But the episode is most suggestive in another sense. Hepburn, who soon joined the order of Minims, eventually made his way to Rome, where he worked as a curator of oriental manuscripts in the Vatican. There, in 1616, he published a lavishly illustrated work of his own, the *Virga aurea,* in which he used kabbalistic materials to praise the Virgin and laid out seventy-two different alphabets, in whose mystical import he clearly believed.[78] Ten years

75. Ibid., 6 recto–verso, 7 recto, 8 recto.

76. Ibid., 4 recto (Hebrew material on AGLA), 3 recto (Latin translation), 4 verso (the signs of the Maccabees, Antiochus, and Constantine). The three signs of the Maccabees, Antiochus, and Constantine resemble those offered by Henry Cornelius Agrippa in *De occulta philosophia* 3.31, Agrippa 1992, 495–496, but Hepburn's comments on them seemingly derive from Johannes Reuchlin's *De arte cabalistica,* Reuchlin 1517, lxviii recto–verso, lxxviiii verso.

77. In his covering text in Latin for the sefirotic roll he translated, Bod MS Add. C 279, 97 recto, Hepburn describes, among the contents of the diagram, "Mercava (visio Ezechielis prophetae, Currus seu Cathedra in cuius 4. rotis 4. alata animalia, 4. Literas magni et ineffabilis nominis cum 4. Evangelistis representantia)"—though the roll contains only Jewish material.

78. This ornate mass of text and images, chiefly the latter, takes the form of five engraved plates. Perhaps its complex layout still reflects Hepburn's Parisian encounter with the sefirotic roll. It is most easily consulted in the facsimile edition, de Mély 1922. Secret 1985, 233–234; Maclean 1980; Stolzenberg 2004, 153.

before, as his own comments show, Hepburn claimed that his reading and copying of the kabbalistic materials now in Oxford gave him access to profound theological truths. Perhaps the task that Casaubon asked Hepburn to perform even helped him choose his intellectual path. But when we turn back, as we now do, to Casaubon's modes and uses of reading his Hebrew books, we will see that gaining access to the contents of this scroll—and conversing with Jacob Hepburn—had no visible impact on Casaubon's beliefs about the Hebrew language or the Hebrew Bible and the best way to read it.

From Mystery to Philology

Casaubon's commitment to Hebrew studies was probably conventional in its origins. Christian Hebraism grew—as many scholars have pointed out—in large part from deeply speculative impulses. Johannes Reuchlin and Pietro Galatino, Egidio da Viterbo and Agostino Giustiniani, disagreed on many points. But all of them saw Hebrew as not only the oldest but the most powerful of languages, the medium with which God had called the world into being. Even those who drew on other sources of power and knowledge as well often accepted this view. Guillaume Postel, for example, believed that he was divinely inspired and that he and a woman he had met in Venice, Mother Jehanne, would somehow bring the world into a new age. But he also held that Jewish texts and the Hebrew language itself harbored profound secrets about the world's earliest history and its immediate future. Many, perhaps most, of those who took up the study of oriental languages in the sixteenth century did so in the hope that they would gain the keys to mysterious intellectual kingdoms. Late in life Scaliger recalled how Postel had convinced him, as they shared the same bed briefly in the house of a Parisian bookseller, that there were "marvelous mysteries" in the Eastern languages, and that "the Hebrews had excellent and very worthwhile authors, who had not yet been translated."[79] The mysteries proved elusive, but

79. Scaliger 1695, 241; 1740, II, 113–114: "Cum prioribus civilibus bellis Lutetiae apud Bibliopolam quendam Postello amicissimum maneret; accidit ut ipse Postellus redux ab exilio in quod relegatus fuerat propter *Joannae Matris* haereses, apud Bibliopolam Scaligeri hospitem diverteretur, et quem antea videre exoptaverat Scaliger, tribus tantum diebus convictorem habuit; statim enim in carcerem a Senatu conjectus est, cum tamen speraret anteactae vitae foedos errores Papistica vita posse obscurari. Is igitur Postellus cum diligentiam Scaligeri in Graecis valde laudaret, persuasit ut eandem operam in Hebraica, Chaldaica, Syriacaque lingua poneret: miranda quippe mysteria in his esse linguis, optimosque lectuque dignissimos auctores apud Hebraeos haberi, qui nondum in alienigenas linguas versi essent, quorum cognitione privaretur, si Graecae modo linguae insudaret." On the details of this encounter, which probably took place around 1561, and possible later ones see Bernays 1855, 263ff.; Secret 1998, 99–108; and

Scaliger was soon able to write Postel a letter in Hebrew—the first milestone of a brilliant career as a student of Jewish history and customs.[80]

Casaubon probably also came to Hebrew with exalted hopes. His Hebrew teacher, Pierre Chevalier, compiled a list of the abbreviations used in Hebrew books. Only a fragment survives, itself copied from Casaubon's copy of the original.[81] But it suffices to reveal something of Chevalier's approach. Chevalier clearly took an interest in Kabbalah and Jewish magic. On the letter א, for example, he wrote: "When dealing with divine matters the Kabbalists use this letter to stand for the divine name El or Adonai. They say it is the sign of the most important and sublime matters, which take shape at the first radiation of divine goodness."[82] In rabbinic texts, a triple א may stand for a formula of reply used in disputation. Chevalier, however, noted only that it appeared on Jewish amulets, followed by a triple ס, and represented an incantation: "Amen, amen, amen, selah, selah, selah."[83]

Whatever faith Casaubon may have cherished in such beliefs and practices, he had lost it by the time he annotated David Kimhi's grammar. The flyleaf of his copy preserves a detailed and irritable critique of traditional forms of Jewish nonsemantic exegesis, often associated with the Kabbalah by Christian scholars:

> The Hebrew masters often not only waste their time, but actually make fools of themselves as they seek out the mysteries of holy letters. They divide the mysteries of letters into three forms.
>
> The first is what they call *notarikon,* in which one considers the letters of a given word not insofar as they made up a single word, but insofar as they think that mysteries are concealed beneath them. They do so, for example, with the first word of Genesis. Some Christians interpret and interrogate this in the same way. Some think the

the important material provided by Calderini De-Marchi 1914 and Simoncelli 1984, 123–124, from Jacopo Corbinelli's correspondence with Gian Vincenzo Pinelli.

80. Scaliger 1695, 241; 1740, II, 114: "Tanto instigatore ac commendatore, animum ad has cognoscendas adjecit, tantumque profecit ut tribus aut quatuor post mensibus, cum esset a Toufou cum D. Castanaeo Rupipozaeo, ad ipsum Postellum litteras Hebraico idiomate scripserit."

81. Universitätsbibliothek Basel, MS Ki Ar 190a, 2 recto–7 recto: "Abbreviaturae quibus Rabbini in suis commentariis utuntur, transcriptae ex Cevallerii autographo, emendante Isaaco Casaubono, Genevae anno 1596 mense Maio" (not in Casaubon's hand). See Burnett 1996, 154 and n. 93.

82. Universitätsbibliothek Basel, MS Ki Ar 190a, 2 recto: "Cabalici in rebus divinis hac litera utuntur pro nomine divino El vel Adonai. Eam ajunt esse notam summarum et altissimarum rerum, quae primo effluxu divinae bonitatis subsistunt."

83. Ibid., 2 verso: "Invenitur et in Amuletis triplex א sequente triplici ס hoc pacto ססאאא id est Amen Amen Amen Selah Selah Selah."

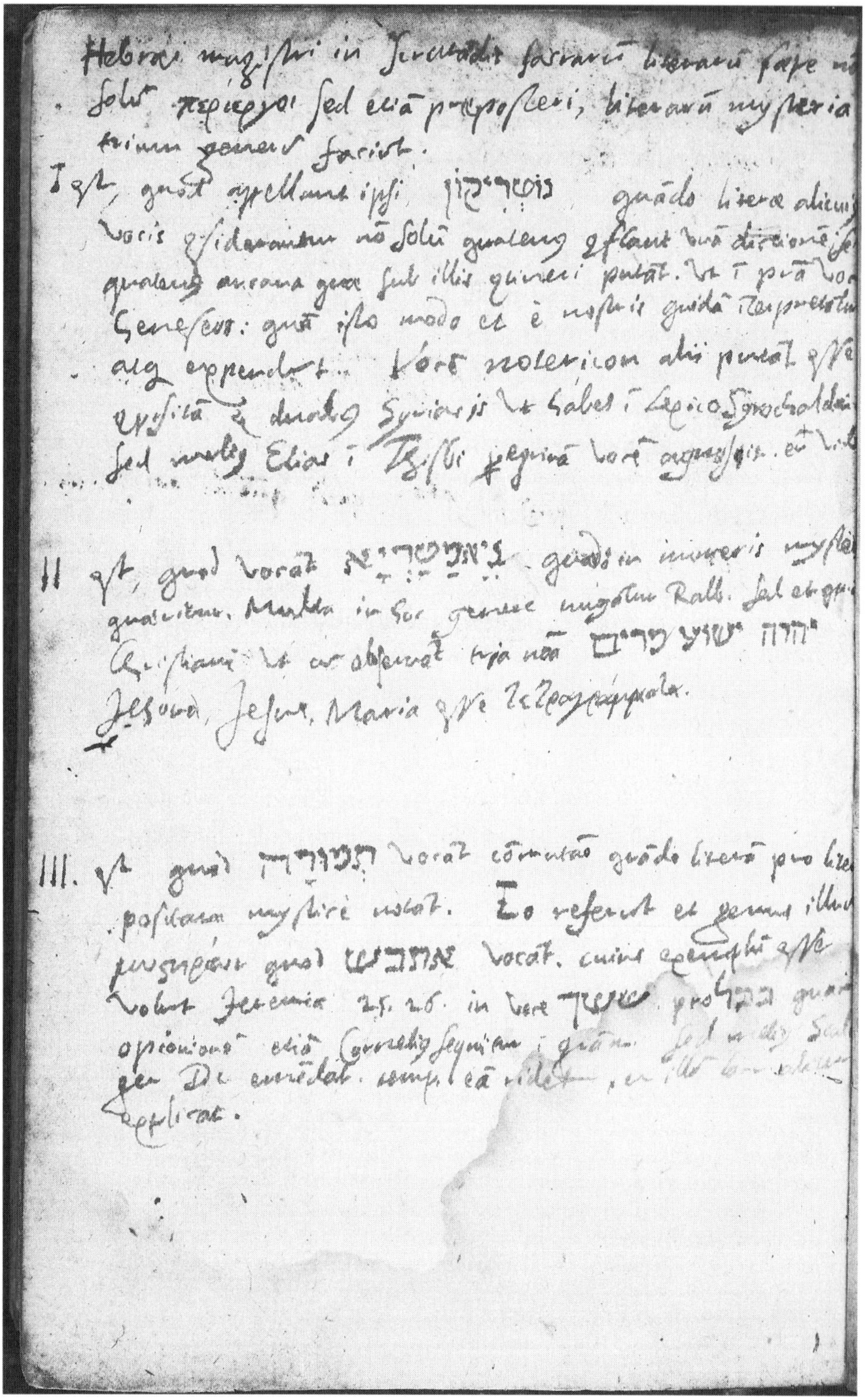

FIGURE 2.9. Notes by Casaubon on Jewish exegetical techniques in David Kimhi's *Sefer Mikhlol*. British Library 1984.a.10.(1).

word *notarikon* is a compound of two Syriac words, but Elijah Levita more correctly sees it as a foreign word in his *Tishbi*. Consult him.[84]

The second is what they call *gematria,* when numbers are treated as having mysterious significance. The rabbis make up many things of this kind, but so do some Christians, as when they note that the three names יהוה, ישוע, and מרים, Jehova, Jesus, and Maria, all are tetragrammata.

The third they call *temurah,* or exchange, when they note that a particular letter is used for mystical reasons instead of another. This is the category to which they assign the sort of mystery that they call *atbash* [a system that substitutes the last word of the alphabet for the first, the second-to-last for the second, and so on]. They believe that an example of this occurs at Jeremiah 25:26, where the text reads Sheshak in place of Babel. Corneille Bertram accepts this view in his grammar, but Joseph Scaliger ridicules this in his *De emendatione temporum* and explains the passage in a different way. And his view is better.[85]

The third part of this note is especially revealing. In the *De emendatione temporum* (1583) of his kindred spirit Joseph Scaliger, Casaubon had found a sharp attack on a notion held by, among others, Corneille Bertram, one of the numerous Swiss Hebraists who took an interest in the Kabbalah.[86] "How

---

84. Levita 1541, 213–214 (misnumbered 113–114): "And I was told by the cardinal that it is Greek. And in the Roman language as well scribes are called *notari,* and therefore in the vocabulary of our rabbis, may their memory be a blessing, they called them *notarin.* And from that comes *notariqon,* which means a form of writing, *Qantzleijsch* in German. For it is the scribes' way of writing shorthand, and they write the letters *bet* or *gimel,* and every one of these amounts to a whole word."

85. Casaubon, note in BL 1984.a.10.(1), recto of second flyleaf before title page:

Hebraei magistri in scrutandis sacrarum literarum saepe non solum περίεργοι sed etiam praeposteri, literarum mysteria trium generum faciunt.

I est, quod appellant ipsi נוטריקון quando literae alicuius vocis considerantur non solum quatenus conflant unam dictionem, sed quatenus arcana quae sub illis contineri putant. Ut in prima voce Geneseos: quam isto modo et e nostris quidam interpretantur atque expendunt. Vocem notericon alii putant esse compositam ex duabus Syriacis ut habes in Lexico Syrochaldaico. sed melius Elias in Thisbi peregrinam vocem agnoscit. eum vide.

II est, quod vocant גיאמטריא quando in numeris mysterium quaeritur. Multa in hoc genere nugantur Rabb. sed et quidam Christiani ut cum observant tria nomina יהוה ישוע מרים Jehova, Jesus, Maria esse τετραγράμματα.

III est quod תמורה vocant commutatio quando literam pro litera positam mystice notant. Eo referunt et genus illud μυστηρίων quod אתבש vocant. cuius exemplum esse volunt Jeremiae 25.26 in voce ששך pro בבל quam opinionem etiam Cornelius sequitur in gramm. sed melius Scaliger De emendat. temp. eam ridet, et illum locum aliter explicat.

86. Bertram 1574, 32: "Multae sunt apud Hebraeorum Rabbinos mutuae literarum in alphabeto inverso oppositiones, quibus fit ut litera in literam transeat, sed vna est omnium antiquissima quam אתבש

is *Sheshak* taken," cries Jeremiah, in the midst of his prophecy about the fate that awaits Babylon (51:41). Bertram and others held that *Sheshak* was another word for the city, derived from manipulation of the letters that spelled Babel. In fact it was the name of a goddess. "All Assyrian and Chaldean names are composed from simple elements," Scaliger wrote, "and more or less all of these are the names of Babylonian gods."[87] In the margin of his copy of Scaliger's book, Casaubon identified the objects of Scaliger's criticism: "In addition to the rabbis, many Christians believe this, including Corneille Bertram."[88] These were some of the materials from which Casaubon developed his critique of the "Hebrew masters." Scaliger's precise, powerfully argued chronology certainly helped to inspire Casaubon with distaste for the Kabbalists' ways of manipulating words.

By 1601, if not before, Casaubon read some Christian Kabbalah: not only the *De arcanis* of Galatino, but also the far more profound *De verbo mirifico* of Johannes Reuchlin. But the experience did not leave much of a mark. Casaubon reflected equivocally in his diary that he was "not ashamed of the time spent on reading" the two men's books.[89] He does not seem to have noticed that Reuchlin's knowledge of the Jewish sources was more profound, or that his mind was more open than Galatino's to Jewish ideas and customs.

Still, in another, more pragmatic, sense, Casaubon cherished the belief that learning Hebrew—not just the Hebrew of the Bible, but that of the rabbis—might enable him to discover wonders. In 1592 he explained to the traveler and diplomat Philippe Canaye de Fresnes why he was working so hard to master "Aramaic and the language of the rabbis." His letter makes clear how excited he was, and why:

---

vocant, ad quam pertinet quod pro בבל Babilon, dicatur Iirm. 25.26. ששך Scheschach. Si enim bipertito diuidas alphabetum, et literas literis opponas, literae ל respondebit כ, et literae ב litera ש. Atque ex Cabalisticis literarum commutationibus hanc praeter caeteras probandam iudicaui, quod ex doctiorum interpretatione ea vsus fuerit eo loci Iirmeja." Bertram drew on the Hebraist Antoine Chevalier's work.

87. Scaliger 1583, 276: "Igitur omnia Assyria et Chaldaea nomina composita sunt ex simplicibus: quae quidem fere omnia sunt Deorum Babyloniorum nomina. ut Mero, Nebo, Bel. Isaiae cap. XLVI. Seschac nomen Deae apud Ieremiam LI. Neque enim Schesach Babylon est per modum, quem ATBASCH ineptissimi Rabbini vocant."

88. Casaubon, marginal note in BL 582.l.9, 276: "hoc praeter Rabb. et nostri plerique censent: in his Cornelius Borauent. in gramm. p. 32."

89. Casaubon 1850, I, 354 (11 June 1601): "In Galatino et Reuchlino fuimus per hosce dies, nec poenitet insumti in illorum lectione temporis, etsi non carent eruditi homines suis magnis naevis, de quibus si voles tu, O Deus, utiliter fortasse aliquando disputabimus." Note also his remark in his copy of Kimhi's *Mikhlol,* BL 1984.a.10.(1), 104 verso, on a reference to *Sefer Yetsirah:* "i. liber in Cabbala: quem nugantur ab Abraamo factum. est versus a Postello." Cf. 108 verso: "Liber Jetsira, caballisticus."

I scarcely dare tell you what my project is. First of all, life is short, and that fact prohibits us from beginning long efforts. Further, a prudent man does not arouse hopes about himself, if he will disappoint them in the future. But I will confess what is the heart of the matter, and I tell this to you alone. I would not work so hard on these languages just to understand the Hebrew rabbis: that is not, I admit, my final goal. It is so that with their help I can understand the Arabic used by the great philosophers, whose excellent writings, in every area of philosophy, are either entirely neglected nowadays because of ignorance of the language, or are read to little or no profit.[90]

At this early stage in Casaubon's Hebrew studies, he saw himself—rather as Scaliger had, a few years before—as preparing for a career in which he would unlock Eastern mysteries. In fact he planned a life of personal as well as intellectual adventure—a life in which rabbinic Hebrew would serve him chiefly as a lingua franca, not so much a treasure-house in itself as a useful tool he could use when he traveled to the East. "If God grants, I have decided to train myself on the writings of the rabbis until I gain the chance of going there. For if I hope to study the Arabic language seriously, I must travel there. I know that many works can be found in those regions, whose very names are unknown here, even in our wildest dreams."[91] These plans, of course, were never carried out, and were probably soon abandoned. Although Casaubon made repeated efforts to master Arabic at a high level, he never achieved his goal, as Alastair Hamilton shows in an appendix to this volume. Still, Casaubon never lost his fascination with Eastern languages and learning. His support for their study made him a valued mentor and interlocutor for younger specialists, like Thomas Erpenius, who far sur-

---

90. Casaubon 1709, 569: "Ego vero quid moliar, quo spectem, vix audeo dicere. Primum, quia vitae summa brevis spes vetat inchoare longas; deinde quia prudentis hominis non est, eam de se spem velle excitare, quam postea sit destituturus. Veruntamen, quod uni tibi dictum sit, fatebor, quod res est; non eo animo tantum studii ponerem in linguis his, ut Hebraeos Rabbinos intelligam; non est, inquam, id ἀρχιτεκτονικὸν meum τέλος. sed ut harum ope Arabicam intelligere queam; qua usi sunt plerique summi Philosophi, quorum scripta in omni sapientiae parte praestantissima, linguae illius imperitia hodie vel ignorantur, vel nulla, certe parva cum utilitate leguntur." As will become clear, Casaubon later modified these views substantially.

91. Ibid.: "Igitur, quod Deus Opt. Max. bene vertat, constitui tantisper in Rabbinicis scriptis me exercere, donec facultas detur isthuc eundi. Isthuc enim ire mihi necesse est, si studium meum Arabicae linguae serio applicare velim. Multa enim in istis locis scio reperiri, quorum hic οὐδ'ἐν ὀνείροις nomina sunt audita."

passed him in mastery of these fields but seem to have deeply appreciated his interest.

No Kabbalist, Casaubon continued to pursue some of the issues central to speculative Hebraism intermittently throughout his life. He found Scaliger's ability to trace connections from one language to another deeply impressive, and noted that his friend had not used the methods of the "Hebrew masters, who are expert only in their own language and pretty much ignorant of all the rest" to arrive at his results, even as he asked for more information about Scaliger's philological method.[92] Like Scaliger and many, many others, he posed the question whether Hebrew was in fact the oldest language and the ancestor of all others; and unlike Scaliger he stated unequivocally that the answer was yes. On the evening of 7 February 1601 Casaubon recorded in his diary that he was working on a "not unpleasant task": "I decided five days ago to investigate in a fairly serious way the Hebrew origins of Greek words."[93] At least some of the notes that he took at this juncture are preserved in one of his Bodleian copybooks. They reveal the simplicity and certainty of his beliefs about Hebrew's place in the complex genealogy of human languages. On the first page of one set of notes he made a strong statement, clearly designed to set the tone for the long series of lexical investigations that followed: "In my view there is no doubt that Hebrew long preceded all other languages. Hence it is not surprising that other languages retain many traces of the original. These include the few points that follow, which I have noted as a byproduct of my studies."[94] Later in these notes Casaubon took the time to explain why he rejected some theories:

> Is the Hebrew language the first one of all? The majesty of the language—or its small lexicon—or the fact that the oldest books of all, those of Moses, are written in it—would any of them be enough to show this. And yet there are some who try to conceal this truest of all truths. I shall ignore the stupidity of the moderns. But I am astonished that Theodoret, a most learned man, made such stupid

92. Casaubon to Scaliger, 15 July 1597, Casaubon 1709, 82: "Et quaeso te, Vir magne, unde illa tibi eruta? . . . non enim ab Hebraeis magistris illa habes: qui suae unius periti, aliarum omnium imperiti fere sunt omnes."

93. Casaubon 1850, I, 328: "Mane per aliquot horas studia: deinde toto die officia amicorum: tum iterum ad pensum rediimus non ingratum. Instituimus enim ante dies quinque paullo diligentius Graecarum dictionum origines in lingua Hebraea quaerere."

94. Bod MS Casaubon 30, 1 recto: "Non est dubitandum, meo judicio, anteire linguas omnes alias HEBRAEAM. Itaque mirum non est, extare in aliis linguis multa vestigia τῆς πρωτοτύπου. Cuiusmodi sunt pauca haec quae observata nobis ὁδοῦ πάρεργον. Omitto nomina literarum: de quibus nemo est monendus."

pronouncements about this point. He thinks that Aramaic is the
oldest language of all, and that the Hebrew language was devised
much later for use in worship. What could be more stupid than the
theory that Aramaic and Hebrew are different languages, and that
Aramaic is the mother tongue, while the other has undergone corruption or simply been invented?[95]

With characteristic pertinacity, Casaubon went on to derive many Greek
words from Hebrew roots. His findings, in his view, yielded something like a
comprehensive history of language. What came into existence after Babel
were not new languages, but new variations on the old one, and new words.

The evidence for this thesis was clear: the patterns of dispersion that Casaubon could descry as he looked over the world's languages, compiling and
analyzing what amounted to an imaginary linguistic atlas, made clear that
the first new languages spoken after the Flood were those most closely related to Hebrew:

> I can prove this with the following fact: it is certain that the peoples
> which were scattered at that time through various regions did not
> suddenly pass to distant parts of the globe, but to places nearer to
> their old fatherland. There, the Assyrians, Syrians, and perhaps also
> the Greeks were doubtless the first born of the Hebrews. Then they
> in turn gave rise to the other peoples, who little by little spread out
> from the place of their origin to the four corners of the world, un-
> til, with the passage of time, the entire inhabited world was in fact
> thronged with inhabitants. If the languages had become totally dif-
> ferent at Babel, then the Chaldeans, Assyrians, and Syrians would
> necessarily have kept those strange languages. But we see that the
> opposite took place. For it is clearly true that in proportion as other
> languages were closer to the ancient and original habitat of man-
> kind, they retained more obvious and visible traces of their He-

95. Ibid., 67 recto: "An Hebraea lingua sit omnium prima. Vel linguae maiestas, vel vocabulorum
paucitas, vel quod antiquissimi libri, Mosis nempe, ea lingua scripti, hoc satis evincant. Et tamen non
desunt qui hanc veriss. veritatem obscurare nitantur. Recentiorum stuporem mitto. At Theodoretum
virum eruditiss. miror tam absurda, tam fatua super hoc pronuntiasse [*Quaestiones in Octateuchum* 60–
62]. Putat Syriacam linguam esse omnium antiquissimam: linguam vero Hebraeam multo post inven-
tam in usum sacrorum. Quid stultius quam putare linguam Syriacam et Hebr. diversas linguas esse
quarum mater sit Syriaca, altera adulterina, aut fictitia?" Cf. Casaubon's note in his copy of Kimhi's
Mikhlol, BL 1984.a.10.(1), verso of flyleaf 2 (of four): "Σηαι inter caeteras laudes linguae Sanctae est haec
quoque vel maxima, quod per annos tam multos hoc est 3420. et amplius mansit incorrupta et
ἄφθαρτος. h. e. a rerum conditu ad captivitatem Babylonicam."

brew origins, and still retain them now. Closeness is relevant in two
senses, in space and time. For the nearer each people was to the Hebrew nation, with respect to both place and time, the closer it came
to the Hebrew language. Distance, in both place and time, gradually
wrought greater changes.[96]

These arguments were less distinctive than Casaubon's rejection of the Kabbalah: comparable genealogies of language, starting with Hebrew as mother
tongue and tracing the spread of Aramaic and other languages in the ancient Near East and beyond, appeared in the Aramaic grammars of Münster
and Bertram.[97]

As more novel evidence for this rational reconstruction, Casaubon offered the case of the Greeks. Starting in Asia, they crossed to Europe, where
they were known as Ionians. Their oldest writings included a relatively large
number of Hebrew words, which gradually fell out of use, although the Asi-
atic Greeks used more of them than the Europeans. The pattern held: peoples and languages had expanded outward, changing as they did so, from
what one might now call a Semitic center.[98] Or so, at least, Casaubon concluded, he must prove—as he tried to with long lists of Greek words and

96. Bod MS Casaubon 30, 68 recto: "Hoc eo probamus: quia certum est eos populos qui tum sparsi
sunt per varias regiones, non in extremas Orbis partes repente transiisse: verum in propiores veteri pa-
triae suae. Itaque ex illis sine dubio Assyrii, Syri, forte et Graeci sunt primo nati: deinde ex istis alii
porro populi, qui paullatim ab ortus primi loco dilatati sunt ad quatuor Orbis cardines: donec progressu
temporis πᾶσα ἡ οἰκουμένη incolis frequentaretur. Igitur si in Babele linguae in totum diversae factae
essent: necessario Chaldaei, Assyrii, Syri ἀλλοκότους illas linguas retinuissent. Atqui contrarium vide-
mus accidisse. Est enim verissimum: Linguas caeteras eo manifestiora et magis expressa originis
Hebraicae vestigia servasse, et nunc servare: quo propius ab antiqua et prima hominum sede abfuerunt.
Propinquitatem hanc duplicem facimus, loci ac temporis: nam proximus quisque populus genti Hebraicae et situs et temporis ratione, proxime ad illius linguam accessit. Longinquitas vero et locorum et temporum, alienationem subinde maiorem intulit."

97. Münster 1527a, 2–3: "Iure igitur inter omnes mundi linguas, Chaldaica post linguam sanctam sibi
primas vendicat. Nec paucos homines linguae huius putes in patria sede relictos, quum mox per suas
generationes occupaverint et repleverint non modo Babyloniam, sed et Mesopotamiam, Assyriam, Ara-
biam et reliqua circumiacentia loca, quorum omnium unam fuisse et hodie esse linguam, quae et Chaldaica et Syriaca vocatur, certissime comprobatur. Tametsi temporis successu (quod omnibus quoque
constat evenisse linguis) ei multa aliena admixta sint vocabula, praesertim Graeca, ubi scilicet cum exteris nationibus Chaldaei ipsi consuetudinem habere coeperunt" (admittedly, Münster separates Aramaic from Greek more sharply than Casaubon); Bertram 1574, ¶i recto–[¶iv recto]; he is especially concerned to trace the interaction of Hebrew and Aramaic.

98. Bod MS Casaubon 30, 68 recto: "Clarum hoc ex comparatione linguarum Syriacae, Chaldaicae,
Arabicae, Punicae, etc. cum Hebr. Clarissimum item, si Graecam linguam diligenter spectes. Graeci
primi in Asia habitarunt: inde Iones vel ut Aeschylus vocat Hebraice, Jauanes, in Europam traiecerunt.
Nos autem observamus, in antiquiss. quibusque Graecorum scriptoribus, multa vocabula Hebraica,
quae postea vel desierunt esse in usu: vel admodum sunt mutata. Observamus etiam, Asiaticos Graecos
magis ἑβραΐζειν quam Europaeos."

their supposed Hebrew roots.[99] Casaubon found these relatively conventional efforts entirely satisfactory. "We have made some progress," he wrote in his diary, "not without great enjoyment, and, I hope, with some utility for the public as well."[100] It seems quite likely that when he collected references to a single God in Aeschylus and other Greek writers, he believed that he was finding traces of the monotheism of their Hebrew-speaking ancestors.[101]

The origins and development of human language were fashionable subjects for literati of many kinds, from grammarians to biblical exegetes, in the sixteenth and seventeenth centuries. Ancient authorities differed enough to give early modern thinkers substantial latitude for debate. The account in Genesis could be taken as suggesting either that linguistic diversity began with Babel, or that its roots lay in the earlier period when the descendants of Shem, Ham, and Japhet moved out into the world. The fathers of the church were also divided. One could argue that all later languages derived from a single, first one—most likely, but not necessarily, Hebrew; or one could assemble them in groups and treat the question of their origins with benign neglect.[102] Casaubon was by no means the only scholar who spent time happily tracing connections between Hebrew and Greek words that sounded alike and had similar meanings—to say nothing of those who dedicated themselves to proving the aboriginal antiquity of Flemish or the Greek origins of French. The German scholar Christian Becmann, for example, argued in 1609 that a rigorous account of the origins of Latin would include a great many Hebrew roots. He stuffed his ample work on the origins of Latin with cases in point, ferociously insisting on the correctness of his thesis and the incorrectness of the views of unnamed adversaries: "*Scala,* σχαλίς, from *sulam,* which means ladder. Those who derive it from the Latin verb *scandere,* to climb, must confess that the Hebrew origin is more correct, whether the meaning or the letters are taken into account."[103]

Others responded to the complexity of the material and the disagreement of ancient authorities in very different ways. The Austrian historian Hieronymus Megiser prefaced his *Thesaurus Polyglottus* (Frankfurt am Main, 1603)—a work he described as useful for everyone from historians to per-

99. Ibid.: "Haec igitur sunt nobis demonstranda."

100. Casaubon 1850, I, 328: "Et jam promovimus aliquantum non sine voluptate magna, utinam cum aliqua utilitate publica."

101. See Fraenkel 1950; Mund-Dopchie 1984.

102. For the background see Borst 1957–1963; Droixhe 1978 and 1992; Considine 2008, esp. 107–109.

103. Becmann 1613, 740: "Scala, σχαλίς, a סלם, quod est scala. Qui Latinum a scandendo faciunt, vel ultro fateantur necesse est, probius ab Hebraeo fieri: sive significatio sive literae etiam ipsae putentur."

fume merchants—with a series of bracketed diagrams that grouped the languages of the world by descent and region, moving from the Old World to the New. He allotted the first of these charts to Hebrew, which he described as "the first and oldest of all the languages, which all the patriarchs used in antiquity," and the dialects of Aramaic and Syriac descended from it.[104] But he did not explain what, if any, linguistic bridges connected this group to the languages descended from Greek and Latin, much less those spoken on the islands of the New World and the Pacific. Megiser's very discretion gave his work an appearance of modernity—at least from the standpoint of a twenty-first-century reader. Unlike a Postel or a Casaubon he insisted that he simply could not trace the lines of descent for all of the world's languages.

In the end, the more mystical and speculative forms of Hebrew and oriental scholarship seem not to have exercised a strong attraction on Casaubon. The same copybook that contains his notes on ancient criticism, much of which dates to the period 1600–1610, also contains his notes on Postel's studies of Eastern languages and alphabets and of the history of the world's languages. Casaubon judged as he read, and his judgments were by no means uniformly negative. He credited Postel with pioneering in the study of Samaritan, Ethiopic, and other tongues and alphabets previously unknown to Europeans.[105] As a well-trained antiquarian, he appreciated the light that Postel had shed on the development of Hebrew script by illustrating it as it appeared on shekels he had obtained in Palestine. By connecting the Samaritan script to Jerome's testimony that the square characters in which Hebrew was written had been devised by the biblical scribe and leader Ezra, Postel had revealed the nature of the original Hebrew script—a major accomplishment, which Casaubon acknowledged by summarizing Postel's discussion at some length.

Ultimately, Casaubon saw little point in pursuing the matter further, especially as Scaliger had gone into the matter at length in his *Thesaurus temporum* of 1606: "It would take a long time to go into the other details, and there is no point. This language differs from Hebrew only in its script. See

---

104. Megiser 1603, I, [)(6 verso]: "Omnium Linguarum Prima et antiquissima est Hebraea vel Hebraica, vel etiam Iudaica: qua nimirum omnes antiquitus usi sunt Patriarchae. Haec Sancta etiam et Biblica appellatur: propterea, quod Vetus Testamentum in ea conscriptum est . . . Mater haec utriusque Chaldaicae, immo omnium pene linguarum Orientis fons est et origo."

105. Bod MS Casaubon 60, 282 recto: "De lingua Samaritana. Primus opinor P. de hac lingua erudite aliquid inter Europaeos nostra memoria scripsit. Quare Jos. Scal. de hoc loquens, rejicit nos ad hanc diatribam P."

Scaliger."[106] Postel's passionate advocacy of the study of Arabic received a similarly dusty answer. The study of Arabic, Postel insisted, was vital. Some of the reasons were purely practical: Arabic was more widely used than any other language; it had already spread through Africa and Asia. When Magellan reached the Moluccas, he found that their inhabitants spoke Arabic. Now the language was beginning to take root in Europe.[107] Arabic was also easy: "This language is so close to Hebrew that anyone who has studied Hebrew intensively can master most of Arabic in two years. I know: I have made the experiment. In fact, I was so quick in comprehension that the Turks who taught me in Constantinople called me a demon, since I seemed to understand everything without working so hard as they thought normal."[108] Most important, though, for Postel was the world of wonders that Arabic promised to those who studied hard enough. Arabic writers, he believed, had progressed beyond the ancients in vital fields of study, and anyone who hoped to pursue the disciplines in a proper, modern way needed access to their work:

> To say nothing about the various disciplines that have been treated in such an excellent way by writers in that language, we owe them astrology and the practice of medicine. Let those self-styled moderns who take delight in tearing down others to gain a reputation for

106. Ibid., 282 verso: "Longum sit reliqua persequi. et nullus est usus. Solis characteribus differt haec lingua ab Hebr. Vide Scaligerum." For Scaliger's use of Postel's material see Grafton 1983–1993, II, 628–630.

107. Postel 1538b, D recto: "Haec est omnibus religionis Muhamedicae cultoribus grammatica, et usque adeo orbem totum occupavit, ut si trifariam inque tria aequalia totam habitabilem dividas, vix una pars extra hanc possit reperiri. Habet totam Affricam, praeter Nubianam illam regionem, quae a Praestano Christiano incolitur. Tota Asia a nostris litoribus per antipodes usque ad illam partem quae in occidua nostri hemisphaerii parte est, hac utitur. Quos enim primos hominum sua navigatione orbem totum ab occidente per antipodes in ortum lustrando Magellanus ultra Americam reperit in maioribus Moluccarum insulis, illi nugas Muhamedis observant. Ad Taschaltical et Curistical ac Temistitan, quamvis praecipua pars Idololatrae sunt, haec pestis pervenit. Praeter quosdam Indos et Narsinganos, quos fabula non est daemonem colere ne saeviat, tota Asia illius dogmata amplectitur. Iam et in Europa haec pestis grassatur, occupatque totam Graeciam, Macedoniam, Thraciam, Daciam, Zagyges seu Hungariae partem, Seruuiam et Bosnam, quae est pars Pannoniae superioris, ut nulla sit hodie lingua, nec usquam olim fuerit, quae in tot orbis partibus locum habeat."

108. Ibid., Dij recto: "Est autem haec lingua [Arabic] Hebraicae adeo affinis ut siquis sit diligenter versatus in Hebraismo, possit ante biennium bonam partem illius linguae intelligere. Scio qui periculum fecerim. Ob illam enim comprehendendi celeritatem illi Turchae qui me docebant Constantinopoli me daemona appellabant, quod viderer praeter consuetam illis diligentiam omnia capere. Id enim sine iactantia de me ausim dicere me plus uno et altero anno in ea lingua profecisse quam multi illorum toto sexennio soleant. In grammaticis enim saepe amplius morantur. Nec mihi mea illud singulari diligentia accidebat, sed quia iuvenis satis diligenter sacras literas iungendo Hebraismo insudaveram."

learning babble as they please. I still venture to claim that there is no learned doctor nowadays, one who has gained experience in practical medicine of the right sort, who, after drawing his splendid training in theory from Galen, has not moved on to grapple with the Arabs. After all, who can deny that each century progresses beyond the last one?[109]

No art, Postel explained, delicately alluding to Cicero, ever came into existence in complete form.[110] And anyone who examined sixteenth-century medicine would see the footprints of the Arabs everywhere, from the myriad new medicaments to whose use they had introduced Europeans to the fine textbooks of Avicenna, each page of which offered more solid content than five or six books of Galen's wordy Greek.[111]

Casaubon's skepticism grew as he read. Postel's claim that Arabic had become the universal language he dismissed as hype: "All this involves some hyperbole. For it is false that all of Asia, Tartary, India, China, and the other peoples in the territories that he defines here as Asian all use this language."[112]

109. Ibid., D recto–verso: "Taceo genera disciplinarum praeclarissime ab illius linguae authoribus pertractata. Astrologiam et rei medicae praxim illis debemus. Nugentur quicquid velint nescio qui neotericistae, qui maledicendi quadam libidine sibi nomen redimere eruditionis volunt. quum tamen, ausim deierare, nullus sit hodie virorum doctorum et in melioris notae praxi exercitatorum, quin postquam egregie a Galeno hausit ipsam theoriam non versetur in Arabibus. Quis enim neget saecula proficere semper?"

110. Ibid., D verso: "Adde neminem unquam artem reperisse et consumasse." Cf. Cicero, *Brutus* 71: "nihil est enim simul et inventum et perfectum," and the important discussion of Gombrich 1960. Postel's use of paired verbs, the former for the discovery of an art and the latter for its completion, indicates the connection between his thought and Cicero's, obscured by his rigorous practice of elegant variation.

111. Postel 1538b, D verso–Dij recto: "Quam multa autem quae felicissime nobis hoc saeculo succedunt, Arabibus solum, non Galeno debemus? Nolo recitare omnium medicinarum temperamentum sacharum, rhabarbarum, nec enim hodie quod nunc habemus antiquorum est, sed a traditione poenorum, turbit, sene, manna praestantissimae medicinae, et composita illa scherab, giulab, suffuf, lohoc, roob, et huius modi, quae ita nobis sunt in usu, et singulari commoditate, ut sine maximo detrimento tolli non possint. At dices, num vis hoc erudito saeculo, nos haurire rem medicam ex tanta barbarie? quum possem illud cum Celso dicere, morbos eloquentia non curari, illud unum requiram a vobis. Quis in melioribus ac latinis disciplinis vel mediocriter versatus, voluisset ante 20. annos in summa illa veteris translationis Galeni barbarie versari? adeo erat interpretum et temporis vitio corruptus, ut a se ad magis barbaros abigeret. Nunc vero ubi illius lingua innotuit, ubi latine a latinis hominibus datus est, omnes allicit, incitat. Nonne censes idem futurum si semel per illius linguae familiaritatem latine loqui inceperint? nonne putas interpretum vitio illic multa admissa minus probe? At in illis sunt errores, nec desunt apud Galenum, Aristotelem, et quemlibet antiquorum quae possint repraehendi, ac falsa ostendi. Sed ubi numerus minor, illic certe citius recurrendum. Quid? quod videas dilucide et clare dictum apud Aben Sina una aut altera pagella tantum, quod vix Galenus cum suo Asiatismo quinque aut sex libris maximis absolvat? Sed missa haec faciamus."

112. Bod MS Casaubon 60, 283 recto: "Haec Postel. non sine hyperbole. nam falsum est totam Asiam, Tartariam, Indiam, Chinam et alias gentes iis finibus inclusas quibus ille Asiam hic definit, hanc linguam usurpare."

Using his favorite pejorative term for intellectual con men, *suaviludius*—a term that he also applied to Hermes Trismegistus—he mocked Postel for claiming that any good Hebraist could learn Arabic easily and rapidly: "Postel is a tricky fellow when it comes to the connection between this language and Hebrew. He writes that it is so close that someone who has studied Hebrew intensively could master the better part of Arabic in less than two years. Does he think that two years is a short time for learning a language? I think that someone who has sampled other studies would find that a long time."[113] Arguments like these were not new to Casaubon: he had even struggled with Francis Bacon's *Advancement of Learning,* from which he had tried to learn English, translating words and expressions into Latin and Greek as he read. Casaubon noted on the title page of his copy that Bacon had done his best to render due credit both to antiquity and to modernity. He even called attention to the lord chancellor's remark that "to speake truly, *Antiquitas seculi Iuuentus mundi.* These times are the ancient times when the world is ancient, and not those which we count antient *Ordine retrogrado,* by a computacion backward from our selues."[114] Accordingly, he met Postel's claims with critical sympathy—and a sense that his own generation of learned humanists understood better how to reconcile the claims of East and West, modernity and antiquity: "Postel argues on behalf of Arabic philosophy, against those who approve only of the Greeks. And one must confess that the Arabic philosophers and medical men have made many learned, clever, and necessary observations. Still, I would not claim that they deserve all the credit that some give them, as I observe."[115]

Casaubon had read Scaliger's preface to his second edition of Manilius, which appeared in 1599, with special care.[116] Scaliger argued there, at length, against the currently fashionable view that all the arts and sciences had originated in the ancient Near East.[117] Casaubon followed his reasoning, pen in

---

113. Ibid., 283 verso: "De affinitate linguae huius cum Hebraica, suaviludius est P. qui scribat, tantam eam esse, ut aliquis diligenter versatus in hebraismo, posset ante biennium, bonam partem illius linguae intelligere. An illi videbatur parum tempus ad linguam aliquam discendam spatium biennii? Ego ei qui alia studia degustarit, id tempus longum censeo."

114. Casaubon, note on the title page of Huntington Library RB56251; "23. Antiquitati quantu[m] deferendum, et de antiquitate hodierna." Casaubon here summarizes Bacon's celebrated discussion of the "peccant humours" of learning (23 verso). For a discussion of Casaubon's linguistic notes see Sherman 2008, 13–15.

115. Bod MS Casaubon 60, 283 recto–verso: "Deinde disputat P. pro Arabum philosophia adversus eos qui solos Graecos probant. Et fatendum est multa docte, acute, necessario animadversa a phi. et med. Arabum. sed non tantum tamen iis tribuerim quantum quosdam video facere."

116. Casaubon's copy is BL 1000.l.3, inscribed on the title page: "Eruditissimo viro Isacio Casaubono suo Ios. Scal. D.D."

117. See Grafton 1983–1993, I, chap. 7.

hand as usual: "The Greeks not only shed light on the arts, but devised them."[118] More generally, Scaliger not only noted that the sciences did not come into being in their finished form; he also offered a subtle formulation of the point: "Great things take a long time to develop, and one age is not enough to work through them systematically. Hence they have certain rude beginnings, and are not passed on to us in their final state. That is why those who come later always devise new things to add to the discoveries of their ancestors, and why the ancestors always leave something to be emended or explicated by those who come after."[119] "Rude beginnings and development of the sciences," wrote Casaubon, showing that he had grasped Scaliger's view.[120] When he read Postel, he remembered this passage and made clear that he found Scaliger's understanding of the development of the sciences superior, although he appreciated the corroborative information about Arabic thought that he could glean from the enthusiastic Postel: "I like Joseph Scaliger's discussion of this point in his preface to Manilius. But Postel adds material that is worth noting."[121] Sadly, Casaubon only summarized, without criticism, the history of peoples and languages that Postel presented in *De originibus* (1551).[122] It would be fascinating to know more about how plausi-

118. Casaubon, marginal note on Scaliger 1600, α2 recto (BL 1000.l.3): "Graeci non solum illustrarunt, sed excogitarunt artes."

119. Scaliger 1600, α2 recto: "Quum enim magnarum rerum tardi sint progressus, et ad earum scrutationem una aetas non sufficiat, earum quaedam primo rudimenta sunt, neque cum perfectione sua ad nos transmittuntur: propterea accidit, ut ad maiorum inventa aliquid procudendo posteriores adiiciant, et posteritati denique semper aliquid relinquatur a superioribus, quod aut emendatore aut illustratore indigeat."

120. Casaubon, marginal note on ibid., α2 recto (BL 1000.l.3): "Rudimenta et progressus scientiarum."

121. Bod MS Casaubon 60, 283 verso: "Placent vero nobis, quae ea de re disputata sunt a Jos. Scal. praef. in Manilium. Sed addit P. quod notare sit operae pretium."

122. Ibid., 290 verso: "Percurrimus et alium P. libellum De originibus: seu de Hebraicae linguae et gentis antiquitate deque variarum linguarum affinitate. Multa in eo libello quae non paeniteat legisse. Primum laudatur loquendi facultas. per quam rationis usum et omnia bona invicem communicamus, etc. ὅτι maxima olim quaestio fuit de prima omnium linguarum, et utrum ex arte an ex natura locutio constet. Pronuntiat omnium primam fuisse Hebr. deque ea sensisse Plinium, cum ait Literas semper arbitror Assyrias fuisse. etc [*Natural History* 7.56.192]. An autem loquimur φύσει an ex compacto hominum? Potest dici a natura accipere hominem habilitatem quandam exprimendi sensa animi sono quodam, stridoreve: quomodo fieri hodieque aiunt a gente quadam in petrae desertis Africae partibus ad Capricorni tropicum. Huic naturali facultati accessit ars, quae loquelam formavit. Haec P. qui optat ut magnates periculum eius rei saepius faciant in pueris extra hominum consortium asservatis. Sequitur longa declaratio chorographiae a Mose exposita, qua hoc docetur plerasque omnes gentes et propagatas et denominatas a filijs Noae." It is curious that Casaubon, who brusquely dismissed Azariah de' Rossi for accepting Annius of Viterbo's fake Berosus and Manetho as genuine, did not criticize Postel for doing the same. See, e.g., Postel 1538a, [Diij recto]: "Iam quum in Graecia literis honos esse inceperat, Berosus qui res Chaldaeorum, quae in aere ac coctis lateribus, etiam ante diluvium, diligenter literis exculptis servabantur, Manethon qui Aegyptiorum, Moses qui res Hebraeorum scripserat, ita erant

ble the speculative philology of the midcentury seemed, half a century later, to the more disciplined, if less imaginative, Casaubon.

Most striking, from the present context, is Casaubon's response to Postel's effort to show that the French language contained many Hebrew words, such as *chiffre* (number). In this case, Postel based his argument not on genealogies of the nations but on well-known facts.[123] Until the time of Philip Augustus, he explained, France had swarmed with Jews, who harassed the French with their usury, and even though Philip had expelled them, they gained reentry only eighty-five years later from Philip the Fair.[124] Casaubon simply summarized Postel's argument. It is curious that he omitted Postel's dialectically elegant point that French had also left a deep impress in the Hebrew of Rashi and other Jews. But this omission probably reflects not disagreement but the fact that Casaubon had noted this phenomenon himself, long before, as he learned to read rabbinical commentary on the prophets.[125] Like Scaliger, the mature Casaubon approached Postel not as a sympathizer

---

vetustate ipsa iam quasi corrosi, ut vix facerent posteris fidem. Hinc, a duobus illis primis quum res olim gestas (Nam ut Mosis lex erat sanctissima, ita summopere cavebatur ne illa profanaretur, ac illis permitteretur hominibus qui nugis divina infercirent) Herodotus ac illius imitator Diodorus Siculus accepisset, tot annexas fabulas immiscuit, ut incredibilis bona pars illius historiae facta sit. Sed nescio quomodo dum volebam de lingua dicere, transii etiam in gentis antiquitatem, unde ne sim prolixior, me recipio."

123. Postel also traced much more speculative and elaborate connections between the French and the Israelites, in the course of which he argued that the very name of the Gauls, *Galli,* which was clearly connected with such words as "Galliah ou Descouverture Divine," indicated their primary position in world history, and informed Charles de Guise that "prisci Hebraeorum characteres sunt Gallorum antiquissimae literae." See Dubois 1994, 139–177 (quotation at 168); and Simoncelli 1984, 89–94 (quotation at 90). Casaubon would presumably have viewed such theories with less sympathy.

124. Postel 1538a [E iiij verso]: "Dicet fortasse aliquis, me omnia ad Hebraismum torquere, requiretque, undenam tam multa nomina Iudaica potuerint in nostrum usum sermonis transire. Miretur ille potius cur tam pauca talia habeamus, quum ipsi Iudaei fuerint aliquando tanta frequentia et potentia apud Parisios, et in tota Gallia, et suis usuris olim Parisios ita divexarint, ut non tantum privata, sed et publica, sacraque ac prophana haberent oppignerata, quamobrem proscripti et expulsi fuere omnes a Philippo Augusto Gallorum rege, anno D. 1220. Illos denuo revocavit, aut quod melius est supplices recepit Philippus Pulcher rex, anno D. 1313. et non ita multum ante haec tempora sunt profligati. Commentariorum illorum multa monumenta testantur apud nos fuisse scripta, ob quamplurimas voces gallicas illic admixtas."

125. For Casaubon's summary of Postel, see Bod MS Casaubon 60, 280 verso: "Nec mirum in sermone Gallico vocabula quaedam Hebr. reperiri: cum constet olim Franciam Hebraeorum fuisse plenam. Legimus in Annal. Franc. aliquando suis usuris sic vexasse Judaeos populum Parisiensem, ut non solum privata, sed et publica, sacra profanaque oppignerata haberent omnia. donec Philippus Aug. rex Fr. anno 1220. Judaeos finibus Franciae expulit. Annis vero 85. circiter post, Philipp. Pulcher eos supplices recepit. Nec multae sunt γενεαὶ ex quo iterum pulsi sunt." On the French words to be found in rabbinical commentaries see Casaubon's note, probably quite early in his career as a Hebraist, on the title page of BL 1942.g.3: "Σηαι et Schelomo Jarhi et David Cimchi Galli fuerunt [added above line: vel Hispani . . .], paret et ex vocibus variis vernaculis quas apponunt ut Schelomo p. 114 Moisir. David p. 75. escume [both are noted on the appropriate pages]."

but as a detective. He wanted just the facts, and by adopting that attitude he revealed the gulf that yawned between his methods and the philology of Christian Kabbalah.

Biblical Exegesis

For the most part, Casaubon seems to have treated Hebrew texts with an expertise and reverence unexpected in one who has never been considered a "Christian Hebraist," and one who certainly did not share the mystical beliefs of Reuchlin and Heinrich Cornelius Agrippa about the mystical powers of the Hebrew letters.[126] As an ascetic Christian humanist who tried to combine his scholarly and devotional lives whenever possible, Casaubon made the close reading of the Hebrew Bible a pious exercise, and he kept scrupulous, minutely detailed records. In an important recent book, Max Engammare has traced the ways in which a guilty consciousness of time's rapid passing burned itself into the consciousness of many Genevan Calvinists.[127] Casaubon's magnificently precise diary entries give rich information about the fascinating, and sometimes unexpected, ways in which he read works in and about Hebrew.

Recovering from an illness in mid-April 1597, Casaubon made clear that he had begun his day, in the private upstairs study that was a special advantage of his position in Montpellier, with the Old Testament: "Since I felt a little better, I rose very early from the bedclothes and buried myself in my study and in my little literary pursuits. I began by falling on my knees, and gave myself over to reading and meditating on the holy Word of God." With impassioned eloquence he expressed his gratitude for that "truly swanlike song of David" which appeared in 1 Chronicles 29. "O pure honey! o true delight! o sweet food for the soul," he exclaimed.[128] But as Casaubon tried to make clear the larger lesson of his experience, the entry took a striking and distinctive turn. Christian scholars, he argued, should read the Bible in the same way as the classics, and even more intensively: "We read the writings of the pagans with great enthusiasm, and we eagerly gather and extract whatever we find there that is smoothly said and has to do with forming the character. And there is nothing wrong with that. But consider how much

---

126. Casaubon read Galatinus and Reuchlin in Paris on 11 June 1601. His diary entry reveals his lack of enthusiasm; see Casaubon 1850, I, 354 quoted in note 89 above. So do his very critical notes on Galatinus in Bod MS Casaubon 27, 200 recto–210 verso. By contrast, he rather enjoyed his encounter with Agrippa in the spring of 1603 (Casaubon 1850, I, 492–493), though his response was not uncritical.

127. Engammare 2004.

128. Casaubon 1850, I, 15: "Cum paullo haberem meliuscule, summo mane surgens e stratis abdo me in literulas et museum. Ac primum γονυπετήσας dedo me lectioni et meditationi sacrosancti Dei Verbi. Inter alia legi Canticum illud vere olorinum Davidis quod habetur 1. Chron. c. ult."

more richly we could furnish ourselves with texts like this drawn from the sacred books!"[129]

Casaubon, in other words, held that Christian scholars should read and make extracts from the Bible, exactly as they learned in school to do with the pagan classics, and that they should make the richest of the extracts in their notes the objects of passionate meditation—the comparison with Erasmus comes to mind. He made no bones about his conviction that the object of such study should be the Hebrew text of the Old Testament. Casaubon disapproved, for example, of ὑπομονή ("remaining behind," "power to endure"), the Septuagint rendering of the word מקוה (*mikveh*) in line 15 of David's poem (*Katsel yameinu al ha'arets veein mikveh*, 29:15; "our days on the earth [are] as a shadow, and [there is] no hope").[130] He consulted not only Junius' Latin version but also the commentaries of Rashi and David Kimhi, in an effort to bring out the full flavor of the Hebrew original's declaration that all life on this earth is transitory. Evidently, then, Casaubon saw not only reading of the Bible but also consultation of Jewish commentators as an integral part of his very Christian reading of the text. When he retreated to his study to heal his soul by plunging into the Old Testament, he did so with the *Mikra'ot gedolot*, the great variorum Bible with its sea of rabbinic commentary, open before him.[131]

Though never satisfied with his progress, Casaubon continued to read, excerpt, and internalize the Hebrew Bible—and to make clear that he read it, as he did the best of the ancient Greeks, as not only a source of sacred truths but also a model of eloquence. In late November and early December 1598, for example, he spent his early mornings reading that "golden little book," the Proverbs of Solomon.[132] He praised the "elegance," as well as the wisdom, of Proverbs, which he studied phrase by phrase, in Hebrew.[133] "Very early," he wrote on 1 December,

> before dawn, in my library, I read one chapter of Solomon's Proverbs. The whole book is golden, and deserves to be memorized. But

129. Ibid.: "O merum mel! o veras delicias! o dulce animae pabulum! Sed nonne praeposteri sumus nos qui literati cluimus? Legimus studiose paganorum scripta, et siquid ibi paullo rotundius invenimus dictum quod ad mores formandos faciat, id avide colligimus et decerpimus. Neque id male. Sed quanto uberiore cum fructu e libris divinis id genus documenta poterant parari: in queis cum omnia sint θεόπνευστα, etiam venustas et elegantia saepe mirabilis."

130. Casaubon 1850, I, 15–16. He does confuse the Hebrew letters in Kimhi's text, reading "cursores" as though the word חרוצים was spelled with *he* rather than *het*.

131. On more than one occasion Casaubon refers to the rabbinic Bible. E.g., in his copy of Mercier's *Libellus Ruth* (BL 1942.g.4, 12 verso) he refers to the marginal note in the first Venetian edition (1517): "ut et in marg. primae edit. Venetae notatur. ועבד ישי."

132. Casaubon 1850, I, 103–104.

133. Ibid., 104: "Eleganter significat Salomon quanto in periculo sint, qui animo elati sunt."

one verse [14:13: ‏גם בשחק יכאב לב ואחריתה שמחה תוגה‎]—"Even in laugh-
ter the heart may ache, and joy may end in grief"] pleased me very
much. I copy it here, not only so that I may memorize it more easily,
but also so that I may translate it into Greek as an enhancement to
my wisdom.[134]

In February 1599 Casaubon was beginning his day with Job 14, and this
text, too, he read as a classic in the best humanistic sense: "In that chapter,"
he remarked, "that wisest of men declares the vanity of mortals in lines that
are most profound and worthy of our meditation."[135] Once again he mea-
sured his understanding of the text against that of a great Jewish authority,
Maimonides, as he insisted that Job should be seen as a historical individual,
and a truly exemplary one:

Before the sermon I was, as long as possible, with Job and Mercier.
O sweet food for the soul! O Job, divine example of all the virtues!
For the opinion of Maimonides, in More Nebukim, that that book
contains not the narration of an event, but, so to speak, the image
and concept of a pious man, is entirely false. There is no doubt that
there was a Job, whom Ezekiel and the Apostles mentioned, and that
everything recorded in that book happened to him. I beseech you,
great God, as a suppliant, that reading this may bring me as much
utility as it does pious pleasure.[136]

By June 1600 Casaubon was spending all the time he could with Isaiah,
whose eloquence he characterized as unique. In July he noted that "this
prophet clearly uses many ornaments in his language that you would not
easily find in other sacred writers."[137]

134. Ibid., 105–106: "Mane πρὸ ἠοῦς in museo caput unum Salomonis Prov. legimus, quod cum sit
totum aureum, et dignissimum, ut caetera illius omnia, quod memoriae mandetur, eximie tamen hic
illius versus mihi placuit, quem hic ascribam, non solum ut tanto facilius eum addiscam; sed ut in Graecum vertam et τροφὴν καὶ αὔξησιν σοφίας."

135. Ibid., 162: "Eo capite vanitatem mortalium praedicat vir sapientissimus gravissimis et meditatione nostra dignissimis sententiis."

136. Ibid., 129–130: "Ante concionem cum Jobo et Mercero fui, quantum licuit. O dulce animi pabulum! O divinum virtutum omnium exemplum Jobum! Nam falsum omnino est quod R. Moseh Ben
Maimon in More Nebukim [3:22–23] putat eo libro contineri non rei gestae narrationem, sed velut
εἰκόνα et ideam aliquam viri pii. Non dubium est Jobum fuisse, cujus Ezechiel et Apostoli meminere,
eique omnia accidisse eo libro contenta. Quorum lectio ut non utilitatis mihi minus afferat, quam piae
voluptatis, supplex te, magne Deus, veneror."

137. Ibid., 285: "Hic propheta perspicue usurpat multa ornamenta orationis, quae in aliis scriptoribus
sacris temere non reperias."

Casaubon, in other words, treated the Hebrew text of the Bible exactly as he did the Latin and Greek texts of the classical authors. He read it in the light of the best commentaries, compared it to ancient and modern versions and commentaries, and made extracts from it which he committed to memory. In order to be sure that he made the Hebrew texts bone of his bone and marrow of his marrow, he resorted to the traditional methods of Western humanism: for example, copying them out, in the distinctively neat and elegant Hebrew script in which he clearly took some pride. Thus in February 1597 he noted that he was "mindful of the many times that Demosthenes, not without reason, copied all of Thucydides in his own hand" when he set out to "to copy one of the sacred Hebrew texts . . . that was the book of Esther."[138] A handsome partial copy of Esther (1:1–15) survives in Bodleian Library MS Casaubon 6—further confirmation, if any is needed, that Casaubon's professions of commitment to *Hebraica veritas* were anything but empty boasts.[139]

In fact the evidence suggests that Casaubon not only marked, but also mastered, the Hebrew Bible and the other Hebrew texts that meant so much to him. Hebrew liturgical words—especially the Hebrew אמן (Amen)—infiltrated the Latin in which he normally cast prayers in his diary. Over and over again, lines of biblical Hebrew received extensive glossing and exegesis in his notes. And the prevalence of Hebrew in this dense but partial record seems to have reflected the larger prevalence of Hebrew in Casaubon's mind.

He savored the literary force of the Bible as well as its divine truth, and brought to its reading the same discriminating hermeneutical sensibility that he brought to understanding the Greeks. When Casaubon read the prophets, for example, he warned himself to bear in mind the many types of prediction and message they had offered. Even as he considered the question why the prophets expressed themselves so obscurely—an ancient exegetical problem, and one that had a direct political bearing in Casaubon's time—he found the answer in the one Greek writer who had even mentioned the Old Testament, the critic known to him and his contemporaries as Longinus:

---

138. Ibid., 2: "Per id tempus die nempe eodem aut priore memores Demosthenem non sine caussa toties Thucydidem manu sua descripisisse librum unum e sacris literis Hebraicis describere cepimus. Is erat Estherae liber." The source for the anecdote about Demosthenes is Lucian, *Adv. indoctos* 4.

139. Bod MS Casaubon 6, 22 recto. Casaubon also copied out the complete book of Daniel and, as we have seen, Psalm 119. Another transcription from the Hebrew Bible is in BL MS Burney 365, 275 recto, where Casaubon copies out Psalm 86. Warm thanks to Malachi Beit-Arié for discussing these materials with us and suggesting that Casaubon may have copied these texts from manuscripts.

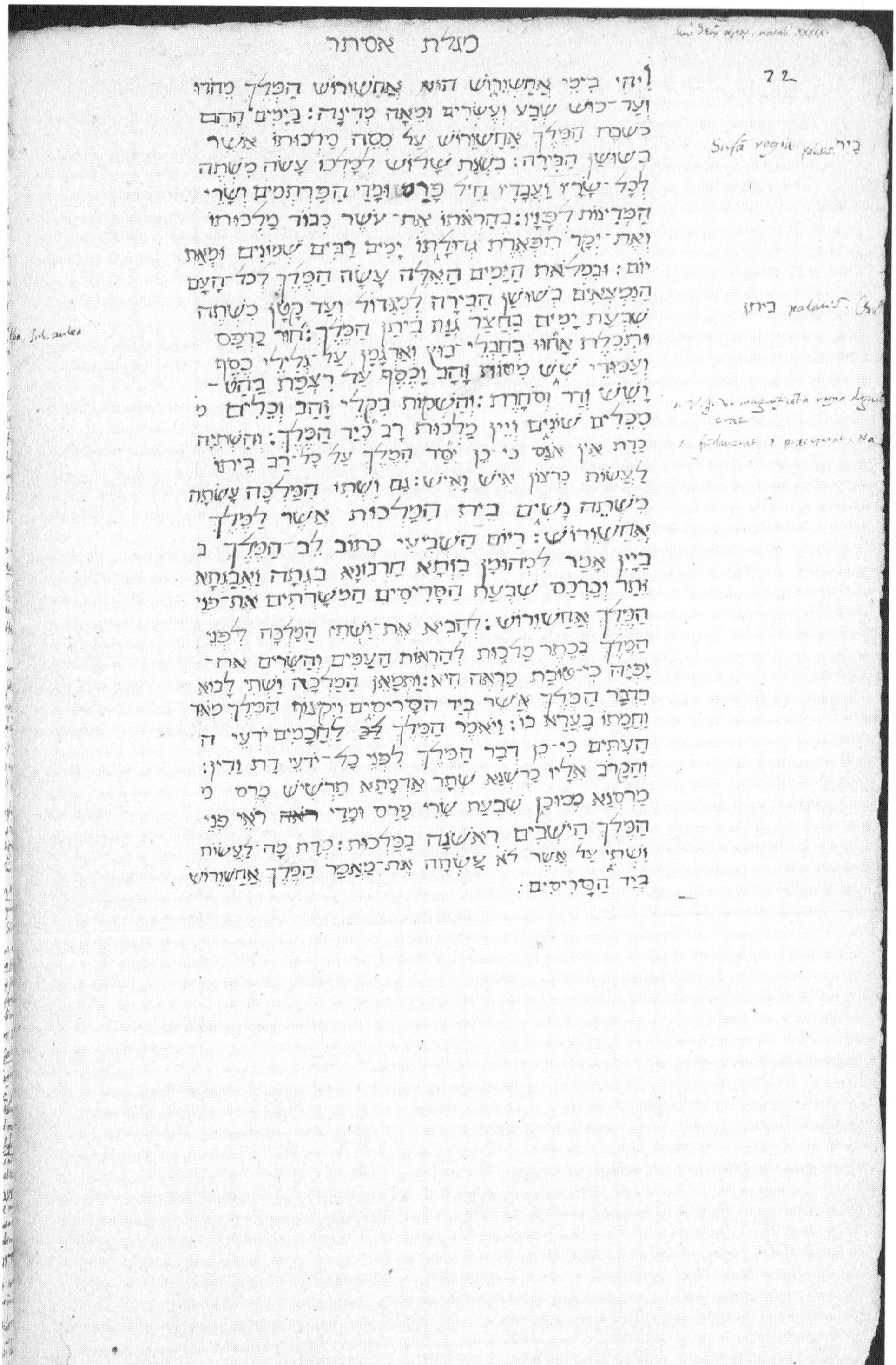

וַיְהִי בִּימֵי אֲחַשְׁוֵרוֹשׁ הוּא אֲחַשְׁוֵרוֹשׁ הַמֹּלֵךְ מֵהֹדּוּ
וְעַד־כּוּשׁ שֶׁבַע וְעֶשְׂרִים וּמֵאָה מְדִינָה: בַּיָּמִים הָהֵם
כְּשֶׁבֶת הַמֶּלֶךְ אֲחַשְׁוֵרוֹשׁ עַל כִּסֵּא מַלְכוּתוֹ אֲשֶׁר
בְּשׁוּשַׁן הַבִּירָה: בִּשְׁנַת שָׁלוֹשׁ לְמָלְכוֹ עָשָׂה מִשְׁתֶּה
לְכָל־שָׂרָיו וַעֲבָדָיו חֵיל פָּרַס וּמָדַי הַפַּרְתְּמִים וְשָׂרֵי
הַמְּדִינוֹת לְפָנָיו: בְּהַרְאֹתוֹ אֶת־עֹשֶׁר כְּבוֹד מַלְכוּתוֹ
וְאֶת־יְקָר תִּפְאֶרֶת גְּדוּלָּתוֹ יָמִים רַבִּים שְׁמוֹנִים וּמְאַת
יוֹם: וּבִמְלֹאת הַיָּמִים הָאֵלֶּה עָשָׂה הַמֶּלֶךְ לְכָל־הָעָם
הַנִּמְצְאִים בְּשׁוּשַׁן הַבִּירָה לְמִגָּדוֹל וְעַד־קָטָן מִשְׁתֶּה
שִׁבְעַת יָמִים בַּחֲצַר גִּנַּת בִּיתַן הַמֶּלֶךְ: חוּר כַּרְפַּס
וּתְכֵלֶת אָחוּז בְּחַבְלֵי־בוּץ וְאַרְגָּמָן עַל־גְּלִילֵי כֶסֶף
וְעַמּוּדֵי שֵׁשׁ מִטּוֹת זָהָב וָכֶסֶף עַל רִצְפַת בַּהַט
וָשֵׁשׁ וְדַר וְסֹחָרֶת: וְהַשְׁקוֹת בִּכְלֵי זָהָב וְכֵלִים מִכֵּלִים
כֵּלִים שׁוֹנִים וְיֵין מַלְכוּת רָב כְּיַד הַמֶּלֶךְ: וְהַשְׁתִיָּה
כַדָּת אֵין אֹנֵס כִּי־כֵן יִסַּד הַמֶּלֶךְ עַל כָּל־רַב בֵּיתוֹ
לַעֲשׂוֹת כִּרְצוֹן אִישׁ וָאִישׁ: גַּם וַשְׁתִּי הַמַּלְכָּה עָשְׂתָה
מִשְׁתֵּה נָשִׁים בֵּית הַמַּלְכוּת אֲשֶׁר לַמֶּלֶךְ
אֲחַשְׁוֵרוֹשׁ: בַּיּוֹם הַשְּׁבִיעִי כְּטוֹב לֵב־הַמֶּלֶךְ בּ
בַּיָּיִן אָמַר לִמְהוּמָן בִּזְּתָא חַרְבוֹנָא בִּגְתָא וַאֲבַגְתָא
זֵתַר וְכַרְכַּס שִׁבְעַת הַסָּרִיסִים הַמְשָׁרְתִים אֶת־פְּנֵי
הַמֶּלֶךְ אֲחַשְׁוֵרוֹשׁ: לְהָבִיא אֶת־וַשְׁתִּי הַמַּלְכָּה לִפְנֵי
הַמֶּלֶךְ בְּכֶתֶר מַלְכוּת לְהַרְאוֹת הָעַמִּים וְהַשָּׂרִים אֶת־
יָפְיָהּ כִּי־טוֹבַת מַרְאֶה הִיא: וַתְּמָאֵן הַמַּלְכָּה וַשְׁתִּי לָבוֹא
בִּדְבַר הַמֶּלֶךְ אֲשֶׁר בְּיַד הַסָּרִיסִים וַיִּקְצֹף הַמֶּלֶךְ מְאֹד
וַחֲמָתוֹ בָּעֲרָה בוֹ: וַיֹּאמֶר הַמֶּלֶךְ לַחֲכָמִים יֹדְעֵי הָ
הָעִתִּים כִּי־כֵן דְּבַר הַמֶּלֶךְ לִפְנֵי כָּל־יֹדְעֵי דָת וָדִין:
וְהַקָּרֹב אֵלָיו כַּרְשְׁנָא שֵׁתָר אַדְמָתָא תַּרְשִׁישׁ מֶרֶס מ
מַרְסְנָא מְמוּכָן שִׁבְעַת שָׂרֵי פָּרַס וּמָדַי רֹאֵי לְאֵי פְּנֵי
הַמֶּלֶךְ הַיֹּשְׁבִים רִאשֹׁנָה בַּמַּלְכוּת: כְּדָת מַה־לַּעֲשׂוֹת
וַשְׁתִּי עַל אֲשֶׁר לֹא עָשְׂתָה אֶת־מַאֲמַר הַמֶּלֶךְ אֲחַשְׁוֵרוֹשׁ
בְּיַד הַסָּרִיסִים:

FIGURE 2.10. Casaubon's transcription of the beginning of the book of Esther. Bodleian Library MS Casaubon 6, 72 recto.

No one who has ever even touched the writings of the prophets in passing has failed to notice their obscurity. The reasons for it are many. It is not for one of my low station to investigate the fundamental reasons why God wished them to speak in this manner. I am firmly convinced that God decided thus because it was best, and it is best because God decided thus. But certain intermediate causes of their obscurity can be noted. Some derive from their subject matter. The matters they deal with are lofty, sublime, and sometimes in the future, so that the prophets had to discuss them obscurely. Others have to do with their style, which is clearly the right one for their subject: a sublime style for sublime things. Whatever Longinus and the other theorists of rhetoric say about how one attains sublimity in speech will all be found, brilliantly expressed, in the writings of the prophets.[140]

Casaubon identified Isaiah as the prophet who most clearly exemplified the sublime style.[141] In a beautiful passage he analyzed the qualities of Isaiah 1: "There the eternal God pleads his case with insignificant mankind, with so much emotion that no greater indication of the divine goodness could be asked for. It is extraordinary that the immortal God deigns to come to court with men and dispute with them, as if on equal terms. That is the meaning of these words, לכו-נא ונוכחה 'come now, let us dispute.'"[142] He went on to list the figures of speech in Isaiah exactly as he might have listed those of a Greek or Latin text.[143] Indeed, Casaubon's heavily glossed copies of the texts and commentaries of Ruth and the minor prophets show him picking out

140. Bod MS Casaubon 51, 19 recto: "Obscuritas prophetarum. Nemo leviter prophetarum scripta attigit quin eorum obscuritatem animadverterit. huius rei multiplex est causa. Ac caussam quidem caussarum investigare cur Deus OPT. MAX. voluerit sic eos loqui non est tenuitatis nostrae: quibus persuasissimum est, ita Deo visum quia ita optimum: ita esse optimum quia sic Deo visum. Sed propiores huius obscuritatis causae multae possunt adnotari. aliae e rebus ipsis proficiscuntur: quae altae, sublimes, interdum etiam futurae: ut de iis non potuerint prophetae nisi obscure loqui. aliae sunt in ipso dicendi genere: quod sane rebus est accommodum, ὑψηλὸν ὑψηλαῖς. Itaque quicquid est apud Longinum et alios rhetoras quod τὸ ὕψος τῷ λόγῳ conciliet, id omne reperietur in prophetarum scriptis luculentissime expressum."

141. Ibid., 19 verso: "has igitur omnes sublimis styli caussas in prophetis posse animadverti maxime in Isaia, legenti planum erit. Quaedam adnotabamus inter legendum illum divinum prophetam."

142. Ibid., 21 recto: "τὸ σφοδρὸν καὶ ἐνθουσιαστικὸν πάθος. In affectibus istis regnant prophetae: sed ex omnibus hic maxime. quid gravius, quid ἐμπαθέστερον, quam totum primum caput? ibi Deus aeternus cum homunculis caussam agit, tanto q. cum affectu ut maior nulla bonitatis divinae significatio possit optari. nam quantum hoc quod Deus immortalis in iudicium venire cum hominibus, et velut ex aequo cum illis disceptare sustinet? Atqui hoc sibi illa praecipere volunt, לכו-נא ונוכחה venite iam, disceptemus. Quae paterna στοργὴ huic comparanda?"

143. Ibid., 24 recto, 28 recto ff.

the rhetorical tropes and the impressive sayings of the rabbis as much as their stupidities.

Casaubon's interests, as we have seen, were not limited to the Bible. Nor were they limited to the rabbinical commentators. His diary, for example, records his interest in the Hebrew text of Matthew: Bishop Jean du Tillet's Hebrew version with the Latin translation of Jean Mercier of the Gospel of Matthew, printed in Paris in 1555. According to Mercier, du Tillet extricated the text from the grip of Roman Jews. Casaubon vividly conveys the excitement that accompanied his reading of the text in an entry in his diary for September 1600: "Today, with great mental pleasure, I began to compare Matthew's Gospel with the Hebrew version edited by du Tillet. With God's help I hope to complete this little task in a few days."[144] The modern reader is unable to fathom Casaubon's state of soul as he set about his "little task," but his copy of the text housed in the British Library provides ample information about the intellectual rigor he employed in comparing the Hebrew and Greek texts. Virtually every verse is annotated: Hebrew printing errors are corrected, divergences from the Greek text are signaled, references to the versions of Tremellius and Münster and postbiblical expressions, such as 'alav hashalom (on him be peace) following a reference to Jeremiah the prophet, are glossed with an X in the margin. Clearly, Casaubon was reading the text with an open mind. His entire painstaking labor was motivated by the desire to come close to the authentic Gospel of Matthew.

At times, however, the revelations of much later Hebrew texts fired Casaubon with almost as much enthusiasm as the Bible itself, and in the same way. One case is especially curious. In 1605 Casaubon published a rich study of ancient satire, in which he gave, for the first time, the correct etymology of the term (usually derived, in the Renaissance, from "satyr"). In the second book of this work, he attacked the question whether satire was a form of true poetry. Plato defined poetry, he noted, as fiction, the invention of *fabulae*. But this was a mistake, if an understandable one, a generalization drawn from the dramatic poetry that Plato and his contemporaries knew best: "In those days poetry found its dominant use in theaters and contests. This sort of poetry consisted more or less in the composition of *fabulae*, tragic, satyric, and comic. That was the origin of the error that little by little possessed the minds of men, so that they spoke and thought about poetry as if it was only for theaters and contests."[145] Satire, with its obdurate connection to

144. Casaubon 1850, I, 300: "Hodie cepi magna cum animi voluptate Evangelium κατὰ Ματθαῖον conferre cum Hebraea versione a Tilio edita, cuius opellae finem paucis diebus visuros nos speramus, volente Domino."

145. Casaubon 1605b, 338: "Erat illis temporibus plurimus poeticae usus in theatris et agonibus: quod

real people and events, also seemed very far from Aristotle's definition, and his sharp contrast between poetry and history.[146]

Where then to look for a more commodious and accurate definition? Horace, Casaubon noted, saw the distinctiveness of poetry as formal, a matter of meter and style, though he too denied that satire could be poetry. And one contemporary, or near-contemporary, Jewish source revised this thought in a useful direction. David ibn Yahya had defined poetry in his work *Shekel haKodesh* of 1506, which was republished with translation as *De metris Hebraeorum* in Paris in 1562, while another Latin translation by Génébrard appeared in his *Eisagoge*.[147] Casaubon had a copy of this work, now preserved in the British Library, and in it he found a definition ("definitio carminis") of a noble utterance, its parts tightly connected, cast in מלות קצרות ערבות שקולות (brief, sweet, balanced words). Casaubon wrote two notes in the margin by this phrase, one noting the presence of a definition and the other that of "librata dictio," literally "balanced diction."[148] In his treatise on satire Casaubon made clear what he only indicated—probably to remind himself of the passage—in his skeletal marginalia. Ibn Yahya's "very beautiful definition," drawn from a Greek source, revealed, unlike those in the standard Greek texts, that poetry must be cast in words that are "short, sweet, and balanced or weighed"—words, that is, that follow a "lex metrica," or metrical rule.[149] By this definition, satire cast in metrical verse definitely

---

genus poeseos fabularum fere compositione constabat, tragicarum, satyricarum, comicarum. inde paulatim irrepsit in animos hominum hic error, ut de poetica sic loquerentur, sic sentirent, quasi aliam nullam agnoscerent, nisi theatralem et agonisticam."

146. Casaubon 1605b, 344–345.

147. The *Libellus de metris Hebraicis e grammatica R. Davidis Iehaiae cuius inscriptio limmudim G. Genebrardo professore regio interprete* is reproduced at pp. 149–162 of Génébrard's *Eisagoge* (Paris, 1587) (BL 622.h.32). Casaubon also glossed this text in a few places. Ibn Yahya's work on prosody, which was printed as part of his work on grammar, was as popular among Jews, particularly Sephardim, as it was among Christians. Three editions appeared in Constantinople. Génébrard appears to have used one of the later sixteenth-century editions.

148. [Ibn Yahya], *Libellus de metris Hebraeorum* (Paris, 1562), BL 1982.c.36, I2 recto; and Casaubon 1605b, 348–349. See esp. Casaubon 1605b, 349: "Vides in hac pulcherrima definitione multas desiderari condiciones ad iustum poema, quarum ultima est lex metri: siquidem שקל quae vox pondus et librationem significat, heic interpretemur de lege metrica."

149. Casaubon 1605b, 348–349. Casaubon did take this Jewish definition as deriving from a Greek source: "non memini usquam apud Graecos invenire definitionem hanc conceptis verbis expressam: sed in Iudaeorum commentationibus de re metrica eam definitionem offendimus, quam cum ipsi fateantur a Graecis se accepisse, pro Graeca huc afferre non verebimur: est enim appositissima ad Horatii mentem." In this respect he followed Génébrard, who noted that David ibn Yahya drew on Aristotle's works and suggested that he might have had access to Hebrew translations of other Greek philosophical texts (Génébrard 1564, 42–43): "Hic existimo citari primum librum Aristotelis de Demonstratione, ex quo intelligitur definitiones antegressas minime exactas esse, et habendas potius descriptionum nomine. Constant enim genere et partim communium, partim propriarum affectionum frequentia, non

belonged in the category of poetry. The assurance with which Casaubon cited his unnamed Hebrew source is breathtaking. He invoked a near contemporary Jew—whom he did not even cite by name—to refute all three of the authorities on which the vast edifice of sixteenth-century literary theory had been reared by Robortello, Vettori, Scaliger, and many others. In this case at least, Casaubon clearly accorded profundity and insight to a modern Hebrew source that dealt not with the Hebrew language or the Bible but with literature.

Moses Maimonides: Jewish Thought, Jewish Law

Like other Christians of the time, Casaubon often accused the old rabbis of speaking "nugae" and "fabulae" in their works. Like them, too, he did, as we will see, subject parts of the Talmud and its commentaries to a critical examination. But Casaubon, like the others, also revered "the incomparable Rabbenu Moses son of Maimon,"[150] although he did not always agree with him: "Moses Maimonides (who is also called Moses the Egyptian) was a man of solid and great learning. I can say of him what Pliny once said of Diodorus Siculus, 'He was the first of his people to desist from playing with words.'"[151] With this classical allusion for initiates Casaubon refers to the preface of the *Natural History*, in which Pliny praises Diodorus for having chosen an appropriate title for his work, thus eschewing the ridiculous habits of his predecessors.[152] The subtle point Casaubon is making is that even if his rabbinic predecessors were unreliable, Maimonides was a man of principle who could be trusted. And his appreciation of Maimonides extended also to the material text on which the immortal words of the master were

autem genere et differentiis, quales nec exactae sunt, nec demonstrationis principia sive media. Quia autem non nisi obiter hoc attingit libro illo priori Aristot. posteriore autem ex professo, fortasse ad alium philosophum (qui multi sunt lingua Hebraica) respexit noster Rabbinus. Nec vero mireris citari Aristotelem ab Hebraeis, cum praesertim illi ut studiosissimi sunt cuiuscunque partis philosophiae, ita et in suam linguam praecipuos philosophos, ut hunc, ut Platonem, ut Ptolomaeum, ut Galenum converterunt. Et certe in bibliotheca Regia extant praedicti philosophi Metaphysica, et Sphaera Ioannis Sacroboscii Hebraice."

150. Casaubon 1709, 231. In a 1605 letter to Scaliger, he refers to "incomparabilis Rabbenu Mosis Maimonis filii Moreh Nebukim."

151. Casaubon 1614, 611; 1654, 538; 1663, 538: "Moses Maimonides (qui et Moses Aegyptius dicitur) solidae atque ingentis doctrinae vir, de quo videor mihi posse id vere dicere, quod Plinius olim de Diodoro Siculo, primum illum inter suos desijsse nugari." The context of this passage will be discussed in Chapter 3.

152. Pliny the Elder, *Natural History*, preface, 25.

inscribed. "The title page is magnificent, in the Jewish manner," Casaubon exclaimed, on gazing at the Bomberg edition (Venice, 1524) of Maimonides' definitive *Code of Law,* the *Mishneh Torah,* also known as the *Yad.* This is but another expression of Casaubon's "voluptas," a term he often used when he wished to convey the almost sensual excitement he experienced upon reading certain texts. It was in London that he came across this particular edition of the *Yad.* He perused its contents carefully, noting the eulogistic tag about Maimonides, "from Moses to Moses there arose none like Moses," framed in the frieze's medallion at the top of the page, constructed in the form of a Roman triumphal arch.[153]

Aaron Katchen has argued that interest in Maimonides diverged in the course of the seventeenth century from a fascination with the *Guide for the Perplexed* to his legal writings, particularly the *Mishneh Torah.*[154] It is of course true that scholars did not produce large-scale Latin translations of the *Code* until the third decade of the seventeenth century—although Géné-brard did translate the *Code's* grand finale, Maimonides' vision of the messianic era, into Latin in 1572.[155] But it is also clear that Casaubon paid as much attention to Maimonides' legal as to his philosophical output, although he appears to have reserved the epithet "divine" for the *Guide.* After having admired the physical features of the Venetian *Yad,* Casaubon set about studying the *Code's* structure, writing out the titles of the books and their division into smaller units of *halakhot* (laws). In yet another notebook he copied out detailed notes from the Latin translation of the *Guide* produced by the Italian orientalist and Hebraist Agostino Giustiniani with the collaboration of the Jewish physician and translator Jacob Mantino.[156]

Casaubon had read and reread these works at different stages in his life. In his notes on the *Guide* he mentions that he had studied the *Yad* intensively as a young man in Geneva and Lyons.[157] From a letter of 1602, it appears that it was Scaliger who had enlightened him about the language

153. He writes out a detailed description of the work in Bod MS Casaubon 30, 82 recto–86 recto. At 82 recto he writes: "Percurrebam Londini librum Mosis ben Maimon Jad inscriptum. Liber editus est Venetiis cum superbo frontispicio more Hebraeorum. Initio est illud elogium, A Mose usque ad Mosem non surrexit ut Moses."

154. Katchen 1984, 4–5.

155. The "Capita R. Mose ben Maiemon de rebus Christi Regis" is printed with other texts in Géné-brard 1572, 46 recto–86 recto, in the Latin translation followed by the Hebrew. Génébrard, unusually, gives the page number, 763, of the text he was using.

156. Maimonides 1520; Casaubon's notes are in Bod MS Casaubon 4, 30 recto–34 verso.

157. Bod MS Casaubon 4, 30 recto: "Vidimus et nos eum librum et multa in eo legimus Genevae et Lugduni."

FIGURE 2.11. Title page of Maimonides' *Mishneh Torah*. Bodleian Library Opp. fol. 777.

(Judaeo-Arabic) in which the *Guide* was written.[158] Indeed, in his notes on the Latin version Casaubon expresses his regret that he did not have the "Hebrew" text in front of him, since "he was unable to grasp the point of the author in many places."[159] Nevertheless, as usual, he persisted, reading "this book of miscellaneous observations on sacred matters" to the end, indicating and signing off his notes with "thanks to God."[160]

Casaubon's reading of this classic of Jewish theology reveals his scholarly, no less than his theological, interests. Thus, intimately familiar with the entire corpus of Aristotle, genuine and inauthentic, this consummate scholar jots down Maimonides' praise of works of Aristotle that "in my opinion are not extant today."[161] As an antiquarian he is also patently interested in Maimonides' famous description of the Sabians—supposedly the patriarch Abraham's pagan contemporaries—a subject that would permeate seventeenth-century treatises on ancient religion.[162]

Casaubon appears to accept Giustiniani's statement, in the preface to his translation of the *Guide,* that the rabbis wished to obliterate Maimonides' writings because "he supported Christian dogmas," a reference to the burning of his works in the thirteenth century.[163] But his notes also seem to reveal an interest not so much in Maimonides' so-called Christian beliefs, but rather in the particular theology and exegesis of scripture that Maimonides was promoting, which on occasion could be used as a comment on contemporary ecclesiastical views. A "golden passage" is Casaubon's assessment of Maimonides' discourse on the limitation of human knowledge. This is ex-

158. Casaubon 1709, 138: "Didici ex literis tuis, opus Rambanii מורה נבוכים Arabice ab Autore fuisse scriptum: quod nos, cum Latinum interpretem ante multos menses legeremus, vel non observaveramus, vel non memineramus. Postea incidi in magni illius Magistri verba in epistola ad Massilienses, qua non obscure de se hoc ipse testatur. Puto enim חבור גדול, quod ait ibi se Arabice scripsisse, de opere illo esse intelligendum." This means that Casaubon must have taken the notes from the Latin version before 1602. He refers here to Maimonides' *Letter to Marseilles* on astrology, which had been published with a Latin translation by Joannes Isaac Levita in Cologne in 1555. Note, too, that he does not understand Maimonides' reference to the *Hibbur Gadol,* which is the *Mishneh Torah,* written in Hebrew not in Arabic. Cf., too, Bod MS Casaubon 52, 43 recto, in which he refers to Samuel ibn Tibbon's Hebrew translation of the *Guide for the Perplexed* in a rather hesitant way: "Samuel ben Tibbon. vidimus huius librum More hannebokim ex alia (puto arab.) lingua translatum et est si memini liber Mosis ben M."

159. Bod MS Casaubon 4, 30 recto: "Doluimus autem persaepe in percurrendo hoc libro, quod textum Hebraicum non haberemus; nam ita versus est ut mentem auctoris assequi multis locis non potuerimus."

160. Ibid., 30 recto–34 verso.

161. Ibid., 30 verso: "Saepe Moses laudat Aristotelem, etiam in ijs quae non extant opinor hodie."

162. Maimonides 1520, III.37.

163. Maimonides 1520, 1 verso: "factum est ut Iudaei omnes Galli . . . in unum conspirarint, librumque incendio devoverint quod sibi videretur nimirum favere Christianorum haeresi." Bod MS Casaubon 4, 30 recto: "Itaque scripta illius RR. conati sunt extinguere ut hominis qui faveret dogmati Christianorum." It is still not clear who were the main perpetrators of the auto-da-fé.

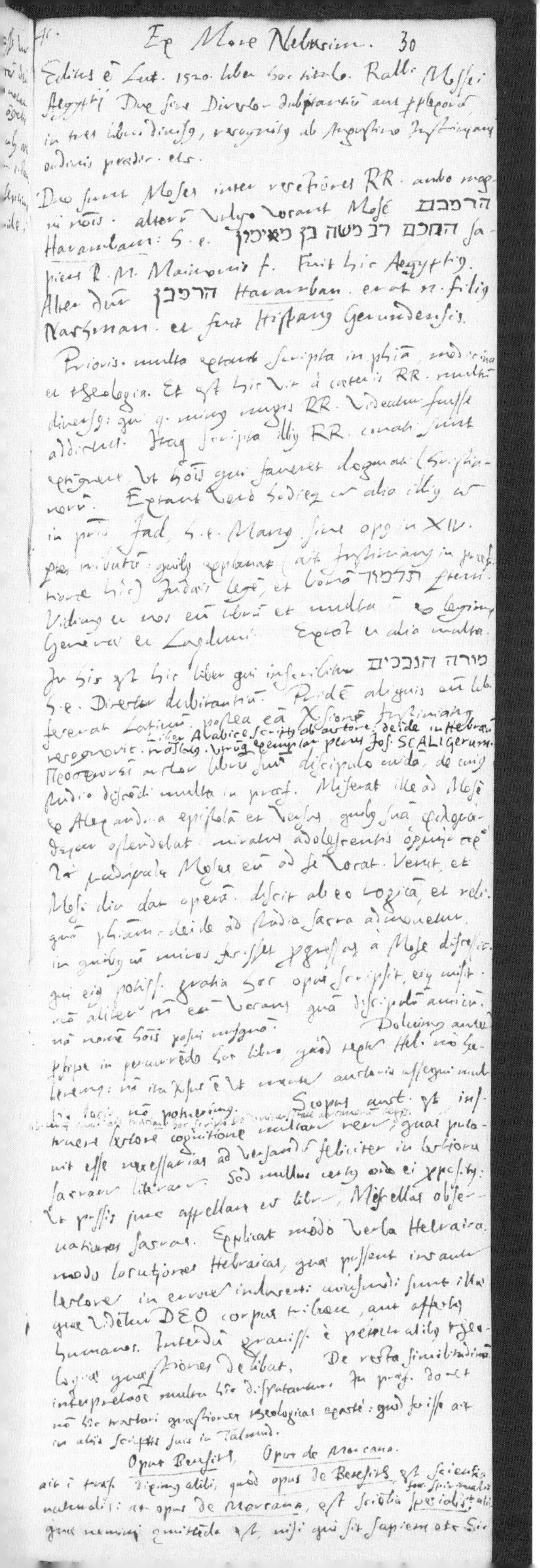

Editus ē Lut. 1520. liber hoc titulo. Rabbi Mose
Aegypti Duce sive Directio dubitantium aut perplexorum
in tres libros divisa, variaq[ue] ab Augustino Justiniano
audivis praedit. etc.

Duo fuere Moses inter veteriores RR. nullo magis
in usu. alteri Vulgo vorant Mose הרמבם
Harambam: s. e. החכם רב משה בן מאימון sa-
piens R. M. Maimonis f. Fuit hic Aegyptius.
Alter dr הרמבן Harambam. erat et filius
Nachman. et fuit Hispanus Gerundensis.

Prioris. multa extant scripta in philo medicina
et theologia. Et est hic vir á ceteris RR. multo
diversus qui quam magis magis RR. videatur fuisse
addictus. Itaq[ue] scripta illius RR. conatus sunt
ephigener[?] ut hos qui faveret dogmati (scriptu-
rani. Extant vero hodieq[ue] et alia illi ut
in prim[o] fad. h. e. Manus sive opus in XIV.
par[tes] in distr[?] quasi ephemas (aut justiniam in par[te]
hac) Judais legi, et totus תורה[?] fuerit.
Vicimus et nos ea libris et multa — so legim[?]
Geneva et Lugduni. Extat et alia multa.

In his est hic liber qui inscribitur מורה הנבכים
s. e. Director dubitantium. Pende aliquis ant lib.
fecerat Latinu[?] postea ea X[?]tione justiniam
recognovit. nostra vir[?] exemplar penes Jos. SCALIgerum.
 Προσφωνει autem librum suu[m] discipulo cuid[a]. de cuius
studio desiderio multa in praef. Miserat ille ad Mose
to Alexandra epistola et versus quib[us] sua philogra-
phiam ostendebat. miratus adolescentis opp[ortun]e[?]
Και [?] Mosen eu[m] ad de Torah. Venit et
Mose dit[?] dam opera. descit ab eo logica, et reliqua philam. deinde ad studia sacra animaverunt.
in quorum cum minus prosset progressus a Mose discessi[t].
qui eio potiss. gratia hoc opus scripsit. eiq[ue] misit
no alliter in ea vorans qua discipulo amico.
no nostra hos populi wspus[?] Dolumus autem
per p[?] in perun[?]redo hoc libro. quod sep[?] sept. Hel. no ha-
bereng. in maxp[?] e[?] ut exeun[?] auctoris assequi uulli[?]
po leg[?] no poticiong. Scopus aut. est inf-
[?]uere lectore cognitione medicani verus quas puto-
uit esse necessarias ad versands feliciter in lectione
sacrarum literarum. Sed multu[m] restat ut[?] ei ypocrit[?]
Et p[ass]is [?] appellant et liber. Misellas obse-
vationes sacras. Explicat modo verba Hebraica.
modo locutiones Hebraicas. qua possent in autho-
lectores in errores inducere. auisundi sunt illa
qua videtur DEO corpus tribuere. aut affectus
humanos. Interdu[m] grauiss. é priecu[m] abilib[us] theo-
logicis quaestiones delibat. De rest[a] simibiludini[?]
interpretose multa[m] h[?]o disputandum. In praef. docet
no hic tractari quaestiones theologias ephuse. quod fuisse ait
in alia scriptis suis in Talmud.

Opus Bereschit. Opus de Mercaua.
ait i[n] praef. dignq[ue] alib[?]i. quod opus de Bereschit, sit scientia
naturalis: et opus de Mercaua, est scientia [?]ophi[?]s[?]ti[?]aliud[?]
q[ua]e nemini q[u?]tenda est, nisi qui sit Sapiens etc Sc[?]

FIGURE 2.12. Notes by Casaubon on Maimonides' *Guide for the Perplexed*. Bodleian Library MS Casaubon 4, 30 recto.

emplified by the famous passage about Rabbi Akiva, who was able to delve into higher speculative matters without being harmed, unlike the apostate Elisha Aher.[164]

Maimonides' invective against popular conceptions of God, with its denunciation of anything that ascribes corporeality to God and that detracts from His essence, concentrating on mere accidents, brings to Casaubon's mind contemporary disputes. And he approves Maimonides' castigation of those who regard the mystery of the letters that constitute the name of God as residing solely in their pronunciation rather than in the meaning that underlies the letters.[165] "O let those who worship bread and divinize words read this," Casaubon exclaims.[166]

Indeed, Casaubon brought Maimonides to bear on a crucial matter that divided reformers from Catholics, the papal claim to apostolic succession through Jesus' conferral of supreme power on Peter: "You are Peter and upon this rock I will build my Church" (Matt. 16:18). The issue arises in the midst of his long and violent attack on Baronio.[167] What is at stake, of course, is the precise meaning of "rock," and in particular its significance in Isaiah 51:1: "Look unto the rock whence ye were hewn." From some illegible scribblings in a notebook that we can date to the time of Casaubon's stay in England, when he was struggling to produce his critique of Baronio, we know that Casaubon scanned all kinds of commentaries on Isaiah.[168] These included the work of Léon de Castro, the highly influential Spanish theologian and opponent of Arias Montano's Polyglot Bible.[169] Maimonides' interpretation of "rock" is given center stage on two occasions in this long dissertation. From this chapter all the definitions of the word are culled: "Rock is an equivocal term. It is a term denoting a mountain . . . It is further a term denoting the quarry from which quarry stones are hewn. Thus, 'Look unto the rock whence ye were hewn' [Isaiah 51:1]."[170] But of course the purpose of

164. Maimonides 1520, I.32 (misnumbered 31 by Giustiniani). Bod MS. Casaubon 4, 31 recto: "R. Aqiba et R. Telixa [the name is Elisha, but Casaubon reproduces what he found in Giustiniani's translation], locus aureus."

165. Maimonides 1520, I.62 (misnumbered 61 by Giustiniani).

166. Bod MS Casaubon 4, 32 recto: "O legant ista ἀρτολάτραι et οἱ τὰ ῥήματα θειάζοντες."

167. Casaubon 1614, 385–401; 1654, 321–366; 1663, 321–366.

168. See Bod MS Casaubon 30, 106 recto. Note the blank page at the beginning of Casaubon's copy of *Sefer Mikhlol* (BL 1984.a.10.[1]), where he lists names for God and adds: "vocatur vere Deus in bibliis et aliis nominibus, ut Deut. 32.4 צור rupis: idem et 31. et saepe." Here, too, Casaubon's preoccupation with the significance of the term "rock" in a theological context is apparent.

169. De Castro 1570.

170. Casaubon 1614, 400; 1654, 353; 1663, 353: "Sed hic titulus longe gloriosissimus, partim caeteris Apostolis communis, partim personaliter Petro est proprius; neque ad eius successores ullo pacto potest pertinere. Quare nihil hoc ad Papam; nihil ad controversias hodiernas. Scio etiam Abrahamum reperiri

Maimonides' minidiscourse on rock is to define not the rock's natural qualities, but rather its meaning in this biblical context when applied to Abraham. Casaubon refers to Maimonides' metaphorical interpretation: "Tread therefore in his footsteps, adhere to his religion and acquire his character," a kind of *imitatio Abrahami.*

At another strategic point in his argument Casaubon then takes up Maimonides' second main point, namely, that "God, may He be exalted, is designated as the Rock since He is the principal and efficient cause of all things other than himself." Noteworthy, here, is that this citation is not culled from Giustiniani's Latin translation, but from Ibn Tibbon's Hebrew translation: כי הוא התחלה והסבה הפועלת לכל אשר זולתו. The insertion at this juncture of the technical medieval Hebrew phrase—so different from the biblical or rabbinic idiom—drives the point home, and the metaphor must therefore win the day: "This metaphor is not meant to express domination, but to indicate the origin of things and the cause of their existence." Casaubon's argument is long-winded, and jam-packed with citations from a variety of sources. Nevertheless, it is patently clear that he invokes Maimonides as the authoritative interpreter of the Bible. His philosophical approach, which tolerates no corporeality, provided the requisite argument in order to vanquish the Catholic position.

---

in Biblijs dictum *petram*, ut dicitur hic Petrus ex istorum sententia. Isaiae LI,1 *Attendite ad petram, unde excisi estis: attendite ad Abrahamum patrem vestrum . . . petra* enim hoc loco nihil aliud significat, nisi originem. et mens Prophetae est; sicut excisus e petra lapis eiusdem est naturae cum rupe unde est excisus: sic vos componite vitam vestram ad exemplum Abrahami, et ut hunc locum explicans ait Maimonides in divino opere More Nebukim, libro 1. cap. xvi., לבו בדרכיו *ite per eius vias.*" Casaubon 1614, 406; 1654, 358–359; 1663, 358–359: "In veteri Testamento Deus locis pene innumeris dicitur צור *Tzur.* quam vocem Graeci interpretes modo vertunt ὄρος, *montem*, modo πέτραν, *petram* aut *rupem.* Moses ben Maimon in More Nebukim, admirandae doctrinae scripto, libro primo, capite XVI. observat, hac voce significari montem vel arcem in rupe sitam; item silicem durum; necnon מקור lapidicinam, unde oriuntur venae lapicidinarum, ut appellat Ulpianus leg. XIII. §. 5. Dig. De usufructu. alibi in libris Iuris vocantur *venae saxorum.* Deum vero appellari *Tzur Petram* כי הוא התחלה והסבה הפועלת לכל אשר זולתו *quia ipse est principium et caussa, per quam facta sunt omnia praeter ipsum.* Non dicit Maimonides, Deum appellari *petram* quia dominetur omnibus rebus creatis; nam etsi verum est, Deum immortalem rerum omnium creatarum dominum esse et absolutissimum Monarcham: haec tamen metaphora non adhibetur ad exprimendam dominationem, sed ad indicandam originem rerum et caussam existentiae: robur etiam significat, ac potentiam et aeternam durationem; denique *Petra* cum metaphorice de Deo dicitur, habito respectu ad naturam et proprietatem verae rupis aut saxi alicuius durissimi, ad significationem nominis Tetragrammati proxime accedit: quod nomen aeternum et perpetuum Dei esse quum designet צור sive *petra*, durationem notat, quae est continuatio τοῦ εἶναι et caussam existendi in creaturas collatam." Casaubon 1614, 407; 1654, 359; 1663, 359: "Haec metonymica appellatio tribuitur Christo Ecclesiae auctori et conservatori, non propter imperium, quod jure obtinet in Ecclesiam: sed ut sciant fideles, inconcussae firmitudinis et durationis aeternae opus esse Ecclesiam, quae fundamento nitatur Petra Christo."

Casaubon did not master the entire corpus of Maimonides' writings, but certainly dipped into a good representative section of the Egyptian Jew's oeuvre. Maimonides articulated the first set of Jewish beliefs known as the "thirteen principles of faith" in the context of his Mishnah commentary on tractate Sanhedrin 10, which begins "All Israel have a share in the world to come." Several centuries later, despite some opposition to the idea of a Jewish creed, and criticism of Maimonides' choice of fundamental beliefs, the thirteen principles *(ikkarim)* became integrated into the Jewish prayerbook. Sebastian Münster translated the principles into Latin (Basel, 1529). This text in turn provided Casaubon with an essential theology of the Jews. According to a note in one of his copybooks he leafed through the work in a moment of God-given leisure. "It contains," he wrote, "as it were [*velut*], the articles of faith on which the religion of the Jews rests."[171] The word "velut" here is well chosen, for it seems to suggest, and quite reasonably, that Casaubon realized that the idea of "articles of faith," the term used by Münster in his preface and by Buxtorf, was somewhat alien to the Jewish religion.[172] Following his usual mode of reading and despite the hasty perusal of the thirteen principles, Casaubon corrected Münster's wrong translation of the philosophical term *sekhel hapoel*, again demonstrating that by 1604 he had mastered some of the basic philosophical terms of medieval Hebrew.[173]

As he reads these principles, the Christian Casaubon comes to the fore. He comments on the Jews' ignorance of "our lord Jesus."[174] Maimonides' declaration of the immutability of the Torah provokes a sharp reaction: "But this is partly false, for the law of grace has partly obliterated the Mosaic law."[175] Similarly, he rejects Maimonides' brief statement on the resurrection of the dead and the implication drawn from other passages that only the

---

171. Bod MS Casaubon 30, 108 recto: "Editus est a Munstero anno 1529. liber continens Mosis ben Maimon libellum . . . Is liber continet velut fidei articulos, quibus tota Judaeorum religio innititur . . . Eum libellum percurrebamus otia faciente Deo, et haec raptim excerpebamus."

172. He refers to Buxtorf's *Synagoga*, which begins with a description of the "articulos tredecim" (Buxtorf 1604, 2–32). In his copy of the *Synagoga* (BL 848.b.19) Casaubon has firmly underlined the words "Fides autem Iudaeorum." The reference to Buxtorf indicates that Casaubon was reading Münster's version after 1604.

173. Bod MS Casaubon 30, 109 recto. Münster had rendered the term used by Maimonides in the sixth principle about prophecy as "intellectus creatoris." Casaubon realized that Maimonides was speaking of the agent intellect *(intellectus agens).*

174. Ibid., 109 verso. With regard to principle 8 Maimonides speaks about going in the footsteps of the Messiah, God of Jacob. Casaubon writes: "Quem obsecro hic vocat Messiam sive Christum? Nam de domino nostro IESU non cogitabat Iudaeus."

175. Ibid., 110 recto: "sed hoc ex parte falsum. nam lex gratiae sustulit ex parte Mosaicam [legem]. sed hoc Iudaeus ignorat."

righteous will be resurrected. Casaubon refers to David Kimhi's interpretation of Psalm 1: "the soul of the wicked will be cut off and perish."[176] Thus, this set of notes reveals another facet of the way Casaubon deciphered Hebrew texts. There is no praise of Maimonides here, but instead a critical assessment of the principles predicated on his own set of beliefs.

The Jewish legal texts served as a quarry for both Baronio and Casaubon as they fought to demonstrate their expertise in Jewish antiquities. For Casaubon, Maimonides' *Code* was a useful point of reference for all manner of subjects. After all, the *Mishneh Torah* was, in effect, the first comprehensive code of Jewish Law. Indeed, the seventeen references to Maimonides' *Code* in his *Exercitationes* are eloquent testimony to the estimation in which Casaubon held the Egyptian Moses.

The historically critical mode of reading that Casaubon applied in his study of the classical literature was equally in play as he read the Hebrew texts or discussed matters of Jewish antiquity. Naturally, Casaubon used Maimonides' work in conjunction with other relevant texts. His wide reading therefore enabled him to select the frozen legal pronouncement from the page and set it in a wider historical context.

The example that best illustrates this occurs, once again, in his critique of Baronio's treatment of the sects of the Second Temple period. The argument centers upon Baronio's misinterpretation of a passage in the fourth and oft-cited letter of Synesius, the fourth-century bishop of Ptolemais.[177] Baronio identifies a Dosithean, a member of a Samaritan sect, in a passage about sabbath observance. This provides the starting point for Casaubon's discussion of sabbath observance in antiquity.[178] The strange story contains a passage about a mixed group of people, including Jews, traveling on a ship on a Friday night. The helmsman and "doctor of the Law," to the despair of those on board, refuses to steer the ship once the sabbath has begun, but at midnight he decides to profane the sabbath rather than risk his life. The aim of Casaubon's attack is to alert the reader not only to Baronio's ignorance of Greek but also to his lack of information about the diversity of Jewish sabbath observance. Casaubon traces the change in sabbath law implemented by Mattathias the Maccabee in the second century B.C.E., in response to the loss of life that resulted from the putting down of arms for the sake of observing the sabbath. This enactment was enforced by the rabbis, and the

176. Casaubon seems to have taken the reference to Kimhi from Buxtorf (1604, 27), who quotes Kimhi's interpretation that both the soul and body of the wicked will perish simultaneously.

177. Baronio 1593–1607, I, 6.

178. Synesius of Cyrene 2000, II, 11. In his own copy of the text, BL 692.f.6.(1), 4, Casaubon writes in the margin: "No. Quando liceat violare sabbatum."

new law is pithily expressed in the dictum quoted by Casaubon, "imminent risk to life takes precedence over the sabbath."[179] Casaubon expresses surprise that Josephus had given the mistaken impression that the law against lighting fires on the sabbath was practiced by Essenes alone. Any examination of Maimonides' codification of the laws on the sabbath clearly demonstrated that this law pertained to all Jews. This was one of the laws that Casaubon copied out in his London notebook.[180]

What emerges is Casaubon's ability to select the passages demonstrating the complexity of an issue that Baronio had treated too cavalierly for his precise mind. Casaubon realizes that the law codified by Maimonides is the official rabbinic statement on the subject. At the same time he is also aware —and not simply because of the way the subject is treated in the Gospels— that people do not necessarily keep to prescribed rules. This realization is illustrated by his citation of a story by the thirteenth-century English chronicler Matthew Paris, not known for his philosemitism.[181] According to his tale, the Jews of Tewkesbury allowed a coreligionist to die when he fell into a latrine on the sabbath, since he refused to let them pull him out until the next day.[182] Alluding to a similar story recounted by Münster in his commentary on Matthew 14, Casaubon concludes that the Jews, flagrantly disobeying Mattathias' decree, not infrequently prefer the letter of the law and death.[183]

From Casaubon's time to the present, some readers have found his *Exercitationes* tedious. Yet a careful examination of his meticulous disquisitions reveals how carefully he read and how cleverly he made connections. In this partial analysis of his attack on Baronio for his misinterpretation of Synesius, we see that Casaubon, by means of a thoughtful reading of Maimonides in his rabbinic legal context, arrives at an impressive understanding of the workings of Jewish law. In this case, his historical acumen does not extend to applying a more critical approach to Matthew Paris. But the ability to see the inconsistencies of life does manifest itself in another context. Casaubon

179. Casaubon 1614, 66; 1654, 61; 1663, 61: "Nam in universum pronuntiant Rabbini, omne periculum praesens vitae amittendae, impellere sabbatum."

180. Bod MS Casaubon 30, 106 verso: "De sabbato, cap. II. habes de periculo animae et de impellentibus sabbatum, p. 78."

181. Paris 1589, 953.

182. Casaubon 1614, 67; 1654, 62; 1663, 62: "Ex hac disciplina illud evenit, ut spreto Matthiae decreto, Iudaei non raro oppetere mortem praeoptarint, quam ad opus digitum exercere. Matthaeus Paris in anno MCCLX: *Eodem tempore apud Theocesbery quidam Iudaeus cecidit in latrinam; sed quia tunc erat sabbatum, non permisit se extrahi, nisi sequente die Dominica, propter reverentiam sui sabbati. quamobrem Iudaeum mori contigit in foetore.*"

183. Casaubon 1587, 215.

owned a copy of Münster's abbreviated edition of Moses of Coucy's volume of positive and negative precepts in Hebrew and Latin.[184] The negative commandment 227 prohibited Jews from returning to live in Egypt. The compiler of the compendium had raised the question why, in that case, Moses ben Maimon had lived in Egypt. Casaubon simply glosses "Maimon in Aegypto."[185] Is Casaubon's deliberate reference to Maimonides then an underhand jibe, a reflection that the great rabbi had transgressed his own negative commandment by making the accursed Egypt his final permanent abode?

184. BL ORB30/5652.

185. Ibid., d4 recto: "Prohibuit deus ne Iudaei revertantur in Aegyptum. Deut. 17. Quod intelligendum est de habitatione non mercantia. Mirum igitur est cur sapientissimus ille Moses filius Maimon habitarit in Aegypto." Casaubon glosses this: "Maimon in Aegypto." On the Latin title page he writes: "Praec. negat 227 Mose. Maimon. in Aeg. habit." In Maimonides' own *Book of Commandments,* the prohibition is listed as number 47. Casaubon also read the Hebrew section, as his interlinear translations demonstrate.

THREE

Wider Horizons in Hebraic Studies

Jews have used many languages over the centuries, from Aramaic and Greek to Yiddish. And many non-Jews, from Alexander Polyhistor in the first century B.C.E. to Johannes Reuchlin in the sixteenth century C.E., have done their best to understand and describe Jewish beliefs and customs. Like all Christians who took a serious interest in Jews and their world, Casaubon followed his passion into languages and forms of scholarship that most of his Jewish contemporaries would have found unfamiliar or even repellent— and, unlike many of them, he maintained an independent, critical attitude as he read. More remarkably still, he also did his best—though with less success—to use one of the most original works of sixteenth-century Jewish scholarship.

Reading a Jewish Text in Greek

At some point after 1603, Casaubon sat down to read a Jewish text, this one written in Greek.[1] He entered his notes not in a copy of the book but in a notebook. As he often did when making formal notes on his reading in his diary or one of his copybooks, he described with striking formality and precision the work he was reading, the progress he made in working through it, and his own response to it.[2] The text that had caught Casaubon's eye was

---

1. The notes in question appear in Bod MS Casaubon 60, 247 recto–253 recto. They are headed "Ex Aristea" and end θεῷ χάρις. A *terminus post quem* is provided by Casaubon's references to his own edition of the *Scriptores historiae Augustae,* which appeared in 1603. See esp. 248 recto: "Quid sit alibi declaramus in Capitol. p. 421"; cf. 251 recto: "Talia exempla multa in Athenaeo et historia Augusta."

2. Good parallels, in format and method, to these notes appear in Bod MS Casaubon 25, e.g., 84 recto: "σὺν Θεῷ. Sollicitus de uxore et liberis, rebusque omnibus meis, dum hic sum Dunamiae ad Eliam, quod superest temporis a sermonibus cum reverendissimo Praesule D. Episcopo Eliensi, et ab aliis huc subinde adventantibus, in lectione librorum pono, et a sensu gravissimae curae animum ᾗ δύναμαί γε avoco. Inter alios libros quos hic sum nactus, fuit Chronologia Ecclesiastica Onuphrii, sed

---

cast in the form of a letter from Aristeas, a courtier of the Alexandrian king Ptolemy II Philadelphus, to his brother Philocrates. Probably written in the second century B.C.E., it explains that Ptolemy's librarian, Demetrius of Phalerum, had convinced him to have a new translation of the Hebrew Bible made (1–40). Aristeas then offers a long narrative of his subsequent mission to Eleazar, the high priest in Jerusalem, which he describes at length and in utopian terms (83–106). In the course of the visit Eleazar gives the philosophical rationale for Jewish law (128–171) and supplies seventy-two experts, six from each of the twelve tribes, to translate the Bible (46–50). On their arrival in Alexandria the king invites them immediately to meet him, violating the custom of the court (174–175) and interrogates them at philosophical banquets that stretch over seven days (187–294). Then he settles them on the island of Pharos, where they produce their translation in seventy-two days (301–307). The text may contain a kernel of historical fact: it is at least possible that Ptolemy Philadelphus commissioned or acquired one of the Greek translations of the Bible. But it is full of legendary material clearly elaborated—like the repetition of the number 72, and the question-and-answer format of the discussions with the king—from the Bible and Jewish ritual and tradition.³

Even the heading of Casaubon's notes shows his desire for precision. Usually in his notebooks he named only the author from whom he drew extracts. Here he wrote: "A book in Greek and Latin was published by the firm of Oporinus, edited by Matthias Garbitius, with the title: 'Aristeas on the

---

versa e Lat. sermone in Italicum . . . In ea Chr. Onufrius id potissimum profitetur, seriem paparum et Impp. ostendere et praecipuas historias adnotare, quae pertinent ad rem Ecclesiasticam"; 105 recto: "Quum per summam imprudentiam nullos domo libros praeter unum aut alterum attulissem coactus sum aliunde petere. Legi igitur οὐδὲν ἐκ προαιρέσεως fere sed casu oblatos libros"; 114 recto: "Quum essem Doninchtoni et Witsbici nullus alius fere liber ad manum esset, legi obiter quaedam in Eunapio Gr."; 121 verso: "σὺν Θεῷ Camerarii epistolae. Rusticanti mihi in hoc secessu et libris plane destituto, missa [MS missae] sunt Cantabrigia cum superiore vita a Camerario scripta [Camerarius' life of Melanchthon, which he annotates 116 recto–121 recto], etiam duo parva volumina Epistolarum illius, quas filii post mortem patris publicarunt. Legi ig. utrunque volumen. nec paenitet operae, neque temporis, quod brevissimum ei lectioni impendimus." For a similar approach to reading a text in Hebrew, see the start of Casaubon's notes on Münster's edition of Josippon, Bod MS Casaubon 27, 169 recto: "Vertere coeperam Genavae Hebraeum Josephum in Lat. sermonem: cum in secundo libro versarer, cognovi Munsterum totum opus pridem fecisse Latinum. Destiti ig. avide cupiens Munsteri editionem nancisci. Ad Lutetiam tandem voti mei compos factus, ubi primum otii aliquantum sumus nacti in praetorio Geruiliano magni Praesidis Thuani, eum librum ἐς πόδας ἐκ κεφαλῆς suscepimus percurrendum: quod tamen maiore cum fructu facturi eramus, si ad manum fuissent nostrae in hoc genere lucubrationes neglectae nobis ab aliquot annis. Liber editus est Basileae apud Henricum Petrum anno 1541. continet praefat. Munsteri de qua mox, et Josephum Hebraice ac Latine."

3. See Wasserstein and Wasserstein 2006; Rajak 2009.

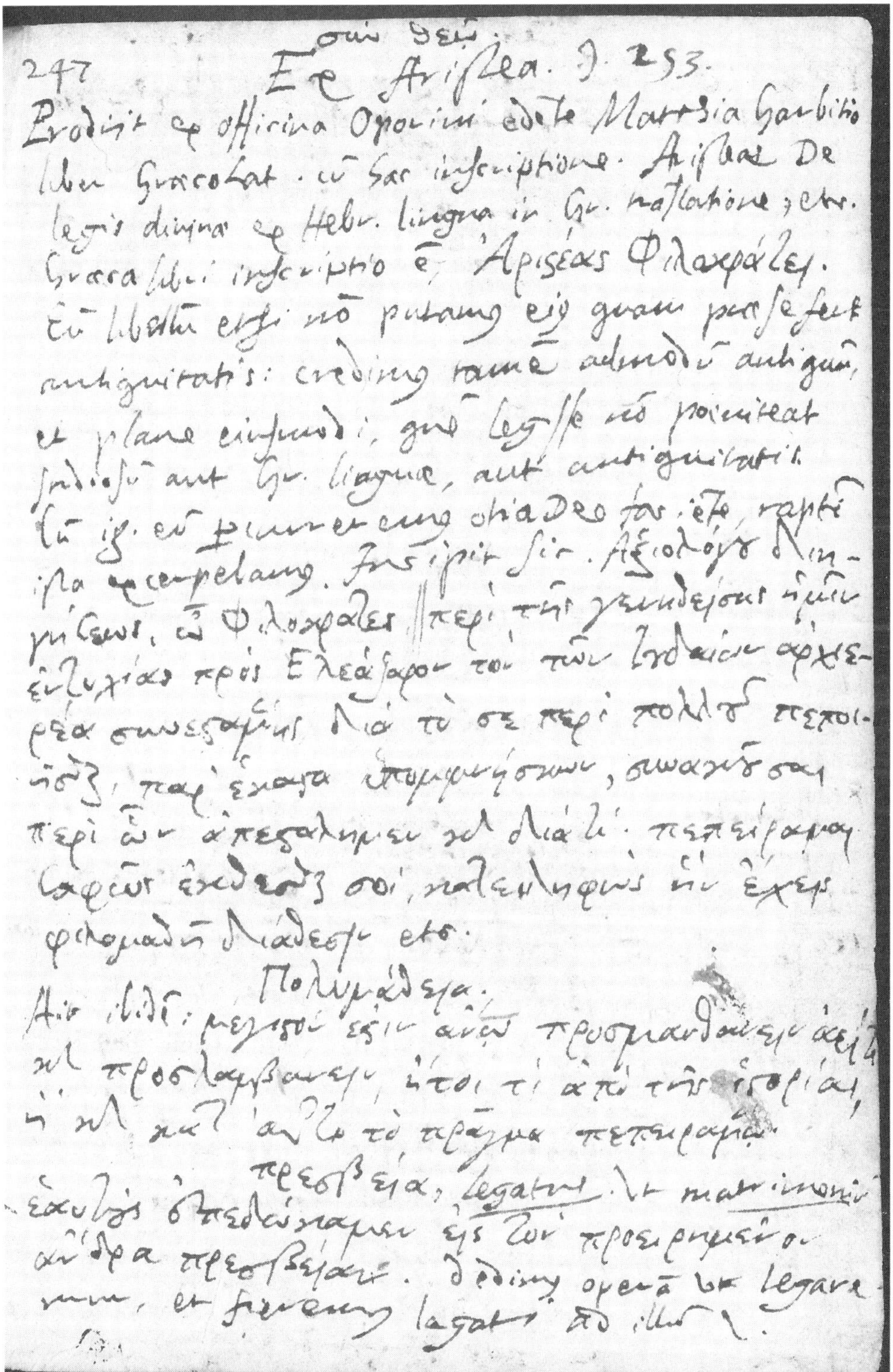

FIGURE 3.1. Beginning of Casaubon's notes on the letter of Aristeas. Bodleian Library MS Casaubon 60, 247 recto.

translation of the divine Law from the Hebrew language into Greek.'"[4] Casaubon took care, in other words, to indicate that he had used the first edition of the Greek text, which—as he failed to mention—had appeared in 1561. He also noted the book's epistolary form, which the Latin title, *Historia,* concealed: "The Greek title of the book is 'Aristeas to Philocrates.'"[5] And he seems to have made the notes as he read the book, working page by page, much as he would have done had he been entering marginal annotations. Inspection of the first page of his notes indicates that Casaubon wrote these pages continuously and at the same time. True, the last sentence of his heading, which is cast in the imperfect, suggests that he might have copied them from an earlier source—a rough draft, for example, or his own marginal notes: "While going through the book when God provided us with free time, we made the following notes in haste."[6] But later notes seem to record the observations of someone reading a text for the first time, as when Casaubon repeatedly writes "ait" (he says). More revealing still are the notes describing what he is about to write. "To clarify this problem," he comments at one point, "we will copy out the passage of Aristeas." At another point, where Garbitius' translation did not match the Greek of his printed text, Casaubon explains: "I have therefore added his [Latin] words." Both notes offer clear evidence that he was thinking his way through the text as he read the 1561 edition, and recording—for his own use or posterity's—his deliberate decisions about which bits to transcribe.[7] Casaubon's passage through this text, then, was highly formal and self-conscious: not a meditation on its meaning, much less an appreciation of its beauty, but a strictly rational and philological effort to note its most historically significant contents and draw out their implications.

It seems clear, moreover, that Casaubon read the letter in his own study. When he drew parallels between Aristeas' usage of terms and that of other ancient texts that he had edited—the geography of Strabo and the *Scriptores historiae Augustae*—he noted the exact page numbers at which the parallels

---

4. Bod MS Casaubon 60, 247 recto: "Prodiit ex officina Oporini edente Matthia Garbitio liber GraecoLat. cum hac inscriptione. Aristeas De legis divinae ex Hebr. lingua in Gr. translatione, etc."

5. Ibid.: "Graeca libri inscriptio est Ἀριστέας Φιλοκράτει." The title page of the edition reads: *Aristeae, de legis divinae ex hebraica lingua in graecam translatione, per septuaginta interpretes, Ptolemaei Philadelphi Aegyptiorum Regis studio ac liberalitate Hierosolyma accersitos, absoluta, Historia nunc primum Graece edita. In qua, praeter multa alia lectu dignissima, et pii Regis imago, et regni optime constituti forma ad unguem expressa demonstratur,* ed. Simon Schard (Basel, 1561).

6. Bod MS Casaubon 60, 247 recto: "Cum igitur eum percurreremus otia Deo faciente, raptim ista excerpebamus."

7. Ibid., 248 recto: "Sed ad illustrationem illius quaestionis describemus locum Aristeae"; 251 verso: "ideo subieci eius verba."

appeared.[8] Providing exact page numbers would have constituted a point-less display of the art of memory if Casaubon had worked without mak-ing reference to the originals. In fact, as he read he presumably consulted his hand-annotated copies of his own editions—works well supplied with printed indices, and which he normally adorned with a fresh coat of margi-nalia, marking his passage through them, as soon as he received them from their publishers.

How then did Casaubon approach the text? In the first instance, with the caution of a herpetologist sneaking up on a cobra. A master critic, he knew that he must assess the genuineness of any text before he relied on it for in-formation. In 1603, for example, he had made clear to readers of the *Scrip-tores historiae Augustae* that these accounts of the lives and quirks of Roman emperors were not, as they stood, the work of individual writers named Ae-lius Spartianus, Aelius Lampridius, Iulius Capitolinus, and so on. Otherwise one would have to accept that all three men had not only begun to write lives of all the Roman emperors, in the same style, at the same time, but also that all of them had come to the end of their enterprises at the same time. In fact some perverse and talented individual had reconfigured the work of a number of writers into a corpus for motives that Casaubon—like most scholars since his time—found indecipherable: "Only a prophet could di-vine what moved the maker of this collection to arrange it in this form."[9] Long before Casaubon set out to read the Greek version of Aristeas, he must have been familiar both with the stories that it told and with the fact that many Protestant scholars dismissed these as pious frauds. In 1605, more-over, his close friend Joseph Scaliger sent him a long letter on forgeries. Scaliger noted such pagan fakes as the Latin accounts of the Trojan War by Dictys of Crete and Dares of Phrygia, and such Christian ones as the "pseudo-Sibylline oracles." And he pointed out with particular venom that the letter of Aristeas, a text old enough that Josephus cited it, was "a false-hood of the Hellenistic Jews."[10] As we will see, Scaliger elaborated on this point in his *Thesaurus temporum,* which appeared in 1606, and a copy of which he sent to Casaubon.

Casaubon's first substantive note on the text suggests that Scaliger's com-ments may well have stimulated him to read the work. Using terms that he

---

8. Ibid., 247 verso: "frequenter utitur, eo sensu quo Strabo n. ed. p. 12"; 248 recto: "Quid sit alibi de-claramus in Capitol. p. 421."

9. Grafton 1991, 147–148, 290.

10. Scaliger 1627, 303: "Quid Aristaeas ille, quam antiquus est, ut etiam a Iosepho citetur? quod est τῶν ἑλληνιστῶν Ἰουδαίων παρεγχείρημα. Quid Ecataeus de Iudaeis, quem ab iisdem Hellenistis an-tiquitus confictum fuisse, manifesto ex Origene colligitur?"

often applied when he recorded reading a work that might seem contentious or of uncertain value, he strikes a properly critical, hesitant note.[11] Yet he also argues from the start that the book cannot simply be classed as a fake to be tossed away: "Though we do not consider this little book to be as old as it pretends to be, we nonetheless believe that it is quite old, and clearly the sort of text that no student of the Greek language or of antiquity must be ashamed to have read."[12] By the time Casaubon had finished reading, moreover, he had convinced himself that his early doubts were unjustified. In the last sentence of his letter, Aristeas tells his brother: "I shall also try to record the rest of the things that are worthy of mention" (322). "At the end," Casaubon reflects, "he promises another text . . . If this was written, I wish we had it. For the author is very old, and I do not doubt that he is the one mentioned by Josephus [*Jewish Antiquities* 12.11–118, esp. 100] . . . Therefore he is the very one who was present at the events that are recorded here."[13]

True, one point still worried Casaubon. At 182 Aristeas sets out to describe the measures taken to give the Jewish visitors to Alexandria their proper places at table. "For this," he writes, "was how it was arranged by the king, which you can see even now"—a clear statement that his embassy to the Jews and the ensuing translation had taken place long before, though elsewhere in the text he described both as recent. "He seems," Casaubon mused, "to hint that this book was written long after those times. But this weapon is not powerful enough [to show that the book was inauthentic.]"[14]

Casaubon took the book as basically reliable for a simple reason: it offered what seemed to him rich and reliable information about the Hellenistic world in general and the court and library of Alexandria and the customs of the Jews in particular. He was fascinated by Aristeas' statement that the Jews had the law of God "written on parchment in Hebrew characters" (4); by the claim of Demetrius of Phalerum, repeated by Aristeas, that the li-

11. Cf., e.g., Bod MS Casaubon 25, 121 verso: "Legi ig. utrunque volumen. Nec paenitet operae, neque temporis, quod brevissimum ei lectioni impendimus"; Bod MS Casaubon 60, 290 verso, on reading a work of Postel's: "Multa in eo libello quae non paeniteat legisse." Casaubon described certain conversations in very similar terms (Casaubon 1850, II, 803, significantly recording events of 31 December 1610): "A prandio fui apud D. Episcopum Bathoniensem, nec me poenitet sermonum quos una habuimus a pietate ut spero non alienos. Atque ita annum hunc, O Deus aeterne, exegi."

12. Bod MS Casaubon 60, 247 recto: "Eum libellum etsi non putamus eius quam prae se fert antiquitatis: credimus tamen admodum antiquum, et plane eiusmodi, quem legisse non poeniteat studiosum aut Gr. linguae, aut antiquitatis."

13. Ibid., 253 recto: "*De auctore.* In extremo pollicetur aliud scriptum . . . Quae si scripta sunt, vellem extarent: nam antiquiss. est auctor nec dubito eum esse de quo Josephus p. 353. [Added between lines: v. argum. praefixum libro Arist.] Itaque ille ipse est qui rebus gestis interfuit quae hic memorantur."

14. Ibid.: "Vnum videtur in dubium hoc posse vocare . . . Videtur enim innuere multo post illa tempora hunc librum scriptum. Sed non admodum firmum hoc telum."

brary already had more than 200,000 books (10); and by Demetrius' remark
that the Jews "supposedly use the Syrian language, but that is untrue, and
they use a different language" (11). And he especially pricked up his ears
when Aristeas described court customs, such as the amount of time that
ambassadors normally had to wait before seeing the king (175) or the gift of
three talents that Ptolemy ordered presented to each of his visitors (294). In
taking this antiquarian approach to the work, Casaubon read more or less as
Simon Schard, the distinguished jurist who edited the editio princeps of
Aristeas in Greek, had recommended: "The desire to read this history has
been stimulated by the very pleasant description of many things that it contains: for example, of vases, of bowls, of the golden table, of the priestly gar-
ments, of places in Judaea, of Jerusalem, of the temple, of the citadel, all of
which are described in such a way that they seem to be laid out before the
reader's eyes: and a cultivated mind must enjoy reading about them."[15] For
both men, the letter of Aristeas served as an invitation to engage in the form
of sacred antiquarianism that Benito Arias Montano and others pursued in
more celebrated works: the systematic effort to recreate the institutions,
customs, and material world of ancient Judaism, mostly from textual evidence.[16]

At one point in the notes, however, the particular, philological quality of
Casaubon's method of reading becomes especially clear. At 297 Aristeas argues that even if his account seems incredible, it deserves credence, since it
would be churlish "to lie about things that have been recorded." "Official diaries of the kings of Egypt," wrote Casaubon, inferring that the Ptolemies,
like Alexander before them, had maintained a detailed official record of
events.[17] Here he showed his belief that he glimpsed, as if in a flash of light-
ning, the lost official sources that Aristeas had exploited in writing his narrative—not blazoned, as a forger would, but simply mentioned in passing
(once again, the similarity between his way of reading the work and Bicker-
mann's is striking). Schard, in his preface, simply portrayed the letter as a
good work of history, based on eyewitness experience and full of high sentence.[18] Casaubon, by contrast, looked behind the preserved text, and in-

15. Aristeas 1561, [α7 verso–α8 recto]: "Auxit porro non parum historiae huius legendae cupiditatem,
iucundissima multarum rerum descriptio: utpote vasorum, phialarum, mensae aureae, vestium pontifi-
calium, locorum Iudaeae, Hierosolymorum, templi, arcis: ita expressa, ut oculis omnia subiecta et exposita videantur, eorumque lectione animus liberalis non possit non affici ac delectari."

16. Miller 2001; Stroumsa 2001a, 2001b; Shalev 2003, 2004; Sheehan 2006; Beaver 2008.

17. Bod MS Casaubon 60, 251 recto: "Ephemerides regum Aegypt."

18. Aristeas 1561, ep. ded., α3 recto: "Quamobrem cum mihi praeterita hyeme, Italiam lustrandi
gratia obeunti, singulari cuiusdam eximij viri humanitate [Antonio Agustín, apparently] (nomini
etenim certis de causis parco) Aristeae libellus ostensus esset, quo, quae a celebratissimo Aegypti rege

ferred that it rested in part on documentary evidence not attested elsewhere.

Aristeas offered information that seemed to come from Jewish as well as Alexandrian sources. Some of this was commonplace. Casaubon did not bother copying out the detailed explanation that Eleazar offered of "the Jewish distinction of foods." He contented himself with remarking, sounding a little discouraged, that "Aristeas questions Eleazar on this point, and he says a great deal."[19] But in at least one passage, Casaubon realized that he had found rare and valuable material. Years before, in his 1587 notes on the New Testament, Casaubon had discussed Pilate's washing of his hands in Matthew 27:24. He could "find no trace of this custom among the Greeks or Romans"; Greeks washed their hands to purge themselves of guilt, not to proclaim their innocence. Accordingly, he concluded that "Pilate, who was living among the Jews, imitated their rules and customs in this respect."[20] In the letter of Aristeas, the king's Jewish guests wash their hands in the sea before explicating the Bible (305–306). Aristeas asks them why they do so, and they reply that they did so "in witness that they had done nothing wrong." "This passage," Casaubon noted, "helps to shed light on the narrative of Our Lord's Passion," since it made clear that Pilate, when he washed his hands, had in fact deliberately followed Jewish custom.[21] His interest in the point is clear: it made its way into his attack on Cesare Baronio, where he not only described in some detail the Jewish elders' custom of washing their hands before working on the text, but also ascribed it to that "most ancient writer Aristeas."[22]

Casaubon, in short, read the text, the first time he went through it, with a humanist's eye for authenticity, derivation, and antiquarian detail. He

---

Ptolemaeo, cognomine Philadelpho, in cura legis divinae transferendae suscepta gestaque fuere, quam elegantissime describerentur, eius obtinendi facultate data, quae ad eius descriptionem pertinerent, perquam lubenter suscepi: maxime cum res verae religionis cultui vicinior, vel liberali benignitate augustior, vel varijs vitae civilis ac gubernationis utilissimis praeceptis refertior, a nullo huius generis historico, meo iudicio, literarum monumentis prodita reperiatur."

19. Bod MS Casaubon 60, 249 verso: "De ciborum diff. Iudaica . . . Aristeas interrogat super hoc Eleazarum, et multa ibi."

20. Casaubon 1587a on Matthew 27:24: "Huius consuetudinis apud Graecos vel Romanos nullum reperio vestigium: Itaque puto Pilatum inter Iudaeos versantem eorum instituta et consuetudinem in hac parte esse imitatum. Nam quod afferunt docti viri ex Sophoclis interprete, id huic loco non convenit. Illi enim lavabant manus, ut scelus a se patratum quoquo modo expiarent: Pilatus ut innocentiam suam testatam faciat."

21. Bod MS Casaubon 60, 252 verso: "Facit hic locus ad illustrandum quod scriptum est in historia passionis Domini nostri."

22. Casaubon 1614, 608; 1654, 536; 1663, 536: "Narrat Aristeas vetustissimus scriptor, Septuaginta Seniores, qui vertendis libris sacris Alexandriae operam posuerunt, solitos prius quam ad lectionem se accingerent, manus lavare."

looked as much for things inadvertently mentioned as for things explicitly discussed—exactly as he would have done in working through a new Greek or Latin text. The most striking fact about his response to the letter is that he did not identify it as Jewish. Scaliger, as we have seen, acknowledged that the letter was ancient, since Josephus had cited it. But he denounced it, to his students, as well as to Casaubon, as a forgery.[23] And although he, too, took the reference to hand-washing as a valid and valuable parallel to the account in the Gospels, he expended most of his energy on noting such evident flaws in the text's veneer of authenticity as its reference to twelve tribes —at a time hundreds of years after the ten tribes of Israel had gone into exile, never to return. For Scaliger, the contradictions and anachronisms that disfigured the text made clear that it was a typical invention of the Hellenistic Jews.[24] Casaubon read the same text, in full awareness of Scaliger's commentary, and found in it indirect testimony of the most valuable kind to the life and rituals of Hellenistic Jewry as well as those of the Alexandrian court.

Vicarious and Direct Knowledge: Casaubon Reads Buxtorf

Like many other Christian scholars, Casaubon desired a richer, more three-dimensional understanding of Jews and their beliefs and customs than he could attain by working his way, line by line, through those Jewish sources to which he had access. Rich lodes of material awaited his pick and shovel. In the course of the sixteenth century, a Christian literature on Jewish life and worship had taken shape. Writing in German, Jewish converts to Christianity described the life cycle of the male Jew and the rituals of the synagogue, especially for the high holy days in the autumn and for Passover. Sharply polemical, written from the standpoint of converts who possessed a "higher wisdom," these texts afforded their readers vivid but incomplete accounts of Jewish practices. Illustrations depicted some of the customs that seemed strangest to outsiders—such as *Tashlikh*, the practice of casting one's sins, symbolically, into running water on the afternoon of Rosh Hashanah; and *Kapparot*, the ritual of atonement performed on the eve of Yom Kippur, which involved moving a live chicken around one's head three times.

---

23. *Scaligerana II*, s.v. "Pilatus," in Scaliger 1695, 313; 1740, II, 504–505: "PILATUS dum lavit manus in signum innocentiae, judaizavit: non enim erat moris nisi caede facta lotione purgari; sed Judaei solebant mali ominis vitandi causa, ut essent innocentes alicujus rei quae se invitis quasi fieret, manus lavare. Vide Thalmud et Casaubonum in locum illum novi Testamenti, et Aristaeam."

24. Scaliger, *Animadversiones in Graeca Eusebii*, in Scaliger 1606, 124; 1658, 134: "Quis nescit Iudaeorum commenta?"

Just at the start of the seventeenth century, a Christian Hebraist, the Basel professor Johann Buxtorf, set out to write a more comprehensive and accurate guide to Jewish life. In 1603 Buxtorf published his material in German, under the title *Juden Schul*.[25] He followed the Jewish male child through the stages of life, from birth and circumcision through education and marriage to divorce and death. His book described the yearly cycle of Jewish worship in rich, precise detail, making continual digs at the Jews' spiritual failings:

> To let you know in part what they pray, and how they do it, I will translate into German some of the morning prayers and explain them. The first prayer starts: *Adon ólam ásher málach.* It is in rhyme, like most of their prayers, and is sung and read standing and in a loud voice. It goes: Lord of the world, who reigned before all things were created, at a time when they were created according to his will, he was called King with his name. After everything is gone, he will still remain King, to whom respect and honor will be given. He was always, he is still, and he will be forever in his beauty. He is alone, there is no one that could be compared with him, or could be placed with him. (With this they deny the divine nature of Christ, and regard him as a bad, common man.) He is without beginning or end; with him is power and dominion. He is my God, and my savior who lives in truth. (Here they scorn our faith that we believe in a savior who died.)[26]

No previous writer had portrayed the lives, works, and worship of Ashkenazic Jews as crisply and precisely as Buxtorf did. An unsatisfactory Latin translation, which appeared in the next year, made his work, retitled *Synagoga,* accessible to scholars across Europe. Scaliger, who read the Latin version within a year or two of its appearance, praised it warmly to his students even though he also complained of unspecified philological failings.[27] When Casaubon happened on the book in 1605 or 1606, he was struck, as he later wrote to Buxtorf, by "your expert knowledge of Hebrew ritual and the con-

25. See in general Cohen 1972; Burnett 1990, 1994, and 1996, 53–102. We use Buxtorf 1604, as Casaubon did.

26. Buxtorf 1604, 158–159; translation from Buxtorf 1603b.

27. See Scaliger's comments in 1695, 73; 1740, II, 248–249: "Buxtorfe a fait Synagogam Judaicam, qui est bonne; mais il n'entend pas beaucoup de mots qu'il explique mal. Buxtorfe est bien un autre homme que Waserus; il est docte. Il faut que j'aye Synagoga Judaica en Aleman, c'est un bon livre. Buxtorfius unicus doctus est Hebraice. Aujourd'huy nous n'avons que luy de grand homme en Hebreu." The comments in *Scaligerana II* date from the years 1603–1606.

temporary synagogue. You seem to know these matters better than anyone who has previously written on this subject for Christian readers."[28]

For some fifteen years, students of Buxtorf and of the other early modern writers who described Jewish mores have called their work "ethnographies," a term introduced in this context by Ronnie Hsia.[29] "Ethnography" conjures up an image of firsthand observation, based on sight and hearing, and it accurately expresses part of what Casaubon admired so much in the *Synagoga*. He believed that Buxtorf wrote from firsthand knowledge, describing what he had seen and what Jews had told him. As we will see, however, Casaubon found much more than ethnography in Buxtorf's book.

The *Synagoga* is a complex text, as loose in exposition as it is systematic in organization, and enriched by long digressions and passages translated from Jewish texts. Casaubon read the book pen in hand, as usual, and he asked a wide range of questions as he did so. He wanted to understand the methods that Buxtorf had applied, to identify his sources, and to evaluate his results. It seems likely that he went through the book no more than once or twice, and he probably had all of his questions in mind as he did so. For the sake of this analysis, however, we will start by separating three of the paths that Casaubon followed in his passage through the text, pulling apart his actual procedures as a reader in order better to appreciate their full complexity. Casaubon, after all, was the most self-aware and articulate of readers. When he began to study a text that he regarded as of special value, as we

28. Casaubon to Buxtorf, 2 February 1610, Universitätsbibliothek Basel, MS G I 62, 99 recto = Casaubon 1709, 606: "Quum ante annos aliquot casu in meas manus tuorum aliquid scriptorum, vir doctissime, incidisset: ita mihi eorum lectione contigit affici, ut semper ex illo tempore et te et tuas vigilias apud omnes praedicaverim. nam quoties huc illuc oculos per Europam circumfero, paucos omnino video qui pari tecum laude in eo genere literarum hodie versentur. Omitto peritiam rituum Hebraicorum et hodiernae Synagogae: quarum rerum notitia videris omnes antecellere, qui inter Christianos de eo argumento libros hactenus ediderunt." Casaubon states that he had read Buxtorf's work some years earlier. In his copy of the *Synagoga*, BL 848.b.19, Casaubon underlined much of a passage on the ritual of hand-washing, at 199: "Inde enim sapientissimi isti res duas didicerunt: quarum una est, quod quando manus ante cibi sumptionem lavantur, tollendae sint in altum, ne videlicet aqua illa, quae prima manibus superfunditur, statimque immunda fit, deorsum labens digitos faciat impuros. Altera deinceps est, quod quamprimum manus lotae sunt, et ita sanctificatae, orandum sit, actioque gratiarum super cibo capiendo dicenda." He also wrote in the margin: "Elenchus Scaligeri, p. 57." Here he referred to Scaliger's *Elenchus* of the Jesuit Nicolaus Serarius, which he read with great care on its appearance in 1605. At 57, Scaliger wrote: "Docti viri adducunt huc ex ritualibus Iudaeorum, quae quamvis ad rem faciunt, non tamen ritum exponunt. A Iudaeo quovis etiam Hebraismi imperito quaeratur quid sit נטילת ידים *elevatio manuum*, χειραρσία, respondebit statim quid sit. Iudaeus lotioni manuum operans quinque digitorum ἄκρα inter se jungit: et quum extremitates digitorum sic inter se commiserit, inde fit, ut manus in pugni speciem collecta sit." Casaubon entered a cross-reference in his copy (BL C.79.a.4.[2]): "Vide Synagog. Judaicam, p. 199." Taken together, the evidence suggests that he read Buxtorf's work in 1605 or 1606.

29. See the pioneering study of Hsia 1994 and the varied responses of Burnett 1994; Carlebach 2001; Deutsch 2004 and n.d.; Walton 2005; and Diemling 2006.

have seen, he sometimes took the time to lay out, in a headnote, the themes that he planned to pursue as he read. In late September 1611, for example, he set out to interpret Psalm 119, a text that he already knew intimately and that meant a great deal to him. "In order that we may profit even more from reading this great psalm," he wrote, "(and may God grant that we read it with profit), we will use a few headings to organize our observations." Then he reminded himself that he should pay special attention to the psalm's "heavenly doctrines," its terminology in Hebrew and Greek, the ways in which the Hebrew, Greek, and Latin texts varied, and other points.[30] In setting out one by one the dominant themes in Casaubon's reading of Buxtorf, we follow his own example.

From the start, Casaubon wanted to know what sort of ethnography he was dealing with. Every time that Buxtorf gave the reader a glimpse into his workshop, Casaubon was there, peering through the window and recording what he saw. On the title page—often, as we have seen, Casaubon's preferred space for singling out what he saw as a book's central points—he wrote that Buxtorf "frequented contemporary rabbis, and to such an extent that he took part in their banquets."[31] Casaubon generalized a little here. What had struck him was Buxtorf's vivid, unkind firsthand description of a single Jew-

---

30. Bod MS Casaubon 28, 14 recto:

σὺν Θεῷ

Ad ψαλμὸν CXIX. observatiunculae. IX. Kal. Oct. 1611.

Vt maiore cum fructu divinissimum hunc ψ. legam (quem Deus det legere cum fructu) observatiunculas nostras ad pauca quaedam capita referemus.

α. Doctrinae coelestis de qua hic ψ. est variae appellationes.

β. φράσεις aliquot aut voces in hoc ψ. valde crebrae.

γ. Notabiles diversitates inter Hebr. textum Graec. et Lat. καὶ ὅτι θείᾳ προνοίᾳ effectum, ut ad summam pietatis οὐδὲν παρὰ τοῦτο. Itaque licet hic illud usurpare Paul. 2. Tim. 2.14. μὴ λογομαχεῖν εἰς οὐδὲν χρήσιμον ἐπὶ καταστροφῇ τῶν ἀκουόντων.

δ. Capita praecipua ad quae doctrina huius ψ. potest referri. et an possit ordo aliquis animadverti et cohaesio, quod saepe facit Ambrosius, ut vers. 3. in ¶. vers. 7. in ¶.

ε.quid sibi in ψ. Graeco sibi velint illae voces saepe insertae, δόξα. κάθισμα. στάσις. quae sunt voces ad praxin Eccliae. Graecae spectantes, de quibus Meursius et nos alibi.

ϛ. Vsus et scopus huius psalmi, ex iis quae pie et docte observat Chrysost. vi. p. 137. et 138. de duobus remediis adversus vitia, λογισμοὶ εὐσεβεῖς, et εὐχαί. No. No.

31. Casaubon, note on the title page of his copy of Buxtorf 1604, BL 848.b.19: "Σηαι p. 94. auctor consuetudinem habuit cum hodiernis Rabb. ut etiam conviviis eorum interesset. Vide p. 121. et 176. 188. 369. 416. 471. 474. 494." Cf. Scaliger's response, in his letter to Buxtorf, 1 June 1606, also stressing Buxtorf's quasi-native fluency and mastery of Jewish matters. Universitätsbibliothek Basel, MS G I 59, 363 recto, printed in Scaliger 1627, 521: "Meum de eruditione tua judicium, quod ex lectione Synagogae tuae Iudaicae amico nostro Iacobo Ad portum exposui, fecit, ut is me non solum in ea sententia confirmaret, sed etiam ut, quem laudabam antea, mirari et amare coeperim. Postquam enim de peritia Hebraismi, de qua etiam cum eximiis Iudaeorum Magistris certare potes, multa praeclara narrasset, adjecit de probitate, humanitate, et comitate, quae me amore tui accenderunt, ut ultro amicitiam tuam ambirem."

ish festivity. "I myself," Buxtorf wrote, "once attended a banquet that they held after a certain ritual circumcision. There a rabbi preached on Solomon's words, 'wisdom is a tree of life to those who hold fast to it' [Proverbs 3:18]. As to this sermon, I can honestly give this verdict: I do not recall ever in my life hearing one so wooden and absurd as this one."[32] Casaubon did not make clear what he thought of Buxtorf's pun. But his note reveals something more important. Like some of Buxtorf's modern interpreters, Casaubon saw the fact that Buxtorf knew Jews and their rituals directly as a central feature of his work, a pillar of his scholarly authority. Inspired by this one cue, Casaubon filled one of the small empty spaces on the title page of his copy with a list of other passages in which Buxtorf clearly described what he had seen.

The contents of the passages Casaubon listed were highly varied. A number of them recorded particular Jewish customs and forms of behavior, more or less straightforwardly. In one of the passages that caught Casaubon's eye Buxtorf noted that German Jews went every year to Spain to purchase citrons to serve as *esrogim,* one of the four species used in the celebration of the autumn holiday Sukkot, and that he had seen a single citron priced at four florins in the autumn before he wrote.[33] In another, he recorded the magical words he had seen written on Jewish houses as a protection against the plague.[34] Buxtorf's language became more charged when he described seeing "a particularly grim chief rabbi, a man of gloomy piety," who wore ritual strings, or *tzitzis,* so long that they hung down to the level of his shoes.[35] And it passed from negative to poisonous when he recorded the Jews' practice of soiling the meat they sold to Christians by having their

32. Buxtorf 1604, 94: "Ego ipse aliquando convivio ipsorum, quod post circumcisionem quandam administratam agitabant, intereram, quando Rabbinus concionaretur verba Salomonis haec: *Sapientia lignum vitae est apprehendentib. illam.* De qua concione vere pronunciare possum, quod tam ligneam tamque ridiculam, quam fuit ista, in vita mea tota audivisse me non meminerim."

33. BL 848.b.19, 368–369: "Mala citrea ex Hispania afferunt; palmae, olivae, denique myrti ramos indidem petentes. Ea est causa, quod annis singulis, Iudaei sedecim in Hispaniam profecti rerum istarum quantumcunque possunt, ex ea secum avehunt; posteaque domum reversi per Germaniam ubi Iudaei commorantur, iterum divendunt universam. Sic ego ipse Septembri hoc malum citreum duntaxat unum florenis quatuor constitisse vidi. In rebus his quatuor mysteria sibi magna constituunt."

34. Ibid., 494: "Tempore pestis grassantis characteres inusitatos, nominaque prorsus admirabilia ad domos, cameras, cubicula, hypocausta, adscribentes, ea angelorum sanctorum, pesti praepositorum nomenclaturas esse dicunt. Ego ipse vidi aliquando domibus istorum literis magnis adscriptum Adiridon, Bediridon, et ita deinceps, ut *Diridon* istud per alphabetum totum ductum, praesentissimum contra pestem remedium esse putaretur."

35. Ibid., 187–188: "Sic ego tetricum quendam morosae sanctitatis Rabbinum, synagogarcham, cum talibus *Zizis* incedentem aliquando vidi tam longis, ut calceos propemodum pedum eius attingerent."

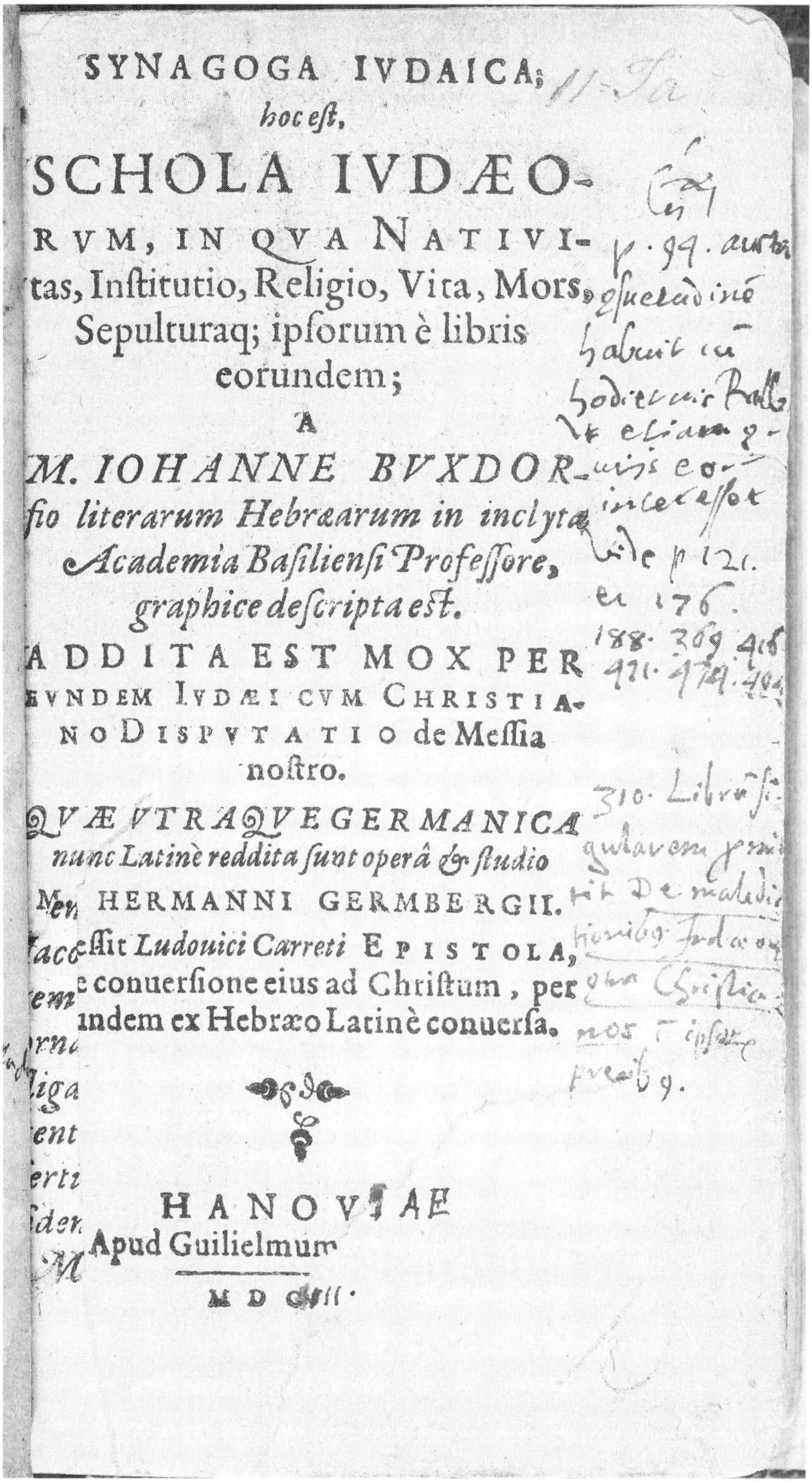

SYNAGOGA IVDAICA;
hoc est,

SCHOLA IVDÆO-
RVM, IN QVA NATIVI-
tas, Inſtitutio, Religio, Vita, Mors,
Sepulturaq; ipſorum è libris
eorundem;

A

M. IOHANNE BVXDOR-
fio literarum Hebræarum in inclyta
Academia Baſilienſi Profeſſore,
graphice deſcripta eſt.

ADDITA EST MOX PER
EVNDEM IVDÆI CVM CHRISTIA-
NO DISPVTATIO de Meſſia
noſtro.

QVÆ VTRAQVE GERMANICA
nunc Latinè reddita ſunt operâ & ſtudio
HERMANNI GERMBERGII.
acceſſit Ludouici Carreti EPISTOLA,
e conuerſione eius ad Chriſtum, per
indem ex Hebræo Latinè conuerſa.

HANOVIAE
Apud Guilielmum
M D CIII.

FIGURE 3.2. Title page of Casaubon's copy of Buxtorf's *Synagoga Iudaica.* British Library 848.b.19.

children urinate on it: "perhaps the Jews are not all equally bad in all places, but this sort of hatred for Christians fits their nature."[36]

A number of the comments that Casaubon listed dealt more specifically with matters of religious observance. Buxtorf remarked that he had seen certain Jews, who aimed at the highest level of piety, stand in one place on Yom Kippur, the Day of Atonement, singing and praying, for twenty-seven hours.[37] More critically, he mentioned seeing relatively recent Jewish prayerbooks from which anti-Christian prayers had been omitted, at the command of Christian authorities in Italy. The Jewish printers, Buxtorf claimed, left blank spaces in the *Aleinu* prayer, to be said at the end of the service, to remind the Jews of the missing words, which were often written in the margins.[38] The same anti-Jewish tone infused Buxtorf's discussion of the Jews' explanation that the silver clasps of the bridegroom's wedding belt and the gold clasps of the bride's reflected the colors of the two sorts of semen emitted by men and women: "This argument is as worthless as everything else that their learning produces." What seems to have interested Casaubon here was less the explanation than the fact, recorded by Buxtorf, that he had received it, at his own request, from a Jew.[39]

36. Ibid., 471–472: "In Italia vero per artem anatomicam (quam ego apud istos super papyro quadam patente impressam conspexi) adinvenerunt, ut per artificiosam subtilemque venarum exemptionem, partes etiam posteriores *muttarim* vel ad edendum licitae fieri possint. Quam artem si Iudaei tempore Mosis cognitam perspectamque habuissent, tunc eum cum cibis quos edi vetuisset, ad latus secedere oportuisset. Quod si magistris his, tam praecellentibus anatomicis, etiam sues committerentur, ut et in istis anatomicam scientiam istam exercerent, invenire possent fortassis et in iisdem, quo ex eis exempto carnes earum Iudaeastris edere liceret. Partes posteriores plerunque Christianis divendunt. Illi vero, qui carnes has libenter ab istis emunt, haec consideranda sibi esse cogitabunt, quod Iudaei omnes, quotquot a fide Iudaica ad Christianam sese converterunt, scribant unanimiter, eos carnes istas prius maculare, et ut liberi ipsorum super eas mingant, curare; maledictionemque super eis dicentes, ut emptor *Goi* carnes illas edens *misa meschunah,* id est, mortem edat, optare. Forte Iudaei non omnes omnibus in locis aeque mali sunt, alias naturae eorum valde consentaneum est, eos animis talibus erga Christianos esse" (Casaubon underlines some phrases and writes "Scelus Judaicum" in the margin of 472).

37. Ibid., 416: "Quidam, qui piissimi omnium esse, poenitentiamque seriam agere volunt, festo illo toto durante surrecti stant, canentes et orantes sine intermissione ulla. quemadmodum ego quosdam vidi, qui per horas viginti septem erecti in loco uno eodemque perstiterunt."

38. Ibid., 175–176: "Hic in libellis Iudaeorum precatoriis verba quaedam omissa sunt, idque mandatu magistratus Italiae, ubi libri ipsorum magna ex parte excusi sunt, et adhuc excudi solent. Omissa autem fuerunt, quod blasphema in Christum essent. In exemplaribus vetustis expressa inveniuntur. Cuius generis exemplar ego habeo Augustae excusum per typographum Iudaicum *Chaiim* vocatum anno Christi 1534. Alias loco verborum istorum omissorum spatium lineae unius dimidiae vacuum relictum est, eum scilicet in finem, ut liberi Iudaeorum aliique ignorantes admoneantur sibi quaerendum esse, quidnam ibi omissum fuerit. qua de re cum quaerunt, tum alii dictant illis verba deficientia: vel scribunt etiam in gratiam illorum in margine libri: quemadmodum ego in libris illorum multis observavi." On the censorhip of prayerbooks see Raz-Krakotzkin 2007.

39. BL 848.b.19, 474: "Cum rei huius ex aliquo Iudaeastro causam tempore quodam quaesiissem, dicebat iste, quod hoc ita fieret, quia argentum semen virile, quod esset album: aurum, semen muliebre,

As Casaubon recognized, Buxtorf's extensive acquaintance with the Jews and their ways had not made him like them, their religion, or their way of life. Even the Jews' scholarship, Buxtorf argued, revealed the deepest flaw of their religion, their preference for the Talmud over the scriptures: "I have encountered many Jews, completely worn out with age, who in all their lives had never read a single prophet from one end to the other."[40] Still, however negative Buxtorf's observations might be, in Casaubon's view they deserved credence. After all, as Casaubon recorded on one of the book's flyleaves, he, too, had seen the Jews take their Torah from its splendid ark and bless and read from it during a synagogue service, exactly as Buxtorf described.[41] Seeing was believing; and a writer who had seen so much deserved belief.

Casaubon was right to infer that Buxtorf had observed the customs of real Jewish communities and synagogues. At times, to be sure, Buxtorf—like everyone else who wrote about the Jews—drew material from earlier texts, some of which he presented without identifying his sources.[42] But one of his working notebooks, which survives in Basel, confirms that he learned much from Jewish informants, with some of whom he worked as an editor and corrector for the press of Conrad Waldkirch.[43] These contacts were especially frequent in the years when Buxtorf was at work on the *Juden Schul.* On 10 May 1600, for example, an unnamed Jew showed him a passage in the *Shulhan Arukh,* the sixteenth-century legal code compiled by Joseph Karo. This directed Jews to burn their nail cuttings lest magicians use them for evil purposes.[44] Two and a half weeks later, a learned rabbi and experienced

---

quod esset rubrum, repraesentaret. quae ratio certe putida est, qualia sunt omnia, quaecunque e schola istorum prodire possunt."

40. Ibid., 121: "Anno quintodecimo pueri Iudaeorum *Gemaram,* quod est, complementum, disputationes ac decisiones et acutas et subtiles super textus Talmudici rebus dubiis comprehendendis intelligendisque discere coguntur omnes. Et in his deinde partem vitae ipsorum maiorem consumunt: libris prophetarum vel rarissime, vel etiam nunquam studium ullum impendunt, quin libros eiusmodi ne legere quidem dignantur: unde fit, quod ego ipse Iudaeos iam senio confectos deprehenderim complures, qui spatio vitae ipsorum toto prophetam ne unicum quidem a capite ad calcem legissent."

41. Casaubon, note on flyleaf, ibid., 3 recto: "236.237. Ceremoniae Judaeorum hodiernorum in proferendo libro Mosis, in Synagogis: quem morem ipsi servatum inter illos vid."

42. See the classic study by Horowitz 1989 with the qualifications made by Burnett, 1994 and 1996.

43. On Hebrew printing in Basel, and Waldkirch in particular, see the classic work of Prijs 1964.

44. Universitätsbibliothek Basel, MS A XII 20, 287: "Iudaei vespera omnium sabbathorum ungues praecidunt, sed non secundum ordinem digitorum: ita ut ne duos quidem digitos secundum ordinem praecidant, semper autem a sinistra incipiunt et quidem a quarto ad secundum, a tertio ad primum, demum quintum. Sic a dextra incipiunt a secundo ad quartum, a tertio ad quintum, inde ad primum. Signum generale habent . . . hoc est, quartus sinistram, dextram incipit digitus secundus. In Orach Chajim aliud habetur signum specialius. Segmenta in ignem projiciunt, quia dicunt, maleficos posse multa mala ijs efficere. A Iudaeo didici 10. Maj anno 1600." Buxtorf used related material in chapter 10 of the *Jüden Schul* (BL 848.b.19, 245): "Econtra, quisquis eos in terram defoderit, is *tzaddik,* id est, iustus et probus est vir. In ignem vero si quis eos iniiciat, ille *chasid,* id est, vir honore quocunque dignus et sanctus est."

corrector, Menachem ben Jacob, pointed out to Buxtorf that a verb in Deuteronomy was a palindrome, and used that fact to explicate the passage in question and its legal import.[45] At the end of January 1602, a well-known Jewish corrector and editor, Jacob Buchhändler, or Mocher Seforim, of Meseritz, lent him a Yiddish tale about two Jewish boys, which he copied.[46] Buxtorf's contacts with Jews were probably more often professional than social, and involved fewer parties than Casaubon imagined. But they did take place, just as Casaubon thought.

In one case, Casaubon's instinct for identifying firsthand information as he read guided him surprisingly well. In chapter 28, which Buxtorf devoted to the Jewish wedding ceremony, he treated *gematria,* the traditional Jewish practice of reading a Hebrew word as a series of numbers. Buxtorf showed that when applied properly, *gematria* could secretly turn a toast into a curse, directed at Christians who attended a Jewish wedding:

> So you should be aware how welcome Christians are at their weddings. If one drinks to the other they respond: *Lechayim tobhim,* to good life, that is, the drink should serve your good health. But if they do not wish well to another person, such as a Christian, then they understand by these words *Qelalah,* that is, a curse, because the word *Qelalah,* counted in the kabbalistic way, has the same numerical value as the previous two words [namely 165], and they understand with it, the person should drink damnation with it. [$l = 30$, $ch = 8$, $y = 10$ (twice), $m = 40$, $t = 9$, $o = 6$, $bh = 2$, $i = 10$, $m = 40$: total $= 165$. $q = 100$, $l = 30$ (twice), $h = 5$: total $= 165$.] These and similar Jewish blessings and secret malice we will bring to light at some other time, God willing.[47]

45. Universitätsbibliothek Basel, MS A XII 20, 314: "Vim vi repellere licere R. Menachem praeclare in lege judaica doctus, mihi ostendit ex eo quod scribitur Deut. 19. 6. והכהו, et percusserit eum, quae vox ordine retrogrado lecta, idem sonat, nempe qui primum percusserit, eum rursus percutere licet. 28 Maij anno 1600." Buxtorf's informant advised on the 1600 Waldkirch edition of Elias Loans' commentary on the Song of Songs. See Prijs 1964, 271–272.

46. Universitätsbibliothek Basel, MS A XII 20, 242–248 ("Die Geschichte von den zwei Judenknaben," beginning: "Ex manuscripto Iudaei libro. Rabbi Aben Haezri ging ein mal spatzieren"). See esp. Buxtorf's subscription at 248: "Ult. Jan. anno 1602 scripsi ex libro chartaceo judaei Poloni, cui nomen Iacob Mocher sephurim, Jacob Buchhandler von Messeritz burtig." On Jacob Buchhändler see Prijs 1964, 254–257, 272–273, 275–277, 517–520.

47. BL 848.b.19, 482–483:
Hinc ergo videre est, quam libenter Christianos interdum nuptiis ipsorum interesse patiantur.
Quando alii aliis propinant, tum *Lechaiim tobhim,* ad bonam vitam, hoc est: haustus hic ad sanitatem tuam tibi prosit, aiunt. Si vero cu[i]piam non bene velint, uti Christianis, per verba praecedentia intelligunt *kelalah,* hoc est, imprecationem. Haec enim vox una secundum compu-

Casaubon found this secret curse very striking. He worked out the *gematria,* wrongly, both on the bottom of the page in question and on the flyleaf before the title page.[48] What he did not know for certain, because Buxtorf did not mention it, was that this information also came from an informant, a Jewish youth who talked to him in the country town of Allschwil on 29 May 1600.[49] Yet the interest that Casaubon showed in Buxtorf's anecdote may well derive from his conjecture that Buxtorf had heard it in conversation.

When Casaubon scrutinized the *Juden Schul,* he approached it exactly as he had approached many other descriptions of foreign cultures, ancient and modern. Most of Casaubon's favorite ancient historians, for example, had been travelers who wrote about societies other than their own, and from the start of his career he probed their work for evidence of how they had gathered information. Reading Herodotus, Casaubon noted the passages in which the Greek historian described his inquiries into the nature of societies outside the Greek world. At the start of book 2, for example, Herodotus told the story of the two children on whom King Psammetichus performed an experiment in order to identify the original language of humanity.[50] He then explained: "Besides this story of the rearing of the children, I also heard other things at Memphis in conversation with the priests of Hephaestus; and I visited Thebes and Heliopolis, too, for this very purpose, because I wished to know if the people of those places would tell me the same story as the priests at Memphis; for the people of Heliopolis are said to be the most learned of the Egyptians."[51] "Note," Casaubon commented in the margin of his copy, "Herodotus' effort to ascertain the truth."[52] Further notes tracked

tationem Cabalisticam, si numerum spectes, tantundem facit, quantum verba superiora duo: innuere volentes, cupere se ut bibens, mortem e poculo bibat. Benedictiones hae, aliaeque complures, quibus Christianos prosequuntur Iudaei, machinationes quoque clandestinae eorundem contra eosdem non paucae, per nos alias Deo volente manifestabuntur.

Translation and commentary adapted from Buxtorf 1604.

48. Casaubon, BL 848.b.19: "קללה [ק changed from ח] חיים טובים *ἰσόψηφα* utrobique 135"; on the verso of the blank before the title page he arrives at the same wrong sum.

49. Universitätsbibliothek Basel, MS A XII 20, 282: "¶ Iudaei propinanti poculum solent respondere לחיים טובים id est ad vitam bonam, hoc est salutare sit vitae poculum istud. At cum Christianis ita respondent, tum intelligunt, Maledictum tibi sit poculum istud. Nam per artem Gematriam idem sunt verba ista quod קללה i. maledictio. A Iudaeo juveni hoc didici 29. Maij. An. 1600 in pago Alswiler [Allschwil]."

50. Herodotus 2.2; cf. Sulek 1989.

51. Herodotus 2.3.1–2 (trans. Godley). Current scholarship would emphasize that Herodotus' accounts of conversations with informants are not to be taken as literal accounts of his working methods: see, e.g., the elegant analysis of references to informants as a sort of performance in Luraghi 2006.

52. Casaubon, marginal note in his copy of the 1570 Henri Estienne edition of Herodotus, Cambridge University Library Adv.a.3.2(1), at [56]: "No. Studium Herodoti indagandae veritatis Helopolitae."

Herodotus' efforts to learn about the past and the world in Egypt, where he went all the way to Elephantine, and in Phoenicia.[53] Strikingly similar annotations established that the more bookish, but still peripatetic, Diodorus Siculus had also seen for himself some of the exotic lands he described, four centuries or so after Herodotus, and collected Polybius' references to his own travels and observations.[54] To Casaubon, in other words, Buxtorf's effort to describe the customs and beliefs of a foreign people represented the latest chapter in the larger story of individuals' efforts to understand foreign peoples, one that had begun at least two thousand years before.

Travel literature, of course, continued to exist, and sometimes flourished, through the Middle Ages and the Renaissance. Sixteenth-century scholars, alerted by the discoveries of Vasco da Gama and Columbus, knew the unique value of direct experience. An older acquaintance of Buxtorf's, the Basel scholar Theodor Zwinger, drew up influential rules for asking the right questions and taking the right notes while traveling, and many younger scholars did their best to employ these as they made their pilgrimages to the great scholars, libraries, and museums of Europe.[55] The categories into which Buxtorf divided the information he offered—birth, education, prayer, religious festivals, cooking, slaughtering, marriage, divorce, sickness, burial —were the very ones that Zwinger advised young scholars to use as they examined the resources and rituals of new cities.

Casaubon, poor and committed to his ascetic regime of reading, enjoyed relatively few opportunities to travel to exotic places. But his diary shows how much he appreciated his visits to picturesque and distinctive towns like Canterbury, Cambridge, and Oxford. When possible, he tried to gain an

53. Casaubon, marginal notes, ibid., 62, on 2.29.1: "Herodotus usque Elephantinem pervenit"; 67, on 2.44.1–3, at 2.44.1: "et hic vide studium Herodoti"; 80, on 2.106.1: "Herodotus in Syriam Palaestinam venit." Cf. the typical note on 68 on the evaluation of Heracles' killings in Egypt at 2.45, at 2.45.3: "Herodoti ingenium pium." Scaliger made similar notes in his copy of the same edition, Cambridge University Library Adv.a.19.2; thus he inscribed on the title page Herodotus' famous statement at 7.152.3: "As for myself, although it is my business to set down that which is told me, to believe it is none at all of my business. This I ask the reader to hold true for the whole of my history"; and on the flyleaf he notes, apropos of 4.81.1–2: "157 Herodotus fuit in Scythia." On Scaliger's esteem for and faith in Herodotus see Momigliano 1968 and Grafton 1983–1993, II, 258.

54. Casaubon, manuscript notes in his copy of the 1559 Henri Estienne edition of Diodorus Siculus (BL C.75.g.11), 3: "Diodorus scripsit hanc histo[riam] annis XXX. lustrata ob id As[ia] et Europa": 30: "Quo tempore Diod. in Aegyptum venerit"; 53: "Diodorus in Aegypto vidit Romanum interfectum ob necem felis"; note on the title page of the Basel 1549 edition of Polybius that served as his heavily used working copy, Bod MS Casaubon 19, 4 recto: "Σηαι Ipse visit Alpes, p. 79. imo Libyam, Galliam, Hispaniam ϑέας χάριν. p. 82. et 228."

55. See Stagl 1983 and 1995; and, for a case study on the impact of the literature of the *ars apodemica*, Grafton 2007.

idea of the "morcs" of exotic lands like Muscovy by conversing with travelers and ambassadors.[56] His library included many works by medieval and Renaissance travelers, whom he followed with the same close attention to their methods of inquiry that he displayed when reading Buxtorf. On the title page of the twelfth-century travel narrative of Benjamin of Tudela—himself a Jew—Casaubon raised a question of credibility: was it really likely that Benjamin had seen great synagogues not far from the ruins of the great cities of Babylon and Persia, where the Jews had been in captivity? Could captives have obtained such privileges?[57]

Similarly acute observations dotted his copies of the travels of Leo Africanus and Pierre Belon.[58] Casaubon did his best, for example, to solve the problem of Leo's religious identity, which has continued to puzzle readers down to the present.[59] His openness to other tribes and cultures—and his sympathy for observers who did not share his erudition—was limited. Casaubon did not hesitate to make fun of Leo when he slipped on a matter of historical learning and confused the Ptolemies with their predecessors, the Pharaohs.[60] All the evidence makes one point clear. Casaubon did not read Buxtorf as an ethnographer because he saw the *Synagoga* as part of a particular ethnographic enterprise, a radically new collective effort to describe contemporary Jewish life from firsthand evidence. He came to Buxtorf's book, as he came to most books, with a framework already in hand: a literary taxonomy into which he planned to fit the book and a strongly developed set of skills to apply to it. Seen through Casaubon's grid, Buxtorf's work belonged to an ancient genre whose practitioners were both ancient and modern, both Christian and non-Christian.

Casaubon's own experience with Jewish matters was not broad enough to

56. For Casaubon's disappointing November 1613 luncheon with the ambassador from Muscovy to England, see Casaubon 1850, II, 1020: "Avebam cognoscere eorum mores, praesertim quod ad religionem pertinet."

57. Casaubon, note on the title page of his copy of Arias Montano's translation of Benjamin of Tudela's *Itinerarium* (Antwerp: Plantin, 1575) (BL 1046.b.2): "Σηαι passim in Persia et Babylonia refert mausolea regum, prope [al]tarum aliorumque τῶν ἐκ τῆς μετοικεσίας. sed an verisimile est captiuis eum honorem habitum."

58. See BL 793.d.2 and BL 972.a.1.(1).

59. Casaubon, note on the flyleaf of his copy of Leo Africanus, BL 793.d.2: "42. Christianum non fuisse sed [Judaeum crossed out] Sarracenum indicat quod passim utitur Hegirae annis. *factum id anno secundum nostram computationem 923. Christi vero anno 1514.* sic passim, ut 44.b. 45. etc. Sed tamen ex p. 238 colligas non fuisse Mahumetanum et p. 270.b. et p. 288 ait feras Nili factas saeviores posteaquam Mahumetani incolunt Aegyptum. fuisse Christianum ex fine ultimo colligas."

60. Casaubon, note in BL 793.d.2, 259 recto (in the account of Egypt). Leo Africanus writes: "Mansit huius regni principatus multis annis penes Aegyptios, nempe Pharaones, quos potentissimos extitisse, mirabilium aedificiorum vestigia testantur, praeter luculenta Historicorum scripta, in quibus celeberrima fit Ptolemaeorum regum mentio." Casaubon comments: "En doctum hominem."

enable him to identify all the elements of Buxtorf's work that actually derived from experience. He was puzzled, for example, by the method Buxtorf
used when transliterating Hebrew into Roman characters: "Note the method
of writing Hebrew. It is very odd in this book, and a beginner will find it
hard to restore them to their original form. I will take down a few examples
[he took only one]: in chapter 4 *tzitzit* is always written *zizis,* as if *zayin* and
tzade were the same. But he always turns *taw* into an *s.*"[61] In fact—as Buxtorf
explained a few years later in his book on the abbreviations used by Jewish writers—he did his best, when transliterating titles, to reproduce the
pronunciation actually employed by Ashkenazic Jews, so that his Christian
readers would be able to understand their Hebrew.[62] For the most part, however, Casaubon did a remarkably precise job of reading over Buxtorf's shoul-
der as his informant sat in synagogues and listened skeptically to rabbis.

Most of the material Buxtorf deployed came from books rather than observation. Casaubon read the *Synagoga* with as sharp an eye for its textual
sources as for Buxtorf's remarks on his own adventures. During the later
Middle Ages, the Jews of western and central Europe found themselves under siege. True, their ancestors had suffered accusations and attacks in the
Middle Ages. But in the late fifteenth century Christian attitudes hardened.
Jews were required to wear badges and other identifying marks. In 1475 the
authorities in Trent executed fifteen Jews for murdering a Christian boy
named Simon. Further ritual-murder trials took place over the next three
decades, and in fairly short order all the imperial free cities except Frankfurt
and Worms expelled their ancient Jewish communities. Meanwhile the convert Johannes Pfefferkorn led a campaign for the suppression of the Talmud
and other Jewish books. Forced to change their habits and habitations, subjected to brutal assaults, threatened with torture and death for imaginary
crimes, Ashkenazic Jews turned from the unbearable present to the past.
Many devoted themselves to collecting the customs *(minhagim)* of their
community or to describing such central practices as circumcision and ritual slaughter. These treatises often began as efforts to identify and extirpate
practices that had no foundation in Halakhah, Jewish law. Over time, however, as Elisheva Carlebach and Dean Phillip Bell have shown, they changed.

61. Casaubon, note on flyleaf before the title page, recto, in BL 848.b.19: "Σηαι super ratione
scribendi Hebraea. Ea vero mira est in hoc libro: ut tironi difficile sit futurum revocare illa ad suam
originem: Pauca notabo. ציצית cap. IV semper *zizis.* Quasi idem esset ז et צ . At ת in s. passim."

62. Buxtorf 1613, 335: "Lectori S. Noveris primo nomina librorum Latine scripta esse ad formam pro-
nunciationis Judaicae, quibus Thau lene sive raphatum semper ut S effertur. Id eo fine, ut si quis eos a
Judaeis petat, sciat eos ipsorum more nominare. Deinde notandum, Judaeos voces polysyllabas fere
semper efferre cum accentu in penultima. Tertio Beth lene quandoque per V consonam, quandoque per
F expressum: in harum enim potestatem incidit." Cf. Prijs 1964, 324.

Authors began instead to look for halakhic justifications for the new practices that had become established over time. The ethnographies of Judaism
written in Latin and the European vernaculars in the sixteenth century and
later often dealt with the same issues—and, when composed by converts,
were often written by the same sort of people—as the existing Jewish literature on Jewish customs and rites.[63]

Christian ethnographies of Judaism were often very bookish, in content
if not in form, for they drew on and adapted existing Jewish sources. Antonius Margaritha, who wrote the first substantive account of Jewish ritual,
was a convert from a rabbinical family. Yet he took care to explain that the
content of his *Der gantz Juden Glaub* came not from his memory but "from
the Jews' own writings and books."[64] At the beginning of his text he identified one of his primary sources as *Sefer haMiddot* (The Book of Ethical
Norms), a fifteenth-century text later known as the *Sefer Orhot Tsaddikim*
(The Book of the Ways of the Just). The second half of Magaritha's work
consisted of a pioneering translation into German of a Jewish prayerbook.[65]
Although he wrote as a Christian by birth, Buxtorf carried on this tradition.
The full title of the *Synagoga,* in the Latin form in which Casaubon encoun-
tered it, made clear that Buxtorf's book, too, rested chiefly on other texts:
"The school of the Jews, in which Johann Buxtorf vividly describes the birth,
education, religion, life, death, and burial of the Jews, from their books."[66]

Buxtorf's letters identify the Jewish books that served as his prime
sources. In September 1606 he gave a retrospective account of his method to
the theologian Matthias Martinius:

> You ask how I managed to collect those Jewish myths. I reply that
> the Jews themselves compiled them for me. They did so in the first
> place by providing me with their book of customs, which is entitled

63. Carlebach 2001; Bell 2007. Still important is the older treatment of this literature by Gilman 1986,
chap. 2.

64. Margaritha 1530, A verso: "Argument, oder innhalt dises Büchleins. In disem nachvolgenden
Büchleyn / findt man klärlich vnd gründtlich alle Ceremonien vnd breüch der Juden / mitt sampt jrem
gantzem wochen gebet / darinn sye all tag. 100 Lobsprechunge zuᵒ Gott thuᵒndt / Das alles durch Antho-
nium Margarithan / Hebreyschen Leser in der löblichen Staat Augspurg / mit der Juden aigen geschrifft
vnnd Bücher bezeüget / Nemlich wye sye sich mit jrem essen / trincken / geschyrren halten / wye vnnd
wenn sye fasten / Kinder beschneyden."

65. Ibid., B recto: "Anfencklich ist zuᵒ wyssen, das die Juden ain Büchlein haben Das sie ספר מידות
Sepher midos nennen / auff Teütsch ain Büchlein darinn jhr ordnunge / vnd Regel begriffen ist / wie sich
ainer halten soll / von dem das er auffsteet / biss er wider nyder gehet / Auch wye er sych imm bethe
halten soll / vonn sollichen sachen will ich ain tayl anzaigen." For analysis of Margaritha's work and his
use of sources see Walton 2005; Diemling 2006; and esp. Carlebach 2001, 176, emphasizing the bookish
character of his text.

66. Buxtorf 1604. On the bookish character of Buxtorf's sources see the full analysis in Burnett 1996.

Minhagim, and is published in Hebrew-German. If you want it, I will give it to you. Then I learned that all of their law, civil, canon, and the rest, can be found stated in *Dinim* [laws], or aphorisms, so to speak, in the book titled *Shulhan Arukh.* The Jews themselves provided this. Later I obtained the Talmud and the further works that I cite, and explored these for amusement. Whatever I found, I added to the *Minhagim.*[67]

Additional letters enable us to put some flesh on the rather dry bones of Buxtorf's narrative. He began the studies that would lead to the *Synagoga* in 1593. At the beginning of August he asked his friend Jacob Zwinger, who was then in Padua, to buy him some typical products of Jewish presses: several copies of the *Chumash*—the five books of Moses, divided into weekly readings—and what he called "a book titled *Sepher*—that means book—*Minhagim,* it is in Hebrew-German, and contains the Jews' rituals for life and worship. It was printed in Venice in 1593 by Giovanni de Gara. It is not big."[68] Three and a half years later, he sent his friend Kaspar Waser, who taught Hebrew in Zurich, a draft of what became the *Synagoga.* Buxtorf's description makes clear that his book took shape as he took notes on the *Minhagim* and related texts: "I am also sending you what I gathered for fun last year on the private and public rituals of the Jews, from the *Minhagim* and some other Jewish books, and threw together on these sheets."[69] In other

67. Buxtorf to Martinius, 4 September 1606, quoted by Burnett 1990, 152 n. 50; Burnett 1996, 64 n. 34: "Quaeris praeterea, quomodo Fabulas illas judaicas congesserim. Respondeo ipsos Judaeos mihi suggessisse. Primo et principaliter oblato libro Rituum, cui *Minhagim* nomen. Et qui hebraeo germanice editus est. Eum si cupis tibi dono mittam. Deinde intellexi totum illorum jus, civile et canonicum et quae praeterea habeant, *Dinim* quasi Aphorismis comprehensum in libro, cui שולחן ערוך nomen. Hunc etiam opera Judaeorum accepi. Postea Talmud ipsum et eos, quos praeterea cito, assecutus sum, in hos animi gratia excurri, et quicquid reperi, ad Minhagim retuli." For an account of Buxtorf's use of these relatively few main sources see Burnett 1996, 63–66.

68. Johannes Buxtorf to Jacob Zwinger, Basel, 4 August 1593, Universitätsbibliothek Basel, MS Fr Gr II 9, 89 (quoted in part by Burnett 1990, 148 n. 7): "Nisi audaculum me judicaveris, aliquid praeterea postulabo precibus intimis. Sunt quinque libri Mosis cum lectionibus propheticis minima forma excusi hebraice absque punctis, quale exemplar proculdubio aliquando vidisti per Pascalem mihi missum: avide ego adhuc quatuor vel sex exemplaria cuperem. Pentateuchum judaei appellant Chimmusch et ei adjunctas illas propheticas lectiones vocitant Haphtaroth, quomodo ibi et tu eos petere poteris. Sunt parvi libelluli, parum ut spero molestiae tibi exhibituri. Pecuniam libenti animo restituam pro libris et vectura expensam: pro officio gratitudinem exhibebo quam possum maximam. Impudens essem si plurib. te onerarem: committam autem tuae insigni humanitati et benevolentiae etiam tertium librum, qui appellatur Sepher (id est liber) Minhagim, estque hebraeo germanicus, continens caeremonias Iudaicas in vita et religione: hoc anno 93 impressus est in urbe majore a Ioanne de Gara. Non est magnus."

69. Buxtorf to Waser, 15 December 1596, Zurich, Zentralbibliothek, MS S-151, 64 recto: "Mitto etiam tibi, quae superiori anno otii fallendi gratia de ceremoniis Iudaeorum privatis et publicis ex libro Minhagim et varijs alijs Iudaicis libris collegi et tumultuarie tantum in eas chartas conjeci."

words, the resemblance between the *Synagoga* and the sort of travel book that Zwinger and his readers produced was anything but accidental. Like Zwinger—and, as we have repeatedly seen, like Casaubon—Buxtorf presumably laid out a series of "loci" (headings) in a notebook, used the *Minhagim* to fill them in, and then added supplements from the section of *Shulhan Arukh* known as *Orah Hayyim* (Path of Life) and other texts as these became available.

Buxtorf's one surviving notebook—which contains a few brief, explicit records of conversations with Jews—confirms this guess.[70] Much of its content consists of Buxtorf's notes on exactly the sorts of texts that provided the rich detail of the *Synagoga*. He took copious notes on the works of converts: Victor of Karben and Johannes Pfefferkorn, whose early, fragmentary treatises began the wave of ethnographies of Judaism.[71] He examined editions of the Jewish prayerbook, collating them, and paying special attention to "the great space left for prayers against the Christians"—a point, as we have seen, to which he would return in the *Synagoga*.[72] He worked through relevant sections of the Talmud, making excerpts, some of which he translated, and paying special attention to tractate *Berakhot* (Benedictions), with its rich information on prayers and rituals.[73] To this already rich mix he added materials from works less often consulted by Christian Hebraists, like the *Sefer haTerumah,* a thirteenth-century legal work by Baruch ben Isaac of Worms, which he combed for evidence of prohibitions against Jews' doing business with Christians.[74] At the same time, Buxtorf inserted passages from contemporary Christian scholars, such as the Hebraist Jean Mercier and Joseph Scaliger, whose work on the rules of the Jewish calendar he excerpted (Scaliger himself had filched part of his exposition from the older humanist Sebastian Münster, possibly after excerpting Münster's text, much as Buxtorf did).[75] Many segments of the notebook reappear either in the *Synagoga* or in other works.[76] Although we do not have the original notes Buxtorf took on the *Minhagim* or the rough draft that he sent to Waser for comment, it is

70. The notebook is Universitätsbibliothek Basel, A XII 20. For a full description see Thomas Willi, "Übersicht über den Inhalt der Kollektaneen von Johann Buxtorf I," in Prijs 1994, 91–98.

71. Universitätsbibliothek Basel, A XII 20, 265–267 (Pfefferkorn); 271–277: "Collectanea quaedam. Ex opere aureo Victoris de Carben, judaei baptizati, in quo Iudaeorum errores manifestantur et redarguuntur. Liber impressus Colo. anno 1509. per Henricum de Nüssia [Neuss]."

72. Ibid., 254–264, at 257: "Vide Machzor in Selichos jom Cippur in precatione quae incipit Schare kodesch hajiom, in qua spacium magnum relictum pro ijs quae contra christianos precantur."

73. Ibid., 231–241.

74. Ibid., 283.

75. Ibid., 227 (from Mercier), 159–170, 173–174, 176 (from Scaliger).

76. Thus Buxtorf records (ibid., 227) a passage from Mercier, which he later cites in full in his treatise on Hebrew abbreviations; Buxtorf 1640, 1.

clear that his primary tool remained not the reporter's notebook, but the humanist's. The *Synagoga* took shape—as its form often suggests—through a largely textual process of accumulation and refinement.

Casaubon—methodologically a kindred spirit, as his own notebooks show—was far less skillful than Buxtorf when it came to excerpting Hebrew texts. He could write only the large square script and the semicursive that he used for blessings, not the smaller cursive that Buxtorf managed fluently; he read a much narrower range of Hebrew works; and he rarely tried to work with texts in Yiddish. Still, he knew more than enough to recognize that Buxtorf drew constantly on written sources. Casaubon viewed the *Synagoga*, accordingly, not only as the record of a personal inquiry, but also as a mosaic of excerpts from books of every kind. As he went through Buxtorf's work, he copied out bibliographical information of all sorts. The flyleaves of his copy bear multiple references to the convert writers Buxtorf cited, Pfefferkorn, Margaritha, and Ernst Ferdinand Hess, as well as to the Jewish sources Buxtorf used.[77] Casaubon paid particular attention to references to Jewish sources to which he had no direct access, noting works as different as the Yiddish *Orah Hayyim* and the Talmud. He seems to have taken a special interest in some of the talmudic passages that he found translated in Buxtorf's book, and which he could not otherwise have read: for example, what he called the "delightful" story of Joseph mokir Schabbas, "Joseph the honorer of the sabbath."[78]

Casaubon did his best to work out which texts Buxtorf had actually used, but neither his library nor his skills quite matched those of his Swiss colleague. Throughout the *Juden Schul,* as we have seen, Buxtorf made extensive use of the *Shulhan Arukh,* drawing on the section known as *Orah Hayyim.* Casaubon owned a copy of a Yiddish book with this title, and he firmly identified it as Buxtorf's source. In a note in the flyleaves of the *Synagoga,* he remarked proudly that "we have this book, in German."[79] On the title page of his copy of the Yiddish *Orah Hayyim,* moreover, Casaubon noted that "the script is Hebrew, the language is German. This is the book from which Buxtorf basically copied the details in his *Synagoga Iuda-*

---

77. Casaubon, notes on flyleaf 1 verso, BL 848.b.19: "[B]en Sira non qualem P. Fagius edidit. [Ora]ch chaiim passim in hoc libr. vide [3]03. [added] nos habemus Germanice. [A printed marginal note on 301 (but the next recto is misnumbered 305) refers to Orah Chaim num. 308 & 312. On this text see below.] [F]erdinandus Hessus recens Judaeus. [Mi]nhagim Germanica. [Co]lbo, lib. 290. ib. Antonius Margarita. [Se]pher Juchasin. Joh. Pfefferkornius."

78. Casaubon, note in ibid., flyleaf 3 recto: "264. Fabula suauiss. super Josepho mokir schabbath, et pisce ab illo empto." For the story see Buxtorf 1604, chap. 10, from Babylonian Talmud, Shabbat 119a.

79. Casaubon, notes on flyleaf 1 verso, BL 848.b.19: "[B]en Sira non qualem P. Fagius edidit. [Ora]ch chaiim passim in hoc libr. vide [3]03. [added] nos habemus Germanice."

ica."[80] Beside a later passage on the ritual washing of hands, he noted the parallels in Buxtorf and in Scaliger's work against Nicolaus Serarius.[81] But Casaubon apparently did not try to read the Yiddish text, which lacks his characteristic underlinings and marginal notes, and he never realized that Buxtorf's occasional marginal references to *Orah Hayyim* were keyed not to his Yiddish book but to the section numbers of *Shulhan Arukh.* In this case at least, although Casaubon glimpsed the vital fact that Buxtorf had compiled the bulk of the material in the *Synagoga* fairly mechanically from a restricted number of sources, he lacked the equipment to track Buxtorf through the forests of Jewish learning.

In other cases, however, Casaubon managed to identify the actual texts Buxtorf had used, and he raised significant questions about his methods. As he read through Buxtorf's account of Jewish prayers, he collated the texts with the collections of *Tefillot* in his own library. At the start of his copy of the Basel 1579 prayerbook, for example, he entered a cross-reference to Buxtorf's account of the hymn *Adon olam,* quoted at the beginning of this section.[82] In the margins of his copy of Buxtorf, he went into more detail, noting differences in order between Spanish and German collections.[83] And at least once Casaubon made clear that he had detected—and disapproved of—Buxtorf's habit of eliding details and differences. In his translation of *Adon olam,* Buxtorf rendered part of the text as "He is without beginning or end; with him is power and dominion. He is my God, and my liberator." "He's omitting a great deal," wrote Casaubon in the margin of his copy. "He is not following the text of the prayers used by the Spanish, but that used by the Germans."[84] In cases like this one, Casaubon read Buxtorf from the standpoint of a critical and expert colleague, a fellow professional reader, scrutinizing an enterprise as up-to-date as his own and judging it by the strictest philological standards.

Complex though this account may already seem, it does not exhaust the range of Casaubon's responses to Buxtorf's text. As Casaubon started work,

80. Casaubon, note on the title page of BL 1935.e.15: "characteres Hebr. lingua Germanica. hic est liber ex quo pene singula descripsit Buxdorfius in Synagoga Judaica."

81. Ibid., A2 recto, on the words נטילת ידים: "Jos. Scal. contra Serar. p. 57. et fuse in Synagoga Jud. Buxd."

82. Casaubon, marginal note in BL 1970.c.2, Aii recto: "Vide Synagogae Judaicae cap. V."

83. Buxtorf 1604, 158–159. In his copy, BL 848.b.19, Casaubon writes: "Tephiloth p. 2.b." just after Buxtorf cites *Adon olam* on 158. On 159, where Buxtorf writes of the 100 blessings, Casaubon notes: "C. beracoth . . . Tephilot p. 50 25 in T. Hisp. At in Germ. p. 2. b."

84. BL 848.b.19, 158: "Ille ut sine principio, sic sine fine est. Apud eum robur et imperium est ∧, Ille Deus meus est, et liberator meus." In the margin, beside the caret after "imperium est," Casaubon writes: " ∧ multa omittit. non sequitur exemplar Tephilloth Hispaniensium: sed Germanicensium."

he noted on the title page that Buxtorf promised to write a separate work "On the Jews' cursing of Christians in their prayers."[85] A little later, a fierce introductory passage led him to draw a general conclusion about Buxtorf's view of the Jews. In his "Preface to the Christian reader" Buxtorf explained that his primary goal in revealing the true religion of the Jews to his fellow Germans had been religious and polemical: "that we may be admonished to set before ourselves as the object of meditation the incredulity of the Jews, and the hardening of God and his equally terrible wrath and severity toward them, and, similarly, to consider his goodness and his mercy toward us, which is beyond all telling." Beside this passage, which he underlined, Casaubon wrote: "On the scope of this work, see pages 461–462."[86] At the pages in question, where Buxtorf noted that Judaism no longer rested on Moses and the prophets, but instead on the false laws and rules introduced by scribes and rabbis, Casaubon noted again that Buxtorf here touched on the "scopus" of his book.[87]

Here Casaubon used yet another method for sophisticated, precise reading, that of formal Protestant hermeneutics, to make clear what was distinctive in the Basel scholar's approach. According to Philipp Melanchthon and Matthias Flacius Illyricus, the South Slav who wrote the first systematic Protestant manual of biblical interpretation, to understand any text or passage one must begin by identifying its true *scopus,* or goal.[88] Only the inter-

85. Ibid., note on the title page: "310. Librum singularem promittit De maledictionibus Judaeorum contra Christianos in ipsorum precibus." At ibid., 309–310, Buxtorf wrote: "Quoniam vero de talibus aliisque rebus aliquammultis, quas isti contra Christianos eorundemque magistratum scribere non verentur, in libello singulari verba facere decrevi." In the margin of 310 Casaubon wrote, simply, "No."

86. Ibid., "Praefatio ad lectorem Christianum Buxdorfiana," [8 verso–9 recto]: "Vt autem Germanis tandem quoque nobis innotescat, an Iudaei vitam agant adeo sanctam; legemque Mosaicam tam strenue, zeloque cum tanto, de quanto gloriantur ipsi, praestent, observent; ideoque soli, sapiens, sanctus, purus, iustus Dei populus sint, prout gestibus externis ostentant, indidemque gloriam quandam aucupantur; ea causa fuit, ut ego fidem et religionem istorum (fabulis prout Apostoli sancti locuti sunt) tanquam lardo quodam infarctam, una cum tota eorum vita et conversatione e libris ipsorum propriis plene vereque declarare, et cuilibet ob oculos constituere aggressus sim. Hoc autem primo praecipueque feci, ut nos per incredulitatem Iudaeorum ingentem, indurationemque non minorem nobis terribilem Dei iram, et severitatem erga eos meditandam proponamus, indidemque ad considerationem bonitatis nec non misericordiae eius erga nos inenarrabilis moneamur." Casaubon wrote: "de scopo operis, i. p. 461. 462."

87. Ibid., chap. 25, 461–462: "Hoc etiam de ceremoniis, quibus Iudaei in feriis et festis inter eos receptis superstitiosam ipsorum fidem exercentes utuntur, dictum adeo sufficit, ut inde quilibet satis perspicere possit, quod religio ipsorum non amplius super Mose et prophetis, sed super mendaciis meris, falsisque Rabbinorum et Scribarum (id quod ab initio libri huius mihi demonstrandum proposui) constitutionibus fundata sit. Sequitur iam praeterea de consuetudinibus nonnullis aliis, secundum quas in vita ipsorum privata se gerunt." Casaubon's note on 461 reads: "Scopus libri."

88. Flacius Illyricus 1968, 90: "Cum igitur aggrederis lectionem alicujus libri: id statim initio, quoad ejus fieri potest, age: ut primum scopum, finem, aut intentionem totius ejus scripti, quod veluti caput aut facies ejus est, protinus vereque notum habeas, qui plerunque paucis verbis notari potest. et non

preter who bore the focus and intention of a work constantly in mind could hope to read its details in the proper light. Casaubon's palette of interpretative methods was too rich and colorful for him to accept any single question as the right one to ask before reading every single text. But he found the notion of the *scopus* useful, and applied it often. When Casaubon read Psalm 119, as we have seen, he reflected at length on how to interpret the text. He laid special emphasis on what he called the "Application and goal [*Vsus et scopus*] of this psalm"—that is, its utility as a remedy against vice.[89] Reading two medieval Hebrew texts, the history of the Second Temple appended to Abraham ibn Daud's *Sefer haKabbalah* and the beginning of the *Sefer haHasidim,* he identified the author's *scopus* in each work.[90] Reading Buxtorf, Casaubon used the same term to describe, in a rigorous way, the author's un-

---

raro in ipso statim titulo notatur: sive is unus est, cum totum scriptum in unum corpus conformatum est, sive plures, cum sunt plures ejus partes, prorsus inter sese non cohaerentes." On the use of the *scopus* in hermeneutics see Büttgen and Thouard's introduction in Flacius Illyricus 2009, 33–38.

89. Bod MS Casaubon 28, 14 recto: "ς. Vsus et scopus huius psalmi, ex iis quae pie et docte observat Chrysost. vi. p. 137. et 138. de duobus remedijs adversus vitia, λογισμοὶ εὐσεβεῖς, et εὐχαί. No. No." Cf. Bod MS Casaubon 51, 17 recto, on Isaiah and the other prophets: "Omnium communis scopus fuit, verum Legis divinae usum demonstrare"; Bod MS Casaubon 4, 30 recto, on Maimonides' *Guide:* "Scopus auct. est instruere lectorem cognitione multarum rerum, quas putavit esse necessarias ad versandum feliciter in lectione sacrarum literarum"; Bod MS Casaubon 25, 100 recto, from notes that Casaubon took on the reading he did while staying with Lancelot Andrewes in August 1611: "Delatus est ad D. Ep. libellus Gallicus, quem in hac inopia librorum percurri. Titulus erat, Le promptuaire des Conciles de Leglise Catholique, et la difference d'iceux. Faict par Jean le Maire de Belges elegant Historiographe. Liber nuncupatur Ludovico XII. Sequitur Prologus, ubi auctor vocat se Indiciaire et alibi hanc vocem usurpat fere pro historiographo. Apparet librum esse scriptum quo tempore bellum erat sive apertum sive tectum inter Ludovicum XII et Papam Julium II. opinor, ac Venetos. Itaque libri scopus est minuere scandalum, quod videtur datum populis Galliae propter illam dissensionem: praesertim cum Papa. Id igitur agit, ut minuat ejus rei admirationem: docens rem esse non novam, ut Papae sint perditissimi nebulones et in Ecclesiam Dei coniurent"; and Bod MS Casaubon 27, 208 recto, where he argues that the Christian Hebraist Pietro Galatino had made a mess of his book *De arcanis Catholicae veritatis* by including material that had nothing to do with his chosen *scopus:* "Acumen Galatini. Mira res: saepe capita integra reperias ubi ne verbum q. invenias, quod titulo respondeat. Exemplo sit cap. ult. lib. vii. cuius ἐπιγραφὴ est: Quod mater Messiae sedes Dei futura erat, super quam divina majestas sedere debebat. Affert locum e More Nebucim, ubi erudite Moses ille explicat quid sit sedes Dei, et sedere Deum. affert tres notiones eius locutionis: sedere in solio, sedere in coelis, et peculiaris sedes solii Domini Exo. 17. has phrases docte explicat. Scopus autem Galatini est probare ex rabb. commentariis, illos habuisse notitiam verae fidei, sed juniores corrumpere doctrinam priorum. Heic ig. quaero qua fine locus [MS locum] e More Neb. afferatur. nam de Maria ne γρὺ quidem ille doctor nisi insani sumus."

90. Casaubon, note in BL 1939.b.63, 131 verso: "Scopus huius libri." Casaubon did not apply the term *scopus* in a mechanically uniform way, but it was central to his approach to many texts. In the introduction to *Sefer haKabbalah,* Ibn Daud does give an account of the *scopus* of his work. But it seems that as Casaubon read his copy, BL 1939.b.63, 52 verso, he was fully occupied in working his way through the text, which is printed in Rashi script, and translating the typical phrases of rabbinic Hebrew, such as the term *Mekubbalim* (recipients of the tradition). Still, at 131 verso, in the third part on the kings of the Second Temple, Ibn Daud speaks again about the chain of tradition that is his core concern, and Casaubon glosses: "scopus huius libri."

bending hatred for the subjects of his work—which clearly, in Casaubon's view, formed the focal point that gave the whole book its shape.

At this point, Casaubon had found a way to focus on what still seems the strangest feature of Buxtorf's work: the unremitting hostility he showed toward the people whose languages, beliefs, and rituals he had studied more intensively than any other Christian before him. It did not take the clear hindsight of the twenty-first century to spot that Buxtorf's values were in some tension with his method of scholarly inquiry. In the same years when Casaubon read Buxtorf's book, Joseph Scaliger remarked to his pupils: "It's amazing how much the Jews like Buxtorf. In his *Synagoga Iudaica* he criticizes them very sharply indeed."[91]

In many ways it seems a pity that Buxtorf never happened to debate the validity of his position with Yuspa Hahn, the Frankfurt rabbi who was his close contemporary and became something like his Jewish counterpart. Hahn asked a Christian scholar in Mainz about the calendar the Christians used, and late in life drew up a set of rules for debating biblical interpretation with Christians (never debate with those who could not read Hebrew; always read lines of disputed meaning in full and in context; know "their books" [the Gospels]).[92] But he devoted himself chiefly to recording the customs of his Jewish community and others, drawing on both his own experience and a wide range of written sources. Hahn's sensitive account of one local form of Jewish life acknowledged its gradual transformation during and after the crisis of the Fettmilch riots, as necessity drove the Jews of Frankfurt to abandon established habits and practices.[93] Like Scaliger, Hahn could have picked a useful bone or two with Buxtorf about ethnographic standards and attitudes. The encounter between Hahn and Buxtorf never took place. Instead, Casaubon noted Buxtorf's prejudices, but did not make clear the extent to which he shared or qualified them. The nature of his ethnographic interest—like so much of his method as a Judaist—remained steeped in ambiguity.

No feature of Casaubon's Judaic studies is more puzzling, finally, than his refusal to knit together the strands of his reading and research. Chapter 2 of Buxtorf's *Synagoga* deals in detail with a ritual designed to prevent the demon Lilith from killing a newborn baby, as well as the related questions of Lilith's identity and the reasons for her destructive impulses:

91. Scaliger 1695, 73–74; 1740, II, 249: "Mirum quomodo Buxtorfius ametur a Judaeis; in illa tamen Synagoga Judaica illos valde perstringit."

92. Fraenkel-Goldschmidt 1997.

93. Bell 2007, 48–65.

When the time of confinement comes for a Jewish pregnant woman, the room in which the child's bed is located will be furnished with all necessary things; and now the man of the house or another holy and pious Jew, if he can be found, takes a chalk and makes a circle in the room and on all walls, and he writes above the door inside and outside, on each wall and around the bed in Hebrew letters: *Adam, Chava, Chutz, Lilith,* that is, "Adam, Eve, out, you Lilith!" This means that if the woman has a son, God should give him a wife like Eve, not like Lilith; but if she has a daughter, then she should be for her future husband like Eve, a helpmate, not like Lilith, who is stubborn and disobedient. What is Lilith? This name is found in Isaiah 34:14 and is sometimes interpreted as Strix [the screech-owl], which is a horrible monstrous bird; some say it is a *Lamia* [Latin: sorceress], a monstrous ghost. The Jews also talk about a devil in the form of a woman, who on the eighth day, the day of their circumcision, would come and kill the babe or take him away. This ghost or night-woman was also called Lilith, from the Hebrew word *Lel,* meaning night.[94]

Buxtorf supplemented this detailed account with a long story about Lilith drawn from Ben Sira, "not as the scholar Paul Fagius has printed and trans-lated it into Latin [1542], but as the Jews have printed it [the spurious *Alpha-bet*]. My copy was printed in Constantinople; and it is the same as Sebastian Münster mentions at the end of his *Cosmographia* . . . I bought this copy from a Jew, who had it from the Münster library, because Münster had been professor of Hebrew here in Basel and is buried here."[95]

Casaubon underlined much of this material and entered brief notes—re-minders rather than summaries—in the margins. But he never mentioned that he had already learned about Lilith from a Jewish source. Elijah Levita included a substantial discussion of Lilith in his lexicon, the *Tishbi,* one of Casaubon's favorite sources. And Casaubon entered extracts from Levita's

---

94. Buxtorf 1604, 74–75; translation from 1603b, modified.

95. BL 848.b.19, 75: "Hac de re legitur historia, in libro *Ben Sira* (non ut vir doctissimus dominus Paulus Fagius et impressit et exposuit in lingua Latina, sed prout Iudaei imprimi fecerunt. Et exemplar sane meum Constantinopoli excusum est idem ipsum, cuius *Sebastianus Munsterus* in fine Cos-mographiae mentionem facit, et ex quo ipse historiam Hebraeam de regione Sacerdotis Iohannis et desumpsit et descripsit; quaeque in fine exemplaris eius, quod ego a Iudaeo quodam horum locorum habitatore, et id e Bibliotheca Munsteriana emptum habente, aere meo redemi, excusa est. Munsterus enim linguae sacrae professor fuit in hac urbe Basiliensi, ubi sepultus etiam est) in *Ben Sira,* inquam, legitur historia talis."

discussion, along with other references to demons, in a notebook.[96] Casaubon learned from Levita that Lilith was discussed in Ben Sira, question 60—Buxtorf gave a less precise reference—and he took down other information as well. He could have found an even more interesting point in the *Tishbi*. Levita disapproved of Ben Sira's long story about Lilith and, apparently, of the practices that it was used to justify: "I find it annoying to give all the details here because I do not believe in them. Still, the custom is widespread among the Ashkenazim to make a circle, going around the walls of the room in which the woman in childbirth is lying, with chalk or coal, and to write Adam, Hauah, Chutz, Lilith on each of the walls . . . The book of Ben Sirah gives a good explanation of the whole matter, and anyone who believes in this affair can consult it."[97] If Casaubon had recalled this passage, he could have used it to call into question Buxtorf's belief that all the Jews of Ashkenaz accepted the same beliefs and practices.

More generally, Casaubon believed in the value of autopsy and of reports that derived from observation. Why, then, did he not refer back to the proverbially learned and reliable Levita, whose scholarship he greatly admired, when reading about a subject about which he clearly spoke from firsthand observation? In fact, though, Casaubon did not refer to the parallel passage in Levita even when he read the Buxtorf only a few years later. As we will see, this was by no means the only occasion on which Casaubon failed to make the sort of systematic use one might have expected of his Jewish resources. Although the evidence is negative, it also suggests that Casaubon's curiosity about the Jews—whether exercised on ethnographic or on textual material—had its limits.

Casaubon's apparent lack of enthusiasm for Buxtorf's more ethnographic

96. Bod MS Casaubon 4, 29 recto: "Miscellae observationes ex Hebraeorum libris. Daemonum nomina quaedam. לליח Multa de Lilith Elias in Thisbi: Est id nomen ϑεᾶς cuiusdam maleficae quae ut Lamia, Gr. pueros devorat. harum Lamiarum et lemurum patrem faciunt Adam qui per illos [C]XX annos quo se ab Eva abstinuit eos genuerit ex daemonum συνουσίᾳ. Alii dicunt matres omnium daemonum esse quatuor istas. אגרת נעמה לילית et מחלת. Vide in libro Ben Sira quaest. LX [in fact VI]. Porro ex ea opinione quam retinent Iudaei quasi pueros intra octavum diem occidat Lilith, nata est superstitio illa Judaeorum praesertim Germanorum inscribendi parietes cubiculi et fores loci ubi decubit puerpera. fuse de ea re Elias. Sed nota apud Josephum Gorionidem col. 7 dici reginam populo suo dilectissimam fuisse illi ללילית quod non potest de dea malefica intelligi."

97. Levita 1541, 182: "qua de re ibidem multa prolixe tractat, quae huc adscribere mihi fastidio fuit quandoquidem illis nullam adhibeo fidem. veruntamen mos inolevit inter Iudaeos praesertim Germanos quod faciunt circulum per circuitum in parietibus cubiculi in quo iacet puerpera cum creta aut carbone, scribuntque in singulis parietibus, Adam, Hauah, Chutz, Lilith. Atque in ostio cubiculi interiori scribunt nomina trium angelorum qui sunt Senoi, Sansenoi, et Sanmangeloph, quemadmodum tradidit illis ipsa Lilith ea hora qua voluerunt eam suffocare in mari. Totum istud bene explicatum habetur in libro Ben Sirah quem ipsum videre potest qui huic rei fidem habet."

approach is striking in a connoisseur of travel writing. In a letter to Protestant nobleman Suffrey de Calignon, Casaubon offered Nehemiah 8:8 ("And they read in the Torah distinctly") as a powerful proof text against the Catholic refusal to allow ordinary Christians to read the scriptures in vernacular translations. The verse describes the way in which Ezra reestablished public reading and explication of the Law after Cyrus ordered that the Jews return to Jerusalem. These exemplary public readings, Casaubon insisted, must have included translations into Aramaic: "The people, who had just returned from captivity, had forgotten the old Hebrew language, and had become accustomed, in their long seventy years of servitude, to the Chaldean tongue. Therefore, they needed a translator in order to grasp the sense of the words of the Law. Accordingly, Ezra used a translator, who gave a literal Chaldean rendering of the words that were recited in Hebrew."[98] Casaubon was certain that this was the right way to understand the verse, not only on philological grounds, but also because he had collected ethnographic evidence to support his reading on his trip to Germany in 1590: "For the custom established by Ezra still survives in the Jewish synagogues, where each pericope is read twice, first in Hebrew and then in Chaldean. We saw this custom being observed with great care at Frankfurt, some years ago."[99] Similarly, in his copy of Génébrard's popular edition of and commentary on the Psalms, Casaubon marked the description of the removal of a Torah scroll without vowels from the ark and its reading with the words "I saw this rite."[100] Despite this appeal to direct experience, Casaubon never seems to have become a full convert to the more empirical approach to Judaism that was slowly spreading in his world.[101] He knew Jews and Judaism very well indeed—through books.

98. Casaubon 1709, 622–623: "Gens illa redux e Captivitate, veteris sermonis Hebraici oblita, Chaldaicae linguae longo annorum septuaginta servitio assueverat. Ideo ut verba Legis caperent, opus erat Interprete. Ergo adhibitus ab Esdra Interpres, qui recitata verba Hebraice παρὰ πόδας verteret Chaldaice." A scribal copy of this letter in BL MS Add. 12,110, 6 recto–7 recto, offers no substantive improvements and quotes Hebrew words in random form without correction. A talmudic tradition, not cited by Casaubon but discussed both by Elijah Levita and by Azariah de' Rossi, stated that "distinctly," in Neh. 8:8, means "translated" (Babylonian Talmud Nedarim 37b; see de' Rossi 2001, 129, 182, 699).

99. Casaubon 1709, 623: "Nam adhuc in Judaeorum Synagogis manet mos ab Esdra institutus, ut ejusdem periochae lectio fiat duplex: Hebraice primum, deinde Chaldaice, quod nos Francofurdi ante aliquot annos vidimus diligenter observatum."

100. BL 1016.d.3 (Génébrard [Lyons, 1607]), I, c recto: "In cuius rei testimonium quando legem Iudaei in Synagogis ostentant solenniter, eam sine punctis, ut nihil humani admixtum habeat, e suo armario, quod היכל Hecal vocitant, proferunt." Casaubon writes: "vidi hunc ritum."

101. See, e.g., Hsia 1994; Carlebach 2001; Deutsch 2001; and the studies in Coudert and Shoulson 2004.

Kindred Spirits in Conflict: Isaac Casaubon and Azariah de' Rossi

In the end, no book about the Jews in any language offered more stimulus for reflection than one written in Hebrew by an older Jewish contemporary, whose work Casaubon possessed for many years, as his diary shows. He records his most intimate and spiritual reflections in his diary, but these pious reflections are often interrupted by deliberate asides relating to everyday matters. Member of a scholarly community for whom the lending of books was a sheer necessity, Casaubon was meticulous in noting the whereabouts of his own precious library. On 7 August 1603 Casaubon records that he had given his "Azarias tout Hebrieu" to M. Du Tiloir.[102] Ten years later he makes a note that he had lent his "R. Azaria to Monsieur Livius."[103]

The "R. Azaria" in question is none other than the Italian Jewish scholar Azariah de' Rossi (1511/12–1577), who in his three pioneering works of critical scholarship, two written in a complex Hebrew, one in an equally complex Italian, had summoned up vast resources of knowledge encompassing pagan, Christian, and Jewish writings in order to provide a reassessment of Jewish history and tradition. Throughout the seventeenth and eighteenth centuries the name "Rabbi Azarias" resounded in the writings of the most learned orientalists. He was even accorded an entry in Richard Simon's catalogue of authors cited in the *Histoire critique du vieux testament*. Simon praised the Jew for having consulted Christian authors.[104]

De' Rossi's reputation rests on his *Me'or Einayim* (Light of the Eyes).[105] This work of outstanding erudition, printed in Mantua between 1573 and 1575—the various printings tell the story of the problems that beset the author in attempting to bring his researches into the public eye—was innovative in many respects. It was de' Rossi who first realized the importance of Hellenistic Judaism for an understanding of the Second Temple period. It was de' Rossi who undermined the chronological structures of rabbinic Judaism by claiming that the traditional computation from the Creation and the calendrical system to which it was connected were unreliable, indeed incorrect. His tripartite work, composed of a description of the earthquake

---

102. Casaubon 1850, I, 509: "Hodie dedi a Monsr Du Tiloir ministre de Sedan deux livres Hebrieux. 1. Kalendarium Hebraeolatinum. 2. Azarias tout Hebrieu."

103. Ibid., II, 972. The identity of the recipient of the book is not known. Casaubon describes the borrower as "professeur en Hebr." (Canterbury Cathedral Archive, Lit MS D/1, 249 verso).

104. Simon 1685, 602.

105. De' Rossi 2001.

which hit Ferrara in 1570, a translation into Hebrew of the letter of Aristeas, and sixty chapters or essays on a wide range of philological and historiographical topics developed by recourse to an impressive array of sources, pagan, Jewish, and Christian. Clearly, then, the book treated subjects close to Casaubon's heart. Given the exceptional nature and scope of de' Rossi's work, it does not seem surprising that Casaubon acquired this monument of Hebrew scholarship and attempted to penetrate de' Rossi's difficult and occasionally convoluted prose.

We cannot know whether Casaubon owned two copies of de' Rossi's book; but it is not implausible that the exemplar in the British Library,[106] which bears his signature, is the volume that Casaubon, already living in England, lent to M. Livius in 1613. One could assume that it takes one great scholar to recognize another, and that Casaubon would have appreciated— as far as he could understand it—the groundbreaking nature of the work. But an inscription on the flyleaf immediately crushes this reasonable assumption: Casaubon indicts de' Rossi for having been taken in by and having cited a best-seller of the day, the histories of ancient Assyria, Persia, Greece, and Rome forged by the Dominican Annius da Viterbo.[107] Casaubon's judgment is unequivocal: "He [de' Rossi] calls this turbulent scoundrel a *hakham*, a 'wise man.' You realize then how one ought to judge the chronology of this author." In other words, de' Rossi's painstaking discussions were compromised because he had availed himself of spurious texts for his reconstruction of Jewish chronology.[108]

And yet, fakes not only demonstrate the fallibility of experts, but also highlight the fact that perception itself is determined by the structure of expectations that underpin it. What, then, were de' Rossi's expectations, which led him to be taken in by Annius' fabrications? In the second chapter of his Light of the Eyes—enlightenment is his goal—de' Rossi lays down the ground rules for his use of sources. Provided they do not hint at heresy or make light of the Torah, any text, whatever its origin, may be employed. This

106. The shelfmark is 1938.f.12. The book is not in good condition, and many of his marginal notes have been erased, but it is clear that Casaubon has leafed through the entire book, usually translating the titles of chapters.

107. Grafton 1991, chaps. 3 and 6.

108. Casaubon, note on the flyleaf of BL 1938.f.12: "Metasthenes pro Megasthenes. et de Annio Viterbiense illo strenuo nugatore. hunc vocat הכחה sapientem illum: ut vel hinc intelligas quid de huius scriptoris chronologia sit judicandum. Et sane ubique pro certis et ratis habet quae illi commentitii scriptores, Berosus, Philo Judaeus in Antiquitatibus Bibl. Metasthenes etc. finguntur ab impuro Annio scripsisse." The same vitriolic attack is made against Baronio, who was likewise taken in by the forgeries, in Casaubon 1614, 145, 204–205; 1654, 131, 183; 1663, 131, 183. Casaubon was less certain about Annius and Berosus at the very start of his career. But by the early 1590s he rejected the Annian texts decisively; see Parenty 2009, 51.

approach gave him carte blanche to quote anything that he regarded as useful for his argument: pagan, Christian, Jewish, ancient, medieval, or modern. The modern included not only books that had just come off the Hebrew printer's press, but also Latin and Italian works that helped him to cut his momentous scholarly path. He took advantage of the latest advances in historical, biblical, and exegetical fields of learning and in turn offered his contributions. Those contributions provided among other things a thorough and incisive critique of traditional Jewish chronology and calendrical history.

Moreover, de' Rossi followed good humanistic practice in assessing the textual authenticity of Hebrew books. In chapter 20, he demonstrates the literary use of numbers in rabbinic texts and, in general, their employment of exaggeration in order to communicate the message in the most effective way possible. In this discussion de' Rossi is able to avoid a potential source of conflict, by passing judgment on the commentary on Chronicles attributed to the favorite medieval exegete Rashi, and pronouncing it inauthentic. In chapter 19, he examines various rabbinic texts that in his view have become corrupt over the centuries. Among the works that he submits to textual criticism is the Jewish classic of Jewish mysticism, the *Zohar*. De' Rossi is unhesitating in his judgment: the work has been subject to interpolations and manipulation of various kinds. Ever watchful for new books, de' Rossi reports his acquisition of Abraham Zacuto's *Sefer Yuhasin*, a Jewish chronology that was mined for historical information by Christian scholars and often cited by Casaubon himself. What caught de' Rossi's attention was the story of the quest for the actual text of the *Zohar*, which Zacuto reports toward the end of his book.[109] Zacuto's narration centered upon a certain Moses de Leon of the thirteenth century and his alleged involvement in the promulgation of the text. Apart from the suggestion that Moses de Leon actually transcribed the book from the original manuscript, other claims were aired: there were innuendos that he had fabricated the text for monetary gain, or that he had written the text down through automated writing, "through the power of the Great Name." Even the wife and daughter of Moses of Leon were called upon to give witness in the case. De' Rossi draws out the moral of the story: "This may help the reader to be receptive only to those writings which accord with reason and to the fundamental texts propagated by our ancestors."[110] And he then proceeds to highlight the dangers of textual fabrication.

109. This story is discussed in Tishby 1989, I, 13–17.
110. De' Rossi 2001, 330.

In other words, de' Rossi and Casaubon were perhaps not soulmates, but they were certainly scholars formed in the same intellectual mold. De' Rossi was an extraordinary polymath, and his curiosity knew no bounds. Like Casaubon, he understood that what was urgently needed was an authentic narration of the events and institutions of Second Temple Judaism and the rise of Christianity. In particular, he singled out Aristeas, Josephus, and Philo as the key eyewitnesses for the period. Shortly before Scaliger and Casaubon had broached the topic of the Greek-speaking Jews, de' Rossi had discussed with a degree of originality the origins of the Septuagint, translating the letter of Aristeas into Hebrew and comparing it to the relevant sources in Josephus and Eusebius.[111] Germane to our discussion here is his pioneering critique of Philo. Reading Sigismund Gelenius' Latin translation of Philo's works, he also was confronted with the patristic tradition, since the editor prefaced the tomes with the relevant ecclesiastical testimonia. De' Rossi renames his subject, hebraizing but not judaizing him: he refers to him throughout his Hebrew works as Yedidyah the Alexandrian. In his Italian work, which he wrote for Christians, the ever tactful or rather politically astute Azariah uses the Italian name Filone, sometimes adding "Alessandrino," but there is no trace of "the Jew."[112]

De' Rossi produced the first comprehensive assessment of the Alexandrian Jew to be undertaken by Jew or Christian. In the first of the four chapters of his critique, he examines the varieties of Judaism in Philo's time in order to set Philo in his proper historical context. In the following chapters he weighs up Philo's good and bad points, carrying out a series of brief investigations into certain facets of Philo's theology, biblical interpretation, knowledge—or rather, ignorance—of Hebrew, and familiarity with Halakhah.

By the end of the sixteenth century Philo and the evidence he presented about the early church had become burning issues. Casaubon, for example, poured scorn on Baronio for arguing that Philo referred to all Jews in his description of the Essenes, and derided him for fantasizing that Philo had documented the change that came about after the birth of Jesus. Scaliger had his own inimitable way of deriding Baronio, whom he scolded for using Philo in such a way that all distinctions between Judaism and Christianity were obliterated. But, as is often the case with intellectual battles such as these, a new scholarship arose from the dregs of the old debate. The identity of the Greek-speaking Jews became a central issue of the day, a subject of discussion, and often, as in more recent times, a matter of fierce debate. The

111. Weinberg 1985.
112. Weinberg 1988.

identity of the Hellenistae mentioned in Acts was discussed.[113] According to Scaliger, these were not simply Jews who lived among Greeks, but Jews who spoke Greek and who, like Philo, were raised on the Greek Bible.[114] In one of the many passages in which Casaubon castigates Baronio for his total incompetence as a scholar of the Second Temple period, he refers to Philo as "Philo Iudaeus Hellenista."[115] This epithet reflects the new history of Hellenistic Judaism.

In his groundbreaking critique, de' Rossi tries to pinpoint the cultural milieu to which Philo belonged. The Alexandrian Philo was far removed from Palestinian and Hebrew tradition. Indeed,

> Philo was even ignorant of Aramaic, the language that was widely used in the land of Israel. The Torah that he studied and wrote about throughout his works was based entirely on his reading of the translation of the elders [the Septuagint]. Since he accepted the view that they translated the Torah from an Aramaic version that they brought to the king, he consequently also believed that Moses had been given the Torah in Aramaic at Sinai. This is evident from his description of the story of the elders and Ptolemy in the second book of *De vita Mosis.* He writes: "In former times, our Torah was written in Aramaic and remained in that language for a long time until the moment came when the nations also desired to acquire its beauty and Ptolemy came."[116] Similarly, in his discourse on the perfect man in his book *De praemiis,* he states: "The Chaldeans call such a man *enosh,* which means 'man.'"[117]

In a similar, though more polemical, vein, Casaubon attacks the Jesuit Franciscus Toletus for his total confusion regarding the Hebrew form of the crucial word *Pesah,* Passover.[118] His errors had stemmed from his failure to discern that Philo thought Hebrew and Aramaic to be the same lan-

---

113. For a discussion of Scaliger's understanding of Hellenistic Judaism see Grafton 1992 and 1983–1993, II, 415–418. See also Canfora 1987, 86–88.

114. Scaliger 1606, 124; 1658, 134: "Hi enim Iudaei sola Biblia Graeca in Synagogis legebant per totam Aegyptum, Graeciam et Italiam: et vix in mille Iudaeis unus reperiebatur, qui Hebraice legeret. Vide Philonem, at quem virum? Quam infans est in Hebraeis? Quam ridiculus?"

115. Casaubon 1614, 66; 1654, 60; 1663, 60.

116. Philo, *De vita Mosis* II.25–29.

117. Philo, *De praemiis* 14: "Hunc Chaldaei nominant Enos quod interpretatur homo." See de' Rossi 2001, 129–130.

118. Toletus 1590–89, I, 383: "Dicitur etiam Pascha quod nomen idem significat, quod Phase, sed hoc Hebraeum, illud vero Chaldaeum est, ut testatur Philo libr. 3. de vita Moysis."

guage.[119] Like de' Rossi, Casaubon illustrates his point by referring to the passage in which Philo characterizes the Hebrew word *enosh* as a Chaldean word for "man."[120] But unlike de' Rossi, Casaubon proceeds to castigate Philo for apparently assuming that the Septuagint was translated from Aramaic: "You have to be a complete beginner in holy scripture not to know that the Seventy [translators] worked from Hebrew."[121] De' Rossi, on the other hand, recognizes Philo's confused ideas about Hebrew and its cognate Aramaic, but forges his own path, constructing a new theory of the Aramaic origins of the Septuagint. De' Rossi's critique of Philo and Casaubon's attack on Toletus thus belong to a single, central debate of the day about Hellenistic Judaism.

Even more illustrative of their similar approach to traditional questions is their treatment of the location of Jerusalem. The verse "who brings salvation in the middle of the earth" (Ps. 74:12), coupled with Jerome's commentary on "I set this Jerusalem in the midst of the nations and the countries round about her" (Ezek. 5:5), had assured Jerusalem a physical and metaphysical centrality for Jews and Christians alike.[122] It was the book of Jubilees, as Philip Alexander has demonstrated, that represented the first clear cartographic image of the world as a whole with Jerusalem as navel.[123] Inspired by anti-Greek political rhetoric, the author of Jubilees wished to challenge Greek occupation of the Jews' land by usurping the traditional position accorded to Delphi as *omphalos* of the world. Subsequently, sacred narrative and medieval maps, typically from the Crusader period, depicted Jerusalem as in the very center of the universe or, in the words of Ezekiel (38:12), as "the navel of the world."[124] But by the end of the sixteenth century

119. Casaubon 1614, 461; 1654, 406–407; 1663, 406–407: "Haec Philonis quum legisset Toletus, scripsit *Pascha* esse nomen Chaldaicum, Hebraicum vero *Phase*: falso et absurde. nam Hebraei פסח *pesah* dicunt, non *phase,* sed non animadverterat Toletus, Philoni linguam Chaldaicam et Hebraicam esse idem. In libro de Abrahamo ita scribit: χαλδαῖοι τὸν ἄνθρωπον ᾽ΕΝΩΣ καλοῦσι. Quis ignorat ENOS pro homine vocem esse Hebraicam? Nam Chaldaei et Syri dicunt ENAS, Arabes ANAS."

120. Casaubon 1614, 461; 1654, 407; 1663, 407. He refers to *De Abrahamo* 8.

121. Casaubon 1614, 461; 1654, 407; 1663, 407: "Atqui puerum in literis sacris esse oportet, qui nesciat versionem Septuaginta Interpretum ex Hebraeo esse desumptam."

122. Jerome, *Commentarius in Ezechielem,* bk. 2, on 5:5 ff. (*Patrologia Latina* XXV, 52): "Jerusalem in medio mundi sitam, hic idem Propheta testatur umbilicum terrae eam esse demonstrans. Et Psalmista nativitatem exprimens Domini . . . Ac deinceps passionem: *Operatus est,* inquit, *salutem in medio terrae* (lxxiii:12). A partibus enim Orientis cingitur plaga quae appellatur Asia. A partibus Occidentis, ejus quae vocatur Europa. A meridie et austro, Libya et Africa. A Septentrione, Scythis, Armenia atque Perside et cunctis Ponti nationibus. In medio igitur gentium posita est, ut qui erat natus in Iudaea Deus (Ps. lxxv) et in Israel magnum nomen ejus, omnes in circuitu nationes illius sequerentur exempla."

123. Alexander 1997.

124. Pilgrims' guides differ widely on cartographic details. Matthew Paris' map, for example, gives Acre, not Jerusalem, pride of place.

the map of the world had changed, and with it the geographical position of Jerusalem.

Each of our two scholars discusses this question in relation to his own particular project. In de' Rossi's case, the point comes up in his extended and wide-ranging discourse on the human fallibility of the rabbis on all matters of science and history. With characteristic discretion he argues that the rabbinic (and Christian) notion of Jerusalem as in the center of the universe had to be amended in the light of the discovery of the New World. He reflects that the rabbis were but men of their own time, who would have readily conceded that their geographical knowledge was deficient, and evokes the explosion of such knowledge in his own day: "Thus nowadays, scientists do not divide up the habitable world into three main sections, Asia, Africa, and Europe, all of which are located in the northern quarter of the globe . . . But now they divide it into four parts by joining the New World to the three zones which were known from antiquity."[125] Like Casaubon, in other words, de' Rossi was a man of the book who appreciated other forms of knowledge as well.

Casaubon's interest in this matter can be traced in various different literary contexts, all of which are brought to bear, not surprisingly, in his arguments against Baronio. His edition of Strabo, a fine work of scholarship written in Geneva, already documents Casaubon's youthful reflections on the concept of "navel." In his *Geographia* (9.3.6), the Greek geographer Strabo had commented on the widespread notion of Delphi as the *omphalos* of the earth. "For it is almost in the centre of Greece taken as a whole, between the country inside the Isthmus and that outside it; and it was also believed to be in the centre of the inhabited world and people called it the navel of the earth, in addition fabricating a myth."[126] In his annotations on this passage Casaubon had already gathered a cluster of sources in which the mythological motif of the *omphalos* is used to denote events of universal significance.[127] Not only Delphi had been accorded this name, but also Enna, where Persephone had been raped by Pluto, and Phlius in the Peloponnese.[128] The same use of the Greek word *omphalos* appears in Josephus' fa-

125. De' Rossi 2001, 215.
126. See Strabo 1949–1954 ad loc.
127. Casaubon 1587, 149.
128. Ibid.: "Porro de nominis huius ratione quae disputat Varro lib. De lingua latina vi. frivola meo iudicio sunt et plerisque eiusdem simillima. [Varro, *De lingua latina* 7.17: Umbilicum dictum aiunt ab umbilico nostro, quod is medius locus sit terrarum, ut umbilicus in nobis; quod utrumque est falsum; neque hic locus est terrarum medius neque noster umbilicus est hominis medius.] Cur enim non probat dictam urbem Delporum ὀμφαλὸν γῆς eam ob causam quam reliqui afferunt? Non ignoro equidem viris mathematicis aegre id grammaticos esse persuasuros: ita tamen sensisse primos huius appellationis

mous description of Jerusalem in book three of the *Jewish War:* "The city of Jerusalem lies at its very centre [of Judaea] for which reason the town has sometimes not inaptly been called the 'navel' of the country" (3.52–53). This passage did not escape Casaubon's eagle eye. In his heavily annotated copy of the first edition of Josephus' *Opera omnia* (Basel 1544), he had underlined the passage, and in the margin he had noted: "Urbs sancta terrae sanctae umbilicus."[129]

Both passages from Strabo and Josephus are brought into play when once again Casaubon raps Baronio on the knuckles for erroneous views. Having declared that the Hebrew word *tabor* (navel) was meant figuratively, he accuses Baronio of having adopted Jerome's view without due consideration. Jerusalem could be said to be in the middle of the world only in the sense that any place on the globe can be said to be the center—a ridiculous idea.[130] The ancients had propounded the view of the seven climes, a scheme according to which Jerusalem could be said to be in the center of their inhabited world. The rabbis, too, had applied the term to Jerusalem.[131] Similarly, the ancient Greeks had applied the same word to Delphi, but this centrality was to be understood in relation to the whole of Greece, as Strabo, "a rather serious writer," had indicated. Similarly, Josephus had understood the phrase "navel of the world," commonly applied to the holy city, as referring to its location within Judaea, "not in the inhabited world, and still less, in the entire universe."[132]

Having dispensed with the literal meaning of the word "navel," Casaubon refers to the symbolic application of the term by Germanus, the eighth-

autores vel ex eo intelligas, quod similem ob causam Peloponnesi locum quendam ὀμφαλὸν appellarunt. Πελοννήσου πάσης μέσον inquit Pausanias [2.13.7]. et in Sicilia quoque prata circa Ennam ubi Proserpina fuisse fertur, cum a Plutone rapta est, quia medium Siciliae occupare credebantur, ideo Siciliae umbilicus appellabantur: autor Diodorus Siculus libro quinto [5.70.4]. Aetoli apud Livium libro XXXV [35.18.4]. umbilicum Graeciae dicuntur incolere."

129. Casaubon, marginal note in BL C.76.g.7, 769.

130. Casaubon 1614, 627–628; 1654, 552–553; 1663, 552–553. Cf. Calvin's pointed remark in his commentary on Dan. 4:16, Calvin 1561, 46 verso: "Quod autem per medium terrae quidam ex Rabbinis vult notari Babylonem, quod fuerit sub eadem linea vel parallelo sub quo sita erat Hierosolyma, nimis est insipidum. Et qui dicunt Hierosolymam esse meditullium terrae pueriliter labuntur, quemadmodum tamen Hieronymus et Origenes et alii ex veteribus tenent hoc quasi certum principium, quod medium terrae sit Hierosolyma. Putant enim sitam esse in medio mundi, sed digni sunt Cynici ludibrio, qui cum esset rogatus ut medium terrae indicaret, tetigit baculo suo terram quae erat sub pedibus: deinde cum alter contra obiiceret non esse umbilicum terrae, Tu metire, inquit, terram. Sed quod ad Hierosolymam spectat certum est nihil posse deprehendi quale illi fingunt."

131. Casaubon distinguishes (1614, 627; 1654, 552; 1663, 552) between the Hebrew words העולם (universe) and החבל (inhabited world): "in scriptis Rabbinorum saepe dicitur, medium העולם *mundi:* melius dicerent החבל τῆς οἰκουμένης."

132. Casaubon 1587b, 149.

century patriarch of Constantinople, in his work on the divine liturgy.[133] According to Germanus, the reenactment of Jesus' crucifixion, burial, and resurrection in the context of the liturgy celebrated by the faithful from India to the Venetian islands had to symbolize the historically true event that salvation was brought about *in the middle of the earth*.[134] Casaubon concludes his discourse with a somewhat casual reference to a crusading text written in the thirteenth century by the Venetian writer Marino Sanuto Torsello (but finally redacted in 1321): "Others point to a certain place in the city that they designate 'the navel'; see Sanuto's *Secreta*."[135] Thus Casaubon ends with an allusion to one of the texts included in the massive tomes edited by his friend and fellow Huguenot Jacques Bongars, whose desire to compile a scholarly compilation of crusader documents was inspired not only by antipapal zeal but also by antiquarian ideals.[136]

This is a cameo of typically Casaubonian scholarship. An unflinching critical spirit applied to classical, scriptural, and ecclesiastical sources is combined with a knowledge, and perhaps a comprehension, of the spiritual dimension of the topic. Casaubon does not do justice to Baronio, who in fact quotes both Jerome and the celebrated passage from Bede:

> But in the middle of Jerusalem, where the dead man came to life when our Lord's cross was placed above him, stands a lofty pillar which at the summer solstice casts no shadow, wherefore it is thought that it is in the middle of the earth. According to this opinion Victorinus, Bishop of the Church of Poitiers, when writing of Golgotha says, "There is a place which we believe to be the centre of

133. There are many variations in this text, but the passage to which Casaubon refers is given in *Liturgiae* 1560, 97 recto (it is not in Meyendorff 1984), where Germanus is describing the *ciborium*: "ut totam terram praefiniunt: quod a quatuor columnis eius quod ciborium appellatur, conclusum aut circumscriptum sacrum solum: in quo completur et propheticus sermo, inquiens: Operatus est salutem in medio terrae Deus. nisi enim ita fuisset actum, quomodo qui in India perficiunt magnum hoc mysterium, et credunt illud corpus Christi et Dei esse nostri crucifixum et sepultum et resurgens, hanc salutem in medio terrae dicerent Dominum operari? quomodo item fideles Veneticas insulas inhabitantes, idem sensu conservato reciperent, omnibus confitentibus, in Hierosolymis circumscriptum esse ipsissimum medium terrae? Aut omnino, quia confinium caeli et terrae cum sancta mensa sit, et item in medio coelestis orbis subsistat, et medium columnarum, quae sunt in circuitu flabella, statione teneat locum, ubi ea cunque fuerit, in medio terrae salutem fieri demonstrat: ubi sunt et omnia quae passionis sunt, Christus subit, proditionem, iudicationem, quae ante crucem quaeque post crucem acta sunt."

134. Once again his reading method is demonstrated by his own copies. In his copy of *Liturgiae* 1560 (BL 692.f.6), 164, he glosses the text.

135. "Alii in ipsa urbe certum locum designarunt in quo ipsum umbilicum constituerent. Vide Sanuti secreta." Casaubon 1614, 628; 1654, 553; 1663, 553, citing *Liber secretorum fidelium crucis* 1611, 253–255.

136. On this edition see the excellent article of Tyerman 1999.

the universe; Jews call it in their native tongue, Golgotha [*De Paschate* 1.2]."[137]

But Baronio also rejects Bede. Like Casaubon and de' Rossi, he alludes to the geographical discoveries of his time and concludes: "Either Jerusalem is situated in the middle of the habitable world or else it is located in the middle of Palestine."[138]

De' Rossi, too, feels no qualms about putting the rabbis right when necessary. In his usual fashion he summons a vast number of sources to demonstrate the whole gamut of views on the subject. In his characteristically discreet manner, however, he fails to mention that the location of Jesus' crucifixion was in the forefront of the minds of Jerome and the fifteenth-century Augustinian Perez (Pharez) de Valencia when they discussed the idea of the centrality of Jerusalem.[139] Rather, he corrects erroneous views of both rabbis and Christians: "Here, then, is presented the unanimous view of theologians of two nations which contradicts the facts that have become clear to the men of science mentioned above, not only through proof, but also from perception and by use of the astrolabe."[140]

Casaubon read the whole of de' Rossi's book. He noticed disapprovingly, as a good Calvinist should, that alternative spelling was used for the divine name, and other minor points. He knew that de' Rossi's learned disquisitions had already been read and appreciated by Christians when Casaubon took possession of his book: his notes, for example, show that he knew that Azariah was also called Bonaiuthus.[141] But there is no evidence that he ever used de' Rossi for higher scholarly ends.

Great scholarship rarely comes in a pure and undiluted form. Casaubon was of course right that de' Rossi should not have used Annius' fakes. He would have approved Arnaldo Momigliano's pronouncement, made in his inimitable style: "One is never simple-minded enough about the condemnation of forgeries. Pious frauds are frauds for which one must show no pi-

137. Bede, *De locis sanctis* 2; Bede 1898, 307.

138. Baronio 1593–1607, I, 177: "Sed profecto fieri non potest quod asserit Beda: nam si id ita esset, necesse omnino foret Hierosolymam ponere intra zonam torridam, et tropico saltem Cancri subijcere: at ab illo longius abesse, omnes qui terras describunt, apertissime tradunt, et certissimis experimentis etiam nunc cognosci potest. Sed illud non male, vel Hierosolymam sitam in medio terrae habitabilis, vel in medio Palaestinae. Animadvertit atque correxit eumdem Bedae errorem noster Thomas Bozius vir cum primis eruditus."

139. De' Rossi 2001, 232.

140. Ibid., 222.

141. Flyleaf, BL 1938.f.12: "Bonaiuth. istius libri author dicebatur."

ety—and no pity."[142] But it can be argued that Casaubon was also probably a little rash in his assessment of de' Rossi, whose critical, philological approach to texts brought him to pose questions and probe traditional presuppositions in ways comparable to and reminiscent of his most ferocious non-Jewish critic.

On 27 September 1620, Thomas Erpenius, one of the foremost orientalists of the early seventeenth century, and a devoted friend of Casaubon, delivered an oration on the dignity of the Hebrew and Arabic languages. He paid homage not only to the languages themselves, but also to those scholars who had worked to promote the study of these noble languages. Among those on whom he lavished praise was the "distinguished ornament of the time, Isaac Casaubon." In particular, Erpenius pointed out, throughout his works Casaubon had strewn learned and truly precious observations that had been obtained from Judaism.[143] Erpenius' perceptive observations on Casaubon's predilection for Hebrew fell on deaf ears—for centuries. Casaubon's library and his notebooks have taught us to understand why the younger orientalist expressed such admiration for an older scholar not known, in modern times, for his expertisc in these fields. We turn now, as Erpenius' comments suggest we should, to the published works in which Casaubon put his Judaic studies to intensive use.

142. Momigliano 1987, 7.

143. Erpenius 1621, 129–130: "hoc tantum dico Clarissimum virum Ishacum Casaubonum, seculi hujus insigne ornamentum, et cui plurimum debent studia mea orientalia, si vitam ei prorogasset qui dederat, editurum fuisse luculentum opus de Graecae linguae ex Ebraea origine, in quo clare satis et nervose (quantum ex ijs quae multa jam indigesta coacervaverat judicare ego potui) demonstraturus erat pleraque Graecorum themata originis Ebraicae esse. Linguis certe reliquis Orientalibus, Chaldaicae imprimis, Syriacae, Arabicae, et Aethiopicae, quae et nobilissimae sunt, et latissime patent, ob magnam quam hae cum sua matre habent affinitatem, mirum quantum adferat lucis, quamque facilem illius cognitio ad hasce addiscendas pariat aditum. Mirandum itaque non est, viros quosdam magnos, etiam non Theologos, ejus studio summopere fuisse delectatos. Inter quos Iosephus Scaliger, singulare hujus Academiae haud ita pridem decus; qui quantum ejus cognitione et sibi, et alijs profuerit, immortalitate dignissimum ejus opus de emendatione temporum, ut de alijs taceam, abunde loquitur, et Ishacus Casaubonus, cujus paulo ante memini, qui scriptis quoque suis doctissimas et vere aureas ex Ebraeismo petitas observationes insparsit."

FOUR

Casaubon and Baronio

Early Christianity in a Jewish Setting

In 1614 Casaubon finished his last book: the *Exercitationes* on the *Annales ecclesiastici* of Cardinal Cesare Baronio, which we have touched upon a number of times already. A vast folio, almost eight hundred pages long, magnificently printed on large sheets of paper by John Bill, printer by appointment to King James, the book is physically splendid.[1] But readers—especially in modern times—have sometimes found its contents off-putting. Casaubon's book is a withering attack on Baronio's work, polemical in content and aggressive in tone. He meant to show that the *Annales*—a comprehensive history of the church from the time of Jesus to the Middle Ages—rested on foundations so shoddy that it could not survive a close reading, much less a serious attack.[2] His copy of the Mainz edition of Baronio, twelve thick double-column volumes long, survives in Archbishop Marsh's Library in Dublin. The rapid underlining that Casaubon left as he read, pen in hand, shows that he went through all twelve volumes, leaving angry notes in large script denouncing "Fooleries," "diabolic deception," and "loathsome falsehood."[3] In the end, though, he managed to write up his critique only of the first half of volume 1, and he abandoned both Baronio and the reader in the year 34, just after the Crucifixion.[4] This immense book, accordingly, is only

1. Casaubon 1614; reprinted with some changes as Casaubon 1654 and 1663. Though unsatisfactory in some ways, the fullest introduction to this work remains Pattison 1892, 323–341. See also Laplanche 1988; Quantin 2009.

2. Baronio did sometimes play fast and loose with textual and material evidence. For a splendid case in point see Bowersock 2006.

3. Casaubon, marginal note in his copy of Baronio, *Annales* (Mainz, 1601), Marsh's Library, II, col. 455: "NUGAE"; IV, col. 390: "O fraudem diabolicam! O mendacium detestandum."

4. For Casaubon's optimistic note recording completion of what he referred to as the first part of his work on the *Annales*, see ibid., I, col. 283, at Baronio 34 n. 233: "Hactenus I parte Exercit. Nostrarum."

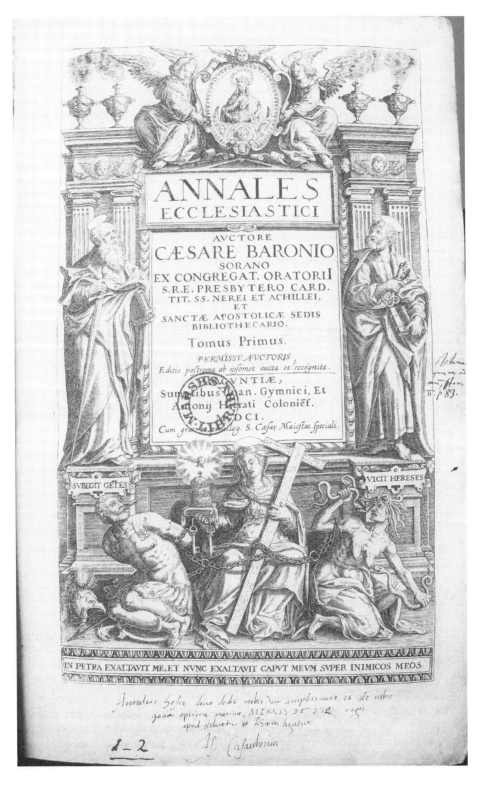

FIGURE 4.1. Title page of volume 1 of Casaubon's copy of Cesare Baronio's *Annales ecclesiastici*. Marsh's Library, Dublin.

ISAACI
CASAVBONI
DE REBVS SACRIS ET
ECCLESIASTICIS
EXERCITATIONES
XVI.

Ad Cardinalis BARONII
Prolegomena in Annales, & primam eorum
partem, de DOMINI NOSTRI
IESV CHRISTI Natiuitate, Vita,
Passione, Assumtione.

AD
IACOBVM, Dei gratia, Magnæ
Britanniæ, Hiberniæ, &c.
Regem Serenissimum.

LONDINI
Ex officina Nortoniana apud Ioan. Billium.
clɔ. lɔ. C. XIIII.
Cum privilegio Regis.

FIGURE 4.2.   Title page of Casaubon's *Exercitationes*. British Library C.24.c.3.

a fragment of what was meant to be the longest book review, and one of the most negative, written in a polemical age.

The book is also densely technical, and devoted to subjects many of which do not—and did not—allure readers. In one of his most sustained and elaborate arguments, for example, Casaubon took up the chronology of the Crucifixion. Baronio argued, in his own relatively brief treatment of the subject, that all four Gospels agreed on the sequence of events in the last days of Jesus' life. In the Jewish calendar, as is well known, the day begins at sunset. On the evening of Thursday, the 14th of the month of Nisan, according to Baronio, Jesus ate the Passover with his disciples. According to Baronio, moreover, "Jesus and the Jews celebrated the Passover at one and the same time."[5] Later that night Judas betrayed him, and on Friday, the 15th of Nisan, he was crucified.[6]

The problem with this argument was simple: although the three Synoptic Gospels agree on the chronology of these events, the Gospel of John seems to differ.[7] Many exegetes found themselves tempted, over the centuries, to see a disagreement here, and some to infer that John meant to correct an error in the other three Gospels. Baronio insisted that it would be impious to infer that the Gospels conflicted with one another, and Casaubon agreed: "we should not even suspect that the evangelists were unable to agree." But Casaubon also noted that one need not adjust John to agree with the Synoptic Gospels.[8] As we will see, a large and complex literature dealing with this subject—and the related problems of how the Jews actually celebrated Passover, and the nature and content of Jewish ritual and law—had grown up over the centuries. Baronio, in Casaubon's view, wrongly dismissed these "noble questions," including whether Passover might have been postponed

5. Baronio 1593–1607, I, 147 (34.25): "Dicimus . . . unum idemque Pascha uno eodemque die a Domino nostro atque Iudaeis esse celebratum."

6. Ibid., Apparatus, 145–150.

7. Key texts include John 13:1: "Now before the feast of the passover, when Jesus knew that his hour was come that he should depart out of this world unto the Father, having loved his own which were in the world, he loved them unto the end"; John 18:28: "Then led they Jesus from Caiaphas unto the hall of judgment: and it was early; and they themselves went not into the judgment hall, lest they should be defiled; but that they might eat the passover"; John 19:14: "And it was the preparation of the passover, and about the sixth hour: and he saith unto the Jews, Behold your King"; John 19:31: "The Jews therefore, because it was the preparation, that the bodies should not remain upon the cross on the sabbath day, (for that sabbath day was an high day,) besought Pilate that their legs might be broken, and [that] they might be taken away."

8. Casaubon 1614, 467; 1654, 412; 1663, 412: "Et vero negari non potest, Matthaei, Marci et Lucae narrationes id videri significare: sed quum clare et perspicue aliud suadeant Iohannis verba, locis aliquam-multis: nefas autem sit, vel suspicari, parum inter se Evangelistas consentire: fuere iam antiquitus, qui caeteros ex Iohanne putarent exponendos."

to the sabbath on the year in question.[9] When dealing with the theological topic of faith and works, Casaubon noted, everything depended on whether one read James through Paul or Paul through James. It seemed to him that in the same way, understanding the chronology of the Crucifixion depended on whether one read John through the Synoptics, as Baronio had, or the Synoptics through John—and John, in turn, through a rich filter of information about Jewish calendars and customs.[10] Casaubon did his best to do justice to all the evidence. He pulled the reader with him over a rough countryside strewn with the shattered remains of rituals and institutions, not all of which he perfectly understood, but some of which had to do with the ways in which Jews actually celebrated Passover and observed the sabbath.

We may already have provided more detail than anyone wants to have about the sorts of questions that engaged Casaubon as he set out to subject his Catholic adversary to a crowd-pleasing public anatomization. Mark Pattison certainly thought so, and treated Casaubon's book as a waste of paper, devoted to arid theological and exegetical games, the rules of which did not allow him to improve dramatically on what Baronio had written: "Many pages e.g. are wasted over the discrepancy as to the day on which the Passover was eaten . . . But Casaubon, equally with Baronius, assumes that it would be 'blasphemous' to suppose discrepancy in point of fact."[11] And he was not the first to be repelled by what Casaubon thought a "quaestio nobilis." When Lancelot Andrewes read a text of the *Exercitationes,* he wrote to his friend: "Although I agree with Padre Paolo [Sarpi] that those *Annales* are of no small importance, yet we all know that you are equal to the task, that you have enough strength and enough words for this duel. But, please, don't spend so much time on those chronological details. Get on to the more important points, the ecclesiastical matters that are worthy of you, quickly. It's to them that the expectations of the literary world summon you."[12]

Casaubon himself claimed to enter this thorny, difficult field of scholarship reluctantly. On 12 September 1612 he recorded in his diary: "I have made some progress in chronology: I wish I did not have to devote part of

---

9. Casaubon, marginal note in Baronio 1601, Marsh's Library, I, col. 191: "Quaestio nobilis An Christus pascha anticipaverit vel cum Judaeis ederit."

10. Casaubon 1614, 467; 1654, 412; 1663, 412: "utrum Iohannes e caeteris tribus Evangelistis exponi debeat, an contra."

11. Pattison 1892, 336.

12. Andrewes to Casaubon, in Casaubon 1850, II, 1203: "Etsi autem cum Patre Paulo non sentio esse opus illud Annalium non magni momenti; at id tamen omnes scimus, parem te oneri, satis jam tibi superque virium esse atque verborum ad hoc duellum. Tantum (amabo) in minutiis illis Chronologicis ne nimium diu haereas: ad illa majora cito te confer, Ecclesiastica te digna, ad quae te vocat expectatio literatorum omnium." Cf. Pattison 1892, 333.

my work on Baronio to this field."[13] On 24 December he noted more explicitly: "I am working on the time of our Lord's Crucifixion, a subject that raises many difficult problems."[14] Yet for all Casaubon's diffidence, in the end he crafted a characteristically detailed, precise, and bitter response to Baronio —whose efforts to solve the same problems he dismissed acerbically as revealing only his incompetence in matters related to Hebrew sources and the Jewish calendar: "he is a blind man making judgments about colors."[15] As we will see, Baronio's ignorance of Hebrew—like his ignorance of Greek—formed a central theme of Casaubon's critique, not only of the *Annales* but also of the entire Catholic culture of erudition, which, in his view, Baronio's massive book exemplified.[16] Casaubon's venture into the territory of chronology was thus unavoidable, even if he feared it was a land from whose bourne few travelers returned. By the time that we return to the chronology of the Crucifixion, its larger place in Casaubon's enterprise, and in the larger world of scholarship he inhabited, will be clear. But before we can examine that issue, we must set Casaubon's critique of Baronio into its larger context.

In fact Casaubon's *Exercitationes* represented more than an injudicious and unproductive foray into a difficult field of scholarship. It was, in the first place, the culmination of his lifelong passion for the early church and the sources that preserved its customs and beliefs. From the start of Casaubon's career, as Pattison observed, "what stirs his soul is Christian Greek."[17] One of his earliest publications was a set of notes on the Greek New Testament that appeared in 1587, when he was only twenty-eight. Precociously, Casaubon insisted on the alienness of this universally familiar text. He noted in his preface that the reader should ignore the already familiar modern divisions into chapter and verse, and wished that one could read the Gospels and Epistles as ancient scholars had left them. Working through the text line by line, he drew on the work of Immanuel Tremellius, an erudite converted

13. Casaubon 1850, II, 944: "In chronologicis aliquid promovimus, quae utinam pars operam nostram non desideraret in Baronio. Deus, ades." As we will see below, Casaubon had in fact read widely in the field of chronology in earlier years, partly—though not entirely—because of his commitment to the works of his close friend Scaliger. A copy of a key ancient work in the field, Censorinus, *De die natali*, Bod Wood 19, bears his signature and the date 1611 on its title page, as well as notes comparing the text to Scaliger's quotations from and discussions of it: a sign that his interest in chronology had not entirely dimmed before Baronio made him enter the field publicly.

14. Casaubon 1850, II, 958: "De tempore Paschatis σταυρωσίμου Domini, in quo multa ardua."

15. Casaubon 1614, 469; 1654, 414; 1663, 414: "Sed iudicat caecus de coloribus."

16. Baronio saw himself as an expert in chronology, and did his best to make the same sorts of chronological distinctions that Scaliger and Casaubon emphasized; see the rich study of Le Gall 2007, esp. 262. As Le Gall remarks there, for all parties "le trébuchet de la critique est la chronologie."

17. Pattison 1892, 441.

Jew, to identify certain words and expressions in the text as "Hebraisms"—linguistic forms that revealed the pressure, on the Greek language, of an underlying Semitic habit of mind and speech. The study of early Christianity, for Casaubon, always involved setting the New Testament in the Jewish world of Jesus and his disciples and opponents.

But early Christianity was a vast subject. By 1597, when Casaubon began keeping his diary, he had already become an erudite and passionate student of the Greek and Latin fathers. Between 19 February and 11 March he read the 698 "exceptionally close-packed" folio pages of Johann Froben's edition of Basil of Caesarea, which had appeared in 1551—an achievement that required him, as Pattison calculated, to maintain a steady pace of 35 folio pages of heavily abbreviated Greek per day.[18] The text and margins of his copy, preserved in Marsh's Library, show the usual signs of his attentive passage. At least once, moreover, Casaubon made clear in a marginal comment that he saw his study of late antiquity as a key to the theologically and liturgically stormy present: "Here is the image of the disturbances that have been stirred up today in the Christian world. The pious should reread this excellent passage often. They will be less surprised by the present state of affairs. This is the fate of the church."[19] Casaubon's copies of Clement of Alexandria, Origen's *Against Celsus,* and Philo, also preserved in Marsh's Library, show similar signs of intense, devoted study.

Casaubon's deep engagement with the Christian writers of late antiquity—like his engagement with the Greek New Testament—would last his whole life. In late April 1612, even as he worked his way through the last volumes of Baronio, he also returned as often as he could to his first love, both as a technical preparation for his assault on the Catholic vision of the early church and as a spiritual exercise: "I spent the day in pious meditation and in reading really good books, especially Chrysostom. May the Lord Jesus grant me to make such progress in knowledge of the truth that my whole life may be imbued with piety."[20] His pleasure was only enhanced by the fact that he could now read Chrysostom, one of his favorite church fathers, in

18. Ibid., 104. For the chronology of Casaubon's turn to the Greek fathers see Parenty 2009.

19. Casaubon, marginal note in his copy of the Basel 1551 edition of Basil of Caesarea, Marsh's Library, title page: "Imago turbellarum quae hodie in orbe christiano sunt excitatae locus eximius et saepe piis legendus. Minus enim mirabuntur praesentem rerum faciem. Haec sunt ecclesiae fata."

20. Casaubon 1850, II, 927: "XI. Kal. Mai. In piis meditationibus et lectione librorum meliorum, praesertim Chrysostomi, diem posui. Atque utinam det mihi Dominus Jesus ita proficere in cognitione veritatis ut vita omnis mea pietatem sapiat." On 23 April 1612 he was still reading Chrysostom "non sine pia voluptate"—a term, as we have seen, that he also applied to reading the Bible in both the Hebrew original text of the Old Testament and the Arabic version of the New.

the new critical edition produced at Eton under the supervision of Henry Savile. For Pattison, Casaubon's love for and mastery of the fathers revealed a "want of classical feeling" that "limited his pleasure in the pure classical writers."[21] To readers in the early twenty-first century, informed by the brilliant work of recent generations of scholars on what we now call late antiquity, Casaubon's efforts reveal his passion for complex and rewarding writers and thinkers—and his belief that scholarship would prove most rewarding when it could directly serve his most profound ideals. To that extent, we are better equipped than Pattison was to appreciate Casaubon as many of his friends did: as an expert on what seemed to them the vital, uniquely valuable world of Christian antiquity and the even larger world of Eastern languages and sources needed to illuminate it.[22]

But wedding truth to passion has always been hard, and it proved especially so for everyone who shared Casaubon's interests in the decades around 1600. The study of early Christianity has never been exactly value free. In the sixteenth century, Protestants and Catholics fought physical, as well as intellectual, battles over which church more faithfully preserved the history and the practices of the earliest Christians.[23] Baronio—a priest from a wealthy and cultured Neapolitan family, who eventually became librarian of the Vatican and a cardinal—was spurred to compile the *Annales* partly by the Protestant challenge. In the 1550s and 1560s, a group of Protestant scholars organized by the South Slav Matthias Flacius Illyricus had prepared and issued a massive, multivolume history of the church designed to expose the pope as a usurper, the Vulgate as an inaccurate version of the Bible, and the Mass and monasticism as corruptions of true Christian life and worship. Baronio set out to refute Flacius. But he also set out—just as Casaubon did —to do more: to recreate the early church and to show that Catholic institutions and practices went back, at least in their origins, to the worlds of Jesus and the church fathers. Inspired by Filippo Neri, whose society of priests,

21. Pattison 1892, 441: "It is almost a paradox that this most successful and most thorough interpreter of the classics, should have been a man who was totally destitute of sympathy for their human and naturalistic element."

22. See Jacques-Auguste de Thou to Lipsius on Casaubon's scholarship, Paris, 6 April 1599, in Burman 1727, I, 406–407 at 407: "Vix tibi enumerare valeam, quae ille in aliquos scriptores Graecos ac Latinos, et praesertim in Patres Graecos paene affecta habet. mitto Hebraicae et aliarum Orientalium linguarum accuratam cognitionem. quibus opibus subnixus quid ille possit, et quid ab ingenio tam fecundo et omni re instructo expectari debeat, tibi, qui harum rerum aequus aestimator es, judicandum relinquo."

23. The most recent comprehensive study of the early modern ecclesiastical history wars is Ditchfield 1995.

the Oratory, he joined, Baronio had spent his youth listening to the Oratorians give moving accounts of the "history of the church, starting with the advent of Christ and narrating what took place, year by year, from the approved writers."[24] To Baronio, it seemed as if the late antique church had come back to life in Neri's circle: "There frequent use of the Eucharist, which had become obsolete, was restored . . . so great was the rush to be there that you would have said that Jerome himself had returned to Rome from his hermitage, and that Paula, Eustochium, Marcella, Fabiola, Blesilla were hastening to him."[25] He found his vocation as a writer of church history in the Oratory, where Neri assigned him to give formal courses on the subject.[26] More important still, Baronio defined church history in Neri's terms: as an effort to trace the genuine continuities between the church of Jesus and that of Jerome and the church of the Counter-Reformation. This approach, which underpinned all twelve volumes of his massive work, was nicely—though not, of course, intentionally—calculated to enrage Casaubon, with his powerful sense that the early Christian past was not a familiar world, one that had known such late and corrupt institutions as the papacy, but another, very distant country to which all Christians must somehow strive to return.

When Casaubon and Baronio first made contact, they addressed each other with warm respect. In 1603, when Baronio wrote to thank Casaubon for the gift of a copy of his edition of the *Scriptores historiae Augustae,* he urged his correspondent to convert, precisely because he would find the Catholic church more to his historicist tastes than the Reformed one: "If examples move you, you have many recent ones given by men of the highest prominence, and a vast number of ancient ones, to imitate. If you are looking for the oldest form of Christian doctrine, then the rich treasures of the fathers and the learned will supply all your needs. By their writings, their

24. Bellucci 1927, 629: "Utque post haec auditores aliquantulum allevarentur, consultum fuit, ut alter fratrum ecclesiasticas repeteret historias, a Christi adventu sumens exordium, quodque per annos singulos utiliter gestum fuerit ex probatis Scriptoribus referret; Aderat postremo qui alicuius Sancti vitam ex probato auctore, paraphrastice magna audientium utilitate enarraret, haecque diu per trium horarum spatium ad minus absque audientium tedio explebantur."

25. Ibid., 628: "illic frequens sacrae Eucharistiae usus iam vetustate dimissus est restitutus, egere id patres verbis, egere et scriptis, qualis illuc statim factus concursus, dixisses ipsum Hieronimum ex haeremo Romam postliminio reversum et illic ad eum properare Paulas, Eustochia, Marcellas, Fabiolas, Blesillas, cursitare ad eum Pammachios et Chromatios, caeterosque ipsum adire, ut bethlehemitico pane satiarentur, verbis instruerentur et moribus inbuerentur, in unoquoque illorum Hieronimum intuentes, Hieronimum venerantes, Hieronimum alloquentes."

26. For Baronio's own account see the dedicatory letter to Sixtus V in Baronio 1593, I, a3 verso–a4 recto.

holy lives, and the power of their miracles they have borne outstanding testimony to the faith to which the Roman Church, the mother of all others, has always held and holds today."[27] The prospects for some sort of meeting of the minds seemed favorable. Meric de Vic, the son-in-law of the great collector Jean Grolier and a prominent royal ambassador who had brought Casaubon to the French court, played the intermediary between them. Baronio not only knew Vic, but sent him a splendid copy of the fourth edition of the *Annales*—perhaps the first copy of the work that Casaubon, who stayed for a time at Vic's house, ever saw.[28] When Vic presented Casaubon with a set of the less grand Mainz edition, he undoubtedly hoped that Baronio's erudition would impress his Huguenot friend, and perhaps that it would show him that the path of true learning led to Rome.[29]

Baronio's hopes were not wholly unrealistic. Casaubon's own religious position during his years at the French court, 1600–1610, gave cause for much gossip to Calvinists and Catholics alike. Called on, in his capacity as a scholarly consultant to the king, to serve as one of three judges in the debate at Fontainebleau over the polemical work of a fellow Huguenot, Philippe Duplessis-Mornay, Casaubon seemingly sided with the Catholics and determined that Mornay had cited sources improperly.[30] Jesuits—especially the erudite and adept Fronton du Duc—swarmed around him, pressing him to convert. Meanwhile, some of his coreligionists began to shock him by their insistence on abandoning all church traditions and returning directly to the teachings of the Bible. In January 1610 Casaubon enjoyed a frisson of horror when he read a handsomely bound copy of what he described as the Catholic *Officium B. Mariae*. With its prohibition against praying in French and its suppression of the biblical injunction against worshiping images, the book, like a little literary Whore of Babylon dressed in leather or vellum,

27. Festa 1911, 269: "Quod si exemplis movearis, habes et recentia quam plurima virorum praestantissimorum, habes et vetera infinita quae imiteris. Si doctrinam antiquiorem quaeras, ecquid non tibi suppeditabunt ditissimi illi thesauri patrum atque doctorum, qui suis scriptis vitaeque sanctitate atque miraculorum virtute eamdem omnes atque omnino fidem, quam semper Ecclesia Romana cunctorum mater tenuit, hodieque tenet, egregie reliquere testatam?"

28. Baronio's dedicatory inscription is in BL C.109.t.2, I, verso of title page: "Sic legas nostra ut memineris orare Deum pro nobis, ut post labores optatam in coelo requiem assequamur. Tu amice lector Vale semper. Mi Vice et pro Catholica fide restituenda labora. Caes. Card. Baronius uti frater amantissimus."

29. Casaubon records the circumstances in a note on the title page of his copy of Baronio 1601, Marsh's Library, I: "Annaleis hosce dono dedit nobis vir amplissimus et de nobis quam optime meritus MERICUS DE VIQ. regis apud Helvetios et Rhaetos legatus."

30. Casaubon's account is in 1850, I, 250–257. See also Pattison 1892; Canfora 2002.

confirmed all the prejudices he had nourished since his youth hiding in the hills with his father to avoid Catholic raiders.[31]

But Casaubon was just as shocked—and considerably more dismayed—in July of the same year, when he heard the Huguenot minister Pierre Du Moulin argue in a sermon that "Scripture needs no interpreter, and although he seemed to wish to give a sort of interpretation of this statement, yet I and others found what he said both false and ridiculous. Most absurd of all was that he cited the example of the words of the Lord's Supper. These, he insisted, required no interpretation."[32] After hearing another of Du Moulin's sermons in September, Casaubon found himself wishing that "we were not so distant from the ancients' beliefs and rituals"—and forced to admit that as a private person he had no standing to demand that his church accept these ancient traditions, since "they do not rest on sufficiently explicit words of God."[33]

Casaubon did not much enjoy combat, and he believed that the vicious religious controversies of his time endangered the Republic of Letters and the fabric of Christendom itself. Sometimes he expressed such thoughts only in the privacy of his margins—as when, in his copy of Calvin's letters,

31. Casaubon 1850, II, 711: "Liber est excellenter compactus, et plures preces pias continens, in his unam Thomae non vulgarem ut erat illius viri admirandum ingenium. In hoc igitur libro quum casu in illum incidissem, et forte aperuissem, duo statim deprehendi quae visa mihi nefanda cum impietate conjuncta. Prius est quod Papa in praefatione diserte vetat omnem precum id genus usum in vernacula lingua. At, Deus bone, quoties mihi contrarium affirmatum est? Quoties dictum moneri viros foemi-nasque ut preces vernacula lingua scriptas usurpent? Sane negari non potest in Gallia hodie multum earum esse usum. Sed hoc profecto nos ab invitis pudore quodam expressimus. Qui si hodie non esse-mus, periret miseris libertas aliquid cognoscendi eorum quae ad pietatem pertinent. Et diserte Papa su-perstitionem id vocat. O monstrum iniquitatis! O vere hac quidem in parte ἀντίχριστον. Alterum fuit, quod sum abominatus, in Decalogo, unde totum de imaginibus praeceptum est sublatum. Euge fidelis Pastor. Hoc est Dei mandata servare." Casaubon's notes on a Venice 1598 edition of the *Missale Roma-num* and Gregorian Calendar are in Bod MS Casaubon 24, 136–144. See esp. 137–138 for Thomas Aqui-nas' *Rythmus ad sacram Eucharistiam* and 139 on the *Missal:* "Hoc igitur opus percurrens pauca adno-tavi, quae mihi cum doctrina Domini nostri Jesu Christi parum convenire videbantur. In primis occurrit passim B. Virginis mentio admodum crebra, et saepe habentur preces ad Deum, ut per illius merita aut intercessionem adjuvemur."

32. Casaubon 1850, II, 753: "Nam hodie quam multa dixit vere nova, potius quam vera; ut, S. Scrip-turam nullo opus habere interprete, quod etsi aliquo modo visus est interpretari velle, tamen vel sic mihi atque aliis visum est tam falsum quam absurdum. Omnium vero absurdissimum quod attulit ex-emplum de verbis S. Coenae Domini, quae si nullam, ut affirmabat, desiderant interpretationem, et ἁπλῶς credendum, quicquid dicitur, credemus panem illum vere esse panem, et vere corpus Domini, quae est haeresis perniciosissima, nisi cum Lutheranis sentiamus."

33. Ibid., 760: "Optaremus minus longe ab illorum [the ancients'] fide et ritibus nostros abiisse: verum quia satis expresso Dei verbo illi antiqui ritus et fides vetus non nituntur, et nos privati sumus, qui sequi, non praeire in Ecclesia Dei debemus, caussam cur aliquid ipsi mutemus nullam satis justam habemus, quum praesertim id agatur ut omnia confirmentur quae vetus superstitio aut nova excogi-tavit."

he wrote, next to a passage on the "poison" of the irenic scholar George Cassander, that "Cassander was a pious man."[34] But sometimes he expressed them publicly, as when he returned to Basil of Caesarea, in the preface to his 1606 edition of Gregory of Nyssa's seventeenth letter, to find a way of describing the current situation of the church in Europe:

> Where, today, can that pious love of other Christians, the sure mark
> of a Christian mind, flourish? Where can harmony? Where can that
> charity that the Apostle Paul called constructive? Basil the Great, in
> his spectacular description of the church, compared it in his own
> day to a ship, hurled about on the deep, with winds, waves, enemies,
> and everything horrible that tends to happen to those who travel the
> deep all conspiring to destroy it. And at the same time, he says, the
> steersmen and sailors, oblivious to their common danger, attack one
> another savagely, raging, each fighting for himself. There is a clear
> image of Christianity today.[35]

Calls for religious peace like these made Casaubon something of a magnet, especially after he arrived in England in 1610, for cosmopolitan, optimistic thinkers like Hugo Grotius and George Calixtus. A few years later, on his deathbed, he harked back to them, telling his young physician, Raphael Thorius, that he regretted that he had not completed his work on church history, which he had begun "for the glory of God and Christian concord."[36] Some well-informed readers agreed that Casaubon was following the path broken long before by irenic figures like Erasmus, Melanchthon, and George

34. Casaubon's copy of Calvin's letters is BL 1084.i.9. On the verso of the title page he noted how much admiration Calvin had aroused: "Σηαι ex epistolis doctorum virorum huic volumini insertis apparet, quantum admirata sit Calvinum sua aetas. Nam et Melanchthon et Martyr et Bulingerus, et Blaurerus, et omnes alij mirifice illum suspexerunt." But on 589, in a letter of 10 September 1561 to Theodore Beza, Calvin wrote of François Baudouin: "Nebulonem excipere cuperem pro merito: sed privatis literis obruor: et si quid alacritatis restabat elanguit. Pergam tamen quoad licebit. Audio etiam nescio quod σύνταγμα Lutetiae fuisse excusum, de historiae coniunctione cum Iurisprudentia: ubi odiose perstringeris. Nunc cum suo Cassandro venenum aliquod coquere dicitur." Casaubon underlined this and commented: "Cassander vir pius."

35. Casaubon 1606, eii recto: "nam ubi hodie inter Christianos amor ille pius, Christianae mentis certus character, viget? ubi concordia? ubi illa charitas Paulo Apostolo aedificans dicta? Magnus Basilius in illa stupenda ecphrasi Ecclesiae, temporibus suis similem eam dicebat navi salo agitatae, in cuius perniciem venti, undae, hostes, et quicquid maxime terribile maria sulcantibus solet occurrere, conspirarunt: cuius interim, ait, vectores et nautae communis periculi obliti, mutuam saevitiam ferro, manu pro se quisque, furore immani, invicem exercent. en hodiernae Christianitatis expressam imaginem."

36. See Patterson 1997, 124–154. Thorius recorded that Casaubon "subinde leviter deplorabat Historiae Ecclesiasticae opus ad Dei gloriam et Christianam concordiam inchoatum, non absolutum relinqui" (Casaubon 1709, 67).

Cassander.[37] As he seemed to wobble on his very public tightrope, delicately balanced between opposing orthodoxies, longing to find a church that really reflected his sense of Christian antiquity, Casaubon certainly must have looked like a strong candidate for counseling and conversion.

In fact, however, as the great Italian scholar Nicola Festa noted almost a century ago, during these years Casaubon was actually becoming more and more determined to direct his energies against Baronio. In 1613 he recalled that he had asked Henri IV ten years before to grant him permission to write a critique of Baronio, only to be informed that the time was not yet ripe.[38] In 1604, when a Protestant scholar in Augsburg, David Hoeschel, asked him to add notes to his edition of Origen's work *Against Celsus* and Gregory Thaumaturgus' oration on Origen, Casaubon remarked to Hoeschel that he had greatly enjoyed becoming acquainted with these texts, which he had not read before. "Nor," he remarked dryly, "I think, have any of those who have written on ecclesiastical matters since the revival of letters. That most diligent man Cesare Baronio could certainly have made his *Annals* both more informative and more correct by reading this speech."[39] By 1606 his project was coming into at least distant focus, and he drew an absolute contrast between his own vocation as a scholar and that of his Catholic opponents. "My intention," he wrote to his friend the Altdorf jurist Conrad Rittershusius, "is to practice truth and illuminate it so far as the stores of my intellect allow. Theirs is to obscure the truth and extirpate it from human memory with their heaps of inventions." Characteristically, Casaubon expressed his seeming confidence in the language of the Psalms as he proclaimed that "there is a God in heaven who sees and laughs at" the devices of these enemies of the truth. At the same time, though, he also resorted to the desperate language of Virgil's Dido, crying out: "Will the day ever come, when someone will arise to serve as a strong champion for the true history of the early church?"[40]

37. See the fascinating anonymous letter to Casaubon from someone in Leiden, perhaps Daniel Heinsius or Petrus Bertius, 18 May 1612, in Burman 1727, II, 446–451.

38. Casaubon to Prideaux, 7 April 1613 (probably Julian), Casaubon 1709, 528, quoted by Festa 1911, 292: "Sunt anni decem, cum ego veniam petii ab Henrico Magno, meo indulgentissimo Mecaenate, ut liceret mihi modeste Baronii mendacia refellere. Responsum tuli ab ore sacro illo, nondum tempus advenisse."

39. Casaubon to Hoeschel, Paris, 18 February 1604, Casaubon 1605c, 497: "Ne illi quidem, opinor, viderunt, qui de rebus Ecclesiasticis hactenus scripserunt post literarum παλιγγενεσίαν. Diligentissimus certe vir Caesar Baronius lectione huius orationis Annales suos poterat locupletiores reddere, et emendatiores."

40. Casaubon to Rittershusius, 28 August 1606, Casaubon 1709, 273: "Mihi propositum est, ἀλήθειαν ἀσκεῖν, et pro ingenii copia illustrare; illis, veritatem obscurare, et sexcentis figmentis aut potius μυρίοις ἐπὶ μυρίοις ex hominum memoria delere. Sed est in coelis Deus, qui molitiones istorum baronum videt ridetque. Ille pro sua bonitate infinita viros excitare velit, scientia literarum et amore verita-

One connection in particular may have helped to bring Casaubon to the point of attacking Baronio in public. He abhorred no Catholic more than the brilliant, vicious pamphleteer Caspar Schoppe, a onetime Protestant who had not only abjured his original faith but become one of the attack dogs of Catholic erudition. In 1607 Schoppe exposed the fact that Joseph Scaliger, who cherished his descent from the della Scala of Verona so much that he wore princely purple on formal occasions at the University of Leiden, was really the grandson of a miniaturist and woodcut artist, Benedetto Bordon. Scaliger's pupils avenged their teacher by portraying Schoppe, in his turn, as obsessed with the salacious bits in Virgil's *Priapeia*.[41] But Schoppe unabashedly continued his attacks on Protestant scholars, including Casaubon. Schoppe ascribed the impulse that had led to his conversion to Baronio's *Annales*. It was, he insisted, a reading of Baronio's work at Prague, which he undertook when advising a friend, Wacker von Wackenfels, about Christian antiquity, that had saved him as a brand from the Protestant fire.[42] Nothing could have done more to induce Casaubon to see Baronio not only as a bad scholar, but also as a bad human being.

When Henri IV was assassinated and Casaubon, fearing the worst for Protestantism in France, accepted the invitation of James I and moved to England, he became solvent for the first time in his life—although ingrained habit and large expenses kept him nervous about his finances until he died in 1614—and he felt himself deeply in the king's debt.[43] But he also admired the king for substantive reasons. James was the sometimes ungrateful beneficiary of a fine humanist education. He appreciated—and shared—Casaubon's expert, critical command of ancient and modern historians, as their first extended conversation in November 1610 made clear: "We happened to speak about Tacitus, Plutarch, Commines, and others. The King said that

---

tis juxta insignes, qui adversus furiosos istos τερατολόγους stylum acuant. En erit unquam ille dies, cum exorietur aliquis [cf. *Aeneid* 4.625: exoriare aliquis nostris ex ossibus ultor], qui patrocinium verae ἀρχαιολογίας ἐκκλησιαστικῆς fortiter suscipiat?"

41. Details in Grafton 1983–1993, II, 747–749.

42. See, e.g., Schoppe's letter to Baronio, Schoppe 1600, 141: "tuorum Annalium aureorum lectio, quam suggerente Illust. Viro Ioann. Matthaeo Wackerio susceperam, in viam me reduxit, et discussa nube in lucem veritatis intueri fecit." See also 142: "Nam si verum dicendum est, sola dulcedine et melle illo antiquorum morum et rituum, quod tu ex scriptoribus variis qua sacris, qua profanis, Graecis et Latinis ad instar apis Hybleae confecisti, illectus primum fui, ut Annales tuos continua lectione absolverem . . . Vere igitur et illud dico, te unum perpetuae salutis meae auctorem exstitisse."

43. The negotiations and passage are well described in Pattison 1892, as is the level of income Casaubon received as a canon of Canterbury and Windsor. James's commitment to him is clear from the note that he saw in August 1612, added in the king's own hand to a letter to Sir Julius Caesar: "Chanceler of my Excheker, I will have Mr. Casaubon paid befor me, my wife, and my barnes, manu ipsius Regis"; Casaubon 1850, II, 942.

those who treated Tacitus as the sole teacher of civil prudence were wrong, and I said that a year ago I had made the same judgment in my preface to Polybius. Then this very learned king said he was delighted that I agreed with him. He criticized Plutarch for his unfairness to Julius Caesar, Commines for his frivolity in judgment, and his mean-spirited verdict on the English."[44] Casaubon was delighted to find himself working for a patron who shared so much of his culture and so many of his values. The assassination of Henri IV—which Casaubon, like so many other Protestants, blamed on the teaching of the Jesuits—helped to crystallize his views.[45] So, of course, did his experience of the hierarchical, sacramental Church of England, which he admired, and sometimes described as the closest existing approximation to the ancient church at its best—even if he found more emotional and religious sustenance in the Huguenot church of his upbringing.

Although James, like Casaubon, knew how to speak an ecumenical language when he wished, he basically saw the Anglican church as the true church, and himself as its defender against its Catholic enemies.[46] For the most part, James wanted Casaubon to read, in an official capacity, the theological treatises and controversial pamphlets in which Catholic and Protestant theologians denounced and mauled one another—and to give James and his bishops such learned assistance as they needed. Often Casaubon dined with the king—a Barmecide feast, in which he and others stood behind their master while he sat and ate, and discussed matters that interested him. These matters, Casaubon soon found, were largely religious. In January 1611, for example, he found himself helping the king to pass judgment over dinner on a new Catholic translation of the Old and New Testaments: "I attended the King as he dined, and throughout the whole course of the meal I heard him give a critique of the notes that appear in the English version of the Holy Bible that recently appeared at Douay. The Bishop of Bath read out passages, the King assessed them. His criticisms found approval

44. Casaubon 1850, II, 786: "Incidit sermo de Tacito, Plutarcho, Commineo, aliis. Quum dixisset Rex errare eos qui Tacitum magistrum civilis prudentiae unicum facerent, atque ego dixissem, ante annum idem judicasse me in praefatione ad Polybium, tum non mediocriter se gaudere Rex doctissimus dixit, quod ego idem secum sentirem. In Plutarcho reprehendebat iniquitatem erga Julium Caesarem, in Commineo levitatem judiciorum et malignum elogium Anglorum. Quid multa? Non sine stupore tantum Regem de literis audivi pronuntiare."

45. For one sample of Casaubon's late views on Jesuits and regicide see his copy of Heraldus (Strasbourg 1612), BL 860.b.19.(1). In a characteristic general note on the title page, Casaubon describes this sharply polemical work as "Opus divinum et Politicis serio legendum," and on the flyleaf he sums up an argument from 131: "Jesuitarum scelere Henricus M. cecidit." For a historical account of the real political views of the Jesuits on these questions see Höpfl 2004, 314–338.

46. For an erudite effort to treat James (and Casaubon) as irenic figures see Patterson 1997. For more balanced accounts, which accept that both men's views were inconsistent at times, see Milton 1995, as well as the classic studies of Malcolm 1984 and Quantin 2009.

with those who were present: the Bishop of Ely, the Bishop of Coventry, and me with them."[47] Casaubon warmly praised "this King's miraculous delight in sacred studies, which can never be sufficiently praised."[48]

Casaubon served the king well. He not only read and judged works of controversial theology for him, but also wrote polemical treatises to order. At the same time, he served not only James, but also the erudite bench of bishops who surrounded the king, and who—like Jacques-Auguste de Thou in the previous decade—felt that a final sanding and varnishing by the hand of this great scholar would make their attacks on Catholic scholars and scholarship gleam very brightly. Soon after his arrival, Casaubon began spending a great deal of time with Lancelot Andrewes, the erudite and eloquent bishop of Ely. The two men developed a deep affection for each other, nourished by a happy trip in summer 1611 to Andrewes' diocese, where Casaubon marveled as the punters in the rivers appeared and disappeared in the reeds, and tried to work out how the Octagon, the spectacular tower of Ely Cathedral, managed to stay aloft.[49] Andrewes' ghost stories of murderous Londoners whose souls were sent back to Earth to confess their crimes and of crosses that fell from the sky on the astonished citizens of Wells seem to have delighted Casaubon's pious soul.[50]

What really brought Casaubon and Andrewes together, however, were their shared interests and the services, the informed reading and criticism, that Casaubon could provide. On 4 December 1610, very soon after his arrival, Casaubon found himself spending the afternoon with the bishop, "listening as he read the eighth chapter of his book. With marvelous elegance the learned man refutes the follies, trivialities, and ineptitudes—and sometimes the downright blasphemies—of Robert Bellarmine. For example, he had denied that Catholics call the Blessed Virgin Diva or Dea. The bishop of Ely cites many passages in which Lipsius refers to her thus."[51] Casaubon

47. Casaubon 1850, II, 809: "Ad Aulam hodie profectus, concioni interfui cujus non multa sane, non tamen plane nihil intellexi. Regem inde conveni serenissimum plane Principem et sui semper simillimum. Prandenti affui, et toto prandio, quam longum illud fuit, audivi examinantem Notas appositas Versioni Anglicae S. Bibliorum quae nuper Duaco prodiit. Legebat Episcopus Bathoniensis, Rex censebat. Censuras approbabant qui aderant Episcopus Eliensis, Episcopus Coventriensis, et ego cum illis."

48. Ibid.: "Dominus Jesus Regem optimum magis magisque lumine suae veritatis velit illustrare. Mira certe hujus Principis in studiis sacris oblectatio, quae satis nunquam laudari poterit."

49. Ibid., 854–878. Some of the notes that Casaubon took on this trip, during July, August, and September 1611, are preserved in Bod MS Casaubon 25.

50. Bod MS Casaubon 25, 115 verso and 128 verso; MS Casaubon 28, 125 recto.

51. Casaubon 1850, II, 793: "Mane aliquid egi in studiis: a prandio apud D. Eliensem fui, et legentem illum audivi caput libri sui octavum. Mira elegantia vir doctissimus quisquilias, naenias et ineptias, imo aliquando impias blasphemias Bellarmini confutat: ut quod negaverat ille Catholicos appellare B. Virginem, vel *Divam,* vel *Deam:* nam profert Eliensis multa Lipsii loca, in quibus ita illam compellat, Lipsii veteris amici mei, qui hac in parte satis vituperari non potest."

claimed to find the bishop's work a revelation, and expressed his shock that his old friend Lipsius had written something so genuinely impious.[52] Soon, however, as Festa pointed out long ago, he was hard at work doing what he called his *pensum* (assignment) at the bishop's house: presumably giving Andrewes' text a range of references and a level of Latinity that would do the Anglican church proud.[53]

In England, Casaubon found a church that seemed to him to follow precisely the via media he had been looking for—a combination of genuinely Protestant theology and genuinely traditional liturgy, richly informed by the study of the fathers and the early church. In the king, in Andrewes, in John Overall, the dean of St. Paul's, and others, he also found conversation partners who shared his interests, admired his learning, and had interesting things of their own to say about difficult passages in the New Testament and the problems of the modern churchman.[54] Meanwhile, as the biggest theological guns on both sides exchanged broadsides and Casaubon himself became more identified as a controversialist, it was almost inevitable that he would turn his attention once again to Baronio.

By late April 1612, Casaubon and James had decided that he would dedicate himself to dismantling the *Annales,* and Casaubon, as usual, described his plans in detail to his diary and his God.[55] He became more and more outspoken in his public polemical writing. As early as 1611 he informed

52. Ibid., 793–794: "Tantine nominis virum tantam ausum esse impietatem? Proh facinus! Ego frivolum putavi utrumque scriptum illius, tamen impium non putavi." The passage the bishop read included what became Andrewes 1610, 174–175:

> Vide vel *Lipsium* (sapientiae utique et literarum Antistitem) atque eius *Divam* geminam, *Hallensem* et *Aspricollem.* Frons ipsa vocem praefert, et vertex cuiusque paginae. Legas ibi plus centies, ne {*imprudenter putes excidisse*} et voce integra, ne capitali litera scriptam, {*ne D. pro B. Typographos quis putet substituisse*} Legas, o *Diva:* et, o *Diva Divarum.* Denique, neque ea voce uti veritus, vel tum, cum ad *Paulum* iam Pontificem scriberet. Atque haec apud *Lipsium:* quem non impune tulisset, qui vivum, vel {*parum prudentem*} vel {*non bene institutum Catholicum*} scripsisset. Puto, nec iam *Scribanio* feret, qui *Divam* et *Lipsium* amat; qui et ipse *Divae* vocem usurpat: qui Illum, qui se, qui censorem *Fabritium,* tum Approbatores *Cameracensem* et *Mechliniensem* Archiepiscopos, ab hac, *male instituti Catholici* calumnia, si vivit, et vir est, vindicabit.
>
> At [*non Dea*]. Imo, nec ea voce abstinuit, in *Hallensi.* [*si vota concepisset Hallensi Deae*].
>
> Tum, in illa altera Dea sua sesquipedali: [*An sudas, Dea, sanguinem? De qua sacra profantur, Hanc fore, quae serpentis conteret caput: fecisti o Dea.*] Et, [*tunc tibi laudes, Dea, dicet omnis, Sexus et aetas.*] Quid videtur?

On Lipsius' devotion to the Virgin see the rich study of Bass 2007 [2008].

53. Festa 1911.

54. For some nice examples see in general Casaubon 1850, II.

55. Casaubon 1850, II, 928: "V. Kal. Mai. Quod Deus Opt. Max. consilium velit fortunare; post longam deliberationem, longam meditationem et praeparationem, hodie accinxi me scriptioni Antibaronianae. Scis tu, bone Jesu, nulla me adduci levitate, nulla inanis gloriolae titillatione, sed sola cupiditate veritatis defendendae, in re praesertim tanti momenti. Nam quum multa sint justa reprehensione digna apud Baronium in Annalibus, nihil tamen est in quo plus ille operae posuerit quam ut Papae Romani tyrannidem in Ecclesiam universam et maxime in Reges et Principes confirmaret. Vident omnes quo

Fronton du Duc that Baronio had really written only to support the papal tyranny, and in 1612 he argued in print that the Anglican, rather than the Catholic, church corresponded best to ancient Christianity.[56] Meanwhile his diary recorded his progress in detail. On 27 July he noted that he had been preparing to write, rather than writing, and was now really buckling down to the work.[57] By August he had begun to compose recognizable passages of the *Exercitationes*.[58] From time to time he encountered setbacks. In December he received the worst bad news any writer can: a rival, the Anglican scholar Richard Mountagu, planned to issue his own work against Baronio —a book that, so far as Casaubon could tell, represented a shameless plagiarism of his own efforts (in fact, Mountagu sharply disapproved of what he saw as Casaubon's savage attacks on the probity and scholarship of the church fathers).[59] When he gave Andrewes a copy of the text, his friend took it, and held on to it—but neither read it nor gave it back.[60] Still, he never lost

---

haec doctrina jam pervenerit, quos progressus fecerit, et quotidie faciat, quot tristia exempla ab illo fonte manantia prodierint. Tibi, magne mundi Rector, eam tyrannidem probari nec credo, nec, ut credam, adduci unquam potero. Putamus eos, qui pro sua virili huic errori sese opponunt, et recte facere, et Deo veritatis vindici gratum offerre sacrificium. Hoc fretus, et spe omni mea in Dei auxilio posita, aggredior polire quae dudum observavi et editioni illa parare. Veneror supremum Numen, adsit conatibus meis, det veritatis notitiam, liberet mentem ab erroribus, servet me, meam et meos ἀπημάντους per Jesum Christum unicum mundi Servatorem, cui una cum Patre et Spiritu Sancto sit laus, honos et gloria in aeternum. Amen."

56. Casaubon 1611, 11–12: "Omnium instar esse queant duo Illustrissimi Cardinales, Baronius et Bellarminus; quorum ille cum Ecclesiasticos Annales, ingens opus et laboriosum, susciperet contexendos, id unum emunctae naris hominibus videtur negotij sibi dari credidisse, ut hanc de infinita Summi Pontificis potentia mirificam doctrinam, per totam seriem temporum εὐκαίρως, ἀκαίρως, confirmaret; qui etiam Paulo V. Pontificatum ineunti, Gregorium VII. ceu perfectam aliquam ideam legitimae administrationis cum proposuit; hoc videlicet non obscure significavit; eum demum se iudicare laude dignum Pontificem, qui dominationis suae caussa caelum terrae miscere, et universam Europam caedibus et parricidijs implere non dubitaret." See Casaubon 1612; Eudaemon-Ioannes 1612; and Prideaux 1614 for the further development of controversy before the *Exercitationes* appeared.

57. Casaubon 1850, II, 938: "Hodie observationes in Baronium serio sum aggressus. Nam hactenus magis paravi praesidia ad scribendum, quam scripsi; nunc Deo duce, ut confido, atque auspice, ad opus manum admovi."

58. Ibid., 940–941 (9 August 1612): "Hodie absolvi disputationem de prophetia Jacobi quam occasione Baronii eram aggressus. Siquid bene dixi, tuum id totum est, Christe Jesu. Si erravi, meum hoc, sed tu da meliora, et miserere languentis. Amen"; ibid., 942 (25 August 1612): "Quaedam hodie de Mercurio Trismegisto, sed quae mox displicuerunt. Deus meae familiae et studiis benedicat."

59. Ibid., 957 (22 December 1612): "Ego modo didici Anglum quendam, ex invidia et improba aemulatione, ausum esse opus, quod jussu Regis aggressus sum. ipsum quoque aggredi, et tradidisse partem edendam hic. Vidi titulos, et vix mihi persuadeo ipsum non grassatum furto in mea scripta, quae tam multi jam viderunt. O invidiam! O improbitatem! Nam si tale quid parabat, cur dissimulavit? Ego illi paratus fui ἐκχωρεῖν. Nunc, illo antevertente, quid consilii ipse capiam, nescio. Puto Savilium, quem mihi olim descripsit Scaliger, esse auctorem consilii." For the further course of this incident see Russell's notes, ibid., 1212–15; Pattison 1892; and Quantin 2009.

60. Casaubon 1850, II, 968 (12 February 1613): "Mihi hodie hoc accidit molestissimum. Chartas meas Baronianas dedi recensendas cuidam amico, viro probo, optimo, et longe doctissimo. Ille jam mensem fere alterum differt reddere, nec legit tamen, de quo mihi certe constat. Repetii ipse saepe; hodie misi

his confidence that—as he wrote to his friend John Prideaux on 13 March 1613—"I . . . have found an infinite number of idiotic mistakes in Baronio and Bellarmine, deriving from shameful ignorance of Greek. For Baronio has never even touched Hebrew or other Eastern languages."[61] At the end of May (old style), after a trip to Oxford, he began writing the final draft.[62] By the end of January 1614 he had finished the enormous text, and although he had only a few months of life left to him, he managed to write substantial prefaces to the king and to the reader, see the book through the press, draw up the indexes—and present completed copies to the king and others.[63]

Casaubon originally planned that his critique would cover a vast range of topics: chiefly what he saw as Baronio's continual effort to support the papacy's claim to universal political authority, but also what he took to be Baronio's efforts to defend the impious self-indulgence and luxury of the contemporary church. "O mores, O tempora," he wrote at one such point in his copy of the *Annales,* treating the Catholic scholar as a combination of Tartuffe and Catiline.[64] Indeed, many of the notes that Casaubon entered in later volumes of the *Annales* show him ranging as widely down the centuries as Baronio, and doing so in a strikingly unecumenical mood: "The martyr-

praeceptorem meorum liberorum, neque ego recepi, neque ille. Atqui vir ille probitate singulari est. Quid igitur? Ego aliud suspicari non possum, nisi virum illum optimum meas lucubrationes amicis suis ostendisse, et jam repetere aut certe recipere non posse. Deum immortalem! Quanta haec est, quae mihi fit injuria? Exspectabo tamen, et me componam ad omnia ferenda."

61. Ibid., 1222: "Scio etiam me in Baronio et Bellarmino infinitos errores asininos deprehendisse e Graecae linguae pudenda ignoratione ortos. Nam Hebraicam aut alias Orientales Baronius ne attigit quidem."

62. Ibid., 986 (29 May 1613): "Hodie, quod faustum esse et felix Deus velit, ad descriptionem operis Baroniani serio me accinxi."

63. Ibid., 1034–35 (21 January 1614): "Jam ante multos annos meditatus eram aliquid adversus Baronii Annales, quod in magna hodie auctoritate esse videbam et sciebam tamen esse errorum plenos. Optabam dari mihi facultatem eos errores, ut equidem existimabam, aperiendi: pertinere enim hoc ad veritatis caelestis defensionem intelligebam; eo impensius optabam posse id a me praestari quod eram meditatus. Nunquam de totius operis refutatione equidem cogitavi gnarus τὸν βίον βραχὺν et me aetate jam provectum. Illud saepe tacitis votis a Deo petii ut ad primum tomum serio possem respondere, quoniam ibi sunt principia omnium hodiernarum controversiarum. Iterum igitur atque iterum imo μυριάκις gratias tibi, Deus aeterne, quod dederis mihi occasionem veniendi in hoc regnum ubi oblata est facultas et otium ad suscipiendum illud inceptum. Suscepi et spatio longe minore quam posse fieri sperabam partem priorem propositi absolvi. Septem mensibus et paucis diebus opus, qualecunque id sit, composui. Oxonium deinde abii, et fui ibi aliquamdiu: fuerunt et alia oblata mihi gravia avocamenta a studiis. Valetudo saepe magnum mihi metum incussit, et tristissima denunciant medici. Veruntamen dedit mihi tua, O Deus, bonitas, ut nullum temere diem propter valetudinem amitterem, quo non lineam saltem aliquam ducerem. Absoluta igitur jam est hujus partis editio. Restant praefationes, in quibus tua cum maxime ope mihi opus, O bone Jesu. Ita prodibit foras opus novum, de quo iniqua multorum judicia me experturum nullus dubito." In fact Casaubon continued to revise the text, at least in parts, after his trip to Oxford.

64. Casaubon, marginal note in his copy of vol. IV of the *Annales,* Baronio 1601, Marsh's Library, col. 247, 367 n. 10: "En pietatem! O mores! O tempora! Nam cur patrocinatur luxui?"

dom of Mary Queen of Scots"—so he wrote in one cold note—"anyone who has read Buchanan's history will take this quite calmly."[65]

In the finished *Exercitationes,* as we have seen, Casaubon concentrated on the earliest years of Christian history, the lifetime of Jesus. But even this limited sphere gave him ample opportunity to argue, as he put it in the preface, that Baronio's failings as a Hebraist mattered as much as his defects as a Hellenist, and that both made it impossible for him to write a scholarly study of the early church:

> For no one can illuminate the institutions of the early Church, shed light on the Gospel History covered in these *Annales,* or illuminate the obscure writings of the Fathers and other writers, if he lacks skill in Hebrew and Greek and perfect mastery of all antiquities. For since this first volume, in particular, is stuffed with the testimonies of Hebrew and Greek writers, one might reasonably ask if Baronio had the linguistic skills and mastery of antiquities appropriate to the task. The *Annales* show, on almost every page, that he did not.[66]

As Casaubon went through Baronio's work, he picked out point after point where the Oratorian revealed his ignorance of all things Jewish. Baronio did not know the bibliography of Jewish scholarship. As he read the first volume of the *Annales,* pen in hand, Casaubon picked up a reference to "the compendium of the Talmud that is called Alfesi." "He means," Casaubon wrote, "the compendium of the Talmud that was written by Rabbi Alphes. He is often cited by other rabbis"—and in his final text he made savage fun of Baronio's mistake.[67] Casaubon took equal pleasure in noting that when Baronio referred to one "Jacob Turim," he showed that he did not actually know the work in question, the *Arba'ah Turim* of Jacob ben Asher.

---

65. Casaubon, note in ibid., V, title page: "Mariae Scotorum reginae martyrium. Hoc aequo feret animo qui Buchanani historiam legerit."

66. Casaubon 1614, A recto; 1654 [f4 verso]; 1663 [f4 verso]: "Nam illustrare nascentis praesertim Ecclesiae instituta, Historiae Evangelicae his annalibus insertae lucem foenerari, scripta Patrum et aliorum scriptorum obscura illustrare et explicare, nemo profecto potest, qui Hebraicae Graecaeque linguae peritia et omnium veterum antiquitatum notitia non sit quam instructissimus. Quum igitur testimonijs scriptorum Hebraicorum et Graecorum hic praesertim tomus primus sit refertissimus: quaerat iure aliquis, an parem tanto incepto cognitionem illarum linguarum et antiquae eruditionis copiam Baronius habuerit. Atqui hoc singulis fere paginis isti Annales clarissime negant."

67. Casaubon, note in vol. I of his copy of the *Annales,* Baronio 1601, Marsh's Library, col. 239, 34 n. 134C, on "ex compendio Thalmud quod dicitur Alphesi": "vult dicere in compendio Talmud quod scripsit R. Alphes. Hic saepe citatur a Rabbinis aliis et in comment. ad pirke 3 . . . R. Mosis sic, כך פסק ר אלפס sic definivit R. Juda vel Joseph. Alphes [e.g., Rabbenu Asher on Gittin 5b]." Baronio had written (1593–1607, I, 183): "Ponendi autem in novo sepulchro Christi corporis quaenam ratio fuerit, colligitur ex compendio Thalmud, quod dicitur Alphesi, et Rabbinis Iacob Turim et Moyse Aegyptio."

Casaubon proudly pointed out that he himself had "recently seen the Cremona edition of that book, in the celebrated Bodleian Library at Oxford, but only in passing, among many other Hebrew books."[68] Baronio, by contrast, "imprudently confused the author's name with the title." This remark was an exaggeration, since perfectly correct references to Jacob ben Asher's book also appeared in Baronio's work.[69] On the other hand, Baronio did seem to suggest, incorrectly, that Maimonides mentioned the practices and implements employed in the Crucifixion—an error that Casaubon took very seriously indeed.[70]

As always in this sort of scholarly skirmish, minor slips gave the critic a pretext to unleash a good bit of small-arms fire, noisy if somewhat inaccurate. But Baronio also tried repeatedly to explicate the Jewish terms and institutions that came up for mention in the Gospels, and in doing so he transgressed on territory that Casaubon considered distinctively his own, and

---

68. Casaubon 1614, 655; 1654, 577; 1663, 577: "Iudica nunc Lector de fide horum Annalium. Praeter Maimonidam laudat Baronius et librum Alphesi et Rabbinum Iacob Turim: etiam haec ex aliena fide, ut res arguit. Putavit Alphesi nomen esse libri, non scriptoris. et verum quidem est, extare inter libros Iudaicos quasi compendium Talmud, ut ait Baronius, sub hoc titulo: sed ignoravit Baronius, id esse nomen eius Rabbini, qui eam syllogen confecit. observo laudari in Commentarijs ad Iad Maimonidae רי אלפס, Rabbi Iudam aut Iosephum Alphes, qui an hic sit, non facile dixerim. Quis autem ille est, quem nominat Baronius Iacobum Turim? Hic vero conditor Annalium hallucinatus est insigniter: perinde enim fecit, ut si quis inter auctores laudaret Tullium de natura, et M. Tullium intelligeret, qui scripsit de natura Deorum. R. Iacob, filius R. Ascher, ante annos trecentos et quod excurrit, librum scripsit ספר ארבע טורים, Liber Arba Turim, sive quatuor ordines: opus est Talmudicum in quatuor partes divisum, quod titulus indicat."

69. Casaubon 1614, 655; 1654, 577; 1663, 577: "nuper eum librum in illustri Bibliotheca Bodlaeana, Oxonij, editum Cremonae, inspexi, sed obiter inter plures alios Hebraicos. Baronius nomen auctoris cum libri titulo imprudenter confudit." For Baronio's use of the text see, e.g., Baronio 1593–1607, I, 183 (34.135–136): "Addimus ad haec insuper quae Rabbi Iacob memoriae prodidit ex Rabbi Moyse Aegyptio: nimirum viros virorum et feminas feminarum curare consuevisse cadavera, in hunc scilicet modum: oculos in primis et ora claudere defuncto, ac stringere fascia, tondere capillos . . . [Babylonian Talmud, Mo'ed Katan 27b] Nec praetermittimus dicere, tantum olim excrevisse apud Hebraeos impensam funerum ut eius magnitudine cognati perterriti, relicto cadavere, se aliquando subducerent. Sed qui haec idem Rabbi Iacob testatur addit ea moderata fuisse a Gamaliele seniore [Iore dea c. 352 (another correct marginal reference)]."

70. Casaubon 1614, 654–655; 1654, 577; 1663, 577: "Solet evenire ijs qui aliena industria scripta sua adornant, ut quae fuerint sibi fideliter suggesta, ea saepe male recitando faciant sua. Hoc fere Baronio accidisse observavimus, quoties ille depromptas è libris Rabbinorum observationes Annalibus suis tanquam emblema aliquod vermiculatum inseruit . . . sed quod ait Mosem Aegyptium auctorem esse, inter caetera Iudaicorum suppliciorum instrumenta, clavos solitos sepeliri, et cruciarios ad lignum excisum fuisse suffixos, non ad arborem: id quia pertinet ad superiorem de cruce disputationem, non praetermittemus. Nam si verum est, Mosem Aegyptium in describendis ritibus suppliciorum Iudaicorum crucifixionis meminisse et clavorum, stare non possunt, quae adversus Baronium in superioribus disputavimus. Sed erravit Baronius, et suggestum sibi locum magni scriptoris malo exemplo in suam sententiam detorsit. Nos vero negamus vel crucifixionis vel clavorum ullam eo loco a Maimonide fieri mentionem. Sententiam Mosis è perek XV illius libri cuius saepe antea meminimus, non eleganter sed fideliter expressam, infra subiecimus." A Latin translation follows of chap. 15 of Maimonides' hilkhot Sanhedrin, which corresponds to Mishnah Sanhedrin 6:4. For further discussion see Chapter 5 below.

that of a few colleagues. At times—especially when Baronio drew on the great Catholic Hebraist Angelo Canini—what he said proved unobjectionable, as when he used Canini's work to explain the meaning of the palm branches that people carried as they went forth to meet Jesus on his way to Jerusalem (John 12:12–13).[71] But when Baronio operated on his own steam, he provoked Casaubon to unlimber bigger guns. In a long note on the publicans who appeared in the Gospels, Baronio explained their function in the Roman Empire. He noted that Zacchaeus was "called the chief of the publicans, for whom the Hebrew term was Gabbe; the other publicans were called Gabbain." And he explained that the "Talmudists," whose views he knew from Canini, regarded the publicans as infamous because they had helped the Romans to destroy the liberty of the Jews. In the margin of the text, Casaubon wrote, with evident irritation, that Baronio did not understand the words he was citing. The standard Hebrew word for publican, he noted, was *mokhes,* and he proceeded to demonstrate this by citing a number of rabbinical texts and a proverb, which also appeared in one of his manuscripts in the Bodleian: "never marry a wife from a family that includes a publican, for they are all publicans."[72] Casaubon drew out the implications of this detailed

71. Baronio's remark appears at Baronio 1593–1607, I, 140–141 (34.5–6): "Nisi dicere velimus esse Hebraismum, idemque sonare, ac si diceretur, Salus nostra a filio David, ut notat Ioannes Drusius [marginal reference: "De voc. Hebr. novi Testa. C. 19"]. Sed magis placent cum quae ipse ex Helia narrat, tum etiam quod Caninius [marginal reference: "Canin. De locis novi Testamen."] rerum Hebraicarum peritissimus, ea refellens, ex Hebraicis fontibus tradit, Hosanna, non duas, sed unam tantum esse dictionem, eandemque significare proprie ramos salicum: verum usurpari consuevisse pro ramis etiam aliarum arborum: atque adeo in Scenophegia moris fuisse portare Hosanna, ac circuire cum Hosanna, hoc est, cum arboris ramo . . . [further evidence] . . . Sed unde accidit, ut arborum rami in ea solemnitate adhiberi soliti, Hosciahnna dicti sint? non aliunde puto, nisi quod sic illi circumeuntes altare et exultantes canerent illud psalmi centesimi decimiseptimi: O Domine salvum me fac: o Domine bene prosperare] ut aperte testantur libri Rituales Hebraeorum, qui extant: inter quae verba, Hosciahnna, vox הושענא expressa habetur, quae repetitur in singulis versibus septem hymnorum, qui septimo die canuntur: quam quoties illi concinerent, ramum illum extollebant, dicentes, Hosciahnna: unde illi nomen est inditum, ut et ut ipse diceretur Hosciahnna." Casaubon lays out a very similar possible interpretation, credited to Canini, at 1614, 448; 1654, 395; 1663, 395.

72. Casaubon, marginal note in his copy of vol. I of the *Annales,* Baronio 1601, Marsh's Library, col. 142, year 31, n. 73 (Baronio 1593, I, 109), on "Hebraice Gabbe":

    videtur nescivisse eam esse formam plur. Publicanus heb. est מוכס ut in proverbio אין לך etc. ne tibi sit uxor e familia מוכס nam sunt [ם]מוכסי כולם [the proverb occurs in many rabbinic texts, including Sifra Ked. 10:10 and B Shevuot 39a].

    Integrum proverbium ita effertur

    אין לך מ

    משפחה ש

    שיש בה מוכס

    שהן כולם

    מוכסים.

Casaubon includes this proverb in a collection preserved in Bod MS Casaubon 17, 1 recto, as the first entry in "Selecta quaedam Hebraica proverbia e scriptis Rabb." On the term *mokhes* see Schürer 1973–1987, I, 376 n. 108.

critique in the *Exercitationes:* "the learned gentleman, suffering from a common failing of the human intellect, apparently wanted to claim credit for knowledge of Hebrew as well, as this passage and others show. But matters fell out in the opposite way. For these passages would more easily lead you to conclude that he did not even know how to read Hebrew, than that he had any real skill in the language."[73]

The issues that divided the two men were sometimes both substantial and traditional. In Genesis 49:10 Jacob predicts that "The scepter shall not depart from Judah, nor a lawgiver from between his feet, until Shiloh come." But Ezekiel seemingly contradicted the patriarch when he wrote (21:27): "I will overturn, overturn, overturn it: and it shall be no [more], until he come whose right it is; and I will give it [him]." Casaubon, like other exegetes before him, worried about the apparent conflict of prophesies. As he wrote in one of his notebooks,

> Many rabbis also agree that Silo is one of the names of the Messiah. I approve of this explanation, because this view is supported by great witnesses. But every time I read Ezekiel 21:27, I have my doubts. For there the prophet predicts the destruction of the Jewish people, or certainly its monarchy, "until he to whom judgment belongs arrives." There can be no doubt that the prophet there refers to Christ. Could it be that the language is full in the other passage and elliptical here?[74]

Baronio tried to reconcile the two passages by arguing that the scepter remained in the tribe of Judah alone until the coming of the Messiah.[75] Casaubon, however, drew on counterarguments put forward by Eusebius in the *Demonstratio evangelica.* He insisted that when Jacob preferred Judah to his

73. Casaubon 1614, 304; 1654, 270; 1663, 270: "Videtur autem vir eruditissimus, humani ingenij vitio usus, etiam e literarum Hebraicarum cognitione laureolam affectasse; quod hic locus arguit et aliquot alij. Sed in contrarium plane res vertit: facilius enim statuas ex eiusmodi locis, ipsum ne legere quidem scivisse Hebraice; quam eius sermonis aliquam peritiam habuisse."

74. Bod MS Casaubon 30, 78 verso: "Gen. 49.10. עד כי יבו שלה [Casaubon misspells יבא]. Exponitur ab accuratioribus interpretibus donec veniat Silo. Etiam multi Rabb. consentiunt Silo esse unum e nominibus Messiae. Probo, quia magnos auctores habet haec sententia. Quoties tamen lego Ezech. versum 27. e cap. 21 [21:32 in the Masoretic text] subdubito. Ibi propheta praedicit destructionem populi Judaici vel certe regiae dignitatis עד בא אשר לו המשפט donec venerit is cuius est judicium. non est dubium de Christo ibi loqui prophetam. An ig. φράσις ibi plena, hic elliptice est enunciata?"

75. Baronio 1593–1607, I, 2: "Tribus enim Iuda in Babylonem, quod sciunt omnes historiae sacrae periti, in servitutem cum sanguine regio fuit adducta; deinde post annos septuaginta in Palaestinam postliminio restituta: cum primum, Iosepho teste, eadem provincia dici Iudaea coepit; quique Hebraei vel Israelitae prius nominabantur, Iudaei deinde sunt appellati. Zerobabel enim, et qui post eum Iudaeos gubernarunt (ut tradit Cyrillus) ex tribu Iuda, ex stirpe David omnes usque ad Herodem Idumaeum fuerunt: quod et Hieronymus testatur, licet alibi aliquando aliter dixerit."

older brother, the first-born Reuben, he awarded him precedence, which the tribe of Judah would retain, and which would make it the appropriate tribe for the Messiah himself to belong to, but not royal power, which was destroyed just as Ezekiel had foreseen.[76] When Petrus Cunaeus, the Dutch scholar whose influential work *De republica Hebraeorum* appeared in 1617, three years after Casaubon's book, he hailed his predecessor's arguments, and those of Eusebius, as the best ones yet advanced—although he maintained that they had not fully understood the nature of the scepter that God had entrusted to the Jewish people.[77] In this and other cases, Casaubon's arguments impressed the community of competent Hebraists as well-informed and weighty, even when they disagreed with him.

The Jesuits who rallied to defend Baronio against Casaubon dismissed these criticisms as pedantic and misguided. Perhaps, Jules-César Bulenger admitted in 1617, Baronio had gone wrong "on chronology, or on some little word in Hebrew, Greek, or Latin," but on matters of faith and doctrine he had never set a foot wrong.[78] But the burrs stuck nonetheless. In a mean-spirited passage, Casaubon ridiculed Baronio for appearing to think that

76. Casaubon 1614, 16; 1654, 15; 1663, 15: "Vis porro decreti huius sive ordinationis ea fuit, ut deinceps inter fratres Iuda semper excelleret, et tribus Iudae inter omnes dignitate potior esset. Stupendam Dei providentiam hic licet admirari; qui illam tribum, ex qua nasciturus erat Messias, voluit ἐπιπολάζειν, et eximio quodam honore insigniri; non quia a primogenito duceret originem, sed ob ipsum, quia Christo originem erat datura. Quis autem piorum dubitare potest, eo potissimum fine haec ita constituta esse, et patefacta, ut populus Iudaicus ex ijs quae videbat oculis suis ad meditationem τῶν μὴ φαινομένων et adhuc latentium excitaretur? dignitas enim tribus Iudae, typus fuit et quasi pignus atque arrhabo regni Messiae. Quae vel maxime ratio videtur impulisse veterum nonnullos, ut figmentum illud excogitarent de regno in tribu Iuda, ad Christi adventum semper mansuro. At longe aliter Iustinus, ut sequentia docebunt. Caesariensis vero Eusebius, vir longe doctissimus et in omni historiarum genere exercitatissimus, in accuratissima huius oraculi explicatione, quae extat libro octavo Demonstrationis [Eusebius, *Demonstratio evangelica* 8.1], figmentum illud validissimis rationibus confutat, ex historia petitis."

77. Cunaeus 1617, 78–79: "Persecutus ea nuper in Exercitationibus Baronianis bene atque feliciter est vir seculi nostri eruditissimus Isaacus Casaubonus, cui placuit Eusebij praeclara de hoc oraculo sententia, quae extat in libro octavo Demonstrationis Evangelicae, in prima demonstratione. Nos ea omnia, quae tam ab Eusebio, quam a Casaubono, recte dicta sunt, praetermittimus, ne actum agamus. Etiam illud fatemur, interpretationum omnium, quae vulgatae hactenus sunt, longe eam esse optimam, cujus autor Eusebius est. Sed quoniam nondum vel Eusebius, vel qui nuper secutus illum est, vir maximus, intellexisse mihi videtur quodnam illud sit sceptrum, aut quando datum Judaeis sit, de quo annosus vates in extremo vitae locutus ad filium est, certe hoc jam expediendum nobis est, sed cum veniae praefatione. Nam nec ab Eusebio dissentire voluptas nobis est, quem in maximis scriptoribus semper numeravimus, et virum, quem nominavimus, seculi nostri primarium, qui secutus Eusebium est, ita penitus veneramur, nemo ut nobis prae illo magnus sit. Est enim is profecto, cujus auspiciis hac aetate admirabilis cursus factus ad omnem doctrinae excellentiam est. Sed nos ingenua simplicitas jubet, quid verum rectumque sit, sine adfectu exquirere."

78. Bulenger 1617, ¶2 verso: "Equidem Illustrissimum Baronium nusquam in tanto opere caespitasse praestare non ausim, sed omnino levia sunt illa, et extra res fidei in quibus allucinatus est. Forte in historia temporum, in vocula Hebraica, Graeca, Latina aliquid peccavit, in re gravi ubi verae et solidae doctrinae caput agitur, inoffenso pede semper ingreditur."

scribes and Pharisees were connected—in fact, a reasonable suggestion: "Baronio thought that the scribes were part of the sect of Pharisees. Nothing more ridiculous than this could be asserted. For the Jews had had an order of Scribes of the Law since very ancient times. They were the ones who read the Law to the people in the Temple and at Synagogues, and interpreted it if necessary."[79] Many Jews, Casaubon believed, traced the origins of the scribal order back to Moses or to David—and thus to periods centuries before the Pharisees and their rivals, the Sadducees, came into being. Not content with making this historical argument, he heaped ridicule on the cardinal's head: "There were scribes who followed the Pharisees, and others who followed the Sadducees, and some who followed the Essenes. Therefore it is no less ridiculous to say that the scribes were one part of the Pharisaic sect than it would be to say that bishops formed one part of the Arian heresy, just because Eusebius of Caesarea, Eusebius of Nicomedia, Paulinus of Tyre, and many other bishops joined Arius."[80] Bulenger struck back with equal violence. Baronio, he pointed out, had followed Jerome. "I think you will not take it on yourself to believe that you are more expert in Hebrew than Saint Jerome, who, as we all admit, was most carefully trained by the Hebrews themselves. Scholars say that you should never have mingled Hebrew words in your writings, since, as they regularly proclaim, you are totally ignorant of them, and they show that you were fooled by the Jew whom you took as your teacher in England."[81] We will return in the next chapter to Casaubon's Jewish teacher. For now, what matters is Bulenger's clear recognition both that when Casaubon denounced Baronio's incompetence in Hebrew, he touched a nerve in his opponents—and that they, in their turn, knew that his claims to mastery of Hebrew had a tinge of exaggeration.

It may seem surprising that Baronio and Casaubon, for all their differ-

79. Casaubon 1614, 57; 1654, 52; 1663, 52: "Existimavit Baronius, Scribas sectae Pharisaeorum esse membrum: quo nihil absurdius dici queat. nam Scribarum Legalium ordo fuit apud Iudaeos ex antiquissimo instituto. ipsi quippe erant, qui Legem populo legebant, in Templo et in Synagogis, ac si opus esset interpretabantur."

80. Casaubon 1614, 57; 1654, 53; 1663, 53: "E corpore Scribarum fuerunt qui sequerentur Pharisaeos, qui Sadducaeos, necnon qui Essenos. quare non minus absurdum est dicere Scribas alteram fuisse partem sectae Pharisaicae; quam si quis dicat Episcopos haereseos Arrianae unam partem confecisse: quia Eusebius Caesariensis, Eusebius Nicomediensis, Paulinus Tyrensis, et plures alij Episcopi Arrio adhaeserunt."

81. Bulenger 1617, 77: "De scribarum antiquitate Illustrissimus Baronius B. Hieronymum auctorem sequutus est, qui eos a Samai et Hillel ortos esse defendit lib. 3. in Esaiam ad cap. 8. Es. Opinor id non tibi sumes, ut Beato Hieronymo te linguae Hebraicae peritiorem esse putes, quem ab Hebraeis ipsis diligentissime institutum fatentur omnes. Te vero docti aiunt Hebraica verba scriptis tuis admiscere non debuisse, quorum te plane rudem esse quotidie clamitant, ostenduntque Iudaeum illum tibi imposuisse, quem in Anglia Doctorem asciveras."

ences in approach, agreed that church historians needed to discuss Jewish institutions and rituals—as well as the Greek and Hebrew texts that described them—in detail. The ancient founder of the genre, Eusebius of Caesarea, offered no precedent for this kind of sustained inquiry in ancient Judaism. Although he touched briefly on the political history of the Jews and the high priesthood in Jerusalem, he emphasized continuity above all, and treated the Christian church as something that had sprung into existence fully formed, already equipped with liturgies, orthodox doctrines, and bishops.[82] He even folded the development of Jewish asceticism into this story by quoting Philo's long account of the beliefs and practices of the Therapeutae, a Jewish ascetic sect, and arguing that they had been the first Christian monks.[83]

But in the 1550s, when Flacius Illyricus and his colleagues set out to write their Protestant history of the church, they adopted a radically different approach—one appropriate to a time when Christian scholars had begun to study Hebrew. From the start of their work, they insisted that one could not hope to understand the church that Jesus created without first surveying the Jewish beliefs and institutions that he had known and worked with: "Christ arrived at a time when the Jewish religion was still in some sense intact. Therefore he used certain ceremonies, especially those that God established through Moses, and did not use others, such as the traditions of the elders, which had elements of superstition. Accordingly, before we go over the new and splendid rituals that Christ established, we will describe the received and customary ceremonies of the Jewish people."[84] This collaborative history, known as the *Magdeburg Centuries,* offered substantial accounts of the three great Jewish sects and of Jewish customs and practices, some of which made ingenious historical use of the Gospels.[85] More generally, the *Centuries*

82. Eusebius, *Historia ecclesiastica* 1.6, 1.10.

83. Ibid., 2.17. Eusebius inserted Philo's account of Christian history into a key passage, ibid., 2.16.

84. Flacius Illyricus et al. 1561–1574, I, col. 237: "Incidit Christus in religionem Iudaicam, adhuc qualitercunque stantem. Itaque et ceremonijs quibusdam communicavit, praesertim a Deo per Mosen institutis: quibusdam vero non, ut traditionib. seniorum, quae aliquid superstitionum habuere. Priusquam igitur ritus novos et insignes a Christo institutos recenseamus, quorum paucissimi sunt, receptas atque usitatas ceremonias populi Iudaici commemorabimus."

85. Ibid., cols. 227–272 (I.i.5–9). A particularly ingenious piece of argument occurs in the passage on synagogues, ibid., col. 240: "Vtrum autem in templo aut prope locus seu auditorium aut lectorium tale, ut nunc vocare possemus, fuerit, non est clare indicatum. Porro in caeteris locis Iudaeae passim synagogae fuerunt: templis vero in universum caruerunt, unico Hierosolymitano (iuxta Dei mandatum) contenti. Sic scriptum est Matthaei 4. IESVM totam circuisse Galilaeam, et docuisse in synagogis eorum. Matthaei 9. Circuibat IESVS omnes civitates et castella, docens in synagogis. Sic synagogae in Capernaum mentio fit Matthaei 12. Marci 3. Lucae 6. in Nazareth, Matthaei 13. Marci 6. Lucae 4. Habuerunt autem in synagogis cathedras, quarum aliae superiores, aliae inferiores habebantur. et taxat Christus

followed Josephus in treating the division of the Jews into rival groups of Pharisees, Sadducees, and Essenes as the basic fact about Judaism in the last centuries B.C.E., and quoted him—rather than Eusebius—as their prime authority. Not all later church historians accepted this approach. The Lutheran scholar Lucas Osiander, who issued what he described as an epitome of the *Centuries* in 1592–1599, suggested that their authors had wasted too much time on Jewish sects. "The countenance of God's Church was sorrowful in those days," he explained, and after a very brief account of Pharisees, Sadducees, and Essenes he passed rapidly on to the life of Jesus.[86] But Baronio, committed to confronting the Centuriators and defeating them, text by text and line by line, followed their lead and investigated Jewish life and institutions with considerable care and seriousness, mostly on the basis of texts in Greek. He, too, examined at length what Josephus had famously identified as the major sects—Pharisees, Sadducees, and Essenes—as well as a host of minor ones, including Samaritans, Hemerobaptists, Ossenes, and Herodians.

Characteristically, Casaubon dismissed Baronio's efforts in general terms as pointless: "Baronio," he wrote, "has a long discourse about the Jewish sects. In this, I must confess, I have not been able to detect a single gleam of truly solid, subtle learning; for as he recites the errors of others he makes them his own, and in addition he makes his own mistakes."[87] From his own point of view, Baronio's errors were especially reprehensible because Hebrew sources offered vital information about the most central, and bitterly controversial, events, in the history of Christianity, such as the Crucifixion itself. Casaubon's desire to come to grips with the vexing problem of the historical circumstances in which Jesus was crucified—a problem that still haunts biblical scholars[88]—is already manifested in the practically illegible

---

scribas et pharisaeos, qui ambitione ardentes, affectarunt in synagogis primas tenere cathedras: Matth. 23."

86. Osiander 1592–1599, I, 2–4 (I.i.2.2). Osiander rejected Eusebius' identification of Jewish ascetics as Christians, using arguments that elegantly wielded historical considerations as his dogmatic convictions dictated (2–4): "Tristis erat ijs temporibus facies Ecclesiae Dei . . . Ceremonias et peculiaria sua dogmata nemini, nisi in ipsorum societatem receptus esset, et silentium per multas execrationes promisisset, revelabant. Quo argumento colligi potest, eos a lucifugo spiritu gubernatos: qui tamen in angelum lucis sese transfigurant. De resurrectione corporum nihil docebant: Animas autem piorum in loca amoenissima, ultra Oceanum, ablegabant: impiorum vero animas locis procellosis et hybernis, plena gemitibus, deputabant. Errant igitur, qui hos homines Christianos fuisse putant: ineptiores autem sunt, qui antiquitatem vitae Monasticae hinc probare nituntur."

87. Casaubon 1614, 53; 1654, 49; 1663, 49: "Sequitur apud Baronium de sectis Iudaeorum sermo prolixus: in quo equidem, fatebor enim, solidioris et exquisitioris eruditionis micam animadverto nullam: nam et peccata aliena recitando facit sua; et praeterea proprijs ipse culpis non caret."

88. For a modern discussion see Bammel 1970, 162–165.

notes that he made in preparation for a public disputation, presumably held in Geneva, in 1593.[89] Clearly, it was to be a well-structured lecture, and the scribblings in the margins of his notebook indicate that he planned to refer not only to relevant classical sources, but also to the first truly antiquarian discussions of the subject, namely Carlo Sigonio's *De republica Hebraeorum* of 1582 and Justus Lipsius' *De cruce* of 1592.[90] Arguing with remarkable historical perspicuity, Casaubon appears to insist that the Romans had granted the Jews sufficient autonomy to enable them to uphold their own ancestral institutions. In his view, the description of the event of Jesus' crucifixion in the Gospel reflected both Jewish and Roman customs. What was typically Roman was the manner of death inflicted on Jesus.[91]

Twenty years later, Casaubon expanded on the question of Jesus' crucifixion in his *Exercitationes* against Baronio.[92] On this occasion Baronio was put in good scholarly company—that of Lipsius and Sigonio—all of whom Casaubon castigated for their misguided views of the Jewish legal institutions encoded in the Bible, Philo, and the writings of the rabbis.[93] Casaubon denounced Baronio for having declared that crucifixion was a death penalty administered by the Jews in antiquity, and for claiming, on the basis of Philo's testimony, that crucifixion was the capital punishment for murderers.[94] According to Casaubon, Jews may have been responsible for the death of Jesus, but they did not crucify him. True, Philo stated in *De legibus spe-*

89. Bod MS Casaubon 25, 41 recto–42 verso: "De passione Domini nostri IESV CHRISTI σὺν θεῷ publice habita disputatio CIƆIƆXCIII."

90. Sigonio 1582, 272–273 (VI.8). Casaubon may be said to have been partly fashioned from the same mold as Sigonio: both had been taught by the Cretan Greek scholar Franciscus Portus. On Lipsius' *De cruce* see de Landtsheer 2000. Casaubon also refers to Bonaventura Cornelius Bertramus, *De politia Judaica*, the 2d ed. of which (Geneva, 1593) is dedicated to Casaubon's mentor Theodor Beza.

91. Bod MS Casaubon 25, 41 recto–verso: "Igitur ut ad rem veniam, illud ante omnia ponendum nobis est: Iudicium quod in urbe Hierusalem de Domino nostro celebratum est, auctoribus q. et actoribus Judaeis esse confectum, caeterum apud magistratus Romanos: qui tamen non ita libertatem Judaicam oppresserant ut nihil illis suo more et secundum majorum suorum instituta facere liceret. Itaque eorum omnium quae in hac historia evenisse leguntur, alia ex Judaeorum institutis facta sunt, alia et ea quidem maxime quae majoris momenti sunt et quae potestatis et ἐξουσίας sint indicia ex moribus Romanorum. Nam ut in eo loco potiss. qui Golgota vocat. Christus crucifigeretur . . . riteque ut crucifixus tolleretur e cruce ante vesperam, aliaque id genus ex iure et instituto Hebr. fuere. At ut morte afficeretur, et tali mortis genere item alia quae deinceps experiretur iure Rom. id factum et moribus eius gentis. Neque hic tamen quaeram habuerintne ius aliquod gladii illis temporibus Judaei an non. Quae graviss. quaestio est non vero huius loci."

92. Casaubon 1614, 610–620; 1654, 537–546; 1663, 537–546.

93. Scaliger also had few good words to say about Lipsius' *De cruce*. See Scaliger 1695, 244; 1740, II, 429: "Lipsius de Cruce n'a rien fait qui vaille. J'en ay traitté en Eusebe, il faudroit qu'il fist un autre livre pour bien faire."

94. Baronio 1593–1607, I, 169: "Erat et apud Iudaeos crux in usu, sed ea poena afficiebantur homicidae, ut Philo tradit."

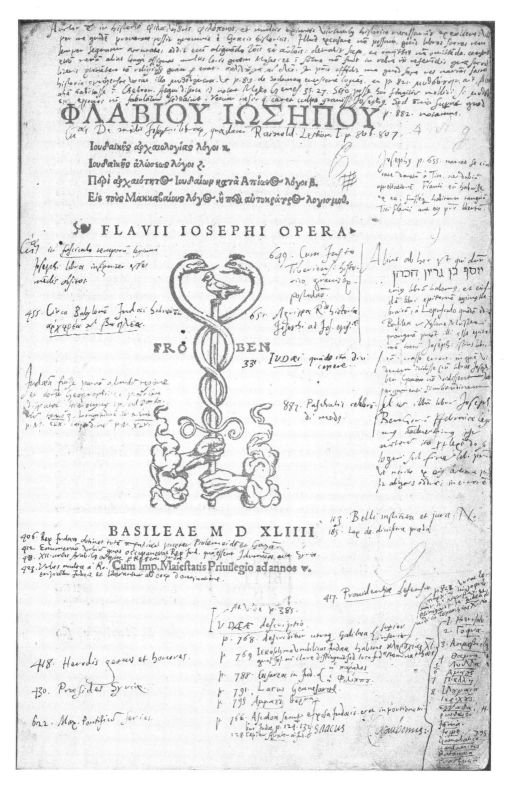

FIGURE 4.3. Title page of Casaubon's copy of Flavius Josephus' *Opera omnia*. British Library C.76.g.7.

cialibus (III.151) that murderers were to be hung. But this was simply a reference to the law in Deuteronomy 21, which ordained that the corpses of murderers who had been first killed by stoning and then hung on the gibbet had to be taken down before nightfall.[95] Casaubon's discussion is long and complicated. He does not really give a fair hearing to Baronio, who had made a genuine attempt to examine whether Jesus' punishment fitted the crime for which he was apprehended. In the final analysis Baronio is more concerned with stressing the divine nature of the event of the Crucifixion.[96] In contrast, Casaubon's study ranges over all kinds of biblical, classical, Hellenistic, and patristic sources, many of which were deemed worthy to be included under the entry for "Cross *(stauros)*" in the *Theological Dictionary of the New Testament*.[97]

One text quoted by Casaubon here as irrefutable evidence is not cited in the modern dictionary. He claims that the "sages of that people had expressly stated that their nation did not know about the Roman cross." This is followed by a Hebrew quotation, accompanied by his Latin translation: "דבר זה לא היה בישראל לתחוב המסמרים ברגלי וידי אדם הנסקלים והנתלים ['It was not Israelite custom to plunge nails into the feet and hands of those who were to be stoned and then hung']." Clarification follows the citation:

> Those unfortunate rabbis use this argument in order to undermine faith in the evangelical account of the Passion of Jesus. But they are easily refuted by truth itself; for the Gospel teaches that it was the Roman Pilate, not the Jews, who inflicted this form of punishment on Christ. Thus the treacherous rabbis do not achieve anything even though what they produce is not false. On the contrary, as will be shown in the following pages, it is absolutely correct.[98]

95. Thus he berates Lipsius for having expressed surprise that Philo should refer to hanging as a punishment.

96. Baronio discusses the problem of the kind of capital punishment meted out: stoning would have been appropriate, if the penalty was inflicted according to Jewish law. Crucifixion was the penalty for robbery according to Roman law, but for murder according to Jewish law, as shown by Philo. The punishment of crucifixion, which was appropriate for Barabbas and for murder resulting from sedition, was transferred to Jesus unjustly. Baronio then transforms the Crucifixion into a divinely wrought act for the redemption of the world and stresses the significance of the *Tau,* or mark, in Ezek. 9:4, the verse usually brought into any discussion of the symbolic significance of the Cross.

97. Kittel 1964–1976, VI, 572–584.

98. Casaubon 1614, 611; 1654, 538; 1663, 538: "Hoc argumento infelices Rabbini utuntur, ut historiae Evangelicae de passione Christi fidem detrahant. in quo facile refelluntur ab ipsa veritate, quae supplicij hanc formam non ab ipsis Iudaeis, sed a Pilato Romano docet fuisse Christo irrogatam. Nihil igitur agunt perfidi Rabbini; etsi falsum non est quod afferunt, sed certissimum, ut ex sequentibus apparebit."

In the context of his own polemical treatise Casaubon asserts that a polemical invective can yield true historical information. The rabbis in this particular case told the truth. Their motives in telling the truth were not honorable, but truth they told. Jews did not use crucifixion as a death penalty. It was not they, but the Romans, who nailed Jesus to the Cross.

Casaubon does not identify his Hebrew source: indeed, he had not found it in a classical rabbinic text. Rather, he had discovered it buried among the annotations with which Sebastian Münster had furnished his Hebrew text of the Gospel of Matthew. Casaubon seems to have prized this Hebrew citation, for in 1600, when he embarked, in a mood of spiritual longing ("cum animi voluptate"), on a reading of Bishop Jean du Tillet's Hebrew text of the Gospel of Matthew (Paris, 1555),[99] he copied down Münster's annotation on the words "and they crucified him" (Matthew 27:35) on the blank page at the front of his copy of the book. The annotation contained the essential evidence. It offered a disparaging comment on the Jews' contradictory approach to Jesus. On the one hand, they call him *talui* (the hanged one). On the other, they disclaim all responsibility for his crucifixion: "In order to weaken our faith, the Jews produce many arguments against the Cross of Christ, which Münster lays out in Matthew 27. They deny that the Beth Din knew or practiced this form of punishment, and they argue at length about the nails in order to undermine God's truth."[100]

Münster had picked this statement, as he had culled many others, from the "virtual anthology of Ashkenazi anti-Christian polemic" compiled in the late thirteenth century, the *Nizzahon vetus*.[101] As both Jews and Christians knew, the Masoretic text of Psalm 22:17 (16) read "like a lion my hands and feet." But both the marginal apparatus of the Hebrew and the Septuagint preserved another reading: "they pierced[102] my hands and feet." Commenting on the former reading, preferred by Christians, the anonymous author of the *Nizzahon vetus* states: "'Like a lion my hands and feet': In their books it says: '*Foderunt* my hands and feet,' and they say this refers to the nails, for he was nailed to the cross through his hands and feet when he was hanged. The answer is: The practice of pushing nails through the hands and feet of

---

99. For a precise description of this text and the manuscript from which the text was transcribed see Rothschild 2006.

100. Casaubon, note on the flyleaf of BL 01901.a.14: "Judaei ut fidem nostram labefactent adversus crucem Christi multa disputant, quae relata sunt a Munst. in cap. 27 Matthaei. Negant id supplicii genus fuisse לבית דין notum aut usitatum. Et de clavis multa scribunt ut veritatem Dei convellant. Atenim iidem illi Judaei Dominum nostrum appellitant תלוי τὸν κρεμασθέντα et crucem eius non vocant lignum ut in lege sed שתי וערב stamen et subtemen. vide ibi M." This corresponds to Münster 1537, 149–150.

101. On this work see Krauss 1995 and bibliography cited, 246–247.

102. The reading is thus כארו for כרו, "they dug."

people who were stoned and hanged did not exist among the Jews."[103] Here, then, is Münster's source, a true disputation with text and response. Moreover, not to be outdone by his imagined Jewish opponent, Münster also appends his own response ("responsio mea") in Hebrew with Latin translation.[104]

When Casaubon came to pen his attack of Baronio on this particular issue, the Jewish pronouncement on crucifixion came in handy. He develops the argument by allusion to what he calls the "talmudic pandects"; the nature and purpose of the Talmud are suggested by his use of the *Pandects,* drawn from Roman law, which designated the *Digest,* an anthology of juridical opinions that forms part of Justinian's *Corpus Iuris.*[105] The four capital punishments administered by the Sanhedrin—stoning, burning, decapitation and strangling—are listed in Hebrew with Greek and Latin renderings. This is followed by a reference to Maimonides' codification of the precepts related to these capital punishments in his *Book of Commandments,* a prime piece of evidence. As we have shown, Casaubon revered Maimonides even if he did not always agree with him. In this case, only praise is reserved for Maimonides, and, as always, Casaubon can call upon this "man of sound and great doctrine" to shed light on the matter at hand. Maimonides had codified the laws of capital punishment in chapter 14 of the Laws Sanhedrin in the *Mishneh Torah,* detailing the exclusive powers of the Sanhedrin, which not even a king could override. In this authoritative and meticulous description of the Sanhedrin's mode of carrying out justice, he had made no mention of the Roman cross. Maimonides is thus summoned as the su-

103. Berger 1979, 150. Ibid., 301, indicates the early Christian readings (Aphtahat, Jerome, Augustine) of this verse as a reference to crucifixion. Kimhi's interpretation of the verse also responds to the Christian reading: see Talmage 1967, 216.

104. Münster 1537, 149–150: "Contradicunt sibiipsis Iudaei in hoc loco, negantes Christum cruci affixum, cum tamen eum ubique contumeliae nomine appellent תלוי suspensum, et ne id de עץ ligno dictum pretexant, sicut lex cadavera occisorum iubet in ligno usque ad solis occasum suspendi, vocant crucem Christi non lignum sed propter formam ipsam שתי וערב idest, stamen et subtegmen. Sed audiant hebraice docti quomodo hic Iudaei impugnent manuum pedumque conclavationem . . . Sensus est: Non fuit mos in Israel, ut clavi figerentur in pedibus et manibus hominum lapidatorum atque suspensorum. Nam tradita sunt quatuor genera mortis iudicibus, lapidatio, combustio, occisio et strangulatio . . . Non autem invenitur quod homo clavis figi debeat ad crucem, sed suspendendus est blasphemus et idololatra et suspenduntur in hunc modum . . . Responsio mea. Etiam rabini vestri asserunt 40. annis ante templi secundi eversionem potestatem iudiciariam sublatam, ob id quod homicidae invaluerunt et enervaverunt iudicia animarum de Israel. Unde non fuit in potestate eorum occidere Christum nostrum, sed convenerunt iudicem Pontium Pilatum, e Romanis terrae Iudaeae praefectum, qui ut ipse voluit, non ut Iudaei, interfecit Christum, sicut et non fuit in potestate eorum auferre corpora crucifixorum nisi ille annuisset."

105. Scaliger had also used the term "Pandects" for the Talmud (Grafton 1983–1993, II, 422), as would John Selden (Toomer 2009, II, 442). This humanistic comparative evaluation of the Talmud effectively subverts the traditional Christian view of the document as a tissue of falsehoods.

preme witness.[106] The Jews did not crucify Jesus, and the cross was not a Jewish form of capital punishment.

In the course of the discussion of hanging in his short overview of capital punishment in ancient Israel, Carlo Sigonio connects a reference to Acts 5 with Psalm 22:17 (21:16): "They pierced my hands and my feet." Casaubon closes his disquisition on the Cross with a reference to the same psalm:

> I should not fail to mention the one passage in which the Roman cross is graphically described with all its own characteristics. David sings in Psalm 22:16[–17]: "They have pierced my hands and feet. They have told all my bones." The pious do not doubt that the Christian reading of the word כארו even according to the Massoretes is the correct one. The piercing denoted perforation with nails. Here, then, are the nails, here are the hands and feet, which belong to the Roman cross. This much I acknowledge. I would further state that these words were enunciated in a spirit of prophecy by the royal seer in a psalm that is virtually entirely dedicated to a historical description of the Passion of Christ, but not according to the laws of his time. Hence it is not relevant.[107]

Having submitted the best antiquarians as well as Baronio to a scathing critique based on historical data that included Jewish sources, Casaubon finally affirms the dominant (Catholic and Protestant) Christological reading of the psalm. This interpretation had been promoted by Génébrard.[108] It was also affirmed by Calvin. Calvin had rejected the rendering of Kimhi, who had attempted to undermine the Christian position in his final reflections on the meaning of the psalm. Explaining that the Christians had misread the Hebrew text, Kimhi had stated: "The uncircumcised explain this Psalm with reference to Jesus—that it relates all the evil that Israel did to him . . . and they mistake the word כארי ('like a lion') for כארו ('they pierced'), as in

106. This is not the end of his discussion. He goes on to deal with other aspects of the question, examining the biblical verses in which "hanging" occurs, various Targumim on the texts, and the use of the various Greek and Latin terms for crucifixion.

107. Casaubon 1614, 619–620; 1654, 546; 1663, 546: "Vnicus restat locus non praetermittendus; ubi crux Romana graphice et quidem proprijs suis notis atque οὐσιώδεσι describitur. Canit enim David Ps. xxi.17. *Foderunt manus meas et pedes meos; dinumeraverunt omnia ossa mea.* nullum apud pios dubium est, כארו vel Massoritarum testimonio recte legi a Christianis; et fodere hic esse, clavis perforare. En igitur clavos, en manus et pedes, quae sunt propria, imo ἰδιαίτατα cruci Romanae. Fateor: sed addo, spiritu prophetico praedici haec a regio vate, in eo psalmo, quo fere historico stylo passio Christi describitur: non ex usu judiciorum sui temporis, quare nihil ad rem."

108. In his heavily annotated copy of Génébrard's edition of the Psalms (BL 1016.d.3) Casaubon had underlined "Totum enim hunc Psalmum ad Christum pertinere etiam docet antiquissima Hebraeorum Glossa, ante 2000. annos fere scripta" and the long discussion of verse 17 (I, 123).

Exodus,[109] and therefore they read 'they pierced his hands and feet with nails when they hung him.'"[110] As a pious Christian Casaubon read the psalm traditionally, exactly as Kimhi had reported; but when he donned his scholar's hat he insisted, against Baronio, and invoking the Jewish authorities, on identifying the perpetrators of the "piercing" according to the historical truth.

The importance of these points remains clear. In other passages, however, Casaubon focused above all on questions so technical that not all of his friends or his later readers have been able to grasp why they mattered to him. Bulenger was not far off the mark when he singled out Casaubon's attacks on matters of chronology and Hebrew as if they were somehow connected. For in fact, just as Lancelot Andrewes unhappily remarked, Pattison vigorously complained, and Casaubon himself sighed, Casaubon approached Baronio within the terms, and with the tools, of the now-forgotten early modern discipline of historical chronology as well as those of church history and biblical exegesis. The existing literature of chronology shaped the questions he asked and determined his choice of texts with which to answer them. By keeping that framework in mind, we can understand both the strengths and the occasional weaknesses of his enterprise.

Casaubon came to chronology as many of his fellow scholars arrived at their interests: by a complex path that combined the spiritual with the philological and the affective with the cognitive.[111] Time, in the first place, was the dimension through which he chose to live his religious life. Casaubon described the vast diary in which he recorded his daily life and work and his religious and scholarly efforts as a single effort to register and assess his soul's accounts: "I decided to establish this diary and account book for my whole life, so that I might rejoice when I spent time well and thank God, and if I wasted time doing nothing or something useless, I might know that as well, and acknowledge my failure or imprudence."[112] He looked everywhere—even in pagan writers—for counsel on how to spend time well, and

109. "If a man digs a pit [יכרה]"; Exod. 21:33.

110. Darom 1967, 58, on Ps. 22:32.

111. On the ways in which these elements intertwined in the learned culture of the sixteenth and early seventeenth centuries, see the richly informative study of Ogilvie 2006, esp. chap. 2.

112. Casaubon 1850, I, 1: "Cum sit πάντων πολυτελέστατον ἀνάλωμα τὸ τοῦ χρόνου, vereque dixerit Stoicus Latinus unius rei honestam avaritiam esse, temporis: quo mihi constaret ratio tam pretiosae rei, nec sera poenitudo unquam invaderet, hanc ἐφημερίδα et totius mei temporis rationarium istud visum instituere, ut et bene collocato gauderem, ac Deo Opt. Max. gratias agerem; et siquid, nihil, aut aliud agenti periisset, id quoque scirem, et meam infelicitatem aut imprudentiam agnoscerem. Te nunc veneror, Deus. Opt. Max. quantumcunque est, quod mihi adhuc necdum actae vitae superest, totum id πάσῃ σπουδῇ καὶ μηχανῇ ad te magis magisque cognoscendum, te colendum impensius, tuam gloriam promovendam, et rem literariam adjuvandam, necnon ad meam et omnium meorum salutem procurandam, assidue conferam."

recorded with admiration Seneca's advice that "it is most useful to go over the day with oneself."[113] Every year Casaubon cast up provisional accounts on his birthday and on 31 December. His efforts at self-discipline, as Max Engammare has recently shown, reflected his insistent belief that "l'étude est le sens même de la vie," that real time was time spent reading.[114] But they also reflected a sense that time was marked by human belief and conduct—the same belief that inspired the vast outpouring of chronological scholarship, Catholic and Protestant, in early modern Europe.

Casaubon's career as a scholar, moreover, brought him into direct contact with the new chronological scholarship of his time in its highest form. For almost twenty years, his closest friend, the man whose respect and interest meant everything to him, was the king of chronologers, his fellow Huguenot scholar Joseph Scaliger. The two men never met. But the long, distinctively detailed letters that they exchanged over the years, with their detailed offerings of bibliographical and interpretative novelties, show how much the relationship meant to both of them. So do the details of their collaborative efforts to obtain for Scaliger the manuscripts he needed to complete his last great work, the *Thesaurus temporum* of 1606.[115] So, above all, do Casaubon's heavily annotated copies of Scaliger's books. He worked his way, pen as always in hand, through both the first and the second editions of Scaliger's densely technical treatise, the *De emendatione temporum;* through every one of the 1500 folio pages of Scaliger's *Thesaurus;* and through many shorter works, such as Scaliger's biting little polemical treatises against the Jesuit Hebraist Nicolaus Serarius and the Reformed theologian David Pareus.[116] Casaubon not only annotated his way through these legendarily difficult books—Scaliger himself remarked that the *De emendatione temporum* had been an intelligence test for his contemporaries, which they had failed—but read them against other works in the field, like Sebastian Münster's *Kalen-*

113. Ibid., 23 (17 May 1597): "Mane preces, τὰ ἐγκύκλια. Legi hodie in Seneca pulcherrimum hoc praceptum. *Utilissimum est diem secum recognoscere. Hoc nos pessimos facit, quod nemo vitam suam respicit. Quid facturi simus, cogitamus, et id raro: quid fecerimus, non cogitamus. Atqui consilium futuri ex praeterito venit. Hodiernus dies solidus est. Nemo ex illo quicquam mihi eripuit: totus inter stratum lectionemque divisus est* [Epistulae 10.83]. Ita profecto est, graviter hac parte peccamus, et tempus misere elapsum non desideramus, saepe non observamus."
114. Engammare 2004, 96–106; quotation from 102.
115. Details in Grafton 1983–1993, II.
116. Casaubon's copy of the first edition of the *De emendatione temporum* (1583) is in the British Library (582.l.9), that of the second edition in Eton College Library. His heavily annotated *Thesaurus temporum* (1606) is in the Cambridge University Library (Adv.a.3.4). His copy of Scaliger 1605 on Serarius is in the British Library (C.79.a.4.[2]), as is his copy of Scaliger 1607 on Pareus (C.75.b.16.[1]). A note on the title page of the latter nicely reveals Casaubon's respect for his friend: "Doctrinam et facundi[am] viri magni hic liber eximi[e] ostendit."

darium Hebraicum of 1527, which he also annotated in detail.[117] Until the end of his life, Casaubon continued to read new chronologies systematically—and to complain bitterly when their authors did not render justice to what they had all learned from his friend in Leiden.[118]

Chronology, as Scaliger practiced it, required constant use of Jewish sources, and focused attention on the Hellenistic and imperial periods—in effect, the background to early Christianity as the new church historians understood it. It is well known that Scaliger insisted on reading the Bible with the same philological method that he applied to the Greeks and Romans, and on correlating the information of ancient historians and the data of astronomy with the Bible. Casaubon agreed with him on both strategies. He filled his copy of the 1575 *Chronicum* of Mathieu Béroalde, a fellow Huguenot who denied the value of pagan sources for ancient history, with disapproving marginalia.[119] And he made clear to his correspondent Hugh Broughton, who largely agreed with Béroalde, that he did not think Scaliger had bothered to criticize the latter's correction of Xenophon.[120] Less well known—but equally central to Scaliger's approach—were his deep interest in the history of intertestamental Judaism, in Greek as well as in Hebrew; his passion for identifying sources as genuine or spurious, and eliminating the latter from chronological scholarship; and his insistence on using everything he could learn about Jewish calendars and associated rituals to understand the events of Christ's life. Each of these features of his approach to the subject left its mark on Casaubon, and taken together they can help to explain some striking, and curious, features of what he wrote.

When Casaubon worked through Baronio's treatment of the three Jewish sects, for example, he used uncharacteristically gentle language about this particular segment of his opponent's work. Yet he made clear that certain unnamed enemies needed to be chastised for their errors on a related point:

> [Baronio] is right to say, at the outset, following Josephus, that the Jews had three main sects, Pharisees, Sadducees, and Essenes, and

117. Casaubon's copy of the *Kalendarium* is BL 481.c.2.

118. See, e.g., his copies of the 1605 *Chronologia* of Seth Calvisius (BL 580.e.14) and of the 1612 chronology of Johann Herwart von Hohenburg (BL C.75.b.15.[1]). A badly cropped note on the title page of the latter reveals Casaubon's view that Herwart dealt unfairly with Scaliger: "cui pleraque sua debet nunquam fere nominat, nisi cum est rep[re]hendendus. At Ba[ro]nius, quem ille scit si quid scit, fatu . . . scriptorem f[uisse], magnifice laudatur."

119. Casaubon's copy is BL C.79.e.12.(1).

120. Casaubon 1709, 600: Τίς ὁ τῷ Βεροάλδῳ περὶ τῆς παρὰ Ξενόφοντι διορθώσεως ἀντειπών; οὐ μέμνημαι γὰρ ἐν τοῖς τοῦ κρατίστου Σκαλάνου περὶ τούτων τι ἀναγνούς. Περὶ δὲ τὰ ταῦτα, γεννναιώτατε Βροχθῶνε, γίγνου ἡμῖν, ταῦτα ἐκπόνει, ταῦτα ἀκρίβωσον.

his account is better than the ones of those who add the Asidaei to the other three. For it would be just as wrong and foolish to name them among the Jewish heretics and sectaries, as it would have been to name Catholics, in the past, among the Christian heretics. Hasidim was the proper name for all pious, holy, and generous people. That name was no more the special one of any particular group, than the word "good." Therefore the Hebrews have a substantial book, titled *Hasidim,* in which the sayings and deeds of pious and holy men are expounded.[121]

The end of the passage is easy to explain. Casaubon here took the opportunity to announce that he owned a book not known to all Christian scholars, the *Sefer Hasidim,* or Book of the Pious. As a proud collector, he did not mention the relevant but discouraging fact that the book is a rich compilation of Jewish anecdotes and prayers from Germany in the decades around 1300, and thus largely irrelevant to the Jews of Josephus' time attested elsewhere.[122]

Why, however, did Casaubon take time out to flagellate unnamed adversaries who took the ancient Asidaei or Hasidaei as a sect? Here Casaubon referred to a controversy in which Scaliger and Johannes Drusius had sided against Serarius, while he and others eagerly urged them on. The Asidaioi were an ancient Jewish group mentioned three times in the first and second books of Maccabees (1 Macc. 2:42, 1 Macc. 7:13, and 2 Macc. 14:6). Drusius admitted that he had not at first been able to identify the Asidaioi, and that the problem had long tormented him.[123] Finally, however, he realized that the *Josippon*—a long Hebrew text based on Josephus, now known to have been written by a southern Italian Jew, which narrated the history of the world—provided the key. As Scaliger noted, the *Josippon* offers a summary in Hebrew of the history of the Jews in the intertestamental period: "without that deceiver, the Jews would be totally ignorant of the history of the Mac-

---

121. Casaubon 1614, 53–54; 1654, 49–50; 1663, 49–50: "Recte tamen illud initio: quod Iosephum secutus, tres ait fuisse Iudaeorum sectas praecipuas, Pharisaeos, Sadducaeos, Essenos. melius quam illi, qui Asidaeos superioribus adiungunt. nam hi inter haereticos et sectarios Iudaeos, non minus inepte atque insulse nominantur, quam Catholici olim inter haereticos Christianos essent nominati. Proprie חסידים pij omnes, sancti et benigni vocantur; neque ea appellatio ulli societati magis fuit peculiaris, quam vox boni aut ἀγαθοῦ. itaque liber extat inter Hebraeos satis magnus, חסידים inscriptus, quo dicta et facta piorum sanctorumque virorum exponuntur."

122. For a fuller account of Casaubon's response to the book see Chapter 1 above.

123. Drusius 1603, 16–18, esp. 18: "Ponam hic quaestionem quae me aliquando torsit. Omnino me explicare non potuissem absque Iosepho Ebraeo fuisset."

cabees and the fall of Jerusalem. For the Jews of today and somewhat older commentators on the Bible narrate Jewish history in exactly the form in which he framed it."[124] This section, rather than the *Josippon's* inexpert excursions into Greek and Roman history, had long interested Christian scholars. The vital passage reads: "And behold the Sadducees said, let us not believe and let us not hear any tradition or any explanation except the law of Moses. And the Cushites followed the Sadducees in those days, and the Sadducees were in Israel one part, and the Hasidaei along with the people that followed them were another part."[125] Drusius knew that the Cushites, or Ethiopians, had not been Sadducees, nor indeed had they lived in the land of Israel. Inspired by a long passage in a twelfth-century chronicle, Abraham ibn Daud's *Sefer haKabbalah,* he emended the text to read "Cuthites," or Samaritans.[126] As corrected, the passage made perfect sense: the Jews had divided into two groups, the Sadducees, who included the Samaritans; and the Hasidaei. The Sadducees, as Drusius and everyone else knew, accepted only the scriptures and rejected the authority of human traditions. The group that the *Josippon* described as opponents—the other sect or part—must accordingly be the Pharisees. The conclusion seemed clear: the Asidaioi of the books of Maccabees formed the Jewish circle from which the Pharisees sprang.

124. Scaliger 1605, 40–41: "Omnem ἀναισχυντίαν καὶ ἀναισθησίαν superat quod quum legisset apud Rufinum cap. xxv. libri II. de excidio Ierosolym. <u>Iosephum filium</u> Gurionis (γωρίωνα Fl. Iosephus vocat) una cum Anano Pontifice praepositum moenium sartis tectis fuisse, et <u>Iosephum filium</u> Mattathiae Galilaeae praefectum: ipse duos illos Iosephos <u>unum Iosephum</u> Gurionis filium esse suspicatus est, eundemque Sacerdotem et excidii Ierosolymitani scriptorem. Hinc splendido mendacio persuasit genti suae se eum ipsum esse scriptorem belli Iudaici, Iosephum filium Gurionis sacerdotem. Certe absque eo impostore esset, Iudaei <u>omnem historiam Maccabaeorum et excidii Ierosolymitani ignorarent</u>. Eodem enim modo, quo ipse interpolavit, omnem historiam illam Iudaei hodierni et paulo vetustiores Bibliorum enarratores referunt." This underlining was entered by Casaubon in his copy, BL C.79.a.4.(2). Scaliger considered the *Josippon* a forgery, as his language here indicates. We return to that point below.

125. Drusius 1603, 45–46.

126. Ibid., 36–39: "*Alterum est* manifestarium in sequentib. Nam ubi nos scripsimus כותים, in ea editione perspicue lectum כושים, contra omnem historiae veritatem. Non enim certe Aethiopes Saducaei erant, sed Chuthaei, qui et Samaritae sive Samaritani. Res est, non conjectura. Abraham Davidis F. Levita in Cabbala sua historica, Quum venisset Alexander Macedo in terram Israel, secessit ad eum Sanaballat Horonites et primores Chuthaeorum, petieruntque ab eo ut liceret Sacerdotibus generis suis et aliis qui duxerant uxores alienigenas, nec dimiserant eas, aedificare domum sanctuarii aliud in monte Garizin. Praecepit autem rex ut sic facerent, et aedificarent domum illam. Tunc divisus est populus Israel in duas partes. Vna dimidia pars sequebatur Simeonem justum et Antigonum discipulum ejus, societatemque ejus, juxta id quod traditum acceperant ab Ezra. Altera pars dimidia ibat post Sanballetum et generos ejus. Qui obtulerunt holocausta et hostias extra domum Domini, et statuerunt statuta judiciaque, quemadmodum commenti fuerant e corde suo. Caeterum in hac aede sacerdotio functus est Manasses filius Iosuae filii Iosadac. Sadoc autem cum Baithos (alias Boetho) socio suo erant primores. Atque hinc sane haeresis initium sumpsit."

In a series of polemical works, Serarius denounced Drusius on multiple grounds. He treated the ancient Jewish sects not as historically defined entities but as perennial formations, which went back deep into history: the Jews in Worms in his own time, he explained, had told him that they were still Pharisees.[127] As to the *Josippon,* the passage in question meant not that the Hasidaei and their followers became a faction, but that the Hasidaei, on their own, became one: became, in fact, the ascetic Essenes.[128] Drusius replied, and Serarius rebutted.[129] And then Scaliger entered the story. He had long taken an interest in the Jewish sects, and in the *De emendatione temporum* he had argued—wrongly, in his current view—that the Karaites still to be found at Constantinople and elsewhere descended from the ancient Sadducees. Now he explained the error of his old ways. He argued, brilliantly, that Drusius' construal of the text in *Josippon* must be correct. And then he added a new ingredient to what was already a complicated textual stew: the *Josippon,* he explained, was not, as Serarius thought, the work of an eyewitness to the fall of Jerusalem, but a medieval patchwork adapted from the Latin Josephus and other standard sources: "There is no need to say so much about Joseph the son of Gurion [the author of the text] . . . It is enough if I show what country he came from, when he lived, and what sort of writer he was. It is not hard to infer that he was a French Jew from the region of Tours, since he treats that area in more detail than other parts of France. The recent place-names that he uses—Tours, Amboise, Chinon—show that he is recent enough."[130] Scaliger's analysis remains impressive—even if he did miss the equally prominent Italian elements that have enabled more recent scholars to pinpoint the origin of the book more precisely.[131]

The relatively brief discussion of the Jewish sects in Casaubon's work does not reveal how closely he followed these debates, or how intensively he prepared himself to take part in them. Contemporaries, however, rightly saw him as an expert on intertestamental Judaism and the relatively few sources

127. Serarius 1604, 135: "Qui apud nos in Germania caeterisque Europae partibus versantur Iudaei, Pharisaeorum fere instituta, leges, caeremonias, perfidiam certe, pertinaciam, avaritiam, et nequitiam retinent. Itaque non invitus aliquando eorum quibusdam assentiebar, cum in Wormaciensi sua Synagoga mihi se Pharisaeos esse dicerent."

128. Ibid., 21–26.

129. See the account in Lebram 1980; and cf. Van den Berg 1988.

130. BL C.79.a.4.(2), 38: "Non opus est tot verbis de Iosepho Gorionide, quibus cap. IX. quaeritur quis fuerit ille. Satis est si ostendero, cujas fuit, quando vixit, cujusmodi scriptor est. Gallum Iudaeum fuisse ex agro Turonensi non difficile est colligere, ut qui plus de illis, quam de aliis Galliae tractibus agat. Recentem admodum fuisse arguunt verba locorum recentia, quibus utitur, *Tours, Amboise, Chinon.* Quae loca post DC annos a natali Christi adhuc *Turones,* Ambasia, Kainon vocabantur."

131. See now Flusser 1978–1980.

that described it.[132] Early in Casaubon's career, while still living in Geneva, he read the *Josippon* and even began to translate it into Latin, but stopped because he did not have a copy of the Hebrew-Latin edition that Sebastian Münster had produced in 1541.[133] In Paris, where he had more time, more money, and at least occasional access to the libraries of the king and de Thou, among others, he made more progress. Finding a copy of Münster's edition at last, Casaubon worked through it with great care. Münster, a remarkable philologist and historian, recognized many of the philological and historical problems that the text raised. Careful comparison between the Hebrew *Josippon* and the better-known texts that covered the same ground —the books of Maccabees and the *Jewish Antiquities* and *Jewish War* that Josephus had written in Greek—revealed small discrepancies and substantive differences. Listing examples, Münster offered an economical explanation for them: Josephus had written "in one way for the Gentiles, in another for the Jews."[134] This "elegant" text, written in a Hebrew very different from that of the rabbis, did not follow the order of Josephus' text in the Greek original or in that of Maccabees either in the original Greek texts or in the

132. See, e.g., Edward Smith to Casaubon, 13 September [no year], BL MS Burney 366, 188 recto–verso: "Hesterna nocte inter convivandum, mihi cum peregrino homine literato magna fuit controversia, de Sadducaeorum origine, unde nomen traxerunt suum; ille ita dictos esse asseruit a Saddoc quodam haeretico inter Judaeos qui vixit circa annum ante Christum a virgine natum quinquagesimum: ego vero probe edoctus fueram ab Epiphanio; dixi nomen habuisse suum ab Hebraea voce צדק quod significat justitiam, illi enim operum suorum justitia freti se tutos et servatos judicarunt, ut idem Epiphanius ait. Sed cum utraque opinio ab Epiphanio recitetur, neutra ab eodem damnetur, ambiguum idcirco etiam adhuc restat, nec poterit dici ex sententia Epiphanij utra verior aut probabilior opinio . . . Quod tuum est pro humanitate tu perage. etenim te sub judice lis est, te judicem fecimus qui litem dirimeres: Idcirco (vir optime) utri parti faveas, literis notum facere digneris. Beabis me si huic quaestioni responsum addideris: praecipue vero si adversarij tui os (quocunque modo fiat) occluseris."

133. Bod MS Casaubon 27, 169 recto: "Vertere coeperam Genavae Hebraeum Josephum in Lat. sermonem: cum in secundo libro versarer, cognovi Munsterum totum opus pridem fecisse Latinum. Destiti ig. avide cupiens Munsteri editionem nancisci."

134. *Josippon* 1541, [A4 verso]: "Iam ut ad obiecta quoque respondeam, sciendum in primis, Iosephum aliter scripsisse gentibus, aliter Hebraeis. Gentibus scripsit antiquitates omnium biblicarum historiarum, et plerumque explicuit eis ritus et consuetudines Iudaeorum, quas secundum legem Mosi observare tenebantur. Vnde libro 17. cap. 12. Antiq. declarat sacrificium paschale in haec verba: Pascha enim illa festivitas vocitatur ad recordationem et memoriam exitus de Aegypto, et sacrificatur ab eis illa die cum alacritate magna pecudum numerosa multitudo, quam in nulla alia solennitate acta. Sic lib. 18. cap. 5. quando Pilatus rector Iudaeae voluit introducere in Ierusalem statuas Caesaris, scribit in hunc modum: Imagines autem aut aliquid huiusmodi facere lex nostra prohibet, et propter hoc ante illum omnes Iudaeae rectores sine signis ingrediebantur moenia civitatis . . . Talia multa in graeca aeditione ubique inculcat, quorum in Hebraico exemplari non meminit, quippe quae Iudaeis ex sacris libris erant manifesta. Graecis autem oportebat declarare, sicut et ipse quodam loco in Antiquitatibus meminit his verbis: Praesens opus assumpsi, credens dignum studium etiam Graecis omnibus apparere . . . Alia ergo ratione Iosephus scripsit gentibus et alia Iudaeis."

Latin Vulgate.[135] Casaubon summarized at length Münster's effort to show that "The man's very elegant style is woven together from the expressions of scripture. The order is reasonable. You can tell that he is not just a translator of the Greek Josephus but an author in his own right."[136]

Despite the care with which he summarized Münster's arguments, Casaubon found them totally unpersuasive: "But the learned gentleman has wasted his time and effort. For in my view he will never persuade anyone of sound judgment that both works could have come from the same source. The Greek Josephus seems consistent, learned, and expert in Greek history. The Hebrew one is always childish and silly when he describes Greek and Roman matters."[137] And no wonder. Casaubon was not very gracious when he used Münster's careful collation of the *Josippon* with Josephus and other, better-known sources to refute Münster's conclusions. His predecessor had already noticed the medieval names that so annoyed Scaliger and Casaubon: he simply diagnosed them differently, as the results of interpolation rather than as signs of spuriousness.[138] But he also had plenty of material of

135. Ibid., [A4 verso–A5 recto]: "Vtitur et stilo hebraico elegantissimo et vere biblico, longe discrepante a stilo modernorum rabbinorum, id quod solum convincere posset lectorem quemque, aeditionem hebraicam Iosephi esse et non interpretis alicuius Iudaei. Si enim esset interpretis alicuius, utique ille in omnibus observasset eum ordinem qui in graeca servatur aeditione. Id autem non fit, sed in hebraica aeditione non raro quaedam integra capita scribuntur, quae in graeca non habentur, id quod in annotationibus nostris signavimus. Nam collationem fecimus utriusque aeditionis. Et rursum multa integra capita in graeca aeditione inveniuntur quae in hebraica non habentur. Et ubi utriusque Machabaeorum libri historiae describuntur, ille ordo quoque non observatur, qui in nostra vulgata editione custoditur, id quod rursum argumentum est, hebraicam editionem non conflatam ex nostra latina aut graeca editione, ut taceam quaedam quoque haberi in Iosepho hebraico, quae in nostris Machabaeis non habentur, aut quaedam hic copiosius tractari quam alibi."

136. Bod MS Casaubon 27, 169 verso–170 recto: "Stylus hominis elegantiss. et ex sacris locutionibus totus conflatus et consutus. Ordo proprius. Scias non esse interpretem Iosephi Graeci, sed sui iuris auctorem."

137. Ibid., 170 recto: "Sed oleum et operam vir doctus perdidit. Nunquam enim cuiquam sano iudice me persuaserit, ab eodem fonte potuisse utrumque opus manare. Ios. Graecus sibi ubique similis ubique doctus et Graecae historiae admodum peritus paret. Hebraeus in Graecorum [MS: Graecae histor, histor deleted] rebus et Romanorum puer et fatuus nusquam non est."

138. See respectively *Josippon* 1541, [A5 verso]: "Caeterum quod quarundam graecarum vocum fit mentio, et citantur quaedam gentes quae longe post Iosephi tempora in mundo surrexerunt, ut sunt Franci, Gothi, Lombardi, Bulgari, etc. haec plane arguunt Iosepho quaedam accessisse per posteros Iudaeos expositionis et praefationis gratia. Nos propterea consulto omisimus ea, quae ab initio huic autori sunt adiecta, eo quod pleraque sunt fabulosa. Quis enim non videt libro 5. cap. quadragesimo primo alium quempiam Iudaeum quam Iosephum loquentem, quando dicitur, Gallos, qui sunt Franci, interfuisse sepulturae Herodis? Galli enim tempore Augusti aut Tiberij nondum assecuti fuerunt appellationem Francorum"; and Bod MS Casaubon 27, 170 recto–verso: "Gallos, Gothos, Francos, et id genus nationes longo tempore post Iosephum notas reperiri in Hebraicis codd. excusat M. affirmatque illa velut emblemata a mala manu esse inserta. neque debere haberi τοῦ ποιητοῦ. quare ipse quoque ea fere praetermisit. Haec M. τὰ μὲν οὖ τὰ δὲ καὶ οὖ."

FIGURE 4.4. Casaubon's working copy of *Josippon*. British Library 1938.f.21.

his own to call into service. Casaubon used his time in Paris to compare the
Josippon with texts that Münster had not known, such as one of the Italian
versions of the Alexander Romance falsely ascribed to Callisthenes, which
he found in the Royal Library. In August 1605 he wrote to Scaliger to describe the fun he had been having as he collated and corrected the two texts:
"I actually admire the deception."[139] He went through his own copy of the
Venice 1544 edition, comparing it with what Scaliger had to say in his attack

139. Casaubon 1709, 246: "Extat in Bibliotheca Pseudo-Callisthenis Historia Rerum Alexandri. Observavi hoc μύθευμα totidem fere verbis in Ebraeum sermonem versum a Pseudo-Gorionide, et sane
cum voluptate quaedam contuli, multaque in textu etiam Italico emendavi; praesertim virorum et locorum nomina. Admiror vero imposturam." See also ibid., 252.

on Serarius and wreathing the Hebrew with his own observations about Pseudo-Callisthenes and many other matters.[140] He noted variations from Münster's abridged version of the Hebrew, took extensive notes on the text's sources, and snorted from time to time with disdain at its pretenses to cover Greek and Roman history. At the same time, he examined or reexamined the short form of the Hebrew text that Sebastian Lepusculus had published in Basel in 1559, comparing it, too, with Scaliger's comments on the text.[141]

Casaubon attacked the *Josippon* with independence as well as with energy. As he read through Scaliger's comments, he relished the vigor with which his friend revealed the author's "stupor," the erudition and penetration that seemingly never failed, and the integrity that he showed as he revealed the Jesuits' "hatred of truth."[142] He also took notes on Scaliger's book in one of his copybooks.[143] In many ways Scaliger's polemic served as a model for Casaubon's. It was no doubt from Scaliger, for example, that Casaubon learned to argue that even when his opponent dealt accurately with a given subject, his treatment showed his ignorance of the real sources in Hebrew or Aramaic.[144] But he also corrected what he took to be the slips that Scaliger had made, in his haste to finish his tirade. Scaliger quoted what he described as a proverb from tractate Sanhedrin of the Babylonian Talmud: "If salt is worth one *sela*, silence is worth two." Casaubon suggested, rightly, that מלח (*Melah;* salt) be corrected to מלה (*Milah;* word).[145] Even as Casaubon picked little flaws in Scaliger's work, though, he learned from it. Scaliger translated the author of the *Josippon*'s reference to books that כתבתי להם, "I wrote for them [the Romans]," as "in libro, quem scripsi ad illos."[146] Casau-

140. Casaubon's copy of the Venice 1544 *Josippon* is BL 1938.f.21.

141. Casaubon's copy of Lepusculus' edition is BL 1982.c.34. This version of the text records the story, also told by Josephus, that Demetrius killed some eight hundred Pharisees at Jerusalem in 88 B.C.E. and drank with the leaders of the Karaites (61). Scaliger recorded the story from Josephus and noted (1605, 96): "Nam et compendium Pseudogurionidae dicit idem, et praeterea addit regem discubuisse cum Sadducaeis, quos ipse Karraim inepte vocat." Casaubon adds a cross-reference to this discussion in his copy of Lepusculus, at 61.

142. For typical comments by Casaubon see, e.g., BL C.79.a.4.(2), 47: "Stupor Pseudog."; 220: "Stupeo ad hanc doctrinam tantam"; 149: "Veritatis odium in istis"; and, at 206, where Scaliger confesses ignorance on a point of etymology: "quis sciet te nesciente?"

143. Bod MS Casaubon 52.

144. See, e.g., Scaliger 1605, 80: "De Doctoribus stantibus honoris caussa non raro et in Talmud, et in Iad Rambam, in Iohasin, et in Germine David legitur. Quae igitur Serarius ex collectione locorum Evangelii argumentatur, habet nostra, quibus ea confirmet, si modo Novatorum odium et ζηλοτυπία ejus judicium non occupaverit."

145. BL C.79.a.4.(2), 105. The proverb actually comes from Babylonian Talmud, Megillah 18a. Casaubon comments: "Scr. מלה dictio, loquela. Vide Buxt. Abbr. p. 258."

146. Scaliger 1605, 48.

bon noted, in his copy of the *Josippon,* that the rendering was inexact.[147] As a gifted and experienced forgery hunter, Scaliger took another such passage as clear evidence that the writer of the *Josippon* had clumsily tried to authenticate his own work: "To prevent anyone from doubting that he was the Josephus whom the Christians called Josephus, he wrote: 'So said Josephus, the son of Gurion, a priest. He is Josiphun, in the diminutive form Iosiphun, who was called Iosephus in Greek and Gushipus in Latin.' Even Crassus, who was nicknamed 'the man who never laughed,' could not have read this without laughing."[148] In a marginal note, Casaubon identified the passage that Scaliger had in mind.[149] And in a second note on the relevant passage in the *Josippon,* he characteristically went a little deeper than his friend had. For Scaliger, as for Casaubon, clumsy statements of authorship revealed a forger at work. But Casaubon, unlike his friend, also took the time to collect a number of these statements, and to note that in some of them "the author seems to distinguish between himself and the true Josephus, since he refers the reader to him."[150] Here—as in his reading of Aristeas—Casaubon showed himself more willing than his friend, at least in the course of reading, to think twice about a text even if he did not think the text itself authentic.

Casaubon developed this point further in the copy of the 1544 Froben edition of the works of Josephus in Greek that he used while preparing the *Exercitationes.* There, too, he took care, in his marginal notes, to distinguish between the *Josippon* and the historical Josephus. Early in his account of the *Jewish War,* Josephus noted that he had translated into Greek a work that he had originally written for the barbarians in his homeland. "This book," Casaubon noted, "was translated from the Hebrew. Some believe that that original text exists as well. But the facts of the matter show that they are very wrong, and Scaliger proved it."[151] But he also made clear, in a note on the title

147. BL 1938.f.21, col. 300: "כתבתי להם sic passim in libris quos scripsi Romanis. vt col. 304, quare minus recte Jos. Scal. in Serar. p. 48."

148. Scaliger 1605, 41: "Ne quis dubitaret se Iosephum esse illum, qui a Christianis Iosephus vocatur, ita scribit: *Sic dixit Ioseph filius Gurion Sacerdos. Ipse est Josiphun, et quidem nomine diminutivo Iosiphun. Ipse est, qui vocatus est Iosiphus, Graece, et* גושיפוס *Guschipus Latine.* Et Crassus ipse qui ἀγέλαστος dictus fuit, haec sine risu non legeret."

149. Casaubon, marginal note in BL C.79.a.4.(2), 41: "locus est columna 225."

150. Casaubon, marginal note in BL 1938.f.21, 49 recto: "Σηαι loca sunt in hoc scriptore ex q. videtur facere discrimen inter se et verum Josephum: cum ad illum reiicit lectorem. Notandum vero col. 191. reiici lectorem ad Josephum qui est penes Ro. col. ali. Σηαι Σηαι locum p. 199. ubi librum magnum historiarum Jos. qui scriptus est Romanis sibi vindicat. confer similes locos omnes, maxime col. 303. ubi videtur sui oblitus."

151. Casaubon, marginal note in his copy of the Basel 1544 Josephus, BL C.76.g.7, 657: "Hic liber versus est de Hebraico: qui etiamnunc extat ut quibusdam placet. sed eos gravissime falli res arguit: et Scaliger probavit."

page, that he did not believe that the author of the *Josippon* had simply claimed to be the historical Josephus:

> This one is not the same as the one called Joseph son of Gorion, the priest, whose books we have, and an epitome of whose book in Hebrew we have read, as published by one Lepusculus at Basel with the translation of Münster. Although they think that that is an epitome of the books of this Josephus. A gross error, into which they seem to have fallen because of the similarity of the subjects, as they had not seen the complete books of Joseph son of Gorion. But when we read the book of Joseph the son of Gorion in Hebrew, we see that he speaks in such a confusing way about himself at the end of the first book that someone could quite reasonably be led into error by reading him.[152]

At this point Casaubon was calling attention to some of the complex features of the text that would prove central, in the twentieth century, to David Flusser's revisionist edition and interpretation.[153]

Casaubon did not always see further than his friend. Like Drusius, and apparently independently of him, Scaliger had emended "Cushim" to "Cuthim" in the key passage "And the Cushites followed the Sadducees in those days." Casaubon, like his friend, took the word "Cushite" in its biblical sense, as a reference to the Ethiopians, and rejected it: "this clearly goes against the historical truth. For what do those foreigners have to do with the domestic affairs of the Jews?" But he did not accept Scaliger's reading either. Instead he proposed to read *harekhushim,* literally "riches," but to transform the substantive into an adjective, "rich," as Casaubon thought the rabbis did. After all, the Greek Josephus had described the Sadducees as attracting the rich.[154] In fact Drusius and Scaliger were right to see the passage as referring

---

152. Ibid., note on title page:

 Alius ab hoc est qui dicitur יוסף בן גריון הכהן cuius librum habemus, et eiusdem libri epitomen legimus Hebraicam, a Lepusculo quodam edita[m] Basileae cum versione Munsteri. quanquam putant illi esse epitomen horum Josephi istius librorum. crasso errore. in quem videntur incidisse (cum libros Josephi ben Gorion non vidissent) ob argumenti similitudinem.

 [new ink] sed cum illum librum Joseph. Ben Gorion Hebraice legimus animadvertimus ipsum auctorem ita perplexe de se loqui sub finem lib. primi ut merito ex eius lectione possit aliquis adduci in errorem.

153. Flusser's interpretations continue to attract discussion and criticism: see, e.g., Sermoneta 1988, 187–188.

154. Casaubon, marginal note in BL 1938.f.21, 48 verso: "והכושים) Munst. legit והבושים vertitque et hi confusi fuerunt. plane contra linguae genium et grammaticam. at Drusius scribit הכותים Cuthaei et ita Scal. emendat contra Serarium pag. 42. plane contra veritatem historiae. nam quid isti peregrini ad res domesticas Judaeorum? Omnino legendum ex vestigiis scriptae lectionis, הרכושים, et divites. Josephus

to the Samaritans as Cuthites. More important, for all his learning and hard work, Casaubon could not add much to what Drusius and Scaliger had worked out about the testimony of the *Josippon* on the ancient divisions of the Jews. And in a crucial passage of the *Exercitationes,* he echoed Scaliger on the most important point of all, the fact that the text was neither authentic nor ancient:

> There is, to be sure, a history elegantly composed in Hebrew, under the name of Joseph son of Gorion. This excellent confidence man crafted his work so that it would seem to have been written by the real Josephus. But cubs smell one way, lions another. This Josephus is so far from being the ancient one, that he is quite a recent writer, and in fact a Frenchman, as Joseph Scaliger recently proved definitively in his *Elenchus.* Moreover, although this faker often follows Josephus, or rather his Latin translator, word for word, the character of his whole work is entirely different.[155]

In the end, then, all of Casaubon's preparatory work left him reiterating, with modest qualifications, what Scaliger had already argued.

What made Casaubon focus so heavily on the *Josippon* and the nature of intertestamental Judaism was not his belief that he had radically new things to say. On the whole, as we have seen, his larger arguments were traditional, and some of his sharpest perceptions on points of detail remained confined to the margins of his book or to his copybooks. Rather, Casaubon had set out to show that Baronio did not know how to negotiate the rocks and labyrinths of chronology, especially now that Scaliger and others had reconfigured the field. And by working so hard to show his mastery of the *Josippon* and the related pagan and Jewish texts, he established a foundation from which he could criticize Baronio on more technical points.

One of these had to do with authenticity. By no means uncritical, Baronio still set out to defend and to use the church's traditions so far as he could.

---

pag. 404 alta voce clamat ita scribi oportere. ait enim τῶν Σαδδουκαίων τοὺς εὐπόρους μόνους πειθόντων [*Jewish Antiquities* 13.298], etc. Vox Hebr. רכוש est apud illos substantivum: apud Rabb. etiam adiectivum, ut heic."

155. Casaubon 1614, 772; 1654, 677; 1663, 677: "Extat quidem historia eiusdem fere argumenti Hebraico sermone eleganter contexta, sub nomine *Iosipon ben Gorion* sive *Iosephi Gorionidae:* qui impostor insignis sic opus suum concinnavit, ut vellet videri a vero Iosepho illud fuisse scriptum. Sed aliter catuli, aliter leones olent. adeo enim antiquus Iosephus hic non est, ut recens admodum sit scriptor, et quidem Gallus, ut certis argumentis demonstravit Iosephus Scaliger in Elencho. Porro etsi planus hic in multis Iosephum sequitur κατὰ πόδας, vel potius eius interpretem Latinum: totius tamen operis textura longe diversissima."

That strategy entailed, as we have seen before, treating Hermes Trismegistus as a pagan prophet who had foreseen the coming of Christianity. But it also entailed trying to defend another ancient document—supposedly the oldest one not by a Christian that tells the story of Jesus. Some manuscripts of the *Jewish Antiquities* of Josephus, all of them presumably deriving from a Christian redaction of the text, contain a summary of Jesus' life, death, and afterlife.[156] From the third century onward, Christian scholars had debated both the wording and the authenticity of this text, now known as the *Testimonium Flavianum*.[157] Baronio treated the passage as reliable, and cited Josephus as the first witness, after the Evangelists, to describe the life of the Savior.[158] By contrast, the Lutheran Osiander dismissed the text as an obvious Christian fake, one "of the same bran," as the Romans had said, as the fake letter of Pontius Pilate to the emperor Tiberius. Neither text fitted its supposed author. "If Pilate had believed these things about Christ," Osiander explained, "he would have been a Christian." Similarly, "If Josephus had felt about Christ as that testimonium holds, he would have been a Christian; but nothing in all of his writings gives off any suggestion of Christianity."[159]

More than one of the scholars who worked on the *Josippon* discussed this issue, and for good reason: the *Testimonium* did not appear in the Hebrew text. Münster, who pointed this out, offered two explanations: either the Jews had excised it, or Josephus had—as he argued in his preface—written

156. Josephus, *Jewish Antiquities* 18.63, trans. L. H. Feldman: "About this time there lived Jesus, a wise man if indeed one ought to call him a man. For he was one who wrought surprising feats and was a teacher of such people as accept the truth gladly. He won over many Jews and many of the Greeks. He was the Messiah. When Pilate, upon hearing him accused by men of the highest standing among us, had condemned him to be crucified, those who had in the first place come to love him did not cease. On the third day he appeared to them restored to life. For the prophets of God had prophesied these and myriads of other marvellous things about him. And the tribe of the Christians, so called after him, has still up to now, not disappeared." Josephus' reference to Jesus in 20.200—"Since Ananus was that kind of person, and because he perceived an opportunity with Festus having died and Albinus not yet arrived, he called a meeting of the Sanhedrin and brought James, the brother of Jesus (who is called 'Messiah') along with some others. He accused them of transgressing the law, and handed them over for stoning"—is taken as genuine even by some of those who deny the authenticity of the other passage.

157. The fullest account of the premodern debate is given by Whealey 2003.

158. Baronio 1593–1607, I, 215 (34.226): "Post sanctos Evangelistas, Iosephus Iudaeus reperitur, qui post annos quinquaginta Graeco sermone res gestas Iudaeorum est prosecutus: qui res etiam gestas Christi addens, eas his paucis perstrinxit."

159. Osiander 1592–1599, 17 (I.ii.7): "Testimonium vero Iosephi de Christo ego omnino supposititium esse credo, et ab aliquo sciolo ipsius libris insertum. Si enim Iosephus ita de Christo sensisset, ut testimonium illud prae se fert, Iosephus fuisset Christianus, cum tamen in omnibus eius scriptis nihil prorsus, quod saltem Christianismum redoleat, reperiri queat. Eiusdem farinae est ficta epistola Pilati ad Imperatorem Tyberium, in Anacephalaeosi Egesippi posita. Si enim Pilatus talia de Christo credidisset, Christianus exstitisset, neque in sua impietate perseverasset et desperasset." Cf. Whealey 2003.

differently for Christians than he did for his fellow Jews.[160] Lepusculus accepted the latter notion, and argued at length that the historic Josephus, who wrote in Greek, but who had read the Bible and interpreted it in Hebrew, had found indications of Christ's coming in the prophets, and that other Jews must have done the same.[161] Unlike Münster, however, he distinguished firmly between this Josephus and the "abbreviator of Josephus" who composed the *Josippon,* and although he, too, suspected dirty work by Jews, he also admitted that this late author might have decided on his own to omit the text.[162]

Casaubon, for his part, denounced the *Testimonium* as an obvious Christian fake, a piece of evidence far too good to be true. In doing so, he carried on part of the chronologer's enterprise as Scaliger understood it. From the start to the end of his career, Scaliger made the authenticity—or lack of it—of sources a central theme of his chronological writing. He denounced the spurious ancient Near Eastern texts forged by Annius of Viterbo, in Latin, under the names of Berosus, Manetho, and Metasthenes. And he offered readers, in their place, the genuine fragments, in Greek, of Berossus, Manetho, and Megasthenes.[163] Although the two men were not in accord on the letter of Aristeas, both agreed that sources must pass the sorts of tests that Scaliger had applied there—highly specific tests of both factual content and biography. And in the first decade of the sixteenth century, they agreed,

160. *Josippon* 1541, 174, on 5.44: "Omittitur hic in Haebraico contextu magnificum illud praeconium, quod Iosephus tribuit servatori nostro Iesu Christo, capite sexto decimi octavi libri Antiquitatum Iudaicarum. Quod an Iudaei ex Hebraico volumine eraserint, aut ipse autor data opera id omiserit ne suis illudere videretur, incertum est. Celebrat autem Iosephus in Graeca aeditione Christum nostrum his verbis: . . ."

161. *Josippon* 1559, 11–12: "Hactenus Iosephus li. 18. cap. 6. de bello Iudaico, quem Iudaei vel maximum putant. Hic igitur, qui et si Graece haec scripserit, Iudaeus tamen fuit, paternarumque traditionum acerrimus aemulator, nisi ea, quae per prophetas ille de Messia praenunciata fuerant, recte intellexisset, neque de Christo tam bene sensisset, neque ea quae de ipso dixerunt, adeo bona fide retulisset. Quare neque dubium est, qui haec de eo Graece scripserit, quin alia quoque longe plura legem et prophetas exponens Hebraice scripserit, quum ipse utranque linguam optime calluerit, et sacris literis ab ipsis incunabulis initiatus fuerit. Vnde et credi quoque par est, alios etiam plurimos, praeter eum, ijsdem temporibus extitisse, qui et de Domino Iesu Christo recte senserint, et prophetarum vaticinia explanantes, vera de eo scripserint. Hactenus ille."

162. Ibid., 10: "Porro quum hic Iosippus noster abbreviator Iosephi sit, ut dictum est, quod illud amplissimum testimonium quod hic Christo servatori nostro tribuit, ille omiserit: an ex perfidia Iudaeorum post Christi adventum factum sit, quae et in alijs locis deprehenditur, scire nequeo. Id itaque in medio relinquo, et in gratiam Christianae iuventutis et omnium quotquot sunt, qui hunc libellum lecturi sunt, subijciam, quae in Iosepho primum Graeco, deinde et Latino, de Domino Iesu habentur, subijciam." The duplicated words underlined here were underlined by Casaubon in his copy (BL 1982.c.34): clear evidence that he saw this passage.

163. Full details in Grafton 1983–1993, II.

in a remarkable exchange of letters, that the early Christians had been terribly wrong to believe that the kingdom of Jesus needed lies to promote it. They also agreed that the only way to right this wrong was to pluck from the record not only the correspondence of Jesus with Abgar of Edessa and the *Acts of Pilate*—relatively low-hanging fruit—but also such complex, durable, and thick-skinned fakes as the *Hermetic Corpus* and the *Sibylline Oracles*. And in their determination to criticize even the early Christian writers whom they loved and whose works they savored, they took a distinctive—and provocative—position, which would never attract many followers.[164]

In the context of this polemic, the *Josippon* and the earlier discussions of the *Testimonium* mattered deeply. Baronio claimed that his long residence in Rome—which he compared to that of the Greek antiquary and historian of Rome, Dionysius of Halicarnassus—endowed his work with authority.[165] He had in mind, among other things, the unlimited access he enjoyed to the rare manuscripts in the Vatican Library. And he took advantage of his position to claim inside knowledge about exactly why the *Testimonium* did not appear in the *Josippon:* "Here at Rome we sent for Josephus' testimony, in a very ancient Jewish manuscript, in which his histories had been copied long, long ago, translated from Greek into Hebrew. We found—O the impudence of those perfidious ones—that it had been excised, and in such a way that the crime could not possibly be excused. The very parchment seemed to cry out."[166] Casaubon did not agree, in general terms, that the resources available to Baronio in Rome had made him a reliable historian: "But it's one thing," he wrote in the margin of his copy of volume 1, "to write the history of the universal church, another that of the Roman people."[167] And he denied that Baronio's specific claims about the *Josippon* deserved any credence: "I am afraid that this author is relying on someone else's credibility when he

164. See Grafton 1991, chap. 6; and Quantin 2009.

165. Baronio 1593–1607, I, [b5 recto]: "sicque triginta circiter annos in his pro viribus, Dei gratia favente, insudavimus: pene enim imberbes eramus, cum haec exordiremur, nunc undique canis aspersi haec scribimus; semperque in Vrbe versati, diversas, quae in ea sunt, bibliothecas nobiles, Vaticanam praecipue, quam ditissimum rerum antiquarum penu promptuariumque dicere consuevimus, perlustravimus, ac cum eruditis viris, quorum magna copia hic esse solet, omnia contulimus, modo consulentes, modo disserentes; unde magna facta est rebus nostris accessio." Note also his clever reference to Dionysius of Halicarnassus, "qui nullo validiori argumento lectoris fidem sibi conciliasse visus est, quam asserens complures se annos Romae versatum, eiusdemque Vrbis vetera monumenta et abdita quaeque sedulo perscrutatum fuisse [*Roman Antiquities* 1.7.2–3]."

166. Baronio 1593–1607, I, 215 (34.226): "cuius testimonium in pervetusto Iudaeorum codice, in quo eius historiae e Graeco in Hebraicum translatae, antiquitus scriptae sunt, cum hic Romae requireretur (o perfidorum impudentiam!) abrasum inventum est, adeo ut nulla ad excusandum scelus posset afferri defensio, cum membrana ipsa id exclamare videretur."

167. Casaubon, note in Baronio 1601, Marsh's Library, I,)()(5 recto: "Sed aliud est ecclesiae universalis historiam scribere aliud populi Ro."

writes about the Hebrew manuscript of Josephus, translated from the Greek, which he says is in the Vatican and preserves clear evidence of the perfidy of the Jews."[168] For the text in question could only be the *Josippon*: and that, as Scaliger and Casaubon had jointly demonstrated, was far too late to lend any credibility to the *Testimonium*. Casaubon's choice of words revealed his contempt for Baronio's lack of critical skills. A late section of the *Hermetic Corpus*, the "Horoi," contains a passage in which the author pretends to be an Egyptian, writing in hieroglyphs, and describes how "in later times" translators would lose the force of his words by rendering them in mere Greek. In his copy of the book, Casaubon signaled that the writer's adverb had been carefully chosen to give his book an air of authenticity: "'Later!' What a tricky fellow [*suaviludius*] it was who wrote this."[169] As to the *Josippon*, "this writer, in my view, cannot possibly be the subject of the story of which some tricky fellow [*suaviludius*] has persuaded Baronio."[170] Evidently, then, Casaubon had not exaggerated in his preface, when he denounced Baronio for his lack of expertise in chronology.

Baronio's failure as a critic affected far more than his treatment of the *Testimonium*. Throughout the early part of the *Annales*, by necessity, he returned again and again to Josephus, whose own *Antiquities* and *Jewish War* offered invaluable details on the history of Judaea and the Jews in the centuries just before the coming of Christ and in the first century of the Common Era. But although Baronio had nothing but praise for Josephus as the transmitter of the *Testimonium*, he took a highly critical position toward him in many other respects, denouncing him as untrustworthy and his work as inaccurate. He shared this view, moreover, with Robert Bellarmine, who distinguished between the Therapeutae, early Christians described movingly by Eusebius, and the Essenes, superstitious Jews described by Josephus.[171] Both men—like Serarius—had received the sharp end of Scaliger's critique on that account. Scaliger ridiculed the idea that Josephus had lied "about the

168. Casaubon 1614, 772; 1654, 677; 1663, 677: "Valde autem vereor, ne ex aliena fide scribat auctor, quae narrat de codice Hebraico Iosephi e Graeco translato, quem ait extare in Vaticana, et servare manifesta vestigia imposturae Iudaeorum, qui locum de Christo, e lib. XVIII. cap. iv. eraserint. Ego vero non puto extare hodie in rerum natura, Iosephi opera e Graeco in Hebraeum, ut ait Baronius, conversa." This critique also held for Serarius, who had summarized Baronio's story about the Hebrew Josephus in his work against Drusius (Serarius 1604, 28): "quod in Hebraea etiam eiusdem versione fuit, sed ab impiis Iudaeis in Codicibus nonnullis abrasum Romae compertum scribit Reverendissimus Baronius Tom. 1. Annalium."

169. Casaubon, note in his copy of the Paris 1554 edition of the *Hermetic Corpus*, BL 491.d.14, 90: "No. ὕστερον. Nae hic homo suaviludius est qui haec scribat."

170. Casaubon 1614, 772; 1654, 677; 1663, 677: "neque in hunc scriptorem, quantum existimo, potest cadere, quod suaviludius aliquis Baronio persuasit."

171. See Serarius 1604, 3.13, 266–267.

Essenes, whom he saw, whose meetings he attended, and whom he wanted to join—though, when he had considered their lives, actions, and mores, he preferred to join the Pharisees."[172] And he heaped scorn on "the founder of the *Annales,* who preferred to trust that inaccurate man Eusebius rather than Josephus, a native writer, who wrote on the basis of what he had seen himself or on that of the Acts of Herod."[173] "Come now," he challenged the Catholics, "which of the ancients wrote history with more credibility than Josephus?"[174] "Iosephi fides," wrote Casaubon in the margin at this point; and he went on, throughout the *Exercitationes,* to argue that Josephus deserved belief far more than Eusebius did. As Casaubon worked on Josephus and related texts, he tried to solve both technical problems that lay at the heart of Christian chronology, such as the dating of Christ's birth, mission, and death, and larger questions that went to the core of early Christianity and its relationship with Judaism, such as the extent to which Essenes and other sectaries had deviated from Jewish practice and belief. In such fields he consistently followed the threads that Scaliger had spooled out behind him as he made his own long march through the centuries around the birth of Christ. Neither simple nor trivial, these chronological questions would remain central to scholarship for centuries.

In some ways, the central question that Casaubon attacked, and the one that led him deepest into the study of Judaism, was that of the Crucifixion— the one with which we began this chapter. The problem was complex, and its relation to Jewish texts and sources had been known for a long time. When Baronio argued that the account in John's Gospel matched those in the other three, he brusquely rejected what he called a solution based on the practices of Jews in recent centuries.[175] Paul of Burgos, a fifteenth-century bishop of Jewish descent, had argued in his *Additions* to the widely influential *Postillae* of Nicholas of Lyra that the Jews had deliberately moved their Passover from the fifteenth of Nisan, a Friday, to the next day, the sabbath. They did so, he claimed, in order to avoid having two days in a row on which

---

172. Scaliger 1605, 199–200: "Profecto omnes auctores mentiuntur, qui ad sociorum argumenta confirmanda nihil conferunt. Vt Iosephus mentitus sit de Essenis? de illis, quos vidit? quorum coetibus interfuit? de quorum numero esse voluit? quorum quum vitam, actiones et mores considerasset, maluerit se ad Pharisaeorum institutum conferre? Ille hos ignoravit?"

173. Ibid., 200: "Certe Bellarminus satis ostendit nullum gustum se habere scriptorum Iosephi, ut neque conditor Annalium, qui in rebus Herodis et belli Iudaici maluit credere homini inaccurato Eusebio quam Iosepho scriptori vernaculo ex fide oculata aut ex Actis Herodis omnia scribenti. Atqui Philo longe superstitiosiora de Essenis retulit quam Iosephus: longe Ἰουδαϊκώτερα. Vnde quis colligere possit, quum Bellarminus illa scriberet, Monachos suos potius, quam Essenos in animo habuisse."

174. Ibid.: "Cedo sis quis veterum fide tanta usus sit in historia conscribenda, quam Iosephus?"

175. Baronio 1593–1607, I, 147: "ex lacunis recentiorum Hebraeorum."

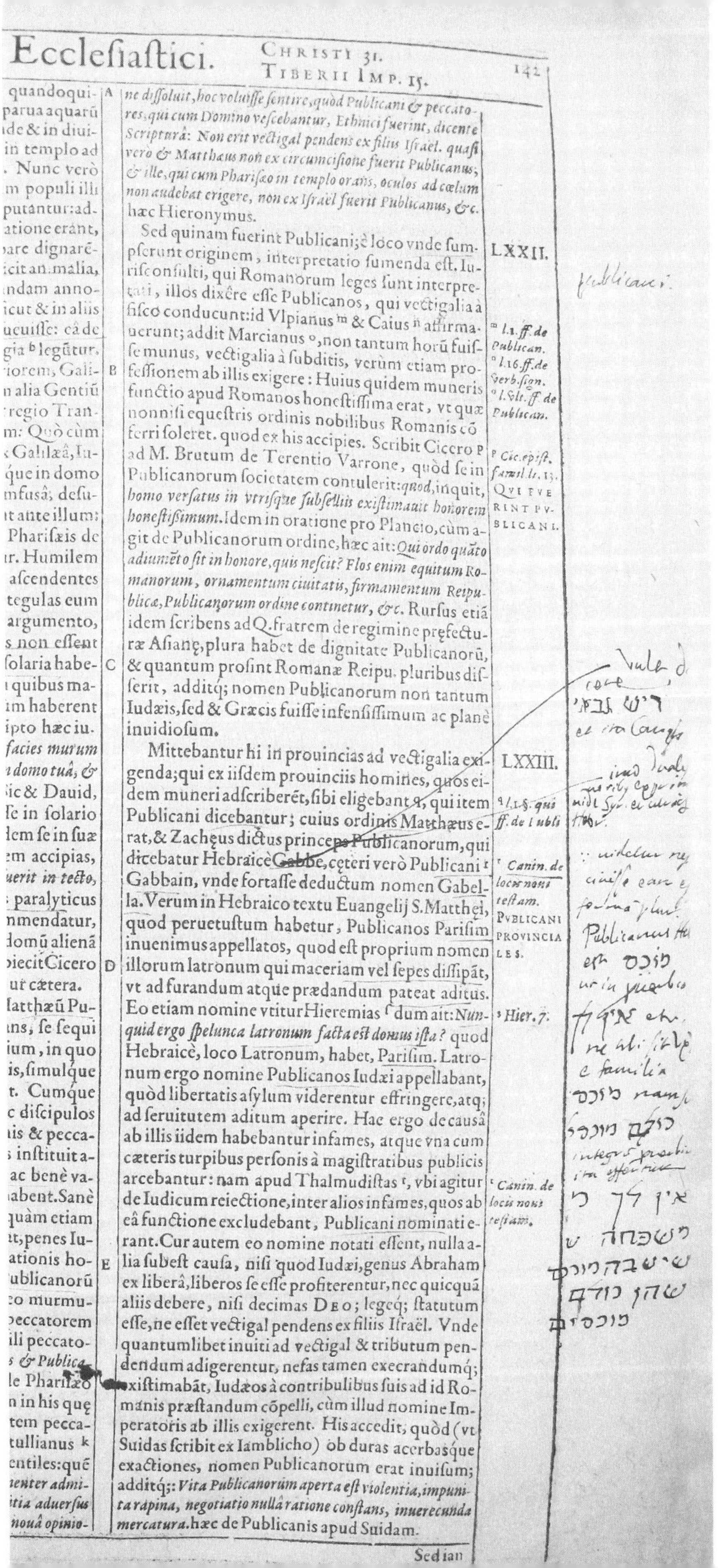

[Left column]

quandoqui-
parua aquarû
ide & in diui-
in templo ad
. Nunc verò
m populi illi
putantur: ad
atione erãt,
are dignarê-
icit an. malia,
ndam anno-
icut & in aliis
ucuisse: eâ de
gia b legitur,
orem, Gali-
n alia Gentiû
regio Tranm:
Quò cùm
x Galilæâ, Iu-
que in domo
mfusâ, desu-
t ante illum:
Pharisæis de
r. Humilem
ascendentes
tegulas eum
argumento,
s non essent
solaria habe-
i quibus ma-
im haberent
ipto hæc iu-
*facies murum
n domo tuâ, &*
ic & Dauid,
se in solario
dem se in suæ
em accipias,
uerit in tecto,
paralyticus
nmendatur,
domû alienã
iiecit Cicero
ut cætera.
atthæu Pu-
ans, se sequi
ium, in quo
is, simulque
t. Cumque
c discipulos
iis & pecca-
s instituit ac
ac bene va-
abent. Sanè
quàm etiam
t, penes Iu-
ationis ho-
ublicanorû
eo murmu-
peccatorem
ili peccato-
s *& Publica*
le Pharisæo
n in his quæ
tem pecca-
tullianus k
entiles: quæ
nenter admi-
itia aduersus
nouã opinio-

[Main column]

ne dissoluit, hoc voluisse sentire, quòd Publicani & peccatores, qui cum Domino vescebantur, Ethnici fuerint, dicente Scripturâ: *Non erit vectigal pendens ex filiis Israel.* quasi verò & Matthæus non ex circumcisione fuerit Publicanus; & ille, qui cum Pharisæo in templo orans, oculos ad cælum non audebat erigere, non ex Israël fuerit Publicanus, &c. hæc Hieronymus.

Sed quinam fuerint Publicani; è loco vnde sumpserunt originem, interpretatio sumenda est. Iurisconsulti, qui Romanorum leges sunt interpretati, illos dixêre esse Publicanos, qui vectigalia à fisco conducunt: id Vlpianus m & Caius n affirmauerunt; addit Marcianus o, non tantum horu fuisse munus, vectigalia à subditis, verùm etiam professionem ab illis exigere: Huius quidem muneris functio apud Romanos honestissima erat, vt quæ nonnisi equestris ordinis nobilibus Romanis co ferri soleret. quod ex his accipies. Scribit Cicero p ad M. Brutum de Terentio Varrone, quòd se in Publicanorum societatem contulerit: *quod,* inquit, *homo versatus in vtrisque subselliis existimauit honorem honestissimum.* Idem in oratione pro Plancio, cùm agit de Publicanorum ordine, hæc ait: *Qui ordo quãto adiumeto sit in honore, quis nescit? Flos enim equitum Romanorum, ornamentum ciuitatis, firmamentum Reipublicæ, Publicanorum ordine continetur,* &c. Rursus etiã idem scribens ad Q. fratrem de regimine præfecturæ Asianæ, plura habet de dignitate Publicanorû, & quantum prosint Romanæ Reipu. pluribus disserit, additq; nomen Publicanorum non tantum Iudæis, sed & Græcis fuisse infensissimum ac planè inuidiosum.

Mittebantur hi in prouincias ad vectigalia exigenda; qui ex iisdem prouinciis homines, quos eidem muneri adscriberêt, sibi eligebant q, qui item Publicani dicebantur; cuius ordinis Matthæus erat, & Zachæus dictus princeps Publicanorum, qui dicebatur Hebraicè Gabbe, ceteri verò Publicani Gabbain, vnde fortasse deductum nomen Gabella. Verum in Hebraico textu Euangelij S. Matthei, quod peruetustum habetur, Publicanos Parisim inuenimus appellatos, quod est proprium nomen illorum latronum qui maceriam vel sepes dissipãt, vt ad furandum atque prædandum pateat aditus. Eo etiam nomine vtitur Hieremias r dum ait: *Nunquid ergo spelunca latronum facta est domus ista?* quod Hebraicè, loco Latronum, habet, Parisim. Latronum ergo nomine Publicanos Iudæi appellabant, quòd libertatis asylum viderentur effringere, atq; ad seruitutem aditum aperire. Hac ergo de causa ab illis iidem habebantur infames, atque vna cum cæteris turpibus personis à magistratibus publicis arcebantur: nam apud Thalmudistas t, vbi agitur de Iudicum reiectione, inter alios infames, quos ab eâ functione excludebant, Publicani nominati erant. Cur autem eo nomine notati essent, nulla alia subest causa, nisi quod Iudæi, genus Abraham ex liberâ, liberos esse profiterentur, nec quicquã aliis debere, nisi decimas DEO; legeq; statutum esse, ne esset vectigal pendens ex filiis Israël. Vnde quantumlibet inuiti ad vectigal & tributum pendendum adigerentur, nefas tamen execrandumq; existimabat, Iudæos à contribulibus suis ad id Romanis præstandum copelli, cùm illud nomine Imperatoris ab illis exigerent. His accedit; quòd (vt Suidas scribit ex Iamblicho) ob duras acerbasque exactiones, nomen Publicanorum erat inuisum; additq; *Vita Publicorum aperta est violenta, impunita rapina, negotiatio nullâ ratione constans, inuerecunda mercatura.* hæc de Publicanis apud Suidam.

Sed ian

[Marginal notes]

LXXII.

m *l.1. ff. de Publican.*
n *l.16. ff. de Verb. sign.*
o *l. Vlt. ff. de Publican.*

p *Cic. epist. famil. li. 13.*

QVI FVERINT PVBLICANI.

LXXIII.

q *l.1.§. quis ff. de l. ubli*

r *Canin. de locis noui testam.*

PVBLICANI PROVINCIALES.

s *Hier. 7.*

t *Canin. de locis noui testam.*

FIGURE 4.5.
Note by Casaubon in his copy of Cesare Baronio's *Annales ecclesiastici.* Marsh's Library, Dublin.

they could not carry out such tasks as burying the dead—just as they did in his own day. Jesus and his disciples, in his view, had celebrated the Passover on the date set in Leviticus, the fourteenth of Nisan—just as the Synoptic Gospels stated. The Jews, by contrast, had celebrated on the sixteenth—just as John's Gospel indicated.[176]

When Baronio rejected what he described as Paul's suggestion, he was knowingly taking a position on an issue that had aroused debate in the church for centuries. And Paul had not been the only participant in these discussions to draw on Jewish sources. As early as the twelfth century, Rupert of Deutz, a theologian who knew, and tried to convert, many Jews, had used his knowledge of the Jewish calendar to explicate the Gospels. He raised a somewhat different problem: "The Jews had eaten the Passover in the evening of the fourteenth day. On the next day, since it was the fifteenth, they would have been obliged to celebrate the feast and, in accordance with the law, to refrain from normal activities. How then could they spend the whole day on the trials by which they condemned the Lord and those whom they crucified with him?"[177] Rupert ignored many problems here: above all the nature of the Jewish calendar and the identity of the legal system that actually condemned Jesus. But he rapidly found a Jewish answer to his profoundly Christian question:

> For among the many traditions that the Jewish elders added to the traditions of God, they established this one: if the day before the sabbath, which we call Friday, happened to be the fifteenth of the month, the feast would not be celebrated then, but put off until the following day, the sabbath. They said it was difficult and inconvenient to have two sabbaths in a row: that is, to refrain from all work on two days. This was the case for many reasons, and one of the most important was that when the corpses of their dead sometimes remained unburied until the fourth day, they produced a troublesome stench.[178]

176. Paul of Burgos, *Additio* to Nicholas of Lyra on Matthew 26, in Paul of Burgos 1477, ii3 recto–[ii5 recto]. See the account in Shuger 1994, 72–73. We are most grateful to Philipp Nothaft, whose dissertation, now nearing completion, treats the history of these problems for the first time in full detail, for his counsel.

177. Rupert of Deutz 1545, 142 verso: "Cum Iudaei quartadecima die ad vesperam pascha celebrando, agnum comedissent, et sequenti die, quoniam quintadecima erat, solennitatem celebrare et secundum legem vacare debuissent, quomodo illis iudicia tractare licuit, quibus tunc totum diem insumpserunt in condemnatione domini et eorum quos cum illo crucifixerunt?"

178. Ibid.: "Nam inter traditiones plurimas quas seniores Iudaeorum superstatuerant traditionibus dei, istud quoque statuerant, ut si diem ante sabbatum, quam sextam feriam dicimus, contingeret esse

Knowledge of these postponements *(dehiyyot)* not only resolved the problem he had raised, but also explained the troubling sentences in John.[179] The problem of the Crucifixion thus forced a Christian exegete to ask new questions, and to consider new sources of knowledge, about the Passover.

Jewish scholars, of course, also discussed at length their calendar and the problems posed by double sabbaths. And they knew that the problems involved were complex, since the Jewish calendar was anything but a fixed body of practices created at a single point. Almost every aspect of the calendar provoked debate.[180] Rupert's Jewish contemporary Abraham ibn Ezra, for example, noted in an extended commentary on Leviticus 23:3 that "in all of scripture we find no evidence of the procedure whereby the Jews established their calendar." True, one of the greatest earlier authorities, Saadia Gaon, who had engaged in heated controversies about the calendar in the first half of the tenth century, had argued that "they relied on the intercalation calculation [that we now employ]." But ibn Ezra insisted that "this cannot be true, as the Mishnah and the Talmud both record that Passover occasionally used to fall on Monday, Wednesday, or Friday. Two stories tell of the occurrence of such events."[181]

In the decades around 1500, Paul of Middelburg, bishop of Fossombrone and astrologer, examined the work of Paul of Burgos and at least some of its Jewish sources in his *Paulina*. This massive treatise on the history and celebration of Easter appeared in 1513, its publication timed to coincide with the Fifth Lateran Council, which Paul and many others hoped would reform the

---

quintamdecimam mensis, non celebraretur solennitas, sed differretur in diem sequentem sabbati, difficile et incommodum esse dicentes, duo sabbata continuare. i. duobus diebus vacare ab omni opere, multas ob causas, quarum ex praecipuis una erat, quod cadavera suorum nonnumquam usque in quartam diem insepulta foetoris molestiam generarent."

179. Ibid.: "Hanc (inquam) quaestionem cognitio cito solvit illius iam dictae traditionis, quia traditum illis fuerat differre solennitatem quum evenisset ante sabbatum legale quintadecima dies mensis, et pro duobus sabbatis unum celebrare sabbatum magnum, solennitate duplici. Vnde cum dixisset Evangelista, Iudaei ergo, quoniam parasceve erat, ut non remanerent in cruce sabbato corpora, causam istam subiunxit: Erat enim magnus dies ille sabbati."

180. Mahler 1916 is the classic manual; Stern 2001 is a very informative recent survey. In chap. 40 of his *Me'or Einayim* (2001, 480–517), de' Rossi discusses the issue of postponements, clearly favoring Maimonides' position. He writes (502): "This difference of view is of great significance, for according to Rabbi Moses, the postponement derives from astronomical principles, whereas the view of his opponents is that it is a convention agreed on authority of a valid Law Court following the scriptural statement, *These are the set times of the Lord, the sacred occasions which you shall celebrate each at its appointed time* [Lev. 23:4]." He takes up the subject again in his *Matsref laKesef* (Refinement of Silver), de' Rossi 1866, II, chap. 7, where he attacks Münster for his use of a late liturgical poem as an authoritative text on the Jewish calendrical system. De' Rossi's sophisticated treatment of this complex topic, drawing upon discussions by numerous medieval Jewish authorities, was not known or used by Casaubon or his contemporaries.

181. Ibn Ezra on Lev. 23:3; Weiser 1976–77, III, 79–80.

ecclesiastical calendar, now in considerable disarray.[182] Paul confessed that—like Ibn Ezra, whom he did not cite—he had originally assumed that the fixed Jewish calendar, with its rules for postponements, came into being long after the lifetime of Jesus. True, Paul knew a *petihah,* a reading that precedes a *piyyut,* which described how the Sanhedrin had created the fixed calendar, as the result of direct divine sanction and inspiration, immediately after the completion of the Second Temple:

> Thus did our rabbis the Sanhedrin, the authorities of the world, decree when the building of the Second Temple had been completed. Then a throne of fire appeared in their place and on it the King of the universe revolving and standing between the portico [and the altar]. And they received a crown, and they took a hidden seal, and they made an irrevocable enactment, and it was given to Rabbi Eliezer, the greatest of them all, and he instituted: "Purim cannot fall on a Monday, Wednesday, or Saturday; Passover on Monday, Wednesday, or Friday, Pentecost on Tuesday, Thursday, or Saturday; New Year on Sunday, Wednesday, or Friday; Day of Atonement on Sunday, Tuesday, or Friday."[183]

Paul not only quoted this impressive charter for the fixed calendar, but also translated it into Latin. For a time, however, he had refused to believe it: "since the Jews, in their perfidy, make a habit of arbitrary invention to enable them to slander the Christian religion, I used to think that they had invented this institution after the Passion of Christ." By doing so, after all, they

---

182. See in general Coyne, Hoskin, and Pedersen 1983.

183. Paul of Middelburg 1513, [Dvi verso–Dvii recto]: "Reliquum iudaeorum argumentum non minus urgere videtur pro quo assumunt quod praecipui ecclesiae doctores perhibent Christum dominum ab eis crucifixum fuisse in die festo paschae iudaeorum. Ex quo sic arguunt: paschalis solemnitas iudaeorum post secundam templi instaurationem nunquam celebrata fuit die veneris, ergo Christus non fuit crucifixus ab eis die veneris in festo paschae. assumptum deducunt ex prisca ipsorum constitutione in secunda templi instauratione longo temporis intervallo ante Christi salvatoris nativitatem aedita, qua cavetur ne festum paschae feria sexta, hoc est, die veneris observari possit: festorum ordine hoc exigente, quam suis linguis maledicis his verbis nobis obiicere solent . . . statuerunt patres nostri iudices aequissimi in templi instauratione secunda quando in templi porta divina eis apparuit maiestas super cathedram igneam ordinem sempiternum. accepta itaque corona et sigillo secreto praesidente Eleazaro legisperito statuerunt ut festum sortis nunquam possit contingere feria secunda, feria quarta, aut sabbato. pascha vero nunquam feria secunda, feria quarta, aut feria sexta celebrari possit et pentecoste nunquam feria tertia, feria quinta aut sabbato accidere possit. caput anni et festum tabernaculorum nunquam feria prima feria quarta aut feria sexta. Ieiunium expiationis nunquam feria prima feria tertia vel feria sexta contingere possit." For this text see Weinberg 2000 (translation at 319). Warm thanks to Philipp Nothaft for pointing out to us that Paul of Middelburg was the first Christian scholar to quote and translate it.

could claim that their ancestors could not have crucified Jesus on a Passover that fell on a Friday. Eventually, however, Paul came across the same rules in a treatise "by the holy Gamaliel, the pupil of Christ and the teacher of Paul," and conceded that they had been in effect in the time of Jesus.[184] Sebastian Münster followed Paul, and even quoted the same impressive *petihah,* at first without giving Paul credit (later he admitted his debt).[185] Other Catholic scholars—notably the biblical scholar Johannes Hentenius and the theologian Cornelius Jansen—followed Münster, although they cited not the work of that convert to Lutheranism but the Jewish chronicle *Seder olam zuta,* which he had incorporated in his work on the calendar.[186]

By the time of Baronio and Casaubon, the majority of exegetes seem to have believed that Christ and his disciples had celebrated Passover on the Thursday evening, the Jews on the Friday evening and Saturday. But some very influential writers disagreed. Robert Bellarmine, for example, devoted a substantial section of his *Disputations* on the Eucharist to showing that all four Gospels agreed on the chronology of the Crucifixion. Although he knew the exegeses of the two Pauls, and recognized that the Jews of his own time followed the fixed calendar, he insisted that "it is false that that tradition, according to which the feast of unleavened bread was never celebrated on a Monday, a Wednesday, or a Friday, was in use in the time of Christ."[187] It was easy to understand how previous Christian expositors had gone wrong. They had naturally believed Paul of Burgos, "on the grounds that he was speaking as an expert in his own art, for he had himself been a rabbi of the Jews."[188] Bellarmine, however, wielded powerful new evidence to prove that the Jewish fixed calendar had come into being relatively recently—and by the same token to disprove Paul's theory about Passover:

> FIRST OF ALL, Rabbi ibn Ezra, in his commentary on Leviticus 23, explicitly asserts that this tradition did not go back to the beginning of the Second Temple, as many pretend, or even to the time when

184. Paul of Middelburg 1513, [Dviiii recto]: "Verum quoniam iudaei perfidia pleni multa pro arbitrio solent confingere, ut christianam religionem calumniari valeant: arbitrabar hanc constitutionem post Christi passionem ab eis confictam fuisse, donec eandem apud sanctum Gamalielem Christi discipulum et Pauli praeceptorem conscriptam invenirem, ad cuius pedes apostolus ipse se legem et prophetas didicisse gloriatur, qui in libro quem de solis et lunae motibus annique ratione conscripsit sic dicit." The Hebrew text that Paul quotes seems to be his own invention.

185. Münster 1527b, 128; 1537, 142.

186. Hentenius in [Eutychius] 1543, [†viii recto]; Jansen 1572–71, IV, 425–426.

187. Bellarmine 1588, 820: "SECVNDO, falsum est tempore Christi fuisse illam traditionem in usu, ut nunquam festum azymorum celebraretur die 2. 4. vel 6. est enim traditio illa multo recentior."

188. Ibid.: "Atque hoc est, quod decepit plurimos scriptores modernos, alioqui eruditissimos: crediderunt enim omnes Burgensi tanquam in sua arte perito: nam et ipse Rabinus Hebraeorum fuerat."

the Talmud was created. For in the Mishnah and the Talmud, as he says, Passover can be found on בדו—that is, on Monday, Wednesday, and Friday. Now it is well established that the Talmud was composed some centuries after the Passion of Christ.[189]

Ibn Ezra made a strong witness—although Bellarmine may not have realized, and certainly did not acknowledge, how isolated his views had been in the Jewish world.

The Jesuit theologian and biblical scholar Franciscus Toletus attacked the same problems in 1589 and 1590, in his own commentary on the Gospels. Like Bellarmine, he found it "astonishing that Catholic teachers believed the fables of the Jews of our time, and did not take into account the testimonies of scripture, or subjected them to violent expositions."[190] Toletus made clear that he rejected any effort to draw on contemporary Jewish practice in order to understand the Crucifixion, even if the Jews claimed that their traditions were ancient.[191] And he argued that the best evidence about ancient practices showed that they had not included the *dehiyyot*. In a complex, difficult sermon by the fifteenth-century Spanish rabbi Isaac Arama, Toletus found a piece of evidence that seemed to prove his point. Arama described the counting of the *Omer,* the interval of forty-nine days between Passover to Pentecost. This began, he explained, with the cutting of a measure of barley to be offered up. The barley must be cut, and the count must begin, on the sixteenth of Nisan. Arama quoted as his authority Mishnah Menahot 10:3, which described the process in detail. The representatives of the law court were to go out after sundown on the feast day and bind a bunch of barley to make it easier to cut. The one deputed to cut should ask the others, three times, if the sun had set, and if they were using the proper implement

189. Ibid.: "Esse autem falsum, traditionem illam tempore Christi in usu fuisse, probo. INPRIMIS Rabbi Abenezra in commentario Levitici, ca. 23. disertis verbis affirmat hanc traditionem non solum non fuisse ab initio secundi templi, ut multi fabulantur, sed nec fuisse eo tempore, quo fiebat Thalmud. Nam et in Misna et in Thalmud, ut ipse dicit, invenitur Pascha in בדו, id est, die 2 .4. et 6. constat autem Thalmud confectum fuisse aliquot annorum centuriis post passionem Christi."

190. Toletus 1590–89, II, 9: "miror autem catholicos hos doctores Iudaeorum nostri temporis fabulis fidem adhibuisse, scripturae testimonijs non consideratis, aut violentis expositionibus adhibitis."

191. Ibid., 10: "Fingunt multa facta fuisse, quae Evangelistae non narrant, sed praeterquam quod haec ab ipsis confingantur et sine auctoritate dicantur, his verbis Evangelistarum numquam accommodabuntur. Opponent nobis Iudaeorum hoc tempore observationem: fateor. Sed interrogati, unde probant eandem fuisse Christi temporibus consuetudinem, respondebunt: id modo affirmare Iudaeos, se antiquissima traditione hanc consuetudinem accipere. Vana est responsio profecto: Iudaeos perfidos, mendaces, et qui nihil fere legis observant, accersere in testimonium tantae veritatis, ubi expressa testimonia scripturae clamant in contrarium."

and in the proper place.[192] Most important, the text made clear that the same rules applied if the sixteenth of Nisan was the sabbath. In these circumstances, the one deputed to cut the barley should "ask the others, is it the sabbath? They answer, It is. He then says: Shall I reap? They answer, reap." But as Toletus noted, if the sabbath could take place on 16 Nisan, then 15 Nisan—the beginning of Passover—could obviously fall on a Friday after all. Here was an authoritative text—one not only far older than Ibn Ezra, but actually drawn from the Jewish code of ritual law—that could not have been formulated as it was if the fixed calendar had been in effect. Menahot, Toletus explained, "is part of the Talmud, which was composed many years after Christ. Here you see that the Jews did not use postponements some years ago, but celebrated the sabbath immediately after the first day of the Feast of Unleavened Bread."[193]

Not every Catholic commentator rejected the views of the two Pauls. Juan de Maldonado, a Jesuit commentator whom some described as a Marrano, drew on all these traditions to support what he called "the opinion that many do not approve: that Christ did not celebrate the Passover in advance, nor did the Jews delay it, and yet they did not celebrate it on the same day. But Christ followed the prescription of the Law, the Jews the traditions of their elders."[194] He noted the dissenting opinion of Ibn Ezra, which he may have known from Bellarmine's work, but he did not see it as reason to amend

192. Ibid.: "Falsa igitur recentiorum Iudaeorum est traditio, et huius sententiae fundamentum. At, ut etiam testimonio ipsorummet Iudaeorum perfidorum nostram veritatem comprobemus, constat aperte ante nonnullos annos talem translationem inter ipsos non fuisse, sed simul celebratum Pascha feria sexta et postea Sabbatum, et manipulum messuisse vespere feriae sextae etiam Sabbato incipiente. Rabbi Isaac Arama auctor libri Achidach Isaac: id est, ligationis Isaac, vir maximae apud Hebraeos auctoritatis, super illud Levit. 23. Cum veneritis in terram, quam ego do vobis, et messueritis, et cetera. habet haec verba: Impossibile est colligere et demetere manipulum, nisi nocte decima sexta lunae, sicut scriptum est in libro Menahoth, id est oblationum farinacearum, in hanc sententiam. Quomodo igitur fit? legati senatus egrediuntur post vesperam diei festi, et colligunt manipulum demetiendum prope radices, ut facilius demeti possit: civitates proximae congregantur, ut maior praecepti merces sit, postquam tenebrae factae sunt, metens dicit adstantibus: occubuitne sol? idque tribus vicibus, quibus respondentibus occubuisse, iterum per tres vices interrogat, an illa falx et area sit in hunc usum destinata? respondentque rem ita se habere." The source is *Aqedat Yitshaq,* gate 67, chap. 4.

193. Toletus 1590–89, II, 10: "quod si fuerit Sabbatum, interrogat eos, estne Sabbatum? Est, inquiunt. Metamne? addit ille: Mete, respondent: et omnia haec tribus interrogationibus absolvuntur. Haec iste. Est autem liber Menahoth pars talmud multis annis post Christum composita, ubi vides Iudaeos ante aliquot annos talem non habuisse translationem, sed celebrasse Sabbatum immediate post primam diem Azymorum, in cuius vespere metebatur manipulus."

194. Maldonado 1607, 559: "Eam ergo probo sententiam, quam multi non probant, neque Christum tempus Paschae anticipasse; neque Iudaeos distulisse, et non eodem tamen die celebrasse, sed Christum legis praescriptum: Iudaeos maiorum suorum traditiones sequutos esse." This is oddly translated in 1888, II, 349–350.

his views: "I know that Rabbi Abraham writes that in the Mishnah and the Talmud it is found that Passover sometimes fell on Monday, Wednesday, and Friday. But I am not certain if he therefore denies that when it fell on Friday it was normally moved to the sabbath; nor if he deserves such great authority that we should depart from the others' opinion for his sake."[195] But Baronio—as he made clear—followed Bellarmine and Toletus in rejecting the whole effort to use what he described as the customs of contemporary Jews to explicate the chronology of the Passion.

One reason that Casaubon set out to debate these chronological points, to which Baronio had devoted relatively little attention or space, was probably tactical. Students of the chronology of the Passion—most of them Catholic—had taken Jewish materials into account for centuries. But Baronio had rejected all such appeals to what he dismissed as the superstitious practices of modern Jews. This made chronology a particularly attractive area in which to demonstrate not only Baronio's general failings as a scholar, but also his ignorance of Hebrew and Jewish customs. Casaubon had worked his way years before through Scaliger's detailed treatment of Passover and the Last Supper. Using the Haggadah, which he analyzed with great intelligence, Scaliger had made clear that the Last Supper described in the Synoptic Gospels must actually have been superimposed on a normal Passover. His arguments evidently excited many Calvinist readers. "Please," wrote the jurist François Hotman to the Zurich theologian Johann Stucki, a few months after Scaliger's work appeared, "read Scaliger's passage on the Lord's Supper in his book *De emendatione temporum,* and let me know your opinion on it whenever it is convenient."[196] Scaliger also argued that the Jews had postponed Passover to the sabbath. In explaining the *dehiyyot,* he called attention not only to the difficulties involved in delaying burials, which Christians had known about for centuries, but also to the further problem that "pot-herbs" would not remain edible for two days on which further cooking was prohibited. Casaubon not only read and annotated both editions of the *De emendatione temporum,* in which these arguments appeared, but also collated them with Scaliger's principal—and largely uncredited—source, Münster's *Kalendarium,* and even made small corrections in the relevant

195. Maldonado 1607, 560: "Scio Rabbi Abraham scribere in Misne et in Thalmud reperiri aliquando Pascha in feriam secundam, quartam, et sextam incurrere, sed nescio, an propterea neget, cum in sextam feriam incurrebat, solitum in sabbatum transferri: aut an tantum auctoritatis mereatur, ut eius gratia ab aliorum sententia discedere debeamus."

196. Hotman to Stuckius, Basel, 14 October 1583, in Hotman and Hotman 1700, 174–175: "Scaligeri locum de Coena Domini in suo de temp. emendat. libro velim legas: tuamque de eo sententiam, ubi commodum erit, perscribas." See more generally Shuger 1994, chap. 1.

passages in Münster. Hebraic learning and the chronology of Christ's last days were intimately linked in Casaubon's understanding. By the time he wrote, after all, it had become normal, even commonplace, for Protestant scholars to claim that the study of Hebrew could be justified by the light it shed on the problems connected with the dating of the Crucifixion.[197]

At the same time, Casaubon drew on a wide range of other sources that he, like Scaliger, saw as basic to the study of chronology: above all Abraham Zacuto's *Yuhasin,* one of the most detailed Jewish chronological texts available to him. Like Scaliger, too, Casaubon applied to particular problems sources that had nothing to do with chronology. Maimonides' *Yad,* which served as his most detailed source for Jewish law, did regular service in his rebuttal of Baronio. Again and again Casaubon argued, drawing on these materials, that the Jews must have postponed Passover. Baronio insisted that the Jews could have condemned and executed Jesus on the day of the feast.[198] Casaubon denied this possibility at detailed length. The Pharisees, he argued, could not possibly have judged Jesus on the holiday itself. Jews, as Maimonides made clear, never held capital trials even on the day before the sabbath or a feast, as it would be impossible to execute a defendant judged guilty on the next day. The Jews' actions could be explained only if—as John indicated—Jesus could have been executed on a weekday.[199]

Casaubon admitted that the most learned chronologers did not agree on every detail of Jewish tradition. One of the most exciting discoveries he made as he worked on these problems had to do with what he recognized as

197. Waser to Buxtorf, in Buxtorf 1610, [):(8 recto]: "Quantum boni, quaeso, praestat haec lingua Chronologo, ut de caeteris sileam? Equidem quod divinus author Plato de sua Geometria magnificentissime pronunciavit, Ἀγεωμέτρητος οὐκ εἰσίτω, innuens ei, qui Geometriae ignarus sit, ad suum Lycaeum aditum et ingressum praeclusum esse: id de Chronologia verissime dixeris, Ἀνεβραῖος οὐκ εἰσίτω: res quandoquidem minime dubia est, sed certa atque concessa apud omnes eos, qui supputationi atque emendationi temporum operam navant. Post investigatum annum Passionis Domini consulendum esse Kalendarium Hebraeorum, ut ex illo mensis Paschalis eliciatur, atque ex situ Plenilunii dies Passionis indicetur. Quomodo autem rudis litterarum Hebraearum Kalendarium isthoc intelligat?"

198. Baronio 1593–1607, I, 150: "Nec aliquem puto dicere iure posse, opera legis festo die esse vetita."

199. Casaubon 1614, 482; 1654, 425; 1663, 425: "Nos interim proferemus hoc loco gravissimi scriptoris testimonium expressum, quo omnes Baronianae coniecturae uno ictu conficientur. Moses ben Maimon libro ultimo Iad, sectione prima, quae inscribitur Sanedrin, capite undecimo, tractans de varijs differentijs inter iudicia Mammonoth, id est, civilia et Animarum, sive capitalia, ait inter caetera . . . *Iudices rerum capitalium non iudicant in parasceve Sabbati, aut in parasceve diei festi: quia non debet id fieri, et reus occidi postridie non potest.* De sindone et myrrha ad Domini pollincturam emptis, mirari subit responsionem Baronij: concedit fieri id non potuisse propter honorem festi, quia Pascha erat: vult die sabbati esse illa empta. At si rapere in ius, caedere, damnare, affigere cruci, die festo Paschatis putat Baronius fuisse licitum: quae malum! importuna religio illum incessit, ut existimet, rei ad opus pium faciendum necessariae emptionem fuisse illo die legibus vetitam? Quod autem arbitratur sabbato illa curare omnia quae ad funus spectabant, licitum fuisse; insigniter fallitur: neque hoc unquam illi concedent istarum politicarum translationum defensores."

a mistake on Scaliger's part. Scaliger had argued that the rules for postponing Passover and Yom Kippur must have been framed under the kings of Israel and Judah, "since the air in Jerusalem was no hotter or more infectious after the Captivity than before."[200] At some point during his stay in England, however, Casaubon came upon an unfinished manuscript chronology by Edward Lively, a professor of Hebrew at Cambridge who had died in 1605.[201] He may have encountered this work during his trip to Cambridge and Ely in 1611. At all events, by 1612 he had realized that Lively's work was of extraordinary quality and interest. As he wrote in his diary on 2 July, "Today I began to copy out some things from the chronological papers of the late Lively. I knew from the writings I had seen that he was a very learned man, but these chronological papers surpass my assessment. I wish this great man had been able to complete them and publish them."[202]

Lively's work survives, in manuscript form, in the library of Trinity College Dublin.[203] And it more than justifies Casaubon's enthusiasm. In a brilliant passage Lively showed that Scaliger himself had misunderstood the talmudic evidence. In fact, the Jews had introduced postponements into their calendar during the Babylonian captivity:

> But the reason for postponing the weekdays was not the climate in Jerusalem, but that in Babylon and Persia. The Jews' Talmud makes this clear in chapter one of Rosh haShanah. For the Jews living in Chaldea say: "the world brings us corruption, but not to them." The commentator explains this as follows: "We Babylonians live in a hotter region, which causes corruption, since Babylon is low-lying, and not a land of mountains and valleys like the land of Israel, which is not subject to the influence of the air. Hence they have no need of intercalation (postponement) there on account of the dead or the herbs, except for our sake alone."[204]

---

200. Grafton 1983–1993, II, 326–328.

201. See the excellent study by Rosenthal 1950; and G. Lloyd Jones, "Lively, Edward," in *ODNB* 2004.

202. Casaubon 1850, II, 935: "Cepi hoc die quaedam describere e chartis chronicis τοῦ μακαρίτου *Livelei.* Sciebam e scriptis, quae videram, virum fuisse doctissimum; sed opinionem meam superant hae chartae chronologicae, quas utinam vir magnus perfecisset, et edere potuisset."

203. A fair copy of Lively's unfinished chronology is Trinity College Dublin MS 126; a rough draft is MS 125.

204. Trinity College Dublin MS 126, 86 recto: "Verum profecto non Ierosolymitanum, sed Babylonicum et Persicum coelum illius reiectionis feriarum instituendae causam fuisse docet Iudaeorum Talmud in רה capite primo. In Chaldaea enim habitantes Iudaei, in hunc modum ibi loquuntur . . . quod ad nos, inquiunt, mundus nobis corruptionem affert: sed illis nequaquam. Id interpres ita declarat . . . Nos Babylonij in calidiore mundi parte versamur, a qua corruptio nobis est; eo quod Babylonia profunda sit, et non terra montium et vallium, ut terra Israelis, cui aer non dominatur. proinde illic nulla intercalatione [translatione] propter mortuos aut olera opus habent, nisi in nostram tantum gratiam."

Yet if Lively corrected Scaliger's causal account, he agreed with him that postponements predated the time of Jesus: "This passage shows that the custom of postponing the weekdays was so old that it seems already to have been established even before, under the Second Temple."[205] Casaubon took Lively's work as a splendid, and unusual, example of critical learning: the work of someone who could build on the achievements of his predecessors while giving them the credit they were due.[206] Accordingly, he printed the passage, and took it as proving that the custom of postponing feasts clearly predated the Passover at which Jesus was crucified.[207] The specialized study of chronology was clearly a necessity, not a pedantic luxury, for the Christian scholar.

In some ways, Casaubon's studies of the Jewish calendar are frustrating. He did not print some of the most challenging passages in Lively's work, in which the English scholar pushed backward, trying to show that Saadia Gaon and the others who created the fixed Jewish calendar toward the end of the first millennium c.e. had actually restored an earlier calendar that the rabbis of the Talmud had misunderstood and mismanaged.[208] But when

205. Ibid.: "Hic igitur locus argumento est illum transferendi ferias morem tam antiquum fuisse ut iam et ante 20 templo institutus videatur."

206. Casaubon 1614, 486; 1654, 429; 1663, 429: "Hactenus ὁ μακαρίτης Liueleus: qui in toto hoc argumento chronologico Iosephum Scaligerum, virum maximum, maxime admirans; non raro tamen ab eo dissentit: verum ita, ut modestiam prius laudes an doctrinam non scias."

207. Casaubon 1614, 485; 1654, 428; 1663, 428: "Vt taceam quae ab alijs viris summis scripta sunt ad refutandam hanc calumniam, quaeque in manibus eruditorum versantur: lectori tantum indicabo, Eduardum Liueleum in opere Chronologico suo, nondum edito, disputationi Cardinalis Toleti, qua doctrinae de translationibus feriarum novitatem probare conatus est, luculente respondisse et docuisse; licet aliquando post destructionem Templi in harum rerum ignoratione versati sint Iudaei, quod Epiphanius ostendit, et scripta quorundam ex ipsis Rabbinis: Kalendarium tamen Iudaeorum, quo hodieque utuntur; cum primis vero hanc de translatione feriarum doctrinam, rem esse antiquissimam, et ante Domini tempora cognitam."

208. E.g., Trinity College Dublin MS 126, 86 recto: "Hoc enim illud contigisse videtur, quod ante in Sabbatis annorum, factum declaravimus. Cum enim rectissimum illorum ordinem Josephus in libris Antiquitatum Judaicarum ostendisset; Quem Talmudici hi magistri veterum temporum ignoratione post secundi templi desolationem perverterunt: Tandem sapientes illi Geonim praecedentium Talmudicorum errore correcto, pristinam eorum veritatem nitori suo restituerunt. Similiter hic, cum ab antiquis usitata feriarum reiectio Talmudicorum inscientia tandem neglecta, et mutata fuisset: succedentes illi excellentes Geonim, antiquam feriarum transferendarum consuetudinem instauraverunt, et quod hic a Talmudicis peccatum fuisset emendaverunt. Hoc de uno atque eo ni fallor R. Saadia testatur Aben Ezra in Levit: 23: cap . . . Dixit Gaon veteres Israelitas computo embolismi nixos fuisse. Nam computum embolismi vocat eam computationis methodum, qua nunc utuntur Judaei. Quae inter alia feriarum reiiciendarum rationem praescribit. Atque antiquissimam quidem fuisse apud Judaeos illam feriarum reiectionem intelligitur ex eo quod Munsterus in calendario suo ex monumentis Hebraeorum memorat, סנהדרין גאוני עולם hoc est iudices antiquissimos Geonim usitati huius computi originem ad reditum a captivitate Babylonica referentes [cf. Münster 1527b, 128; and Weinberg 2000]. Idem ipse Munsterus indicavit eodem libro ubi scribit Judaeos feria 6a. a praetorii ingressu abstinuisse: ut eo die ad vesperam pascha comederent, iuxta patrum decreta. Decreta enim ea intelligit quibus statuerant pascha: a 2: 4: 6: feria in sequentem esse differendum."

matters of textual exegesis came to the fore—when the question at issue was less the date when Jesus actually died than how, more generally, to make sense of the details of the Gospel texts—Casaubon drew deftly on the material Lively had assembled, and added independent observations to it.

The various Gospel testimonies about the chronology of Jesus' last days are the pieces of a maddeningly complex puzzle. For centuries, as we have seen, scholars have arranged and rearranged them—and sometimes tried to push one or more of them off the board entirely. Casaubon's efforts to examine and classify each bit of evidence reveal even more about the character of his mind and method than do his larger efforts to frame the Gospel history as a whole. At 19:14, for example, John writes: "And it was the preparation [*parasceve*] of the Passover [παρασκευὴ τοῦ πάσχα], and about the sixth hour: and he [Pilate] saith unto the Jews, Behold your King!" Here he seems to say explicitly that Christ suffered not on Passover but on the day before, the day of preparation for the feast. No verse presented more obstacles to those who—like Bellarmine and Baronio—rejected the theory that John's chronology differed from that of the Synoptic Gospels. Bellarmine, however, insisted that John had meant nothing of the sort. His argument was muddy, as befitted the violence to which he had to subject John's words. But his meaning was clear. Despite what seemed John's clear testimony, the Jews had not called the day before Passover παρασκευὴ τοῦ πάσχα—"*parasceve, or preparation for the Passover*." They had only had a "preparation for the sabbath"—their term for Fridays, including the Friday on which Christ suffered, which coincided with Passover, and on which, as on any other Friday, food had had to prepared for the sabbath.

> I REPLY: The Jews had no *parasceve,* except for the sabbath. For before the sabbath a preparation was necessary—a preparation of foods, that is, for on the sabbath food could not be prepared. That is why we read at John 19[:31]: "The Jews therefore [besought Pilate], because it was the preparation, that the bodies should not remain upon the cross on the sabbath day, (for it was the great day of the sabbath)" . . . Here you see that the preparation was not for the Passover, but for the sabbath, which was even more solemn in that year, and was called the great sabbath, because it fell during the week of Passover, all of which was sacred, though the first and last days were more sacred.[209] That is why Mark expresses the same point in

---

209. Bellarmine, like many Christian expositors before and after him, seemingly assumed that the "great day of the Sabbath" referred to by John in 19:31 (ἦν γὰρ μεγάλη ἡμέρα ἐκείνου τοῦ σαββάτου) was also the Jewish "great Sabbath," which is in fact the sabbath before Passover.

15[:42]: "It was the preparation, that is, the day before the sabbath"; and Luke in 23[:54]: "And that day was the preparation, and the sabbath drew on." Accordingly, the term "preparation of the Passover" there referred not to a preparation for Passover, but for a preparation that took place at the Passover: as if we might say, it was the Friday of Passover.[210]

Toletus agreed: the *parasceve* mentioned by John referred only to the preparations for the sabbath, not to preparations for Passover.[211]

Lively, however, sharply disagreed: "The Gospel of John supplies so many proofs," he argued, that the day of the Crucifixion was also the *parasceve* for Passover "that, so far as I am concerned, this point is to be classified as one of those about which there can be no doubt."[212] He rejected the theory—which he ascribed to Toletus, although Bellarmine seems to have devised it—that the *parasceve* applied only to the sabbath.[213] In fact, he argued, "It is easy to establish how ridiculous their assertion is. For the Greek word $\pi\alpha\rho\alpha\sigma\kappa\epsilon\nu\grave{\eta}$ is the same as the Hebrew term ערב [*erev*], that is, evening."[214]

210. Bellarmine 1588, 823: "*Erat autem Parasceue Paschae hora quasi sexta*. RESPONDEO: Parasceue non erat apud Hebraeos, nisi propter Sabbatum: siquidem ante Sabbatum necessaria erat Parasceue, id est, praeparatio ciborum, quia in Sabbato cibi parari non poterant. Quare Ioan. 19. sic legimus: *Propter Parasceuen Iudaeorum, ut non remanerent in cruce corpora Sabbato: erat enim magnus dies ille sabbathi*. Ubi vides, Parasceuen fuisse non ad Pascha, sed ad Sabbatum, quod illo anno celebrius erat, et magnum Sabbatum dicebatur, quia incidebat intra hebdomadam Paschalem, quae tota solennis erat, licet primus et ultimus dies solenniores essent. Hinc etiam Marcus cap. 15. ita illud idem expressit: *Erat Parasceue, quod est ante Sabbatum*, et Lucas cap. 23. inquit, *Erat autem Parasceue, et Sabbatum illucescebat*. Illud igitur Parasceue Paschae non significat Parasceuen ad Pascha, sed Parasceuen in Paschate occurrentem: quomodo si nos diceremus, Erat feria VI. Paschae."

211. Toletus 1590–89, II, 11: "Tertius locus est eiusdem Ioannis: *Erat autem parasceue Paschae*. Si igitur erat parasceue Paschae, quando Christus crucifixus est, igitur nondum erat celebratum Pascha: nam Parasceue praeparationem significat. Hoc argumentum debile valde est: non enim dicitur parasceue Paschae, quia erat parasceue ad ipsum Pascha: sed quia erat Sabbati Parasceue, et simul erat unus ex diebus Paschae. Nullius enim festi in tota scriptura dicitur Parasceue, nisi Sabbati: quia in solo Sabbato non licebat praeparare, quae ad esum necessaria erant: proptereaque feria sexta praeparabantur, et idcirco Parasceue dicta est. In die autem Azymorum primo, non erat talis prohibitio, immo expressa concessio. Exo. 12. non erat igitur Parasceue ipsius Paschae, quasi praeparatorius ad Pascha, sed quia erat unus ex diebus illis Paschae, et simul praeparatorius Sabbati, quod satis aperte indicat Marc. cap. 15."

212. Trinity College Dublin MS 126, 81 recto: "Tot vero argumenta ex evangelio Johannis suppeditantur ad probandum parasceven fuisse, ut quod ad me attinet, inter ea illud ponendum censeam de quibus dubitari non debet. Joh: 19: v: 14 crucifixionis dies disertis verbis parasceve paschatis fuisse dicitur. Erat autem parasceve paschae, hora quasi 6a cum Pilatus Judaeis diceret, ecce rex vester, illi vero clamarent, tolle, tolle, crucifige eum."

213. Ibid.: "Toletus quem Bellarminus et Baronius sequuntur, contendit parasceven paschatis eo loco dici parasceven illius sabbati, quod in festum paschatis 7. dierum incidit; negans eam vocem aliter usurpari quia praeparationem (inquit) proprie significat, quae tantum feriae 6ae convenit. Eo quod in solo sabbato, non item in aliis festis diebus azymorum, parare ad esum necessaria prohibitum fuerit."

214. Ibid.: "Quam hoc absurde dicatur ex eo facile constare potest, quod Graece *paraskeue* idem sit cum eo quod Hebraice ערב id est vespera dicitur."

Lively quoted a passage from a central Jewish source, one which no previous commentator had quoted, and which made clear that the Jewish calendar included a day of preparation for Passover: "in tractate Sanhedrin, chapter 6, the authors of the Talmud say: 'There is a tradition that Jesus was hung up בערב פסח [be'erev pesah; on the eve of Pesach], that is, on the *parasceve* of Passover.'"[215] Lively did not claim that he was the first to understand the Gospel text properly: "everyone knows that the word *erev* stands for what is called the *parasceve* in the Gospel of John."[216] In fact, many previous expositors had taken John's phrase as referring to a day of preparation for the Passover; both Paul of Burgos and Paul of Middelburg understood the relevant line in that sense.[217] But when Lively read the Greek of the Gospels—especially when he encountered expressions of time—he heard undertones that his predecessors had missed. He vividly sensed the presence of Hebrew and Aramaic beneath the Greek, and he used Jewish texts to identify the words and phrases in question.

Casaubon agreed with Lively, passionately. In the detailed argument in which he developed Lively's thesis, he invoked "the Talmud, Maimonides' *Yad*, Zacuto's *Yuhasin*, and other rabbinical writings" to prove that John had described Friday as the formal day of preparation for Passover.[218] As so often, the sources Casaubon quoted were late, and one of them, Zacuto, was a writer whom no Jew would have cited in this context. But he added to the materials that Lively cited a highly relevant passage from the Mishnah,

215. Ibid.: "Ut in tractatu sanhedrin cap: 6: Traditum est Jesum fuisse suspensum בערב פסח inquiunt Talmudici id est in parasceve paschatis."

216. Ibid.: "ערב enim ibi positum esse pro eo quod in evangelio Johannis *paraskeue* dicitur, omnes noverunt."

217. Paul of Burgos 1477, ii3 recto: "johan. xix. expresse dicit. Erat autem parasceve pasche etc. Cum enim parasceve alicuius festi idem est quod preparatio ad illam diem. et non dicit parasceve sabbati sed pasche. manifeste ostendit quod in illa die pascha parabatur quod est propositum. Item si sexta feria in qua cristus fuit passus fuisset xv. sequeretur quod res non corresponderent proprie figure quod est valde inconveniens in hac materia"; Paul of Middelburg 1513, E verso–Eii recto: "si enim dicere voluisset ipsum parasceue fuisse pascha posuisset pascha in casu nominativo identice et non in genitivo casu et dixisset erat autem paraskeue ipsum pascha et non ipsius paschae. Iam autem in originali legitur ἦν δὲ παρασκευὴ τοῦ πάσχα, hoc est erat autem paraskeue paschae. apparet ergo christum non fuisse crucifixum in die festo paschae Iudaeorum, sed in vigilia sive profesto paschae."

218. Casaubon 1614, 477; 1654, 420–421; 1663, 420–421: "Post haec ait Baronius, solum fuisse Sabbatum, quod Parasceven haberet: Paschatis vero aut reliquorum festorum, nullam fuisse parasceven. Qui si Commentarios Rabbinorum a limine saltem salutasset, non potuisset nescire, passim facere illos mentionem ערב יום טוב hoc est, τῆς παρασκευῆς τῆς ἑορτῆς. Unicuique enim טי diei bono sive festo attribuitur sua vespera προεόρτιος, parandis rebus ad festum necessarijs destinata. Leges igitur in Thalmud, Iad Rambam, Iuchasin Zachuthi, et alijs scriptis Rabbinicis, ערב ראש השנה, *parasceven capitis anni*, sive Kalendarum novarum: ערב עצרת *parasceven Pentecostes*; ערב פסח *parasceven Paschatis*: vel distinctius, *parasceven primi diei boni Paschatis*: et *parasceven posterioris diei boni Paschatis*. hoc est, ultimi diei totius solemnitatis cum Paschatis, tum Azymorum."

which stated that "from all the crafts, three do their work on the eve of Pass-over [בערב פסח] up to noon."[219] This second apposite quotation from an authoritative and relevant source clinched the case, in his view.

Although Casaubon and Lively read the New Testament in similar ways, their approaches to the Hebrew materials with which they sought to illuminate it differed. Lively, it seems, could read the Talmud—or at least the Mishnah—without difficulty. Casaubon presumably could not. Nor did he claim that he could do so. Instead, he stated that he had found his passage not in the original context but as one of dozens of grammatical examples quoted by David Kimhi in his *Sefer Mikhlol* (Book of Completeness).[220] Casaubon's copy of the work has a marginal note at the passage in question, in which he identified the text from which the quotation came and the three crafts that it mentioned.[221] Here Casaubon treated Kimhi as he would have treated a late antique or medieval grammarian or lexicographer, writing in Latin or Greek: as a source of quotations from earlier and more valuable texts.

For all the weight that Casaubon rested on his quotation, he did not discuss it exhaustively or, indeed, with complete accuracy. It comes from Mishnah Pesahim—a text that offers a great deal of additional material that he could have used to describe and explicate the observance of Passover (and that all of the Christian exegetes who studied these passages, including Casaubon, could have studied to their profit, though only Scaliger actually did so). More significantly, it does not say exactly what Casaubon claimed, as he would have seen had he tracked it to its original context and examined it as scrupulously as he did the Greek of the New Testament. Both in his marginal note in Kimhi and in the *Exercitationes*, Casaubon identified the three crafts allowed to work on the eve of Passover as tailors, shoemakers, and scribes. In both places, he interpreted the unvocalized Hebrew word for the third craft, ספרים, as *soferim* (scribes).[222] In fact Mishnah Pesahim 4:6 reads: "R. Meir says: Whatsoever work a man has begun before the four-

---

219. Mishnah Pesahim 4:6.

220. Casaubon 1614, 477; 1654, 421; 1663, 421: "In Michlol Kimchi quo loco agit de forma nominum in *ut*, editionis Venetae, fol. 221. dictum huiusmodi affertur e Misna [the first two words do not come from the Mishnah]: מן אומנות שלש אמניות עושין מלאכה בערבי פסחין עד חצות *ex omnibus artibus tres artifices faciunt* (exercent) *artem in parascevis Paschatum, ad medium ipsius Parasceves. Tres autem illos artifices volunt quidam esse istos:* חיטים *sartores;* רצענים *cerdones, calceolarios;* et ספורים *scribas.*"

221. Casaubon, marginal note in his copy of Kimhi's *Sefer Mikhlol* (Venice, 1545), BL 1984.a.10.(1), 221 verso: "Tal. No. 3. artes possunt opus facere die ante pascha, sive parasceve. hae a. sunt 1. חיטים sartores 2. רצענים coriarii sive cerdones 3. ספרים scribae."

222. Casaubon 1614, 477; 1654, 421; 1663, 421: "Tres autem illos artifices volunt quidam esse istos: חיטים *sartores;* רצענים *cerdones, calceolarios;* et ספרים *scribas.*" In his copy of Kimhi, Casaubon vocalized and pointed out the word as *sapparim,* but he did not rethink his interpretation.

teenth he may finish on the fourteenth; but he may not begin it from the beginning on the fourteenth even though he was able to finish it. But the sages say: three craftsmen may do work until midday on the eve of Passover, and these are they: tailors, barbers [*sapparim*], and washermen. R. Jose b. R. Judah says: Shoemakers also." The craftsmen who could work on the eve of Passover were all specialists whose ministrations would enable others to celebrate the holiday properly, a point Casaubon never took on board. Passages like this—and there are others—suggest that his vaunted command of Hebrew and Jewish sources sometimes had as much to do with rhetoric as with substance. Like many of the Christian scholars who shared his interests, Casaubon drew much of his information from a narrow range of texts, most of them late, and used their quotations from extant earlier sources rather than examining the originals—as he would certainly have done had Greek or Latin texts been involved.[223]

Still, Casaubon clearly saw—as Lively did—that one could not explicate the language of the Gospels without drawing on the rich evidence of the Mishnah and the Talmud. Even in his marginal note, he identified the source of the passage that Kimhi cited, as Kimhi himself did not, writing the abbreviated word "Tal.," Talmud, beside it in the margin of his copy of *Mikhlol*. As our next chapter will show, moreover, he discussed this and other passages from the Talmud with a live informant, a Jewish one, as he polished the draft of his attack on Baronio. The debate about the date of the Crucifixion seemed grimly technical to Lancelot Andrewes and even, at times, to Casaubon himself. To one who came to the Gospels as he did, however, it provided a natural occasion for elaborating what amounted to a new approach to the New Testament and to early Christianity.

223. Any modern Jew must wonder why none of these learned men ever asked a Jew or a convert what the preparation for Passover actually requires (removing *hamets,* or leavened products, from the house, for a start). A simple answer would have spared everyone much exhausting study of texts with little relevance to the question at hand.

FIVE

The Teller and the Tale

What Casaubon Learned from Jews

One of the passages in which Casaubon disputed Baronio's scholarly credentials is especially revealing. Baronio suggested in the *Annales* that Jesus had used the Greek word *Apostolos* to refer to his disciples.[1] Like the Catholic painters and sculptors of his day, the cardinal consistently tried to show that Jesus and his followers had already formed a recognizable, Catholic church—one that closely resembled the post-Tridentine Ecclesia Triumphans in language, liturgy, and customs as well as doctrine.[2] Christian authorities, moreover, had his trust, even when he reconstructed a Jewish practice. In this case he followed Epiphanius and Eusebius, who seemed to say that Jews had used the term.[3] Like most Protestants, Casaubon insisted that a great distance separated the world of Jesus and his followers from his

1. Baronio 1593–1607, I, 112–113: "Ascendens deinde in montem ut oraret, elegit mox duodecim ex discipulis, ut mitteret eos ad praedicandum; quibus et dedit potestatem curandi morbos, et eijciendi daemonia; eosque Apostolos nominavit. Vsitatum nomen fuit apud Hebraeos, ut Apostolos illos nominarent, qui assidue versarentur cum summo sacerdote consulendi gratia, qui et ad ipsum referrent ea quae sunt in lege; quos etiam ipse sibi legare consuevisset ad componendos optimos mores sacerdotum, ipsas synagogas inspiciendas, pravos mores corrigendos, atque ipsos denique ministros, qui non secundum legem vixissent, in ordinem redigendos; ut ex his colligitur quae Epiphanius de Iosepho apud Iudaeos Apostolo, agens contra Ebionaeos, conscribit. Perseveravit eadem functio ordinis apud eosdem etiam ad tempora Arcadij et Honorij Impp. in quorum rescripto de ijsdem habetur mentio, quod mitterentur ab eorum Patriarcha certo tempore ad exigendum aurum et argentum a singulis synagogis, exactamque summam ad eumdem reportarent."

2. On the scholarship of Baronio and his colleagues and followers and its rich connections to the larger world of the Counter-Reformation—subjects to which we cannot do justice here—see the classic works of Cochrane 1981 and Ditchfield 1995. In recent years the historiography of this area has expanded with vertiginous speed; see, e.g., Le Gall 2007; Herklotz 2008; Vélez 2008; Olds 2009; and Sawilla 2009.

3. Epiphanius, *Panarion* 30.4.2–3; Eusebius on Isaiah 18:1–2 (*Patrologia Graeca* XXIV, 213 A–B); cf. Jerome on Galatians 1:1 (*Patrologia Latina* XXVI, 311 D).

own day. Unlike most of his coreligionists, however, he imagined Jesus and his followers not only as far holier than modern Christians in their worship and conduct, but also as very different in other crucial respects. Most of the first Christians, he argued, had been Jews, and had retained many Jewish customs long since abandoned by Christianity.

It was certain, Casaubon informed his readers, that Jesus had spoken Aramaic. He "called his 12 disciplines *Shelihin,* in Aramaic. The Evangelists, who wrote in Greek, called them apostles." Maimonides and other Jewish writers regularly used the term *Shelih* (properly *Shaliah*) when describing Jewish rituals: "In the descriptions of their rites there is mentioned the *Shelih Tzibbur,* or apostle of the synagogue, as in the *Yad* of Maimonides, Tractate Tahanioth, book three, chapter four." In fact, Casaubon noted, Jews still used the term: "Nowadays, too, synagogues have their own *Shelihim,* whom they appoint as cantors, who pray to God on behalf of the congregation as a whole." On this point, Casaubon emphasized, he did not rely only on books, but also had a human source for his information: "For that is how Jews answered us when we asked about the duties of the *Schelichim.*" Baronio, Casaubon clearly implied, not only failed to match his mastery of Jewish texts, but also lacked his access to Jewish informants. Therefore he deserved no credence.[4] As we have seen, Casaubon repeatedly exaggerated his mastery of Jewish texts.[5] But he did not wholly exaggerate when he claimed that he had found his way to living sources of Jewish tradition. In this case, he may well have learned what he wrote from the Jews of the Frankfurt synagogue,

4. Casaubon 1614, 311; 1654, 275–276; 1663, 275–276: "Epiphanius igitur, ut ad propositum redeamus, de Patriarchis Tiberiadensium Iudaeorum aetatis suae loquens, adsessores quosdam ipsos scribit habuisse, qui APOSTOLI nominarentur. Baronius vero ad summum Sacerdotem et Domini nostri tempora eam historiam refert; errore, quod nemo queat negare, prorsus immani. Nam quid habuit commune summus Pontifex stantis Reip. Iudaeorum, cum praefectis tenuium reliquiarum, quae urbe deleta varijs in locis Asiae atque Europae sunt collectae? Quare falsum est, Dominum nostrum discipulis suis eam appellationem indidisse, vocem mutuatum ex communi usu Iudaicae Synagogae. Atqui nullum dubium est, Dominum nostrum, quum Syriace loqueretur, voce Syriaca usum, et שליחין SCHELICHIN suos xii. Discipulos appellasse, quos Evangelistae, qui Graece scribebant, ἀποστόλους dixerunt. Itaque Syriaca Paraphrasis, quam constat esse antiquissimam, et quae dubio procul verbum Graecum ea voce expressit, quae in Syriae Ecclesijs primis illis temporibus fuit in usu, Apostolos sempter nominat שליחא. Si, ut putat Baronius, iam inde a Christi tempore, vox Graeca a Iudaeis civitate fuisset donata; cur illam Ecclesiae Palaestinae et Syriae non retinuerunt? Verba Lucae, quae suadere contrarium videntur, mox interpretabimur. Nos in Iad Mosis Aegyptij, et alibi apud Rabbinos, in descriptione rituum Iudaicorum, mentionem variorum ministrorum fieri observamus, qui שליחים id est *Apostoli* nominantur. Invenitur etiam in illorum ritibus, qui שליח ציבור ἀπόστολος τῆς συναγωγῆς nominatur, quasi dicas, legatum Synagogae: ut in perek quarto, tractatus Tahanioth, libro III. Iad Maimonidae [*Hilkhot Ta'aniyyot* 4.5]. Habent et hodiernae Synagogae suos Schelichim, quos volunt esse cantores, qui pro universo coetu preces ad Deum mittunt. Ita enim quaerentibus nobis de eorum officio Iudaei responderunt."

5. Casaubon noted in his copy of the Hebrew text of the Gospel of Matthew (BL 01901.a.14) that the term *shelihim* was used there for the Apostles. He wrote in the margin of 37, at Matt. 10:2: "XII apost."

which he visited in 1590.[6] At other times as well, as we will see, he came closer to living sources of Jewish tradition.

A generous, supremely articulate man, Casaubon had great gifts for scholarly friendship, which was very close to his heart.[7] His circle of friends and close acquaintances included prickly, polymathic correspondents whom he never met, like Scaliger, as well as a wide range of scholars, churchmen, and courtiers with whom he exchanged formal visits and conversed on theology and philology. Though almost entirely Christian, this circle included two men born as Jews. One of them, a convert with whom Casaubon exchanged warm letters, in Hebrew, piqued his interest, although little came of their connection in the end. The other, who lived with Casaubon for a month, endured dramatic and painful experiences in which Casaubon himself played no small part. He also offered Casaubon information vital to his scholarship. The stories of Casaubon and these two Jews show more vividly than textual analysis can how much he knew and how hard he thought about Judaism. They also suggest that he could be surprisingly open to individual Jews, but at the same time they confirm that his openness to Judaism as a larger world had certain limits.

Julius Conradus Otto: Casaubon Corresponds with a Convert

Early in 1606 Isaac Casaubon received a letter in Hebrew from Julius Conradus Otto (1562–?), a convert and extraordinary professor of Hebrew, Syriac, and Aramaic at the Altdorf Academy—the institution that offered the patricians of Nuremberg, which had no university, a sophisticated humanistic education for their sons in the decades before and after 1600.[8] Otto, a scion of the distinguished Margolioth family (his original name had been Naph-

---

6. Casaubon 1709, 623: "Nam adhuc in Judaeorum Synagogis manet mos ab Esdra institutus, ut ejusdem periochae lectio fiat duplex: Hebraice primum, deinde Chaldaice, quod nos Francofurdi ante aliquot annos vidimus diligenter observatum."

7. Cf. Casaubon's meditation on the earlier friendship of Philipp Melanchthon and Joachim Camerarius, Bod MS Casaubon 25, 116 recto: "Inter felicia amicorum exempla non dubitaverim ponere par amicorum nobile Ph. Melanchthonem et Joachimum Camerarium: qui in studiis, inque rebus religionis mirifice congruentes, amoris mutui fructum perceperunt quam diutiss. ut est vita hominum. et postquam morte Philippi usus amicitiae est sublatus, nihil praetermisit Camer. quo de memoria amici fato functi bene mereretur. Haec vera est amicitia, quae est inter idem sentiente[s], quae longo usu firmatur, quae ne morte quidem dissolvitur." For Casaubon's thoughts on Melanchthon's friendship with Camerarius see ibid., 121 verso.

8. See in general Stopp 1974 and Mährle 2000. Other letters in Hebrew received by Casaubon include those of Johannes Drusius the younger (BL MS Burney 363, 275 recto) and, more surprisingly, one of the doctors of the Ambrosiana Library and eminent historian of Milan, Giuseppe Ripamonti (BL MS Burney 365, 272 recto, this last in a rather incomprehensible Hebrew). See discussion by Galbiati 1956. On Drusius as Hebrew correspondent see Fuks 1969.

thali Margolioth), came from Vienna. The Altdorf authorities had appointed him in 1603 to teach Hebrew, as an experiment.[9] After a salutation in somewhat garbled Syriac, Otto's letter devolved into a flurry of conventional phrases and compliments, devoid of precise information about himself but replete with misinformation about Casaubon.[10]

> May the honorable scholar enjoy health and peace.
>
> Verily, I have initiated this discourse;[11] yet I beseech my lord not to suspect me of being willful, nor let my lord say, "Who asked anything of you, and who appointed you as a spokesman in a place to which you were not invited?" Rather, with abounding love and in great humility I have come knocking on the door of my lord to see where you graze and where you make your flock to rest [Song of Songs 1:7]. For I heard about you, my lord, and rejoiced as one rejoices in the harvest [Isaiah 9:2]. I give thanks to God, who has enabled you to scale the highest peaks of wisdom [Deuteronomy 32:13] in order to disseminate Torah, and the holy tongue in particular.[12] Blessed be the Lord, who has shown you wonderful kindness [Psalm 31:22]. May He not cease to extend His kindness to you. Furthermore, my lord, I have heard that you are ready [literally, hand stretched out] to disseminate[13] works written in the holy tongue, and specifically the works of the rabbis, for the greater good. May the Lord be a help and support for you.

This blizzard of stock phrases—with its natural, but incorrect, assumptions that its recipient must be a professor and a specialized teacher of Hebrew—might have bewildered a lesser man than Casaubon. And what followed might have astonished an ordinary Christian scholar even more. For Otto

9. Mährle 2000, 267–269, esp. 267: "uf ein versuchen." Casaubon was not the only Christian scholar whom Otto contacted. A letter from a "learned rabbi" to Buxtorf, quoted and partly translated by Prijs 1964, seems to be from Otto. See also Ioannes Moltherus' 1603 letter to Buxtorf, Universitätsbibliothek Basel, MS G I 60, 214 recto: "Scripsit ad me superioribus mensibus ex Academia Julia doctus quidam Iudaeus ad Christianismum conversus, consulens de quibusdam testimonijs, quibus adversus Judaeos usus sum: quem hortatus sum, ut Hebraice in Iudaeos scriberet, quod viderent eum eximia Styli Hebraei facultate pollere. Vocatur Christianus Gerson." Despite the difference in names, this seems to be Otto.

10. The Syriac salutation, in Serto characters, appears to say "Strength and grace from my God of wisdom to a great man." We are grateful to Sebastian Brock for helping us to decipher the Syriac headings in the letters discussed here.

11. A formula based on Job 33:2.

12. The word beferat, "in particular," has not been understood by the Latin translator (see below).

13. The use of the hiphil conjugation for the verb prsh is inexplicable.

went on not only to list Hebrew books in his possession that might be of interest—always a subject to make Casaubon prick up his ears—but also to describe his own studies, in the mystical, grandiose terms that had bewitched early Christian scholars for two generations:

> It is your wish to know the titles of the Hebrew works that I own. You should know that those books which are in my possession are described in this letter, which has been inserted within this document. At this time I should also inform you about a product of my own hands, the book that is called *Sefer haKabbalah* in the Holy Tongue. Whoever sets eyes on it will say that nothing like it has ever been seen in all our generations. Indeed, it will appear amazing to all those who see it, for in it are revealed the mysteries of the godhead. I declare that in my opinion this book should be published and the secret mysteries of the wisdom of the Kabbalah, which are more pleasant than gold and precious gems and sweeter than honey and the drippings of the honeycomb, should be brought to light. I shall see to it that they are set in type[14] so that their fountains will spread abroad in order that the many may profit therefrom. I therefore pray that it could be published in your press that is situated in the famous and wonderful city [Paris]. Should my lord desire to speak to the owner of the press in the city of Paris, and should you decide to publish this book and reward me for my labor with an adequate payment, you would establish the ties of friendship with me. Rejoicing in your letter I would then send you two or three pages of this book. This suffices for now.
>
> Your servant
> 5 December[15]
> Julius Conradus Otto, professor of Hebrew at Altdorf[16]

---

14. Cf. Exod. 32:16.

15. He uses an inexplicable date, אמה לפק.

16. BL MS Burney 365, 270 (257) recto; there is a Latin translation, apparently done for Georges Babou de la Bourdaisière, on whom see ibid., 269 recto: "Gratia et misericordia a Deo meo (cuius est sapientia) viro Magno; Ac dignitati gloriae religionis (vel dispositionis) tuae vita et pax. Ecce aperui os meum, loquere lingua mea cum palato [marginal note: Syre, risu] meo. Obsecro Dominum meum ne reputet me tanquam temerarium, neque dicat Dominus meus, quis petiit a te, aut quis constituit te virum verborum (id est iussit te loqui in loco cui non invitatus fuisti). Veruntamen prae multitudine amoris, inque humilitate magna veni ad pulsandum hostium domicilii Domini mei, ad videndum ubi pascas, ubi cubes. Cum audivi nomen tuum Domine mj gavisus sum quasi gaudio in messem, egique gratias potenti Deo, qui insedere fecit te super excelsa sapientiae ad cubare faciendum legem (id est Gymnasii praesidem) et praesertim (lectorem) linguae sanctae; benedictus sit Dominus qui mirificavit naturam suam tibi, et benignitatem suam a te non prohibet et amplius Domine mi audivj quod est

A fragment of Otto's work on the Kabbalah survives, copied out by Casaubon in one of his Hebrew grammars.[17] Apparently the book described non-standard Hebrew alphabets, their letters supposedly even more charged than the normal characters with mystical meaning—rather like the magical and mystical alphabets that Heinrich Cornelius Agrippa had included in his *De occulta philosophia* of 1533.

Casaubon was not an enthusiast about promises of magical power or paeans to the mystical secrets of ancient Near Eastern languages. He had already decided that the dialogues of Hermes Trismegistus, with all their claims for the profundity of the ancient Egyptian hieroglyphs, were forged—an argument that he would make public, at great length, in his attack on Baronio.[18] And he dismissed as absurdities the methods of exegesis, based on Jewish precedents, that involved substitutions of letters and numbers. Reuchlin and other Christian Hebraists had claimed that gematria and related techniques could yield the names of angels and even the secret names of God. Casaubon rejected these practices with contempt: "The Hebrew masters often not only waste their time, but actually make fools of themselves as they seek out the mysteries of holy letters."[19] Yet Otto's letter fascinated him. He showed it to Georges Babou de la Bourdaisière, Comte de

---

manus tua extensa (id est parata) ad interpretandum libros linguae sacrae, et particulariter libros Rabinorum, quatenus ad colandum in eis plurimos; Dominus sit tibi auxilio et fulcimento. Et cum voluntas tua sit ad cognoscendum nomina librorum sacrosanctae linguae qui in manibus meis (id est penes me sunt) sciendo scies quod ipsi libri qui in facultate mea sunt, inscripti sunt in Epistola quae collocata est in medio epistolae istius: et etiam certiorem te reddo quod tempore presenti sunt opera manuum mearum liber qui nuncupatur idiomate sancto Liber Cabbalae: omnisque qui viderit istum dicet, non fuit talis in omnibus generationibus nostris: et certe mirabilis liber iste in oculis omnium ipsum contemplantium: quoniam in eo detecta est secretorum Theologia, et opinione fui imprimere librum istum et in lucem edere occulta mysteria sapientiae Cabbalae desiderabilia prae auro, auroque optimo multo, suaviaque prae melle et fluxu favorum: et induxi eorum exarationem super tabulas ut foras erumpant eorum scaturigines ad purificandum multos. Ac propterea Quis det (id est faxit Deus) ut impressus esset typis vestris, essetque in urbe laudabili et gloriosa (parisiorum) et si placeat domino meo alloqui Typographum in civitate par. si sciat imprimere librum hunc, ut det mercedem laboris mei sufficientem. Itaque pangas mecum amicitiae pactum, ac laetifices cor meum Chirographo tuo, et tunc remittam tibi duas aut 3. paginas istius libri, et ita verborum finem facio. Julius Conradus Octo professor Hebraeae linguae Altorph."

17. The notes appear in BL 621.i.9. On the blank before the title page Casaubon writes out the tetragrammaton in a peculiar form of lettering and notes: "Inter varias scripturas a Rabinis excogitatas est haec quam usurpabat Otho Fridericus Judaeus in literis ad D. de la Bourdeziere et me . . . Ex hac methodo ita scribes nomen יהוה." Casaubon also gives samples of the peculiar angular characters that Otto used, and another cipher for the divine name ק ב (the Holy One, Blessed be he), an abbreviation often used in kabbalistic works.

18. For this whole debate see now Mulsow 2002 and Chapter 1 above.

19. BL 1984.a.10.(1), recto of second flyleaf before title page: "Hebraei magistri in scrutandis sacrarum literarum saepe non solum περίεργοι sed etiam praeposteri, literarum mysteria trium generum faciunt."

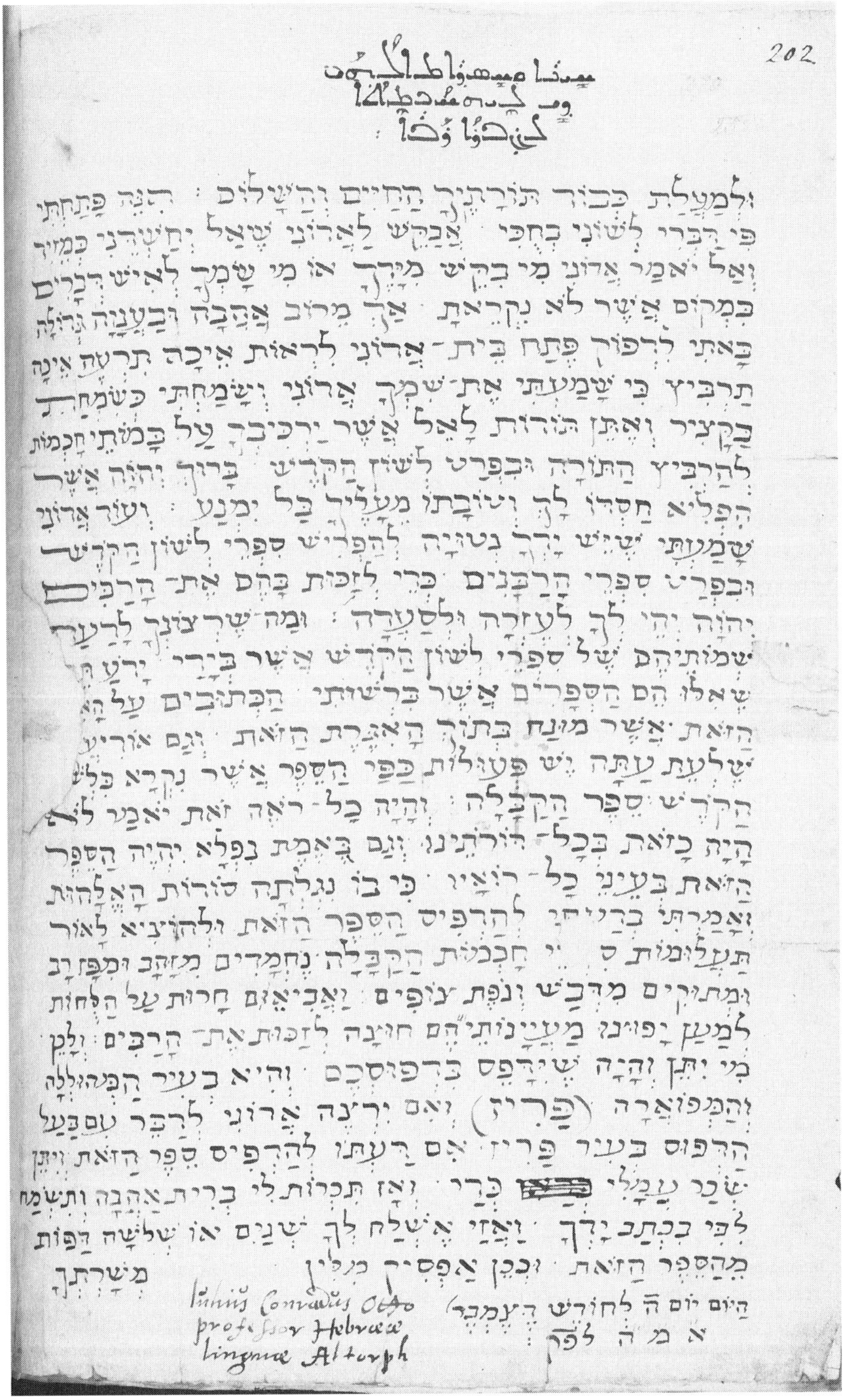

ܡܝܢܐ ܡܫܝܚܐ ܘܐܠܗܐ ܝܫܘܥ
ܘ... ܟܬܒ ܩܕܝܫܐ
ܟܝ ܚܕܘ ܘܙܕܩ

וּלְמַעֲלַת כְּבוֹד תּוֹרָתְךָ הַחַיִּים וְהַשָּׁלוֹם : הִנֵּה פָּתַחְתִּי
פִּי דְּבָרַי לְשׁוֹנִי בְחִכִּי אֲבַקֵּשׁ לַאדוֹנִי שְׁאַל יַחְשְׁרֵנִי כָּמִיר
וָאֹמַר אֲדוֹנִי מִי בִקֵּשׁ מִיָּדֶךָ אוֹ מִי שָׂמְךָ לְאִישׁ דְּבָרִים
בִּמְקוֹמִים אֲשֶׁר לֹא נִקְרֵאתָ אַךְ מֵרֹב אַהֲבָה וּבְעִנְיָן גְּדוֹלָה
בָּאתִי לִרְפוֹק פֶּתַח בֵּית אֲדוֹנִי לִרְאוֹת אֵיכָה תֵרְעֶה אֵיפֹה
תַּרְבִּיץ כִּי שָׁמַעְתִּי אֶת שִׁמְךָ אֲדוֹנִי וְיִשְׂמַחְתִּי כְּשִׂמְחַת
בַּקָּצִיר וָאֶתֵּן הוֹדוֹת לָאֵל אֲשֶׁר יִרְכִּיבְךָ עַל בָּמֹתֵי חָכְמֹת
לְהַרְבִּיץ הַתּוֹרָה וּבִפְרָט לְשׁוֹן הַקֹּדֶשׁ בָּרוּךְ יְהֹוָה אֲשֶׁר
הִפְלִיא חַסְדּוֹ לָךְ וְיוֹבָתוֹ מֵעָלָיו בָּל יִמָּנַע : וְעוֹד אֲדוֹנִי
שָׁמַעְתִּי שֶׁיֵּשׁ יָדְךָ נְטוּיָה לְהַפְרִישׁ סִפְרֵי לְשׁוֹן הַקֹּדֶשׁ
וּבִפְרָט סִפְרֵי הָרַבָּנִים כְּרֵי לִזְכּוֹת בָּהֶם אֶת הָרַבִּים
יְהֹוָה יְהִי לָךְ לְעֶזְרָה וּלְסַעֲדָה : וּמַה שֶּׁר צֹנֶךָ לָרֶעֶךָ
שִׂמְחוֹתֵיהֶם שֶׁל סִפְרֵי לְשׁוֹן הַקֹּדֶשׁ אֲשֶׁר בְּיָדִי יָדַע ...
שֶׁאֵלּוּ הֵם הַסְּפָרִים אֲשֶׁר כְּרְשׁוּתִי הַכְּתוּבִים עַל ...
הַזֹּאת אֲשֶׁר מֻנַּח בְּתוֹךְ הָאִגֶּרֶת הַזֹּאת : וְגַם אוֹרִיעַ
שִׁלַּעַת עַתָּה יֵשׁ פְּעֻלּוֹת כַּפֵּי הַסֵּפֶר אֲשֶׁר נִקְרָא כֶּלֶת
הַקֹּדֶשׁ סֵפֶר הַקַּבָּלָה : וְהָיָה כָל רֹאֶה זֹאת יֹאמַר לֹא
הָיָה כָזֹאת בְּכָל דּוֹרוֹתֵינוּ וְגַם בֶּאֱמֶת נִפְלָא יִהְיֶה הַסֵּפֶר
הַזֹּאת בְּעֵינֵי כָל רוֹאָיו כִּי בוֹ נִגְלְתָה סוֹדוֹת הָאֱלֹהוּת
וְאָמַרְתִּי בְרַיְחִי לְהַדְפִּיס הַסֵּפֶר הַזֹּאת וּלְהוֹצִיא לָאוֹר
תַּעֲלוּמֹת ס יְיָ חָכְמוֹת הַקַּבָּלָה נֶחְמָדִים מִזָּהָב וּמִפַּז רָב
וּמְתוּקִים מִדְּבַשׁ וְנֹפֶת צוּפִים וַאֲבִיאֵם חָרוּת עַל הַלֻּחוֹת
לְמַעַן יָפוּצוּ מַעְיְנֹתֵיהֶם חוּצָה לִזְכּוֹת אֶת הָרַבִּים וְלָכֵן
מִי יִתֵּן וְהָיָה שֶׁיֻּדְפַּס בִּדְפוּסְכֶם וְהִיא בְּעִיר הַמְהֻלָּלָה
וְהַמְפֹאָרָה (פָּרִיז) וְאִם יִרְצֶה אֲדוֹנִי לְדַבֵּר עִם בַּעַל
הַדְּפוּס בְּעִיר פָּרִיז אִם רַצַּתוֹ לְהַדְפִּיס סֵפֶר הַזֹּאת וְיֵן
שָׂכָר עֲמָלִי ... כְּרִי וְאָז תִּכְרוֹת לִי בְּרִית אַהֲבָה וְתִשְׂמַח
לִבִּי כִּכְתָב יָדְךָ וַאֲנִי אֶשְׁלַח לְךָ שְׁנַיִם אוֹ שְׁלֹשָׁה דַּפּוֹת
מֵהַסֵּפֶר הַזֹּאת וּבְכֵן אַפְסִיק מִלִּין מְשָׁרֶתְךָ
הַיּוֹם יוֹם ה' לַחֹדֶשׁ דֶּעֶמְבֶּר
א מ ה לפ"ק

Iulius Conradus Otto
professor Hebraeæ
linguæ Altorph

FIGURE 5.1. Letter from Julius Conradus Otto to Casaubon, 1605. British Library MS Burney 365, 270 (257) recto.

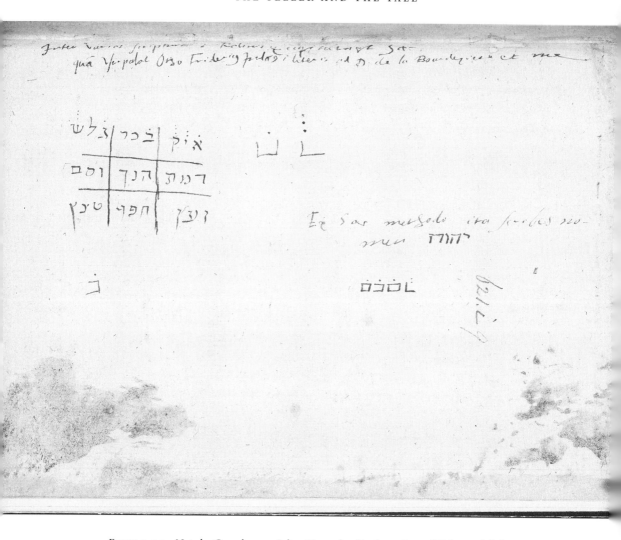

FIGURE 5.2. Note by Casaubon on Julius Conradus Otto's versions of Hebrew alphabets and the divine name, in Antoine Chevalier's *Rudimenta hebraicae linguae*. British Library 621.i.9.

Sagonne, an erudite aristocrat and counselor to Henri IV, who had it translated into Latin and expressed enthusiastic interest in Otto's kabbalistic book.[20] He also took the time to reply, in a Hebrew as allusive, if not as natural, as his correspondent's. And he, too, played the orientalist, prefacing the letter with a series of salutations in Arabic and Syriac and concluding it with

20. On Georges Babou de la Bourdaisière (1531–1607) see the article by A. Martin in *Dictionnaire de Biographie Française*. Casaubon said that Babou had Otto's first letter translated into Latin, and in the note that he entered on the leaf he preserves the translation, BL MS Burney 365, 269 recto: "Vir illustris D. de la Bourdaisiere, cum Hebraei hominis epistolam videre optasset, mox a se versam Latine in hac charta transmisit: usus opera Scoti viri doctissimi quem secum habebat." The learned Scot was James

the word "Amen" in Ethiopic characters.[21] Casaubon made clear that he was neither head of a school nor a teacher of Hebrew, but a humanist whose chief interest lay in making the Greek and Latin classics useful in his own time—in particular, in providing a new and accurate Latin translation of the Greek historian Polybius, whose expert understanding of warfare he thought vital for his contemporaries.[22]

> Blessed be my lord, who, being mindful of me, has written to me and not cast me aside.[23] Indeed I was overjoyed by your letter. You should, however, realize that I have not set myself the task nor committed myself to the dissemination[24] of works written in the holy tongue; I am not an expert in Torah, nor do I scale the highest peaks of wisdom as my lord thinks. For few and evil have been the years of my life. Yet I have happened upon goodness, and blessedness has fallen to my lot, for the Lord is my share and portion [Psalm 16:6]. Until now I have been absorbed in gaining proficiency in various disciplines and acquainting myself with languages, and I am intending to write some books. In your letter you informed me about *Sefer haKabbalah,* but I was not the only recipient of your news. For I showed it to the great nobles of France, and in particular to the sieur de Labrousière, the chevalier of two legions of the king, may the Lord keep him, *conseiller d'état, capitaine des cent gentilshommes de*

Hepburn, for whom see Chapter 2 above. The note, in Casaubon's hand, is identified as his and transcribed more legibly by an anonymous reader. Babou's scholarly and antiquarian interests are described in the postscript to one of Casaubon's letters to Scaliger, Casaubon 1709, 261 (19 January 1606): "Est in aula vir nobilitatis praecipuae, M. De la Bourdaiziere, quicum mihi familiaritas et amicitia non vulgaris intercedit; est enim earum literarum amantissimus et intelligentissimus, quas pauci, non dicam e Proceribus ejus Amplitudinis, sed ex iis, qui literarum notitia sunt celebres, norunt, nedum tenent. Cum eo multus mihi de tua praestantia sermo: nuper vero, cum mihi κειμήλια sua ἀξιάγαστα ostenderet, jaspidem unum inter caeteras antiqui operis gemmas spectandum exhibuit, itemque achatem unum, quorum lapillorum alterum ait tibi quondam fuisse visum, et prodiisse a te doctissimum scriptum ad illustrationem ejus gemmae. *Falaiseau,* opinor, fuit Medicus Turonensis, cui illa scripseras. Is igitur vir nobilissimus te plurima salute impertit; oratque, ut si forte in adversariis tuis vestigium aliquod superest ejus scriptionis, velis eam secum communicare; et hoc beneficio ipsum demereri. Idem nos quoque a te contendimus, quod tuo commodo fiat."

21. The Arabic salutation, appropriate to a convert, reads: "The Lord answers your call on a day of misfortune. The name of the Lord of Jacob gives you victory. God sends you help from His divinity and from His awesome majesty in order to seal a covenant with you." We are grateful to Alastair Hamilton for his advice and to Arnoud Vrolijk, who suggested this rendering. Strangely, the Syriac has one line in Serto characters and the other in Estrangela, with which Casaubon was less familiar. For Casaubon's Arabic studies at this time see Appendix 1 below and Hamilton 2009.

22. For the Renaissance rediscovery of Polybius as an authority on military affairs see Momigliano 1974; for Casaubon's work on Polybius see Casaubon 1999 and Parenty 2009.

23. Literally, "behind his back"; cf. Isa. 38:17.

24. Like Otto, Casaubon uses להפריש.

la maison du Roi and comte de Sagonne. He is a wise nobleman and learned in various languages. He is particularly proficient in the holy tongue; indeed, his knowledge of this language surpasses that of all other French nobles. He is very fond of all scholars. He said that I should write to you with regard to the Kabbalah. If my lord should desire to publish the book here in our press, he should send me some pages of the book. I shall certainly speak to the owner of the press and tell him to publish it and give you, honorable rabbi,[25] a reward for your labor. I would not dare to assure you that the reward would be appropriate. But I shall not fail to do what I can. And if it meets with my lord's approval, let him state his price.[26] There is no news; but there is a powerful rumor that war is about to break out between His Majesty[27] our king and the king of Spain. This is why I am currently engaged in translating Polybius from Greek into Latin. He is a historian, a military man; from his work we can all gain expertise in and experience of wars. May the merciful, compassionate, long-suffering one who loves kindness and truth divert His anger from upon us and turn the sadness into joy, the evil into good for the sake of the glory of His Messiah. May there be peace on you as you so desire and as I, Isaac Casaubon,[28] do also desire. Amen.[29]

Casaubon, in short, not only did not reject Otto's offer of kabbalistic secrets, but responded to it with considerable enthusiasm, even as he tried to clarify his own position in the world and the nature of his own scholarly enterprise.

It is not hard to explain why Otto received so kind an answer. Casaubon had in fact encouraged him to open a correspondence. As early as September 1601, he had written to a friend at Altdorf, the Italian émigré jurist Scipione Gentili, expressing his interest in what Gentili had evidently told him about a Jewish scholar—possibly Otto—and his own wish to become a better Hebraist: "What you wrote about your Jew was very pleasing to me. I wish we were together. I would play his student, and in such a way that I might be able to do something for him as well. I love Hebrew letters, but the

---

25. He uses the conventional rabbinic abbreviation here.

26. The Hebrew is not totally comprehensible.

27. He uses the conventional rabbinic abbreviation for "His Majesty."

28. His name transliterates phonetically "Casaoobon." The formula used here may reflect an effort to translate from a vernacular language.

29. BL MS Burney 365, 271 (258) recto. The word "Amen" is transcribed in Ethiopic characters.

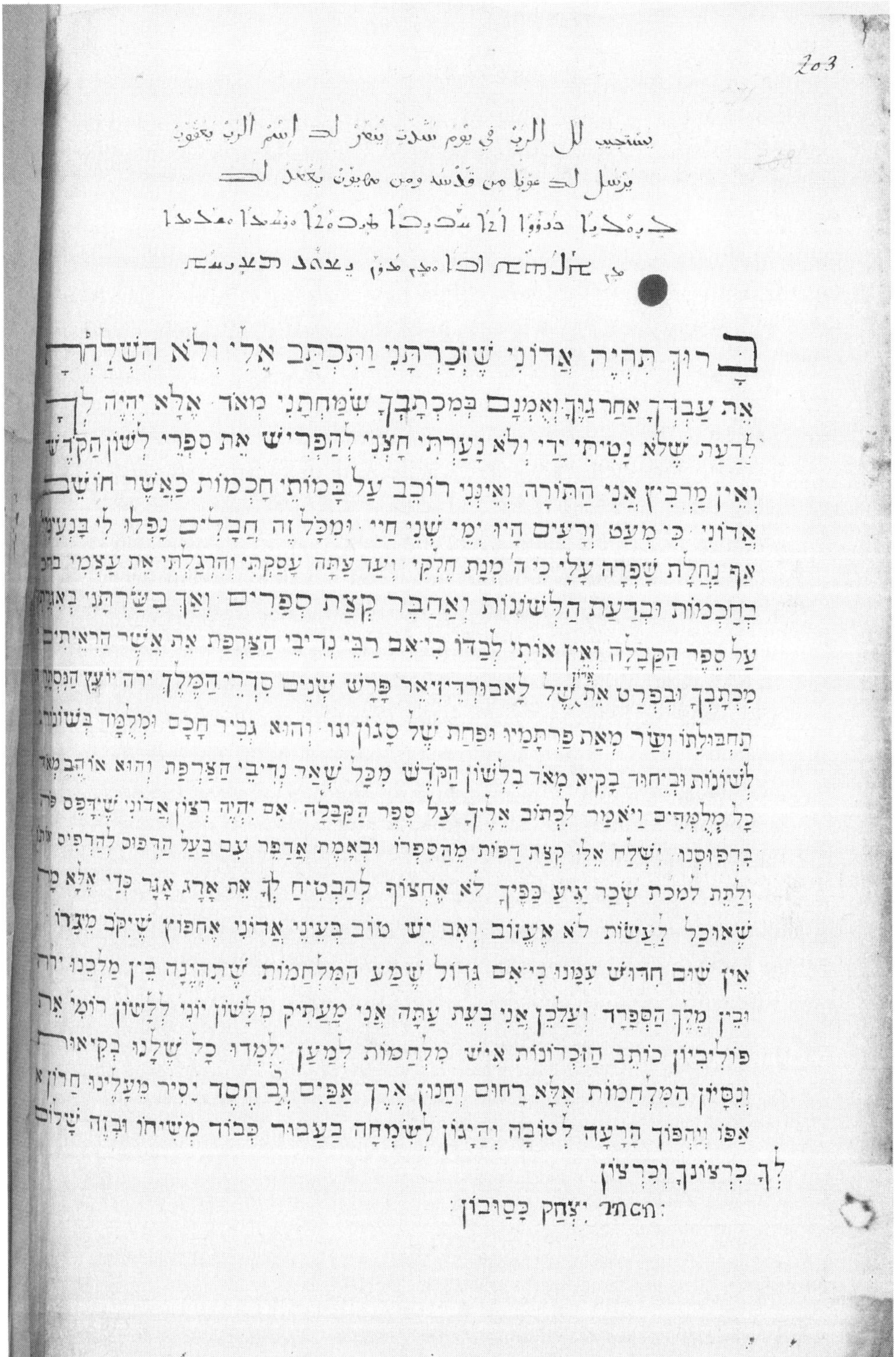

بستجيب لل الرب في يوم شدت نصر لـ اسم الرب يعقوب

يرسل لـ عونا من قدسه ومن صهيون يعضد لـ

ܟܪܝܟܐ ܕܢܘܢ ܐܙܐ ܣܟܝܟܐ ܚܟܝܟܐ ܐܪܟܐ ܣܟܠܪܐ

ܝ ܐܠܚܣܡ ܐܕܐ ܣܝ ܐܢ ܝܨܚܩ ܟܣܘܒܢ

בָּרוּךְ תִּהְיֶה אֲדוֹנִי שֶׁזְּכַרְתַּנִי וַתִּכְתָּב אֵלַי וְלֹא הִשְׁלַלוֹהְ

אֶת עַבְדָּךְ אַחַרַגְוּךְ וְאָמְנָם בְּמִכְתָּבָךְ שָׂמַחְתָּנִי מְאֹד אֶלָּא יִהְיֶה לְךָ

לָדַעַת שֶׁלֹּא נָטִיתִי יָדַי וְלֹא נָעַרְתִּי חָצְנִי לְהַפְרִישׁ אֶת סְפָרַי לְשׁוֹן הַקֹּדֶשׁ

וְאֵין מַרְבִּין אֲנִי הַתּוֹרָה וְאֵינֶנִּי רוֹכֵב עַל בָּמוֹתֵי חַכְמוֹת כַּאֲשֶׁר חוֹשֵׁב

אֲדוֹנִי כִּי מְעַט וְרָעִים הָיוּ יְמֵי שְׁנֵי חַי וּמִכָּל זֶה חֲבָלִ"ב נָפְלוּ לִי בַּנְעִימ

אַף נַחֲלַת שָׁפְרָה עָלַי כִּי ה' מְנָת חֶלְקִי וְעַד עַתָּה עָסַקְתִּי וְהִרְגַלְתִּי אֶת עַצְמִי

בַּחָכְמוֹת וּבְדַעַת הַלְּשׁוֹנוֹת וְאָחַבֵּר קְצָת סְפָרִים וְאַךְ בְּשֵׁרַתַּנִי בְּאַ

עַל סֵפֶר הַקַּבָּלָה וְאֵין אוֹתִי לְבַדּוֹ כִּי אָב רַבִּי נְדִיבֵי הַצָּרְפַת אֵת אֲשֶׁר הֶרְאֵיתִים

מִכְתָּבָךְ וּבִפְרָט אֶתְ שֶׁל לָאבּוּרִדִיזַאר פָּרַשׁ שְׁנִים סִדְרֵי הַמֶּלֶךְ ירה יּעֵץ הַנִּסְתָּר

תַּחְבּוּלָתוֹ וְטַר מֵאַת פַּרְתָּמָיו וּפְתַח שֶׁל סָגוֹן וְגוֹ וְהוּא גְבִיר חָכָם וּמְלֻמָּד בְּשֵׁווֹנ

לְשׁוֹנוֹת וּבֵיחוּד בָּקִיא מְאֹד בִּלְשׁוֹן הַקֹּדֶשׁ מִכָּל שְׁאַר נְדִיבֵי הַצָּרְפַת וְהוּא אוֹהֵב מְא

כָּל מְלָמְּדִים וַיֹּאמַר לִכְתּוֹב אֵלֶיךָ עַל סֵפֶר הַקַּבָּלָה אִם יִהְיֶה רְצוֹן אֲדוֹנִי שֶׁיַּדְפֵּס פֹה

בְּדְפוּסֵנוּ וְשָׁלַח אֵלַי קְצָת דַּפּוֹת מֵהַסִּפְרוֹ וּבֶאֱמֶת אֲדַבֵּר עִם בַּעַל הַדְּפוּס לְהַדְפִּיס זֹה

וְלָתֵת לְמֶכֶת שָׂכָר גָּיעַ כַּפָּיךְ לֹא אֶחְצוּף לְהַבְטִיחַ לָךְ אֵת אֶרֶץ עָנָר כְּדִי אֶלָּא כָּר

שָׁאוּכַל לַעֲשׂוֹת לֹא אֶעֱזוֹב וְאָב יֵשׁ טוֹב בְּעֵינֵי אֲדוֹנִי אֶחְפּוּץ שֶׁיַּעֲקֹב מִצְרוּ

אֵין שִׁיב חִדּוּשׁ עִמָּנוּ כִּי אָם גָּדוֹל שֶׁמַע הַמִּלְחָמוֹת שֶׁתִּהְיֶנָה בֵּין מַלְכֵּנוּ ירה

וּבֵין מֶלֶךְ הַסְּפָּרַד וְעַלְכֵן אֲנִי בְּעֵת עַתָּה אֲנִי מַעֲתִיק מִלְּשׁוֹן יוֹנִי לְלָשׁוֹן רוֹמִי אֶר

פּוֹלִיבִּיוֹן כּוֹתֵב הַזִּכְרוֹנוֹת אִישׁ מִלְחָמוֹת לְמַעַן יְלַמְּדוּ כָּל שֶׁלָּנוּ בְּקִיאוּת

וְנִסָּיוֹן הַמִּלְחָמוֹת אֶלָּא רַחוּם וְחַנּוּן אֶרֶךְ אַפַּיִם וְרַב חֶסֶד יָסִיר מֵעָלֵינוּ חָרוֹן א

אַפּוֹ וְיַהֲפוֹךְ הָרָעָה לְטוֹבָה וְהַיָּגוֹן לְשִׂמְחָה בַּעֲבוּר כְּבוֹד מְשִׁיחוֹ וּבְזֶה שָׁלוֹם

לָךְ כִּרְצוֹנָךְ וְכִרְצוֹן

נאמ יִצְחָק כַּסוּבּוֹן

FIGURE 5.3. Letter from Casaubon to Julius Conradus Otto, 1606. British Library MS Burney 365, 271 (258) recto.

level of my progress in the field makes me ashamed."[30] He also noted his puzzlement at the format of what was apparently a specimen of a dictionary planned by Otto. The empty sheets between testimonia struck him as likely to yield an unnecessarily expensive end product.[31] In the winter of 1605, the Frankfurt Book Fair catalogue announced that Otto was publishing a "dictionary to help in understanding the rabbis." Casaubon put this information together with Gentili's descriptions of the new professor at Altdorf. His head filled with hopes for a major program of rabbinical publication aimed at Christian scholars, he wrote ardently to Gentili:

> Your letter informed me that there is a converted Jew there who has set out to publish the books of the rabbis. Your news came to me as a blessing, my Gentili. When I read in the Frankfurt catalogue about the book that he has announced, and could find no one who had seen the book or knew anything about it, I was in a dreadful state of torment. For that book is such that I could not wish for anything more, or enjoy anything more, than to read it. I beg you, by all the Muses, to urge him, using my words, to publish as soon as possible whatever he has of that master whom they call Our Rabbi Hakadosh. Then I would like to see it followed by the *Bahir* of R. Nechonija, the son of Hakkana, and the *More Nebukim* of the incomparable Maimonides . . . In my view publication of authors like these would be an extraordinary help to the study of letters.[32]

Casaubon also wrote to another friend at Altdorf, the jurist and humanist Conrad Rittershusius, asking for information about the professor of Hebrew. Rittershusius passed this letter along to Gentili, who warned Casau-

---

30. Casaubon to Scipione Gentili, 3 September 1601, Casaubon 1709, 126: "De Judaeo vestro gratissimum fuit quod scripsisti. Utinam una essemus: sic agerem ejus discipulum, ut fortasse aliquid opera mea posset uti: non possum negare, amare me illas literas: etsi quantum adhuc profecerim, poenitet me."

31. Casaubon 1709, 126: "Miratus sum in inchoato Dictionario cur tantum vacuae chartae interponerentur, inter auctorum τὰς χρείας: nam si ad hoc exemplum opus procedit, quis par erit tantis sumptibus? atque parci poterat dimidio hujus impensae."

32. Casaubon to Gentili, 4 January 1605, Casaubon 1709, 231: "Ex tuis didici, esse isthic Judaeum gente, professione Christianum, qui edendis Rabbinorum libris det operam. Beasti me, mi Gentilis, hoc nuntio. Nam ego, qui in elencho Francofurdiensi libri ab eo promissi titulum legeram, cum neminem invenirem, qui aut librum illum vidisset, aut de eo quidquam haberet compertum, miris modis angebar. Est enim ejus generis liber ille, ut nihil mihi possit ejus lectione aut optatius, aut jucundius contingere. Quare te per omnes Musas oro, obsecro, horteris illum meis verbis, ut quicquid nactus fuerit Magistri illius, qui ipsi Rabbenu Hackados nominatur, publici juris quam primum faciat. Sequantur velim R. Nechonijae, filii Hakkanae בהיר, et incomparabilis Rabbenu Mosis, Maimonis filii מורה נבוכים. Habet divinus Scaliger hoc opus et Hebraicum et Arabicum, quomodo est ab Autore editum. Horum, et similium Autorum editione mirifice literarum meliorum studia iri adjutum, nos quidem judicamus."

bon in April 1605 that his expectations were exaggerated: "How much he has achieved in these two works, or can in his others, I don't know. Given that he is quite ignorant of Greek and Latin letters and learning, I am sorry that the letter I wrote you long ago excited such great expectations. I fear that a sight of the books will serve to diminish that."[33]

In another letter a year later, Gentili tried even harder to dampen Casaubon's considerable enthusiasm, which had evidently found expression in other communications that do not survive:

> To tell you the truth, I do not know what of significance he can achieve, since he is so ignorant of Latin that he can barely read it or scrawl it. He uses the help of two students—and not the best ones— for translation. I am sorry that I made your mouth water with my letter, and fear that he will scarcely live up to your expectations. The man is completely ignorant of our learning and all the writings that Christians have published in this sort of interpretation, and takes his own works as marvelous.

Evidently Casaubon had asked for Otto's help in obtaining rabbinical texts, and here, too, Gentili felt obliged to warn his friend not to hope for too much: "At Frankfurt he bought those rabbinical commentaries through what he calls an amazing trick; but they are not manuscripts, but printed, I think, at Venice." Gentili also enclosed a "little sheet" from Otto—presumably his first Hebrew letter to Casaubon—and the introduction to the rabbinical dictionary—evidently the only part of it to be printed.[34]

33. Gentili to Casaubon, 20 April 1605, BL MS Burney 364, 126 recto: "Heri misit mihi literas tuas ad se scriptas coll. meus Rittershusius, in quibus mihi adscripta salus iucundissima fuit, sed eadem indicabat, perijsse forte literas meas, quas non ita pridem ad te dederam, Doctorique Remo, id petenti, commiseram. Erant autem pleraque scriptae de Hebraeo illo nostro Professore, a quo et Titulum operis impressum misi, id est Dictionarij ad Rabinos praecipue intelligendos, ut videtur, elaborati: sicut et Grammatica, quae his nundinis prodijt. sed quid in utroque opere ille praestiterit, aut praestare in caeteris possit, ignoro: nisi quod cum et linguae latinae ac graecae omnisque doctrinae sit ignarus, doleo me tantam expectationem meis literis ad te olim scriptis concitavisse: quam vereor, ut minuat adspectus librorum." The lost letter to which Gentili refers is not in the Burney MS.

34. Gentili to Casaubon, 23 February 1606, BL MS Burney 364, 127 recto: "Mandatum illud de libris Rabbinorum mihi curae fuit sed non licuit citius per absentiam professoris nostri Hebraei. Is reversus dedit mihi hanc schedulam, quam ad te mitterem, unaque principium Dictionarij sui, quod iam sub praelo est. Vt vere dicam, nescio quid praestare magnum possit, cum plane rudis sit linguae latinae, vix ut legere eam et pingere possit. Vtitur autem duorum studiosorum, neque eorum doctissimorum, in interpretando opera. Doleo commotam tibi salivam literis meis: vereor enim, ne ulla ex parte respondeat expectationi tuae. Homo eruditionis omnis nostrae imperitus et scriptorum, quae a Christianis in hoc genere interpretandi edita sunt, omnia sua pro praeclaris accipit. Emit Francofurti commentarios istos Rabbinorum mira techna, ut dicit: neque scripti manu sunt, sed impressi, opinor, Venetiis. His nundinis nihil eorum proditurum dicebat, sed Autumnalibus."

Casaubon took less interest in Otto's reported failings as a Latinist than in his demonstrated mastery of Hebrew, and brushed these warnings aside. In March 1606 he told Gentili that he had found Otto's letters "delightful." In fact, he hoped that the conversion of such a man might benefit the entire Republic of Letters. It was with this reply to Gentili that Casaubon enclosed what he described as his "very rough" Hebrew letter to Otto, "not to show off my learning but to declare my friendship."[35]

Casaubon meant what he said. In August, Otto wrote again.[36] This time he offered Casaubon another project, one very different from his proposed book on the secrets of the Kabbalah. Now he wanted to revise the polyglot New Testament, including a Hebrew version of the entire work, which the Leipzig professor Elias Hutter had published in 1599:

> My lord and master, do not be surprised that I am now circulating yet another letter. As you know I had already written to my honorable doctor[37] about certain matters. But please accept this one, too. Do not withdraw your hand from this [letter], my beloved lord. You should know that previously the book called *Berit hadashah* [New Testament] in the Holy Tongue was published in the city of Nuremberg by the author Elias Hutter, and its cost was defrayed by the worthy lord and distinguished Hieronymus Keller [Kähler]. The book was printed in twelve languages, as you can see with your own eyes.[38] One of the languages [in which it is written] is the Holy Tongue, for he translated the New Testament from Greek into the Holy Tongue. Since the Hebrew [text] is not altogether correct, it serves no useful purpose for those who love the Holy Tongue. It has therefore been removed; the book does not sell, and the above-

---

35. Casaubon to Gentili, 29 March 1606, Casaubon 1709, 263: "Et literae tuae gratissimae mihi fuerunt, ut semper, clarissime Scipio; et illae quoque jucundissimae, quas a Conrado Ottone, viro eruditissimo, mihi misisti. Spero fore utilem Ecclesiae Dei et Reipublicae literariae hominis tam docti conversionem ad Christianismum. Atque utinam ita viveremus nos veteres Christiani, ut probitas nostra miseram gentem ad expetendam veritatis notitiam alliceret! Huic certe viro optimo [e scriptis videor cognoscere] opto laeta omnia, ut quae orsus est ad illustrationem earum literarum, ad umbilicum brevi possit perducere. Scripsi ad illum sane quam παχυμερῶς, non ostentandae eruditioni, sed benevolentiae declarandae. Eas literas tibi mitto, teque oro, ut de meo erga ipsum animo prolixe omnia polliceris, quae ab homine tanto intervallo terrarum separato potest exspectare."

36. Otto acknowledged Casaubon's letter and sent greetings via Rittershusius in June 1606; BL MS Burney 365, 362 recto: "Rabbinus noster Jul. Conrad. Otto gratissimo animo tuam salutis dictionem accepit, et te officiose resalutat."

37. Casaubon's Latin translation, given below in note 42, shows that he realized that this is an honorific title, but it is not clear whether he really knew which words the Hebrew letters תק stand for.

38. Cf. Psalm 17:2.

mentioned lord Hieronymus Keller has been unable to cover the cost and has incurred financial loss. Consequently, certain scholars decided to translate that book and to compensate for its deficiencies for the sake of the greater good. They also thought of asking me to translate it. I took into account the usefulness of the book and the losses incurred by lord Keller, who is a wise, intelligent, decent, and upright man. All that he does is for the sake of the glory of the blessed Lord and for the benefit of His creation. Therefore I took pity on him and decided to comply with their idea. So I am the translator, and I will ensure that my Hebrew rendering, being accurate and without deficiencies, will be on a par with the other eleven[39] languages, as is proper. So I decided to write to my lord and to request my lord to show this letter to my lord the distinguished George Babon [Babou] de Labrouzière. Thus for the sake of the honor of the blessed Lord and that of His creation the noblemen will make every effort to sell copies of the book in your own province and domain. For I know and have been told that many French noblemen love the Holy Tongue and have expert knowledge and understanding of it. So magnify the Lord with me, and let us exalt His name together [Ps. 34:3]. If you do this, you will undoubtedly shine forth with the radiance of the firmament and the stars of heaven for eternity. I entreat you, my lord, to respond both to this letter and to the previous one. Please do not send me away empty-handed. May the blessed Lord be with you and grant peace to us and to you, Amen

    Your friend and servant, the humble and lowly Julius Conradus
      Otto, teacher of the Holy Tongue in the Academy of Altdorf
    I wrote this on Monday, 28 August [אמו][40]
    I also wrote to the worthy lord Jacques Bongars about this.[41]

The evidence suggests that Casaubon took Otto's new proposal very seriously indeed. He took the time to translate Otto's letter into Latin.[42]

39. Casaubon corrects the text silently to read "eleven."

40. In this letter, too, the Hebrew date does not make sense.

41. BL MS Burney 367, 82 recto.

42. BL MS Burney 365, 276 (263) recto: "Domine mi <u>doctor</u> mi ne mireris super revolutione manus meae, postquam scripsi ad מכה celsitudinem gloriosam laudis tuae, de parte harum rerum, ut scis: sed apprehende etiam hoc: et in hoc ne cesset manus tua. dilecte domine mi scito, quod antea editus est liber qui vocatur in lingua Sta ברית חדשה in urbe Noriber. auctore Elia Hutero, sumtibus domini τοῦ κλειζομένου magnifici Hieronymus Kerler. Atque iste liber editus est in XII. linguis, ut videbunt oculi tui recte. estque [Read atque?] una e linguis illis est lingua sancta, quia translatum est N. T. e lingua

Only a few days after Otto wrote, Babou took a measure that shows how much hope he reposed in Otto. In an exuberant, even phosphorescent, official letter he begged Otto to come to Paris and teach the holy language, as a royal professor. "I have read many of your excellent and erudite essays," he wrote, "and they recalled to my mind that truest of true prophecies: ואמרו רק עם חכם ונבון הגוי הגדול הזה [and say, surely this great people is a wise and understanding people; Deut. 4:6]. For from all other peoples, you will find one who rivals a Jew in wisdom and intelligence to be rarer than a white raven or phoenix."[43] It seems likely that Casaubon and Babou were working together in the hope of attracting Otto to Paris.

Gr. in L. S. et quia L. S. non est tota כהוגן ut decet: propterea non est utilis studiosis L. S. propterea מונח jacet, et non venditur hic liber. et dictus D. Hier. Cerler non potest pervenire ad sumtus suos. (h.e. recipere quod impendit) et stat in damno. Et propter hanc caussam dederunt ei consilium quidam discipuli sapientes ut verteret (denuo vertendum curaret) dictum librum: et impleret quae deficiunt, ad multo-rum utilitatem. atque etiam de me eum monuerunt, ad vertendum. qui ubi vidi utilitatem huius libri, et damnum dicti D. Cerler, qui est vir sapiens et intelligens et commodus, rectus, perfectus: qui quicquid fecit, ad gloriam Dei et utilitatem הבריאה. creaturae ἀντὶ hominum, fecit. itaque cor meum συμπαθὲς ἐγένετο ὑπὲρ αὐτοῦ: et assensus sum sententiae ipsorum, ut verteretur: et ipse sum qui verti: verti autem ipsum, ut etiam lingua S. sit cum reliquis XI. linguis: sicut oportet et rectum est: neque deficiat in eo quicquam. et hoc non implevi ἀντὶ simul ac susceptum opus perfeci, cum animo meo, scripsi ad dominum meum et rogavi Dominum meum ut tradat hanc epistolam etiam illustri D. G. Babon de la B. legendam: ut DD. proxenetae sint (יטרחו) ad gloriam Dei et utilitatem creaturae ipsius (ἀντὶ publicam) quo vendantur aliis libri dicti in urbe vestra et vicinis. Scio enim atque audivi multos principes Gallos amare literas S. et sunt in ea docti atque eius intelligentes. magnificate Deum mecum: et extollemus nomen eius una. quod si hoc feceritis, lucebitis tanquam luminaria firmamenti, et stellae caeli in aeternum sine fine. Et oro DD. ut mittatis responsum. et obsecro ne avertatis faciem vestram longe ab hac epistola: et ea quam antea scripsi. Pax Domini sit vobiscum: detque is pacem nobis et vobis. Amen. Amator vester et minister vester, humilis et parvus Jul. Conr. O. doctor L. S. in schola Alt. Scripsi hodie, die 2. mensis Augusti."

43. Babou to Otto, 11 August 1606, BL MS Burney 365, 45 recto (a very handsome and regular scribal copy): "D. Georgius Babou Dominus de Laboudezier, Comes de Sagon, Eques auratus, Consiliarius secreti consilii Regis, Dux Nobilium veteranorum, etc. R. Julio Conrado amico suo S.P.D. Quandoquidem humanae dux vitae, virtutis magistra, vitiorum expultrix, omnium omnino hominum consensu et iudicio, coelestis sit sapientia; hanc vero in sacris characteribus [above line: id est codicibus seu Bibliis] minime contineri nullus affirmabit: hos autem sine cognitione לשון הקדש intelligi nemo dixerit: fatendum igitur autumo, nisi ingrati simus, plurimum debere ingenuos nos omnes, istius linguae peritis, tibique praecipue, vir doctissime, qui in egregio divini huius idiomatis studio tempus contrivisti, operam navasti, industriam contulisti, oleum impendisti, maximeque profecisti; ita ut nunc latentes arcanorum latices oraculorum recludas, et sitientes sacrosanctis scaturiginibus, lympidissimisque caelestis sapientiae fontibus, non turbidis rivulis potes. passimque nectareis plena liquoribus pocula petentibus propines, esurientes autem et famelicos ambroseo aeterni faminis manna cibes ac saties. Silentio hic lubenter hebraeae linguae dignitates enarrare (quod omnium linguarum princeps et parens sit; quod ea usi sunt protoplasti et patriarchae; quod in ea divina data sunt edicta omnia; quod eam Sanctus B.I.O.M. suo ore sanctissimo consecravit; etc.) praetermittam; cum quia tacere potius, quam pauca de eius encomio nunquam satis laudando fari praestet: Tum quia, ut verum fatear, res mihi sit perardua, onusque meis imbellibus humeris impar valde. Nihil enim in me est quod Ciceronis aut Demosthenis lucernam oleat, oratorium siquidem munus, dicendique facultatem, non modo non primoribus labiis attigi, sed ne a limite [read limine?] quidem salutavi. hoc enim ad te vir litteratissime potissimum pertinet, te

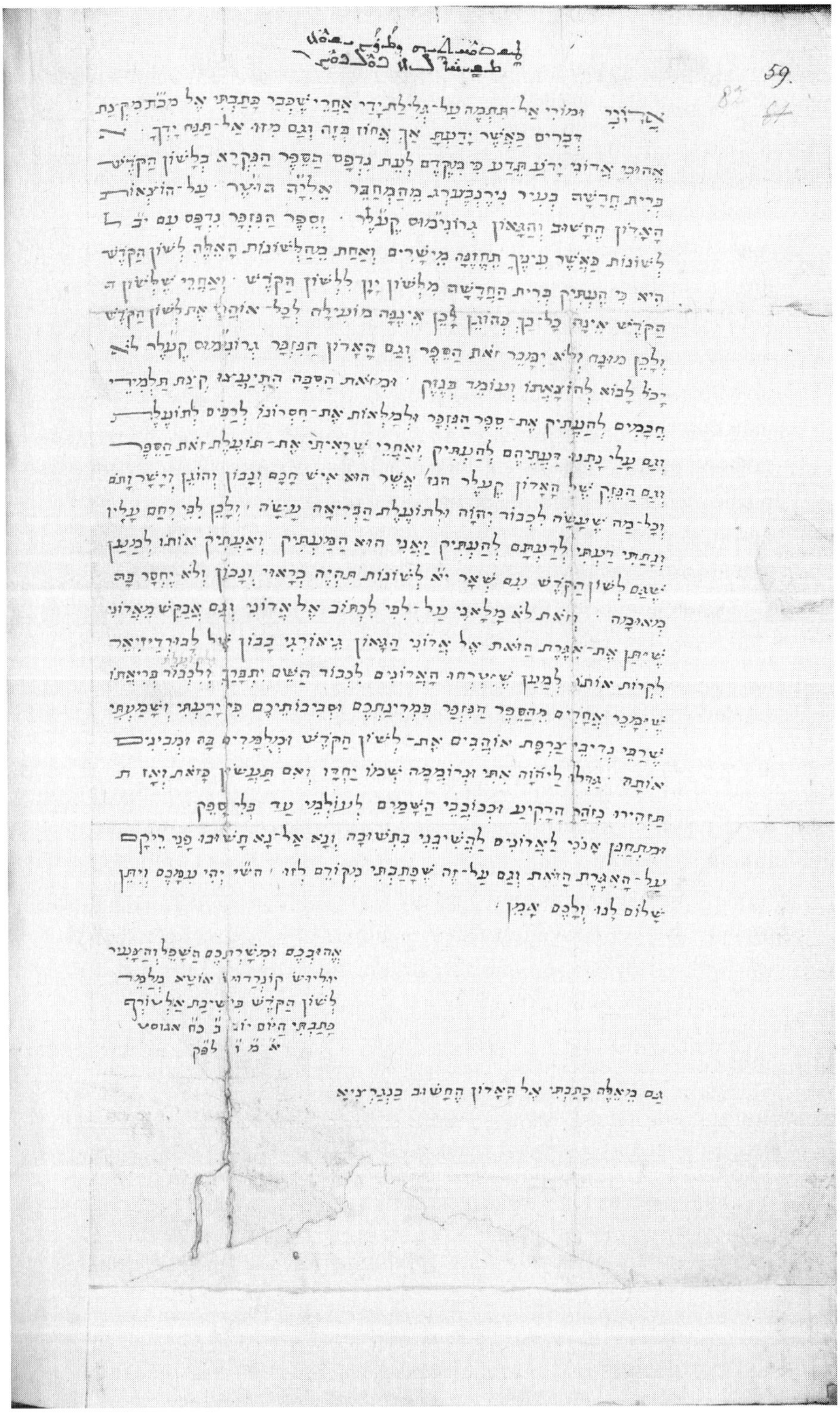

FIGURE 5.4. Letter from Julius Conradus Otto to Casaubon, 1606. British Library MS Burney 367, 82 recto.

Otto replied at eloquent length. Again he urged the potential value of Hutter's polyglot New Testament:

> Greetings to those far and near.
>
> I shall mention the Lord's kindness on account of the great goodness He has extended to us. His righteousness prevails like the powerful mountains [Ps. 36:7], for He is our Messiah and redeemer. Lift your eyes on high and reflect deeply. Has He not given us a mind to enable us to explore and discover how the heavenly bounty shows us which direction to take? With the Lord we shall ascend on the path that leads heavenward; we shall be implanted in a place of holiness and purity. There we can take delight and pleasure in the higher resplendence and glory, reside in the highest realm, and dwell in the first dominion.[44] Therefore, my lord and master, you who are wise and magnificent, a priceless jewel,[45] incline your ear and listen to my riddle and give ear to the words of my mouth. I wrote previously to your honor and to the worthy, distinguished, and honorable George Babon [Babou] de la Bourdaisière, my lord, on this matter. It concerns the book that is called *Berit hadashah* [New Testament] in the Holy Tongue and *Neue Testament* in German. Elias Hutter translated it from Greek into the Holy Tongue to the best of his ability. If you happen to find errors and untenable mistakes in this work, you should nevertheless realize and declare that "there is no just person on earth who does good and does not sin" [Ecclesiastes 7:20]. As for my humble self, I have translated each part in its correct place, as you will rightly see for yourselves. Thus its fountains may spring forth into your streets as streams of living water, honeysuckle, pleas-

---

spectat, et expectat. cuius eximiae eruditionis fama omnium pervenit ad aures, quaque percussus est ipse Galliarum Rex, eaque ita impulsus est, ut te professorem suum sanctaeque lectorem linguae ardenter aveat. cuius ergo, mihi idem vehementer desideranti imperavit ipse haut parva, nec pauca pollicens, ut te litteris certiorem facerem, quod quidem hisce factum velim. Plurimas praeclaras ac pereruditas lucubratiunculas tuas perlegi, quae mihi in animum verissimum illud veritatis vaticinium revocarunt: ואמרו רק עם חכם ונבון הגוי הגדול הזה [Deut. 4:6]. Ex omnibus enim gentibus corvo albo aut phoenice rariorem qui in sapientia et intelligentia cum Judaeo conferri queat invenies. O fortunatam et beatam Galliam, si te solo, imo Sole frueretur. Tunc phoebeo nobis lumine praeluceres, cunctasque imperitiae, inscitiae, et ignorantiae nebulas in quibus continuo caecutientes incedimus, nitidissimis ac purissimis coruscantium radiorum tuorum fulgoribus, fulgidissimisque luminum tuorum splendoribus, splendidissimisque lucis tuae flammulis, flammarumque caloribus penitus discuteres, dissipares, et annihilares. At ut verbis finem faciam, si tibi ipsi recte consulas, statim huc commigres. מלה להחכם די. Salve atque vale. Lutetiae Parisiorum, a.d. xxii Kal. Sep. Ἀπὸ τῆς τοῦ λόγου ἐνσαρκώσεως CIↃ IↃ CVI. la bourdaiziere."

44. Cf. Micah 4:8.

45. Otto uses the Aramaic form of the popular expression.

ant words, balm for the soul, and healing for the bones. For I know
that you are worthy leaders, honored princes. Your reputation ex-
tends throughout the world, and particularly in your own environs.
So you, the seed of the blessed Lord, do not withdraw your hands.
It is time to acquire, for the day is short and the work is onerous
and the worthy lord Hieronymus Keller, who funded the work, has
incurred losses; but by means of your plans, a buyer may present
himself.[46]

    Your servant—I have written this in very great haste,

        15 December 1606

        Julius Conrad Otto, Professor of the Hebrew language in
        Altdorf[47]

May all those who care for my welfare plead my cause; especially the
great worthy and splendid George Babon de la Bourdaisière should
also read this letter.

[On obverse (in Hebrew)]
Again I would inform my learned teacher that the wise Scipio Gen-
tilus [sic] spoke to the nobles of Nuremberg with regard to my fee.
You, too, my distinguished teacher, also wrote to him, and as a result
of his intervention and your justifiably good word on my behalf, I
received a good fee. So may you and all Christians [Meshihim] be
granted peace and life.

    Isac Causabon [sic][48]

    Just at this promising point, with Otto and Casaubon in active contact,
the story breaks off. For unknown reasons, Otto abandoned his wife, his
debts, and his position in Altdorf in December 1607.[49] According to a persis-
tent report, he also left the Christian faith. At all events, he never reached
Paris or published the series of rabbinical works that Casaubon so eagerly
hoped he might make accessible to Christian scholars.

    Gentili's pessimistic estimate of Otto's scholarly potential was probably

46. There appears to be an abbreviation in relation to the date, but again the reference is not clear.

47. This last phrase is in Latin.

48. BL Ms Burney 365, 274 (262) recto. The address on the obverse reads, in Hebrew: "To the worthy
and distinguished, pure upright true and wise lord, a shining light, a great man, the noble and princely
master and teacher Isaac Casaubon. May His rock and redeemer protect him. To the city of Paris."
Otto added the ban in mnemonic form attributed to Rabbenu Gershom against other people's opening
the letter. Buxtorf gives the mnemonic with explanation in his *Institutio epistolaris Hebraica* (Buxtorf
1610, 59).

49. Mährle 2000, 268.

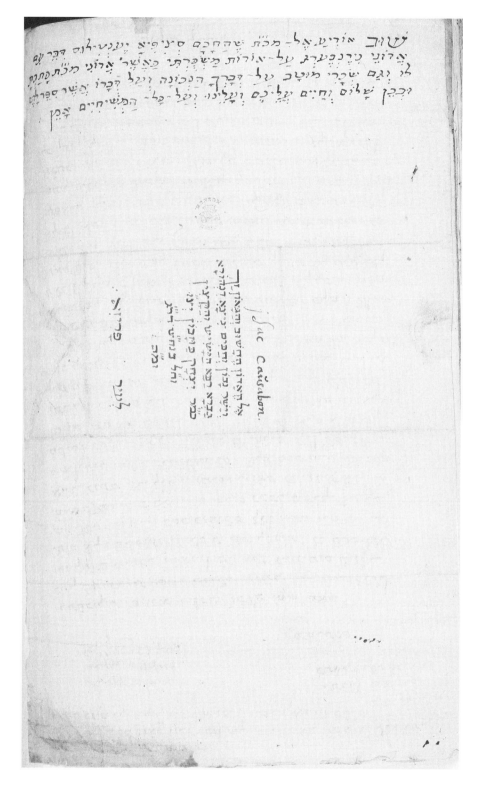

FIGURE 5.5. Obverse of letter from Julius Conradus Otto to Casaubon, December 1606. British Library MS Burney 365, 274 (262) recto.

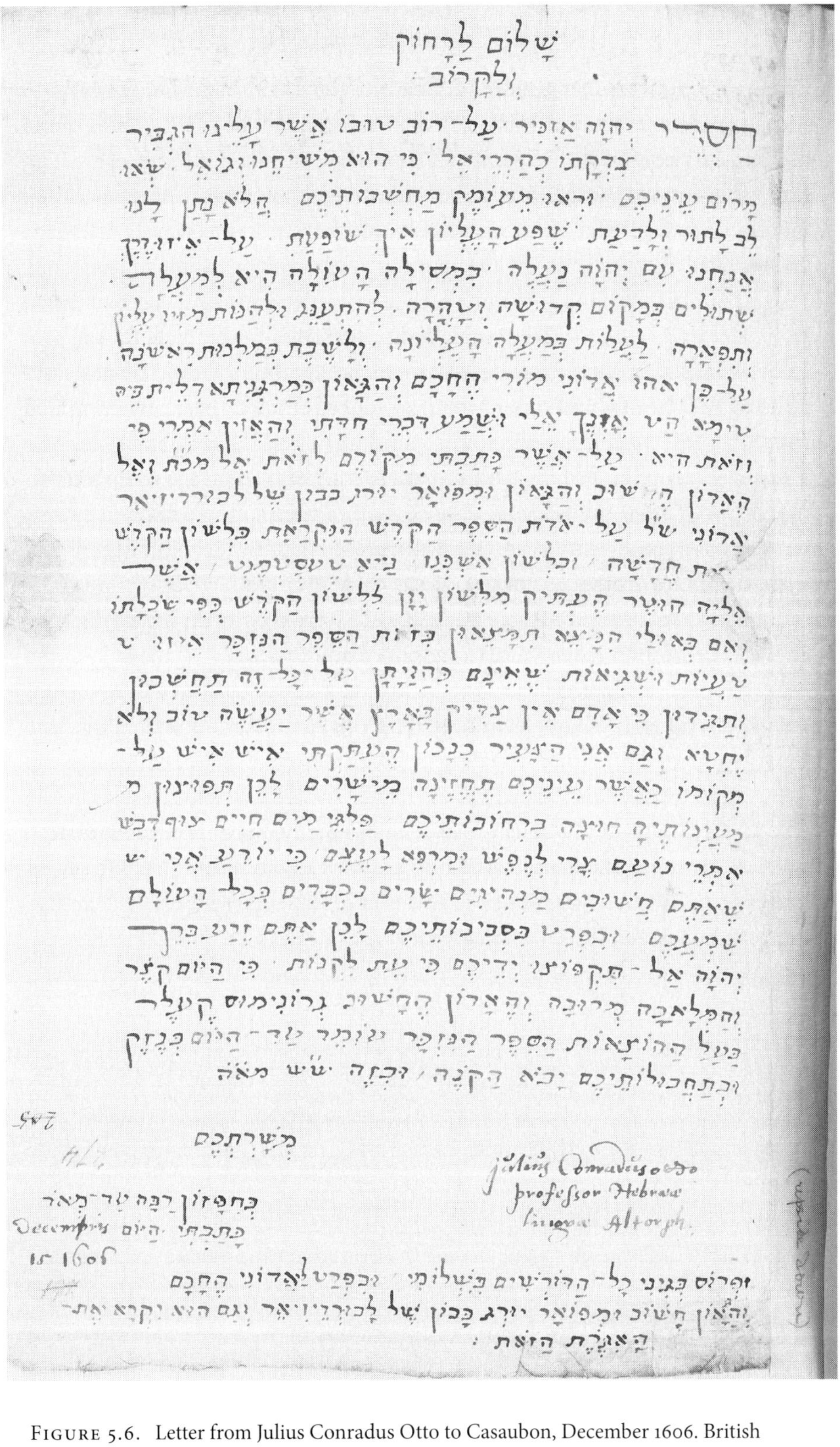

שָׁלוֹם לְרָחוֹק
וְלְקָרוֹב

חֶסֶד יְהוָה אַזְכִּיר עַל־רוֹב טוּבוֹ אֲשֶׁר עָלֵינוּ הַגְבִּיר
צִדְקָתוֹ כְּהַרְרֵי־אֵל כִּי הוּא מְשִׁיחֵנוּ וְגֹאֲלֵנוּ שֶׁאוּ
מְרוֹם עֵינֵיכֶם וּרְאוּ מֵעֹמֶק מַחְשְׁבוֹתֵיכֶם חֲלֹא נָתַן לָנוּ
לֵב לָתוּר וְלָדַעַת שֶׁפַע הָעֶלְיוֹן אֵיךְ שׁוֹפֵעַ עַל־אֶזוּרֶךָ
אֲנַחְנוּ גַם וְהָיָה נַעֲלֶה בִּמְשִׁילָה הָעֹלָה הִיא לְמַעְלָה
שְׁתוּלִים בִּמְקוֹם קְדוּשָׁה וְטָהֳרָה לְהִתְעַנֵּג וּלְהָנוֹת מִזִּיו עֶלְיוֹן
וְתִפְאָרָה לַעֲלוֹת בְּמַעֲלָה הָעֶלְיוֹנָה וְלֹא יֵשֵׁב בְּמַלְכוּת רִאשׁוֹנָה
עַל־כֵּן אֵהוּ אֲדוֹנִי מוֹרִי הֶחָכָם וְהַגָּאוֹן כְּמַרְגָּנִיתָא דְלֵית לַהּ
טִימָא קִיט וְאֵזְנֶךָ אֵלַי וּשְׁמַע דִּבְרֵי חֲדָתִי וְהָאֵין אִמְרֵי פִי
וְזֹאת הִיא עַל־אֲשֶׁר כָּתַבְתִּי מִקֹּדֶם לְזֹאת אֶל מִכַּת וְאֶל
הָאָדוֹן הֶחָשׁוּב וְהַגָּאוֹן וּמְפֹאָר יוּרְג כַּבֵּן שֶׁל לְכוּרְדִי וִיאַר
אֲדוֹנִי שֶׁלֹּא עַל־אֹדוֹת הַסֵּפֶר הַקֹּדֶשׁ הַנִּקְרָאַת פְּלִישׁוֹן הַקֹּדֶשׁ
אֵת חֲדָשָׁה וּכְלָשׁוֹן אֲשֶׁפְּנוּ נִיא טֶעסְטוּמֶעט אֲשֶׁר
אֵלֶיהָ הוּעַר הָעַתִּיק מִלָּשׁוֹן יָוָן לַלָּשׁוֹן הַקֹּדֶשׁ כְּפִי שִׂכְלָתוֹ
וְאִם כָּאֵלֶּי הַנִּמְצָא תִּמָּצֵאִין בְּזֹאת הַסֵּפֶר הַנִּזְכָּר אֵיזוּ ט
טָעֻיּוֹת וּשְׁגִיאוֹת שֶׁאֵינָם כְּהַנְּיָתָן עַל־כָּל־זֶה תַּחְשְׁבוּכֶן
וְתַגְמְרִין כִּי אָדָם אֵין צַדִּיק בָּאָרֶץ אֲשֶׁר יַעֲשֶׂה טוֹב וְלֹא־
יֶחֱטָא וְגַם אֲנִי הַצָּעִיר כְּנִכֵּן הֶעֱתַקְתִּי אִישׁ אִישׁ עַל־
מְקֹּחוֹ כַּאֲשֶׁר עֵינֵיכֶם תֶּחֱזֶינָה מֵיְשָׁרִים לָכֵן תִּפְנִיּוֹן מ
מַעְיְנוֹתֶיךָ חוּצָה בִּרְחוֹבוֹתֵיכֶם פַּלְגֵי מַיִם חַיִּים אוֹף דְּבַשׁ
אִמְרֵי נֹעַם צֳרִי לְנַפְשׁוֹ וּמַרְפֵּא לְעֶצֶם כִּי יוֹדֵעַ אָנִי יֵשׁ
שֶׁאַתֶּם חֲשׁוּכִים בֵּנֵיהֶן גַּם שָׂרִים נִכְבָּדִים בְּכָל־הָעוֹלָם
שְׁמִיעֲכֶם וּבִפְרָט בְּסְכִיבוֹתֵיכֶם לָכֵן אַתֶּם זְרַע בֶּרֶךְ
יְהוָה אַל־תִּקְפְּצוּ יְדֵיכֶם כִּי עֵת לַקְּנוֹת כִּי הַיּוֹם קָצֵר
וְהַמְּלָאכָה מְרֻבָּה וְהָאָדוֹן הֶחָשׁוּב גְּרוֹנִימוּס קַזַלֵר
בַּעַל הַהוֹצָאוֹת הַסֵּפֶר הַנִּזְכָּר יַעֲמֹד עוֹד הַיּוֹם בְּנֶזֶק
וּבְתַחְבּוּלוֹתֵיכֶם יָבֹא בַּקָּנָה וּבְזֶה שֵׁשׁ מֵאָה

מְשָׁרֶתְכֶם

Julius Conradus Otto
professor Hebraeae
linguae Altorph.

בְּחֶזְיוֹן רַבָּה שֵׂר מְאֹר
December כָּתַבְתִּי הַיּוֹם
15 1606

וּפֵרוֹס בְּגִינֵי כָּל־הַדּוֹרְשִׁים בִּשְׁלוֹמִי וּבִפְרָט לַאֲדוֹנִי הֶחָכָם
וְהָאָדוֹן חָשׁוּב וּמְפֹאָר יוּרְג כַּבֵּן שֶׁל לְכוּרְדִי וִיאַר וְגַם הוּא יִקְרָא אֶת־
הָאִגֶּרֶת הַזֹּאת ׃

FIGURE 5.6. Letter from Julius Conradus Otto to Casaubon, December 1606. British
Library MS Burney 365, 274 verso.

more accurate than Casaubon's optimistic view from afar. Evidently Otto was a competent Hebrew teacher: Daniel Schwenter, one of his pupils, wrote a poem in Hebrew for the front matter of one of his books and succeeded him in his chair.[50] But Otto's publications were no more impressive than Gentili suggested. His Hebrew grammar, though described on its title page as "handled methodically in the manner of the rabbis," was conventional. His rabbinical dictionary never reached completion.[51] And his *Gali razia* (Revealer of Secrets) of 1605, a detailed scrapbook of rabbinical passages in Hebrew and Latin that supposedly supported the divinity of Jesus, the doctrine of the Trinity, and other Christian doctrines, was basically compiled from an early sixteenth-century compendium of rabbinic aggadah, the *Ein Ya'akov* of Jacob ibn Habib[52]—although Otto accompanied the main anthology of proof-texts pulled from context with a useful chronology of Jewish writers to which he added entries down to his own time.[53] Nothing in *Gali razia* or in Otto's other writing suggests that he could have lived up to Casaubon's expectations. Otto's career seems to have continued for a long time after his correspondence with Casaubon came to an end. A decade and a half after Otto contacted Casaubon, he was still active in both Christian and Jewish circles, still of indeterminate religious identity, and still infuriating those who relied on him. According to Johann Buxtorf, who gathered gossip about Otto from Jewish as well as Christian sources, he set himself up as a teacher in Bremen and elsewhere and fooled many students. Unfortunately, Buxtorf gives no further details, but he does make clear that Otto lived longer than scholars have realized, and that his later career bore out not Casaubon's hopes, but Gentili's warnings.[54]

50. Ibid., 268–271.

51. Otto 1605b.

52. In a note at the end of the preface, Otto states that the page numbers in his references to the tractates of the Talmud refer to Jacob ibn Habib's work (1605a): "Quicquid in margine huius operis de Rabbinis dicitur, illud omne in libro עין יעקב qui totum Talmud continet, scriptum reperitur." The references indicate that Otto used the 1600 Kraków edition.

53. Otto 1605a.

54. Buxtorf to Waser, 3 February 1619, Zurich, Zentralbibliothek, MS F 167, 46 recto: "Es ist zu Sultz, ein tagreise von hinnen, ein Jud welchen die andere Juden uberaus rhümen von grosser geschickligkeit und wissenschaft, und wie er die Christen an vielen Orten mit diskuteren uberwunden hab. Sol etwas Latin konnen und weiss vil von der Christen Religion thun und lassen zu sagen. Daher mir von meinem Judischen mit Corrector alhie, in ein Ohr vertrawet worden, als wen man denselben im argwohn halte, es seye der, welcher sich bei uns hat tauffen lassen. Deswegen bete Ich, Ihr wölten mir denselbigen etwas beschreiben, so wil Ich nachforschen, ob er dem worigen gleichförmig sehe. Ich möchte auch wol wissen, ob er sich bei uns nicht vermercken lassen, dass er meiner durch Schreiben oder Briffe etwas kundschafft hab, oder Ich einmahl an ihn geschriben hab, dessen sich diser Jud zu Sultz daselbs berhümet, und meine briffe herfur gezeigt dass auch meine hand von anderen Juden seye erkennet worden. Von diesem also, so is er kein anderer, als der Julius Conradus Otto, getauffter Jud, so vor etlich Jahren

For all its gaps and despite its dim ending, the story reveals much about Casaubon. It makes clear his passion for Jewish literature—including the works of medieval and later rabbis. It demonstrates his respect and sympathy for an individual Jew—admittedly one who had converted. Above all, it proves that he could read and translate letters in contemporary Hebrew, and even answer one of them in correct if sometimes awkward Hebrew of his own. Although Casaubon's contact with Otto proved abortive, it could not have taken place at all if he had not made himself a Hebraist more adept than many of those who taught the language for a living in Christian universities.

Jacob Barnet: Casaubon Confronts a Jewish Scholar

Only a few years after Casaubon's negotiations with Otto collapsed, he found himself engaged in a second encounter with a living Jew, Jacob Barnet—an encounter more direct, more provocative, and more productive than the first.[55] This meeting of minds and interests left traces in more than one passage of the *Exercitationes,* and the signs of it in Casaubon's notebooks are in some ways even more impressive. In 1613, as Casaubon prepared the final version of his critique of Baronio, he visited Oxford under the kindly if fussy guidance of Henry Savile.[56] Far more than the Paris where Casaubon had spent the years 1600–1610, London, Cambridge, and Oxford were nurseries of serious, if limited, Hebraic scholarship.[57] At Oxford he discussed Hebrew questions with Richard Kilbye, rector of Lincoln, professor of Hebrew, and author of a detailed commentary on Exodus, steeped in material drawn

---

zu Altorff ist Professor linguae Hebraeae gewesen, und Anno 1605 zu Nurrenberg ein Buch in hebraisch und Teutscher Sprach wider die Juden trucken lassen, גלי רזיא Revelator occultorum getituliert. Dieser ist darnach ausgerissen und heimlich davon gezogen, Ich halte auch denselbigen eben fur den, der vor wenig Jahren zu Bremen die studiosos und andere herrn betrogen hat, und bedunckt mich, eben der selbig auch bei uns [Ms auch] gewesen seyhe. Er hat sich disen winter zu Sultz fur ein Judischen Schulmaister aufgehalten, und sich weder auf kunftigen Summer aufs neue verdingt. Es mochte nicht unrhatsam seyen, disem Buben etwas nachzu forschen." Otto was still active two years later. See Buxtorf to Waser, Basel, 28 March 1621, ibid., 55 recto: "Hujus mei epistolii causa est, judaeus ille apud vos ultimo baptizatus. Is nunc Argentinae per aliquot septimanas est, et pro more suo linguas orientales fraudulenter vendit. Est inquam ille Julius Conradus, qui Bremae studiosos defraudavit. Quod si idem ille is fuit, qui et vos decepit, tunc ille nunc Argentinae est. An de hoc aliquis amicorum ibi monendus, tu noveris. Ego de eo te monere intermittere non potui."

55. On Barnet see, in addition to the account in Pattison 1892, 367–371, Roth 1950; and Shapiro 1996, 162–164.

56. On Casaubon's relations with Savile see William Carr, "Savile, Henry," in *DNB* 1885–1901; and Robert Goulding, "Savile, Henry," in *ODNB* 2004.

57. See the lively and informed review of English Hebraists in this period in Daiches 1941.

from Hebrew biblical commentaries.[58] Their discussions were evidently precise. Kilbye knew he could turn to Casaubon when he wanted to borrow a copy of the Jewish chronological work *Sefer Yuhasin,* which he had never seen.[59]

Casaubon reached Oxford on 18 May. He toured the handsome colleges, met the local good and great, ate rich meals, especially at Magdalen, and evaded efforts to give him an honorary degree. Above all, he admired and worked in the Bodleian Library.[60] What struck him most about Thomas Bodley's creation was not its ancient codices. As he told a correspondent, perhaps de Thou, the manuscript collection could not bear comparison with the far richer royal one in Paris.[61] But the Bodleian did offer something Casaubon had not seen before: a unique scholarly community, called into being by the library's distinctive collection of recent literature and refusal to allow borrowing:

> The collection of printed books is remarkably large, and will increase every year. For Bodley left a rich annual income to see to that. So long as I was at Oxford, I spent whole days in the library. For the books cannot be taken out, but the library is open to all scholars for seven or eight hours a day. You would always see a goodly number

58. On Kilbye see Gordon Goodwin, "Kilbye, Richard," in *DNB* 1885–1901; David Wilson, "Kilbye, Richard," in *ODNB* 2004; and Feingold 1997, 454–455. Kilbye's unpublished commentary on Exodus is Lincoln College Oxford, MS lat. 121, housed in the Bodleian Library. An anonymous scribal copy, it has corrections in Kilbye's unmistakable handwriting.

59. Kilbye to Casaubon, 13 July 1613, BL MS Burney 364, 323 recto: "doctissime vir nunquam vidi ספר יוחסין audio te illum habere, si modo digneris velis illum ad me mittere per mensem, ego illum ad te sartum tectum cum maximis gratiis remitterem." Note also Casaubon to Erpenius, 13 June 1612, Casaubon 1709, 537, where he mentions that he has seen only two copies of Raphelengius' *Lexicon,* "unum in manibus Eliensis [Andrewes], alterum Oxonii apud Professorem Hebraeum [Kilbye]."

60. Casaubon wrote more than one brief account of what he saw in Oxford that did not mention his meeting Jacob. In addition to the letter quoted in the text, there is an informative preface to the notes he took in Oxford in Bod MS Casaubon 28, 116 recto: "Σὺν Θεῷ Excerpta Oxoniensia. Anno 1613. mense Maio cum ἡ φιλτάτη iter in Galliam instituisset, atque ego finem primae parti mearum in Baronium animadversionum ferme imposuissem: ad Oxonium invisendum id tempus opportunum ratus, die xv. post uxoris profectionem dedi me in viam: et die altero cum D. Savilio huc perveni, χάριτι τοῦ θεοῦ. Hic primum aedificia collegiorum spectavi omnia: deinde cum doctoribus huius Acad. viris humanitate et doctrina excellentibus notitiam contraxi, sumque familiariter cum praecipuis eorum, praesertim cum D. Abotio, D. Decano, D. Kilbie, D. Prideaux et aliis primariis viris, versatus. Die Lunae x. Maii, Bodleianam bibliothecam caepi inspicere et libros eius B. tractare. Atque interea, domum reversus, quia libros B. efferre nefas, alios libros lectitavi. imprimis illum qui de adventu Regis in hanc Academiam scriptus est et inscribitur, Rex Platonicus. lectu sane dignissimus, propter admirandam Regis maximi doctrinam et φιλομάθειαν, quarum eximia hic dedit specimina."

61. Casaubon 1709, 537, quoted in Casaubon 1850, II, 1229: "Noli cogitare similem hic reperiri librorum MSS. copiam, atque est in Regia: sunt sane et in Anglia MSS. non pauci, sed nihil ad Regias opes." Russell suggests that the recipient was de Thou.

of scholars greedily enjoying this feast prepared for them, a sight that gave me great pleasure.[62]

Bodley's first librarian, Thomas James, saw the library as an arsenal of weapons to be deployed against Catholic scholars in historical and philological controversy. Although his larger enterprises eventually failed, he did succeed, with Bodley's endowments, in making the library a kind of counterpart to such contemporary centers of collaborative erudition in the Catholic world as the Vatican and the Biblioteca Ambrosiana. Casaubon's encounters with his Jewish informant—like his conversations with other scholars in Duke Humfrey's library—formed part of his exposure to this new form of scholarly community. No wonder that after Casaubon returned to London, he told another friend that he had been "buried through my whole stay in the excellent library, which I left with great regret."[63]

On 23 May Casaubon recorded in his diary: "I spent several hours on Hebrew studies with a Jew, a most learned man, whom I found here."[64] This was the first of his many meetings with Jacob Barnet. A letter to John Prideaux, written some weeks later, fills in a few details: "From the first time that I happened to meet him, in your lodgings, I recognized from just a few words how expert he was in talmudic learning."[65] Evidently, then, Casaubon met Barnet at Exeter College, of which Prideaux, soon to become professor of divinity, had been elected rector in 1612.[66] Evidently, too, they found common ground in talmudic studies. It seems certain that their discussions continued. Though Casaubon did not say that his later Hebrew sessions in Oxford involved Barnet, the inference seems reasonable, for henceforth, by his own testimony, he devoted much of his time in Oxford to the reading of Jewish texts.

62. Casaubon 1709, 537–538: "At librorum editorum admirandus est numerus, et qui incrementum quotannis est accepturus: reliquit enim Bodlaeus annuos reditus sane luculentos in eam rem. Quamdiu Oxonii fui, totos dies in bibliotheca posui, nam libri efferri non possunt; patet vero bibliotheca omnibus studiosis per horas septem aut octo quotidie. Videres igitur multos semper studiosos paratis illis dapibus cupide fruentes, quod me non parum delectabat."

63. Casaubon to Edmondes, 6 July 1613, BL MS Stowe 174, 112 verso: "J'ai este logé ches Monsieur le Doien aedis Christi, personnage de singuliere pieté et doctrine. J'ai grandement admiré la grandeur et richesse de vos Colleges, et par dessus tout l'excellente Bibliotheq qui est la, dans laquelle j'ai este enseveli tant qu'ai esté a Oxford, et l'ai quittée a grand regret."

64. Casaubon 1850, II, 981: "Dedimus et plures horas studiis Hebraicis cum Judaeo, quem hic invenimus, viro doctissimo."

65. Casaubon to Prideaux, 23 June 1613, Casaubon 1709, 538: "Jam tum, quando primum apud te mihi contigit ipsum alloqui, ex paucis verbis cognovi, quantum ipse usum in illa Thalmudica doctrina haberet."

66. See E. G. Hawke, "Prideaux, John," in *DNB* 1885–1901; and A. J. Hegarty, "Prideaux, John," in *ODNB* 2004.

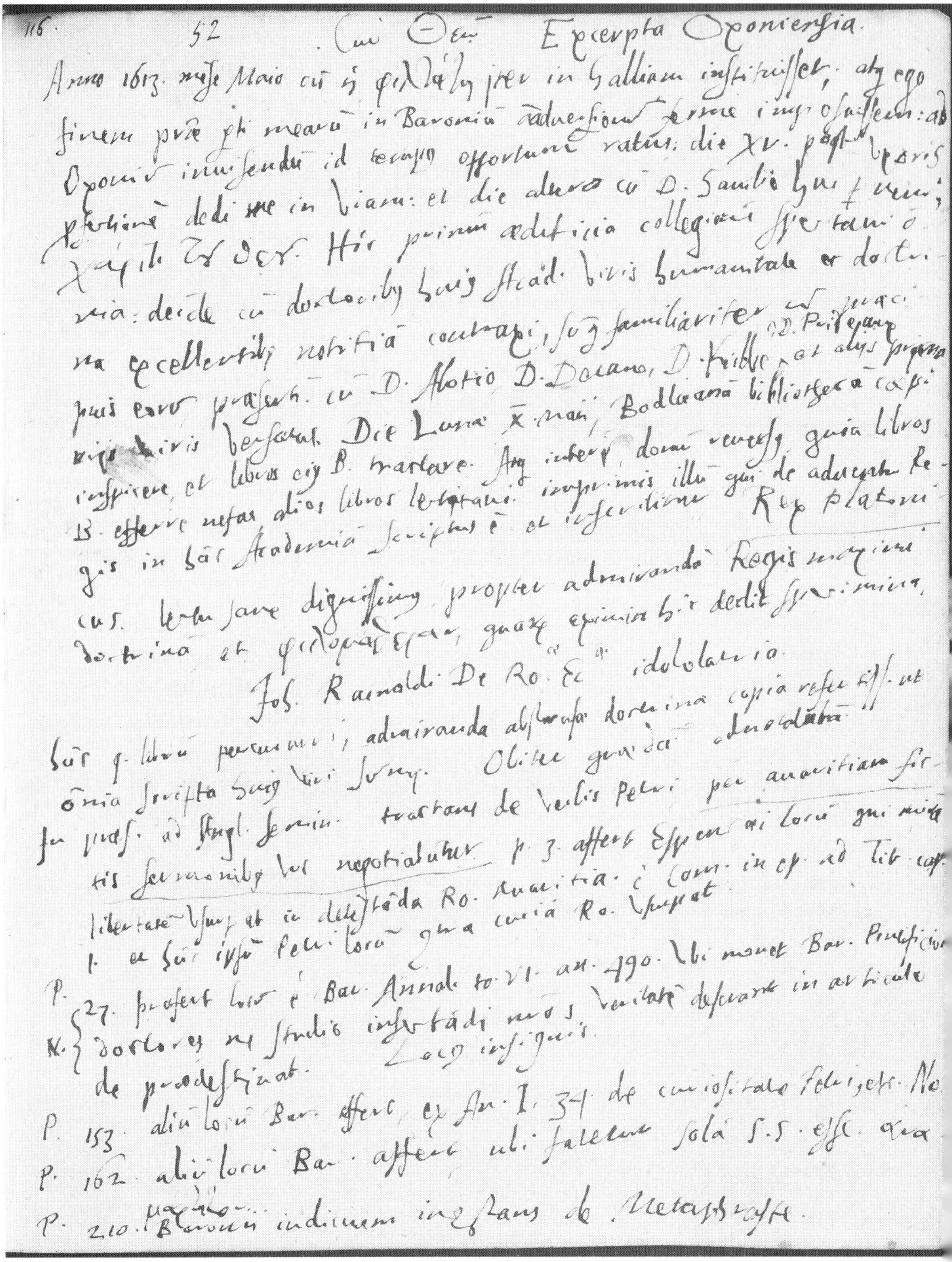

[Handwritten Latin manuscript notes in Casaubon's hand — largely cursive and difficult to read]

Cui Θεῶ Excerpta Oxoniensia.

Anno 1613. mense Maio cum in ... iter in Galliam instituissem, atq̃ ego finem prae... meum in Baronium adversionem ... in...

...

Jos. Rainoldi De Ro. Ec̃. idololatria.

...

P. 527. ...

N. ...

P. 153. ...

P. 162. ...

P. 210. ...

FIGURE 5.7. Beginning of Casaubon's notes taken in the Bodleian Library, May 1613. Bodleian Library MS Casaubon 28, 116 recto.

On 24 May, while still at Oxford, Casaubon recorded that he had "spent the morning hours on reading the Talmud." On 25 May, he noted that "today I studied Hebrew and Basil's Commentary on Isaiah, and I don't regret it."[67] When he left for London—where he began, in early June, to write up his work against Baronio—Barnet came with him. During June Casaubon, now in London, mentioned twice that he had spent substantial amounts of time on Hebrew even as he worked on the Baronio manuscript.[68] It seems likely that these notes record sessions with Barnet. Casaubon's son Meric tells us that Isaac and Jacob usually conversed during meals, although he does not say what Jacob was willing to eat at Casaubon's table.[69]

Later we will see that their conversations ranged over many issues; but first, the rest of Barnet's story. Before long Casaubon decided that he must send Barnet away. "Today," Casaubon noted on 23 June, "Jacob the Jew, whom I had brought from Oxford, left me. I would not regret this plan if my other projects had left me the time to work with him. But my poverty always obstructs my enterprises."[70] During these early summer days, Casaubon had come to feel that he could not spend substantial amounts of time working with Jacob if he was also to complete in a timely fashion the work on Baronio that James expected him to write. Apparently he also concluded that he could not afford to keep Jacob with him if they would have little time together for work. So he sent Jacob back to Oxford, armed with nine letters of recommendation to his friends there.

It is not surprising that Barnet won Casaubon over. We have few reports about him, and all of them come from Christian sources—many of which, for reasons that will soon become clear, were biased against him. Nonetheless they suggest that Barnet was very appealing. The first British divine to give him shelter and support was the Cambridge-educated Puritan Andrew Willet.[71] According to Willet's son-in-law, Peter Smith, in 1610 or a little afterward he spent a month or more disputing with Barnet about "Whether

67. Casaubon 1850, II, 982: "Horas matutinas lectioni Talmud impendimus. A prandio Choniaten absolvimus. Leonem a Castro in Isaiam percurrimus . . . In Hebraeis hodie et in Commentario Basilii in Isaiam fui, nec poenitet operae." Casaubon also referred to his reading of Leon di Castro's commentary on Isaiah in Bod MS Casaubon 30, 106 recto.

68. Casaubon 1850, II, 987 (7 June 1613): "Hebraica studia hodie nos habuerunt"; 988 (10 June 1613): "Studia fere non inspexi praeter Hebraica."

69. Meric Casaubon, Pietas, in Casaubon 1709, 103: "Quamdiu una cum Patre fuit, possum ego testari rarissime eos esse collocutos, nisi inter epulas, non quidem quod non multa Pater ab eo se doceri cuperet, sed quia aliis tum necessariis occupationibus distinebatur."

70. Casaubon 1850, II, 990: "Hodie discessit a me Jacobus Judaeus, quem Oxonio adduxeram. Non poeniteret consilii si per alia studia licuisset opera illius uti. Sed nostris semper conatibus obstat res angusta domi. Scripsi novem epistolas ut Oxoniensibus amicis illum commendarem."

71. On Willet see J. F. Wilkinson, "Willet, Andrew," in DNB 1885–1901; and Anthony Milton, "Willet, Andrew," in ODNB 2004.

Christ be already come, and whether hee was the same who suffered once upon the crosse, which the Jewes deny." At length, Barnet "confessed his sight was cleared, and the veile was now removed from his eyes." He agreed to convert. After a visit to Cambridge, he set out for Oxford, equipped by Willet with "letters . . . to commend him to some Professors there, and by these he gaines kinde entertainment."[72] At Oxford, according to a later source, he "read Hebrew to divers young students."[73]

Smith draws a vivid portrait of Jacob. He notes that Barnet was "borne (as he said) in Italy, and I thinke in Venice," and that he had a deep mastery of Jewish learning: "He was no stranger in the Old Testament, but most familiarly acquainted with the letter of it, and knew everie Criticism of the Hebrew Dialect." More remarkable, he spoke Latin fluently enough to make a favorable first impression on Willet, as he later would on Casaubon: "It was his hap to light upon this reverend Doctor, who after a word or two in Latine enterchanged betwixt them, invites him into his house." Evidently, Barnet was not only learned but charming: "a young man of a comely presence, a smiling countenance, and of gracefull behaviour"—not the terms in which Christians described many Jews in this period.[74] Casaubon added one more detail, this time from the Jew's own report: Barnet, he told Prideaux, came from a rich and affectionate family.[75]

Yet another source tells us that the English subsidized Barnet for two years.[76] We are not absolutely certain what he did to earn his keep in Oxford. But a letter from Peter Goldman, a young Scot to whom we will return, to Patrick Young, the learned and energetic royal librarian, gives a sense of how eagerly and intensively he worked with the more willing of those "divers young students": "As boys need the help of a nurse when they learn to walk, so, when I totter, the Jew holds me up; when I fall, he lifts me; when I am running into the wall, he changes my course. To confess the whole truth, he is everything to me. Believe me, this language is harder than I suspected. Some parts of it are impenetrable, and many points require hard work, a fair number of them require intelligence, and a great many require the presence of a teacher."[77] Clearly, Barnet's pupils appreciated his goodwill—even if not

72. Peter Smith, "The Life and Death of Doctor Willet," in Willet 1634, c recto–verso.

73. Clarke 1683, 14.

74. Smith 1634, c recto.

75. Casaubon 1709, 538: "memoria parentum, quos habet sui amantissimos et divites."

76. Vanini 1615, 66: "quem per 2. annos magnificis impensis aluerunt, ut Christianam religionem amplecteretur." On Vanini's testimony see further below.

77. Bod MS Smith 75, 27: "nam ut pueri cum discunt incedere, nutricum opera indigent, ita me Judaeus nunc nutantem fulcit, nunc lapsum erigit, nunc in parietem impingentem avertit; et ut ingenue fatear, ille mihi omnia est. maior est, mihi crede, in his literis, quam suspicabar, difficultas, nec omnia pervia: multa diligentiam, non pauca ingenium, plurima praeceptorem postulant."

all of them emerged from his tuition with a strong command of Hebrew or Aramaic.

Casaubon was impressed by Barnet's expressed desire to convert. He recommended his Jewish friend to every possible patron. Casaubon described Barnet to the king himself, and recommended him to both the Archbishop of Canterbury and Lancelot Andrewes, "both of whom showed him great generosity."[78] The main point Casaubon noted, as they spent their month together and he and Barnet discussed scholarly problems more intensively, was that Barnet was even more expert in the Talmud than he had at first realized.[79] Others confirm this judgment. After Barnet had left Oxford in disgrace, for reasons to which we will return, Kilbye, perhaps the most expert Hebraist in the university, wrote to Casaubon that "it will be a long time before a Jew like him, and with his skills, reaches our shores. If only he had converted to Christianity he could have been of help to many members of the university, so that they could have attained a modest knowledge of rabbinical learning, if not a profound mastery of it. For no one can ever understand the Hebrew masters perfectly on his own, but one must also use the help of a Jew."[80] Evidently, the most learned Christians saw Barnet as the very model of a learned Jew.

By the time that Barnet returned to Oxford, as Casaubon knew, his fate had become a public issue. He had already promised Willet that he would convert. In 1613 he attracted the attention of the king and the great prelates, who came to see him as a prize catch for the Church of England. Though generally enthusiastic, Casaubon worried. To Prideaux, of whose liking and esteem for "our rabbi" Casaubon felt certain, he described what already

78. Casaubon to an unidentified bishop (wrongly identified by Janson van Almeloveen as Benjamin Carier), 11 November 1613, Casaubon 1709, 547–548: "Reverendissime Domine, Accidit mihi ante aliquot menses, cum essem Oxonii, ut Judaeum quendam ibi offenderem, adolescentem in literis Judaicis et Thalmudicis supra fidem doctum. Vastam enim illam molem totius doctrinae Thalmudicae ita habet in numerato, ut longo intervallo superet omnes quos unquam vidi Judaeos. Accedit cognitio plurimarum linguarum, et in his Latinae, quod in Judaeo rarum est. Hic cum velle se fieri Christianum diceret, de sententiis virorum clarissimorum, qui illustrem illam Academiam regunt, venit Londinum una mecum, et apud me mensem et amplius mansit. Cum videretur serio velle nomen Christo dare, ausus sum de illo sermonem habere apud serenissimi Regis Majestatem: commendavi etiam illum illustrissimo Praesuli, Domino Archiepiscopo, et reverendissimo Domino Eliensi; quorum uterque liberaliter admodum cum Judaeo egit: atque ille sic postea discessit a me, Oxonium repetens, ut magno Baptismi desiderio videretur affici."

79. Casaubon 1709, 538: "Sed multo magis id sum expertus, quoties mihi per gravissimas occupationes meas licuit cum ipso de illa studiorum meorum parte conferre."

80. Kilbye to Casaubon, 20 December 1613, BL MS Burney 364, 322 recto: "vix talis ac tam peritus Judaeus propere ad nostra littora appellet, et si modo Christum induisset plurimis in academia opi et adminiculo fuisset, ut Rabbinorum intelligentia ac scientia saltem leviter tincti, si non plane imbuti essent, nam nemo doctores hebraeorum unquam perfecte intelligere potest proprio marte ac studio, qui non ultra Judaei alicuius opera usus sit."

seemed to him an awkward situation: "The most serene King and the most illustrious Archbishop are very committed to our rabbi's becoming a Christian." Casaubon, however, had urged Barnet "to see to it that he was very fully instructed on the question of religion before being baptized. Better to have it be a little more solid and take place a little bit later." For Barnet, as he explained, "with his incredible command of talmudic learning, is beset by many doubts," and the thought of his family also gave him pause. Casaubon felt that Barnet genuinely wanted to convert, but he also clearly saw that the young man was not yet ready to do so in a wholehearted way. He urged Prideaux to see to it that all ended well, and that Barnet became the adornment to Oxford that he could and should be.[81]

Over the next few months, Casaubon followed Barnet's career sympathetically from a distance. At first at least some of his colleagues in Oxford accepted the view that Barnet was not quite ready to convert, and like Casaubon they nevertheless showed affection for him. Kilbye, for example, wrote to Casaubon in June, while Barnet was with him in London, asking him "to give warm greetings for me to Jacob the Jew, my dear friend, and, as I hope, one who will be a faithful disciple of Christ."[82] In July 1613, after Barnet's return to Oxford, Kilbye reported that some "rash" men were pushing Barnet to be baptized. Kilbye himself, however, "thought it entirely foreign to right reason and religion for Barnet's body to undergo Christ's holy baptism before his soul is imbued with knowledge of and faith in Christ."[83] But by September a decision had been made. Oxford's vice-chancellor, Kilbye reported, wanted Barnet to undergo a public baptism in the University Church of St. Mary at the start of the Michaelmas term. Kilbye himself cherished high hopes that "Jacob will be another James, a faithful disciple of Christ, and I pray that as he rejoices in splendid natural gifts, so he may abound more and more in spiritual gifts, and be confirmed over time in His

81. Casaubon 1709, 538: "Redeo ad nostrum Rabbinum; quem serio fieri Christianum, serenissimus Rex et illustrissimus Archiepiscopus vehementer optant. Ego illi auctor fui, ut curaret se in negotio Religionis ante baptismum diligenter instituendum. Praestat paulo serius, modo firmius. Video ipsum in Thalmudica doctrina mire versatum, multis tentari dubitationibus; quas evelli ex ipsius animo pretium fuerit operae. Accedit quod memoria parentum, quos habet sui amantissimos et divites, reflectere oculos ipsum aliquando cogat. Hoc ego non semel animadverti, qui tamen videor posse affirmare, ipsum voluntate jam Christianum esse. Opto ipsum Oxonii manere; persuasus posse olim ejus operam illustrissimae Academiae vestrae decus aliquod afferre. Iterum igitur atque iterum te oro, ut pro tua pietate negotium hoc tua cura indignum ne existimes."

82. Kilbye to Casaubon, 13 June 1613, BL MS Burney 364, 325 recto: "Salutes quaeso benigne nomine meo Jacobum Judaeum mihi amicissimum, et ut spero christi discipulum futurum fidelem."

83. Kilbye to Casaubon, 13 July 1613, ibid., 323 recto: "Siquidem prorsus alienum putavi a recta ratione ac religione corpus suum sacro christi baptismo tingi, antequam animus eius Christi scientia ac fide imbuatur."

grace and faith."[84] In turning to Casaubon now, he asked for liturgical information that even the greatest Anglican experts lacked, since England lacked Jews: "If you have ever seen a Jew baptized, please give me an account by letter of any ceremonies that you have seen or have heard about from others."[85]

What followed was the catastrophe that Casaubon had clearly feared. Samuel Clarke tells the story: "But the very day before he was to be baptized, this dissembling Jew ran away. Dr. Lake being informed hereof, sent some on horseback, others on foot to pursue him, who overtaking him, brought him back, though against his will, to Oxford, where, on his own accord, he professed that he was returned to his old Judaism, which he had forsworn: he jeared at Christ and despised Baptism, for he had now filled his purse." William Twisse, who had prepared a sermon to celebrate Barnet's baptism, put it aside and preached another, which he prepared in only a few hours, "wherein he shewed Gods just judgment upon that perverse nation and people . . . with great applause and to the admiration of the whole University."[86] Barnet was placed in Bocardo, the university prison. Enraged by what they saw as his skillful and deliberate plot to deceive them, the dons railed and preached at him by turns, uncertain what they could achieve but none the kinder for that. As Kilbye explained on 18 October, "he is kept in prison. I often send my servant, to bring him to me and then take him back. He promises many things, he inclines toward faith and baptism; but whether he does this from the soul, or by pretense, only God knows, Who knows men's hearts." "I do not think it safe to believe him too rapidly." Kilbye explained, with a significant choice of proverb, "lest he return again, with the dog, to his vomit."[87]

84. Kilbye to Casaubon, 6 September 1613, ibid., 326 recto: "Optime spero de Jacobo, quod futurus sit alter Jacobus christi discipulus fidelis, et ut praeclaris naturae dotibus pollet, sic precor ut donis spiritalibus magis magisque abundet, ac ut cum eius gratia et fide indies confirmetur."

85. Ibid.: "si vero aliquem Judaeum baptizatum videris, oro ut caeremonias quas vel ipse videris vel ab aliis intellexeris, literis tuis denunties." In fact there were English precedents for the ceremony to be held at Oxford. See, e.g., "The confession of faith, which Nathanael a Iewe borne, made before the Congregation in the Parish church of Alhallowes in Lombard streete at London, whereupon he was according to his desire, received into the number of the faithfull and so baptized the first of April. 1577," in Foxe 1578, Bi recto–[Ciii verso]. According to a printed note on the verso of the title page, Nathanael or Nathaniel's confession, with its denunciation of Spanish and Portuguese idolatry, was "vvritten first by him selfe in the Spanish tongue, and novv translated into English for the more benefite of the godlie Reader." This incident and its context are discussed in Achinstein 2001, 114–115.

86. Clarke 1683, 14, repeated in Wood 1813–1820, I, 316. On William Twisse (spelled Twiss by Clarke and Twyss by Wood) see E. C. Vernon, "Twisse, William," in ODNB 2004.

87. Kilbye to Casaubon, 18 October 1613, BL MS Burney 364, 327 recto: "in carcere detinetur, saepe autem famulum meum mitto, ut illum ad me adducat, et postea reducat, iam vero plura spondet, ad fidem et baptismum facit, sed sive ex animo id fit, sive simulate deus καρδιογνώστης novit, nec tutum

Even before Kilbye wrote to describe Barnet's apostasy and his current wretched condition, Casaubon tried to intervene. He used the normal harsh language to describe Barnet: "I hear," he wrote to Prideaux, in whose goodwill toward Barnet he believed, "that the wretched Jew has ruined himself, and I am not sure whether it is more correct to say from stupidity or from perfidiousness." But he refused to judge Barnet's actions: "On the matter itself I cannot speak, for it is unknown to me." And he urged Prideaux to be as gentle as possible, in a plea whose language revealed both Casaubon's conventional anti-Semitism and his magnificent, wholly unconventional intellectual honesty:

> I shall be quite shameless, and in my love of letters I shall beg you
> not to whip him forward in his rush to doom. Please, don't pass too
> severe a sentence on him. Let the obstinate Jew recognize the kind-
> ness of Christ in the clemency of those who profess Christ's name.
> Perhaps my boldness will shock you. But please, reverend sir, allow
> me to put off all shame before you on behalf of that man, whom it
> was my lot to have as a teacher.[88]

Reports of Barnet's condition continued to reach Casaubon. They were disquieting, or even worse. On 7 November Peter Goldman, a humanist and Greek scribe who had taken a medical degree in Leiden and who had a Scot's distrust for the English dignitaries who governed Oxford, contacted Casaubon for the third time to urge him to take some action on behalf of the Jew who had taught him so well.[89] He himself, he claimed, felt no sympathy for

---

fore censeo cito fidem adhibere, ne forte iterum cum cane ad vomitum redeat." The proverb that Kilbye used here (Proverbs 26:11, quoted in 2 Peter 2:22) was often used in invectives against heretics and converts. When the Catholic ex-Carmelite Vanini promised to convert to the Church of England, he used the same phrase that was later turned against Jacob (and Vanini himself): that is, he swore not to return to his vomit. Evidently Kilbye's locution referred only to Barnet's refusal to convert from Judaism, not to his being a Jew. For an account of Vanini's oath and the dazzlingly clever equivocation he used to nullify it, see Abbot to Carleton, 16 March 1613/14, edited in Christie 1902, 204–205. The letter is reprinted less accurately in Namer 1965, 74–75.

88. Casaubon to Prideaux, 4 October 1613, Casaubon 1709, 545: "Audio miserum Judaeum ivisse se perditum, stultitia sua nescio dicam an perfidia. De re nihil possum dicere, quae mihi est ignota. Perfricabo tantum frontem, et pro meo erga literas amore, te rogabo ut ruentem ne impellas; neve sententiae adversus illum asperioris auctor esse velis. Agnoscat Judaeus obstinatus Christi mansuetudinem ex illorum clementia, qui nomen Christi profitentur. Miraberis fortasse audaciam meam; sed liceat mihi, Vir εὐσεβέστατε, pro eo viro pudorem apud te ponere, quo uti mihi contigit Praeceptore."

89. Goldman, unknown alike to *ODNB* and Gamilschegg and Harlfinger 1981, was the scribe of BL MS Royal 16 D VII and 16 D IX. In his subscription to the former (154 recto) he identifies himself, in Hebrew, as "Cephas, son of Gold, a Scot, from Dundee, the great city" (כתב כיפא בן-זהב סכוטוס מן דאידונם עיר הגדולה). He apparently completed this MS, which he copied from an original in the Bodleian, on 9 November 1613, the same date on which his name appears in the Bodleian register, where he is described as

Barnet, about whose perfidy he had already warned Casaubon in person in London; and he clearly wished that Barnet had been willing to convert. But this erudite man from what he liked to call, in Hebrew, "the great city of Dundee" was shaken by the terrible conditions of Barnet's imprisonment and the fury displayed by the Oxford dons.[90] Goldman painted a moving picture of the Jew, counting his few coins and barely able to buy food for the next few days, while the vice-chancellor railed, Kilbye tried to persuade him to forsake his original faith, and Bodley's librarian, Thomas James—whom Goldman dismissed as fit only to make catalogues—demanded that the Jew be punished "by the custom of our ancestors"—that is, presumably, killed, as the Jews of medieval York had been massacred. Like Casaubon, moreover, Goldman hated to see a true scholar suffer, even if he deserved it: "The man's learning moves me."[91] Goldman's plea was evidently sincere. He also wrote to Patrick Young, begging him even more urgently to intervene: "If you can do anything for the Jew, do it, no differently than if I were in his place. I weep for his wretchedness. The long imprisonment has made him filthy, and the poor thing has no money with which to buy food. He fears even worse things, for all the professors are furious with him."[92]

"Anglus peregrinus": Clark 1887, 276. He had defended *Theses medicae de melancholia* (Leiden: Basson, 1610) for an M.D. degree at Leiden on 12 July 1610. Goldman's Latin verse appears in Burggravius 1611, 45; and in *Delitiae* 1637, 364–376.

90. Cf. also the notes in Casaubon's copy of the *Variae* of Cassiodorus, BL C.80.a.1, to which Arnaldo Momigliano called attention long ago (Momigliano 1977). In the central position on the title page, he wrote: "Religionem imperare non possumus" and "66. Theodoricus ad Judaeos: quia nemo cogitur ut credat invitus. sic p. 348 cum divinitas patiatur multas esse religiones, nos non audemus unam imponere." One wonders if Casaubon remembered these remarks when he defended Jacob Barnet against what he saw as the cruelty of Christians bent on converting a Jew.

91. Goldman to Casaubon, 7 November 1613, BL MS Burney 364, 150 recto: "Ignosce, vir maxime, si te jam tertio interpello: nam invitus hanc provinciam subij. novi enim te non nisi religiose adiri solere. rogavit, ac tantum non ursit Judaeus ὃς δὴ δηθὰ φίλων ἀπὸ πήματα πάσχει, in teterrimo carcere, ubi, Κλησταὶ σανίδες πλεῖαι μέλανος θανάτοιο. καὶ ἡ κακὴ βούβρωστις ἐπὶ χθόνα δῖαν ἐλαύνει. φοιτᾷ δ᾽οὔτε θεοῖσι τετιμένος, οὔτε βροτοῖσι. nam cum rationes cum crumena subduceret, proxime, videbat sibi paucorum dierum reliquias reliquas. et ad miserias corporis, accedit insanabile et cacoethes ulcus animae: nam superstitiones Judaicas mordicus retinet, nec ad clarissimum solem oculos attolere sustinet. memini me quum londini essem, tibi dicere, ἠπεροπῆα τ᾽ἔμεν καὶ ἐπίκλοπον, οἷά τε πολλοὺς βόσκει γαῖα μέλαινα πολυσπερέας ιουδαίους, ψεύδεα τ᾽ἀρτύνοντας, ὅθεν κέ τις οὐδὲ ἴδοιτο [*Od.* 11.364–366, substituting *ioudaious* for *anthropous*]. movet me tamen hominis eruditio. τῷ δ᾽ἔνι γὰρ μορφὴ ἐπέων, ἔνι δὲ φρένες ἐσθλαὶ. Vicecancellarius οὔτι κατακτείνει, πλάζει δ᾽ἀπὸ πατρίδος ἄτης. Kilbius ἀεὶ καὶ μαλακοῖσι καὶ αἱμυλιοῖσι λόγοισι θέλγει, ὅπως πάτρης ἐπιλήσεται. Jamesius insulsissimus antiquitatis amator, et hic publicum famae cymbalum ἀσπερχὲς μενεαίνει ἀντιθέῳ. et hominem more majorum puniendum censet. sed nosti hominem. facit hic quod se facere dignissimum est, syllabos et indices conficit. Vale vir maxime. e ferricrepinis insulis [Plautus, *Asinaria* 1.1.18]. 7 Novemb."

92. Kemke 1898, 20: "Si quid pro Judaeo poteris, age, non aliter, quam si ego eius loco essem. Ego eius miseriam defleo: nam diuturno carcere situm et squalorem contraxit; nec miser habet, unde prandium emat. Graviora etiam metuit: nam et omnes professores male volunt."

A few days later Casaubon wrote at length to an unidentified bishop, to whom he told the whole story.[93] He begged his powerful acquaintance to see the king and ask for Jacob's release. Barnet, he pleaded, had been brought up in the Talmud, enmeshed since early childhood in superstitions and blasphemies against Jesus. No wonder that he could not manage to convert: to do so he would have had to extricate himself from the whole clinging, tight-meshed net of his upbringing and culture. Even during their study sessions, he had sometimes startled Casaubon with reminders that he had been "brought up entirely on texts that contain dreadful blasphemies against the Savior."[94] True, he had practiced dissimulation upon his return to Oxford, and that was a great fault. But his refusal to convert, Casaubon insisted, was not evil in itself: "the fact that he did not wish to become a Christian is not, in my view, a crime punishable by law: only the fact that he pretended."[95] In any event, Casaubon was horrified by Goldman's account of the cruelty with which the authorities had treated Barnet. He asked the archbishop of Canterbury himself to intervene. In the end, the value of sheer erudition and the requirements of Christian pity outweighed even the charge that he thought valid: "Although I detest his perfidy from the

93. In Casaubon 1709, 547, the addressee of this letter is identified as Benjamin Carier, the man who conducted Casaubon to England. But in the spring of 1613 Carier left for the Continent and was reconciled to the Catholic church; see Anthony Charles Ryan, "Carier, Benjamin," in *ODNB* 2004; and Questier 1996. Casaubon knew all about the scandal, since King James used him as his intermediary in an effort to induce Carier to return. Casaubon addresses his correspondent as "Praesul εὐσεβέστατε," so he was clearly a bishop, but one with whom Casaubon was on less intimate terms than he was with Andrewes, and not George Abbott, the archbishop of Canterbury (in the letter Casaubon refers to both men in the third person). Perhaps his correspondent was Tobie Matthew, archbishop of York, to whom Casaubon gave a copy of Casaubon 1611, the book in which he published materials about Henry Garnett's use of dissimulation (York Minster Library).

94. Casaubon to an unidentified bishop, 11 November 1613, Casaubon 1709, 547–548: "Reverendissime Domine, Accidit mihi ante aliquot menses, cum essem Oxonii, ut Judaeum quendam ibi offenderem, adolescentem in literis Judaicis et Thalmudicis supra fidem doctum. Vastam enim illam molem totius doctrinae Thalmudicae ita habet in numerato, ut longo intervallo superet omnes quos unquam vidi Judaeos. Accedit cognitio plurimarum linguarum, et in his Latinae, quod in Judaeo rarum est. Hic cum velle se fieri Christianum diceret, de sententiis virorum clarissimorum, qui illustrem illam Academiam regunt, venit Londinum una mecum, et apud me mensem et amplius mansit. Cum videretur serio velle nomen Christo dare, ausus sum de illo sermonem habere apud serenissimi Regis Majestatem: commendavi etiam illum illustrissimo Praesuli, Domino Archiepiscopo, et reverendissimo Domino Eliensi; quorum uterque liberaliter admodum cum Judaeo egit: atque ille sic postea discessit a me, Oxonium repetens, ut magno Baptismi desiderio videretur affici. Quod cum ego mirifice optarem, vereri tamen subiit non semel, ne infelici Judaeo sua doctrina cederet in perniciem: enutritus enim iis scriptis, quae blasphemias contra Salvatorem horrendas continent, ita animi mentem dissimulare non poterat, ut non aliquam interdum metuendi occasionem mihi praeberet."

95. Ibid., 547: "Ne multis Reverentiam tuam morer, eventus docuit non fuisse metum meum inanem. Oxonium reversus, et longa simulatione usus, ubi ad rem ventum est, et dies instabat, quo erat baptizandus, repente Judaeus urbe aufugit, et itineri se accinxit, ut huc veniret. Retractus a fuga, rejectus est in carcerem, ubi etiam nunc haeret, justas suae perfidiae poenas pendens. Nam quod nolit fieri Christianus, crimen legibus puniendum, opinor, hoc non est; sed tantum, quod simulaverit."

bottom of my heart, I cannot but feel some pity for him, given his great learning."[96]

The Oxford scholars who responded to Barnet's disaster explained it by reference to the uniformity, permanence, and unchangeability of his entire nation's character. William Twisse, in his sermon on the occasion, blamed "that perverse nation and people," and his audience agreed.[97] Arthur Lake, warden of New College Oxford and one of the translators of the King James Bible, took so serious an interest in Hebrew that he endowed a lectureship in the subject at Oxford. After he sent men on horse and foot to capture Barnet, he preached a revealing series of sermons in the church where the Jew was to have been baptized. Lake admitted that "euerie Countrie may haue Pharisees and Saduces," the Jewish villains of the Gospel narratives.[98] But he also used his knowledge of Hebrew and Judaism to denounce the Jews, who "in their Holy Synagogues" thanked God for making them Jews rather than Gentiles. The Jews, he insisted, were the worst enemies of Christianity: "The *Turkes* though they doe not receiue him for the Sonne of God, yet doe they reuerence him for a great Prophet . . . Only the *Iew* is in direct opposition, and the most desperate impugner of our Sauiour Christ, witnesse their *Talmude*." These features were universal: centuries of conditioning had made the Jews an evil race. "Neither is this sinne personall to some few of them, but nationall, the same malice is found in them all. Neither is it only nationall, but naturall also; they haue for many generations brought vp their children in it; so that wee may well say that sinne is growne in them to the highest, amongst them there is neither good egge nor bird; they fill vp the measure of their fathers iniquitie; nay, they farre exceed them."[99] What

96. Ibid., 547–548: "Audio tamen esse quosdam, qui justo odio accensi, dirum aliquod in miserum hominem supplicium cupiunt statui. Haec causa est, cur alterum jam mensem in carcere haereat sine spe dimissionis. Egi de illo cum illustrissimo et reverendissimo Archiepiscopo, qui confirmavit mihi, se daturum operam, ut ei negotio finis semel imponeretur. Sed audio esse aliquem, qui impediat quo minus hoc fiat. Et scribitur ad me Oxonio, periculum esse ne homo infelix fame et paedore pereat in illo duro carcere. Ego, etsi detestor ex animo illius perfidiam, non possum tamen non aliqua ejus tangi commiseratione, propter excellentem ejus doctrinam; quam et Dominus Kilbius, Regius Professor Linguae Sanctae Oxonii, vir praestantissimus, non minus admiratur quam ipse faciam. Habes, reverendissime Domine, causam hujus meae scriptionis; nam quia nulla spes meliorum affulget, nisi a clementia optimi Regis, peto a te obnixe, ut meo nomine, si placet, ipsam Majestatem convenias, et significes hoc unum cupere me ab illo impetrare, ut semel tandem statuatur de captivo, et quoquomodo finis imponatur ejus durae sane captivitati. Oro, obsecro, obtestor tuam Reverentiam, Praesul εὐσεβέστατε, ut tuo patrocinio miserum ne judices indignum. Spero illam immensam Domini Regis bonitatem, quam in ejus Majestate etiam hostes admirantur, mihi veniam daturam hujus audaciae, et humillimas preces meas non aspernaturam."

97. Clarke 1683, 14; repeated in Wood 1813–1820, I, 316.

98. Lake 1629, 490.

99. Ibid., 479. See Shapiro 1996, 163; and, for the larger development of ideas about race in this period, Martínez 2008.

makes Goldman and Casaubon stand out in this dismal record is not the negative view of Jews and Judaism in general that that they shared with their contemporaries but their ability to see Jacob Barnet as an individual, and to feel for him.

Casaubon's pleas—and perhaps those of others—were heard, and counsels of moderation prevailed. On 7 November the Privy Council ordered that Barnet be released from Bocardo and brought to London "under safe custody," and nine days later it directed that he "be presently conveyed to the seaside, to be sent out of the realm."[100] This was done, and Barnet—like Otto—disappeared from Casaubon's life. Unlike Otto, however, he did not disappear from history. A man of parts, he seems to have made his next stop after Dover the French court in Paris. So, at least, we hear from Giulio Cesare Vanini. Vanini had learned about Jacob during his own difficult stay in England during the years 1612–1614.[101] A onetime Carmelite, he, too, told the authorities that he wished to convert to the Church of England, and he, too, experienced the rough side of clerical tongues—not to mention imprisonment and threats—when he reneged on his promise. In Paris the two men discussed their English hosts' savage hatred of the Jews. True, they had shown Jacob uncommon liberality while they still thought he planned to convert—a judgment, like many of Vanini's, couched in many levels of irony, and all the more appropriate to Jacob Barnet.[102] Young and Goldman, by

100. *Acts of the Privy Council* 1921, 257, 272–273. By the end of 1613, when Goldman wrote again to Patrick Young, Jacob had left England; see Kemke 1898, 20: "Judaeum, si Londini est, officiosissime saluta, et ad me quamprimum rescribe: nam impatienter fero, te tanto temporis intervallo nihil ad me literarum scripsisse."

101. It is at least possible that Vanini knew Casaubon, and even that he learned from him that the works ascribed to Hermes Trismegistus were spurious. See Foucault 2003, 293–296. On Vanini's life see most recently Raimondi 2005; for his time in England see also Paola 1979 and Mas 2003.

102. Vanini 1615, 65–66, reproduced in Vanini 1990, 189: "Si sub eodem Arietis signo utraque provinciarum constituta est, cur cometes in Britannia non vero in Iudaea futurum schisma antenunciavit? deinde cur vatiniano quasi odio Angli Iudaeos prosequuntur, ita ut in Principes Italos, qui illis domicilia stationesque concedunt, quotidie, licet immerito, debacchentur: contra vero cur Iudaeis Angli invississimi infensissimique sunt? Fuit quidam temporibus meis Iudaeus in Anglia, ut Christi fidem susciperet, et ab Oxoniensi Academia perhumaniter fuit exceptus. Cum vero ad sacrum lavacrum deducendus esset, aufugit, captus est. Rex ex benignitate dimisit. offendi eum aliquo tempore post Lutetiae Parisiorum in aula Regia, ubi in sermone mutuo quem duximus, Anglorum avaritiam mirum in modum sugillabat, ut tum prae caeteris nationibus vel maxime dediti sint uni liberaliti, illamque quibuscunque possunt rationibus erga extraneos ostendant, praecipue vero in ipsum Hebraeum, quem per 2. annos magnificis impensis aluerunt, ut Christianam religionem amplecteretur." This text was noted by Pattison 1892—perhaps thanks to information from R. C. Christie—at 371 n. 2, but has since been forgotten by writers on Barnet (not, of course, by writers on Vanini; but they have strange things to say about Barnet: see, e.g., Foucault 2003, 296–297). This is curious, since Christie, in his classic article of 1895 (1902), compared Vanini's English experiences to those of Barnet, suggested that the two men met while in England, and called attention to Pattison's "entertaining" account of Barnet's "stay at Oxford and simulated conversion" (Christie 1902, 197; see also 208).

contrast, had by now lost all sympathy with the man whom Young called "that vile and ungrateful circumcised one," and both believed him to be writing some sort of polemical text—though in the end it never appeared, perhaps, so Young thought, because he could not write Latin. On 26 October 1614 Goldman wrote to Young from Paris: "By the custom of my ancestors, I have renounced his friendship."[103] The personal story of Jacob Barnet dwindles into vain threats and inexplicable fury.

More than a year before that, however, Casaubon and Barnet had their discussions, in Oxford and then in London. In early July 1612 Casaubon wrote to Thomas Erpenius that he was hard at work on Baronio, and spending his spare time on rabbinic studies.[104] At the beginning of August he told Erpenius that if he only had a companion, he would steep himself "in the books of the rabbis."[105] The evidence suggests that he now found his companion in Barnet—and that when he did so, he saw that the rabbis were not a sideline, but vital to his work against Baronio. Two of Casaubon's surviving notebooks probably record some of their study sessions. One of them contains a long series of notes that Isaac, as he himself made clear, took in the Bodleian during his stay in Oxford.[106] In the middle of this series appears

103. Young to Goldman, late summer/fall 1614, Kemke 1898, 24: "Infamis et ingrati illius recutiti libellos famosos libenter viderem; rogo itaque te obnixe, ut per primum internuncium ad me transmittas"; Goldman to Young, Paris, 26 October 1614, ibid., 27: "Judaei schedas ad te misissem, si lucem vidissent; sed bene est, quod Latine scribere non possit. Ego ei more majorum amicitiam renuntiavi." Goldman remained in Paris for some time, as the colophon of BL MS Royal 16 D IX, 263 verso, attests. But we hear nothing more of contact with Barnet.

104. Casaubon to Erpenius, 9 July 1612, Casaubon 1709, 477–478: "Habemus in manibus, mi Erpeni, opus arduum, cujus finem si dederit Deus videre, fructum, ut spero, non mediocrem e vigiliis nostris Ecclesia Dei percipiet. Animadversiones enim scribimus in Annales Baronii, et fraudes illius atque imperitiam stupendam orbi patefacimus. Non tamen a studiis linguarum Orientalium ita sumus alieni, ut non aliquando de illis quoque cogitemus. In Rabbinis praesertim succisiva temporum nostrorum, quoties licet, collocamus."

105. Casaubon to Erpenius, 1 August 1612, ibid., 479: "Quod si studiorum socium haberem, non leviter me in libros Rabbinorum immergerem, quos aliquando coeperam diligenter evolvere. Sed me aliae curae inde revocarunt."

106. Bod MS Casaubon 28, 116 recto: "Σὺν Θεῷ Excerpta Oxoniensia. Anno 1613. mense Maio"; 117 recto: "σὺν Θεῷ Vidi in illustri Biblioth. Bodleana Oxonij librum ex Hispania nuper allatum cuius est hic titulus"; 121 recto: "Σὺν Θεῷ Vidi in Bibl. Bodleana Oxonii librum recenti manu descriptum, sed eleganter et in maxima et crassissima papyro quam unquam meminerim vidisse"; 131 recto: "haec raptim. Θεῷ χάρις. Oxonii."; 143 recto: "σὺν Θεῷ Percurrebam in eadem B. Bod. Harmoniam IIII. Evangel. ab Andrea Osiandro editam Gr. et Lat. Adiecit et Annotationes in quibus aliquam linguae Hebraicae et Rabb. peritiam ostendit, sed sane non magnam"; 154 recto: "σὺν Θεῷ Diu optatum librum Suiseth Calculatoris inveni Oxonii in B. B."; 154 verso: "Libri σὺν Θεῷ parandi, quos in B. B. percurri ex parte"; 155 recto: "σὺν Θεῷ Servatur in Bibl. Bodl. liber in 4° Graecus satis q. ille vulgaris hodie, sed propter vetustatem editionis insignis. est Ζηνοβίου ἐπιτομὴ τοῦ Ταρραίου καὶ Διδύμου etc. παροιμιῶν. Editus est valde informi charactere, Florentiae, anno MCCCCLXXXVII. non memini multos libros legere Graecos antiquioris editionis. Ibi in ea quae omnium prima pag. nullus est libri titulus. pag. 4. est praefatio quam sequentur emendationes quaedam: sed Graece prorsus scriptae, cum hoc titulo, ἐπανορθώσεις τοῦ παρόντος βιβλίου ἐν τῷ πρώτῳ τετραδίῳ. hactenus Oxonii. Θεῷ χάρις."

one page of notes on two Jewish texts. "Among the Hebrew books that I saw in the Bodleian library was the *Arba Turim*, which is titled *Sefer Arba'ah Turim le-rabbenu Yaakov ben Rabbenu Asher zal* [*The Four Rows* of Rabbi Jacob ben Asher of blessed memory]. It was printed in Cremona and is a type of talmudic epitome."[107] Casaubon was reading—perhaps with Barnet by his side—one of the most authoritative codes of Jewish law, compiled by Jacob ben Asher in Spain in the early fourteenth century. Among the many editions printed in the sixteenth century was the Cremona version produced in 1558. Casaubon had apparently never cast eyes on this monumental code, commonly designated by its short title, *Tur*. But he had come across several references to the *Arba'ah Turim* in Baronio's *Annales ecclesiastici*. These include one passage in which "Jacob Turrim" is cited alongside another important rabbinic authority, Isaac Alfasi, the author of the "little Talmud." In his working copy of the *Annales*, Casaubon had stopped at this juncture to cast a sneering remark in the margin about Baronio's illiterate reference to Alfasi, but he passed no comment on Baronio's mention of "Jacob Turrim."[108]

As we have seen, Casaubon had a knack of making immediate use of recently acquired knowledge for his censorious attacks on Baronio. Thus, when he came to pen his mighty critique, he clearly took great pleasure in noting that Baronio's designation of the author Jacob Turrim indicated that he did not actually know the latter's work. Casaubon smugly pointed out that he himself had "recently seen the Cremona edition of that book, in the celebrated Bodleian Library at Oxford, but only in passing, among many other Hebrew books"; Baronio, by contrast, "imprudently confused the author's name with the title."[109] Intent on exposing Baronio's ignorance, Casau-

---

107. Ibid., 132 verso: "σὺν Θεῷ. Inter alios libros Hebraicos quos vidi in Bibl. Bodleana erat lib. Arba Thurim cuius est inscriptio: ל"ז רשא וניבר ןב בקעי וניברל םירוט העברא רפס. editus est Cremonae. Est quaedam velut Epitoma Talmud. Prima pars vocatur Ora Chaiim. Post brevem summam 4 librorum sequitur tabula primae partis םייח חרוא ינמיס חול Habes ibi inter alia halachot zizit, halachot tephilin, item halacoth םיפכ תואישנ. Item alii multi tituli in Talmud et Mose ben Maimon iidem."

108. Casaubon, note in his copy of Baronio 1601, Marsh's Library, I, 239, on 34 n. 134: "Vult dicere in compendio Talmud quod scripsit R. Alphes. Hic saepe citatur a Rabbinis aliis et in comment. ad pirke 3 . . . R. Mosis sic, סאפלא ר קספ ךכ, sic definivit R. Juda vel Joseph. Alphes." But in the margin of the introduction in his copy of *Sefer Hasidim* (BL 1934.f.13, * ij verso), he notes the mention of the name Isaac Alfasi. Casaubon hits upon the wrong personal name of Alfasi, suggesting that the letter *yod* stood for Joseph or Judah rather than Isaac.

109. Casaubon 1614, 655; 1654, 663; 1663, 577: "nuper eum librum in illustri Bibliotheca Bodlaeana, Oxonij, editum Cremonae, inspexi, sed obiter inter plures alios Hebraicos. Baronius nomen auctoris cum libri titulo imprudenter confudit." For Baronio's use of the text see, e.g., 1593–1607, I, 183: "Addimus ad haec insuper quae Rabbi Iacob memoriae prodidit ex Rabbi Moyse Aegyptio: nimirum viros virorum et feminas feminarum curare consuevisse cadavera, in hunc scilicet modum: oculos in primis et ora claudere defuncto, ac stringere fascia, tondere capillos . . . [Babylonian Talmud, Mo'ed Katan 27b]

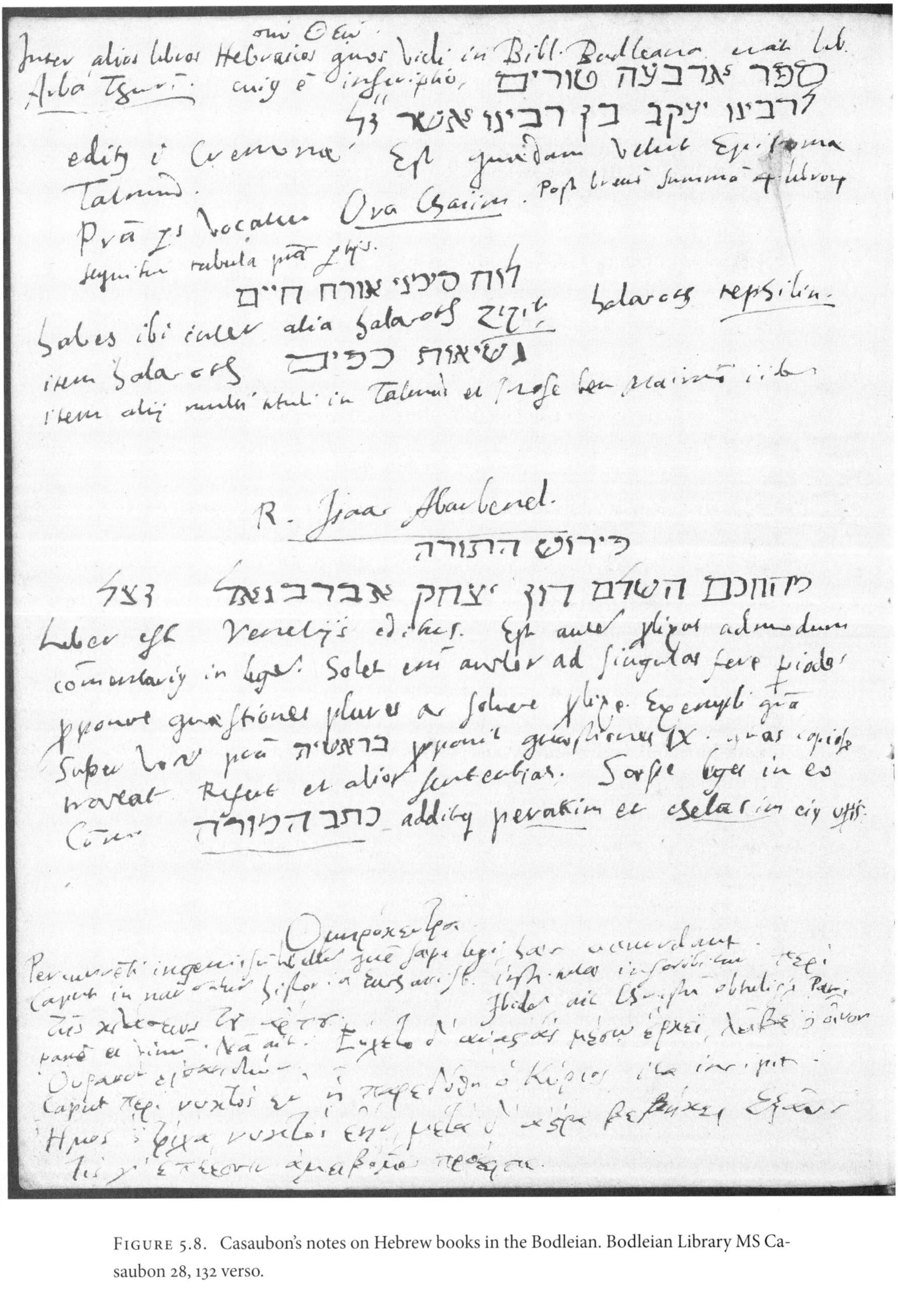

Inter alios libros Hebraicos quos vidi in Bibl. Bodleiana erat lib.
Alba Tzuri cuius e inscriptio, ספר ארבעה טורים
רבינו יעקב בן רבינו אשר 73

edito i Cremona. Est quidam velut Epitoma
Talmud.
Prima pars vocatur Ova Chaim. Post breve summario capitulorum
sequitur tabula prima pag. 45.
לוח סימני אורח חיים
habes ibi inter alia halaroth ציצת halaroth repsilia
item halaroth כפים שאות
item alij multi intul in Talmud et Prose ben rlaino liber.

R. Jsaac Abarbenel.
פירוש התורה
73   מחוכם השלם דון יצחק אברבנאל
Liber est Venetijs editus. Est autem plipas admodum
commentarij in leges. Solet enim author ad singulas fere piades
pponere quaestiones plures ac solvere plipe. Exempli gra
super lor prae בראשית pponit quaestiones IX. quas ipise
trovat. Refut et alior sententias. Sorpe leges in eo
Commentario כתב המורה addito perakim et ecselarum cuius ups.

Omporseerja
Percurrebi ingeniis ... illu que sape legi ben vacundant.
Capiet in natura hij Bijtor i tures... ... ... regi
... ... Hudor aic ... obtulisi Petri
pane et vini. Na ... Εγετο δ' αμφιρος μρω ερκει, λαβε ο αιναν
Ουρανον εsουσαν. ... ...
Capiet περ. νυκτος τε ... η παρελθεν ο Κυριος ... incipit.
Ημος δ'ηρι νυκτος εγενμετα δ' εξρα βεβηκει Εραεω
τις γ' ετικτεν αιμαβριοσ πεrσαι.

FIGURE 5.8. Casaubon's notes on Hebrew books in the Bodleian. Bodleian Library MS Casaubon 28, 132 verso.

bon made no effort to give serious consideration to the actual citation from Rabbi Jacob's work, nor did he credit Baronio for what appears to be an attempt—admittedly unsuccessful—to follow the Jewish practice of referring to an author by the title of his work.[110]

But why did Baronio single out Jacob ben Asher's code for information about first-century Judaea? As we have seen, Baronio (or an anonymous adviser) was sufficiently familiar with Jewish writings that in describing Jewish funerary customs he was able to cite the one minor talmudic tractate devoted to the subject, *Evel Rabbati.* Clearly, as Casaubon pointed out time after time, there were limitations to Baronio's understanding of the Jewish sources. And yet it does seem likely that Baronio's interest in Jacob ben Asher's *Tur* must have been generated by the popularity that the code enjoyed among Jewish readers, particularly those of Germany, Italy, and Poland.[111] Likewise, Casaubon, casting his gaze on Bodley's Hebraica collection, picked out the *Tur,* or talmudic epitome as he called it, noting its similarity to the *Mishneh Torah* of Maimonides. It stands to reason, however, that he would have been incapable of assessing the legal authority of the *Tur.* Rather, he carefully copied down some of the contents of the first section of the code, the *Orah Hayyim,* "which deals with *Zizit* [prayer shawls], *Tefillin* [phylacteries], and *Nesiut Kappayim* [priestly benediction], among other matters."[112] Not surprisingly, given Casaubon's fascination with Jewish prayers and Jewish modes of worship, it was the ritual section of Jacob ben Asher's code that caught his attention. It should also be remembered that he had read Buxtorf's *Synagoga,* in which the work was often mentioned. Moreover, Casaubon himself owned an anonymous book about Jewish customs in Yiddish,

---

Nec praetermittimus dicere, tantum olim excrevisse apud Hebraeos impensam funerum, ut eius magnitudine cognati perterriti, relicto cadavere, se aliquando subducerent. Sed qui haec idem Rabbi Iacob testatur, addit ea moderata fuisse a Gamaliele seniore [marginal note: Iore dea c. 352 (another correct reference)]."

110. Casaubon 1614, 655; 1654, 577; 1663, 577: "Iudica nunc Lector de fide horum Annalium. Praeter Maimonidam laudat Baronius et librum Alphesi et Rabbinum Iacob Turim: etiam haec ex aliena fide, ut res arguit. Putavit Alphesi nomen esse libri, non scriptoris. et verum quidem est, extare inter libros Iudaicos quasi compendium Talmud, ut ait Baronius, sub hoc titulo: sed ignoravit Baronius, id esse nomen eius Rabbini, qui eam syllogen confecit. observo laudari in Commentarijs ad Iad Maimonidae רי אלפס, Rabbi Iudam aut Iosephum Alphes [in fact, Isaac], qui an hic sit, non facile dixerim. Quis autem ille est, quem nominat Baronius *Iacobum Turim?* Hic vero conditor Annalium hallucinatus est insigniter: perinde enim fecit, ut si quis inter auctores laudaret *Tullium de natura,* et M. Tullium intelligeret, qui scripsit de natura Deorum. R. Iacob, filius R. Ascher, ante annos trecentos et quod excurrit, librum scripsit, ספר ארבעה טורים, *Liber Arba Turim,* sive quatuor ordines: opus est Talmudicum in quatuor partes divisum, quod titulus indicat."

111. See Elon 1994, 1277–1302.

112. See note 107 above.

also titled *Orah Hayyim*.[113] It is not unlikely that he picked out the section whose title stirred vague memories of his other encounter with Jewish books.

The other Hebrew book selected for inspection in the Bodleian was a commentary on the Pentateuch written by the famous Iberian scholar and statesman Isaac Abravanel, which was printed in Venice in 1579.[114] Abravanel's prolix style called for comment. Casaubon, not unreasonably, slightly disparaged the author's scholastic method of posing many questions about specific words, which he then "proceeds to treat at great length." Casaubon read the text as though he had never encountered the name of Abravanel before, but he had read, and possibly also possessed, Abravanel's commentary on the minor prophets,[115] and he would certainly have come across his name (rendered as Barbinel) in his reading of Calvin's Bible commentaries.[116] The short visit to the Bodleian did not allow for in-depth reading of these texts. But the two Hebrew works chosen for examination, belonging to two discrete parts of Jewish tradition—the one legal, the other exegetical—reveal again the catholic nature of Casaubon's quest for Jewish learning.

A second set of notes—scrawled in a hand even less regular, and less attractive, than Casaubon's usual chicken scratch, which may reflect his efforts to keep up with oral instruction—records more elaborate inquiries into a whole series of Hebrew and Aramaic texts. One or two of these notes Casaubon places in London, apparently in the period just after his return from Oxford—the period when Jacob Barnet was staying with him.[117] By examining these materials and comparing them to the *Exercitationes,* we can tease out something of what Barnet and Casaubon did, and what Casaubon learned from him, in their few weeks together.

At first glance the materials collated in the copybook appear to be a

113. *Sefer Orah Hayyim* (Basel, 1602) (BL 1935.e.15). According to Prijs 1964, 176, Joseph ben Eliezer Halfan, whose name is given as the printer, was also the author of the text.

114. Bod MS Casaubon 28, 132 verso: "פירוש התורה מהחכם השלם דון יצחק אברבנאל זצל Liber [of Abravanel] est Venetijs editus. Est autem prolixus admodum commentarius in legem. Solet enim auctor ad singulas fere periodos proponere quaestiones plures ac solvere prolixe. Exempli gratia super vocem primam בראשית proponit quaestiones IX. quas copiose tractat. Refert et aliorum sententias. Saepe leges in eo Commentario כתב המורה additque perakim et chelacim eius operis." Casaubon does not seem to recognize Abravanel's reference to Maimonides' *Guide.*

115. Bod MS Casaubon 30, 112 verso: "modo scribunt אלקים ut in praefatione Abarbinel in 12 proph."

116. See, e.g., Calvin 1561, 46 verso, on Dan. 4:16.

117. Bod MS Casaubon 30, 82 recto: "σὺν Θεῷ Percurrebam Londini librum Mosis ben Maimon Jad inscriptum"; notes on talmudic and other problems continue to 106 recto. It is especially telling that on 106 recto Casaubon writes: "vide Int. et Leonem a Castro." For on 24 May 1613, while working in the Bodleian, Casaubon noted that he had gone through "Leonem a Castro in Isaiam." See Casaubon 1850, II, 982. This is de Castro 1570.

hodgepodge of talmudic texts.[118] On closer inspection, however, it becomes clear that a specific agenda informs the selection of sources.[119] Among the various subjects treated in these pages—which, as usual, were inscribed "with God"—are rabbinic discussions of the dimensions of sepulchral cham-

118. Bod Ms Casaubon 30, 105 recto–107 verso:

σὺν Θεῷ. Locus e Talmud, in Baba batra, cap. sexto, ed. Bas. p. Cᵃ in secunda columna, in sectione רנה 255.

Misna sic incipit:

מתני

המוכר מקום לחברו לעשות לו קבר וכן המקבל מחברו לעשות לו קבר עושה תוכה שלמערה ד אמות על שש
ופותח לתוכה שמונה כוכין שלש מכאן ושלש מכאן ושנים מכנגדן וכוכין ארכון ארבע אמות ורומן שבעה ורחבן
ששה רבי שמעון אומר עושה תוכה של מערה שש אמות על שמונה ופותח לתוכה שלשה עשר כוך ארבעה
מכאן וארבעה ושלשה מכנגדן ואחד מימין הפתח ואחד מן השמאל ועושה חצר על פי המערה שש על שש
כמלא המטה ופותח לתוכה שתי מערות אחת מכאן ואחת מכאן רבי שמעון אומר ארבע לארבע רוחותיה רבן
שמעון בן גמליאל אומר הכל לפי הסלע

Qui vendit locum socio suo ad faciendum ei sepulcrum et sic (huiusmodi) qui suscipit (ὁ ἐργολάβος) a socio suo ad fac. ipsi sepulcrum, faciet intra speluncam 4. cubitorum supra 6. (h.e. 4. in lat. et 6. in long.) et aperiens in medio 8. foramina (sedes cuiusque cadaveris) 3. hinc et 3. inde, et duo e regione. et foraminum longitudo 4. cubitorum altitudo 7. cubitorum et latitudo 6. cubitorum. R. S. dicit faciet intra speluncam 6. cub. in 8. (h.e. pro long. et lat.) et aperiens in medio 13. foramina 4. hic, 4. illic, et 3. e regione unum ad dextram introitus et unum ad sinistram et faciat atrium ante speluncam 6. et 6. (lati. et longit.) iuxta spatium feretri et aperit in medio 2. speluncas, unam hinc, alteram inde. R. S. ait 4. (speluncas) in 4. lateribus. Raban S. F. G. ait, omnia secundum magnitudinem ipsius petrae.

Confer cum R. Moses Ben Maimon Halacot [Hilkhot] Mecira, cap. 21 lib. xii. liber possessionum.

Notat R. Samuel ben Meir nepos ipsius R. Salomonis, notat in superiora verba Misnae. Non fuit mos in Is. ut sepelirentur singuli separati, sed tota familia in spelunca una, et unus quisque in foramine pro se. כל אחד בכוך בפני עצמו. sed vide totum illum locum. Nam videtur 2. speluncas ponere uno atrio disiunctas.

Locus e Talmud de D. Jesu.

In Tract. Sanhedrin, cap. 6 quod incipit et vocatur Nigmar hadin. fol. 43. in Misna. post misnam Motzeu lo Zacut.

in edit. [Bas. crossed out] Ven. [added above line] est script. sic: sed in eorum libris est לישו הנצרי

Tania

בערב פסח תלאוהו לישו והכרוז יוצא לפניו מ' יום (ישו הנוצרי) יוצא ליסקל על שכישף והסית
והידיח את ישראל כל מי שיודע לו זכות יבא וילמד עליו ולא מצאו לו זכות ותלאוהו בע''פ

In parasc. pasch. suspenderunt Jesum Naz. et κῆρυξ praecedebat eum per 4[0] dies. Jesus Naz. exit ut lapidetur quia ἐμαγεύσατο et persuasit et expedit (extra leg.Mosis) Israelem. Quicunque sciverit aliquid de eius innocentia, veniat et doceat pro eo. Et non inventa est pro eo innocentia et susp. in parasc. pasch.

Tzur est nomen aequivocum nomen montis, nomen lapidis duri

nomen originis unde exscidi solent lapides inde translat. sunt lapides originales. inde transtulerunt ad radicem omnium rerum . . . Sequitur locus de Abrahamo valde appositus ad locum N. T.

Locus a. ille est Isaiae e cap. Li. ubi vide Int. et Leonem a Castro.

See de Castro 1570, 15–16.

119. In addition to the notable examples discussed here, other cases of Casaubon's selective reading of Talmud occur on several pages in Bod MS Casaubon 30. On 107 recto Casaubon transcribes a passage from tractate Sanhedrin (2:1), and refers to Maimonides' *Mishneh Torah,* which deals with the laws

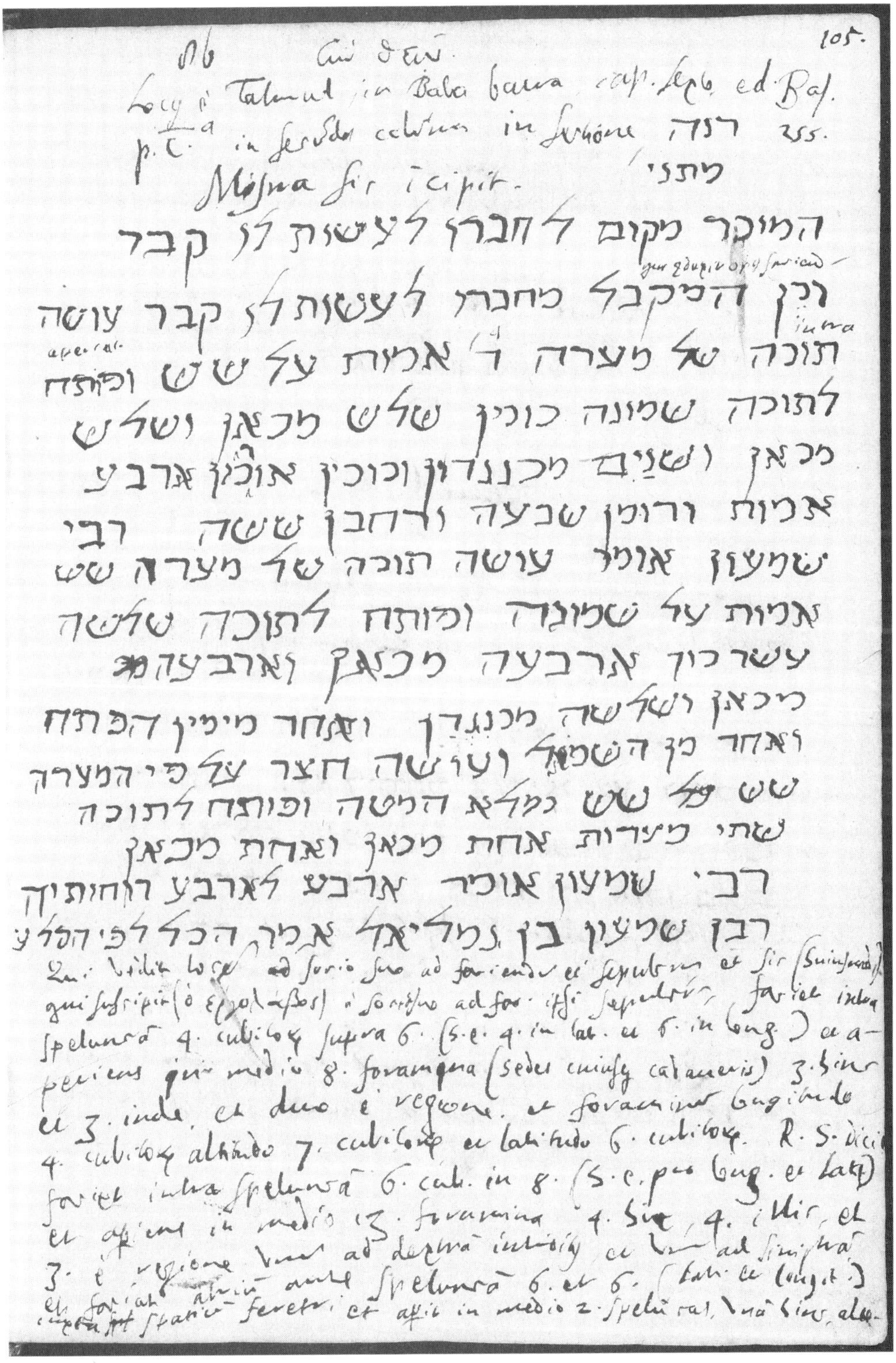

אלו לא אמרו

Locus è Talmud in Baba bava cap. ... ed. Bas.
p.ᵃ in secunda columna in sermone רזה ... us.
Misna sic incipit. מתני׳

הַמוֹכֵר מקום לְחברוֹ לַעֲשׂוֹת לוֹ קבר

וְכן הַמְקַבֵּל מחברוֹ לעשׂוֹת לוֹ קבר עושׂה

תוכה של מערה ד' אמות על ש ש ומוצא

לתוכה שׁמוֹנה כוכין שׁלשׁ מכאן ושׁלשׁ

מכאן ושׁנַיִם מכנגדן וכוכין אוֹרכן אַרבע

אמות ורומן שׁבעה ורחבן ששׁה רבי

שׁמעון אומר עושׂה תוכה שׁל מערה שׁ

אמות על שׁמונה ומוצא לתוכה שׁלשׁה

עשׂר כוּך ארבעה מכאן וארבעה מ

מכאן ואַחד מימין הפתח ואחד מכנגדן

ואחד מן השׁמאל ועושׂה חצר על פי המערק

שׁש על שׁש כמלא המטה ופותחה לתוכה

שׁתי מערות אחת מכאן ואחת מכאן

רבי שׁמעון אומר ארבע לארבע רוחותיה

רבן שׁמעון בן גמליאל אמר הכל לפי הסלע

Qui vendit locum ad forium suo ad faciendum ei sepulcrum et sic (quinque)
qui suscipit (o exolator) à socio ad fac. ipsi sepulcrum, faciet intra
speluncam 4. cubitos supra 6. (s. e. q. in lat. et 6. in long.) et a-
periens per medio 8. foramina (sedes cuiusq cataneris) 3. hinc
et 3. inde, et duo è regione. et foramen longitudo
4. cubitos altitudo 7. cubitos et latitudo 6. cubitos. R. S. dicit
faciet intra speluncam 6. cub. in 8. (s. e. per long. et latit)
et aperiens in medio 13. foramina 4. hinc 4. illinc, et
3. è regione. unum ad dextra introitus et unum ad sinistra
et faciat atrium ante speluncam 6. et 6. (latit et longit.)
instar spatii feretrici et aperit in medio 2. speluncas, una hinc, alia

FIGURE 5.9. Collaborative notes by Casaubon and Jacob Barnet, in Casaubon's hand, on a passage on graves from the Talmud. Bodleian Library MS Casaubon 30, 105 recto.

bers, references to Jesus in tractate Sanhedrin of the Babylonian Talmud, and a list of essential talmudic terms. Casaubon's impressive ability to surf the complex web of rabbinic texts, unprecedented in his earlier work, must lead us to conclude that a prompter was near at hand. Two massive sets of Talmud are called up for this topic: the censored Basel Talmud of 1578–1581 and the Venetian Bomberg edition of the 1520s. Evidently this Protestant reader of Talmud knew that information about Jesus' death, excised from the Basel edition, was to be located in the Venetian Talmud.[120] Perhaps Casaubon had also heeded the warning given by his erstwhile correspondent, the convert Julius Conradus Otto, that for correct presentation of talmudic materials it was necessary to return to the "old authentic Talmud."[121]

The reason for Casaubon's remarkable plunge into the "sea of the Talmud" is not difficult to discern. Unlike his investigation of other rabbinic and Jewish works, this was not reading for its own sake. Indeed, all the texts were selected with a view of reconstructing "the history of the Jewish people in the time of Jesus Christ."[122] On one page, the section is titled "A Talmudic Passage about Lord Jesus."[123] In this case, the censored Basel edition had to be removed from the table to make way for the Venetian (Bomberg) text,[124] which records: "*Tanya* [it is taught]: On the eve of Passover they hung Jesus.

---

of the high priest and king. The same material is brought into play in Casaubon 1614, 244–245; 1654, 218; 1663, 218, where he attacks Baronio for failing to understand the relative powers of the Sanhedrin and the king (Baronio's view rested on a faulty reading of Josephus). Casaubon also transcribes a strange story from Babylonian Talmud, Pesahim 57a–b, which he reads as illustrating the issue of the respective authority of the high priest and king. The text recounts an argument between a king and queen (presumably Hasmoneans), in which the king asserts that goat's flesh is better for sacrifice than the lamb's flesh that the queen favors. The high priest Issachar of Kefar Barkai is brought in to intervene, but his decision is regarded as suspect, and in the end both his hands are cut off. This dénouement is assessed by R. Joseph: "Praised be the Merciful one who caused Issachar to receive his reward in this world." On this story Casaubon notes: "Apparet istum Rab. mag. approbasse facta Regis." Indication of his search for material on the same topic is demonstrated by his transcription on 107 verso of a passage from "Talmud in tractatu הוריות cap. 3., pag. 13. [Babylonian Talmud, Horayot 13a] regarding the preeminence of a king over a high priest. This text, too, is put to polemical use in Casaubon 1614, 362–363; 1654, 320; 1663, 320.

120. The first Venetian editions of the Talmud did not contain Rashbam's commentary on Bava Batra, which provided Casaubon with important information.

121. Otto 1605a, B verso–Bii recto: "Praefatio ad lectorem": "Tandem etiam benevolum lectorem monendum duxi, me omnia illa, quae scripsi, non ex recentiore illa editione Talmud Basileae excusi, quem librum Judaei ex veteri Talmud congesserunt, et Christianis hodie obtrudunt, excerpsisse, sed ex veteri, vero, et genuino, quem etiam librum ut et alia Rabbinorum praeclara et utilissima scripta non sine magno labore et praesentissimo vitae periculo, in usus meos comparavi." On the idea of the "Old Talmud" and its esoteric use by Flavius Mithridates in his *De passione Domini* see Wirszubski 1963, 19–18.

122. This is the title of the important German work (1886–1890) of Emil Schürer, translated as Schürer 1973–1987.

123. Bod MS Casaubon 30, 105 verso: "Locus e Talmud de D. Jesu."

124. Casaubon excised the reference to the Basel Talmud, writing Venice in its place (Bod MS Casaubon 30, 105 verso): "in edit. [Bas. crossed out] Ven. est script. sic: sed in eorum libris est."

For forty days a herald went out before him proclaiming: '(Jesus the Naza-rene)[125] is going forth to be stoned because he performed witchcraft, and perverted Israel, and led them astray. Anybody who can speak up in his de-fense may come and state it.' But no defense was brought, and they hung him on the eve of Passover."[126] The passage, from tractate Sanhedrin of the Babylonian Talmud, is presented as a *baraita* (a tradition attributed to the sages of the Mishnah, but not included in the official Mishnah of ca. 200 C.E.). It is in fact only a part of a larger talmudic discussion.[127] On the fac-ing page Casaubon lists various terms that are used to denote the different voices or strata of the Talmud. The list is titled *baraita*, which he bizarrely writes as two words (the term literally means "that which is outside").[128] These are the notes of a tyro, and apparently one taking down oral instruc-tion: hence the spelling error. Although Casaubon possessed all manner of books—Génébrard's *Eisagoge,* for example—from which he could have learned the meaning of the common technical talmudic vocabulary, it is clear that here we witness him inquiring about the meaning of the term *tanya* in the Sanhedrin passage. Under the guidance of a good pedagogue, Casaubon not only received an explanation of the term *baraita,* but also was initiated into the meaning of the standard signposts on the talmudic page.

Of a rather more unusual nature are Casaubon's transcription and Latin translation of a passage in tractate Bava Batra, which he took down from the Basel edition of the Babylonian Talmud.[129] Casaubon transcribed the fourth Mishnah of chapter 6 and then translated it:

> If a person sells his fellow a plot in order to make a grave . . . the in-side of the cave must have an area of four by six cubits, and open-ing into it eight niches, three on each side and two at the top and bottom. The niches must be four cubits long, seven handbreadths high, and six wide. R. Simeon says: "He must make the inside of the

125. Casaubon writes the Hebrew words for "Jesus the Christian" in parentheses. Did he have the manuscript, now in Munich, in which these words are excised? See Schäfer 2007, 168 n. 13.

126. Babylonian Talmud, Sanhedrin 43a. Bod MS Casaubon 30, 105 verso: "In Tract. Sanhedrin, cap. 6 quod incipit et vocatur Nigmar hadin. fol. 43 in Misna. post misnam Motzeu lo Zacut." Edward Lively cited this passage in his treatise on the Jewish calendar, which Casaubon in turn cited with enthusiastic praise in his *Exercitationes.*

127. For a recent discussion of this text see Schäfer 2007, chap. 6.

128. Bod MS Casaubon 30, 106 recto:

> e Bar aitha. Secunda pars in Talmud, q.d. extra scholam, quia proponebatur et docebatur extra scholam.
>
> מתני׳ גמי׳ דתניא
>
> מתנתין.vel מתנין.
>
> In Talmud hae voces occurrunt saepe in ipso corpore textus. Prima vox indicat sequentia esse e Misna. sequens, esse e Gemara. tertia esse e Bar aitha.

129. Babylonian Talmud, Bava Batra 100b–101a.

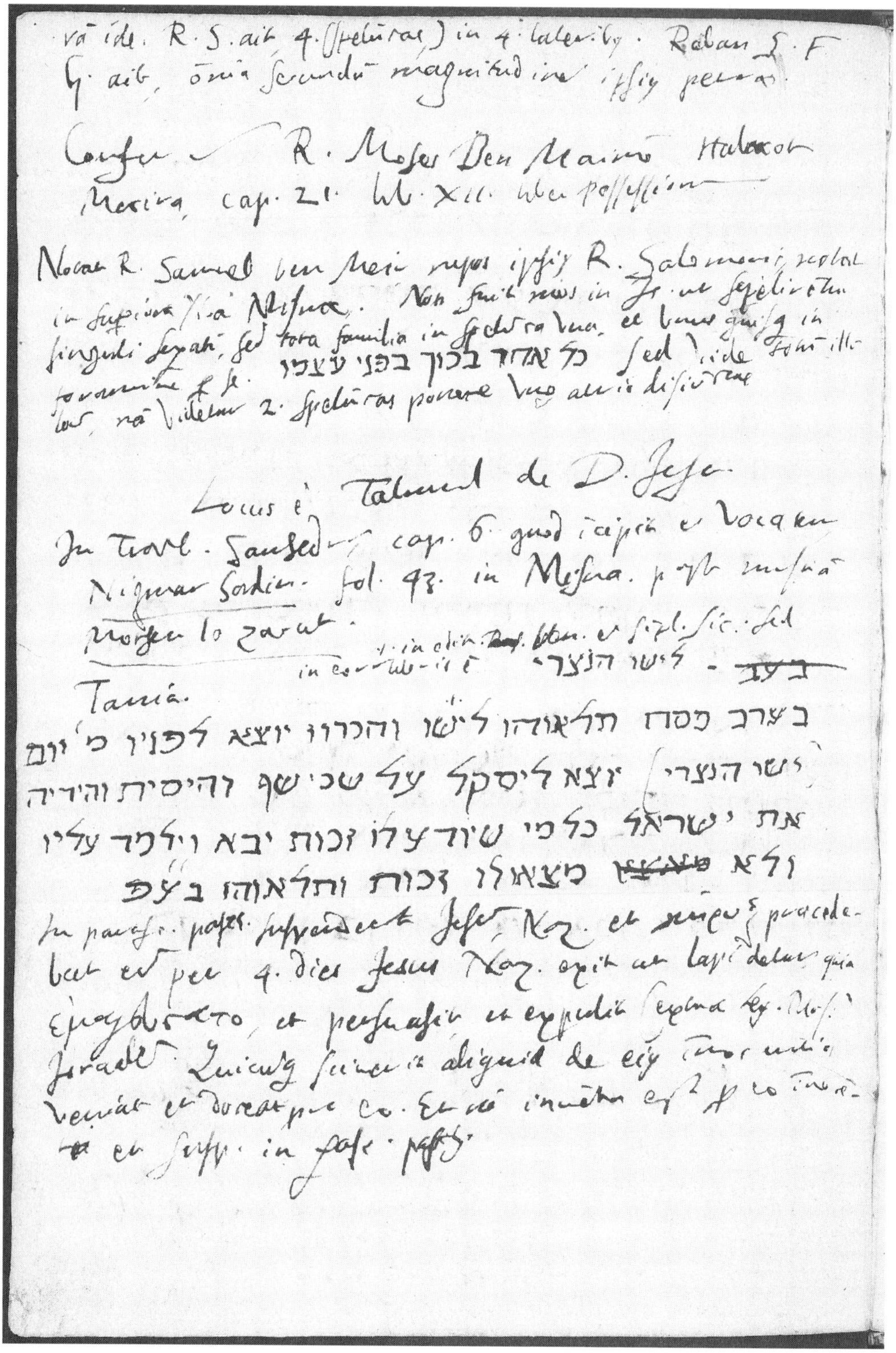

FIGURE 5.10. Collaborative notes by Casaubon and Jacob Barnet, in Casaubon's hand, on a passage on the Crucifixion in the Talmud. Bodleian Library MS Casaubon 30, 105 verso.

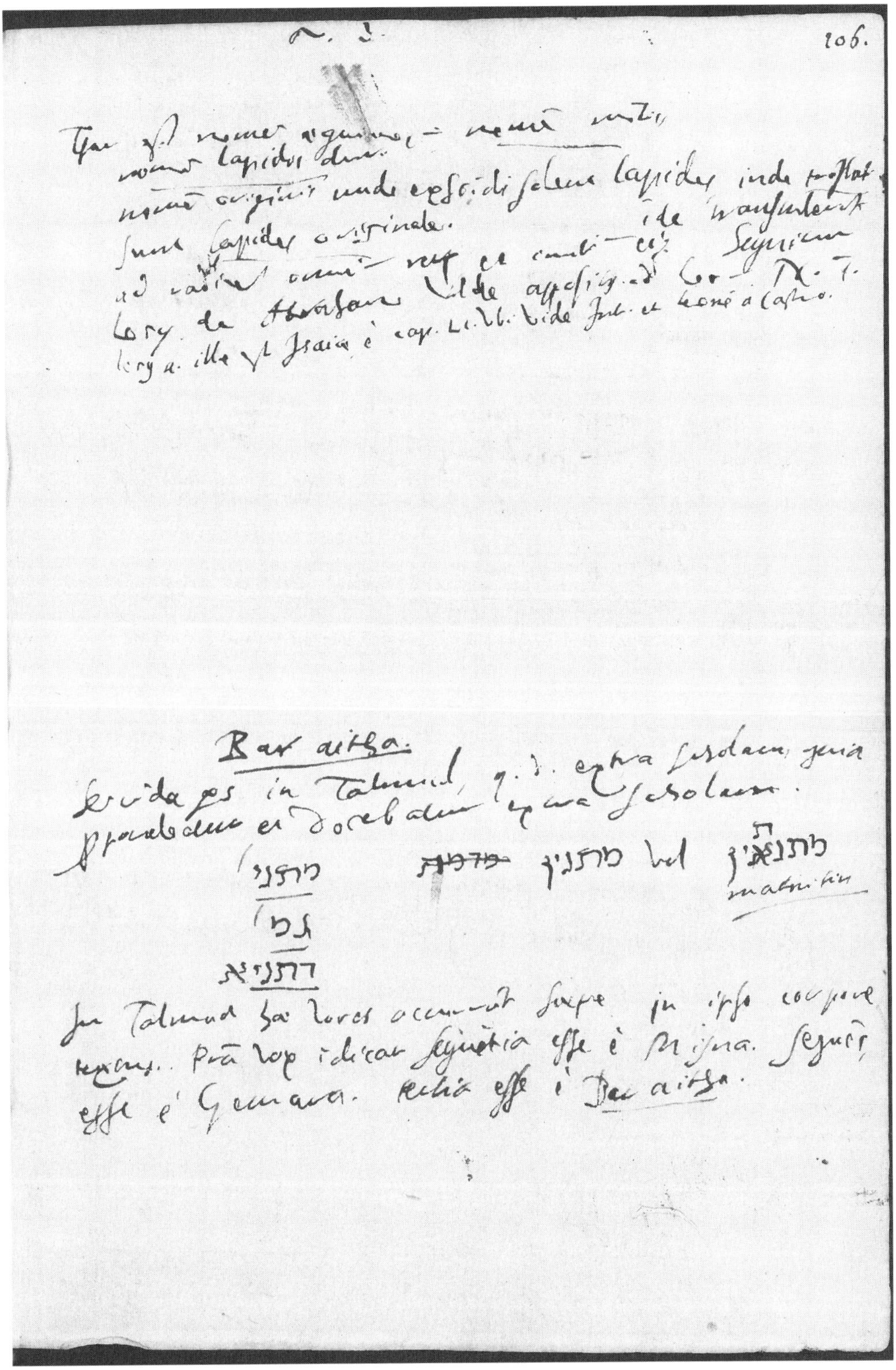

[handwritten Latin notes in Casaubon's hand, largely illegible]

Bar aitza.

[handwritten Latin notes]

מתני׳ | vel | מתניין | אגדה | ברייתא | ברייתי

matnitin

בר | מתניא | דתניא

[handwritten Latin notes]

FIGURE 5.11. Collaborative notes by Casaubon and Jacob Barnet, in Casaubon's hand, on exegesis and talmudic terminology. Bodleian Library MS Casaubon 30, 106 recto.

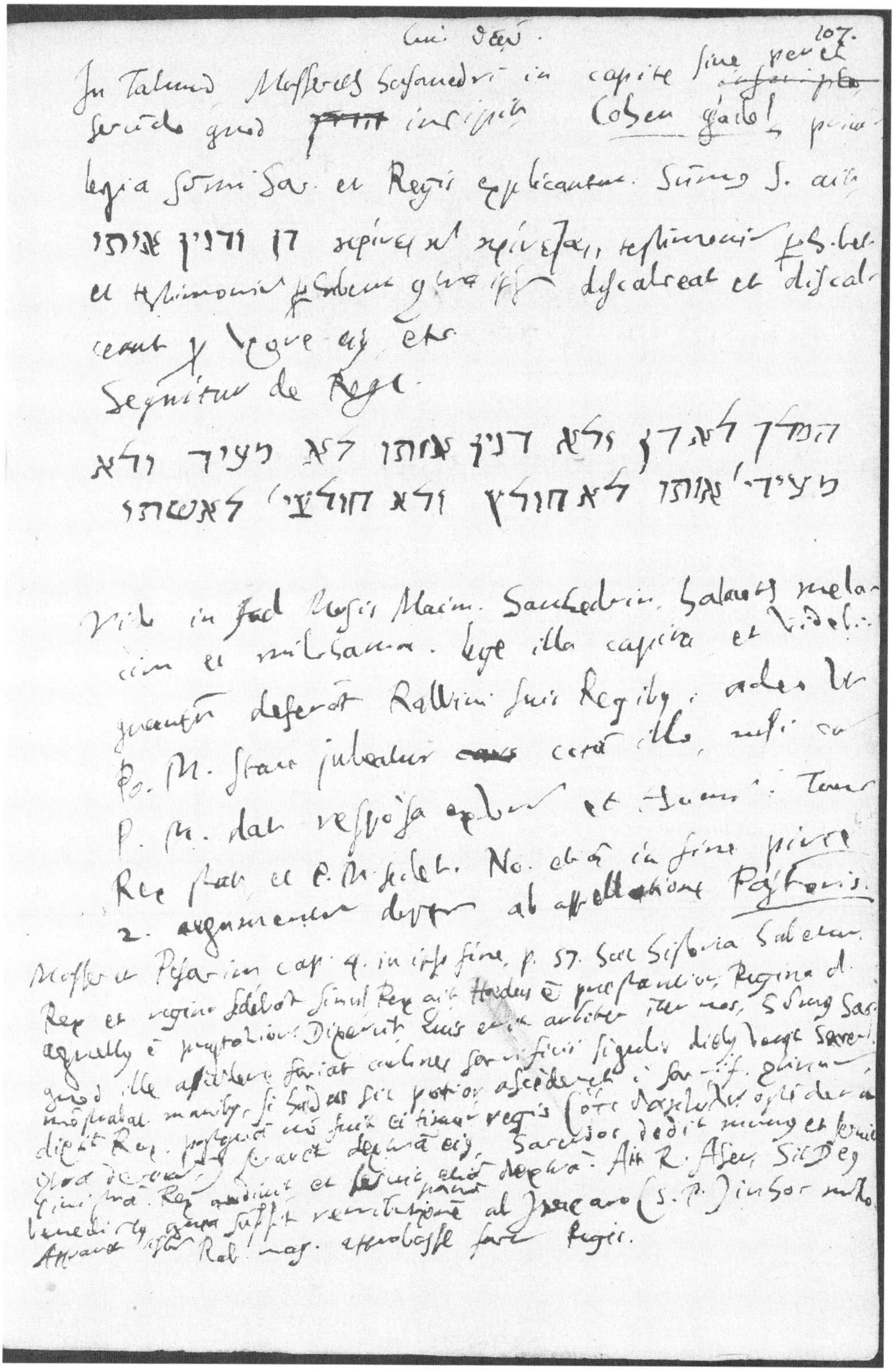

FIGURE 5.12. Further collaborative notes by Casaubon and Jacob Barnet, in Casaubon's hand, on the Talmud. Bodleian Library MS Casaubon 30, 107 recto.

vault four cubits by eight and an opening within it thirteen niches, four on this side, four on that side, three opposite and one to the right of the doorway and one to the left" . . . He also makes a court-yard at the mouth of the cave six cubits square, as much as the coffin with its bearer needs. He may open up within it two other caves, one on either side. R. Simeon, however, says: "four to all its four sides." R. Simeon b. Gamaliel, however, maintains that all must be done according to the rock.[130]

An experienced reader of rabbinic texts will know that a new ordering and exposition of the talmudic material is to be found in the medieval codes and commentaries. At first glance, then, one can only be impressed by the non-chalance with which Casaubon notes down the relevant section in Maimo-nides' *Code:* chapter 21 of the laws of buying and selling in the "Book of Ac-quisition" (21:6). True, on the fringes of the talmudic page lay the reference to the Maimonidean text. But only a scholar possessing considerable famili-arity with rabbinic texts could find his way to the edge of the page.

The probing of the text did not end with the Maimonidean reference. Rather, like a well-trained yeshivah student, Casaubon then retrieved a clar-ification of the Mishnah by means of a gloss by R. Samuel ben Meir (also known as Rashbam), which lies buried in the thicket of commentary on the same talmudic page (Bava Batra 100b). Before transcribing the text Casau-bon noted the identity of Samuel ben Meir as the grandson of Rabbi Solo-mon, namely, Rashi, the preeminent commentator on the Talmud, indicat-ing an awareness of the connection between the two rabbis as expositors of the talmudic text.[131] That established, Casaubon transcribed the passage and translated it into Latin: "It was not Israelite custom to bury individuals sepa-rately. Rather, the entire family was placed in one cave, and each individual in his own niche [*kokh*]." Casaubon then indicated that the entire passage should be examined, since "it seems that they put two cavities in one cham-ber."[132] Rashbam's gloss, according to Casaubon, provided evidence of an

130. A common form of tomb was the natural cave, sometimes resculpted to permit better access. The word *kokh (loculus)* was used to mean a cavity or chamber cut out into a rock, giving rise to man-made tombs and buildings. The *kokhim,* with their various forms of individual interment and primary burial, could easily be associated with familial occupation. For a recent discussion see Hachlili 2005.

131. There is no commentary by Rashi on this part of the Talmud. Rashbam's commentary serves in lieu. On Rashbam as commentator on the Talmud and in particular on Bava Batra, see Urbach 1980, 45–54.

132. Bod MS Casaubon 30, 105 verso: "Notat R. Samuel ben Meir nepos ipsius R. Salomonis, notat in superiora verba Misnae. Non fuit mos in Is. ut sepelirentur singuli separati, sed tota familia in spelunca una, et unus quisque in foramine pro se כל אחד בכוך בפני עצמו. sed vide totum illum locum. nam

Israelite custom of burying in familial tombs, while "each individual was placed in his own niche or chamber." It may have been an association of ideas that led Casaubon to scrawl on the next page of his notebook, after this study of Jewish tombs, niches, and crypts, a somewhat illegible note about the Hebrew word for "rock," although he actually used that material elsewhere, in a discussion of what Jesus meant by calling Peter his "rock."[133]

It will come as no surprise that Casaubon's selection of these passages was not fortuitous. The amassing of knowledge was important, but it all served a greater purpose. Where was Jesus placed when he was taken down from the Cross? This is one of the innumerable questions that Casaubon confronted in his encounter with the Catholic Baronio, and it had a particular contemporary significance. The discovery of the Vigna Sanchez catacomb in 1578 had unleashed fervent displays of devotion.[134] This and other Christian burial sites became renewed centers of pilgrimage.[135] Filippo Neri organized visits to the catacombs, which came to represent the earliest expression of Christian faith, symbolized by the bones of the Christian martyrs who were allegedly interred there. The evidence of the catacombs, with their primitive inscriptions, murals, and reliefs, became the hallmark of true Christianity. Antonio Bosio, the author of the first detailed material description of the Roman catacombs (including one Jewish catacomb), the *Roma sotteranea*, celebrated them in text and image.[136] In the short preface to Bosio's posthumously published work, the Oratorian priest Giovanni Severano took it upon himself to drive home the book's message: it contained "arsenals from which they could take up the arms with which to fight the heretics, and in particular, the iconoclasts."[137] Baronio, who had accompanied Bosio on a tour of the catacombs, was deeply impressed by the subterranean city, with its network of galleries and burial chambers. He proceeded to use these material, iconic remains of the Christian past for the sake of the Catholic faith. Baronio claimed that the Roman catacombs reflected the ancient practice of

---

videtur 2. speluncas ponere uno atrio disiunctas." The printed text reads: "They were not accustomed." It appears that Casaubon wishes to stress the antiquity of Jewish practice. The Hebrew reads: והם לא היו רגילים ליקבר אחד אחד בפני עצמו אלא כל בני משפחה נקברין במערה אחת כל אחד בכוך בפני עצמו הלכך המוכר לחברו קבר מכר לו מקום לשתי מערות וחצר ביניהם... i.e., one who sells somebody a grave should sell him space for two caves separated by an atrium.

133. Ibid., 106 recto: "Tzur est nomen aequivocum nomen montis, nomen lapidis duri."

134. See Grafton 2001, 31–61; Ditchfeld 1995; Rutgers 1995, 5–14.

135. For a recent account of the exploration and use of the catacombs before the sixteenth century see Oryshkevich 2003.

136. For a short description of Bosio's account of the Jewish catacomb see Rutgers 1995, 9–14.

137. Bosio 1632–1634, preface: "Arsenali, donde si pigliano le armi da combattere contra gli Eretici e particolarmente contra gl'Iconoclasti, impugnatori delle sacre Imagini, delle quali sono ripieni i cimiterij." His work was published posthumously. On some of the vagaries of the printing of the work see Finocchiaro 1995, 189–193.

"burying the dead in crypts and in niches hollowed out in them, which was apparently derived from the Jews: that is why Abraham, the father of all believers, bought a double sepulchre from Ephron [Genesis 23]."[138] His impressionistic mode of excavating the past, which included a sprinkling of Jewish sources, aroused Casaubon's ire.

At the outset, Casaubon admitted that the topic was not without its problems.[139] But his solution was to extract all the rabbinic passages that, under Jacob Barnet's supervision, he had painstakingly written out in his copybook, and, in one fell swoop, to transfer them into his anti-Baronian monument. The Talmud, Rashbam, and Maimonides were now all invoked. A discreet rewording of Rashbam's statement—from "they were not accustomed [lo hayu regilim likaber]" to "the custom of the ancient Jews was not to"—strengthened Casaubon's argument, implying that the medieval commentator's gloss referred to first-century Judaea:

> Rabbi Samuel ben Meir writes that the custom of the ancient Jews was not to bury people in individual graves separated from their own family; rather, the entire family would be placed in one cave and each corpse in separate niches. This is what is meant by "Each person in his own niche." Moreover, if an individual head of a family had not inherited his own grave from his parents for his own and his family's use, he would acquire a plot for that purpose.[140]

It is at this juncture that we see the experienced scholar of antiquity show himself in all his colors. Having summoned up the rabbinic evidence, Ca-

---

138. Baronio 1593–1607, II, 346: "Ex Hebraeis namque accepta videtur eiusmodi consuetudo sepeliendi mortuos in cryptis, loculis in eisdem excavatis: ad hoc namque opus Pater credentium Abraham ab Ephron speluncam duplicem emit. In interiori quoque spelunca diximus fuissse sepulchrum Domini excisum in petra."

139. Casaubon 1614, 656; 1654, 577; 1663, 576–577: "De forma sepulcrorum Iudaicorum observationes e scriptis Iudaeorum": "Historia sepulcri in quo repositum est corpus Domini de cruce depositum, difficultatibus non caret: de quibus prius quam dicimus, iuvat commemorare hoc loco, quae de forma sepulcrorum Iudaicorum in Thalmudicis et Rabbinicis scriptis observavimus."

140. Casaubon 1614, 656; 1654, 577–578; 1663, 577–578: "Scribit R. Samuel ben Meir, priscis Iudaeis fuisse in more, ut non sepelirentur singuli separatim a suis, sed tota familia in spelunca una, conditis singulis corporibus in separatis foraminibus. hoc enim volunt haec illius verba כל אחד בכוך בפני עצמו. Propterea solebant singuli patresfamilias, si proprium monumentum sibi et suis non accepissent a parentibus pretio locum sibi parare in eum usum. In Talmud seder Nezikin, sive parte quarta, libro III. Baua Batra, cap. sexto, ubi de rerum acquisitionibus disseritur, discimus, fuisse hoc ius apud Iudaeos, ut si quis monumentum ab aliquo emere vellet, aut locare faciendum, venditor aut manceps operae teneretur cavernam in petra excavare שש על אמות ד quatuor cubitorum supra sex, id est, ut videtur, longam sex, latam quatuor cubitos: in ea autem caverna octo (alij volunt tredicim) cavanda erant foramina, ad singula corpora reponenda. Addunt ante os speluncae fuisse faciendum חצר atrium. Eadem habentur apud Mosem Aegyptium in Iad, lib. XII., sectione Mecira, cap. XXI."

saubon applied it to the context of the Gospels. The evangelists wrote that "Joseph laid it [Jesus' body] in his own new tomb, which was hewn out in the rock: and he rolled a great stone to the door of the sepulchre, and departed" (Matthew 27:60), and that "he took it down, and wrapped it in linen, and laid it in a sepulchre that was hewn in stone, wherein never man before was laid" (Luke 23:53).[141] Casaubon attempted to understand the significance of the hewn-out rock. He recalled another contentious issue: the exact place of Jesus' birth. His favorite author, Strabo, had described the terrain in the area around Jerusalem as rocky.[142] Casaubon used Strabo to uphold his own view on where the birth took place.[143] The evidence of the ancient geographer thus supported his view that the cave or grotto into which Mary put Jesus was not a subterranean gallery, but instead a natural grotto. The description in both Gospels thus conjured up the actual physical characteristics of the terrain with its hewn-out rock—all of which was confirmed by the rabbinic texts.[144] "The body of our Lord," he concluded, "was placed in one of the eight or thirteen niches which as, we said, were usually hewn into each grave. In the talmudic texts the niches are called *kokhim,* and they refer to a stone or rock that they call *golel,* because the rock is rolled against the opening of the grave or tomb."[145] Here we see the historian and antiquarian Casaubon at work. Beginning and ending with the historical and geological evidence, Casaubon rightly places the burial in caves hewn out of the rock. Baronio, in contrast, had one big idea in mind, that of the continuity of Catholic practice, and he recreated the burial of Jesus according to that pic-

141. Casaubon 1614, 656; 1654, 578; 1663, 578: "in historia Christi . . . *monumentum in saxo incisum,* Lucae xxiii.53 . . . et Matth.xxvii.60."

142. Strabo, *Geographia* 16.2.32. Casaubon tries to qualify Strabo's negative assessment of the nature of the terrain of Judaea by insisting that Strabo was referring to the Judaea of his own time (Casaubon 1587, 215): "Ait Iudaeam non esse foelici solo . . . verum dubium non est, quin Strabonis temporibus multo deteriorem agrum Iudaei colerent, quam coluissent olim: quod ex iisdem sacris literis probare posse mihi videor, si id ageretur."

143. See Casaubon 1614, 161–162; 1663, 145, where he quotes the same passage from Strabo 16.2.32: "Porro stabulum in quo natus est Dominus, passim Graeci Latinique Patres appellant σπήλαιον, *speluncam:* nec mirum: nam quum esset Bethlehem in saxeo colle sita, videntur pleraeque domus in saxis fuisse excisae. Strabo observat, totam regionem circa Ierosolyma, ad sexagesimum usque lapidem, esse . . . *petrosam.*"

144. Casaubon 1614, 656; 1654, 578; 1663, 578: "Igitur in historia Christi . . . *monumentum quod Iosephus inciderat in petra* est ille locus qui dicitur in scriptis Rabbinorum קבר *keber,* sepulcrum, a fine, et מערה *mahara,* spelunca, sive antrum a forma: quoniam, ut modo dicebamus ex Evangelistis, cavabatur locus in petra sive saxo: cuius rei petenda ratio est ex eo quod observabamus in disputatione de loco ubi natus Dominus, totum circa Ierusalem solum esse saxosum et ὑπόπετρον, ut appellatur a Strabone."

145. Casaubon 1614, 656; 1654, 578; 1663, 578: "Locus vero ubi positum est corpus Domini, unum erat ex illis octo vel tredecim foraminibus, quae diximus cavari solita in quoque monumento. כוכים ea vocantur in Talmudicis scriptis. in quibus fit etiam mentio lapidis, sive saxi, quod vocant גלל *golel* quia advolvebatur ori monumenti vel conditorij. quo pertinent verba Matth. XXVIII.2 . . . *devolvit lapidem a foribus.* et Luc. XXIV.2. . . . *invenerunt lapidem devolutum a monumento.*"

ture. He imagined Jesus as buried in one of the niches incised in the wall of the catacomb.

Having collated all the relevant Jewish sources, in the next section of the *Exercitationes* Casaubon proceeded to the heart of the matter. The question with which the section opens, "Whether the custom of burying in the sides of crypts originated with the Lord's sepulchre," was clearly purely rhetorical.[146] Baronio had asserted that Christians in Rome copied the ancient Jewish burial customs of the land of Israel. Jews buried their dead "not underneath the earth, but above, in the niches in the sides of the crypts surmounted by arches."[147] Casaubon's correct response was to reassert his contention that neither scripture nor the rabbinic texts could sustain such a view. Rather, Jesus was buried according to the widespread Jewish practices of the time: "Then took they the body of Jesus, and wound it in linen clothes with the spices, as the manner of the Jews is to bury" (John 19:40).

To win this argument mattered, in ecclesiastical terms in the first instance. The importance of the catacombs, as both a model for contemporary Catholic spirituality and practice and a weapon against Protestant iconoclasm, had to be minimized. Casaubon set out to demonstrate the flaws in Baronio's argument, and in this polemical context his flamboyant display of rabbinic learning was not just for show. But a larger issue was also at stake, in more complex ways. Casaubon read the New Testament in its Jewish setting, and condemned Baronio for failing to do so. In fact, as we have seen, Baronio made more serious use of Jewish sources than Casaubon ever admitted. But Casaubon stood for a more systematic approach, one that had become de rigueur for many Christian scholars in the course of the sixteenth century. As early as 1554, the Italian scholar Angelo Canini appended to his Aramaic grammar a monograph titled *Novi Testamenti multorum locorum historica enarratio*: a collection of observations on various obscure passages in the New Testament, which he expounded by means of Hebrew, Syriac (that is, Aramaic), Arabic, and Ethiopic. What distinguished Canini's treatment of this subject was his direct recourse to Jewish texts and history, which enabled him to identify and expound certain "Semitic" passages in the New Testament.[148]

---

146. Casaubon 1614, 657; 1663, 578–579: *"An mos sepeliendi in lateribus cryptarum ortus sit e sepulcro Domini."*

147. Baronio 1593, I, 183: "In petra autem excidi solitas sepulturas apud Iudaeos, iam superius dictum est: eamdemque consuetudinem ad Christianos esse dilapsam, coemeteria quae tum Romae, tum alibi in cryptis arenarijs sunt antiquitus instituta, fidem faciunt: in his enim, non in terra deorsum, sed desuper in lateribus cryptarum fornices sustinentibus, in excavatis ibi loculis reponi cadavera, moris fuit. Quaenam vero in reliquis esset Iudaeorum in mortuis sepeliendis consuetudo, quam in Christi sepultura esse servatam Ioannes [19] affirmat, eam ex parte in defuncto Lazaro idem insinuat."

148. See Weinberg 2006.

Canini's was the first word in this area, not the last. Later scholars, from the Protestant converts Immanuel Tremellius and Joseph Scaliger to the Italian Jew Azariah de' Rossi, set out, in their different ways, to demonstrate that a philologically sound and historically rich interpretation of the New Testament required systematic use of rabbinic texts. A generation after Casaubon, the influential commentator and theologian Johannes Cocceius exaggerated when he claimed, in the preface to his translation of the Mishnah tractates Sanhedrin and Makkot, "What I am doing is new: for I am trying to show that understanding of the Talmud and talmudic writings sheds a brilliant light on the New Testament."[149] In fact, Cocceius stood out not for the novelty of his method but for the learning and precision with which he pursued it. A century after Cocceius, as David Ruderman has taught us, William Wotton fought to convince his contemporaries that knowledge of the Mishnah was essential to proper study of the New Testament.[150] He drew up a history of systematic Christian study of the Mishnah, which began with Cocceius. But Wotton traced the roots of this approach to the humanism of the later sixteenth century. Scaliger, he recalled, "knew the worth" of Maimonides as a guide to Jewish law; "however Joseph Scaliger did not stop there: he had read the *Misna* carefully, as appears from many places of his Writings."[151] Wotton knew that even though Scaliger had never devoted a full-scale work to the Mishnah, he deserved a place in this story. So does Casaubon.

Although many Christian scholars attacked these questions in the decades after 1600, Johann Buxtorf the elder surpassed all the rest, including John Selden, in his impressive command of Jewish tradition. Exegesis of the Judaic parts of the New Testament, he showed, could not be achieved only by systematic study of Moses Maimonides and occasional excursions back to the Talmud. Rather, the Christian exegete must do his best to follow the development of Jewish tradition in the postbiblical period, from Josephus to the Mishnah and from there to the Babylonian and Palestinian Talmuds and their interpreters.[152] Buxtorf's surviving research notes offer impressive evidence not only of the pertinacity with which he questioned Jews about their ways, but also of the range of his Jewish learning and the fluency with which

149. Cocceius 1629: "Sed novum est quod molior ostendere nempe cognitionem Talmudis, Thalmudicorumque scriptorum ad Novi Testamenti illustrationem insignem lucem affere." Cocceius' approach was novel in other ways, for which see Yoffie 2004.

150. Ruderman 2007, esp. 77–93, 105–110.

151. Reprinted in ibid., 109; for Cocceius see ibid, 107.

152. A prime example of Buxtorf's ability to scan the Jewish sources and select the relevant material for his exegesis is provided in his dedicatory letter to his *De abbreviaturis* (Buxtorf 1613), where he discusses Paul's flagellation by the Jews in the light of Jewish sources.

he read, excerpted, and translated texts, the mysteries of which other Christians could not explore unless someone who had undergone a traditional Jewish education was willing to play the role of Virgil.[153]

One way to describe what Casaubon accomplished is to compare his work with that of Buxtorf. During his precious hours of study with Jacob Barnet, Casaubon dipped his toes into the sea of the Talmud. He did so in order to understand, as he saw it, some of the customs of the ancient Jews relevant to the life and death of Jesus. And the late talmudic evidence provided him, in this instance, with the apposite material to emend Baronio's ideological reconstruction. Yet Casaubon's Jewish learning, as we have seen, was eclectic. He himself acknowledged that he could not rival Buxtorf's command of the core Jewish materials. Considered as a "Christian Hebraist"—to use the category that has become accepted in modern scholarship —Casaubon falls short of the highest standards both in range of reading and in technical virtuosity. Many of the texts that he knew best—from Kimhi's grammar to the *Yuhasin,* and from Galatino to the *Josippon*—were relatively common. Like so many of his colleagues, he often contented himself with late intermediary sources even when he could have replaced them with the older, more rebarbative originals. No wonder, then, that he has never found a place in modern lineages of Christian Hebraism.

Yet Casaubon's approach to the Jewish world had distinctive qualities, some of which Buxtorf's lacked. Another comparison will help to bring these out. Joseph Scaliger, Casaubon's most honored friend and partner in philological discussion, also devoted himself to using Jewish sources to explicate the New Testament. Like Casaubon, Scaliger knew, as he told the students who lived in his house in Leiden, that "there is just no way to read the Talmud without the living voice of a Jew."[154] Scaliger had even more experience to go on. For six months or so he read the Talmud with a Jew named Philippus Ferdinandus, who had been made professor of Arabic at Leiden on his recommendation. These lessons proved transformative. Scaliger informed his students that many of Jesus' teachings in the Gospels were not attacks on Jewish beliefs but standard Jewish precepts, also attested in the

153. For the history of talmudic studies in the German world in the century after Buxtorf—and some striking comparisons with the situation in the Netherlands—see Wilke 2000. Katchen 1984 offers much information on Jewish studies in the seventeenth-century Netherlands.

154. Scaliger 1695, 384; 1740, II, 590–591: "THALMUD. On ne sçauroit l'entendre sans la vive voix d'un Juif: le Juif qui lisoit icy, m'en a appris quelque chose, nous y leusmes ensemble. Je fus auteur qu'on le mist Professeur en Arabe; il le parloit bien, mais il ne sçavoit pas les regles, le les luy formois; il avait assez d'auditeurs; Junius luy portoit grand'envie. Les Chrestiens ont terriblement chastré le Thalmud. J'ay cette edition là, les Juifs n'en veulent point acheter. Le Thalmud imprimé à Basle parce qu'il est chastré, les Juifs n'en veulent point."

Talmud: "I have noted many things in the New Testament, which are in the Talmud. Christ brings them forth from the normal speech of the Jews. A case in point is the proverb 'New wine is not put in old vessels,' which indicates that nothing should be changed too violently."[155] Scaliger would not have needed Ferdinand's help to identify this Jewish text, from Avot 4, since many Christian scholars already knew it. Moreover, it did not provide a perfect parallel to Mark 2:22. Still, Scaliger clearly saw that the Talmud offered information, not only about the rituals and beliefs Jesus condemned, but also about those that he accepted. He went so far as to say: "I approve of certain Jewish ceremonies that Christ took over." Moreover, Scaliger made clear that Jesus had dressed and worshiped as a Jew: "A certain Norman denies that Jesus went about in Jewish clothing. He celebrated the Supper by Jewish custom; he would not have dared to do otherwise."[156] Like Scaliger's insistence, decades before, that the Passover ritual shed light on the Last Supper, these were strong statements. As Scaliger must have known, the Portuguese Inquisition long before had charged that the Scottish historian and poet George Buchanan told the king of Scotland that a Christian must eat the paschal lamb in order to win salvation.[157]

Scaliger's statements were sharper, more forthright, and more consistent than Casaubon's—a fact that may reflect the differences in their direct experience of Jews and Judaism, as well as the differences in their temperaments.

155. Scaliger 1695, 328; 1740, II, 522: "Talia multa annotavi in Novo Testamento, quae sunt in Thalmud, et Christus affert illa ex communi sermone Judaeorum. Item illud est proverbium *Vinum novum non ponitur in vasis veteribus* et notatur nihil esse violenter faciendum." See further de Jonge 1975, 84.

156. Scaliger 1695, 221; 1740, II, 410: "Cerimonias quasdam probo Judaeorum, quas Christus usurpavit. Quidam Normannus negat Christum incessisse vestibus Judaicis; celebravit Coenam ut Judaei solebant, non ausus fuisset aliter. Ego multa praeclara de Judaeis habeo quae egregie sumpsit Plessaeus. Habui multa ex Chaldaicis libris scriptis ante Christi tempora."

157. James Laing, doctor of the Sorbonne and controversialist, spread the accusation against Buchanan, and told the story of John Major's refutation of his heresy, in 1581—a date close enough to the publication of Scaliger's *De emendatione temporum* in 1583 to underline the intrepidness of Scaliger's use of the Passover Haggadah in that work. See Laing 1581, 39 recto: "Homo sacrarum literarum imperitissimus, simulque impudentissimus ita regi respondit tu domine similiter debes agnum paschae comedere, si vis salutem consequi"; 39 verso–40 recto: "Itaque maister Iohannes maior de quaestione proposita ita Regi respondit, ille qui dicit Rex christianissime te debere comedere agnum paschae, vellet te Iudaeum esse, sive more Iudaeorum vivere, qui negant christum adhuc venisse, aut de virgine Maria natum esse. Agnus enim paschae est aliquid caeremoniale ut loquuntur doctores theologi, sed omne caeremoniale, christo iam passo fuit mortuum, id quod etiam videtur satis clare dicere apostolus quinto capite ad Galatas: testificor autem cursus omni homini circumcidenti se, quoniam deditor est universae legis faciendae. Et mox postea, Nam in christo Iesu neque circumcisio aliquid valet, neque praeputium. Caeterum Georgius bucananus, tanti sceleris inauditi et incogniti convictus, clanculum aufugit (sociis eius captis atque combustis) alioqui ille cum caeteris combustus fuisset. Deinde profectus est in lusitaniam, ubi pro haeretico captus et accusatus fuit, et nisi celeri fuga sibi salutem quaesivisset, de illo actum fuisset." Before the Inquisition, Buchanan simply dismissed the accusation: Aitken 1939, 36: "De Iudaismo nunquam cogitavi." The court seems to have accepted his testimony. See in general McFarlane 1981, 68–69; and, for a different view, Williamson 1994, 99–100.

At some point between 1583 and 1593, Scaliger visited Avignon. There he came to know a Jewish woman, who was poor but decently dressed—a fact that led him to admire Jewish charity. She ate with him: only fish and bread, no meat. And she impressed him with her ability to read Hebrew. Scaliger's friend told him many interesting things—including the story that the Jews of Avignon, in order to save their best scholars from papal tyranny, had sent them away and made their most incompetent circumcised Jew become their rabbi. When Scaliger laughed at this tale, she replied: "Don't laugh, my lord: your Jesus was circumcised, too." After that encounter, it seems, Scaliger never ceased thinking about the Jewish elements in the Gospels.[158]

Scaliger's *De emendatione temporum* of 1583 won the admiration of the world of learning for many reasons—not least for his use of Jewish material to recreate the Last Supper. But he knew that some of his other ideas would not find ready assent. In 1591 he wrote to his friend Jacques-Auguste de Thou that he could not complete his planned notes on the New Testament "without my books, for it is vital to have the Talmud and several other books. If we were together, engaged in informal conversation, I could speak to you about many things relevant to this, and in my view that would be enough to make you happy. With someone else, I would neither want to do this, nor dare to."[159] The happy accident of a research post in Holland gave Scaliger

158. On the Jews of Avignon and their small, closely regulated community see Ruderman 1981, 4–11; and Benbassa 1999. For Scaliger's visit see Scaliger 1695, 220–221; 1740, II, 409–410: "Eram Avenione, et novi pauperem Judaeam, sed honeste indutam, non mendicant Judaei, et melius subveniunt suis quam Christiani, nec patiuntur suos mendicare. Mihi dixit, nos sumus tantum tres Tribus mixtae, ut vix possimus scire ex qua simus, reliquae Tribus sunt perditae; perierunt nescio quomodo: et dixit mihi causam, quare non haberent doctos Rabbinos, nam Rabbinum eorum contra quem disputaveram, vocabant Asinum. Nempe Pius V. semel voluit ejicere Judaeos Avenione; tum quidam monuit Papam, Judaeos multa debere Christianis, ideo suasum ut relinqueret quosdam qui manerent ibi ut persolverent saltem foenus. Ergo dimiserunt praestantissimos suos Rabbinos. Agnoverunt quendam ex suis occisum, quem ideo agnoverunt quia habebat suum Berit. Cum riderem, dixit illa, ne ride, mi Domine, nam et vester Jesus fuit circumcisus. Dicebat mihi, nullos habemus Sacerdotes, nam multi se dicunt, sed non possunt probare, sumus confusi, et si haberemus Sanctuarium, non sacrificaremus, sed oraremus, quia non habemus Sacerdotes; non possunt extra templum sacrificare. Ego illi mulieri dedi panes, volebat quidem mecum edere pisces, sed non carnem. Mirum est quam ibi doctae sunt mulieres, multa tenent Hebraice; legunt sua scripta Provincialia characteribus Hebraicis, et in Germania etiam. Habeo librum Avenionensem Characteribus Hebraicis." This visit took place before Scaliger left France for Holland in 1593. In his edition of the *Canon Paschalis* of Hippolytus, Scaliger thanked the Jews of Avignon for helping him reach a deeper understanding of the Jewish calendar (Scaliger 1595, *4 recto). It is possible that they helped him gather the talmudic extracts on calendrical matters that he left behind in France, to his regret (Grafton 1983–1993, 421–424). Philipp Nothaft, whom we thank for his advice, will examine this question in his forthcoming study of the chronology of the life of Jesus.

159. Scaliger to Jacques-Auguste de Thou, 13 April 1591, in Scaliger 1879, 284: "Les notes du Nouveau Testament ne se peuvent faire sans mes livres, car il fault avoir le Talmud et plusieurs aultres livres. Mais si nous estions ensemble, en discours familiers, je vous pourrois encores entretenir de beaucoup de choses sur ce, qui vous contenteroient à mon advis. À un aultre, je ne le vouldrois ni oserois." See de Jonge 1975, 84.

the chance to pursue these adventurous thoughts in good company. As an aged professor in Leiden, he welcomed the arrival of Portuguese and other Jews in Holland. He liked to see the women of the Portuguese community in Amsterdam sitting in front of their houses, observing the sabbath, and he contrasted the enlightened policy of the Estates of Holland with that of Swiss cities like Basel, which had exiled their Jews: "The Jews should never be expelled; they bring us profit, and we learn from them."[160] Casaubon spent far less time with Jacob Barnet than Scaliger did with Philippus Ferdinandus. Their conversations took place in isolation and under a kind of spotlight as religious and secular authorities planned Barnet's conversion, not in the easier circumstances that Scaliger and Ferdinandus enjoyed. And Casaubon, as we have seen again and again, lacked Scaliger's taste for facts and texts that seemed to call fundamental truths into question.

Yet the differences, in the end, seem less striking than the similarities. Both Scaliger and Casaubon devoted much of their lives to the study of early Christianity, which they saw as part of a larger ancient culture. Both believed that that culture could be understood only by scholars who took Jewish texts, histories, and customs into account—especially the culture of the Hellenistic and imperial periods, when so many Jews had spoken, written, and worshiped in Greek.[161] More radically still, both argued that no modern scholar could understand Christianity itself without mastering a wide range of difficult Jewish sources. Both learned Hebrew well enough to write letters in it (although the surviving draft of Scaliger's letter to the Samaritan community in Cairo, asking for information about manuscripts, is less fluent than Casaubon's surviving letter to Julius Conradus Otto).[162]

Both carried out these intellectual journeys at least as much in the pri-

160. Scaliger 1695, 218; 1740, II, 406: "Les Juifs viendront à Harlem, et y auront Synagogue et privilege des Estats, erit magna in his regionibus commoditas, ils seront plus libres qu'ailleurs, ils renient ouvertement J. C. Cela ostera le profit aux Lombards. Il y a plus de 200 Juifs Portugais à Amsterdam, et vous verrez le Samedy les femmes bien habillées s'asseoir devant leurs portes, sans rien faire. Ils ont enlevé tous les volumes Hebreux qu'ils ont peu trouver, et ont fait venir des Rabins"; 1695, 218–219; 1740, II, 407–408: "Friburgi Brisgoiae sunt docti Judaei, distant Basilea uno die. In Helvetia non credo fuisse ullam Synagogam Judaeorum; statim post Lutherum, Protestantes expulerunt Judaeos, iverunt in Bohemiam et Poloniam. Non sunt expellendi, lucrum afferunt, deinde ab illis discimus. Raro Judaeus aliquis Christianus factus, fuit bonus, semper sunt nequam . . . Erat Basileae praestantissima Judaeorum Synagoga. Extant adhuc sepulchra Hebraica."

161. Casaubon saw Scaliger as *the* authority on these matters: see Casaubon 1710, 124: "Hieron. De Scriptor. Eccles. in *Petrus* dicit, Petrum praedicasse Evangelium $\tau\hat{\eta}$ $\delta\iota\alpha\sigma\pi\sigma\rho\hat{\alpha}$ Judaeorum per Asiam et Pontum. Expende locum Josephi p. 426. sed ante omnes vid. Jos. Scaligerum in Euseb. sive Canones Isagog. 278. ubi breviter rem expedit docta distinctione." Here he refers to Scaliger 1606, *Isagogici canones*, 278–279.

162. Scaliger's draft is preserved in Leiden University Library MS Or. 6882; reproduced in Vrolijk and van Ommen 2009, 50.

vate role of readers, working for their own instruction and that of an intimate circle, as in the public one of writers seeking to address a wider readership. Jewish learning had much to teach Christians; but some of the lessons evidently called for private rumination rather than public presentation. At times, however, both men extended their webs of reading, annotation, and meditation from the margins of their books and notebooks into their publications. At times, too, their weaving became for a time a shared, or collaborative, activity. The strands touched not only texts but human beings: Jews, whom they could see as complex individuals, and for whom they could feel, as they showed in different ways, a protective affection that did not depend on the Jews' willingness to convert. Private men who lived intensive, even obsessive, lives of silent study, Scaliger and Casaubon also cared deeply about the social dimension of intellectual inquiry, which they would probably have called "civil conversation."[163] When they embarked on their journeys into the labyrinths of tradition, Jews were among the companions whom they prized, and whose help, as they acknowledged, they needed.

In the end, though, the comparison yields one very important difference. Casaubon showed at times a striking personal openness, not only to Jews, but also to Jewish beliefs and practices. Like Casaubon, Scaliger owned collections of Jewish prayers; but no surviving evidence attests that he shared Casaubon's appreciation for the beauty and variety of the Jewish liturgy of his own day, or even his warm interest in the details of synagogue ritual.[164] Like Casaubon, Scaliger owned a copy of *Sefer Hasidim*. But whereas Casaubon saw something of the beauty of the lives the book recorded, Scaliger dismissed it as "a book of no great age, which contains some of the sayings of the Jewish masters."[165] Buxtorf, for all his vast Judaic learning, used language that dripped with contempt to describe his voyages into Jewish communities in search of texts; and Scaliger—for all the quizzical humor with which he encountered the great Judaist's Judaeophobia—sometimes did the same. Like Scaliger, Casaubon found it easy to make demeaning remarks about the ignorance of the Hellenistic Jews and the fantasies and pedantry of the rabbis. But he also found his way, rather like the seventeenth-century Dutch Talmudists who knew Jews and Judaism far better than he could, to a

163. For this side of Casaubon see esp. Considine 2003.

164. Bonaventura Vulcanius' inventory of Scaliger's manuscripts includes this entry (Leiden University Library MS Vulc. 108, part 5, reproduced in Vrolijk and van Ommen 2009, 26): "Egregium volumen, continens hymnos et alia omnia quae Judaei in Synagoga canunt. estque alius liber ab Euchalogio Judaeorum sive Diurnali."

165. Scaliger 1627, 298: "Librum חסידים habeo; opus non vetustum, quaedam γνωμολογικὰ Iudaeorum Magistrorum continens."

warm appreciation of the Jewish tradition as hard to define as it is impossible to ignore.[166]

It is not easy to state what Casaubon hoped to achieve, or to work out the extent to which he realized his aspirations. The terms that he and Scaliger used for their work—and the actors' categories that these embody—were complex and sometimes contradictory. Their full range of meanings still eludes us. When these men called themselves "grammarians" or "critics," they did not mean that they were classical scholars in a sense now easily recognized.[167] They did not claim to be "Christian Hebraists," or indeed "patristic scholars." Yet their project was at once classical, Hebraic, and patristic, in complex combinations, and the depth and interest of what they achieved are clear. It seems a pity that their enterprise lacks a modern name, especially given the many ways in which it adumbrates the discoveries of the last half century. At least, though, we can now see that when Casaubon studied Calvin's catechism in Hebrew, he labored in the same vocation that had occupied him for most of his lifetime.

166. See Wilke 2000.
167. See Parenty 2009.

APPENDIXES

GLOSSARY

BIBLIOGRAPHY

ACKNOWLEDGMENTS

INDEX

The Long Apprenticeship:
Casaubon and Arabic

Alastair Hamilton

In August 1592, while he was still living in Geneva, Isaac Casaubon told his friend Philippe de La Canaye de Fresnes that he was about to embark on the study of Arabic. In order to prepare himself, he said, he was busy reading Hebrew, and would then proceed to the language which had been used by many of the very "greatest philosophers" to have contributed to every branch of learning.[1]

For a student of antiquity with an interest in the eastern Mediterranean, the decision to tackle the most widely spoken language in the area was understandable. Apologies for the study of Arabic were plentiful.[2] In the thirteenth century Roger Bacon had already emphasized its value for the increase of knowledge,[3] and, three hundred years later, other scholars were warmly recommending that it be studied and taught—Juan Luis Vives, Nicolas Clenardus, Richard Argentine, Robert Wakefield, Ruthger Spey, and Guillaume Postel. Postel, who dwelled on its importance for missionaries, doctors, and astrologers, also stressed its use for the discovery of the physical world. Arabic, he wrote in 1538, was understood throughout Africa and Asia, from the Atlantic to the eastern coasts of the Indian Ocean.[4] It thus seemed invaluable for travelers, diplomats, merchants, topographers, and explorers.

Yet, despite the many reasons advanced for studying it, the instruments for learning Arabic were limited in 1592. There was no serviceable dictio-

---

1. Casaubon 1709, 569.
2. For a survey see Hamilton 1985, 69–85.
3. Bacon 1897, I, 92.
4. Postel 1538b, D1 recto—D2 verso; Postel ca. 1538, D1 verso, D2 recto—D3 recto.

nary in print. The only grammar of any use was the one published by Postel
in about 1538, but that was short and hardly adequate for anyone wanting to
make proper progress. Most of the works that had appeared on Arabic went
no further than a discussion of the alphabet, and there were few Arabic texts
available in the West. Students such as Casaubon had one great advantage,
and that was the knowledge of Hebrew; they were thus already acquainted
with the structure of a Semitic language. Yet, as Casaubon soon discovered,
the distance between Arabic and Hebrew remained large, and he dismissed
Postel's claim that the mastery of Hebrew could lead to an easy mastery of
Arabic within two years. In order to bridge the gap between Hebrew and
Arabic, prospective Arabists had a restricted choice: they could depend on
the few native Arabic speakers who found their way to Europe; they could
approach Europeans who had either spent some time in the Arab world or,
in even rarer cases, had somehow managed to learn the language on their
own; or, best of all, they could go to the Arab world themselves.[5]

It was several years before Casaubon made any significant advance in his
studies. In 1596 he moved from Geneva to Montpellier and began to form
his collection of Arabic material.[6] And in 1600 he settled in Paris. There,
when he was already over forty, he at last got to grips with the language. In
Paris, where he was immediately allowed the run of the library of his patron
Jacques-Auguste de Thou and access, though limited, to the royal library, he
found books and manuscripts in, and on, Arabic, as well as scholars who
knew it.[7] His first teacher was Etienne Hubert, physician to the French king
and professor at the Collège Royal, who had spent a year in Morocco serving as physician to the ruler, Aḥmad al-Manṣūr, and, while he was in Mar-
rakesh, had assembled a collection of manuscripts.[8] Casaubon could benefit,
too, from the society of Arnoult de l'Isle, Hubert's predecessor at the Collège
Royal, who had also once been the physician of the king of France and then
of Aḥmad al-Manṣūr. He had returned to Paris in 1599 and would go again
to Morocco as French ambassador in 1606. And there were other men of letters in Paris who shared Casaubon's interest: Jean Martin, likewise a physician, who probably lectured in Arabic at the Collège Royal;[9] and the councilor Etienne Fleury.[10]

5. R. Jones 1988, 13–24, 64–123.

6. Bod MS Casaubon 22, 43 verso, 46 recto.

7. For Casaubon's impressions of Paris see Pattison 1892, 115–121.

8. Casaubon 1709, 132. For Hubert and Arnoult de l'Isle see Balagna Coustou 1989, 114–117; for the
Arabists in Paris, Toomer 1996, 26–35.

9. Lefranc 1893, 383.

10. Casaubon 1850, I, p. 374.

295

Above all Casaubon sought inspiration from a man no longer in Paris: Joseph Justus Scaliger, who had moved to Leiden in 1593 and with whom Casaubon had exchanged his first letters in 1594. By the time Casaubon arrived in Paris, Scaliger had completed a Latin-Arabic glossary, destined to remain in manuscript,[11] and had acquired a justifiably high reputation as an Arabist.[12] It was to him that Casaubon confided the details of his own progress.

Casaubon soon had a sizable collection of books on Arabic. When acquired by the British Museum long after his death, they would form the basis of the Arabic collection at what is now the British Library.[13] From these we can catch a glimpse of how he proceeded.[14] The first, in a mixed volume containing grammatical texts, is the *Alphabetum arabicum* of Jacob Christmann, professor at Heidelberg, who discussed the different elements—the number, name, shape, and phonetic value—of the Arabic consonants and provided an Arabic version of the Lord's Prayer and a passage from the Epistle to the Philippians as exercises. It was published in 1582.[15] This is followed by the *Specimen characterum arabicorum,* issued in 1592 by Franciscus Raphelengius, the son-in-law of the printer Christophe Plantin, who had moved from Antwerp to Leiden to manage the local branch of his father-in-law's publishing firm and who was himself appointed professor of Hebrew at the university.[16] Intended mainly as a specimen of the firm's Arabic types, it contained only the Arabic alphabet and an Arabic version of Psalm 50 (51). Then comes a mutilated edition (lacking the introduction) of the *Introductio in linguam arabicam,* by Bartholomeus Radtmann, professor at Frankfurt an der Oder. This, too, came out in 1592 and was only about the Arabic alphabet. Since no Arabic types were available in Frankfurt, the Arabic characters had to be filled in by hand.[17] The fourth booklet is the *Alphabetum arabicum,* produced in 1592 by Giambattista Raimondi, the director of the Typographia Medicea in Rome, one of the first presses to print with Arabic types. Although this work, like the others, focuses upon the alphabet, it also includes a syllabary illustrating the vocalization, as well as sample texts of the Lord's Prayer, the Ave Maria, Psalms 112 (113) and 116 (117), and the first

11. Leiden University Library, MS Or. 212.

12. See Fück 1955, 47–53.

13. Birrell 1980, 64.

14. Hamilton 2009.

15. Casaubon's copy is BL 622.h.2.(4). For a discussion of the book see R. Jones 1988, 161–162, 265–266.

16. BL 622.h.2.(3).

17. Casaubon's copy, BL 622.h.2.(2), lacks the title page and was identified by R. Jones 1988, 72–74, 167–169, 241–242.

verses of the Gospel of John.[18] Although Casaubon seems to have owned the *Compendium grammatices arabicae,* published by Ruthger Spey in Heidelberg in 1583 and based on Postel's Arabic grammar,[19] and even though he knew Postel's work, none of the books he owned would have enabled him to go very far. Nevertheless, he initially made swift progress. In November 1601 he informed Scaliger that he had started to compile a word list,[20] and he scoured the books in his possession for Arabic words.[21] Like Scaliger, however, he was under no illusions about the difficulties of the language.[22]

Casaubon's enthusiasm for his new subject was such that Marcus Welser, the classical scholar in Augsburg, feared that it might distract him from his other studies.[23] But in fact Casaubon remained loyal to his other commitments, more demanding and more urgent. For Arabic, he relied on the presence of his teachers. Casaubon seems to have abandoned his Arabic studies, however briefly, when Etienne Hubert had to leave Paris. He resumed them when Adriaen Willemsz arrived in France with a letter from Scaliger in March 1602.

Adriaen Willemsz, from the Dutch seaport of Flushing, had matriculated at the Faculty of Letters of Leiden University in 1595 at the age of eighteen and subsequently switched to the study of medicine.[24] He probably received some instruction in Arabic from the Polish convert from Judaism Philippus Ferdinandus, who, on the insistence of Scaliger, was appointed to the chair of Arabic in Leiden for a trial period in August 1599 but died before the year was out.[25] Adriaen was also taught by Peter Kirsten, a physician from Breslau who was traveling across Europe in the hope of finding someone to teach him enough Arabic to read the works of Avicenna in the original and who had met an Arabic-speaking Christian who assisted him. While visiting the Low Countries to seek out Scaliger, he encountered Adriaen.[26] Adriaen

18. BL 622.h.2.(2). For an extensive discussion of Raimondi's work see R. Jones 1988, 169–172, 268.

19. Bod MS Casaubon 22, 119 recto. For Spey see R. Jones 1988, 163–166.

20. Casaubon 1709, 132.

21. See, for example, his notes on the flyleaf of his copy of Johannes Stoeffler's *Elucidatio fabricae ususque astrolabii* (Paris, 1585), BL 531.f.14.

22. Casaubon 1709, 143 (27 March 1602): "Video longum esse iter, non dicam, ad cognitionem ejus linguae perfectam, sed vel mediocrem notitiam. Nam quod venuste sic, ut nihil possit magis, scriptum a te, in aditu blandiri hanc linguam; cum vero intus admissus fuerit aliquis, commendatitiis esse opus; id, inquam, experti reapse nos sumus. Initio cum huic curae primum adjecimus animum, comparationem quandam institueramus Hebraicae Arabicaeque linguae: quo incepto, fatebor enim ingenue, visi sumus nobis per dies aliquammultos belli homines, qui eramus saperdae meri. Fruantur illi sane opinione sua, qui ex aliquot pagellarum intuitu, non enim lectione, satis scio, repente prodierunt Arabes."

23. Casaubon 1709, 146.

24. Du Rieu 1875, 42.

25. See Alastair Hamilton, "Ferdinand, Philip (1556–1599)," in *ODNB* 2004.

26. BL MS Burney 364, 332 recto–verso. See also Kirsten 1608, 5, 7. For Kirsten as an Arabist see Fück 1955, 57–59.

thus arrived in France with some grounding in Arabic. He became Casaubon's most trusted teacher and collaborator.

Casaubon was devoted to Adriaen. He and his wife regarded him as an adopted son, and the two men worked their way through the Arabic texts that Casaubon had acquired.[27] Nearly all of these were publications of the Typographia Medicea in Rome. There was the *Kitāb nuzhat al-mushtāq,* an excerpt from the large work on geography by the twelfth-century topographer al-Idrīsī, who was born in Morocco but spent much of his life in Sicily. In Europe al-Idrīsī was known as "Geographus arabs" or "Nubiensis" until John Selden identified him in 1646.[28] Casaubon and Adriaen started to translate the work.[29] Then there was the Roman edition of the Arabic Gospels, which had appeared in 1591. Casaubon acquired it in 1601, but he did not start reading it properly, with Adriaen, until 1603.[30] They also read the Typographia Medicea editions of Avicenna's great medical work, *al-Qānūn,*[31] and of *al-Ajurrūmiyya,* by the fourteenth-century Moroccan grammarian al-Sanhājī. Casaubon's marginalia to this last book survive in the British Library.[32] They also started studying the Koran.[33]

Casaubon and Adriaen planned a joint publication. In 1602 David Rivault de Fleurance, the future tutor of Louis XIII, presented Casaubon with an Arabic manuscript of two hundred proverbs mainly attributed to Abū 'Ubayd in the eighth century, but in fact of various origin. Rivault accompanied the manuscript with a Latin translation by a Maronite. Casaubon thought that the translation was poor. He and Adriaen set about copying out the Arabic text, and Casaubon dispatched Adriaen's transcription of the first 177 proverbs to Scaliger in October 1602,[34] suggesting that he translate and annotate them. Scaliger did so, and Adriaen then copied out the rest of the manuscript; but Scaliger never managed to complete his work.[35]

At about this time Casaubon also drew up an Arabic word list. It is in his interleaved copy of the *Dittionario novo Hebraico,* a Hebrew-Italian-Latin

27. Casaubon 1709, 213–214.

28. Toomer 1996, 23, 65, 68; 2009, II, 619.

29. Casaubon 1709, 111. See also Casaubon 1850, I, 481–482, 509, 510, 525. For the translation see Bod MS Casaubon 17, 81 recto–96 recto.

30. BL Or.72.c.5. Casaubon recorded his acquisition of the book in 1601 on the flyleaf, but subsequently changed the date to 1603, adding that he had taken it up again later.

31. Casaubon 1709, 168.

32. BL 14593.b.31.

33. Casaubon 1850, I, 481–482; Hamilton 2009, 148–149.

34. Leiden University Library 874.D.7:3. Vrolijk and van Ommen 2009, 98–99.

35. The episode is recounted by Casaubon in his preface to Scaliger 1610, i3 verso–i4 recto, and is reconstructed by Erpenius in his edition of the proverbs, Erpenius 1614, *3 verso–*4 recto. For a discussion of the proverbs themselves see Sellheim 1954, 56–89.

זה ספר הנקרא על אשר חבח בשם בבהרותו

צמח דוד

הישיש והנעלה דוד רופא מובהק ופילוסוף מעיר ספוליטי
הלא הוא משבט יהודה ממשפחת התפוחים א'מד' בתי אבות המיוחסות שהגלה טיטוס מירושלם
לרומה העיר המהוללה׃ בוהצ יח ופרש באר היטב בקצור בשלש ל'לשונות כל שורש מלה
ומלה שמצא בספר הערוך הגדול ובשרשים והעקריות הנמצאות בספר המתרגמן
ובספר התשבי ומלות אחרות זולתן אין מספר כאשר למראה
עיניו ישפוט כל הקורא בו׃

חבור באה עם רב התועלת להבין כל מה שנכתב בלשון הקדש ובלשון גמרא ורז"ל ברכות ובמדרשים
על דרך כל ועל דרך חלק באופן שכל מי שיקראהו לא יטרדך כמעט כי בכל פתרון המלה הנם הושמו

DITTIONARIO NOVO

Hebraico, molto copioſo, Dechiarato in tre lingue; con bel-
liſſime annotationi, e con l'indice latino, e volgare; de tutti li ſuoi ſignificati.

LEXICON NOVVM HAEBRAICVM;
locupletiſſimum quantum nunquam antea; triplici
lingua perſpicuè explanatum.

Cum externarum vocum, in quibus tum priſci, tum recentiores
Rabini, hactenus verſati ſunt, ac paſſim vbique verſan-
tur, ab AruK, Meturgeman, Tisbi, fideliter
excerptarum; additione.

Cum duplici indice copioſiſſimo, latino nempe, nec non vulgari ſermone conſcripto,
ſingularum vocum hic repertarum ſignificationes dilucidiſſimè oſtendente; ad hoc,
vt quiſque conceptum ſuum hæbraicè eleganter exprimere, ſcripturaſq;
ſingulas ſacras interpraetari perfacilè valeat.

Cum characteris quoque hebraici circumſcriptione, Italicus index per pulcrè, & quàm dilucidè or-
natus: tali etenim pacto, docilis fiet magis in altera lingua, qui-
cunque eam prius ignorabat.

Cum annotationibus innumeris ſcitu perpulcris, æq; atq; neceſſariis.

Cum quaedam Margaritarum, Vnicornis, Ambræ, Hyacinti, nec non cæterorum lapidum precioſorum noua, & minimè ob-
ſcura vniuerſali cognitione; quæ tamquam arcana à quam plurimis exiſtimabitur.

Cum quibuſdam abreuiationibus quibus hebræi frequenter vtuntur in calce appoſitis.

Dauid de Pomis Medico Hebræo, atq; Phyloſopho, de Tribu Iuda, ex Ingenua Pomaria
Familia, quàm Titus ab Hieroſolima Romam in captiuitatem duxit, Autore.

Cum licentia Superiorum, & cum Priuilegio Sereniſſ. D. Venet. & quorundam aliorum
Principum, in annos 20. Venetijs, apud Ioannem de Gara. 1587.

FIGURE APP. 1. Title page of Casaubon's copy of David de' Pomis's *Dittionario novo Hebraico.* British Library C.79.d.6.

dictionary published in 1587 by the Italian Jewish scholar David de' Pomi.[36] On the flyleaf Casaubon lists his sources—the publications of the Typographia Medicea (which were solely in Arabic), the polyglot psalter (in Latin, Greek, Hebrew, Aramaic, and Arabic) published by Agostino Giustiniani in Genoa in 1516, the Arabic passages in the 1598 edition of Scaliger's *De emendatione temporum,* the manuscript of proverbs attributed to Abū 'Ubayd, and a Koran.

The lack of a published dictionary compelled all Casaubon's fellow Arabists, such as William Bedwell in England and Franciscus Raphelengius and Scaliger in Leiden, to compile word lists of their own. Casaubon's use of an interleaved copy of de' Pomi's Hebrew dictionary—a method also employed by Scaliger—raised the question of the Arabic alphabetical order. This was a problem faced by a number of European Arabists at the time. Their familiarity with the Hebrew alphabet led them to prefer the "Aramaic" order in Arabic, in which the letters were arranged according to their numerical value, rather than what is now the standard *hijā'* order, an arrangement according to shape. Casaubon, however, violated even the numerical order by joining Arabic characters that had no Hebrew equivalent to those that did— the *dhāl* to the *dāl,* the *hā* to the *khā,* the *zā* to the *tā,* the *ghain* to the *'ain,* the *dād* to the *sād,* the *shīn* to the *sīn,* and the *thā* to the *tā.*[37]

Soon Casaubon was also applying his Arabic in his publications. Arabic was never central to his studies, yet he was determined to exploit his knowledge of it to the utmost. His Arabic quotations are particularly striking on account of the large and ungainly Arabic types provided by Guillaume Le Bé, and his use of the language corresponds to what we would expect of a contemporary antiquarian. He applied it above all in the domains of topography, medicine, etymology, and biblical criticism. But he often approached it with the same critical sense with which he approached the texts that he edited. In his notes to the *Historiae Augustae scriptores* of 1604 he provided two Arabic spellings for the name of Libyan Tripoli in connection with the birthplace of Britannicus, and corrected an error in Avicenna's use of the term *conditum,* a pharmaceutical preparation.[38] He also discussed the Arabic word for elephant, the etymology of the name Heliogabalus (a subject about which he had corresponded with Scaliger), and the gender of the Arabic word for the crescent moon.[39] A year later he published his *De satyrica Graecorum poesi et Romanorum satira libri duo* and quoted Avicenna in Ar-

36. BL C.79.d.6.

37. For a further discussion see Hamilton 2009, 154–155.

38. Casaubon 1603, 266, 337.

39. Ibid., 97, 316, 401. Cf. Casaubon 1709, 132; Scaliger 1627, 209 (Ep. 66).

abic on priapism, correcting a mistake in the Typographia Medicea version of *al-Qānūn*.[40] In 1606 there followed his edition of Gregory of Nyssa, in which he speculated on the identity of al-Idrīsī and quoted from an Arabic version of the Epistle to the Galatians.[41]

The assistance of Adriaen Willemsz had been essential. Casaubon was overcome by grief when Adriaen died after a brief illness in July 1604. Casaubon described to Scaliger his desperate ride to Adriaen's lodgings and the scene at his deathbed.[42] For a while he abandoned the studies that continued to remind him of his tutor. Not until March 1605 does he seem to have again taken up his translation of al-Idrīsī, and in November to have been reading Avicenna.[43] Although he continued to provide Arabic words in his publications, it is clear from his correspondence with Scaliger, in which discussions of Arabic had once held a central place, that his keenness had waned. In March 1607 he told Sebastian Tengnagel, the Dutch imperial librarian in Vienna, that he had all but relinquished Arabic.[44]

Casaubon suffered again with the death of Scaliger in January 1609, but in the same month there arrived in Paris one of Scaliger's pupils, Thomas Erpenius. Erpenius was destined to become the greatest Arabist of his generation, and it was in France that he made his extraordinary progress. Casaubon helped him from the outset. He lent him his Arabic material. He introduced him to Josephus Abudacnus, a Copt from Cairo who had himself gotten in touch with Casaubon in the previous year; and Abudacnus gave Erpenius some tuition in Arabic to supplement what he had learned from William Bedwell in London in December 1608.[45] Encouraged by Erpenius' presence, Casaubon returned to his earlier studies, and in October 1609 he entrusted Erpenius with the manuscript of the proverbs attributed to Abū ʿUbayd in Adriaen's transcription and with Scaliger's annotations (as well as his own), asking him to retranslate the text, then edit and publish it.[46]

In November Erpenius left Paris for Saumur, where he spent the best part of a year before again returning to Paris.[47] It was during his second stay in the French capital that he encountered, in Conflans, Aḥmad ibn Qāsim al-Hajarī, an Arab of Andalusian origin who was in France in the service of the

40. Casaubon 1605b, 90.

41. Casaubon 1606, 66–67, 140.

42. Casaubon 1709, 213–214.

43. Ibid., 234, 255.

44. Ibid., 286.

45. On Abudacnus see Hamilton 2006, 127–136; 1994. On Erpenius and Bedwell's lessons see Hamilton 1985, 31–33.

46. Casaubon 1850, II, 694. Cf. Casaubon 1709, 339.

47. For Erpenius' life see Juynboll 1931, 59–118.

ruler of Morocco.[48] Although their meeting seems to have been relatively brief, al-Hajarī gave Erpenius the most satisfactory lessons in Arabic he had ever received and enabled him to perfect the Arabic grammar on which he was working and which, after its publication in 1613, would remain unsurpassed until the nineteenth century. At first Erpenius was attracted by Casaubon's proposal that he have it published, together with the proverbs, by Le Bé in Paris. Yet in March 1611 Casaubon, who had himself left Paris for London at the end of 1610, had to tell him that Le Bé now refused to publish books by "heretics."[49] By then, moreover, Erpenius had embarked on a journey that he hoped would take him to Istanbul, where he could buy Arabic manuscripts. He was disappointed. No boats were sailing from Venice, and he had to make do with material purchased in Venice and the Arabic collections in the libraries of Milan, Basel, Geneva, and, above all, of Heidelberg, which held most of the manuscripts that Guillaume Postel had collected in the Levant.

While Erpenius was traveling Casaubon had approached, through William Bedwell, the heirs of Franciscus Raphelengius in Leiden, and had urged them to publish Erpenius' Arabic grammar with his corrections of their father's Arabic dictionary.[50] He also wrote to Hugo Grotius and Daniel Heinsius to enlist their support in appointing Erpenius professor of Arabic at the university.[51] When Erpenius at last returned to Holland in the summer of 1612 the Leiden chair was his, and he remained grateful to Casaubon for the rest of his life.[52]

Though deprived of teachers and with ever less time to devote to Arabic, Casaubon made the most use of it in his last—and arguably greatest—publication. This was his attack on Baronio, the *Exercitationes,* which appeared in London in 1614. In it Casaubon quotes al-Idrīsī on the distance from Bethle-

48. The event is described in al-Hajarī 1987, 195, 263, 268–269; and by Erpenius in Casaubon 1709, 660–662. See also Wiegers 1988, 45–63.

49. Casaubon 1709, 375.

50. Juynboll 1931, 72.

51. Casaubon 1709, 478–479; Hamilton 1988–89, esp. 580–584.

52. See his statement in the dedicatory epistle to Casaubon's son Meric in Erpenius 1623, *2 recto–verso: "Is [sc. Casaubon] autem simul ac me vidit, et Linguarum Orientalium studiosissimum esse cognovit, vehementer et me amare, et studiis meis favere caepit, ita quidem ut, cum Arabicae linguae desiderio, magni Scaligeri hortatu, jam totum me flagrare, et libris omnibus destitui animadverteret, supellectilem suam Arabicam, quam satis habebat luculentam, ultro mihi offerret, et concederet. quod quidem beneficium tanto me gaudio affecit, ut me beatiorem crederem vivere neminem: et tantum Arabismi studium in me excitavit, ut majori cum ardore atque animi alacritate neminem unquam illas literas aggressum esse persuasum habeam." See also his oration on Hebrew delivered at Leiden University on 27 September 1620 (Erpenius 1621, 129): "hoc tantum dico Clarissimum virum Ishacum Casaubonum, seculi hujus insigne ornamentum, et cui plurimum debent studia mea orientalia."

hem to Jerusalem,[53] but above all he refers to the Typographia Medicea edition of the Arabic Gospels. For much of the time he simply uses the Arabic to confirm a reading in Syriac in Tremellius' 1569 edition of the Peshitta.[54] Yet he is also critical of the Roman edition of the Gospels. We do not know with certainty from what manuscripts the Arabic text was drawn, but it corresponded mainly to the so-called Alexandrian Vulgate, the origin of which can be traced back to the thirteenth century, when a Coptic (Bohairic) version of the New Testament was supplemented by passages from Syriac and Greek versions. A hybrid product, which was to form the basis of all published editions of the Gospels in Arabic from 1591 to the twentieth century, it is of hardly any use for critical purposes.[55] Casaubon was probably unaware of the genealogy of the edition, but he was clearly aware of its defects. Certain passages, moreover, offended him deeply as a Protestant. The most striking is Matthew 16:18, "Thou art Peter, and upon this rock I will build my church"—the text most frequently used to justify papal supremacy. The Arabic in the Typographia Medicea edition (but not of subsequent editions) goes further still, and instead of "Thou art Peter" gives "Thou art the rock," which was even better suited to Roman claims.[56]

One book in particular in Casaubon's library points to his intention of using Arabic material in the continuation of his attack on Baronio—the *Brevis orthodoxae fidei professio,* a Maronite confession of faith printed entirely in Arabic by the Typographia Medicea in 1595.[57] Although the Maronites had long claimed to have always been in communion with Rome, there were doubts about this thesis, and the Protestants looked at them with only slightly less interest than at the other Arabic-speaking Christians who, they held, had resisted with heroism the overtures of the papacy. In the confession of faith Casaubon marked those points that Protestants would have regarded as contentious—the Catholic claim, for example, that the Maronites believed both in the seven sacraments and in purgatory, and the passages on the church councils in which the Eastern Christians played an important role: Nicaea, Chalcedon, Constantinople, and Florence. Baronio, elated by what seemed to be decisive signs of the conversion to Roman Catholicism of the Coptic church of Alexandria, had boldly announced an imminent

53. Casaubon 1614, 162.

54. Ibid., 178, 250, 288, 289, 624, 714.

55. Metzger 1977, 265.

56. Casaubon 1614, 388. See also 638.

57. Casaubon's copy of the *Brevis orthodoxae fidei professio* (Rome, 1595) is BL 753.g.72.(2). Bod MS Casaubon 22, 121 recto, provides an indication that he owned the work when he was in London.

union, and the Protestants of Europe reacted robustly against this procla-
mation.[58]

When he was in England Casaubon at last met William Bedwell, with
whom he had corresponded for so long, and formed with him a friendship
that lasted until his death. Bedwell showed him the Arabic lexicon he was
compiling, wrote to him from Leiden when he went there briefly in 1612,
and informed him of details of his own Arabic studies.[59] Casaubon wrote
querulously to Etienne Hubert, complaining about the hostility he believed
he had encountered in England. Two men, however, remained loyal and affectionate: Bedwell, and Bedwell's patron Lancelot Andrewes.[60]

In England, however, Casaubon was above all a spectator of the great advances made by Erpenius, who kept him abreast of the stages of his progress. And it was thanks to Erpenius that Casaubon's interest in Arabic was
rewarded. In 1613 Erpenius sent him an inscribed copy of his Arabic grammar,[61] and in March 1614 a copy of the *Kitāb al-amthāl seu Proverbiorum arabicorum centuriae duae*.[62] This was the published edition of the proverbs
attributed to Abū 'Ubayd. It was dedicated to Casaubon and contained Erpenius' own translation of the proverbs added to notes by Scaliger and Casaubon. In his preface Erpenius gave full credit to the gifts of Adriaen Willemsz, expressed his infinite gratitude to Casaubon, and presented the work
as a monument to the collaboration among the four friends, Casaubon,
Scaliger, Adriaen, and himself. A few months later Casaubon was dead.

If we look back at what Casaubon actually achieved as an Arabist the results are disappointing. He set out with bold plans, but he never had time to
bring them to fruition or to reach the standard of Arabists such as Raphelengius and Scaliger, let alone Erpenius. Dependent on the help of others, he
was repeatedly frustrated by their departure or their death. He composed
two lines of appropriate Arabic for his letter to Julius Conradus Otto—but
nothing comparable to the Hebrew of the letter itself.[63] Nevertheless he is
entitled to a place of distinction among contemporary orientalists. Why?

Casaubon's high reputation as a scholar meant that news of his interest in
Arabic soon spread through the Republic of Letters, and his own energy as a
letter writer made him something of a focal point among its orientalists. All
the main Arabists of the time wrote to him as one of the few men who could

58. Hamilton 2006, 75, 123–124, 141.

59. Hamilton 1985, 33–34, 37–38.

60. Ibid., 54.

61. BL 622.h.5.(2).

62. Casaubon 1709, 556.

63. BL MS Burney 365, 27 recto; see 238–239 above.

understand their problems, appreciate their progress, and answer their questions. Not only did he correspond consistently with Scaliger and Erpenius, but he exchanged letters with Etienne Hubert in Paris,[64] William Bedwell in England,[65] Jacob Christmann in Heidelberg,[66] and Peter Kirsten in Breslau.[67] They sent him their publications and thirsted for his opinions. Georg Michael Lingelsheim, the councilor of the Elector Palatine, spontaneously lent him an Arabic manuscript from the Heidelberg library.[68] The Copt Josephus Abudacnus, who was always in search of intellectual celebrities and begged Scaliger to take him on as his assistant, also wrote to Casaubon in the hope of making his acquaintance.[69] In 1613, when he was in London, Casaubon was approached by the Arabic-speaking Christian Murqus Du'ābilī al-Kurdī, known in Europe as Marco Dobelo, who had lectured in Arabic at the Maronite College in Rome, had then moved to Spain, and was searching for employment in England.[70] Casaubon's fame had extended across Europe, and he must be regarded as one of the scholars who made the use of oriental languages in learned correspondence fashionable.

Then there were Casaubon's plans, a number of which display an approach far ahead of his time. His plan to edit the proverbs attributed to Abū 'Ubayd after he had received them in 1602 was in itself highly original. Just then the only Arabic texts that had been edited or translated in the West were either devotional—parts of the Koran, excerpts from the scriptures, Christian prayers, and confessions of faith—or scholarly—on history, topography, medicine, mathematics, and grammar. What Casaubon proposed was the introduction of a completely different genre, a literary text. This idea would have a glorious future. After Erpenius had edited Casaubon's proverbs, he went on to publish other collections of Arabic sayings. Soon works of literature, such as the *Maqāmāt* in rhyming prose and pieces of poetry, would broaden European knowledge of Arabic culture.

Casaubon can also claim to have been the first Western Arabist to propose a study of Arabic poetry. He did so in his 1605 edition of the satires of Persius,[71] and his interest in the matter is confirmed by a number of the passages he underlined and annotated in his copy of Leo Africanus' *De totius Africae descriptione*.[72] That he never actually managed to carry out his plan

64. BL MS Burney 364, 299 recto–303 recto.
65. Hamilton 1985, 97–101.
66. BL MS Burney 363, 224 recto.
67. BL MS Burney 364, 334 recto, 336 recto–verso.
68. BL MS Burney 365, 106 recto, 123 recto; Casaubon 1709, 210, 217, 233, 454, 462, 540.
69. BL MS Burney 367, 200 recto.
70. Bod MS Or.298.3. See Levi della Vida 1939, 282.
71. Casaubon 1605a, 133–134: "De Arabum rhythmica poësi, qua fere contextum est Muhammedis Alcoranum, si clementissimo Deo fuerit visum, alias disseremus."
72. BL 793.d.2, 19 recto–20 verso, 42 verso, 132 recto.

may have been due to the shortage of time and the lack of texts available in the West. Again it was Erpenius who would follow his lead, and defend Arabic poetry in his public orations at Leiden University in 1613 and 1620.[73]

That Casaubon should have expended so much time and energy on Arabic testifies to his tireless quest for knowledge as an antiquarian. Nor was it only the language that interested him. Even if most of his comments on the Koran were disparaging and smacked of traditional anti-Islamic rhetoric,[74] he owned at least three manuscripts of the work in Arabic, besides the so-called *Epitome Alcorani*, edited by Johann Albrecht Widmanstetter, and the Latin translation edited by Bibliander in 1543.[75] With Scaliger, who had advised him to read it, he discussed the text dispassionately[76] and was clearly eager to understand it in the same way as he wished to understand the rabbinic works to which he once compared it.[77]

We may well wonder what would have happened had Casaubon had the chance to fulfill his plans—to complete his Arabic dictionary, to discuss Arabic poetry, and to delve further into Arabic culture. And indeed, we can extend the question to the other oriental languages in which he showed an interest. For Casaubon owned material in Ethiopic and Armenian,[78] neither of which he managed to study even though he started listing the Ethiopic words he found in Francisco Alvarez's account of the quest for Prester John.[79] He went further in the study of Coptic. He had consulted a couple of manuscripts with Coptic texts in Paris, and we see from his notes that he had started to work on the alphabet.[80] This was some twenty years before Athanasius Kircher introduced the study of the language into Europe.[81]

It would be unfair—and somewhat misleading—to compare Casaubon's knowledge of Arabic with his knowledge of Hebrew. Hebrew was central to much of his work, and the time invested in learning it was repaid with interest. It was being studied increasingly in Europe in Casaubon's day. Adequate grammars and dictionaries were available, and Jewish converts to Christian-

---

73. Erpenius 1621, 33; R. Jones 1988, 15–25, esp. 19.

74. Casaubon 1606, 132.

75. Bod MS Casaubon 22, 44 recto (nos. 51, 53, and 55), 60 verso, 69 recto.

76. Casaubon 1709, 184, 666.

77. Casaubon 1614, 100: "Nam si valet haec ratio, ut credi omnia debeant, quae aliquis haereticus aut fanaticus finxerit, quia Deus illa potest facere: quid est cur deliria Rabbinorum, aut etiam Mahometis, respuamus? etsi enim stupenda sunt, et insana figmenta, quae in libris Rabbinorum aut in Alcorano recitantur: nihil tamen est adeo portentose excogitatum, quod, si omnipotentiam Dei respicimus, fieri a Deo non posse credi debeat." See also 211.

78. Ethiopic: Bod MS Casaubon 22, 34 recto, 120 recto: Armenian: ibid., 44 recto.

79. Bod MS Casaubon 30, 75 recto–77 verso.

80. Bod MS Casaubon 11, 51 recto–52 verso.

81. On the early history of Coptic studies see Hamilton 2006, 197–199.

ity could be found as teachers and advisers. Arabic was a very different matter. The European city in which it was easiest to meet native speakers of Arabic was Rome, where Gregory XIII had founded the Maronite College in 1584. But Casaubon never went to Rome. He found Paris stimulating, but, if we except occasional visitors such as Abudacnus and al-Hajarī, it was only some years after Casaubon had left Paris for London that Arabic-speakers arrived in any number, mainly learned Maronites invited to collaborate on the Polyglot Bible, to serve as royal interpreters, and to teach at the Collège Royal.[82] The difficulties, therefore, were enormous, and it took the genius of Erpenius, his fortunate encounter with al-Hajarī, and his single-minded concentration on the language to break through the constrictions that weighed on the study of Arabic. Casaubon helped him, and this fact gives him an added importance in the history of Arabic studies in Europe.

Additional note (July 2010): The dispersal of Casaubon's manuscript collection is likely to be a lasting source of surprises. One manuscript which it is possible to identify as his is a bilingual copy of part of the Koran, the Arabic on the left pages and, on the right, the Latin translation made in Spain by Johannes Gabriel Terrolensis for Egidio da Viterbo in 1518. The manuscript, MS Mm v 26, probably dating from the 1530s, is in Cambridge University Library, and is discussed in detail by Thomas E. Burman in his *Reading the Qur'ān in Latin Christendom, 1140–1560* (Philadelphia: University of Pennsylvania Press, 2007), 168–173, 277–279. Burman identified the annotator as the Biblical scholar William Tyndale. In fact, however, the notes, written, some interlineally and others alongside the Latin translation from sura 2: 46 to 231 (fos. 7–39), are unmistakably in the hand of Casaubon. The name *Wilyām Tindalun,* transcribed in Arabic on a blank folio near the beginning of the manuscript, is not, in my view, in the same hand as the annotations. It would seem to be a mark of ownership, but William Tyndalls or Tindales were common enough at the time: no fewer than four of them matriculated at Cambridge between 1545 and 1595. The annotations have been analyzed thoroughly by Burman. They were meant as corrections to Terrolensis, and they all endeavor to convey the literal meaning of the Arabic, whereas Terrolensis tends to paraphrase. Though some suggestions are less felicitous, they are, by and large, fine improvements and testify to their author's expertise in Arabic. The annotations were probably made in Paris between the summer of 1602 and the summer of 1604, when Casaubon was reading the Koran together with Adriaen Willemsz. They should consequently be regarded as yet another fruit of their collaboration.

82. Hamilton and Richard 2004, 47–50.

APPENDIX 2

Casaubon on the Masoretic Text

Early in 1603, Casaubon wrote an unexpectedly generous letter to the Catholic scholar Jean Porthaise. A member of the aggressively orthodox Franciscans, who led many of the public demonstrations of the Catholic League in Paris during the Wars of Religion, Porthaise made his name as a writer producing polemics against Protestant theology and astrology. To the amusement of Huguenot observers, he prudently changed his style when Henri IV assumed the throne.[1] Porthaise's mastery of Hebrew may not have been profound, if Isaac Vossius' account deserves credence: "Speaking in [Poitiers], with shameless deceitfulness he recited long passages in Bas-Breton, his mother tongue, to his audience, and pretended they were Hebrew. But he was exposed by Scaliger, who went to hear him one day out of curiosity. Knowing both Hebrew and Bas-Breton, he exposed Porthaise's deceit to those who had taken him to the man's sermon."[2] Nonetheless he asked Casaubon's advice about the Masorah—the spiky thicket of letters, numbers, and signs that appeared on the tops and bottoms of pages, and between the Hebrew text of the Bible and the Aramaic translation, in most editions of the Rabbinic Bible.[3] Casaubon replied confidently and in detail, counseling Porthaise on the nature, value, and uses of the biblical apparatus. He used an

1. Scaliger 1695, 322; 1740, II, 514: "Ce Predicateur avoit esté aussi des plus animez contre le Roy Henry IV. avant que Dieu l'eust affermy sur le throsne; mais depuis les choses ayant changé, Porthaise changea aussi de note, et entre autres, estant à Saumur, il vint faire sa Cour à Monsieur du Plessis, qui en estoit Gouverneur; duquel ayant obtenu permission de prescher à saint Pierre, à la charge d'exhorter bien le peuple à estre fidelle au Roy, le Compagnon m'y manqua pas."

2. Scaliger 1695, 322; 1740, II, 513–514: "Le mesme, preschant au mesme lieu [Poitiers], debitoit impudemment à ses Auditeurs de grandes periodes en Bas Breton, son langage maternel, qu'il leur faisoit passer pour de l'Hebreu; mais il fut decouvert par Monsieur de Lescalle, qui l'ayant esté ouyr un jour par curiosité, et n'ignorant ny l'Hebreu, ny le Bas Breton, fit connoistre sa fourbe à ceux qui l'avoient mené au sermon de Porthaise."

3. For the character of Porthaise's inquiry see Casaubon 1709, 173, which makes clear that he asked about the "orbiculi" to be found in the Masorah. The first edition to offer a full version of this apparatus, and the model for most later ones, was the second Bomberg Rabbinic Bible of 1524–25, edited by Jacob b. Hayyim.

oft-cited but enigmatic Hebrew phrase to express his sense that the makers of the Masorah had done their job well. "The criticism of the Hebrews," Casaubon explained, "which they call the Masorah, is a wholly divine thing. The rabbis generally use the very clever term 'Fence for the law' to refer to it, as you clearly know, for I see that you have learned to exercise in this gymnasium."[4] For all the hyperbole of Casaubon's praise, as we will see he took the Masorah as something quite historical: a critical apparatus, devised and developed by men, that had preserved the text of the Old Testament in a reliable form.

Casaubon derived this overview of Masoretic tradition from the third preface to the *Massoret haMassoret* (Tradition of the Tradition), the groundbreaking study of the textual apparatus of the Hebrew Bible written by the Jewish scholar Elijah Levita. This short, tightly packed book, which appeared in 1538, offered the first detailed account of the origins and nature of the Masorah. It became, and remained for more than a century, a desk reference for any Christian scholar interested in the Hebrew Bible.[5] Most Jews, Levita noted, believed that "Ezra the scribe, and his associates, who were the men of the Great Synagogue, made the Masorah, the vowel points, and the accents through all the scriptures."[6] Others—notably the author of the *Zohar*, which Levita may not have read at this point, and many other Kabbalists—held "that they were given on Sinai" by Moses himself.[7] For his part, Levita maintained that the entire apparatus had been added by the Masoretes—the Jewish grammarians who worked both in Palestine and in Iraq from the seventh through the eleventh centuries C.E. With striking historical insight—and a little exaggeration—Levita described these men as consummate philologists, who had had to restore not only the text, but the Hebrew language itself, which had long since yielded to Aramaic in everyday life. After the destruction of the Second Temple, he explained, "the sacred tongue began gradually to disappear, till the time of the Masoretes, who are the men of Tiberias, which is Mouzia. They were great sages, and thoroughly

---

4. Casaubon 1709, 173: "De proposita quaestione sic paucis habe. Plane divina res est Hebraeorum Critica, quam ipsi Massoram vocant. Septem Legis solent Rabbini hanc indigetare πάνυ εὐστόχως: quod tu non ignoras, qui, ut video, in hac palaestra te exercuisti." Casaubon was fond of Akiva's saying, "The tradition is a fence around the law" (Avot 3:14). See Casaubon 1621, epistola ad lectorem, [† 5 recto] (first published 1600): "Sed studij huius necessitatem Hebraeorum doctores verbo indicant, qui Legis divinae (quanto igitur meliore iure humanorum scriptorum?) sepem esse Criticam non minus vere quam eleganter pronunciant"; and cf. Bravo 2006, 164–166.

5. On Levita see Ginsburg's still standard introduction to Levita 1867; and Weil 1963. For the reception of his views, Ginsburg remains very informative. See also Allen 1949; Muller 1980; and Malcolm 2002.

6. Levita 1867, 103.

7. Ibid., 121; see Ginsburg's introduction, 48; and Penkower 1989.

conversant with the scriptures and the structure of the language, more so than all the other Jews who lived in that generation, and none like them have existed since."[8] Levita believed that the Masoretes had drawn on "traditions" that went back to the authors of the biblical books as they did their work, even when they reported variants in the Pentateuch. But he insisted that they had assembled and sifted these materials as scholars, collating manuscripts, not as beneficiaries of direct revelation.[9]

Casaubon concentrated on one aspect of the Masoretes' work: the textual corrections they proposed in hundreds of cases, using the system known as *Ketiv* (what is written) and *Kere* (what is read). The Masoretes left the transmitted text, or *Ketiv,* intact, and used the margin and their system of vocalization to indicate what they thought the better readings, which were to be used when the Torah was read. Casaubon never said so explicitly, but it seems very likely that he saw the analogy between the Masoretes' way of proposing emendations without altering the transmitted text and the methods of Aristarchus and other Alexandrian critics of Homer. They, too, had respected the transmitted text, and had devised a system of marginal signs to identify particular verses as spurious or unworthy of Homer.[10]

Casaubon laid out the development of this system, which he thought had begun not with Moses, but with Ezra, when he reconstituted the text of the Torah after the exile:

> The Jewish Masters offer varied explanations for the origins of the Masorah. You have seen, I believe, what Elijah Levita wrote on this matter in the preface to his *Massoret haMassoret* . . . It is certainly true that Moses was not the author of the *Ketiv* and *Kere,* and it is absurd to think that the matters taught in that art go back to the authors themselves. More plausible is the opinion of those rabbis who ascribe the invention of the *Ketiv* and *Kere* to that profoundly wise scribe of the law, Ezra. But this can hold only for the books of Moses and the other older ones. For as Elijah rightly argues, there was hardly any need for correctors to work on the writings of the more

---

8. Levita 1867, 131.

9. Ibid., 110–112. On 120 he argued that even Ezra and his associates had had to collate manuscripts when they could not find the author's autograph of a given biblical book. In such cases, he thought, "they undoubtedly followed the majority of codices, which they had collected from different places."

10. Friedrich August Wolf made explicit use of this analogy in his 1795 *Prolegomena ad Homerum.* He planned, but wrote only two chapters of, a second part of this work, which he intended to dedicate to a comparison between the transmission of the two texts. See Wolf 1985. In the twentieth century, Saul Lieberman made the same comparison, and argued that the Jews had drawn their critical methods in part from Alexandrian criticism (Lieberman 1942 and 1950).

recent prophets. I think that this opinion is either true, or close to the truth, and that Ezra, or others around his time, created the Criticism of the Hebrews. Afterward, the most learned members of the Jewish schools treated it. For just as we read that the Greeks had schools of philosophers and grammarians, so also there were schools and, as it were, families of the Masoretes. For the synagogues that remained in the East followed the major author of this form of learning, Jacob, son of Naftali. Those who returned to the West and their fatherland cite Aaron, son of Asher, as the creator of their Masorah. And so this form of study was divided into two sects, so to speak, Ben Naftali and Ben Asher. Those who think that the Masorah shows the corruption of the divinely inspired books of scripture become guilty of a great crime. In fact, this art attests to the certainty and accuracy of the divine Word. If God grants, someday I will prove this with a very precise commentary.[11]

Although Casaubon cited Levita, he also criticized him for hemming and hawing at vital points in his argument: "That most learned and judicious man clearly had the right opinion on this matter, though what he wrote was not perfectly correct. For in the end he seems to come back to the opinion of those who hold that the authors of the sacred books also passed on the Masorah, which is not only false, but also absurd. And it is patently clear from Elijah's own words that he saw this: but nothing is harder than either to recognize or to reject a mistake, once it has become established."[12]

Levita, Casaubon argued, believed that the Masoretes had actually recon-

11. Casaubon 1709, 173–174: "Originem Massorae varie explicant Judaeorum Magistri. Vidisti, credo, quae super ea re scripsit Elias Levita, in Praefatione suae Massoreth Hammassoreth . . . Atqui omnino verum est, Autorem non esse Mosem τοῦ כתיב et קרי: estque παγγέλοιον existimare, ab ipsis autoribus esse profecta, quae in arte illa docentur. Similior veri est eorum Rabbinorum opinio, qui inventionem τοῦ כתיב et קרי ad sapientissimum illum Legis Scribam Ezram referunt. Sed hoc verum fuerit in Libris duntaxat Mosaicis et aliis antiquioribus. Nam ut disputat Elias recte, in scriptis recentiorum Prophetarum vix opus adhuc fuit correctorum diligentia. Horum sententiam putamus nos aut veram, aut verae proximam; neque dubitamus, vel Ezram, vel alios circa illa fere tempora, initium dedisse huic Hebraeorum Criticae; quam postea doctissimi quique e Judaeorum Scholis tractarunt. Quemadmodum autem Philosophorum apud Graecos atque etiam Grammaticorum Sectas legimus fuisse, ita et Massoretarum diversae Scholae, ac velut familiae extiterunt. Nam quae in Oriente remanserunt Synagogae, praecipuum hujus eruditionis autorem secuti sunt Jacobum, Nephtali filium. Qui in Occidentem et veterem patriam redierunt, conditorem Massorae suae laudant Aaronem, filium Ascher. Ita scissa est haec disciplina in duas ὡς εἰπεῖν αἱρέσεις, נפתלי בן אשר et בן נפתלי. Qui existimant Massoram corruptorum Librorum θεοπνεύστων esse argumentum, nae illi magni criminis se obligant; cum potius certae fidei et integrae testimonium divino Verbo haec ars praebeat. Quod aliquando, Θεοῦ διδόντος, nostro quodam exactae diligentiae commentario sumus probaturi."

12. Ibid., 173: "Vir ille doctissimus et acerrimi judicii haut dubie sensit recte hac de re; etsi scripsit non satis recte. Videtur enim tandem eo revolvi, ut eorum accedat sententiae, qui putant traditam Massoram Librorum Sacrorum ab ipsis eorum Auctoribus: quod non solum falsum, sed et ridiculum est.

structed a system first given by Moses on Sinai, and Casaubon—who seems to have been one of the few Christian readers to grasp how conservative Levita's central position was—condemned this concession to the notion that the text was inspired. He thought it absurd to suggest that Moses himself had introduced variants into the text. At the same time, though, Casaubon approved the history of the later Masoretic tradition that Levita had sketched. He followed Levita in describing the two Masoretic schools of Ben Naftali and Ben Asher in tenth-century Tiberias, in Palestine, both of which introduced further refinements into their different versions of the text. Unlike many earlier Christian writers, who treated Jewish efforts to correct the Old Testament text as evidence of their perfidy, of their desire to conceal its prophecies of Jesus, Casaubon inferred that the Jews had done their best, over the centuries, to preserve the Hebrew Bible intact—just as the ancient Greek and Roman critics had tried to preserve their canonical texts.

What Casaubon gave Porthaise was not a full conspectus of Levita's argument, even so far as the *Qere* and *Ketiv* were concerned, but a summary of one of his prefaces. The text he used, moreover, seems not to have been that of the printed edition, in which Levita's Hebrew original was accompanied by a Latin translation of the third preface. Rather, it was a Latin translation, ascribed to Casaubon's Genevan Greek teacher, Pierre Chevalier, which survives, in part, in the Bodleian Library.[13] In the margins of this manuscript, Casaubon noted the existence of "Oriental" and "Occidental" Masoretes, followers of Ben Naftali and Ben Asher, just as he would in his letter to Porthaise.[14] More important, he also recorded the same responses to Levita's arguments that he would pass on to the Catholic scholar. Casaubon picked out for criticism the points where, he thought, Levita qualified his true views about the age of the Masorah. At one point, for example, Levita quoted a passage from the Talmud which others had seen as proving that the vowel points came from Sinai: "What I find very difficult is what they say in the

---

Neque hoc non videbat Elias, quod facile ex ejus verbis apparet: sed nihil difficilius est, quam usu confirmatum errorem vel agnoscere, vel libere repudiare."

13. The manuscript begins with the third preface, which runs from 1 recto–11 recto and corresponds to the text in Levita 1867, 102–143. On Casaubon's work with Chevalier see Casaubon to Scaliger, Casaubon 1709, 206: "Sed quotusquisque nostrum est, qui de eo vel cogitet, vel qui eum usum τῆς ῾Ραββινικῆς διαλέκτου habeat, ut par sit tanto incepto? Olim in eo studio aliquid operae atque olei consumpsimus, usi Magistro Petro Cevallerio Genevensi, quo nihil probius, nihil ἁπλοϊκώτερον. Verum amisso morte immatura amicissimo Praeceptore, non multum post illa profecimus"; Meric Casaubon, *Pietas*, in Casaubon 1709, 103: "Scito autem, Bulengere, illum mature ad illas literas animum applicuisse, et adhuc juvenem Rabbinorum sacris initiatum a Petro Cevallerio: a quo tamen non tantum didicit, quantum optabat, propter viri illius optimi et doctissimi immaturam mortem."

14. Bod MS Casaubon 10, 4 recto = Levita 1867, 113: "Orientales Occidentales . . . Aser et Nephthali"; 4 verso = Levita 1867, 116: "Liber ab Aser correctus in Aegypto, cui innituntur Occidentales . . . Nephthalitae Orientales."

same chapter, thus: R. Isaac says that the variant readings in scripture were passed on to Moses at Mount Sinai."[15] "Nugae," wrote Casaubon in the margin: "nonsense, that the Masorah was passed down to Moses."[16] The remark was hardly fair: Levita had cited the passage only in order to show that it could hardly refer to the Five Books of Moses, since none of the readings cited by R. Isaac came from them. Elsewhere Casaubon's critique had more substance. Casaubon thought Levita must be hedging when he recorded that "All the men of the great synagogue noted down the variant readings in the law, as they had received them from Moses of pious memory, and that which is in the prophets and the sages according to the Kabbalah received from the prophets and their writings."[17] "It is stated here," Casaubon wrote, "that the cabala of the individual books was received from their authors. This is false."[18] Casaubon could not accept that Levita, who described himself as planning to "do battle against those who say that they [the points] were given on Sinai," honestly believed that much of the Masorah represented a restoration of the text's true form, rather than a set of innovations.[19]

When Casaubon insisted on the late origin of the Masorah, he departed from the views of his teacher. Even though Chevalier had provided the version of Levita's work that Casaubon used, he did not agree with the *Massoret haMassoret*. In his edition of an older Hebrew grammar, Chevalier argued that Moses must have equipped the Pentateuch with vowel points. After all, he asked, "If the Law was set out without points, who besides Moses could at first have read and recited it correctly?"[20] Scaliger described Chevalier's "diatribe," in a typically malign marginal note in his own copy of Antoine Che-

15. Bod MS Casaubon 10, 3 recto = Levita 1867, 109: "Sed adhuc maiorem difficultatem id habet apud me, quod dicunt in memorato capite his verbis [Babylonian Talmud, Nedarim 37b]. Dicit R. Isaac, Diversitas Lectionis et Scripturae tradita est [MS: in] Mosi in monte Sinai vt Legitur et non Scribitur quod est in voce [פרת]: *Euphrates*, quod est *in versu* בלכתו [2 Sam. 8:3] *cum iret ipse*." The tradition in the talmudic text is described as *halakhah leMoshe misinai* (a law given to Moses at Sinai); this is the term given to a number of laws, which are accorded biblical authority although they are neither stated in scripture nor derived from hermeneutical principles.

16. Bod MS Casaubon 10, 3 recto = Levita 1867, 112: "Nugae. ὅτι Massora tradita Mosi."

17. Bod MS Casaubon 10, 3 verso–4 recto = Levita 1867, 112: "CANON. Omnes viri magnae synagogae annotarunt diversam lectionem in lege, iuxta quod acceperant a Mose piae memoriae: eam autem quae in prophetis et hagiographis iuxta Kabbalam acceptam a prophetis et sapientibus aetatum: in libris vero captivitatis iuxta interpretationem ipsorum authorum, qui adhuc superstites erant non propter ullam dubitationem ut multi putarunt. Et ecce cum applicui animum meum ad quaerendum et scrutandum quicquid factum est circa negotium Scripti et Lecti, inveni diversam lectionem (quae hebraice vocatur קרי et כתיב *lectum et scriptum*) non inveniri in *Deficientibus* et *Plenis*."

18. Bod MS Casaubon 10, 3 verso = Levita 1867, 112: "ὅτι cabala singulorum librorum accepta ab auctoribus ipsorum libr. hoc falsum."

19. Levita 1867, 130–131.

20. Pierre Chevalier, note in A. Chevalier 1590, 24: "Si sine punctis lex proposita fuit, quis praeter Mosem eam recte legere et recitare initio potuit?"

valier's grammar, as "silly, false, and the work of an ignorant man; let scholars beware."[21] He had read the *Massoret haMassoret* in full, in Hebrew, and knew that Levita had refuted this rebuttal in advance. Anticipating the objection that unpointed texts were unreadable, Levita vividly described three Syrian Christians who had visited Rome at the invitation of Leo X: "I then saw in their hands the book of Psalms, written in Syriac characters, as well as translated into Syriac . . . Now I saw them reading this Psalter without points, and asked them, Have you points, or any signs to indicate the vowels? And they answered me, 'No! But we have been conversant with that language from our youth till now, and, therefore, know how to read without points.'"[22] Casaubon, who seems not to have read Levita's whole text, still clearly freed himself from his teacher's influence and decided that Levita was generally right.[23]

Casaubon did not limit himself to reading the translated preface to the *Massoret haMassoret.* In fact he looked for evidence both about Jewish ways of correcting the biblical text and about their wider historical context. As Benedetto Bravo has shown, during his Paris years, from 1600 to 1610, Casaubon pursued a larger project of which his inquiry into the Masorah formed only one chapter: a full-scale study of ancient critics and their work, in which he planned to compare Greek, Roman, and Jewish methods of textual criticism.[24] As early as 1601, he wrote to Scaliger about his plans and asked his friend for help finding sources: "It is my intention to lay out the full critical method of the Hebrews in the book I have written about criticism. Could you please let me know if you have seen any rabbis who wrote something worthwhile on this subject? As for me, I know nothing of this kind beyond the notes in the Venice Bibles and the little book of the most learned Elijah."[25] As Casaubon's curious slide from future plans to the perfect tense indicates, this account of his progress was more than a little optimistic. Still, he wrote to Porthaise—who was in fact already dead—in January 1603. It seems likely that Casaubon had studied Levita's work by then.

Casaubon's notes on the criticism of the ancient Jews, or some of them, survive in the Bodleian Library. They include a reference to Levita's "most

21. Scaliger, note ad loc., in Leiden University Library 873 B 12: "Haec diatriba asinina, falsa et idiotae hominis. Caveant studiosi."

22. Levita 1867, 130–131.

23. See below for a discussion of Chevalier's interest in Kabbalah and Jewish magic—subjects in which Casaubon soon lost interest.

24. Bravo 2006. See also the fragments and critical discussion in Casaubon 1710, 38–39, 248–250.

25. Casaubon 1709, 127: "Cum in eo libro, quem de Critica fecimus, omnem Hebraeorum Κριτικὴν explicare sit animus, σύν γε τῷ Θεῷ εἰπεῖν, velim indices mihi, si quem Rabbinorum vidisti, qui in eo argumento operam non poenitendam posuerit. Ego praeter notas Bibliorum Venetorum, et eruditissimi Eliae libellum, novi nihil huius generis."

elegant work" on the Masorah, as well as definitions of Hebrew terms for schools and scholars given by Levita in the *Tishbi.*[26] Casaubon knew, of course, that in order to undertake a serious investigation of Jewish criticism he would have to bring many more sources into play. As in his letter to Porthaise, he reminded himself in his notes that in addition to the *Massoret haMassoret,* "there are many other disparate things in the books of the rabbis relevant to this," and that he must "add in the notes on the Bible"—that is, glean evidence from a direct study of the Masorah itself.[27] No notes by Casaubon on the Masorah itself survive—a point to which we shall return. Still, he harvested evidence about the terms that Jewish critics used from an unexpected Jewish source, the *Sefer Hasidim* of Judah ben Samuel of Regensburg, a book he owned by 1605.[28] Casaubon remarked on the flyleaf of his copy that the text contained a section on scribes and books, teachers and pupils.[29] His notes in Oxford discuss a term for old texts, ספר ישן נושן, which he found and underlined on the book's title page.[30]

Casaubon's most detailed notes on Jewish criticism, however, come from a sprawling, messy product of Christian Hebraism, a book that, as we have already seen, he thought both untrustworthy and chaotic: Pietro Galatino's *De arcanis Catholicae veritatis.* Twenty years before Levita, Galatino had offered a crude, negative history of the text of the Hebrew Bible. In one chapter, he analyzed the eighteen standard *tikkunei soferim* (corrections of the scribes). These were changes made in very ancient times to remove anthropomorphic terms from the biblical text.[31] Galatino ascribed these corrections to "talmudists" working in the Christian era. The Jews who claimed that they went back to Ezra himself were clearly wrong, since they would in that case have been labeled *tikkunei Ezra.*

More important, Galatino explained why the Jews had changed the text.

26. Bod MS Casaubon 60, 26 verso: "elegantiss. opus Eliae"; 12 recto: "schola et doctores Heb. Helias in Tisb. rad. רבץ. ait scholas vocari ישיבה q. d. habitationem nempe τῶν תלמידים. i. discipulorum. at professores vocant iidem מרביצי תורה q. facientes accubare leg. i. explicantes . . . הגא διορθοῦν. Criticorum Hebr. proprium hoc est vocabulum. Vide Eliam in Thisbi. מגיה ὁ διορθωτής etc." Here Casaubon draws on the article *rbts* from Levita's *Tishbi,* partly underlined in his own copy (BL 1936.e.5)

27. Bod MS Casaubon 60, 26 verso: "<u>Massora</u> sive <u>Critica</u> Hebraeorum. Praeter elegantiss. opus Eliae sunt alia multa per libros RR. sparsa huc pertinentia. Adde Notas biblicas."

28. For this *terminus ante quem* see Casaubon 1709, 246, and Chapter 1 above.

29. Casaubon, note on flyleaf in BL 1934.f.13: "Pag. צד sive 94. et seqq. agit de scribis et libris eorum scriptione ac descriptione: item de off. doctorum et discipulorum, etc. Quaedam inibi φιλόλογα." Casaubon noted the topics of sections, e.g., 94 recto: "De scriptoribus librorum"; 101 recto: "De doctore et discipulis." But he did not take detailed notes.

30. Bod MS Casaubon 60, 12 recto; "ספר ישן נושן sic vocant codicem antiquiss. ut in libro Hachassidim."

31. For a study of the tradition of the *tikkunei soferim* down to Ramon Martí, who in turn was Galatino's source, see McCarthy 1981. See also Azariah de' Rossi's discussion in *Me'or 'Einayim,* chap. 19, de' Rossi 2001, 325–328.

The Talmudists wanted to remove from the Bible prophecies that Christianity clearly fulfilled and mysteries that clearly confirmed its truths. But they also removed from the scriptures many things that they did not understand, or that in their view seemed absurd, and might bring the text into discredit either with infidels or with "ignorant and simple Jews." This was a rational way to explain such changes as the notorious one that had supposedly taken place in Genesis 18:22 ("And Abraham was still standing before the Lord"). According to tradition, the original text had described God as standing before Abraham. The scribes found the roles of the two parties improper and changed the text so that Abraham stood before God. The Jews, Galatino inferred from this and other cases, had corrupted scripture, and violated their own commandments in doing so: but they had done so "not for the sake of hiding the truth, or with any other evil intention," but to protect their scripture from the ridicule of infidels and Christians. In his view, the stages of this process of corruption could still be seen, first in the Septuagint, as the Talmud suggested, and then in the Talmud itself, which preserved the evidence about the *tikkunei soferim*.[32]

One reason Galatino felt sure that the Jews had not meant to deceive was simple: they had left all the evidence in plain sight. When they emended the text, "they did not actually change the letters, but dared to point them in a way different from what scripture naturally demands."[33] As usual, Galatino's

32. Galatino 1603, 27–28 (I.8): "GAL. Innumera profecto in sacra pagina erant mysteria admodum inclyta, atque Christianae fidei plurimum consentanea, quae veteres Iudaeorum gentilibus omni studio occulere nitebantur. Hinc septuaginta interpretes (ut de eis primum dicam) multa, teste Talmud, Ptolomaeo regi transferre omiserunt, et plurima mutaverunt, ne divina arcana gentilibus tunc indignis, nota fieri contingeret. Hinc etiam et ipsi סופרים *sophrim,* id est, scribae sive sapientes, multa tanquam absurda, et tanquam ea quae apud gentium nationes, nefas erat vel somniare, de divinis scripturis abraserunt, tanquam ij, qui adhuc divini consilij celsitudinem super humani generis salute, plene non perpendebant: aut quia timebant divinas scripturas propter talia a suis et ab aliis infidelibus irrisum iri: aut quia suspicati sunt, Iudaeis ignaris atque simplicibus, ex huiusmodi impiae credulitatis scandalum generari. Eapropter non veritatis occultandae gratia, aut alio quovis malo animo, eas mutationes quibus scripturam sacram depravari contigit, eos fecisse constat: cum et in his et aliis in locis pene infinitis, sibi invicem veritatem reserare non praetermiserint, ut in Talmudicis libris liquido patet."

33. For the sources of Galatino's material and even much of his wording on the *tikkunei soferim* see Martí 1651, 222–223 (II.iii.9), 547–550 (III.iii.4.11), 669–670 (III.iii.16.27) (and cf. McCarthy 1981, 52–54). It is revealing to compare, e.g., 549 with the passage from Galatino I.8 quoted above: "sic quoque vel tunc vel postea scribae saepius memorati eraserunt quae dicta sunt de Scripturis divinis tanquam absurda, et tanquam illa quae apud gentium sapientes nefas videbatur etiam somniare: vel quia suspicati sunt posse de facili per huiusmodi Iudaeis simplicibus impiae credulitatis scandalum generari: vel quia timebant scripturas divinas propter talia a suis et ab aliis infidelibus irrideri: vel forte quia celsitudinem divini consilii super salute generis humani minime perpendebant." For the Masoretes, see III.iii.21.1, 696: "Caeterum sciendum quod nec Moyses punctavit legem, unde Iudaei non habent eam cum punctis, i. cum vocalibus scriptam in rotulis suis; nec aliquis ex prophetis punctavit librum suum; sed duo Iudaei, quorum unus dictus est *Nephtali,* alter vero *Ben Ascher,* totum vetus Testamentum punctasse leguntur: quae quidem puncta cum quibusdam virgulis sunt loco vocalium apud eos." Still, Galatino wove

learning was not his own. His information about the corrections of the scribes came from Ramon Martí's thirteenth-century *Pugio fidei,* as Casaubon eventually learned. Still, Casaubon seems to have felt that Galatino, with his paradoxical mixture of anti-Jewish polemic and rich information about the history of Jewish learning, offered vital material that he could not readily find elsewhere, and he identified Galatino as a prime source of information about the *tikkunei soferim.*[34]

Galatino did not quench Casaubon's curiosity. In 1613, when he spent time in Oxford, he took detailed, extensive notes on the *Syntagma* of the early sixteenth-century Hebraist Robert Wakefield. Like Galatino's book, the *Syntagma,* published by Wynkyn de Worde in London in 1534, predated the *Massoret haMassoret.*[35] Unlike Galatino, however, Wakefield based his evaluation of the Hebrew text on direct study of the two Bomberg editions of the Rabbinic Bible, as well as the psalters edited by Felix Pratensis and Agostino Giustiniani.[36] Casaubon rightly found Wakefield's discussion of the Masorah—by far the most detailed one produced by a Christian Hebraist before the appearance of Levita's book—very impressive.[37] But he did not integrate these detailed notes with his other notes on ancient criticism.

For our immediate purposes, the fact that Casaubon relied so heavily on secondary sources, the works of Christian Hebraists, is most suggestive. It seems likely that he never carried out—or even tried hard to carry out—his proposed direct investigation of the Masorah. In the letter to Porthaise, Casaubon went on to describe the Masorah, revealing that he had used Rabbinic Bibles, and even to offer some help with deciphering its tightly encrypted information:

> The little circles that you asked about serve only to indicate to the reader that he should look at the margin of the book, where he will find a Masoretic note. But in the great Bibles printed in Venice the

---

the material into a seamless narrative, and, harsh though his condemnations of the Jews were, he did not quite match Martí's bile (223): "Per ista quidem satis patet Iudaeos esse falsigraphos, fures, atque mendaces."

34. Bod MS Casaubon 60, 12 recto: "Loci correcti in bibliis. Loci XVIII. dicuntur a Masoritis correcti de q. vide Galatinum et Mercerum in Job, cap. 32."

35. The publication date was established by Rex 1990. On Wakefield's Hebrew studies see in general Wakefield 1989, although the introduction is very general.

36. Carley 2001 is a splendid study of Wakefield's library, including his Hebrew books, and his habits as a reader. For a study of Wakefield's biblical scholarship see Grafton forthcoming.

37. Bod MS Casaubon 28, 143 verso: "Vixit hic vir in Acad. Oxon. temporibus Henrici VIII. et eo tempore quo disputabatur de jure repudii quod ille Rex cum uxore sua fecit. Qua de causa extat initio libelli disputatio: ibidem sequitur libellus de incoru. codd. Heb. sane eruditus." For a much fuller study of Casaubon's extracts and Wakefield's own work see Grafton forthcoming.

notes of the Masoretes are not printed, as is the normal way, at the margin of the text, but partly in the space between the Hebrew text and the Chaldean Targum, and partly beneath each column. The marginal notes of the critics are usually written in single letters, as you will see in the spaces I mentioned. For example, the little circle over *bara* refers to the note that you will find in that place; but what those numbers mean is explained in the other place I mentioned. When the little circle appears between two words, you should know that the critical note refers to both of them. There is no small difficulty involved in arriving at a correct understanding of all the forms of annotation in this art. Jean Mercier, doubtless the greatest Christian Hebraist of our time, was especially skilled at this. I hope that my work will someday shed no small light on studies of this kind, but that lies in the lap of the gods, for I need time and leisure, and other concerns busy me at present.[38]

Casaubon's description of the *mise-en-page* of the Masorah shows that he had used it in the form given in Rabbinic Bibles. But it remains very general: he does not point out, for example, that the notes at the top and bottom of the page belong to the so-called Masora Magna, those between the Hebrew text and the Targum to the Masora Parva. Casaubon's elaborate deference to Mercier suggests that he did not feel confident when it came to actually working with the Masorah. So does the one example of a Masoretic note that he chose to discuss, the circle superscribed between the first two words of Genesis 1:1. This came directly from Casaubon's rather tatty Rosetta Stone for the Masorah, Chevalier's unpublished Latin translation of Levita.[39] Through 1603, in other words, Casaubon's knowledge of the Maso-

---

38. Casaubon 1709, 174: "Orbiculi, de quibus scripsisti, nullum alium usum habent, nisi ut Lectorem admoneant, ut oram libri consulat, inventurus ibi notam Massoreticam. In magnis Bibliis tamen Veneticis notae Massoretarum, non ut fieri amat, ad contextum in margine sunt adnotatae: verum partim in eo intervallo, quod est inter Hebraicum textum et Chaldaicum Targum; partim utrique illi pagellae subijcitur. Solent marginales Criticorum notae singulis fere literis scribi; ut videbis eo, quod diximus, interstitio. Exempli gratia: Circulus τῷ ברא impositus rejicit ad notam, quam illo loco habes: quid autem illi numeri significent, declaratur in altero, quem indicavimus, loco. Cum hic orbiculus duabus dictionibus interjicitur, scire licet, ad utrumque verbum adjectam notam criticam pertinere. Non minima sane difficultas est, omnes has notationes ejus artis recte intelligere: qua re excelluit olim divinus vir Joannes Mercerus, omnium Christianorum nostri seculi sine controversia Hebraice doctissimus. Speramus non mediocrem aliquando lucem opera nostra accessuram huic studiorum generi: verum hoc Θεοῦ ἐν γούνασι κεῖται, χρόνου γὰρ δεῖ καὶ σχολῆς. Nunc quidem aliae curae nos habent."

39. Bod MS Casaubon 10, 10 recto = Levita 1867, 139: "Super autem omnem dictionem in quam aliquid tradiderunt, fecerunt circulum in medio dictionis quae est in contextu, ad notandum aliquid tradi de ea in margine . . . Quando vero circulus ille collocatur inter duas dictiones, signum est annotationem Masoreticam ad utramque dictionem pertinere, ut אלהים ° ברא."

rah remained relatively superficial. Nothing in the surviving evidence indicates that he ever worked his way through Levita's tabulation and analysis of the various forms of Masoretic correction—much less that he could have investigated the Masorah on his own.

One reason for Casaubon's apparent failure to pursue his promised line of research may have been a gradual loss of faith in the quality of Jewish—or, indeed, of ancient—textual criticism. In his miscellaneous notes on ancient criticism, he remarks that the text of the *Phaenomena* of Aratus, an ancient didactic poem on astronomy, "shows by itself how much liberty the ancient critics allowed themselves in editing and emending—or rather transfiguring, so to speak—their books. Astronomers, grammarians, and geometers read or corrupted practically every verse of this in different ways. More intolerable still is that various fools added a composite prologue to it on their own authority . . . And the same liberties were sometimes taken, even by the orthodox, with the New Testament."[40] Some leaves later appear detailed treatments of what Casaubon called "remarkable errors derived from false readings"—in these cases, Jewish ones. He argued at length that the Jews had been wrong to infer from Exodus 3:15 (זה שמי לעלם, "this is my name forever") that it was forbidden to speak aloud the name of God. Their error, moreover, rested on a change introduced into the text by an ancient "Hebrew master." This anonymous scribe revocalized לעלם from *leolam* (forever) to *lealam* (properly *lealem*, "concealed"). So emended, the verse meant "this my name is hidden," and it became a charter for Jewish superstitions about the pronunciation of the divine name.[41] Casaubon found all of this information, as he duly noted, in Galatino.[42]

40. Bod MS Casaubon 60, 8 recto: "Quantum sibi critici veteres permiserunt in libris recensendis et emendandis imo transfigurandis (ut ita dicam) unius Arati Φαινόμενα declarant. cuius singuli paene versus varie lecti aut depravati fuere, ab astronomis, grammaticis et geometris. sed nihil intolerabilius quam quod Prooemium illi multiplex varii nugatores affinxerunt de suo. vide ad Achillem Statium p. 109 . . . Eadem licentia alicubi usurpata in Novo Test. etiam ab orthodoxis proh nefas! Epiphan. 482."

41. Ibid., 24 verso: "Exodi 3.15. postquam dixit Deus ad Mosem sibi esse nomen Jehovae, addit: זה שמי לעולם וזה זכרי לדור ודור τόδε μοι ὄνομα εἰς αἰῶνα· καὶ τόδε μοι μνημόσυνον εἰς γενεὰς γενεῶν. Locus nihil habet obscuri: et tamen repertus olim quidam magister Hebraeorum qui pro לעלם legens לעלם ut celetur, auctor fuit superstitionis illius quae tam severe servatur a Judaeis, ut nomen istud nunquam legant: idque putent summum nefas. Neque enim verentur pronuntiare, qui secus faxit, nullam ei fore partem in vita aeterna. En quantum errorem in vitam induxerit prava lectio voculae unius. Porro istius errorem multa confutant: sive ipsum illum locum accurate perpendas: sive alios, ut Isaiae 63.16. Porro quod dicto loco Exodi 3.15 לעלם sine ו est scriptum, id nihil est: etsi non nescio RR. in eo latere velle mysterium, quasi oblique indicaretur nomen Jehovae occultum futurum usque ad Messiae adventum."

42. Galatino 1603, 94 (II.14), quoting the *libellus* of R. Abraham Picus: "In quibus quidem nominibus et in nominibus patrum fit mentio divinitatis, quoniam dicit, dii Abraham, dii Ishac, et dii Iacob. Et

In a second case, Casaubon argued even more sharply that one of the greatest Jewish scholars had either followed a corrupt text of the Pentateuch or corrupted it himself:

> Rabbi Akiva, a man of great reputation, lived at the time of Jesus Christ, or certainly that of the apostles. But it was his stupidity, not his learning, that made him prominent. For when by chance he happened on corrupt texts of Moses—or perhaps had corrupted them himself—he read, at Numbers 24:17 ["There shall come a star out of Jacob"], in place of *cohav,* star, *cozab,* lie. This led him to believe, and to persuade others, that the man who claimed that he was the Messiah, under the name *Barcozab,* was the true Messiah.[43]

In this case, the ice on which Casaubon skated was paper-thin. Without knowing it, he was discussing a bitterly controversial episode from Jewish history—one so controversial that the tradition retained vivid, and in part conflicting, records of it.[44] It is possible that Akiva did—but also that he did not—see Bar Kochba as the fulfillment of the prophecy of Numbers 24:17.

Casaubon, however, could not know of any of these complications, since he encountered the texts not directly, but as interpreted by Galatino:

> For as it is written in the Jerusalem Talmud, in the tractate titled Taanith, that is, "On fasts," in the chapter that begins "In three chapters," R. Akiva expounded the passage from Numbers 24:17, "A star shall step forth from Jacob" as "Barcozba will step forth from Jacob." And when he saw Barcozba himself, he said: "This is the King Messiah." This is also clearly contained in the commentary on Jeremiah's lament titled *Echa rabbethi,* on Lamentations 2:2. For it is said there that R. Judah the son of Elai said that R. Akiva, when he expounded

---

quando speculatus fueris, in nomine אלהי *Elohe,* invenies divinitatem pluraliter signatam, et qui intelligit, intelligat. Et hoc est quod dicit, Hoc est nomen meum in aeternum: et scriptum est sic לעלם (hoc est sine vau litera) quod occultum significat. Non enim licet hoc sacramentum patefacere, nisi homini miti, et qui incumbat doctrinae Cabalae."

43. Bod MS Casaubon 60, 25 recto: "Vixit temporibus Jesu Christi vel certe apostolorum Rabbi Akiba vir ingentis nominis: sed quem sua stultitia nobilem fecit potius quam eruditio. Hic enim cum forte incidisset in depravatos Mosis codices, aut forte ipse depravasset, et Numerorum cap. [24:17] pro stella כוכב mendacium, כוזב, inductus est ut crederet atque aliis persuaderet, eum qui pro Messia se jactabat sub nomine Barcozab, verum esse Messiam. pro quo etiam diu est habitus. vide Galat. 4.21. p. 263. Drus. No. T. 125 [the last reference added later]."

44. See Palestinian Talmud, Ta'anit 4, 68d; Eikha Rabba 2:2; Schäfer 1978, 86–90; 1980, 117–119.

the verse, "A star shall step forth from Jacob," said that one should not read *cohav,* star, but *cozab,* that is, lie, because it was the name of his false Messiah.[45]

As usual, Galatino had borrowed his erudition from Ramon Martí.[46] Casaubon, drawing on Galatino in his turn, pressed the evidence to confirm his view that Akiva had been a fool. The sequence of Galatino's account, though not perfectly clear, suggests a simple and basically logical series of developments. In his enthusiasm for Bar Kochba, Akiva expounded Numbers 24:17 in a directly messianic sense. Bar Kochba's failure then led Akiva's pupil Judah bar Ilai to suggest that *cozab,* lie, would have been a more appropriate reading than *cohav,* star. Casaubon, by contrast, not only made Akiva responsible for high-handed play with the wording of the Bible; he also went so far as to claim that Akiva or someone else corrupted the text of Numbers before Akiva applied it to Bar Kochba. Even Galatino had not portrayed Akiva as attacking the text in this manner. Casaubon acted in this case, distinctively, less as a philologist than as yet another interpreter in the chain, and a violent one—at least as violent as Akiva himself. He did not explain why anyone would have changed the line before Bar Kochba came on the scene. Only one point seems clear: Casaubon had now begun to think, as many Christian polemicists had argued in the past, that the early rabbis had dealt in a fast and loose way with the biblical text.

When Casaubon addressed the question of the variants in the Hebrew text and the form of ancient textual criticism they reflected, he trod, as he knew, on dangerous ground. In 1604 he wrote to the Leiden scholar Petrus Scriverius to explain that the need to cover Hebrew criticism would delay the completion of his projected larger work, since he could not do so with-

45. Galatino 1603, 262–263 (IV.21): "Nam ut legitur in Talmud Ierosolymitano, in libro qui תענית *Taanith,* id est, de ieiunio nuncupatur, in ca. quod incipit בשלשה פרקים *Bislosa perakim,* id est in tribus capitulis, R. Akiba scripturam illam Numer. 23 [24:17]. מיעקב דרך כוכב [quoted in this form by Galatino] Id est, Orietur stella ex Iacob, ita exponebat, Orietur *Barcozba* ex Iacob. Et cum videret ipsum *Barcozbam,* dicebat: en hic est Rex Messias. Id idem quoque in expositione planctus Ieremiae, quae איכה רבתי *Echa rabbethi* appellatur, clare habetur, super illud Thren. 2. dictum, Dissipavit Dominus, et non est misertus: ibi enim dicitur R. Iudam filium Elai dixisse, quod R. Akiba exponens dictum illud, Orietur stella ex Iacob, dicebat: Non esse legendum כוכב *cochab,* id est, stella, sed כוזב *cozab,* id est, mendacium, quod sui falsi Messiae nomen erat."

46. Martí 1651, 598 (III.iii.9.2): "*Dixit R. Juda, R. Akiba erat exponens illud Num. 24.v.17,* Egressa est stella de Iacob: *Non legas* כוכב *stella; sed* כוזב *mendacium,* vel falsitas: *Cumque videbat R. Akiba Bar kosba,* dicebat, Iste est rex Messias. Hucusque Glossa Threnorum. Idem quoque scribitur in *Talmud Hierosolymitano in libro* Taanit, *in distinctione* quae incipit *Scheloscha perakim . . . R. Akiba erat exponens,* Et egredietur stella de Iacob; *non legas* stella; *sed* mendacium. *Et quando videbat Ben kosba, dicebat, iste est Rex Messias. Haec in Talmude."

out entering into polemics: "This investigation is particularly difficult, both because it bristles with technical problems, and because it contains certain rather unrestrained arguments against those who, committing a terrible crime, have the audacity to demean the holy scriptures."[47] The status of the Hebrew text had long been controversial in the Christian world. Some—above all Jerome—described it as "Hebraica veritas," the authoritative, original text. Others denounced it as a tissue of fabrications, woven by Jews determined not to acknowledge that Christ was the Messiah whose coming the prophets had predicted. These debates revived in the fifteenth and sixteenth centuries as humanists turned their philological tools to the Bible, demanding a return to the pure sources of tradition.[48] The Reformation recast the arguments in a still sharper key. Luther and other early Protestants, supersessionists by profound conviction, were delighted to find that they need not trust the Jews to correct and explicate the Old Testament. Levita's book seemed to many to confirm these views. Most Catholic scholars also embraced the thesis that the Masorah and the variant readings it contained were late. By doing so they could argue—to the fury of the few Jews who paid attention to Christian scholarship—that the Hebrew text of the Old Testament was too unreliable and corrupt to serve as an authoritative basis for theology. Only the magisterium of the Catholic church, informed by divine help, could determine what the Bible actually said.

By the end of the sixteenth century, however, many Calvinists and Lutherans realized that Protestantism needed a principle of authority as solid as the Catholic magisterium—and that this must logically consist in an absolutely reliable text of scripture. Some began to insist that the Hebrew Old Testament and the Greek New Testament were both literally flawless—not only in the original versions, divinely inspired but long lost to human readers, but even in those transmitted by scribes and printers.[49] No philologist gave literalist theologians more aid and comfort than Johann Buxtorf, the Basel Hebraist with whom Casaubon exchanged letters, and for whom he had deep respect. Buxtorf knew—as he admitted, in private, to Louis Cappel—that the evidence about the history of the Masorah was complex, and largely contradicted his view that it went back to Ezra and the men of the Great Synagogue. Neither the talmudic nor the targumic evidence proved

---

47. Casaubon to Scriverius, 29 June 1604, Casaubon 1709, 213: "Illa autem lucubratio peculiarem habet difficultatem, cum et spinosa sit tota, et quaedam in eo contineantur liberius adversus eos disputata, qui scelere immani de Sacra Pagina audent detrahere."

48. Schwarz 1955; Botley 2004.

49. See Muller 1980; Goshen-Gottstein 1987; Burnett 1996. For the more normal (and rational) forms of biblical literalism in this period see Yoffie 2009.

that the vowel points were known to their authors. If the ancient Hebrew text had had vowel points, Jerome should at least have mentioned them, and he did not. And the later history of the text suffered from so grave a lack of definite dates and information that it could not be reconstructed in detail.[50] On the other hand, Buxtorf asked, "If their inventors are recent, and R. Asher and R. Naftali or others not long before them devised the points, what certainty and authority can they have?"[51] Given the dangers that the subject posed, Buxtorf argued that it would be better simply to refrain from airing "this most subtle and profound" problem in public.[52] In his writings, however, Buxtorf insisted staunchly that the vowel points were ancient. Only the appearance of Levita's book and the partial translation by Sebastian Münster, he argued, had provoked Christian scholars to call their age and authenticity into doubt.[53] These debates were anything but academic. They had radical implications for everything from the standard of authority in the Christian world to the proper method for Christian chronology—a very fashionable area of study at the time. The decision to choose the Septuagint in preference to the Masoretic text of the Old Testament, for example, solved

50. Buxtorf to Louis Cappel, Basel, 1 January 1623 (copy), Zurich, Zentralbibliothek, MS F 45, 247 verso: "In locis Talmudicis, quae punctorum vocalium et accentuum videntur facere mentionem, illud me semper (ante longe quam scriptum tuum legi) perplexum tenuit, de potestate potius quam figuris ea intelligenda esse. In Targum centena loca notavi, quae indicant eos authores ex textu non punctato notasse. Difficile est explicatu quod, si ante Hieronymum punctata exemplaria exstiterunt, ne minimo quidem rumore id a Iudaeis praeceptoribus unquam cognoverit, et posteritati revelaverit, etiamsi vel propter raritatem, vel propter authoritatem non licuisset exemplar videre, famam tamen non tacuisset. Si vero recentes sunt authores, et vel R. Ascher, et R. Naphtali, aut alii non diu ante eos ipsorum authores sunt, quae tunc punctorum certitudo vel authoritas, si inter ipsa exordia de iis capita Doctorum litigarunt et dissenserunt. Operae pretium magnum esset nos habere de his duobus ipsorum tempore, loco, doctrina, scriptis certam historiam habere; item de primis Grammaticis R. Iona, et R. Abraham Chijugs forte ex illis aliquid posset peti certius. Sed horum scripta Davidi Kimchio visa, qui forte produxisset si quid solidius et verius de punctorum principiis ipsi docuissent. Quid multis? laboramus defectu historiae Hebraicae unde veritatem inde demonstrare."

51. Ibid.: "Si vero recentes sunt authores, et vel R. Ascher, et R. Naphtali, aut alii non diu ante ipsorum authores sunt, quae tunc punctorum certitudo vel authoritas, si inter ipsa exordia de iis capita Doctorum litigarunt et dissenserunt."

52. Ibid.: "Hinc probe agnosco, difficile esse argumentum de antiquitate punctorum. Interea etiam pessimas et periculosissimas consequentias ex novitate punctorum non satis ex animo meo evellis, quae etiam eo me pertrahunt ut putem non expedire publice hanc quaestionem subtilis. et profundis. in scholis vel voce vel editis libris tractari."

53. Buxtorf 1620,):(2 verso: "Paucissimi enim hactenus deprehensi sunt, qui vel mediocrem in hac materia cognitionem aut scientiam adepti fuere, non quod discendi defuerit voluntas, sed quod occasio. Unus Elias Levita, genere judaeus, gente Germanus, superiori seculo, suis hanc viam praeivit, edito libro *Masoreth hammasoreth,* qui brevis in Masoram Commentarius. Ejus exemplaria tam inter judaeos quam Christianos hodie rarissima, pares cultores habent. Inter Christianos etiam eo rariores, quod nunquam Latine iste Liber conversus sit, ut et alibi dixi. At quod paucula inde Sebastianus Munsterus aliquando transtulit, id causam praebuit, quare plurimi doctrina praecellentes viri Theologi et Philologi, de Masora et Masorethis, sinistra nimium conceperunt praejudicia."

one problem that bedeviled all chronologers. It extended the period between the Creation and the Flood by over 1,200 years, making room for Chaldean, Egyptian, and, eventually, Chinese dynasties that the shorter Hebrew chronology could not accommodate.[54]

One might have expected Casaubon to stand with Buxtorf. In his view, Catholic scholars' efforts to show that the Vulgate was, as the Council of Trent had proclaimed, the authentic text of the Bible, merely served to reveal "how wickedly the Papists treat those who use the true texts in Hebrew or Greek to correct translations."[55] Casaubon knew his opponents and did not underestimate them. He read a 1607 edition of Gilbert Génébrard's commentary on the Psalms with care, even pronouncing it "Opus eruditissimum."[56] But he also noted the Catholic Hebraist's general tendency to favor the Septuagint unduly.[57] When other Catholic expositors—Bellarmine, for example, whose mastery of patristic exegesis Casaubon respected—went even farther in the same direction, Casaubon treated them with contempt:

> Once they decided to treat the Latin translation as authoritative, they were prepared to say anything, however absurd, foolish, and ridiculous, in its defense: indeed, they do say anything. Bellarmine's entire commentary on the Psalms is only one long defense of the mistakes that time has introduced into the old translation. And they defend not only the Latin, but also the Septuagint, which is defended because the Latin more or less derives from it.[58]

54. For these problems and the protracted debates they caused see Allen 1949 and 1970; Klempt 1960; Van Kley 1971; P. Rossi 1984; Bietenholz 1994; Laplanche 1994; Malcolm 2002; Jorink 2006; and Weststeijn 2007.

55. Bod MS Casaubon 30, 79 recto: "σὺν Θεῷ. Iniquitas Pontificiorum erga eos qui e veritate Hebraica vel Graeca interpretationes corrigunt."

56. Casaubon, note on title page of BL 1016.d.3.

57. Ibid.: "Σηαι Gen. etsi mire deditus LXX. quos fere ubique non excusat sed laudat, et certo judicio ac spiritu prophetico variasse ab Heb. contendit. aliquando tamen fontem Hebraeum, et ad illum torquet verba τῶν 70. ut 736 [735]. 781."

58. Bod MS Casaubon 30, 79 recto: "Postquam constitutum est ab istis habere pro authentica versionem Latinam, nihil tam absurdum, fatuum, ridiculum est, quod pro ejus defensione dicturi non sint, imo quod non dicant. Totus Bellarmini Comment. in Ψαλ. nihil fere est aliud, nisi perpetua defensio omnium errorum, quos invexit longa dies in veterem interpretem. Neque vero solum Latinam defendunt, sed etiam τὴν 70. quae dicitur quia ex illa fere pendet Latina. Quaedam obiter adnotamus." For a very different response to Bellarmine's exegesis, from Casaubon's last years, see his note on the title page of BL 3089.g.20: "Liber est scholasticus et ad explicationem huius divini operis Davidici ex mente Patrum, item ad conciliandas versiones cum origine apprime utilis. Singularis etiam B. est cura revocandi τὸν τύπον ad rem significatam, id est Christum." But even here Casaubon's negative verdict reappears on the flyleaf, apropos of Bellarmine's treatment of Psalm 40:7: "277. Latina versio etsi diversa ab Hebr. et Gr. codd. non potest reprobari, quia sit approbata per concilium Trid. ô vanitatem argumenti!"

Even in the matter of chronology, Casaubon rejected any effort to make the Septuagint rather than the Masoretic text the standard. In his notes on ancient criticism, he complained that the passionately Catholic chronologer Christophe Lauret, a former follower of the Duc de Guise, had systematically undermined the authority of the Hebrew Old Testament. Casaubon's criticism was just. Lauret had argued that the Septuagint represented the true, uncorrupted text of the Old Testament, as publicly attested by the Jews, while the rabbis who later created the Mishnah and the Talmud had also deliberately conspired to corrupt the Hebrew so that Jesus would not seem to be the Messiah called for by the prophets.[59] As a good Calvinist and a staunch upholder of the principle of scriptural authority against such outlandish and ill-informed arguments, Casaubon might well have accepted Buxtorf's simple principle: if the points were not original, then the text they clarified lacked all authority.[60]

In fact, Calvinist scholars already disagreed sharply on these issues. Scaliger, whom Casaubon took as an authority on all matters Hebraic, agreed in general that the Masoretic text was the closest surviving approximation to the original Old Testament. But he regarded the Septuagint as superior in the passages where its redactors' wider knowledge of the non-Jewish world had helped them: for example, on the orthography of the names of Near Eastern monarchs. Scaliger wrote to Buxtorf in the late spring of 1606 to deny the antiquity of the Masoretic vowel points. He believed without question that they were added late, after the text was translated into Greek—probably, he argued, in the early centuries of the common era. The same dating would hold, by extension, for the Masoretes' efforts at textual emendation. Scaliger warned Buxtorf that the *Zohar,* the great kabbalistic work

59. Bod MS Casaubon 60, 25 recto: "Σηαι Christoph. Lauretus in sua Chronologia omnibus viribus convellit auctoritatem Hebraici textus." See esp. Lauret 1598, 70 recto: "Les Iuifs, Scribes et Pharisiens s'estans obstinez contre Iesus Christ, et s'estans rendus ennemis à outrance d'iceluy, se voyans pressez de la plenitude des temps que l'on tenoit estre advenue au temps du Roy Herodes Ascalonite, si que plusieurs s'eslevoient, et se disoient estre le Messias; comme Iudas Gaulonite, Theudas Caphedon, Cozba, Barcozba et autres, ont eu occasion, voire ont esté contraints ayans le moyen de ce faire, de corrompre la Chronique du texte Hebraic, dont les Scribes seuls avoyent la garde et entiere charge; depuis le temps d'Esdras, et de mettre en avant les mensonges contra Iesus Christ, qui sont en leurs Talmuds et livres Cabalistiques: ainsi que les Prophetes avoyent predict." He develops the argument further in the still more visionary and bizarre Lauret 1610, e.g., 44–51.

60. For Casaubon's general position see, e.g., Casaubon 1710, 67: "Ad quaestionem de corrupt. Sacri codicis ita respondet Casaubonus: Literae quidem sacrae h.e. ὁ νοῦς utriusque testamenti ἄφθαρτα sunt, et nulli depravationi obnoxia: at lingua, quae literarum illarum veluti φόρημα est, quin aliquam labem aut labeculam sed sine detrimento τοῦ νοῦ acceperit longi temporis tractu, non est, ut puto, dubitandum. In Graeco res manifesta: multa leviter immutata, quaedam gravius tentata, sed sic, ut veritas inconcussa maneret. In Hebr. cur dubitemus? nonne tota Masora certissimum ejus rei testimonium praebet? Vide Augustin. de C. D. p. 825."

that assumed the antiquity of the vowel points, was actually not so old as the Talmud.[61] Some years later, the Franeker Hebraist Johannes Drusius wrote Buxtorf to similar effect. He claimed that he had called Scaliger's attention to the material about the promulgation of the *Zohar* presented in Abraham Zacuto's *Yuchasin,* which proved the work's late origin. "Here," he pointed out, "you have the testimony of a Jew, which is not to be despised."[62] In other words, the Calvinist scholars whom Casaubon admired most disagreed with Buxtorf.

Casaubon's original position, the one he presented to Porthaise, resembled the one most visibly espoused by Scaliger: the Masoretic text, a product of the industry of learned, responsible men, was basically reliable. Yet it seems that both men, in the years after 1603, came to have their doubts—not about the humanity of the Jewish critics, but about their reliability. Scaliger wavered. On one day he told the French students who boarded with him at Leiden: "For more than 1,300 years, the Hebrew Bible has been well kept by the Jews and the Masoretes. They put in the marks of punctuation, the accents, and the letters, marking them with great care, with their exact numbers. It would be hard to prove that it is corrupt."[63] In other moods, however,

---

61. Scaliger to Buxtorf, 1 June (Julian) 1606, Universitätsbibliothek Basel, MS G I 59, 363 verso, printed in Scaliger 1627, 523–524: "De apicibus vocalibus Hebraeorum, tam mihi constat rem novam esse, quam eos falli, qui natos una cum lingua putant, quo nihil stultius dici potuit aut cogitari. Nam praeceptiones Grammaticae alicujus linguae tunc instituuntur, non quando vernacula est illa lingua, sed postquam in usu vulgi esse desiit. Quis hoc negare potest? Arabismi puncta vocalia est recens inventum, id est, multis annis post obitum impostoris Muhammedis. Hodie tamen pueri Turcarum, Arabum, Persarum, ac omnium denique Muhammedanorum sine punctis legere discunt. Eodem modo Samaritani et Judaei sine ullis punctis in Synagogis suis Legem ἐν ταῖς διφθέραις legunt. Neque est, quod qui contra sentiunt, locum illum objiciant ex Zohar, quem in epistola tua produxisti. Ille liber est recentior quam Talmud. Nobis plura argumenta ex versione LXX interpretum suppetunt, ut probemus nulla puncta olim fuisse, quam Judaeis, qui illud tantum ex paucis aliquot Targum locis probare possunt. Sed haec disputatio majoris otii est, quam nostri, addo etiam melioris ingenii." For his position see more generally Grafton 1983–1993, II, 736–737.

62. Drusius to Buxtorf, 8 February 1613, Universitätsbibliothek Basel, MS G I 59, 260 recto: "Judicium Scaligeri de libro Zohar valde probo. Puto me eum monuisse ea de re. Ego autem primum didici ex Salmanticensi Judaeo, qui de hac re ita scribit in libro Johasin: Videtur quod R. Eliezer Haccaphar fuerit ex posterioribus, licet citetur in Pirke R. Eliezer. Jam enim cognitum est, quamvis tribuatur liber ille R. Eliezero, tamen a posterioribus eum factum esse, ut liber hazoar, qui tribuitur R. Simeoni: et sic invenitur liber Jetzira, qui falso tribuitur Abrahamo Patriarchae, cum scriptus sit ab aliis. En testimonium Judaei, quod spernendum non est. Miror autem te in Grammatica tua, ubi de punctis vocalibus agis, maluisse sequi sententiam indoctorum, quam illorum qui eruditionis nomine clari sunt. in queis Mercerus, Veltuickus, Johannes Jsahac et alii, qui omnes in ea sententia sunt puncta ascripta fuisse a Masoritis. Quas autem rationes pro contraria sententia producis ex Amando Polano, sunt rationes Illyrici: quae hactenus nihil me moverunt."

63. Scaliger 1695, 59; 1740, II, 234: "Il y a plus de 1300 ans que la Bible Hebraique a esté bien gardée par les Juifs et les Massoreths, qui ont marqué les distinctions, poincts, lettres, qui ont esté soigneusement marquées, en quel nombre elles sont. Il seroit bien difficile à prouver qu'elle soit corrupue."

he took a more critical position. Casaubon read Scaliger's 1607 reply to the biblicist chronology of David Pareus, which rested on an absolute faith in the perfection of the text, with amusement and approval. He found it an exemplary defense of humanism against what Scaliger termed "fanaticism." "This book," Casaubon wrote on the title page, "gives an excellent view of this great man's learning and eloquence."[64] And he understood and summarized, without critical comment, Scaliger's argument that errors in the numbers in the Masoretic text required correction.[65]

It was perhaps in the same period that Casaubon came back to Galatino, and began to worry that the Masoretic fence around the Law, however solid its joinery, had been erected on swampy ground.[66] Datable evidence shows that he continued to ponder the problems until almost the end of his life: to his account of Akiva and Bar Kochba, for example, he appended a reference to Drusius' commentary on the New Testament, which appeared only in 1612.[67] For all his criticisms of Galatino, moreover, he had some reason to think he could rely on the material in the *De arcanis Catholicae veritatis*, at least where the history of Jewish textual criticism was concerned. Galatino's work did amount to a kind of history of the biblical text, however perverse it now looks. The Hebraists whom Casaubon respected most, moreover, used Galatino's work in exactly this way, and encouraged others to do so as well. Drusius, in the passage Casaubon noted down, cited Galatino with apparent approval as an authority on Akiva and Bar Kochba.[68] More important still was another, earlier witness. As we have seen, Casaubon respected Mercier's Hebrew scholarship implicitly. In particular, he believed that Mercier possessed special expertise in interpreting the Masorah. In his notes on ancient criticism, when he mentioned the eighteen *tikkunei soferim*, he referred to two authorities: Galatino and Mercier. In doing so, however, what he offered potential users of his collection was less complementary accounts than a

64. Casaubon, note on title page of BL C.75.b.16.(1) (Scaliger 1607): "Doctrinam et facundi[am] viri magni hic liber exim[ie] ostendit."

65. Casaubon, notes in BL C.75.b.16.(1), 26 (Scaliger 1607): "Scalig. putat Hebraea corrigenda"; 27: "Errores in Hebr. textu e notis numerorum"; 77 (on Scaliger's argument that biblical chronology, which had no eclipses to provide absolute dates, was actually harder than secular chronology to establish): "Chronologia S. S. difficilior quam in exotica h."

66. Casaubon also derived his survey of the contents of the Talmud, Bod MS Casaubon 52, 71 recto–73 recto, from Galatino.

67. Bod MS Casaubon 60, 25 recto: "vide Galat. 4.21. p. 263. Drus. No. T. 125 [the last reference added later]."

68. Drusius 1612, 125, on John 5:43 ("I am come in my Father's name, and ye receive me not: if another shall come in his own name, him ye will receive"): "Si venerit alius nomine suo qualis erat Barchocheba, quem omnes fere Iudaei et inter eos R. Aquiba, qui ejus armiger erat, ut Messiam receperunt. Historia nota. Vide Petrum Galatinum de arcanis catholicae veritatis IX.184. Impostor iste grave bellum gessit cum Romanis, quo confecto cum se deceptos viderent Iudaei, non amplius Barchochebam, id est filium stellae, sed Barchozibam eum vocarunt, id est filium mendacii."

feedback loop. Job 32:3 says of Elihu: "Also against his three friends was his wrath kindled, because they had found no answer, and [yet] had condemned Job." Numerous Jewish sources describe the verse as a *tikkun* and indicate that in the original form of the verse, the friends condemned God. The passage is puzzling in many ways, and none of the versions reflects the supposed original form.[69] Mercier, in his commentary on the verse, expressed strong doubts as to whether it had actually been altered. If the change had been made, however, he denounced it, in terms that help us to understand why Casaubon relied so heavily on the *De arcanis:* "In this matter, I think that they acted most rashly when they dared to change the text. And if this is the case, I would agree with Galatino that the text should be restored to its original state. Why did they not simply give their judgment in the margin, as with variant readings?" For further information on the *tikkunei soferim* he referred readers to the Masorah at the beginning of Numbers, and to Galatino.[70]

It is just possible that Casaubon's thinking about both Galatino and early Jewish criticism began to change again in the summer of 1613, when he encountered Wakefield's book. For Wakefield, who actually knew the primary evidence, Christian and Jewish, had made war on those who held that the rabbis and Masoretes had corrupted the biblical text. His exceptionally lucid and well-documented book represented the only Christian effort of the sixteenth century, before or after Levita's book appeared, to work through the primary evidence, verse by verse. Casaubon's summary should not be over-interpreted, but at the very least it suggests that he paid respectful attention to Wakefield's effort to defend the Masorah, and to set it into a larger context within the world of ancient scholarship:

It is clear that he was deeply grounded in Hebrew and rabbinic books and had some knowledge of Arabic as well. To sum up his ar-

69. McCarthy 1981, 115–120.

70. Mercier 1651, 254: "Hebraei constanter affirmant hunc locum esse e numero octodecim quae a scribis sint correcta, de quibus vide Galatinum et Masoram initio Numer. in quibus ante erat aliquid quod durius videbatur et indignum Dei majestate, scribae autem id temperarunt nonnihil immutantes: qua in re temere eos fecisse judico quod contextum ausi sint mutare. ac si ita est, contextum cum Galatino reponendum putarem uti erat antea. Cur enim non potius suum ad marg. judicium, ut in varia lectione, adjiciebant? putant ergo hic scriptum fuisse, damnarunt Dominum silentio scil. suo, quia Iobum atrociora loquentem in Dominum non satis coercuerant, in eo causam Domini non satis defendentes, condemnasse Dominum videbantur, quasi juxta verba Iobi ille injuste Iobum innocentem affligeret. Sane Aben-Ezra dicit illos qui hunc locum putant a scribis emendatum, plus videre quam ipse sciat, quia causam non intelligat. Sed causa est, si res ita habet, quod hoc durum de Deo videbatur, ideo loco Dei Iobum posuerunt, quod sensui optime quadrat. Quod si ita est mirum est neque Hier. neque Chaldaeum interpretem aut Septuaginta aut alios interpretes veteres ad hunc locum aut alios septemdecim advertisse."

gument: it is not true that the Hebrews treacherously corrupted the sacred scriptures. They did not corrupt them before the birth of the Lord: for he never accused them of this crime. They did not corrupt them afterward, as he proves from Origen, Jerome, Augustine. He shows that the Hebrews far outdid all the Greeks and Romans in their passion to preserve their holy books.[71]

Casaubon paid careful attention to Wakefield's close analysis of passages in the Talmud and bits of the Masorah, noting his conclusion that the rabbis might have changed the occasional vowel, but that they had rarely resorted to such expedients and had done little or no harm to the text.[72] By now, however, Casaubon's time was running out, and his *Critica* never took final shape. His work on the Masoretic text, in the end, sheds less light on the problems of ancient criticism than it does on Casaubon's aspirations, achievements, and limits as a student of Jewish tradition.

71. Bod MS Casaubon 28, 143 verso–144 recto: "Apparet illum valde fuisse versatum in libris Hebraicis et Rabbinicis et Arabicas etiam literas non plane ignorasse. Summa disputationis est: non esse verum, Hebraeos dolo corrupisse S. S. Non corrupisse ante Domini nativitatem apparet: quia nunquam D. hoc scelus illis obiicit. Non corrupisse postea probat ex Origene, Hieronymo, Augustino. Ostendit Hebraeos studio conservandi incorruptos libros sacros superasse longe omnes Graecos et Romanos."
72. Ibid., 144 recto:

Obiectiones postea quasdam proponit. I. est ex ipso Talmude in Masseceth Ieuamoth, id est, tractatu fratriarum, distinctione quae incipit Herel [Arel], ad eius extremum prope, ubi dicunt Rabbini (ipse apponit literis Latinis) Mutaf shettehaker oth achath mittora vaijthkaddosh shem shamaijm bepharhesia. i.e. Bene sit si e Lege evellatur character unus, seu litera una, ut Dei benedicti nomen in publico sanctificetur, in pretioque habeatur et non in gentibus blasphemetur.

Summa disp. est. Fatetur Rabbinos aliquot apices et vocales alicubi corrupisse. fortasse etiam vocem aliquam. sed hoc parcissime inveniri factum: et id ipsum, nihil admodum summae rei nocere. nam depravationes illas in paucis duntaxat exempl. reperiri, et ex ipsis Rabb. aut interpretibus posse emendari, vel e libris emendatioribus, vel e Com. Rabb. vel e Massora.

APPENDIX 3

Casaubon's Hebrew and Judaic Library

Bibles and Commentaries

Bellarmine, Robert. *Explanatio in Psalmos.* Lyons: H. Cardon, 1611. British Library 3089.g.20.

Hosee cum Thargum, id est Chaldaica paraphrasi Ionathan, et commentariis R. Selomo Iarhi, R. Abraham Aben Ezra, et R. D. Kimhi [Minor prophets with Rashi, Kimhi, and Ibn Ezra], ed. Jean Mercier. Paris: Robert Estienne, 1556. British Library 1942.g.3.

Libellus Ruth cum scholiis Masorae ad marginem; item in eundem succincta expositio nondum in lucem emissa, cuius in manu scripto exemplari auctor praefertur R. D. Kimhi, ed. Jean Mercier. Paris: Robert Estienne, 1563. British Library 1942.g.4. The commentary is in fact not by Kimhi but by Isaiah de Trani.

Psalmi Davidis variis calendariis et commentariis genuinum sensum et Hebraismos fusissime aperientibus a Gil. Genebrardo . . . instructi. Lyons: H. Cardon, 1607. British Library 1016.d.3, 4.

Grammars and Lexica

Buxtorf, Johann. *Epitome radicum Hebraicarum et Chaldaicarum.* Basel: C. Waldkirch, 1607. British Library 621.d.2.

Chevalier, Antoine Rudolphe. *Rudimenta Hebraicae linguae.* Geneva: F. le Preux, 1590. British Library 621.i.9. Presentation copy from the author.

de' Pomi, David. *Tsemah David, Dittionario novo Hebraico . . . Lexicon Novum Hebraicum.* Venice: G. di Gara, 1587. British Library C.79.d.6.

Kimhi, David. *Sefer Mikhlol.* Venice: D. Bomberg, 1545. British Library 1984.a.10.(1).

Levita, Elijah. *Grammatica Hebraica, absolutissima . . . nuper per Sebastianum Munsterum iuxta Hebraismum Latinitate donata . . . Institutio elementaria in Hebraicam linguam eodem Sebast. Munstero autore.* Basel: Io. Froben, 1525. British Library 621.d.11. [Bound with *Sefer haBahur, Sefer haHarkavah,* and *Luah haBinyanim.*]

———. *Sefer haTishbi.* Basel: C. Waldkirch, 1601. British Library 1936.c.5.

Münster, Sebastian. *Dictionarium Chaldaicum.* Basel: Io. Froben, 1527. British Library 621.g.1.

Miscellaneous Hebrew Texts

Avkat Rokhel. Venice: Z. di Cavalli, 1566. British Library 1968.a.16.

de' Rossi, Azariah. *Me'or 'Einayim.* Mantua: G. Rufinelli, 1574. British Library 1938.f.12.

Joseph ben Eliezer Halfan? *Sefer Orah Hayyim* [Yiddish]. Basel: [C. Waldkirch?], 1602. British Library 1935.e.15.

Judah ben Samuel. *Sefer haHasidim*. Basel: A. Froben, 1580. British Library 1934.f.13.

Mahzor Sefardim miyamim nora'im [Sephardi prayerbook for high holy days]. Venice: D. Zanetti, 1598. British Library 1972.c.14.

Samuel di Uceda. *Midrash Shemuel*. Venice: G. di Gara, 1585. British Library 1952.f.9.

Seder Tefillot mikol haShanah. Basel: A. Froben, 1579. British Library 1970.c.2 (formerly 481.a.11).

Temunot Tehinot Tefillot Sefarad [Sephardi prayerbook]. Venice: D. Zanetti, 1598. British Library 1972.c.1.

Jewish Chronologies

Josippon. Venice: C. Adelkind, 1544. British Library 1938.f.21.

Josippus de bello Iudaico: deinde decem Iudaeorum captivitates et Decalogus cum eleganti commentariolo Rabbi Aben Ezra. Hisce accesserunt Collectanea aliquot, quae Sebastianus Lepusculus Basiliensis colligebat, de quibus videre poteris verso folio. Omnia Hebraicolatina. Basel: Petri, 1559. British Library 1982.c.34.

Seder Olam Rabbah, ve-Seder Olam Zuta, Megillat Ta´anit, ve-Sefer haKabbalah le-haRabad. Basel: A. Froben, 1580. British Library 1939.b.63.

Hellenistic Jewish Authors

Josephus, Flavius. *Opera omnia*. Basel: Io. Froben, 1544. British Library C.76.g.7. *Editio princeps* of the Greek text.

Philo. *Opera*. Paris: Turnèbe, 1552. Marsh's Library, Dublin.

———. *Opuscula tria*, ed. David Hoeschel. Frankfurt am Main: J. Wechel, 1587. British Library 1012.a.12.

[Ps.]Hegesippus. *Hegesippi scriptoris gravissimi De bello Judaico et urbis Hierosolymitani excidio, libri quinque*. Cologne: M. Cholinus, 1559. British Library 1112.b.1.

Christian Hebraica, Including Translations of Hebrew Works

Abraham bar Hiyya, Mizrahi, Elijah. *Sphaera mundi, autore rabbi Abrahamo Hispano filio R. Haijae* [Abraham bar Ḥiyya], *Arithmetica secundum omnes species suas, autore Rabbi Elija Orientali* [Elijah Mizrahi], *quos libros Osvualdus Schreckenfuchsius vertit in linguam latinam, Sebastianus vero Munsterus illustravit annotationibus*. Basel: H. Petri, 1546. British Library 532.f.1.

Benjamin of Tudela. *Itinerarium Beniamini Tudelensis ex Hebraico Latinum factum Bened. Aria Montano interprete*. Antwerp: C. Plantin, 1575. British Library 1046.b.2.

Buxtorf, Johann. *Institutio epistolaris hebraica, cum epistolarum Hebraicarum familiarium centuria*. Basel: C. Waldkirch, 1610. British Library 1085.k.12.

———. *Synagoga Iudaica*. Hanau: G. [Antonus], 1604. British Library 848.b.19.

Calvin, Jean. *Sefer Hinukh behire Yah* [Calvin's catechism, translated into Hebrew by Immanuel Tremellius]. Geneva: Robert Estienne, 1554. Houghton Library, Harvard University, Heb. 7103.978.5/*FC5,C2646Zz554c.

Chaldaea Ionathae in sex prophetas . . . interpretatio per Iohannem Mercerum. Paris: C. Stephanus, 1559. [Bound with other Targumim and Latin translations.] British Library Or.70.b.2.1. The volume contains Casaubon's notes, but was probably not owned by him.

Drusius, Johannes. *Responsio ad Serarium De tribus sectis Iudaeorum. Accessit Josephi Scaligeri Elenchus Trihaeresii Nicolai Serarii* etc. Franeker: A. Radaeus, 1605. British Library C.79.a.4. Presentation copy from Scaliger.

Evangelium Matthaei ex Hebraeo fideliter redditum, trans. Jean du Tillet. Paris: M. Iuvenis, 1555. British Library 01901.a.14.

Fagius, Paulus. *Exegesis sive Expositio dictionum Hebraicarum literalis et simplex in quatuor capita Geneseos, pro studiosis linguae ebraicae.* Isny, 1542. British Library 481.c.4.(2).

Génébrard, Gilbert. *Eisagoge ad legenda et intelligenda Hebraeorum & orientalium sine punctis scripta.* Paris: Ae. Gorbinus, 1587. British Library 622.h.32. Presentation copy from Pierre Chevalier.

[Ibn Yahya, David ben Solomon]. *Libellus de metris Hebraeorum ex Grammatica R. Davidis Iehaiae.* Paris: Guil. Morelius, 1562. [Bound with David ibn Yahya, *De Poetica Hebraeorum,* trans. Gilbert Génébrard, Paris: Guil. Morelius, 1563; Hai ben Sherira, *Cantica eruditionis intellectus,* Paris, 1559; and Joseph Ezobi, *Paropsis argentea,* ed. and trans. Jean Mercier, Paris: Guil. Morelius, 1561.] British Library 1982.c.36.

Isaac, Johannes. *Defensio veritatis hebraicae scripturarum, adversus libros tres Reveren. D. Vvilhelmi Lindani S.T. Doctoris, quos de optimo Scripturas interpretandi genere inscripsit.* Cologne: Ia. Soter, 1559. British Library 1020.c.5.

Münster, Sebastian. *Catalogus omnium praeceptorum legis mosaicae, quae ab Hebraeis sexcenta et tredecim numerantur, cum succincta rabinorum expositione et additione traditionum, quibus irrita fecerunt mandata dei.* Basel: H. Petrus, 1533. British Library ORB30/5652 (formerly 01950.a.41).

———. *Kalendarium Hebraicum.* Basel: Io. Froben, 1527. British Library 481.c.2.

Veltwyck, Gerard. *Shwile tohu, Itinera deserti. De Judaicis disciplinis et earum vanitate autore Gerardo Veltvycko Ravesteynensi.* Venice: D. Bomberg, 1539. British Library 1932.b.1.

Glossary

Aggadah (pl. *aggadot*). The nonlegal material in rabbinic writings.

Avot. An anomalous tractate of the *Mishnah,* beginning with a chain of tradition, and containing wisdom and ethical sayings.

Baraita (pl. *beraitot*). A tradition attributed to the sages of the *Mishnah* but not included in the official *Mishnah.*

Gaon (pl. *Geonim*). Title of the leaders and teachers in the rabbinic academies of Babylonia in the post-talmudic period, from the seventh to the eleventh centuries. The title was also used as a purely honorific designation.

Gemara. A term for the talmudic commentary on the *Mishnah.*

Halakhah (pl. *halakhot*). The legal material in the classical rabbinic corpus.

Judah haNasi. See *Mishnah.*

Kabbalah. Tradition; frequently used as a term to denote the mystical and esoteric tradition.

Masorah. The traditional text of the Hebrew Bible, which was systematized, established, and transmitted by a school of scholars known as the Massoretes in the early Middle Ages.

Men of the Great Synagogue. The body of sages who, according to rabbinic tradition, were authoritative during the prerabbinic period, in the first years of the Second Temple.

Midrash (pl. *Midrashim*). Rabbinic exposition of scripture. The term is applied both to the method of exegesis and to the actual product(s), incorporated in the Talmuds and in the various collections of *Midrashim.*

Mishnah. The authoritative corpus of Jewish law compiled about 200 C.E. and attributed to Rabbi Judah the patriarch.

Mitsvah (pl. *mitsvot*). Commandment or precept of the Torah.

Sefirot. A fundamental term of the Kabbalah denoting the divine manifestation in creation through ten emanations or attributes.

Talmud. Corpus of Jewish learning presented as a commentary on the Mishnah, of which there are two compilations: the Palestinian Talmud (redacted in the first half of the fifth century C.E.) and the later and more authoritative Babylonian Talmud (redacted in the sixth century C.E.).

Yeshivah. School or academy for study of Talmud and other texts of the Jewish tradition.

Bibliography

Manuscripts

Basel, Universitätsbibliothek Basel
A XII 20
Fr Gr II 9
G I 59
G I 60
G I 62
Ki Ar 190a

Canterbury Cathedral Archive
Lit MS D/1

Dublin, Trinity College Dublin
125
126

Leiden, Leiden University Library
874.D.7:3
Or. 212
Or. 6882
Vulc. 108

London, British Library
Add. 12,110
Burney 363
Burney 364
Burney 365
Burney 366
Burney 367
Burney 368
Egerton 1570
Royal 16 C XV
Royal 16 D VII
Royal 16 D IX
Royal 16 D XIII
Stowe 174

Oxford,
Bodleian Library
Add. C 279
Casaubon 3
Casaubon 4
Casaubon 6
Casaubon 7
Casaubon 8
Casaubon 10
Casaubon 11
Casaubon 16
Casaubon 17
Casaubon 19
Casaubon 21
Casaubon 22
Casaubon 23
Casaubon 24
Casaubon 25
Casaubon 27
Casaubon 28
Casaubon 30
Casaubon 51
Casaubon 52
Casaubon 53
Casaubon 57
Casaubon 60
Huntington Add.E.(R.)
Or.298.3
Pattison 57
Rawlinson Letters 76[a]
Smith 75

Vatican City, Biblioteca
Apostolica Vaticana
Vat. lat. 5684

Zurich,
Zentralbibliothek
F 45
F 167
S-151

335

BIBLIOGRAPHY

Printed Books with Manuscript Annotations
(by Casaubon except Where Otherwise Noted)

Cambridge, Cambridge University Library

Adv.a.3.2(1). Herodotus. *Historiae,* ed. Henri Estienne. Geneva: Estienne, 1570.

Adv.a.3.3. Estienne, Henri, ed. *Poetae Graeci principes heroici carminis.* 2 vols. Geneva: Estienne, 1566.

Adv.a.3.4. Scaliger, Joseph. *Thesaurus temporum.* Leiden: Basson, 1606.

Adv.a.19.2. Herodotus. *Historiae,* ed. Henri Estienne. Geneva: Estienne, 1570. Joseph Scaliger's copy.

Cambridge, Wren Library, Trinity College Cambridge

Adv.d.1.30. Julian. *Opera.* 4 parts. Paris: Duval, 1583.

Adv.d.1.31–32. *Examinis Concilii Tridentini per Dom. D. Martinum Chemnicium scripti, opus integrum.* 4 vols. in 2. Frankfurt am Main: Ruland and Roth, 1606.

Cambridge, Massachusetts, Houghton Library, Harvard University

*FC5.C2646.Zz578p. Plautus. [*Comoediae*], ed. Denys Lambin. Lyons: Hertman, 1578.

Heb. 7103.978.5/*FC5.C2646.Zz554c. Calvin, Jean. *Sefer Hinukh behire Yah* [Calvin's catechism, translated into Hebrew by Immanuel Tremellius]. Geneva: Robert Estienne, 1554.

Dublin, Marsh's Library

Baronio, Cesare. 1601. *Annales ecclesiastici.* 14 vols. Mainz: Gymnicus et Hieratus.

Basil of Caesarea. 1551. *Opera.* Basel: Froben.

Clement of Alexandria. 1592. *Opera,* ed. Friedrich Sylburg. Heidelberg: Commelin.

Philo. 1552. *Opera.* Paris: Turnèbe.

Ptolemy. 1538. *Almagest.* Basel: Walder.

Thucydides. 1564. *Historiae.* Geneva: Estienne.

Eton, College Library

Scaliger, Joseph. 1598. *Opus novum de emendatione temporum.* 2d ed. Leiden: Plantin/Raphelengius.

Leiden, Leiden University Library

759 B 16. Suidas. *Lexicon.* Basel: Froben, 1544.

873 B 12. Chevalier, Antoine Rodolphe. *Rudimenta hebraicae linguae.* Geneva, 1592. Annotated by Joseph Scaliger.

London, British Library

C.24.c.3. Casaubon, Isaac. *De rebus sacris et ecclesiasticis exercitationes XVI. Ad Cardinalis Baronii Prolegomena in Annales, et primam eorum partem, de Domini Nostri Iesu Christi natiuitate, vita, passione, assumptione.* London: Norton, 1614.

C.28.f.12. Kepler, Johannes. *De stella nova in pede Serpentarii.* Prague: Sessius/Kepler, 1606. Presentation copy to King James.

C.45.i.15. Strabo. *Rerum geographicarum libri xvii,* ed. Isaac Casaubon. Lyons: Vignon, 1587.

Annotated by Philip Cluverius and presented by him to Casaubon as material for a revised edition.

C.72.f.2. Seneca, Lucius Annaeus. *Scripta quae extant.* Paris: Beys, 1587.

C.73.g.3. *Pausaniae accurata Graeciae descriptio, qua lector ceu manu per eam regionem circumducitur,* ed. William Xylander, with commentary by Xylander and Friedrich Sylburg. Frankfurt an Main: Heirs of Andreas Wechel, 1583.

C.75.b.15.(1). Herwart von Hohenburg, Johann Georg. *Novae, verae et ad calculm* [*sic*] *astronomicum revocatae chronologiae, seu temporum ab origine mundi supputationis, capita praecipua, quibus tota temporum ratio continetur et innumerabiles omnium chronologorum errores deteguntur.* Munich: Henricus, 1612.

C.75.b.16.(1). Scaliger, Joseph. *Elenchus utriusque orationis D. Davidis Parei: quarum secunda operis calci addita; prior vero Commentariis auctoris in Hoseam Heydelbergae excusis prostat.* Leiden: Elzevir, 1607.

C.75.g.11. Diodorus Siculus. *Bibliothecae historicae libri quindecim de quadraginta.* Geneva: Estienne, 1559.

C.76.g.7. Josephus, Flavius. *Opera omnia.* Basel: Io. Froben, 1544.

C.77.f.2. Livy. *Historiae.* 2 vols. Frankfurt am Main: Feyerabend, 1578.

C.77.g.12. Aristophanes. *Comoediae novem cum commentariis antiquis admodum utilibus.* Basel: Froben, 1547.

C.78.a.9.(1). Mercuriale, Girolamo. *Variarum lectionum libri.* Basel: Perna, 1576.

C.78.a.9.(2). Themistius. *Orationes XIIII,* ed. Henri Estienne. Geneva: Estienne, 1562.

C.79.a.4. Drusius, Johannes. *Responsio ad Serarium De tribus sectis Iudaeorum. Accessit Josephi Scaligeri Elenchus Trihaeresii Nicolai Serarii* etc. Franeker: A. Radaeus, 1605. Presentation copy from the author.

C.79.a.4.(2). Scaliger, Joseph. *Elenchus Trihæresii N. Serarii.* Franeker: Radaeus, 1605.

C.79.b.16.(1). Scaliger, Joseph. *Elenchus utriusque Orationis Chronologicæ D. D. Parei.* Leiden: Elzevier, 1607.

C.79.d.6. de' Pomi, David. *Tsemah David, Dittionario novo Hebraico . . . Lexicon Novum Hebraicum.* Venice: G. di Gara, 1587.

C.79.e.12.(1). Béroalde, Matthieu. *Chronicum, Scripturae sacrae autoritate constitutum.* Geneva: Chuppin, 1575.

C.80.a.1. Cassiodorus. *Variarum libri xii. et chronicon, ad Theodoricum regem.* Paris: Nivellius, 1583.

C.109.t.2. Baronio, Cesare. 1593–1607. *Annales Ecclesiastici.* 12 vols. Rome: Oratory. Copy of Meric de Vic.

Or.72.c.5. [The Four Gospels in Arabic, with an interlinear Latin translation], ed. G. B. Raimondi. Rome: Typographia Medicea, 1591.

ORB30/5652 (formerly 01950.a.41). Münster, Sebastian. *Catalogus omnium praeceptorum legis mosaicae quae ab Hebraeis sexcenta et tredecim numerantur, cum succincta rabinorum expositione et additione traditionum, quibus irrita fecerunt mandata dei.* Basel: H. Petri, 1533.

481.c.2. Münster, Sebastian. *Kalendarium Hebraicum, opera Sebastiani Munsteri ex Hebraeorum penetralibus iam recens in lucem aeditum: quod non tam Hebraice studiosis quam Historiographis et Astronomiae peritis subservire poterit.* Basel: Io. Froben, 1527.

481.c.4.(2). Fagius, Paulus. *Exegesis sive Expositio dictionum Hebraicarum literalis et simplex in quatuor capita Geneseos, pro studiosis linguae ebraicae.* Isny, 1542.

491.d.14. Hermes Trismegistus. *Poemander, seu de potestate ac sapientia divina. Aesculapii definitiones ad Ammonem Regem,* ed. Adrianus Turnebus. Paris: Turnebus, 1554.

497.h.6. Budé, Guillaume. *Annotationes . . . in quatuor et viginti Pandectarum libros.* Paris: Vascosan, 1543. [Bound with *Altera editio annotationum in Pandectas,* Paris: Vascosan, 1542; *De asse et partibus eius libri quinque,* Paris: Vascosan, 1542.]

513.f.14. Stöffler, Joannes. *Elucidatio fabricae ususque astrolabii.* Paris: Marnef and widow of Cavellat, 1585.

525.a.10. Theophrastus. *Characteres ethici, sive descriptiones morum Graece,* ed. and trans. Isaac Casaubon. 2 vols. Lyons: F. le Preux, 1592.

531.f.14. Stoeffler, Johannes. *Elucidatio fabricæ ususque Astrolabii.* Paris: Marnef and Cavellat, 1585.

532.f.1. Abraham bar Hiyya, Mizrahi, Elijah. *Sphaera mundi, autore rabbi Abrahamo Hispano filio R. Haijae* [Abraham bar Hiyya], *Arithmetica secundum omnes species suas, autore Rabbi Elija Orientali* [Elijah Mizrahi], *quos libros Osvualdus Schreckenfuchsius vertit in linguam latinam, Sebastianus vero Munsterus illustravit annotationibus.* Basel: H. Petri, 1546.

536.b.4. Bodin, Jean. *Universae naturae theatrum.* Lyons: Roussin, 1596.

580.e.14. Calvisius, Seth. *Chronologia, ex autoritate potissimum sacrae scripturae et historicorum fide dignissimorum, ad motum luminarium coelestium, tempora et annos distinguentium, secundum characteres chronologicos contexta et deducta . . .* Leipzig: Apellus, 1605.

582.l.9. Scaliger, Joseph. *Opus novum de emendatione temporum.* Paris: Mamert Patisson, 1583.

586.c.4. Caesar, Julius. *De bello gallico commentarii vii.* Lyons: Vincentius, 1574.

589.a.15.(1). C. *Velleius Paterculus cum Aldi Manutii scholiis; Iusti Lipsii Animadversionibus; Iacobi Scegkii notis; Vincentii Acidalii variis lectionibus.* Lyons: F. le Preux, 1594.

589.a.15.(2). Censorinus. *De die natali,* ed. L. Carrio. Lyons: F. le Preux, 1593.

589.a.15.(3). Martial. *Epigrammata in Caesaris Amphitheatrum,* ed. Theodorus Marcilius. Lyons: F. le Preux, 1593.

589.a.15.(4). Justin. *Trogi Pompeii historiarum Philippicarum epitoma.* Lyons: Carterius, 1593.

621.g.1. Münster, Sebastian. *Dictionarium Chaldaicum.* Basel: Io. Froben, 1527.

621.i.9. Chevalier, Antoine Rudolphe. *Rudimenta hebraicae linguae, accurata methodo et breuitate conscripta.* Geneva: F. le Preux, 1590. Presentation copy from the author.

622.h.2.(2). *Alphabetum Arabicum.* Rome: Medici Press, 1592.

622.h.2.(3). Raphelengius, Franciscus. *Specimen characterum Arabicorum Officinæ Plantinianæ Franc. Raphelengij.* Leiden: Plantin/Raphelengius, 1595.

622.h.2.(4). Christmann, Jacob. *Alphabetum arabicum cum isagoge scribendi legendique Arabice.* Neustadt: Harnisch, 1582.

622.h.5.(2). Erpenius, Thomas. *Grammatica Arabica quinque libris . . . explicata.* Leiden: Raphelengius, 1613.

622.h.32. Génébrard, Gilbert. *Eisagoge ad legenda et intelligenda Hebraeorum & orientalium sine punctis scripta.* Paris: Ae. Gorbinus, 1587. Presentation copy from Pierre Chevalier.

692.f.6. *Liturgiae sive missae sanctorum patrum.* Antwerp: Plantin, 1560.

692.f.6.(1). *Synesius, de regno ad Arcadium imperatorum Dion, sive de suæ vitæ ratione. Calvitii laudatio. De providentia, seu Ægyptius. Concio quædam panegyrica. De insomniis, cum Nicephori Gregoræ explicatione. Ejusdem Synesii epistolæ.* Paris: Turnèbe, 1563.

698.a.22. Jewell, John. *Apologia ecclesiae Anglicanae.* Amberg: Forster, 1606.

704.f.4. Horapollo. *De sacris notis et sculpturis libri duo,* ed. Jean Mercier. Paris: Wechel, 1548.

753.g.72(2). *Brevis orthodoxæ fidei professio.* Rome: Typographia Medicea, 1595.

793.d.2. Leo Africanus, Joannes. *De totius Africæ descriptione, libri IX.* Antwerp: Latius, 1556.

802.d.1.(1.–3.). Ctesias. *Fragmenta,* ed. Henri Estienne. Geneva: Estienne, 1554. [Bound with Appian, *Hispanica et Annibalica,* Geneva: Estienne, 1560; Aristotle and Theophrastus, *Scripta quaedam,* Geneva: Estienne, 1557.]

832.h.12. Oppian. *De piscatu libri V. De venatione libri IIII.* Paris: Turnebus, 1555.

848.b.19. Buxtorf, Johann. *Synagoga Iudaica.* Hanau: G. [Antonus], 1604.

852.h.3. Du Moulin, Pierre. *Defense de la foye catholique contenue au livre de trespuissant et serenissime Roy Iaques I. Roy de la grand' Bretagne et d'Irlande. Contra la Response de F. N. Coeffeteau Docteur en Theologie et Vicaire general des Freres Prescheurs.* Paris, 1605.

860.b.19.(1). Heraldus, Desiderius. *Davidis Leidhresseri super doctrinae capitibus inter academiam parisiensem et societatis Iesu patres controversis dissertatio politica, duobus libris comprehensa.* Strasbourg: Gesner, 1612.

972.a.1.(1). Belon, Pierre. *Plurimarum singularium et memorabilium rerum in Graecia, Asia, Aegypto, Iudaea, Arabia, aliisque exteris Provinciis ab ipso conspectarum observationes, tribus libris expressae,* trans. Carolus Clusius. Antwerp: Plantin, 1589.

1000.l.3. Manilius, Marcus. *Astronomicon,* ed. Joseph Scaliger. Leiden: Plantin-Raphelengius, 1600.

1016.d.3, 4. *Psalmi Davidis variis calendariis et commentariis genuinum sensum et Hebraismos fusissime aperientibus a Gil. Genebrardo.* Lyons: H. Cardon, 1607.

1020.f.2. Abdias. *De historia certaminis apostolici libri decem, Iulio Africano (cuius subinde D. Hieronymus meminit) interprete,* ed. Wolfgang Lazius. Paris: Guillard and Warancore, 1560.

1068.b.2.(1). Claudian, ed. Theodore Pulmannus. Antwerp: Plantin, 1571.

1068.i.15. Juvenal. *XVI Satyrae. Item Persii Satyrae. Ad exemplar Aldinum.* Basel: Th. Wolff, 1522.

1084.i.9. Calvin, Jean. *Epistolae et responsa, quibus interiectae sunt etiam insignium in ecclesia Dei virorum aliquot epistolae. Eiusdem Ioan. Calvini vita a Theod. Beza Genevensis Ecclesiae ministro, accurate descripta.* 3d ed. Hanau: Guilielmus Antonius, 1597.

1089.h.7.(1). Scaliger, Joseph. *Emendationes ad Theocriti, Moschi et Bionis Idyllia.* Isaac Casaubon, *Theocriticarum lectionum libellus.* Heidelberg: Commelin, 1596.

1089.h.7.(2). Theophrastus. *Notationes morum,* ed. and trans. Isaac Casaubon. Lyons: de Harsy, 1599.

1112.b.1. [Ps.]Hegesippus. *Hegesippi scriptoris gravissimi De bello Judaico et urbis Hierosolymitani excidio, libri quinque.* Cologne: M. Cholinus, 1559.

01901.a.14. *Evangelium Matthaei ex Hebraeo fideliter redditum,* trans. Jean du Tillet. Paris: M. Iuvenis, 1555.

1934.f.13. Judah ben Samuel. *Sefer haHasidim.* Basel: A. Froben, 1580.

1935.e.15. Joseph ben Eliezer Halfan? *Sefer Orah Hayyim* [Yiddish]. Basel: [C. Waldkirch?], 1602.

1936.c.5. Levita, Elijah. *Sefer haTishbi.* Basel: C. Waldkirch, 1601.

1938.f.12. de' Rossi, Azariah. *Me'or 'Einayim.* Mantua: G. Rufinelli, 1574.

1938.f.21. *Josippon.* Venice: C. Adelkind, 1544.

1939.b.63. *Seder Olam Rabbah, ve-Seder Olam Zuta, Megillat Ta'anit, ve-Sefer haKabbalah le-haRabad.* Basel: A. Froben, 1580.

1942.g.3. *Hosee cum Thargum, id est Chaldaica paraphrasi Ionathan, et commentariis R. Sel-

omo Iarhi, R. Abraham aben Ezra, et R. D. Kimhi [Minor prophets with Rashi, Kimhi, and Ibn Ezra], ed. Jean Mercier. Paris: Robert Estienne, 1556.

1942.g.4. *Libellus Ruth cum scholiis Masorae ad marginem; item in eundem succincta expositio nondum in lucem emissa, cuius in manu scripto exemplari auctor praefertur R. D. Kimhi,* ed. Jean Mercier. Paris: Robert Estienne, 1563. The commentary is in fact not by Kimhi but by Isaiah de Trani.

1952.f.9. Samuel di Uceda. *Midrash Shemuel.* Venice: G. di Gara, 1585.

1970.c.2 (formerly 481.a.11). *Seder Tefillot mikol haShanah.* Basel: A. Froben, 1579.

1972.c.1. *Temunot Tehinot Tefillot Sefarad* [Sephardi prayerbook]. Venice: D. Zanetti, 1598.

1972.c.14. *Mahzor sefardim miyamim nora'im* [Sephardi prayerbook for high holy days]. Venice: D. Zanetti, 1598.

1982.c.34. *Josippus de bello Iudaico: deinde decem Iudaeorum captivitates et Decalogus cum eleganti commentariolo Rabbi Aben Ezra. Hisce accesserunt Collectanea aliquot, quae Sebastianus Lepusculus Basiliensis colligebat, de quibus videre poteris verso folio. Omnia Hebraicolatina.* Basel: Petri, 1559.

1982.c.36. [Ibn Yahya, David ben Solomon]. *Libellus de metris Hebraeorum ex Grammatica R. Davidis Iehaiae.* Paris: Guil. Morelius, 1562. [Bound with David ibn Yahya, *De Poetica Hebraeorum,* trans. Gilbert Génébrard, Paris: Guil. Morelius, 1563; Hai ben Sherira, *Cantica eruditionis intellectus,* Paris, 1559; and Joseph Ezobi, *Paropsis argentei,* ed. and trans. Jean Mercier, Paris: Guil. Morelius, 1561.]

1984.a.10.(1). Kimhi, David. *Sefer Mikhlol.* Venice: D. Bomberg, 1545.

3089.b.8. Arnobius. *Commentarii pii iuxta et eruditi in omnes psalmos,* ed. Desiderius Erasmus. Basel: Froben, 1560.

3089.g.20. Bellarmine, Robert. *Explanatio in Psalmos.* Lyons: H. Cardon, 1611.

14593.b.31. *Grammatica Arabica in compendium redacta quæ vocatur Giarrumia, auctore Mahmeto filio Davidis Alsanhagii.* Rome: Medici Press, 1592.

Oxford, Bodleian Library

Auct.S.2.9. *Supplementum linguae latinae, seu dictionarium abstrusorum vocabulorum a Rob. Constantino collectum.* Lyons: Vignon, 1573.

Opp. fol. *777.* Maimonides, Moses. *Mishneh Torah.* Venice, 1524?

Wood 19. Censorinus. *De die natali,* ed. Louis Carrion. Paris: Beys, 1583.

San Marino, Huntington Library and Art Gallery

RB 56251. Bacon, Francis. *The Tvvoo Bookes of Francis Bacon, of the Proficience and Aduancement of Learning, Diuine and Humane.* London: Henrie Tomes, 1605.

York, York Minster Library

Casaubon, Isaac. 1611. *Ad Frontonem Ducaeum S.J. Theologum epistola, in qua de Apologia disseritur communi Iesuitarum nomine ante aliquot menses Lutetiae Parisiorum edita.* London: Norton. Tobie Matthew's copy.

Primary Sources

Acts of the Privy Council of England (1613–1614). 1921. London: His Majesty's Stationery Office.

Agrippa, Henry Cornelius. 1992. *De occulta philosophia libri tres,* ed. V. Perrone Compagni. Leiden: Brill.

Aitken, James. 1939. *The Trial of George Buchanan before the Lisbon Inquisition.* Edinburgh: Oliver and Boyd.

Andrewes, Lancelot. 1610. *Responsio ad apologiam Cardinalis Bellarmini, quam nuper edidit contra praefationem monitoriam serenissimi ac potentissimi principis Iacobi, Dei Gratia Magnae Britanniae, Franciae, et Hiberniae Regis, Fidei Defensoris, omnibus Christianis monarchis, principus atque ordinibus inscriptam.* London: Barker.

———. 1892. *The Greek Devotions of Lancelot Andrewes Bishop of Winchester,* ed. Peter Goldsmith Medd. London: Society for Promoting Christian Knowledge.

Aristeas. 1561. *De legis diuinæ ex Hebraica lingua in Graecam translatione, per septuaginta interpretes, Ptolemæi Philadelphi Aegyptiorum regis studio ac liberalitate Hierosolyma accersitos, absoluta, historia,* trans. Matthias Garbitius, ed. Simon Schardius. Basel: Oporinus.

Bacon, Roger. 1897. *Opus majus,* ed. John Henry Bridges. 2 vols. Oxford: Clarendon Press.

Bang, Thomas. 1657. *Caelum orientis et prisci mundi triade exercitationum literariarum repraesentatum.* Copenhagen: Haubold.

Baremius, Martin, ed. 1608. *Inscriptio vetus graeca.* Goslar: Vogdius.

Baronio, Cesare. 1593–1607. *Annales ecclesiastici.* 12 vols. Rome: Oratory.

Becmann, Christian. 1609. *De originibus linguae latinae.* Wittenberg: Helwichius.

———. 1613. *De originibus linguae latinae.* New ed. Wittenberg: Helwichius.

Bede. 1898. *De locis sanctis.* In *Itinera Hierosolymitana,* ed. Paulus Geyer. Prague: F. Tempsky.

Bellarmine, Robert. 1588. *Disputationum . . . de controversiis Christianae fidei, adversus huius temporis haereticos, tomus secundus.* Ingolstadt: Sartorius.

———. 1872. *Opera omnia.* 8 vols. Naples: C. Pedone Lauriel.

Béroalde, Matthieu. 1575. *Chronicum, Scripturae sacrae autoritate constitutum.* Geneva: Chuppin.

Bertram, Corneille. 1574. *Comparatio grammaticae Hebraicae et Aramicae, atque adeo dialectorum Aramicarum inter se: concinnata ex Hebraicis Antonii Ceualerii praeceptionibus, Aramicisque doctorum aliorum virorum observationibus: quibus et quamplurimae aliae in utraque lingua adiectae sunt.* Geneva: Vignon.

Beza, Theodore. 1960–. *Correspondance,* ed. Hippolyte Aubert et al. 30 vols. to date. Geneva: Droz.

Bodley, Thomas. 1926. *Letters of Sir Thomas Bodley to Thomas James, First Keeper of the Bodleian Library,* ed. G. W. Wheeler. Oxford: Clarendon Press.

Bosio, Girolamo. 1632–1634. *Roma sotterranea.* Rome: G. Facciotti.

Bulenger, Jules-César. 1617. *Diatribae ad Isaaci Casauboni Exercitationes adversus illustrissimum Cardinalem Baronium.* Lyons: Heirs of Rovilius.

Burggravius, Dan. Ernestus. 1611. *Biolychnium, seu lucerna; cum vita ejus, cui accensa est Mystice, vivens jugiter; cum morte ejusdem expirans, omnesque affectus prodens.* 2d ed. Franeker: Balck.

Burman, Peter, ed. 1727. *Sylloges epistolarum a viris illustribus scriptarum tomi quinque.* 5 vols. Leiden: Luchtmans.

Buxtorf, Johann. 1603a. *Synagoga Iudaica: das ist, Juden-Schul: darinnen der gantz Jüdische Glaub und Glaubens vbung / mit allen Ceremonien / Satzungen / Sitten und Gebräuchen / wie sie bey ihnen offentlich und heimlich im Brauche: Auss ihren eigenen Bücheren und Schrifften / so den Christen mehrtheils vnbekandt vnnd verborgen*

sind / mit vermeldung jedes Buchs ort vnd blat/grundlich erkläret . . . Basel: Sebastian Henricpetri.

——. 1603b. *Juden-Schul*, trans. Alan Corré. Available at http://www.uwm.edu/~corre/buxdorf/index.html.

——. 1604. *Synagoga Iudaica*. Hanau: G [Antonus].

——. 1610. *Institutio epistolaris Hebraica, cum epistolarum Hebraicarum familiarium centuria, ex quibus, pro auspicato incipientium subsidio, quinquaginta punctis vocabulis animatae, versione Latina et notis illustratae sunt*. Basel: C. Waldkirch.

——. 1613. *De abbreviaturis Hebraicis liber novus et copiosus: cui accesserunt operis Talmudici recensio, cum ejusdam librorum et capitum Indice. Item Bibliotheca Rabbinica nova, ordine Alphabethico disposita*. Basel: Waldkirch.

——. 1620. *Tiberias sive commentarius Masorethicus triplex, historicus, didacticus, criticus ad illustrationem operis biblici Basileensis conscriptus*. Basel: König.

——. 1640. *De abbreviaturis Hebraicis liber novus et copiosus: cui accesserunt operis Talmudici recensio, cum ejusdam librorum et capitum Indice. Item Bibliotheca Rabbinica nova, ordine Alphabethico disposita*. 2d ed. Basel: König.

Calvin, Jean. 1556. *Secunda defensio piæ et orthodoxæ de sacramentis fidei, contra Ioachimi Westphali calumnias*. Geneva: Crespin.

——. 1561. *Praelectiones in librum prophetiarum Danielis Joannis Budaei et Caroli Ionvillaei labore et industria exceptae*. Geneva: Laonius.

Calvisius, Seth. 1605. *Chronologia, ex autoritate potissimum sacrae scripturae et historicorum fide dignissimorum, ad motum luminarium coelestium, tempora et annos distinguentium, secundum characteres chronologicos contexta et deducta*. Frankfurt am Main: Apelius.

Camerarius, Joachim. 1566. *De Philippi Melanchthonis ortu, totius vitae curriculo et morte, implicata rerum memorabilium temporis illius hominumque mentione atque indicio, cum expositionis serie cohaerentium, narratio diligens et accurata*. Leipzig: Voegelin.

Casaubon, Isaac. 1583. *Notae ad Diogenis Laertii libros de vitis, dictis et decretis principum philosophorum*. Geneva: Sylvius.

——, ed. 1587a. *Novum testamentum*. Geneva: Vignon.

——, ed. 1587b. *Strabonis Rerum geographicarum libri XVII*. Geneva: Vignon.

——, ed. and trans. 1592. Theophrastus. *Characteres ethici, sive descriptiones morum Graece*. 2 vols. Lyons: F. le Preux.

——, ed. 1593. *Diog. Laert. De vitis, dogm. et apophth. clarorum philosophorum libri X*. Geneva: Estienne.

——, ed. 1597. *Athenaei Deipnosophistarum libri xv*. Heidelberg: Commelin.

Casaubon, Isaac, ed. and trans. 1599. Theophrastus. *Notationes morum*. Lyons: de Harsy, 1599.

Casaubon, Isaac. 1600. *Animadversionum in Athenaei Dipnosophistas libri xv*. Lyons: de Harsy.

——, ed. 1603. *Scriptores historiae Augustae sex*. Paris: Drouart.

——, ed. 1605a. *Avli Persi Flacci Satirarum liber*. Paris: Drouart.

——. 1605b. *De satyrica graecorum poesi et romanorum satira libri duo*. Paris: Drouart.

——. 1605c. "In Greg. Thau. ΛΟΓΟΝ notae." In *Origenis contra Celsum libri VIII. Et Gregorii Neocaesar. Thaumaturgi Panegyricus in Origenem*, ed. David Hoeschel. Augsburg: ad insigne pinus, 497–506.

——, ed. 1606. *B. Gregorii Nysseni ad Eustathiam, Ambrosiam et Basilissam epistola*. Paris: Estienne.

———, ed. 1606? *Inscriptio vetus graeca.* N.p.

———, ed. 1607. *B. Gregorii Nysseni ad Eustathiam, Ambrosiam et Basilissam epistola.* Hanau: de Marne and Heirs of Aubry.

———, ed. 1609. *Polybii Lycortae F. Megalopolitani Historiarum libri qui supersunt.* Paris: Drouart.

Casaubon, Isaac. 1611. *Ad Frontonem Ducaeum S.J. Theologum epistola, in qua de Apologia disseritur communi Iesuitarum nomine ante aliquot menses Lutetiae Parisiorum edita.* London: Norton.

———. 1612. *Ad epistolam illustr. et reverendiss. Cardinalis Perronii, Responsio.* London: Norton.

———. 1614. *De rebus sacris et ecclesiasticis exercitationes XVI. Ad Cardinalis Baronii Prolegomena in Annales, et primam eorum partem, de Domini Nostri Iesu Christi natiuitate, vita, passione, assumtione.* London: Norton.

———. 1620. *Notae ac emendationes.* In *Historiae Augustae Scriptores VI,* ed. Claude Saumaise. Paris: Drovart.

———. 1621. *Animadversionum in Athen. Dipnosophistas libri xv.* Lyons: Widow of Ant. de Harsy and Rivaud.

———. 1654. *De rebus sacris et ecclesiasticis exercitationes xvi, ad Cardinalis Baronii Prolegomena in Annales et primam eorum partem, de D.N. Iesu Christi nativitate, vita, passione, assumptione, cum prolegomenis auctoris, in quibus de Baronianis annalibus candide disputatur.* Geneva: De Tournes.

———. 1663. *De rebus sacris et ecclesiasticis exercitationes xvi, ad Cardinalis Baronii Prolegomena in Annales et primam eorum partem, de D.N. Iesu Christi nativitate, vita, passione, assumptione, cum prolegomenis auctoris, in quibus de Baronianis annalibus candide disputatur.* Geneva: De Tournes.

———. 1709. *Epistolae,* ed. Theodore Janson van Almeloveen. Rotterdam.

———. 1710. *Casauboniana,* ed. Io. Christophorus Wolf. Hamburg: Libezeit/Stromer.

———. 1774. *De satyrica Graecorum poesi et Romanorum satira libri duo.* Halle.

———. 1850. *Ephemerides,* ed. John Russell. 2 vols. Oxford: Oxford University Press.

———. 1999. *Polibio,* ed. and trans. Guerrino Brussich, with a note by Luciano Canfora. Palermo: Sellerio.

Casaubon, Meric. 1624. *Vindicatio patris adversus impostorem, qui librum ineptum et impium De origine idololatriae, etc., nuper sub Isaaci Casauboni nomine publicavit.* London: Norton and Bill.

Chevalier, Antoine Rudolphe. 1590. *Rudimenta hebraicae linguae, accurata methodo et breuitate conscripta.* Geneva: F. le Preux, 1590.

Chevalier, Pierre. 1592. *Rudimenta hebraicae linguae.* Geneva.

Clarke, Samuel. 1683. *The Lives of Sundry Eminent Persons in This Later Age.* 2 parts. London: Simmons.

Cocceius, Joannes. 1629. *Duo tituli Thalmvdici Sanhedrin et Maccoth: quorum ille agit de Synedriis, judiciis, suppliciis capitalibus Ebræorum; hic de pœna falsi testimonii, exsilio et asylis, flagellatione: cum excerptis ex utriusque Gemara, versa, & annotationibus, depromtis maximam partem ex Ebræorum commentariis, illustrata.* Amsterdam: Jansson.

Critici Sacri. 1660. Ed. John Pearson, Anthony Scattergood, Francis Gouldman, and Richard Pearson. 9 vols. London: Bee.

Cunaeus, Petrus. 1617. *De republica Hebraeorum libri III.* Leiden: Elzevir.

———. 1631. *De republica Hebraeorum libri III.* 2d ed. Leiden: Eickhoutius.

———. 1725. *Petri Cunaei, Eloquentiae et Juris Romani quondam Academia Batava Professo-ris, et doctorum virorum ad eum epistolae,* ed. Peter Burman. Leiden: vander Aa.

———. 1996. *De republica Hebraeorum (The Commonwealth of the Hebrews),* ed. Lea Campos Boralevi. Florence: Centro editoriale Toscano.

———. 2006. *The Hebrew Republic,* ed. and trans. Peter Wyetzer. Jerusalem: Shalem Center.

Davy du Perron, Jacques. 1612. *Lettre de Monseigneur le Cardinal du Perron, envoyée au Sieur Casaubon en Angleterre.* Paris: Pierre Durand.

de Castro, Leon. 1570. *Commentaria in Esaiam prophetam.* Salamanca: Gastius.

———. 1585. *Apologeticus pro lectione apostolica et evangelica, pro vulgata Diui Hieronymi, pro translatione LXX virorum, proque omni ecclesiastica lectione: contra earum obtrec-tatores.* Salamanca: Heirs of Gastius.

Delitiae Poetarum Scotorum hujus aevi Illustrium. 1637. Amsterdam: Blaeu.

de' Rossi, Azariah. 1866. *Matsref laKesef.* Vilnius: Joseph Reuben bar Menahem.

———. 2001. *The Light of the Eyes,* ed. and trans. Joanna Weinberg. New Haven: Yale University Press.

Drusius, Johannes. 1599. *Quaestionum Ebraicarum libri tres.* 2d ed. Franeker: Radaeus.

———, ed. 1600. *Liber Hasmonaeorum qui vulgo prior Machabaeorum, Graece ex editione Romana, et Latine ex interpretatione I. Drusii, cum notis sive commentario eiusdem.* Franeker: Radaeus.

Drusius, Johannes. 1603. *De Hasidaeis, quorum mentio in Libris Machabaeorum, libellus.* Franeker: Radaeus.

———. 1605. *Responsio ad Serarium De tribus sectis Iudaeorum. Accessit Iosephi Scaligeri Elenchus Trihaeresii Nicolai Serarii etc.* Franeker: A. Radaeus.

———. 1606. *Ad Minerval Serarii responsio, libris duobus comprehensa cum appendice.* Franeker: Radaeus.

———. 1612. *Annotationum in totum Jesu Christi Testamentum, sive Praeteritorum libri decem.* Franeker: Radaeus.

Du Moulin, Pierre, ed. 1607. *B. Gregorii episcopi Nyssae de euntibus Ierosolyma epistola, Latine versa et Notis illustrata a Petro Molineo, cum eiusdem Tractatu de Peregrina-tionibus et altero de Altaribus et Sacrificiis Christianorum.* Hanau: de Marne and Heirs of Aubry.

Du Rieu, Willem Nicolaas. 1875. *Album studiosorum Academiae Lugduno Batavae MDLXXV–MDCCCLXXV: accedunt nomina curatorum et professorum per eadem sec-ula.* The Hague: Nijhoff.

Erpenius, Thomas, ed. 1614. *[Kitāb al-amthāl.] Seu Proverbiorum Arabicorum centuriae duae, ab anonymo quodam Arabe collectae & explicatae.* Leiden: Raphelengius.

Erpenius, Thomas. 1621. *Orationes tres de Linguarum Ebraeae atque Arabicae dignitate.* Leiden: Erpenius.

———, ed. 1623. *[Kitāb al-amthāl.] Seu Proverbiorum Arabicorum centuriae duae, ab anon-ymo quodam Arabe collectae & explicatae.* 2d ed. Leiden: Erpenius.

Eudaemon-Ioannes, Andreas. 1612. *Responsio ad epistolam Isaaci Casauboni.* Cologne: Kinckius.

———. 1617. *Defensio annalium ecclesiasticorum Caesaris Baronii S. R. E. Cardin. adversus falsas calumnias, errores ac mendacia Isaaci Casauboni, quas in exercitationibus suis inferciit, in SS. Patres, scriptores vetustos, et totam Ecclesiae antiquitatem; atque etiam contra SS. Scripturarum et S. Theologiae interpretationes eiusdem impias et ineptas.* Cologne: Kinchius.

[Eutychius Zigabenus]. 1543. *Commentaria in sacrosancta quatuor Christi Evangelia ex Chrysostomi aliorumque veterum scriptis magna ex parte collecta.* Louvain: Rescius.

Fagius, Paulus. 1542. *Precationes Hebraicae quibus in solennioribus festis Iudaei, cum mensae accumbunt, adhuc hodie utuntur, & quo modo, ordine, & ritu eas dicant, ex quo uidere licet uestigia qu[a]edam ritus ueteris populi, quem & Christus saluator noster in sacrosancta coena sua, ut eam Euangelistae, praesertim Lucas describunt, in quibusdam observauit.* Isny.

———. 1660. *In paraphrasin Chaldaicam Pentateuchi succinctae annotationes.* In *Critici Sacri* 1660, I. First printed in *Thargum, hoc est, paraphrasis Onkeli Chaldaica in Sacra Biblia, ex Chaldaeo in Latinum fidelissime versa, additis in singula fere capita succinctis annotationibus.* Strasbourg: G. Machaeropoeus, 1546.

Flacius Illyricus, Matthias. 1968. *De ratione cognoscendi sacras literas. Über den Erkenntnisgrund der Heiligen Schrift,* ed. and trans. Lutz Geldsetzer. Düsseldorf: Stern–Verlag Janssen.

———. 2009. *La clé des écritures: Clavis scripturae sacrae,* ed. and trans. Philippe Büttgen and Denis Thouard. Villeneuve d'Ascq: Presses Universitaires du Septentrion.

Flacius Illyricus, Matthias, et al. 1561–1574. *Ecclesiastica Historia, integram Ecclesiae Christi ideam quantum ad locum, propagationem, persecutionem, tranquillitatem, doctrinam, haereses, ceremonias, gubernationem, schismata, synodos, personas, miracula, martyria, religiones extra Ecclesiam, et statum Imperii politicum attinet, secundum singulas centurias, perspicuo ordine complectens: singulari diligentia et fide ex vetustissimis et optimis historicis, patribus, et aliis scriptoribus congesta per aliquot studiosos et pios viros in urbe Magdeburgica.* 7 vols. Basel: Oporinus.

Flusser, David, ed. 1978–1980. *The Josippon [Josephus Gorionides], Edited with an Introduction, Commentary, and Notes* [Hebrew]. 2 vols. Jerusalem: Bialik.

Foxe, John. 1578. *A Sermon Preached at the Christening of a Certain Iew, at London,* trans. James Bell. London: Barker.

Galatino, Pietro. 1603. *De arcanis Catholicae veritatis libri XII.* Frankfurt am Main: de Marne and Aubry.

Garetius, Joannes. 1565. *Mortuos viuorum precibus adiuuari, ex Sanctis Patribus, assertio.* Antwerp: Plantin.

Gassendi, Pierre. 1641. *Viri illustris Nicolai Claudii Fabricii de Peiresc, senatoris Aquisextiensis, vita.* Paris: Cramoisy.

Génébrard, Gilbert. 1564. *R. Davidis Iehaiae, de poetica Hebraeorum,* trans. Gilbert Génébrard. Paris: Morel.

———. 1569. *Symbolum fidei Judaeorum e R. Mose Aegypto. Praecationes eorumdem pro defunctis e lib. Mahzor . . . Sexcenta tredecim legis praecepta e More Nebuchim.* Paris: M. le Jeune.

———. 1572. *Hebraeorum breve chronicon.* Paris: M. le Jeune.

———. 1608. *Chronologia Hebraeorum maior quae Seder Olam Rabba inscribitur, et minor, quae Seder Olam Zuta, De mundi ordine et temporibus ab orbe condito usque ad annum Domini cum aliis opusculis ad res Synagogae pertinentibus.* Lyons: Pillehotte.

Goldast, Melchior, ed. 1610. *Philologicarum epistolarum centuria una diversorum a renatis literis doctissimorum virorum, in qua veterum theologorum, iurisconsultorum, medicorum, philosophorum, historicorum, poetarum, grammaticorum libri difficillimis locis vel emendantur vel illustrantur.* Frankfurt am Main: Emmelius.

Goldman, Peter. 1610. *Theses medicae de melancholia.* Leiden: Basson.

Gretser, Jacob. 1606. *De sacris et religiosis peregrinationibus libri quatuor. Eiusdem de Cath-*

*olicae ecclesiae processionibus seu supplicationibus libri duo. Quibus adiuncti de volun-
taria flagellorum cruce, seu de disciplinarum usu libri tres.* Ingolstadt: Sartorius.

Grotius, Hugo, 1687. *Epistolae, quotquot reperiri potuerunt.* Amsteram: Blaeu.

al-Hajarī, Ahmad ibn Qāsim. 1997. *Kitâb nasir al-dīn 'ala 'l-qawm al-kafirīn (The Supporter
of Religion against the Infidels),* ed. and trans. P. S. van Koningsveld, Q. al-Samarrai,
and G. A. Wiegers. Madrid: Consejo Superior de Investigaciones Científicas, Agencia
Española de Cooperación Internacional.

Hepburn, James. 1922. *La virga aurea du Fr. J. B. Hepburn,* ed. Fernand Dusaussay de Mély.
Paris: Ernest Leroux.

Heredia, Paulus de. 1487? *Illustrissimo ac sapientissimo Domino D. Enigo de Mendocza
Comiti Tendiliae Legato Sacre Maiestatis regis Hispaniae Paulus de Heredia salutem
perpetuamque foelicitatem.* Rome.

———. 1998. *The Epistle of Secrets,* ed. J. F. Coakley, trans. Rodney Dennis. Oxford: Jericho
Press.

Herwart von Hohenburg, Joannes Georg. 1612. *Novae, verae et ad calculm [sic] astronomicum revocatae chronologiae, seu temporum ab origine mundi supputationis, capita
praecipua, quibus tota temporum ratio continetur et innumerabiles omnium chronologorum errores deteguntur.* Munich: Henricus.

Hess, Ernst Ferdinand. 1600. *Flagellum Iudeorum: Juden Geissel, das ist: Ein Newe sehr nütze
und gründtliche Erweisung, das Jhesus Christus Gottes und der heiligen Jungfrawen
Marien Sohn der ware verheissene und gesandte Messias sey.* Erfurt: Wittel.

Hotman, François. 1603. *Antitribonian.* Paris: Perier.

Hotman, François, and Jean Hotman. 1700. *Francisci et Joannis Hotomanorum patris ac filii
epistolae.* Amsterdam: Gallet.

Ibn Ezra, Abraham ben Meïr. 1986. *The Commentary of Abraham ibn Ezra on the Pentateuch.*
Vol. 3: *Leviticus,* trans. Jay Schacter. Hoboken: Ktav.

———. 1988. *Commentary on the Pentateuch: Genesis (Bereshit),* trans. H. Norman Strick-
man and Arthur Silver. New York: Menorah Publishing.

Jansen, Cornelius. 1572–71. *Commentariorum in suam concordiam ac totam historiam evan-
gelicam, partes IIII.* 4 vols. Louvain: Zangrius.

Josippon. 1541. *Josephus Hebraicus diu desideratus, et nunc ex Constantinopolitano exemplari
iuxta Hebraismum opera Sebastiani Munsteri versus et annotationibus atque collationibus illustratus.* Basel.

———. 1559. *Josippus de bello Iudaico: deinde decem Iudaeorum captivitates et Decalogus cum
eleganti commentariolo Rabbi Aben Ezra. Hisce accesserunt Collectanea aliquot quae
Sebastianus Lepusculus Basiliensis colligebat, de quibus videre poteris verso folio. Omnia Hebraicolatina.* Basel: Petri.

Kemke, Johannes, ed. 1898. *Patricius Junius (Patrick Young), Bibliothekar der Könige Jacob I.
und Carl I. von England. Mitteilungen aus seinem Briefwechsel.* Leipzig: M. Spirgatis.

Kirsten, Peter. 1608. *Grammatices arabicae Liber I.* Breslau: published by the author.

Laing, James. 1581. *De vita et moribus atque rebus gestis haereticorum nostri temporis etc.*
Paris: de Roigny.

Lake, Arthur. 1629. *Sermons, with some Religious and Diuine Meditations.* London: Butter.

[Laurence, Richard]. 1834. *On the Existence of the Soul after Death.* London: Rivington.

Lauret, Christofle. 1598. *La doctrine des temps et de l'astronomie universelle.* Paris: du Pré.

———. 1610. *Hazoar sive illustratio prophetarum de plenitudine temporis Messiae.* Paris:
Cramoisy.

Levita, Elijah. 1541. *Tishbi,* trans. Paulus Fagius. Isny.

———. 1867. *Massoreth haMassoreth*, ed. and trans. Christian Ginsburg. London: Longmans, Green, Reader and Dyer.

Lettere. 1744. *Lettere d'uomini illustri che fiorirono nel principio del secolo decimosettimo, non più stampate.* Venice: Baglioni.

Liber secretorum fidelium crucis. 1611. *Liber secretorum fidelium crucis super terrae sanctae recuperatione et conservatione.* Hanau: Aubry.

Liturgiae. 1560. *Liturgiae sive missae sanctorum patrum.* Antwerp: Plantin.

Maimonides, Moses. 1520. *Dux seu director dubitantium aut perplexorum*, ed. and trans. Agostino Giustiniani. Paris: Badius Ascensius.

Maldonado, Juan de. 1607. *Commentarii in quatuor Evangelistas.* Lyons: Cardon.

———. 1888. *A Commentary on the Holy Gospels*, trans. George Davie. 2d ed. 2 vols. London: Hodges.

Margaliot, Reuven, ed. 2004. *Sefer Hasidim shehibber Rabbeinu Yehudah heHasid.* Jerusalem: Mossad haRav Kook.

Margaritha, Antonius. 1530. *Der gantz Jüdisch glaub mit sampt ainer gründtlichen und warhafften anzaygunge, Aller Satzungen, Ceremonien, Gebetten, Haymliche und offentliche Gebreüch, deren sich dye Juden halten, durch das gantz Jar, mit schönen und gegründten Argumenten wider jren Glauben.* Augsburg: Steyner.

Martí, Ramon. 1651. *Pugio fidei*, ed. Joseph de Voisin. Paris: Henault and Henault.

———. 1687. *Pugio fidei*, ed. Joseph de Voisin, int. Johann Benedikt Carpzow. Leipzig: Heirs of Lanckisius.

Megiser, Hieronymus. 1603. *Thesaurus polyglottus*, 2 vols. Frankfurt am Main: published by the author.

Mercier, Jean. 1651. *Commentarii in Iobum et Salomonis Proverbia, Ecclesiasten, Canticum canticorum.* Amsterdam: Elzevir.

Morel, Frédéric, ed. and trans. 1583. Theophrastus. *De notis morum liber singularis.* Paris: Morel.

Mountagu, Richard, ed. 1610. *Sancti Gregorii Nazianzeni in Iulianum invectivae duae. Cum scholiis Graecis nunc primume ditis, et ejusdem Authoris nonnullis aliis quorum syllabum sequens Pag. continet. Omnia ex Bibliotheca Clarissimi viri D. Henrici Savilii.* Eton: Norton.

Mountagu, Richard. 1622. *Analecta ecclesiasticarum exercitationum.* London: Pro Societate Bibliopolarum.

———. 1635. *Apparatus ad origines ecclesiasticas.* Oxford: Lichfield.

———. 1636. *De originibus ecclesiasticis commentariorum tomus primus.* London: Flesher and Young.

———. 1640. *ΘΕΑΝΘΡΩΠΙΙΚΟΝ seu de vita Jesu Christi, Domini nostri, originum ecclesiasticarum libri duo.* London: Kirton and Warren.

Münster, Sebastian. 1527a. *Chaldaica grammatica.* Basel: Io. Froben.

———. 1527b. *Kalendarium Hebraicum, opera Sebastiani Munsteri ex Hebraeorum penetralibus iam recens in lucem aeditum: quod non tam Hebraice studiosis quam Historiographis et Astronomiae peritis subservire poterit.* Basel: Io. Froben.

———, ed. 1537. *Evangelium secundum Matthaeum in lingua Hebraica cum versione latina atque succinctis annotationibus Sebastiani Munsteri.* Basel: H. Petri.

———, ed. 1541. *Josephus Hebraicus diu desideratus, et nunc ex Constantinopolitano exemplari iuxta Hebraismum opera Sebastiani Munsteri versus, et annotationibus atque collationibus illustratus.* Basel: H. Petri.

Novum Testamentum. 1599. *Novum testamentum Domini Jesu Christi Syriace, Ebraice,*

Græce, Latine, Germanice, Bohemice, Italice, Hispanice, Gallice, Anglice, Danice, Polonice, ed. Elias Hutter. Nuremberg.

Osiander, Lucas. 1592–1599. *Epitomes historiae ecclesiasticae centuria I.II.III.–Septima.* Tübingen: Gruppenbachius.

Otto, Julius Conradus. 1605a. *Gali razia occultorum detectio: hoc est, monstratio dogmatum quae omnes rabbini recte sentientes de unitate essentiae divinae, Trinitate personarum et de Messia posteritati reliquerunt.* Nuremberg: Koerberus; reprinted, Stettin: Duberus, 1613.

———. 1605b. *Grammatica hebraea, methodice tractata pro more rabbinorum.* Nuremberg: Theodoricus.

Paris, Matthew. 1589. *Historia maior a Guglielmo Conquaestore ad ultimum annum Henrici tertii.* Zurich: Froschauer.

Paul of Burgos. 1477. *Additiones,* in *Postilla Nicolai de Lira super quatuor evangeliis cum Additionibus domini Pauli Burgensis episcopi et cum Replicationibus fratris Mathei Doringk ordinis minorum.* Mantua: Puzpach.

Paul of Middelburg. 1513. *Paulina de recta Paschae celebratione: et de die passionis domini nostri iesu Christi.* Fossombrone: Ottaviano Petrucci.

Perroniana. 1669. *Perroniana sive Excerpta ex ore Cardinalis Perronii per F. F. P. P.* Geneva: Columesius.

Persius. 1812. *Satirae,* ed. Nicolas Louis Achaintre. Paris: Firmin Diot.

Pignoria, Lorenzo. 1608. *Characteres Aegyptii.* Frankfurt am Main: Becker and de Bry.

Postel, Guillaume. 1538a. *De originibus seu de Hebraicae linguae et gentis antiquitate deque variarum linguarum affinitate.* Paris: Lescuier.

———. 1538b. *Linguarum duodecim characteribus differentium alphabetum, introductio, ac legendi modus longe facilimus.* Paris: Lescuier and Vidovaeus.

———. Ca. 1538. *Grammatica arabica.* Paris: Gromorsus.

Prideaux, John. 1614. *Castigatio cuiusdam circulatoris, qui R. P. Andream Eudaemon-Iohannem Cydonium e Societate Iesu seipsum nuncupat, opposita ipsius calumniis in Epistolam Isaaci Casauboni ad Frontonem Ducaeum.* Oxford: Barnes.

Ramus, Petrus. 1577. *Commentariorum de religione Christiana libri quatuor. Eiusdem vita, a Theophilo Banosio descripta.* Frankfurt am Main: Wechel.

Reuchlin, Johannes. 1517. *De arte cabalistica libri tres.* Hagenau: Thomas Anshelm.

Ricci, Agostino. 1521. *De motu octavae sphaerae, opus mathematica atque philosophia plenum. Vbi tam antiquorum quam iuniorum errores luce clarius demonstrantur. In quo et quam plurima Platonicorum et antiquae magiae (quam Cabalam Hebraei dicunt) dogmata videre licet intellectui suavissima. Eiusdem de astronomiae autoribus epistola.* Paris: Colin.

Rittershusius, Conrad, ed. 1609. *Liber commentarius in epistolas Plinii et Trajani.* Amberg: Schönfeld, 1609.

Rosweyde, Heribert. 1614. *Lex talionis XII. Tabularum Cardinali Baronio ab Isaaco Casaubono dicta: retaliante Heriberto Ros-vveydo Societatis Iesu Theologi.* Antwerp: Plantin.

Rupert of Deutz. 1545. *Opera duo, ut egregia sane, ita diu desiderata, multoque labore perquisita, ac sumptu haud ita modico excusa. In Matthaeum de gloria & honore filij hominis. Lib. XIII. De glorificatione Trinitatis, & processione Spiritus sancti, lib. IX.* Paris: Boucher.

———. 1602. *Opera omnia.* 2 vols. Cologne: Birckmann.

———. 1979. *De gloria et honore Filii hominis super Mattheum,* ed. Hrabanus Haacke. Corpus Christianorum, Continuatio Medievalis, 29. Turnhout: Brepols.

Samuel di Uceda. 1951. *Derashot Rabbi Shmuel de Uceda al haTorah*, ed. Samuel Yerushalmi. Jerusalem: privately printed.

Scaliger, Joseph. 1583. *Opus novum de emendatione temporum*. Paris: Patisson.

———, ed. 1595. *Hippolyti episcopi Canon Paschalis*. Leiden: Plantin/Raphelengius.

———, ed. 1600. *Manilius, Astronomicon*. Leiden: Plantin/Raphelengius.

Scaliger, Joseph. 1605. *Elenchus Trihaeresii Nicolai Serarii. Ejus in ipsum Scaligerum animadversiones confutatae. Eiusdem delirium fanaticum et impudentissimum mendacium, quo Essenos Monachos Christianos fuisse contendit, validissimis argumentis elusum*. Franeker: Radaeus.

———. 1606. *Thesaurus temporum*. Leiden: Basson.

———. 1607. *Elenchus utriusque orationis D. Davidis Parei: quarum secunda operis calci addita; prior vero Commentariis auctoris in Hoseam Heydelbergae excusis prostat*. Leiden: Elzevir.

———. 1627. *Epistolae omnes quae reperiri potuerunt*, ed. Daniel Heinsius. Leiden: Elzevir.

———. 1658. *Thesaurus temporum*. 2d ed. Amsterdam.

———. 1695. *Scaligerana, ou Bons mots, rencontres agreables, et remarques judicieuses & sçavantes de J. Scaliger*. Cologne and Amsterdam: Chez les Huguetans.

———. 1703. *Elenchus*. In *Trium illustrium scriptorum de tribus Judaeorum sectis Syntagma*, ed. Jacobus Triglandius. 2 vols. Delft: Beman.

———. 1740. *Scaligerana, Thuana, Perroniana, Pithoeana et Colomesiana*, ed. Pierre Des Maizeaux. 2 vols. Amsterdam: Cóvens & Mortier.

———. 1879. *Lettres françaises inédites*, ed. Philippe Tamizey de Larroque. Paris: Picard.

Schoppe, Kaspar. 1600. *Epistola de sua ad Orthodoxos migratione et de veritate interpretationis et sententiae Catholicæ in ambiguis Scripturarum locis, et controversis fidei capitibus*. Ingolstadt: Sartorius.

Serarius, Nicolaus. 1604. *Trihaeresium, seu de celeberrimis tribus apud Iudaeos, Pharisaeorum, Sadducaeorum, et Essenorum sectis, ad varios utriusque Testamenti veterumque Scriptorum locos intelligendum, et ad nupero Io. Drusii De Hasidaeis libello respondendum, libri tres*. Mainz: Lippius.

———. 1605. *Minerval divinis Hollandiae Frisiaeque grammaticis, Ios. Scaligero et Io. Drusio, Trihaeresii auctati ergo, e Grammatico, Ethico, Theologicoque saccello, libra librorum quinum Paraenetica et Antirrhetica depensum*. Mainz: Lippius.

———. 1611. *Commentarij in sacros Bibliorum libros, Iosuæ, Iudicum, Ruth, Tobiæ, Iudith, Esther, Machabæorum, etc*. Paris: Martin.

Sheringham, Robert, ed. 1696. *Yoma, codex Talmudicus, in quo agitur de sacrificiis caeterisque ministeriis Diei expiationis*. Franeker: Wibiumbleck.

Sigonio, Carlo. 1582. *De republica Hebraeorum libri VII*. Bologna: Giovanni de' Rossi.

Simon, Richard. 1685. *Histoire critique du Vieux Testament*. Rotterdam: Leers.

Smith, Peter. 1634. "The Life and Death of Doctor Willet." In Willet 1634, a recto–[c 4 verso].

Strabo. 1949–1954. *Geography*, trans. Harold Lloyd Jones. 8 vols. Cambridge, Mass.: Harvard University Press.

Synesius of Cyrene. 2000. *Correspondance*, ed. Antonio Garzya and Denis Roques. 2 vols. Paris: Les Belles Lettres.

———. 2003. *La mia fortunosa navigazione da Alessandria a Cirene*, ed. Petro Janni. Florence: Olschi.

Thevet, André. 1554. *Cosmographie de Levant*. Lyons: De Tournes and Gazeau.

Toletus, Franciscus, S.J. 1590–89. *In sacrosanctum Ioannis evangelium Commentarii*. 2 vols. Rome: Typographia Vaticana.

Tolosani, Giovanni, O.P. 1537. *Ioannis Lucidi Samothei viri clarissimi Opusculum de emenda-tionibus temporum ab orbe condito ad usque hanc aetatem nostram.* Venice: Giunti.

Valla, Lorenzo. 2007. *On the Donation of Constantine,* ed. Glen Bowersock. Cambridge, Mass.: Harvard University Press.

Vanini, Giulio Cesare. 1615. *Amphitheatrum aeternae providentiae divino-magicum, christiano-phisicum, nec non astrologo-catholicum.* Lyons: Widow of de Harsy.

———. 1990. *Opere,* ed. G. Papuli and F. P. Raimondi. Galatina: Congedo.

Vettori, Pier. 1582. *Variarum lectionum libri XXXVIII.* Florence: Giunti.

Vives, Juan Luis, ed. 1555. *Divi Aurelii Augustini Hipponensis Episcopi De civitate Dei libri xxii. ad priscae venerandaeque vetustatis exemplaria denuo collati, eruditissimisque in-super Commentariis per undequaque doctiss. virum Ioann. Lodovicum Vivem illustrati et recogniti.* Basel: Froben.

Wakefield, Robert. 1524. *Oratio de laudibus et utilitate trium linguarum Arabicae Chaldaicae et Hebraicae, atque idiomatibus Hebraicis quae in utroque Testamento inveniuntur.* London: Winkyn de Worde.

———. 1534. *Syntagma de Hebraeorum codicum incorruptione. Item eiusdem oratio Oxonii habita, una cum quibusdam aliis lectu ac annotatu non indignis.* [London: Winkyn de Worde.]

———. 1989. *On the Three Languages* [1524], ed. and trans. G. Lloyd Jones. Binghamton, N.Y.: Medieval and Renaissance Texts and Studies in association with the Renaissance Society of America.

Weiser, Asher, ed. 1976–77. *Peirushei haTorah leRabbenu Avraham ibn Ezra.* 3 vols. Jerusa-lem: Mossad haRav Kook.

Welser, Marcus. 1682. *Opera historica et philologica, sacra et prophana.* Nuremberg: Mauri-tius and sons of Endter.

Willet, Andrew. 1634. *Synopsis papismi.* London: Haviland and Allot.

Wistinetzki, Jehudah, ed. 1969. *Sefer Hasidim.* Reprint, New York: Ktav.

Wolf, Friedrich August. 1884. *Prolegomena ad Homerum,* ed. Rudolf Peppmüller. 3d ed. Halle: Orphanotropheum.

———. 1985. *Prolegomena to Homer,* trans. Anthony Grafton, Glenn Most, and James Zetzel. Princeton: Princeton University Press.

Wood, Anthony à. 1813–1820. *Fasti Oxonienses, or, Annals of the University of Oxford,* ed. Philip Bliss. 2 vols. London: Rivington.

Zacuto, Abraham. 1580/81. *Sefer Yuhasin.* Kraków: Prostitz.

Secondary Sources

Achinstein, Sharon. 2001. "John Foxe and the Jews." *Renaissance Quarterly* 54: 86–120.

Alexander, Alexander. 1997. "Jerusalem as the 'Omphalos' of the World: On the History of a Geograpical Concept." *Judaism* 47, no. 2: 147–158.

Allen, Don Cameron. 1949. *The Legend of Noah: Renaissance Rationalism in Art, Science, and Letters.* Urbana: University of Illinois Press.

———. 1970. *Mysteriously Meant: The Rediscovery of Pagan Symbolism and Allegorical Inter-pretation in the Renaissance.* Baltimore: Johns Hopkins Press.

Allony, Nehemia. 1991. *Studies in Medieval Philology and Literature. Collected Papers,* IV. Jerusalem: Reuben Mass.

Altmann, Alexander. 1952. "William Wollaston (1659–1704)." *Transactions of the Jewish His-torical Society of England* 16: 185–211.

Assmann, Jan. 1997. *Moses the Egyptian: The Memory of Egypt in Western Monotheism.* Cambridge, Mass.: Harvard University Press.

Awerbach, Marianne. 1997. "Alltagsleben in der Frankfurter Judengasse im 17. und 18. Jahrhundert." In Grözinger 1997, 1–24.

Balagna Coustou, Josée. 1989. *Arabe et humanisme dans la France des derniers Valois.* Paris : Maisonneuve et Larose.

Bammel, Ernst. 1970. *The Trial of Jesus: Cambridge Studies in Honour of C. F. D. Moule.* London: SCM Press.

Bass, Marisa. 2007 [2008]. "Justus Lipsius and His Silver Pen." *Journal of the Warburg and Courtauld Institutes* 70: 157–194.

Beaver, Adam. 2008. "A Holy Land for the Catholic Monarchy: Palestine in the Making of Modern Spain, 1469—1598." Ph.D. diss., Harvard University.

Bell, Dean Phillip. 2001. *Sacred Communities: Jewish and Christian Identities in Fifteenth-Century Germany.* Leiden: Brill.

———. 2007. *Jewish Identity in Early Modern Germany: Memory, Power and Community.* Aldershot: Ashgate.

———. 2008. "The Little Ice Age and the Jews: Environmental History and the Mercurial Nature of Jewish-Christian Relations in Early Modern Germany." *AJS Review* 32: 1–27.

Bellucci, Antonio. 1927. "Il 'De origine Oratorii': Opuscolo inedito del Cardinale Cesare Baronio." *Aevum* 1: 625–633.

Benbassa, Esther. 1999. *The Jews of France: A History from Antiquity to the Present,* trans. Malcolm DeBevoise. Princeton: Princeton University Press.

Ben-Jacob, Yitshak. 1880. *Otsar haSefarim.* Vilna: Romm.

Berg, J. van den. 1988. "Proto-Protestants? The Image of the Karaites as a Mirror of the Catholic-Protestant Controversy in the Seventeenth Century." In *Jewish-Christian Relations in the Seventeenth Century: Studies and Documents,* ed. J. van den Berg and Ernestine G. E. van der Wall. Dordrecht: Kluwer, 43–64.

Berger, David, ed. 1979. *Nizzahon vetus: The Jewish-Christian Debate in the High Middle Ages.* Philadelphia: JPS.

Bernays, Jacob. 1855. *Joseph Justus Scaliger.* Berlin: Hertz.

Bickerman, Elias J. 1951. "The Maxim of Antigonus of Socho." *Harvard Theological Review* 44: 153–165.

Bietenholz, Peter. 1994. *Historia and Fabula: Myths and Legends in Historical Thought from Antiquity to the Modern Age.* Leiden: Brill.

Birrell, T. A. 1980. "The Reconstruction of the Library of Isaac Casaubon." In *Hellinga Festschrift/Feestbundel/Mélanges.* Amsterdam: Nico Israel, 59–68.

Blair, Ann. 1992. "Humanist Methods in Natural Philosophy: The Commonplace Book." *Journal of the History of Ideas* 53: 541–551.

———. 1996. "Bibliothèques portables: Les recueils de lieux communs dans la Renaissance tardive." In *Le pouvoir des bibliothèques: La mémoire des livres en Occident,* ed. Marc Baratin and Christian Jacob. Paris: Albin Michel, 84–106.

———. 1997a. "Bodin, Montaigne and the Role of Disciplinary Boundaries." In Kelley 1997, 29–40.

———. 1997b. *The Theater of Nature: Jean Bodin and Renaissance Science.* Princeton: Princeton University Press.

———. 2000a. "Annotating and Indexing Natural Philosophy." In Frasca-Spada and Jardine 2000, 69–89.

———. 2000b. "The Practices of Erudition according to Morhof." In *Mapping the World of Learning: The Polyhistor of Daniel Georg Morhof,* ed. Françoise Waquet. Wiesbaden: Harrassowitz, 59–74.

———. 2003. "Reading Strategies for Coping with Information Overload, ca. 1550–1700." *Journal of the History of Ideas* 64: 11–28.

———. 2004a. "Note-Taking as an Art of Transmission." *Critical Inquiry* 31: 85–107.

———. 2004b. "Scientific Reading: An Early Modernist's Perspective." *Isis* 95: 64–74.

———. 2005. "*Historia* in Zwinger's *Theatrum Humanae Vitae.*" In Pomata and Siraisi 2005, 269–296.

———. 2010. *Too Much To Know: Managing Scholarly Information before the Modern Age.* New Haven: Yale University Press.

Borelli, Mario. 1964. *Opere e documenti sul Baronio presso la British Museum Library.* Naples: Gennaro d'Agostino.

Borst, Arno. 1957–1963. *Der Turmbau von Babel: Geschichte der Meinungen über Ursprung und Vielfalt der Sprachen und Völker.* 4 vols. in 6. Stuttgart: Hiersemann.

Bos, Jacques. 1998. "Individuality and Inwardness in the Literary Character Sketches of the Seventeenth Century." *Journal of the Warburg and Courtauld Institutes* 61: 142–157.

Botley, Paul. 2004. *Latin Translation in the Renaissance: The Theory and Practice of Leonardo Bruni, Giannozzo Manetti, and Desiderius Erasmus.* Cambridge: Cambridge University Press.

Bowersock, Glen. 2006. "Peter and Constantine." In *St. Peter's in the Vatican,* ed. William Tronzo. Cambridge: Cambridge University Press, 5–16.

Bowersock, Glen, Peter Brown, and Oleg Grabar, eds. 1999. *Late Antiquity: A Guide to the Post-Classical World.* Cambridge, Mass.: Harvard University Press.

Boyce, Benjamin. 1947. *The Theophrastan Character in England to 1642.* Cambridge, Mass.: Harvard University Press; reprinted, London: Frank Cass, 1967.

Bravo, Benedetto. 2006. "*Critice* in the Sixteenth and Seventeenth Centuries and the Birth of the Notion of Historical Criticism." In *History of Scholarship,* ed. Christopher Ligota and Jean-Louis Quantin. Oxford: Oxford University Press, 135–195.

Burnett, Stephen. 1990. "The Christian Hebraism of Johann Buxtorf (1564–1629)." Ph.D. diss., University of Wisconsin–Madison.

———. 1994. "Distorted Mirrors: Antonius Margarita, Johann Buxtorf and Christian Ethnographies of the Jews." *Sixteenth Century Journal* 25: 275–287.

———. 1996. *From Christian Hebraism to Jewish Studies: Johannes Buxtorf (1564–1629) and Hebrew Learning in the Seventeenth Century.* Leiden: Brill.

Calderini De-Marchi, Rita, 1914. *Jacopo Corbinelli et les érudits français d'après la correspondance inédite Corbinelli-Pinelli (1566–1587).* Milan: Hoepli.

Campagnolo, Matteo. 2007. "Entre Théodore de Bèze et Érasme de Rotterdam: Isaac Casaubon." In *Théodore de Bèze (1519–1605): Actes du colloque de Genève (septembre 2005),* ed. Irena Backus. Geneva: Droz, 195–217.

Canfora, Luciano. 1987. *Ellenismo.* Rome: Laterza.

———. 2002. *Convertire Casaubon.* Milan: Adelphi.

———. 2007. *Ellenismo.* Rome: Laterza.

Carlebach, Elisheva. 2001. *Divided Souls: Converts from Judaism in Germany, 1500–1750.* New Haven: Yale University Press.

Carley, James. 2001. "Religious Controversy and Marginalia: Pierfrancesco di Piero Bardi, Thomas Wakefield, and Their Books." *Transactions of the Cambridge Bibliographical Society* 12, pt. 3: 206–245.

Cerbu, Thomas. 1986. "Leone Allacci (1587–1669): The Fortunes of an Early Byzantinist." Ph.D. diss., Harvard University.

Christie, Richard Copley. 1902. "Vanini in England." In *Selected Essays and Papers,* ed. William A. Shaw. London: Longmans, Green, 172–208. Originally printed in *English Historical Review* 10 (1895): 238–265.

Clark, Andrew. 1887. *Register of the University of Oxford.* Vol. 1: *Introductions;* vol. II: *1571–1622.* Oxford: Clarendon Press.

Cochrane, Eric. 1981. *Historians and Historiography in the Italian Renaissance.* Chicago: University of Chicago Press.

Cohen, Mark. 1972. "Leone de Modena's *Riti:* A Seventeenth-Century Plea for Toleration of Jews." *Jewish Social Studies* 34: 287–321.

Colomiès, Paul. 1665. *Gallia Orientalis.* The Hague: Vlacq.

———. 1730. *Italia et Hispania Orientalis.* Hamburg: Felginer.

Considine, John. 2003. "Philology and Autobiography in Isaac Casaubon, *Animadversionum in Athenaei Deipnosophistas libri XV* (1600)." In *Acta conventus neo-latini Cantabrigiensis,* ed. Rhoda Schnur. Tempe: Arizona Center for Medieval and Renaissance Studies, 155–162.

———. 2008. *Dictionaries in Early Modern Europe: Lexicography and the Making of Heritage.* Cambridge: Cambridge University Press.

Copenhaver, Brian, ed. 1992. *Hermetica.* Cambridge: Cambridge University Press.

Coudert, Alison, and Jeffrey Shoulson, eds. 2004. *Hebraica veritas? Christian Hebraists and the Study of Judaism in Early Modern Europe.* Philadelphia: University of Pennsylvania Press.

Coyne, George, Michael Hoskin, and Olaf Pedersen, eds. 1983. *Gregorian Reform of the Calendar: Proceedings of the Vatican Conference to Commemorate Its 400th Anniversary, 1582–1982.* Vatican City: Pontificia Academia Scientiarum, Specola Vaticana.

Cozzi, Gaetano. 1978. *Paolo Sarpi tra Venezia e l'Europa.* Turin: Einaudi.

Craster, H. H. E. 1926. "Casaubon's Greek Manuscripts." *Bodleian Library Record* 5: 97–100.

Daiches, David. 1941. *The King James Version of the English Bible.* Chicago: University of Chicago Press.

Dan, Joseph. 1997. *The Christian Kabbalah.* Cambridge, Mass.: Harvard College Library.

Darom, Abraham, ed. 1967. *R. David Kimhi (Redaq) haPerush haShalem al Tehillim.* Jerusalem: Mossad Harav Kook.

Décultot, Élisabeth. 2000. *Johann Joachim Winckelmann: Enquête sur la genèse de l'histoire de l'art.* Paris: Presses Universitaires de France.

———, ed. 2003. *Lire, copier, écrire: Les bibliothèques manuscrites et leurs usages au XVIIIe siècle.* Paris: Centre National de la Recherche Scientifique.

Deissler, Alfons. 1955. *Psalm 119 (118) und seine Theologie.* Munich: Zink.

de Jonge, Henk Jan. 1975. "The Study of the New Testament." In *Leiden University in the Seventeenth Century: An Exchange of Learning,* ed. T. H. Lunsingh Scheurleer and G. H. M. Posthumus Meyjes. Leiden: Universitaire Pers Leiden and Brill, 65–109.

De Landtsheer, Jeanine. 2000. "Justus Lipsius' *De cruce* and the Reception of the Fathers." *Neulateinisches Jahrbuch* 2: 99–124.

Delisle, Léopold. 1868. *Le Cabinet des Manuscrits de la Bibliothèque Impériale.* Vol. 1. Paris: Imprimerie Impériale.

de Mély, F. 1922. *La Virga Aurea du Fr. J.-B. Hepburn d'Écosse.* Paris: Ernest Leroux.

Derenbourg, J, 1895. "L'édition de la Bible rabbinique de Jean Buxtorf." *Revue des Études Juives* 30: 70–78.

Deutsch, Yaacov. 2001. "'A View of the Jewish Religion': Conceptions of Jewish Practice and Ritual in Early Modern Europe." *Archiv für Religionsgeschichte* 3: 273–295.

———. 2004. "Polemical Ethnographies: Descriptions of Yom Kippur in the Writings of Christian Hebraists and Jewish Converts to Christianity in Early Modern Europe." In Coudert and Shoulson 2004, 202–232.

———. N.d. "Introduction to The Jewish Synagoge." In *Early Modern Workshop: Jewish History Resources*. Available at http://www.earlymodern.org/workshops/2006/deutsch/text01/intro.php?tid=20 (accessed 15 July 2008).

Dickey, Eleanor. 2007. *Ancient Greek Scholarship*. New York: American Philological Association.

Diemling, Maria. 2006. "Anthonius Margaritha and His 'Der Gantz Jüdisch Glaub.'" In *Jews, Judaism and the Reformation in Sixteenth-Century Germany,* ed. Dean Phillip Bell and Stephen G. Burnett. Leiden: Brill, 303–333.

Diggle, James, ed. 2004. *Theophrastus, Characters*. Cambridge: Cambridge University Press.

Ditchfield, Simon. 1995. *Liturgy, Sanctity and History in Tridentine Italy: Pietro Maria Campi and the Preservation of the Particular*. Cambridge: Cambridge University Press.

DNB. 1885–1901. *Dictionary of National Biography*, ed. Leslie Stephen and Sidney Lee. 63 vols. London: Smith, Elder. Digital version: http://www.oxforddnb.com.

Droixhe, Daniel. 1978. *La linguistique et l'appel de l'histoire (1600–1800): Rationalisme et révolutions positivistes*. Geneva: Droz.

———. 1992. "La crise de l'hébreu langue-mère au XVIIe siècle." In *La république des lettres et l'histoire du Judaïsme antique, XVIe–XVIIIe siècles,* ed. Chantal Grell and Francois Laplanche. Paris: Presses de l'Université de Paris–Sorbonne, 65–99.

Dubois, Claude-Gilbert. 1994. *La mythologie des origines chez Guillaume Postel*. Orléans: Paradigme.

Dunbar, Nan, ed. 1995. *Aristophanes, Birds*. Oxford: Clarendon Press.

Elon, Menahem. 1994. *Jewish Law: History, Sources, Principles,* trans. B. Auerbach and M. J. Sykes. Vol. 3. Philadelphia: JPS.

Engammare, Max. 2004. *L'ordre du temps: L'invention de la ponctualité au XVIe siècle*. Geneva: Droz.

Epstein, A. 1900. "Die Wormser Minhagbücher, Literarisches und Culturhistorisches aus denselben." In *Gedenkbuch zur Erinnerung an David Kaufmann,* ed. M. Brann and F. Rosenthal. Breslau: Schles. Verlags-Astalt; Jerusalem: Mekor, 288–317.

Epstein, Morris. 1973. "Simon Levi Ginzburg's Illustrated Customal (Minhagim-Book) of Venice and Its Travels." In *Proceedings of the Fifth World Congress of Jewish Studies, Jerusalem, 3–11 August 1969*. Jerusalem: World Congress of Jewish Studies, IV, 197–218.

Feingold, Mordechai. 1997. "Oriental Languages." In *The History of the University of Oxford*. Vol. 4: *Seventeenth-Century Oxford,* ed. Nicholas Tyacke. Oxford: Clarendon Press, 449–503.

Ferreri, Luigi. 2007. *La questione omerica dal Cinquecento al Settecento*. Rome: Storia e letteratura.

Festa, Nicola. 1911. "Note per un capitolo della biografia d'Isacco Casaubon." In *Per Carlo Baronio: Scritti vari nel terzo centenario della sua morte*. Rome: Athenaeum, 261–294.

Feuchtwanger-Sarig, Naomi. 2000. "How Italian Are the Jewish Minhagim of 1593? A Chapter in the History of Yiddish Printing in Italy." In Graetz 2000, 177–205.

Finocchiaro, Giuseppe. 1995. "La Roma sotterranea e la Congregazione dell'Oratorio. Inediti e lacune del monoscritto vallicelliano G. 31." In *Messer Filippo Neri, santo, l'apostolo di Roma*. Exhibition catalog. Rome: De Luca, 188–198.

———. 2005. *Cesare Baronio e la tipografia dell'Oratorio: Impresa e ideologia.* Florence: Olschki.

Fisher, Nick. 2000. "Symposiasts, Fish-Eaters and Flatterers: Social Mobility and Moral Concerns." In *The Rivals of Aristophanes: Studies in Athenian Old Comedy.* London: Duckworth and the Classical Presses of Wales, 355–396.

Fishman, Talya. 2004. "Rhineland Pietist Approaches to Prayer and the Textualization of Rabbinic Culture in Medieval Northern Europe." *Jewish Studies Quarterly* 11, no. 4: 313–331.

———. 2006. "The Rhineland Pietists' Sacralization of Oral Torah." *Jewish Quarterly Review* 96, no. 1: 9–16.

Flusser, David. 1978–1980. *Sefer Yosifon: . . . sadur u-mugah 'al-pi kitve-yad be-lvyat mavo, be'urim ve-hilufe girsa'ot.* 2 vols. Jerusalem: Mosad Byalik.

Foucault, Didier. 2003. *Un philosophe libertin dans l'Europe baroque: Giulio Cesare Vanini (1585–1619).* Paris: Champion.

Fowden, Garth. 1986. *The Egyptian Hermes: A Historical Approach to the Late Pagan Mind.* Cambridge: Cambridge University Press.

Fraenkel, Eduard, ed. 1950. *Aeschylus, Agamemnon.* Oxford: Clarendon Press.

Fraenkel-Goldschmidt, Chava. 1997. "Jüdische Religion und Kultur in Frankfurt am Main im 16. und 17. Jahrhundert—Yuzpa Hahn und sein *Yosif omez.*" In Grözinger 1997, 101–121.

Frasca-Spada, Marina, and Nick Jardine, eds. 2000. *Books and the Sciences in History.* Cambridge: Cambridge University Press.

Fubini, Riccardo. 2003. *Storiografia dell'umanesimo in Italia da Leonardo Bruni ad Annio da Viterbo.* Rome: Storia e Letteratura.

Fück, Johann. 1955. *Die arabischen Studien in Europa bis in den Anfang des 20. Jahrhunderts.* Leipzig: Harrassowitz.

Fuks, L. 1969. "Het Hebreuwse brieveboek van Johannes Drusius jr. Hebreuws en Hebraisten in Nederland rondom 1600." *Studia Rosenthaliana* 3: 1–52.

Galbiati, Enrico. 1956. "Lettere del Ripamonti e dell'Olgiati ad Isaac Casaubon." In *Studi Storici in memoria di mons. Angelo Mercati.* Milan: A. Giuffrè Editore, 185–194.

Gamilschegg, Ernst, and Dieter Harlfinger. 1981. *Repertorium der griechischen Kopisten, 800–1600.* Vol. 1: *Handschriften aus Bibliotheken Grossbritanniens. A: Verzeichnis der Kopisten.* Vienna: Verlag der Österreichischen Akademie der Wissenschaften.

Garin, Eugenio. 1988. *Ermetismo del Rinascimento.* Rome: Editori Riuniti.

Garshowitz, Libby. 1992–1993. "Shemtov ben Isaac ibn Shaprut's Gospel of Matthew." In *The Frank Talmage Memorial Volume 1,* ed. Barry Walfish. Haifa: Haifa University Press, 297–322.

Geison, Gerald. 1995. *The Private Science of Louis Pasteur.* Princeton: Princeton University Press.

Gentile, Sebastiano, and Carlos Gilly. 1999. *Marsilio Ficino e il ritorno di Ermete Trismegisto / Marsilio Ficino and the Return of Hermes Trismegistus.* Florence: Centro Di.

Gilly, Carlos, and van Heertum, Cis. 2002. *Magia, alchimia, scienza dal' '400 al '700: L'influsso di Ermete Trismegisto / Magic, Alchemy and Science, 15th–18th Centuries: The Influence of Hermes Trismegistus.* 2 vols. Florence: Centro Di.

Gilman, Sander, 1986. *Jewish Self-Hatred: Anti-Semitism and the Hidden Language of the Jews.* Baltimore: Johns Hopkins University Press.

Ginsburg, Christian. 1966. *Introduction to the Massoretico-Critical Edition of the Hebrew Bible.* New York: Ktav.

Goldschmidt, E. Daniel. 1978. *On Jewish Liturgy: Essays in Prayer and Religious Poetry* [Hebrew]. Jerusalem: Magnes.

———. 1980. "The Liturgy of the Jews of Rome." In *On Jewish Liturgy* [Hebrew]. Jerusalem: Magnes, 153–176.

Gombrich, E. H. 1960. "Vasari's Lives and Cicero's Brutus." *Journal of the Warburg and Courtauld Institutes* 23: 309–311.

Goshen-Gottstein, M. 1987. "Foundations of Biblical Philology in the Seventeenth Century: Christian and Jewish Dimensions." In *Jewish Thought in the Seventeenth Century,* ed. Isidore Twersky and Bernard Septimus. Cambridge, Mass.: Harvard Center for Jewish Studies, 77–94.

Goulding, Robert. 2006. "Method and Mathematics: Peter Ramus's Histories of the Sciences." *Journal of the History of Ideas* 67: 63–85.

Graetz, Michael, ed. 2000. *Schöpferische Momente des europäischen Judentums in der frühen Neuzeit.* Heidelberg: Winter.

Grafton, Anthony. 1981. "Prolegomena to Friedrich August Wolf." *Journal of the Warburg and Courtauld Institutes* 44: 101–129; reprinted in Grafton 1991, chap. 9.

———. 1983. "Protestant versus Prophet: Isaac Casaubon on Hermes Trismegistus." *Journal of the Warburg and Courtauld Institutes* 46: 78–93; reprinted in Grafton 1991, chap. 7.

———. 1983–1993. *Joseph Scaliger: A Study in the History of Classical Scholarship.* 2 vols. Oxford: Clarendon Press.

———. 1990. *Forgers and Critics: Creativity and Duplicity in Western Scholarship.* Princeton: Princeton University Press.

———. 1991. *Defenders of the Text.* Cambridge, Mass.: Harvard University Press.

———. 1992. "Joseph Scaliger et l'histoire du Judaïsme Hellénistique." In *La république des lettres et l'histoire du Judaïsme antique, XVIe–XVIIe siècles,* ed. Chantal Grell and François Laplanche. Paris: Presses de l'Université de Paris–Sorbonne, 51–63.

———. 2001. *Bring Out Your Dead: The Past as Revelation.* Cambridge, Mass.: Harvard University Press.

———. 2007. *What Was History? The Art of History in Early Modern Europe.* Cambridge: Cambridge University Press.

———. Forthcoming. "Robert Wakefield, Masorete."

Grossman, Abraham. 2004. *Pious and Rebellious: Jewish Women in Medieval Europe,* trans. Jonathan Chipman. Waltham, Mass.: Brandeis University Press.

Grözinger, Karl, ed. 1997. *Jüdische Kultur in Frankfurt am Main von den Anfängen bis zur Gegenwart.* Wiesbaden: Harrassowitz.

Hachlili, Rachel. 2005. *Jewish Funerary Customs, Practices and Rites in the Second Temple Period.* Leiden: Brill.

Hamilton, Alastair. 1985. *William Bedwell the Arabist, 1563–1632.* Leiden: Leiden University Press.

———. 1988–89. "'Nam tirones sumus': Franciscus Raphelengius' *Lexicon Arabico-Latinum* (Leiden 1613)." *De Gulden Passer* 66–67: 557–589.

———. 1994. "An Egyptian Traveller in the Republic of Letters: Josephus Barbatus or Abudacnus the Copt." *Journal of the Warburg and Courtauld Institutes* 57: 123–150.

———. 2006. *The Copts and the West, 1439–1822: The European Discovery of the Egyptian Church.* Oxford: Oxford University Press.

———. 2009. "Isaac Casaubon the Arabist: 'Video longum esse iter.'" *Journal of the Warburg and Courtauld Institutes* 72: 143–168.

Hamilton, Alastair, and Francis Richard. 2004. *Andre Du Ryer and Oriental Studies in*

Seventeenth-Century France. London: Arcadian Library; Oxford: Oxford University Press.

Harl, Marguerite, with Gilles Dorival. 1972. *La chaîne palestinienne sur le psaume 118 (Origène, Eusèbe, Didyme, Apollinaire, Athanase, Théodoret).* Paris: Éditions du Cerf.

Hartrup, Karen. 2004. *"On the Beliefs of the Greeks": Leo Allatius and Popular Orthodoxy.* Leiden: Brill.

Heide, Albert van der. 2008. *Hebraica veritas: Christopher Plantin and the Christian Hebraists.* Antwerp: Plantin-Moretus Museum/Print Room.

Henke, Ernst Ludwig Theodor. 1853–1860. *Georg Calixtus und seine Zeit.* 2 vols. Halle: Verlag der Buchhandlung des Waisenhauses.

Herklotz, Ingo. 2008. *Die Academia Basiliana: Griechische Philologie, Kirchengeschichte und Unionsbemühungen im Rom der Barberini.* Rome: Herder.

Hess, Jonathan. 2002. *Germans, Jews, and the Claims of Modernity.* New Haven: Yale University Press.

Holmes, Oliver Wendell, and Harold Laski. 1953. *Holmes-Laski Letters: The Correspondence of Mr. Justice Holmes and Harold J. Laski, 1916–1935.* 2 vols. Cambridge, Mass.: Harvard University Press, 1953.

Höpfl, Harro. 2004. *Jesuit Political Thought: The Society of Jesus and the State, c. 1540–1630.* Cambridge: Cambridge University Press.

Horowitz, Elliott. 1989. "The Eve of the Circumcision: A Chapter in the History of Jewish Nightlife." *Journal of Social History* 23: 45–69.

Hsia, Ronnie Po-chia. 1994. "Christian Ethnographies of Jews in Early Modern Germany." In *The Expulsion of the Jews: 1492 and After,* ed. Raymond B. Waddington and Arthur H. Williamson. New York: Garland, 223–236.

Jardine, Lisa, and Anthony Grafton. 1990. "'Studied for Action': How Gabriel Harvey Read His Livy." *Past and Present* 129: 30–78.

Jones, H. S. 2007. *Intellect and Character in Victorian England: Mark Pattison and the Invention of the Don.* Cambridge: Cambridge University Press.

Jones, Robert. 1988. "Learning Arabic in Renaissance Europe (1505–1624)." Ph.D. diss., School of Oriental and African Studies, London University.

Jorink, Eric. 2006. *Het "boeck der natuere": Nederlandse geleerden en de wonderen van Gods Schepping, 1575–1715.* Leiden: Primavera Pers.

Juynboll, Wilhelmina Maria Cornelia. 1931. *Zeventiende-eeuwsche beoefenaars van het Arabisch in Nederland.* Utrecht: Kemink en Zoon.

Kampen, John. 1988. *The Hasideans and the Origin of Pharisaism: A Study in 1 and 2 Maccabees.* Atlanta: Scholars Press.

Katchen, Aaron L. 1984. *Christian Hebraists and Dutch Rabbis.* Cambridge, Mass.: Harvard University Press.

Katz, David. 1982. *Philo-Semitism and the Readmission of the Jews to England, 1603–55.* Oxford: Oxford University Press.

Kelley, Donald, ed. 1997. *History and the Disciplines: The Reclassification of Knowledge in Early Modern Europe.* Rochester: University of Rochester Press.

Kittel, Gerhard. 1964–1976. *Theological Dictionary of the New Testament,* ed. Gerhard Friedrich. 10 vols. Grand Rapids: Eerdmans.

Klempt, Adalbert. 1960. *Die Säkularisierung der universalhistorischen Auffassung; zum Wandel des Geschichtsdenkens im 16. und 17. Jahrhundert.* Göttingen: Musterschmidt.

Krauss, Samuel. 1995. *The Jewish-Christian Controversy from the Earliest Times to 1789,* ed. William Horbury. Vol. 1. Tübingen: J. C. B. Mohr (Paul Siebeck).

Kristeller, Paul, ed. 1937. *Supplementum Ficinianum.* 2 vols. Florence: Olschki.

Laplanche, François. 1986. *L'écriture, le sacré et l'histoire: Érudits et politiques devant la Bible en France au XVIIe siècle.* Amsterdam: APA–Holland University Press.

——. 1988. "À propos d'Isaac Casaubon: La controverse confessionnelle et la naissance de l'histoire." *History of European Ideas* 9: 405–422.

——. 1994. *La Bible en France entre mythe et critique (XVIe–XIXe siècles).* Paris: Albin Michel.

Lasker, Daniel. 2006. "Karaism and Christian Hebraism: A New Document." *Renaissance Quarterly* 59: 1089–1116.

Lebram, J. C. H. 1980. "De Hasidaeis: Over Joodse studiën in het oude Leiden." In *Voordrachten Faculteitentag 1980.* Leiden: n.p.

Lefranc, Abel. 1893. *Histoire du Collège de France depuis ses origines jusqu'à la fin du premier empire.* Paris: Hachette.

Le Gall, Jean-Marie. 2007. *Le mythe de Saint Denis: Entre renaissance et révolution.* Seyssel: Champvallon.

Leithart, Peter. 2001. "Nabal and His Wine." *Journal of Biblical Literature* 120: 525–527.

Leu, Urs, Raffael Keller, and Sandra Weidmann. 2008. *Conrad Gessner's Private Library.* Leiden: Brill.

Levi della Vida, Giorgio. 1939. *Ricerche sulla formazione del più antico fondo dei manoscritti orientali della Biblioteca Vaticana.* Vatican City: Biblioteca Apostolica Vaticana.

Levine, Joseph. 1977. *Dr. Woodward's Shield: History, Science, and Satire in Augustan England.* Berkeley: University of California Press.

——. 1999. *The Autonomy of History: Truth and Method from Erasmus to Gibbon.* Chicago: University of Chicago Press.

Lieberman, Saul. 1942. *Greek in Jewish Palestine: Studies in the Life and Manners of Jewish Palestine in the II–IV Centuries C.E.* New York: Jewish Theological Seminary of America.

——. 1950. *Hellenism in Jewish Palestine: Studies in the Literary Transmission, Beliefs and Manners of Palestine in the I Century B.C.E.–IV Century C.E.* New York: Jewish Theological Seminary of America.

Lloyd Jones, Gareth. 1983. *The Discovery of Hebrew in Tudor England: A Third Language.* Manchester: Manchester University Press.

Lossky, Nicolas. 1991. *Lancelot Andrewes, the Preacher (1555–1626): The Origins of the Mystical Theology of the Church of England,* trans. Andrew Louth. Oxford: Clarendon Press.

Luraghi, Nino. 2006. "*Meta-historiê*: Method and Genre in the Histories." In *The Cambridge Companion to Herodotus,* ed. Carolyn Dewald and John Marincola. Cambridge: Cambridge University Press, 76–91.

Luzzatto, Samuele Davide. 1966. *Mavo le-Mahzor Benei Roma.* New ed., with supplement by D. Goldshmidt and a bibliography of the printed *mahzor* and *siddur* by J. J. Cohen. Tel Aviv: Devir.

Lyon, Gregory. 2003. "Baudouin, Flacius, and the Plan for the Magdeburg Centuries." *Journal of the History of Ideas* 64: 253–272.

Maclean, Adam. 1980. "The Virga Aurea—Seventy-two Magical and Other Related Alphabets." *Hermetic Journal,* digitized at http://www.levity.com/virga_aurea.html (consulted 16 August 2009).

Mahler, Eduard. 1916. *Handbuch der jüdischen Chronologie.* Leipzig: Fock.

Mährle, Wolfgang. 2000. *Academia Norica: Wissenschaft und Bildung an der Nürnberger Hohen Schule in Altdorf, 1575–1623.* Stuttgart: Steiner.

Malcolm, Noel. 1984. *De Dominis (1560–1624): Venetian, Anglican, Ecumenist and Relapsed Heretic.* London: Strickland & Scott.

———. 2002. *Aspects of Hobbes.* Oxford: Clarendon Press.

———. 2004. "Thomas Harrison and His 'Ark of Studies': An Episode in the History of the Organization of Knowledge." *Seventeenth Century* 19: 196–232.

———. 2006 [2007]. "Jean Bodin and the Authorship of the *Colloquium Heptaplomeres.*" *Journal of the Warburg and Courtauld Institutes* 69: 95–150.

Manuel, Frank. 1992. *The Broken Staff: Judaism through Christian Eyes.* Cambridge, Mass.: Harvard University Press.

Marcus, Ivan. 1981. *Piety and Society: The Jewish Pietists of Medieval Germany.* Leiden: Brill.

Marr, Alexander, 2004. "'Curious and Useful Buildings': The Mathematical Model of Sir Clement Edmondes." *Bodleian Library Record* 18: 108–149.

Martínez, María Elena. 2008. *Genealogical Fictions: Limpieza de Sangre, Religion, and Gender in Colonial Mexico.* Stanford, Calif.: Stanford University Press.

Mas, Enrico de. 2003. "Vanini nell'ambito del Seicento anglo-veneto." In *Giulio Cesare Vanini: Dal tardo Rinascimento al libertinisme érudit,* ed. Francesco Paolo Raimondi. Galatino: Congedo, 215–234.

McCarthy, Carmel. 1981. *The Tiqqune Sopherim and Other Theological Corrections in the Masoretic Text of the Old Testament.* Freiburg/Schweiz: Universitätsverlag; Göttingen: Vandenhoeck and Ruprecht.

McFarlane, I. D. 1981. *Buchanan.* London: Duckworth.

Merchavia, Ch. 1965. "The Talmud in the *Additiones* of Paul of Burgos." *Journal of Jewish Studies* 16: 115–134.

Metzger, Bruce. 1977. *The Early Versions of the New Testament: Their Origin, Transmission and Limitations.* Oxford: Clarendon Press.

Meyendorff, Paul, ed. 1984. *On the Divine Liturgy: The Greek Text with Translation, Introduction and Commentary.* Crestwood, N.Y: St. Vladimir's Seminary Press.

Miller, Peter. 2000. *Peiresc's Europe: Learning and Virtue in the Seventeenth Century.* New Haven: Yale University Press.

———. 2001. "The 'Antiquarianization' of Biblical Scholarship and the London Polyglot Bible (1653–57)." *Journal of the History of Ideas* 62, no. 3: 463–482.

———, ed. 2007. *Momigliano and Antiquarianism: Foundations of the Modern Cultural Sciences.* Toronto: University of Toronto Press.

Millet, Olivier. 2006. "Le stoicisme au quotidien: Le journal de Casaubon." In *Stoïcisme et christianisme à la Renaissance,* ed. Alexandre Tarrête. Paris: Cahiers V. L. Saulnier, 145–162.

Millett, Paul. 2007. *Theophrastus and His World. Proceedings of the Cambridge Philological Society,* suppl. vol. 333. Cambridge: Cambridge Philological Society.

Milton, Anthony. 1995. *Catholic and Reformed: The Roman and Protestant Churches in English Protestant Thought, 1600–1640.* Cambridge: Cambridge University Press.

Momigliano, Arnaldo. 1950. "Ancient History and the Antiquarian." *Journal of the Warburg and Courtauld Institutes* 13: 285–315; reprinted in Momigliano, *Contributo alla storia degli studi classici,* Rome: Edizioni di Storia e Letteratura, 1955, 67–106.

———. 1968. *Studies in Historiography.* London: Weidenfeld and Nicolson.

———. 1974. *Polybius between the English and the Turks.* The Seventh J. L. Myres Memorial

Lecture. Oxford: n.p.; reprinted in Momigliano, *Sesto contributo alla storia degli studi classici e del mondo antico,* 2 vols., Rome: Storia e Letteratura, 1980, I, 125–141.

———. 1977. "Un appunto di I. Casaubon dalle 'Variae' di Cassiodoro." In *Tra Latino e Volgare: Per Carlo Dionisotti.* 2 vols. Padua: Antenore, II, 615–617; reprinted in Momigliano, *Sesto contributo alla storia degli studi classici e del mondo antico,* 2 vols., Rome: Storia e Letteratura, 1980, I, 187–189.

———. 1987. "Biblical Studies and Classical Studies: Simple Reflections upon Historical Method." In *Pagans, Jews, and Christians.* Middletown, Conn.: Wesleyan University Press, 3–10.

Montague, Francis Charles. 1934. "Some Early Letters of Mark Pattison." *Bulletin of the John Rylands Library* 18: 1–21.

Muller, R. A. 1980. "The Debate over the Vowel Points and the Crisis in Orthodox Hermeneutics." *Journal of Medieval and Renaissance Studies* 10: 53–72.

Mulsow, Martin, ed. 2002. *Das Ende des Hermetismus: Historische Kritik und neue Naturphilosophie in der Spätrenaissance. Dokumentation und Analyse der Debatten um die Datierung der hermetischen Schriften von Génébrard bis Casaubon (1567-1614).* Tübingen: Mohr (Siebeck).

Mulsow, Martin. 2004. "Ambiguities of the *Prisca Sapientia* in Late Renaissance Humanism." *Journal of the History of Ideas* 65: 1–13.

———. 2006. "Practices of Unmasking: Polyhistor, Correspondence, and the Birth of Dictionaries of Pseudonymity in Seventeenth-Century Germany." *Journal of the History of Ideas* 67: 219–250.

Mund-Dopchie, Monique. 1984. *La survie d'Eschyle à la Renaissance: Éditions, traductions, commentaires et imitations.* Louvain: Peeters.

Namer, Emile. 1965. *Documents sur la vie de Jules-César Vanini de Taurisano.* Bari: Adriatica.

Nötscher, F. 1961. "Bar Kochba, Ben Kosba: der Sternsohn, der Prächtige." *Vetus Testamentum* 11: 449–451.

Nuttall, A. D. 2003. *Dead from the Waist Down: Scholars and Scholarship in Literature and the Popular Imagination.* New Haven: Yale University Press.

ODNB. 2004. *Oxford Dictionary of National Biography,* ed. H. C. G. Matthew and Brian Harrison. 60 vols. Oxford: Oxford University Press. Digital version: http://www.oxforddnb.com.

Ogilvie, Brian. 2006. *The Science of Describing: Natural History in Renaissance Europe.* Chicago: University of Chicago Press.

Olds, Katrina. 2009. "The 'False Chronicles' in Early Modern Spain: Forgery, Tradition, and the Invention of Texts and Relics, 1595–c.1670." Ph.D. diss., Princeton University.

Oryshkevich, I. T. 2003. "The History of the Roman Catacombs from the Age of Constantine to the Renaissance." Ph.D. diss., Columbia University.

Pachter, Mordechai. 1994. *From Safed's Hidden Treasures* [Hebrew]. Jerusalem: Merkaz Zalman Shazar le-toldot Yisrael.

Paladini, Alba. 2004. *Il De arcanis di Pietro Galatino: Traditio giudaica e nuove instanze filologiche.* Lecce: Congedo.

Paola, Francesco de. 1979. *Vanini e il primo '600 anglo-veneto.* Cutrofiano: Toraldo & Panico.

Parenty, Hélène. 2009. *Isaac Casaubon, helléniste: Des studia humanitatis à la philologie.* Geneva: Droz.

Patterson, W. B. 1997. *King James VI and I and the Reunion of Christendom.* Cambridge: Cambridge University Press.

Pattison, Mark. 1892. *Isaac Casaubon, 1559-1614.* 2d ed. Oxford: Clarendon Press.

Penkower, Jordan. 1989. "A Reconsideration of 'Sefer Massoreth haMassoreth' of Elijah Levita: The Late Origin of Vowel Markings and Criticism of the Zohar" [Hebrew]. *Italia* 8, nos. 1–2: 7–73.

Peritz, Moritz. 1894. "Ein Brief Elijah Levita's an Sebastian Münster." *Monatsschrift für Geschichte und Wissenschaft des Judentums* 2: 252–267.

Pettegree, Andrew. 2005. *The Reformation and the Culture of Persuasion.* Cambridge: Cambridge University Press.

Pocock, John, 1999—. *Barbarism and Religion.* 4 vols. to date. Cambridge: Cambridge University Press.

Pomata, Gianna, and Nancy Siraisi, eds. 2005. *Historia: Empiricism and Erudition in Early Modern Europe.* Cambridge, Mass.: MIT Press.

Popper, Nicholas. 2005. "The English Polydaedali: How Gabriel Harvey Read Late Tudor London." *Journal of the History of Ideas* 66, no. 3: 351–381.

Popper, William. 1899. *The Censorship of Hebrew Books.* New York: privately printed.

Prijs, Joseph. 1964. *Die Basler hebräischen Drucke (1492–1866),* ed. Bernhard Prijs. Olten: Urs-Graf Verlag.

———. 1994. *Die Handschriften der Universitätsbibliothek Basel. Die Hebräischen Handschriften. Katalog auf Grund der Beschreibungen von Joseph Prijs,* ed. Bernhard Prijs and David Prijs, with Stephen G. Burnett and Thomas Willi. Basel: Universitätsbibliothek.

Purnell, Frederick, Jr. 1976. "Francesco Patrizi and the Critics of Hermes Trismegistus." *Journal of Medieval and Renaissance Studies* 6: 155–178.

Quantin, Jean-Louis. 2009. *The Church of England and Christian Antiquity: The Construction of a Confessional Identity in the 17th Century.* Oxford: Oxford University Press.

Questier, Michael. 1996. "Crypto-Catholicism, Anti-Calvinism and Conversion at the Jacobean Court: The Enigma of Benjamin Carier." *Journal of Ecclesiastical History* 47: 45–64.

Raimondi, Francesco Paolo. 2005. *Giulio Cesare Vanini nell'Europa del Seicento.* Rome: Istituti Editoriali e Poligrafici Internazionali.

Rajak, Tessa. 2009. *Translation and Survival: The Greek Bible of the Ancient Jewish Diaspora.* Oxford: Oxford University Press.

Raz-Krakotzkin, Amnon. 2007. *The Censor, the Editor and the Text: The Catholic Church and the Shaping of the Jewish Canon in the Sixteenth Century,* trans. Jackie Feldman. Philadelphia: University of Pennsylvania Press. Hebrew version, Jerusalem: Magnes, 2005.

Reinhartz, Adele. 1989. "Rabbinic Perceptions of Simeon bar Kosiba." *Journal for the Study of Judaism* 20: 171–194.

Reverdin, Olivier. 1961. "Isaac Casaubon et Genève de 1596 à 1614." In *Mélanges offerts à M. Paul-E. Martin par ses amis, ses collègues et ses élèves.* Geneva: Comité des Mélanges P.-E. Martin, 503–521.

Rex, Richard, 1990. "The Earliest Use of Hebrew in Books Printed in England: Dating Some Works of Richard Pace and Robert Wakefield." *Transactions of the Cambridge Bibliographical Society* 9, pt. 5: 517–525.

Rosenblatt, Jason. 2006. *Renaissance England's Chief Rabbi: John Selden.* Oxford: Oxford University Press.

Rosenthal, Erwin I. J. 1950. "Edward Lively: Cambridge Hebraist." In *Essays and Studies Presented to Stanley Arthur Cook,* ed. D. Winton Thomas. London: Taylor's Foreign Press, 95–112.

Rossi, Paolo. 1984. *The Dark Abyss of Time: The History of the Earth and the History of Na-*

tions from Hooke to Vico, trans. Lydia G. Cochrane. Chicago: University of Chicago Press.

Roth, Cecil. 1950. "Jews in Oxford after 1290." *Oxoniensia* 15: 63–80.

Rothschild, Jean-Pierre. 2006. "Les éditions hébraïques de Jean Mercier." In *Jean (c. 1525–1570) et Josias (c. 1560–1626) Mercier: L'amour de la philologie à la Renaissance et au début de l'âge classique.* Paris: Honoré Champion, 43–75.

Ruderman, David. 1981. *The World of a Renaissance Jew: The Life and Thought of Abraham ben Mordecai Farissol.* Cincinnati: Hebrew Union College Press; New York: Distributed by KTAV.

———. 2007. *Connecting the Covenants: Judaism and the Search for Christian Identity in Eighteenth-Century England.* Philadelphia: University of Pennsylvania Press.

Rusconi, Roberto. 1992. "An Angelic Pope before the Sack of Rome." *Prophetic Rome in the High Renaissance Period,* ed. Marjorie Reeves. Oxford: Clarendon Press, 157–187.

Rutgers, Leonard. 1995. *The Jews of Late Ancient Rome: Evidence of Cultural Interaction in the Roman Diaspora.* Leiden: Brill.

Sawilla, Jan Marco. 2009. *Antiquarianismus, Hagiographie und Historie im 17. Jahrhundert: Zum Werk der Bollandisten. Ein Wissenschaftshistorischer Versuch.* Tübingen: Niemeyer.

Scanlon, T. F. 2002. *Eros and Greek Athletics.* Oxford: Oxford University Press.

Schäfer, Peter. 1978. "R. Aqiva und Bar Kokhba." In *Studien zur Geschichte und Theologie des rabbinischen Judentums.* Leiden: Brill, 65–121.

———. 1980. "Rabbi Aqiva and Bar Kokhba." In *Approaches to Ancient Judaism,* vol. 2, ed. W. S. Green. Ann Arbor: Scholars Press, 113–130.

———. 2007. *Jesus in the Talmud.* Princeton: Princeton University Press.

Schechter, Solomon. 1896. *Studies in Judaism.* London: Black.

Schoeps, Hans Joachim. 1952. *Philosemitismus im Barock: Religions- und geistegeschichtliche Untersuchungen.* Tübingen: J. C. B. Mohr (Paul Siebeck).

Scholem, Gershom. 1946. *Major Trends in Jewish Mysticism.* Jerusalem: Schocken.

———. 1954. *Major Trends in Jewish Mysticism.* 3d ed. New York: Schocken.

Schürer, Emil. 1973–1987. *The History of the Jewish People in the Age of Jesus Christ (175 B.C.–A.D. 135),* trans. T. A. Burkill et al., rev. ed. Geza Vermes and Fergus Millar. 3 vols. Edinburgh: Clark.

Schwarz, Werner. 1955. *Principles and Problems of Biblical Translation: Some Reformation Controversies and Their Background.* London: Cambridge University Press.

Secret, François. 1966. "*L'Ensis Pauli* di Paulus de Heredia." *Sefarad* 26: 79–102, 253–272.

———. 1985. *Les Kabbalistes chrétiens de la Renaissance.* New ed. Milan: Archè.

———. 1998. *Postel revisité: Nouvelles recherches sur Guillaume Postel et son milieu.* Paris: Société d'Étude de l'Histoire de l'Alchimie.

Sed-Rajna, Gabrielle. 1980. "Un diagramme kabbalistique de la Bibliothèque de Gilles de Viterbe." In *Hommage à Georges Vajda: Études d'histoire et de pensée juives,* ed. Gérard Nahon and Charles Touati. Louvain: Peeters, 365–376.

Sellheim, Rudolf. 1954. *Die klassisch-arabischen Sprichwörtersammlungen, insbesondere die des Abū-'Ubaid.* The Hague: Mouton.

Sermoneta, Giuseppe. 1988. "L'incontro culturale tra Ebrei e Cristiani nel Medioevo e nel Rinascimento." In *Ebrei e cristiani nell'Italia medievale e moderna: Conversioni, scambi, contrasti. Atti del VI Congresso internazionale dell'AISG, S. Miniato, 4–6 novembre 1986,* ed. Michele Luzzati, Michele Olivari, and Alessandra Veronese. Rome: Carucci, 183–207.

Shalev, Zur. 2003. "Sacred Geography, Antiquarianism, and Visual Erudition: Benito Arias Montano and the Maps of the Antwerp Polyglot Bible." *Imago Mundi* 55: 56-80.

———. 2004. "*Geographia Sacra:* Cartography, Religion, and Scholarship in the Sixteenth and Seventeenth Centuries." Ph.D. diss., Princeton University.

Shapiro, James. 1996. *Shakespeare and the Jews.* New York: Columbia University Press.

Sheehan, Jonathan. 2005. *The Enlightenment Bible: Translation, Scholarship, Culture.* Princeton: Princeton University Press.

———. 2006. "Sacred and Profane: Idolatry, Antiquarianism, and the Polemics of Distinction in the Seventeenth Century." *Past and Present* 192: 37–66.

Sherman, William. 2008. *Used Books: Marking Readers in Renaissance England.* Philadelphia: University of Pennsylvania Press.

Shuger, Debora Kuller. 1994. *The Renaissance Bible: Scholarship, Sacrifice, and Subjectivity.* Berkeley: University of California Press.

Simoncelli, Paolo. 1984. *La lingua di Adamo: Guillaume Postel tra accademici e fuorisciti fiorentini.* Florence: Olschki.

Siraisi, Nancy. 2000. "Anatomizing the Past: Physicians and History in Renaissance Culture." *Renaissance Quarterly* 53: 1–30.

———. 2007. *History, Medicine, and the Traditions of Renaissance Learning.* Ann Arbor: University of Michigan Press.

Smet, Ingrid de. 2006. *Thuanus: The Making of Jacques-Auguste de Thou (1553–1617).* Geneva: Droz.

Soll, Jacob. 2005. *Publishing The Prince: History, Reading, and the Birth of Political Criticism.* Ann Arbor: University of Michigan Press.

Stagl, Justin. 1983. *Apodemiken: Eine räsonnierte Bibliographie der reisetheoretischen Literatur des 16., 17. und 18. Jahrhunderts.* Paderborn: Schöningh.

———. 1995. *A History of Curiosity: The Theory of Travel, 1550–1800.* Chur: Harwood.

Stein, Siegfried. 1942. "Philippus Ferdinandus Polonus: A Sixteenth-Century Hebraist in England." In *Essays in Honour of the Very Rev. Dr. J. H. Hertz,* ed. Isidore Epstein, Ephraim Levine, and Cecil Roth. London: Goldston, 397–412.

Stenhouse, William. 2005. *Reading Inscriptions and Writing Ancient History: Historical Scholarship in the Late Renaissance.* London: Institute of Classical Studies.

Stern, Sasha. 2001. *Calendar and Community: A History of the Jewish Calendar, Second Century B.C.E.–Tenth Century C.E.* Oxford: Oxford University Press.

Stolzenberg, Daniel, ed. 2001. *The Great Art of Knowing: The Baroque Encyclopedia of Athanasius Kircher.* Stanford: Stanford University Libraries.

Stolzenberg, Daniel. 2004. "Four Trees, Some Amulets, and the Seventy-two Names of God: Kircher Reveals the Kabbalah." In *Athanasius Kircher: The Last Man Who Knew Everything,* ed. Paula Findlen. New York: Routledge, 149–169.

Stopp, F. J. 1974. *The Emblems of the Altdorf Academy: Medals and Medal Orations, 1577–1626.* London: Modern Humanities Research Association.

Storey, Ian. 2003. *Eupolis: Poet of Old Comedy.* Oxford: Oxford University Press.

Stow, Kenneth. 1986. "Conversion, Christian Hebraism, and Hebrew Prayer in the Sixteenth Century." *Hebrew Union College Annual* 47: 217–236.

Strack, Hermann, and Paul Billerbeck. 1922–1961. *Kommentar zum Neuen Testament aus Talmud und Midrasch.* 6 vols. in 7. Munich: Beck.

Stroumsa, Guy. 2001a. "John Spencer and the Roots of Idolatry." *History of Religions* 40: 1–23.

———. 2001b. "Richard Simon: From Philology to Comparativism." *Archiv für Religionsgeschichte* 3: 89–107.

————. 2003. "*Antiquitates Judaicae:* Some Precursors of the Modern Study of Israelite Religion." In *Jews, Antiquity, and the Nineteenth Century Imagination,* ed. Hayim Lapin and Dale Martin. Bethesda: University Press of Maryland, 17–32.

Sulek, Antoni, 1989. "The Experiment of Psammetichus: Fact, Fiction, and Model to Follow." *Journal of the History of Ideas* 50: 645–651.

Sutcliffe, Adam. 2003. *Judaism and Enlightenment.* Cambridge: Cambridge University Press.

Talmage, Frank. 1967. "R. David Kimhi as Polemicist." *Hebrew Union College Annual* 38: 213–235.

Tishby, Isaiah. 1989. *The Wisdom of the Zohar,* trans. D. Goldstein. 3 vols. Oxford: Oxford University Press for the Littman Library.

Toch, Michael. 1997. "Wirtschaft und Geldwesen der Juden Frankfurts im Spätmittelalter und in der Frühen Neuzeit." In Grözinger 1997, 25–46.

Toomer, G. J. 1996. *Eastern Wisedome and Learning: The Study of Arabic in Seventeenth-Century England.* Oxford: Clarendon Press.

————. 2009. *John Selden: A Life in Scholarship.* 2 vols. Oxford: Oxford University Press.

Tournoy, Gilbert. 1998. "'*Ad ultimas inscitiae lineas sumus*': Justus Lipsius and Isaac Casaubon in the Changing World of Classical Scholarship." In *The World of Justus Lipsius: A Contribution toward His Intellectual Biography,* ed. Mark Laureys. Brussels: Belgian Historical Institute in Rome, 191–208.

————. 2000. "Erycius Puteanus, Isaac Casaubon and the Author of the *Corona Regia.*" *Humanistica Lovaniensia* 49: 377–390.

Trevor-Roper, Hugh. 2006. *Europe's Physician: The Various Life of Sir Theodore de Mayerne.* New Haven: Yale University Press.

Tuck, Richard. 1993. *Philosophy and Government, 1572–1651.* Cambridge: Cambridge University Press.

Turniansky, Chava. 2000. "The Events in Frankfurt am Main (1612–1616) in *Megillas Vints* and in an Unknown Yiddish 'Historical' Song." In Graetz 2000, 121–137.

Tyerman, Christopher. 1999. "Early Modern Views on Medieval Christendom." In *The Medieval Church: Universities, Heresy, and the Religious Life. Essays in Honour of Gordon Leff,* ed. Peter Biller and Barrie Dobson. Woodbridge, N.Y.: Boydell Press for the Ecclesiastical History Society, 293–307.

Urbach, Ephraim E. 1980. *The Tosafists, Their History, Writings and Methods.* 4th ed. [Hebrew]. Jerusalem: Bialik Institute.

Van Boxel, Piet. 1980. "Cardinal Santoro and the Expurgation of Hebrew Literature." In *The Roman Inquisition, the Index and the Jews: New Perspectives for Research,* ed. Stephen Wendehorst. Leiden: Brill, 19–34.

Van den Berg, J. 1988. "Proto-Protestants? The Image of the Karaites as a Mirror of the Catholic-Protestant Controversy in the Seventeenth Century." In *Jewish-Christian Relations in the Seventeenth Century: Studies and Documents,* ed. J. van den Berg and Ernestine G. E. van der Wall. Dordrecht: Kluwer, 33–49.

Van Kley, Edwin. 1971. "Europe's 'Discovery' of China and the Writing of World History." *American Historical Review* 76, no. 2: 358–385.

Vasoli, Cesare. 1984. "Giorgio B. Salviati, Pietro Galatino e la edizione di Ortona—1518— del '*De arcanis catholicae fidei.*'" In *Cultura umanistica nel Meridione e la stampa in Abruzzo.* L'Aquila: Deputazione Abruzzese di Storia Patria.

Vélez, Karin. 2008. "Resolved to Fly: The Virgin of Loreto, the Jesuits and the Miracle of Portable Catholicism in the Seventeenth-Century Atlantic World." Ph.D. diss., Princeton University.

Veltri, Giuseppe, and Gerold Necker, eds. 2004. *Gottes Sprache in der philologischen Werkstatt: Hebraistik vom 15. bis zum 19. Jahrhundert.* Leiden: Brill.

Vivanti, Corrado. 1963. *Lotta politica e pace religiosa in Francia tra Cinque e Seicento.* Turin: Einaudi.

Vrolijk, Arnoud, and Kasper van Ommen, eds. 2009. *"All My Books in Foreign Tongues":* *Scaliger's Oriental Legacy in Leiden, 1609–2009.* Leiden: Leiden University Library.

Walker, D. P. 1988. "The Cessation of Miracles." In *Hermeticism and the Renaissance: Intellectual History and the Occult in Early Modern Europe,* ed. Ingrid Merkel and Allen Debus. Washington, D.C.: Folger Shakespeare Library; London: Associated University Presses, 111–124.

Walton, Michael. 2005. "Anthonius Margaritha—Honest Reporter?" *Sixteenth Century Journal* 36: 129–141.

Wasserstein, Abraham, and David Wasserstein. 2006. *The Legend of the Septuagint: From Classical Antiquity to Today.* Cambridge: Cambridge University Press.

Weil, G. E. 1963. *Élie Lévita, humaniste et massorète.* Leiden: Brill.

Weinberg, Joanna. 1985. "Azariah de' Rossi and Septuagint Traditions." *Italia* 5, no. 1–2: 7–35.

———. 1988. "The Quest for the Historical Philo in Sixteenth-Century Jewish Historiography." In *Jewish History: Essays in Honour of Chimen Abramsky,* ed. Ada Rapoport-Albert and Steven Zipperstein. London: Halban, 163–187.

———. 2000. "Invention and Convention: Jewish and Christian Critique of the Jewish Fixed Calendar." *Jewish History* 14: 317–330.

———. 2006. "A Hebraic Approach to the New Testament." In *History of Scholarship: A Selection of Papers from the Seminar on the History of Scholarship Held Annually at the Warburg Institute,* ed. Christopher Ligota and Jean-Louis Quantin. Oxford: Oxford University Press, 238–247.

Wertheim, Gustav. 1896. *Die Arithmetik des Elia Misrachi: Ein Beitrag zur Geschichte der Mathematik.* Braunschweig: Friedrich Vieweg & Sohn.

Weststeijn, Thijs. 2007. "*Spinoza sinicus:* An Asian Paragraph in the History of the Radical Enlightenment." *Journal of the History of Ideas* 68: 537–561.

Whealey, Alice. 2003. *Josephus on Jesus: The Testimonium Flavianum Controversy from Late Antiquity to Modern Times.* New York: Peter Lang.

Wiegers, G. A. 1988. *A Learned Muslim Acquaintance of Erpenius and Golius: Ahmad b. Kāsim al-Andalusī and Arabic Studies in the Netherlands.* Leiden: Documentatiebureau Islam-Christendom, Faculteit der Godgeleerdheid, Rijksuniversiteit Leiden.

Wilke, Carsten. 2000. "Splendeurs et infortunes du talmudisme académique en Allemagne." In *Les Textes judéophobes et judéophiles dans l'Europe chrétienne à l'époque moderne, XVIème–XVIIIème siècles,* ed. Daniel Tollet. Paris: Presses Universitaires de France, 97–134.

Williamson, Arthur. 1994. "British Israel and Roman Britain: The Jews and Scottish Models of Polity from George Buchanan to Samuel Rutherford." In *Jewish Christians and Christian Jews from the Renaissance to the Enlightenment,* ed. Richard Popkin and Gordon Weiner. Dordrecht: Kluwer Academic, 97–117.

Wirszubski, Chaim, ed. 1963. *Flavius Mithridates, Sermo De passione Domini.* Jerusalem: Israel Academy of Sciences and Humanities.

Wolfthal, Diane. 2001. "Remembering Amalek and Nebuchadnezzar: Biblical Warfare and Symbolic Violence in Italian Renaissance Yiddish Books of Customs." In *Artful Armies, Beautiful Battles,* ed. Pia Cuneo. Leiden: Brill, 181–212.

———. 2002. "Imagining the Self: Representations of Jewish Ritual in Yiddish Books of Cus-

BIBLIOGRAPHY

toms." In *Imagining the Self, Imagining the Other: Visual Representation and Jewish-Christian Dynamics in the Middle Ages and Early Modern Period,* ed. Eva Frojmovic. Leiden: Brill, 189–211.

Yates, Frances. 1964. *Giordano Bruno and the Hermetic Tradition.* London: Routledge and Kegan Paul.

Yoffie, Adina. 2004. "Cocceius and the Jewish Commentators." *Journal of the History of Ideas* 65: 383–398.

———. 2009. "Biblical Literalism and Scholarship in Early Modern Northern Europe, 1630–1700." Ph.D. diss., Harvard University.

Zen, Stefano. 1994. *Baronio storico: Controriforma e crisi del metodo umanistico.* Naples: Vivarium.

Zinguer, Ilana, ed. 1992. *L'Hébreu au temps de la Renaissance.* Leiden: Brill.

Ziskind, Jonathan. 1978. "Petrus Cunaeus on Theocracy, Jubilee and the Latifundia." *Jewish Quarterly Review,* n.s., 68: 235–254.

Acknowledgments

This book first took shape in the form of the Carl Newell Jackson Lectures, which we delivered at Harvard University in December 2008. Exactly forty years before we spoke at Harvard, Arnaldo Momigliano delivered his Jackson Lectures on the development of Greek biography. Both of us had the good fortune to study with him in the 1970s and to benefit from his teaching, his counsel, and his generous encouragement until his death in 1987. Many years ago, when Joanna Weinberg first turned up a Hebrew volume annotated by Isaac Casaubon and showed it to Momigliano, he immediately saw the significance of the subject and urged her to pursue it. Like so much of what both of us have done as scholars and teachers, our lectures and the book that has grown from them owe their inspiration to his example and his teaching. It was moving, as well as exciting, to speak about Casaubon's life of scholarship in a great university that Momigliano loved.

We are most grateful to Harvard's Department of the Classics, and especially to Professors Kathleen Coleman and Jan Ziolkowski, for the invitation to speak, and to the members and students of the department for their willingness to welcome two ex-classicists into what has traditionally been a classical venue and to allow us to address the history, rather than the current practice, of scholarship. We are also grateful to many friends at Harvard, old and new, for their gracious hospitality. Special thanks go to Vera Keller, Arthur Kiron, Eric Nelson, the late Ihor Sevcenko, and Ben Weiss, who posed particularly helpful and difficult questions after our lectures.

Many friends, colleagues, and institutions made our research both possible and pleasant. The bulk of our work was done in the British Library and the Bodleian Library, and we owe far more than we can ever repay to the hard-pressed but endlessly generous and gracious staffs of these two great institutions. They allowed us to piece together Casaubon's archive in the best imaginable conditions, produced films, scans, and photographs, and showed a heartening interest in what we were doing. The libraries of Princeton University, the University of Pennsylvania, and the Warburg Institute provided us with printed and digital materials of every kind, from Casaubon's biographies, correspondence, and diaries to the burgeoning literature on Christian Hebraism and ecclesiastical scholarship in early modern Europe.

As we pursued the scattered remains of Casaubon's library and followed the branches of his scholarly interests, we ran up further debts to the staffs of the Universitätsbibliothek Basel; the Beinecke Library, Yale University; the Bibliothèque Nationale de France; the Cambridge University Library; the Canterbury Cathedral Archive; the Houghton Library, Harvard University; the Leiden University Library; the Library of Lambeth Palace; Marsh's Library, Dublin; the Wren Library, Trinity College Cambridge; York Minster Library; and the Zentralbibliothek Zürich. Special thanks to Giles Mandlebrote and Barry Taylor at the Brit-

368

ACKNOWLEDGMENTS

ish Library, to Dominik Hunger at the Universitätsbibliothek, Basel, and to Muriel McCarthy, Urs Leu, Kasper van Ommen, and David McKitterick for their kindness and hospitality in Dublin, Zurich, Leiden, and Cambridge.*

At Princeton, as always, Judy Hanson and Barb Leavey made the impossible easy. Practical support for our research came from the Center for Advanced Judaic Studies at the University of Pennsylvania, which jump-started our work by inviting both of us to join the group assembled to study The Jewish Book during the academic year 2005–06, and from Princeton University, the Swiss National Fund, and the Faculty of Pedagogy of the University of Zurich, the Scaliger Institute of the University of Leiden, Trinity College Cambridge, Merton College Oxford, and the Warburg Institute. The extraordinary generosity of the Andrew W. Mellon Foundation, which gave Anthony Grafton the means to do his part of the research and the freedom to pursue it, also made it possible to equip this book with an unusual wealth of illustrations and apparatus.

From the beginning, our friends David Ruderman and Peter Schäfer have followed and supported the project that led to this book. Both of them offered advice and criticism at every step of the way, and both gave us essential opportunities to present our findings to expert and critical audiences. Many other friends offered expert scholarly counsel, provided vital information, or asked challenging questions: Jean Baumgarten, Malachi Beit-Arié, Ann Blair, Paul Botley, Stephen Burnett, Henk Jan de Jonge, Simon Ditchfield, Theo Dunkelgrün, Moti Feingold, Anja Goeing, Joseph Hacker, Arthur Kiron, Jill Kraye, Peter Lake, Scott Mandlebrote, Suzanne Marchand, Peter Miller, Philipp Nothaft, the late Tony Nuttall, Jason Rosenblatt, Wilhelm Schmidt-Biggemann, Bill Sherman, Peter Stallybrass, Piet van Boxel, Kate Elliott van Liere, and Dirk van Miert. Alastair Hamilton not only advised us on Casaubon's work in Arabic—a passion of his, and one as unexplored as his Hebrew studies—but investigated the documents in depth, and generously provided a summary of his findings, which appears here as Appendix 1.

Two of our long-dead predecessors have provided continual stimulus: Mark Pattison, whose biography of Casaubon remains the most engaging and eloquent book on any early modern scholar, and Eduard Fraenkel, who became Pattison's fiercest critic as he worked his way into the fascinating labyrinths of Casaubon's annotated books and notebooks. So have our contemporaries. Hélène Parenty allowed us to see an early draft of her book on Casaubon's philology before it appeared. We are grateful to her—as to Ingo Herklotz, Jean-Marie Le Gall, Jean-Louis Quantin, Jan Marco Sawilla, and G. J. Toomer—for their exemplary studies of subjects closely connected to our own. Lindsay Waters of Harvard University Press has been committed to this project since it was only an idea. He, Phoebe Kosman, Hannah Wong, Donna Bouvier, Ann Hawthorne, and Harvard's anonymous referee greatly aided us in planning our work and revising our draft. Our warmest thanks of all, of course, are owed to Louise Grafton and Piet van Boxel, *sine quibus non.*

*A preliminary discussion of our findings appears as "Isaac Casaubon's Library of Hebrew Books," in *Libraries within the Library: The Origins of the British Library's Printed Collections,* ed. Giles Mandelbrote and Barry Taylor (London: British Library, 2009), 24–42.

Index